Personality Disorders
in Childhood
and Adolescence

Personality Disorders in Childhood and Adolescence

Edited by

Arthur Freeman

and

Mark A. Reinecke

BICENTENNIAL
1807
WILEY
2007
BICENTENNIAL

John Wiley & Sons, Inc.

Published by John Wiley & Sons, Inc., Hoboken, New Jersey.
Published simultaneously in Canada.

Wiley Bicentennial Logo: Richard J. Pacifico

This publication is designed to provide accurate and authoritative information in regard to the subject matter covered. It is sold with the understanding that the publisher is not engaged in rendering professional services. If legal, accounting, medical, psychological or any other expert assistance is required, the services of a competent professional person should be sought.

Designations used by companies to distinguish their products are often claimed as trademarks. In all instances where John Wiley & Sons, Inc. is aware of a claim, the product names appear in initial capital or all capital letters. Readers, however, should contact the appropriate companies for more complete information regarding trademarks and registration.

For general information on our other products and services please contact our Customer Care Department within the United States at (800) 762-2974, outside the United States at (317) 572-3993 or fax (317) 572-4002.

Wiley also publishes its books in a variety of electronic formats. Some content that appears in print may not be available in electronic books. For more information about Wiley products, visit our web site at www.wiley.com.

Library of Congress Cataloging-in-Publication Data:

Personality disorders in childhood and adolescence / edited by Arthur Freeman and Mark Reinecke.
     p. ; cm.
  ISBN: 978-0-471-68304-9 (cloth : alk. paper)
 1. Personality disorders in children. 2. Personality disorders in adolescence. I. Freeman, Arthur, 1942– II. Reinecke, Mark A.
  [DNLM: 1. Personality Disorders. 2. Adolescent. 3. Child. WS 350.8.P3 P467   2007]
  RJ506.P32P47   2007
  618.92'8581—dc22

                                                        2006036777

Printed in the United States of America.

10 9 8 7 6 5 4 3 2 1

This volume is dedicated to
Aaron T. Beck, MD, and to Albert Ellis,
PhD, heros, mentors, colleagues, and friends.
Psychology and psychiatry have been enriched by
their contributions. Their work has ameliorated the pain of
emotional problems for many people over the past 50 years.

Contents

Preface

THIS VOLUME began as a discussion between the editors almost 10 years ago. We were actively discussing (maybe debating) the possibilities of diagnosing personality disorders in children. Both of us had worked with youth for many years and had seen innumerable children who certainly seemed similar in behavior to adults we had encountered with personality disorders. We had both had the experience of adult patients describing childhood experiences and circumstances that were both precursors and de facto exemplars of the criteria set out in *DSM* for the range of personality disorders. Because we believed that it would be important to understand the developmental psychopathology of these disorders, and that prevention would be desirable goal, we discussed the possibility of inviting a number of colleagues to contribute to an edited volume on the development and clinical reality of personality disorders in children and adolescents.

Many of the colleagues with whom we discussed the idea were shocked by the proposed project. For some, the reaction was incendiary—they were appalled that we would even *consider* such a project. A smaller number agreed that these were important questions, but were discomforted by making the issue so open. We spoke to editors of several major publishing houses who presented the idea to their editorial consultants. Here again, the answer was, "Thanks, but no thanks." With the publication of volumes by Kernberg, Weiner, and Bardenstein (2000) and Bleiberg (2004), however, the environment changed. The development and treatment of personality disorders during childhood had come into the open. Uncomfortable as it might be, as debatable as it was, there it was in front of us.

Though we have, over the past decade, both worked independently and collaborated on other volumes, this book idea kept surfacing in our discussions. We decided that it was time to bring this project to fruition. We took the proposal to John Wiley & Sons, who were enthusiastic and supportive. Their consultants were positive about the need for an open and comprehensive discussion. We spoke to a number of experts in the area, and the present volume is the result. It still wasn't easy. Well-controlled empirical research on personality disorders during childhood is limited. Case studies and clinical speculation abound. Although braver colleagues had described personality disordered patterns among adolescents (Flynn, 2004; Kernberg, 1984), most writers approached the topic obliquely. Clinicians and theoreticians described patterns of "severe emotional disturbance," or "pathological interactions." Still others chose to speak euphemistically, though on a spectrum (e.g., a child was not an avoidant personality, he or she was "painfully shy"). The shyness spectrum might be that the child was quiet, shy, quite shy, very shy, extremely shy, painfully shy. Similarly, a child might be self-focused, self-absorbed, selfish, very selfish, extremely selfish. All of this without using the term *narcissistic*. Part of the problem stems from a desire to be kind to children and not use pejorative taxonomic labels that might follow them throughout their lives. Yet, we must do that with many disorders (e.g., Asperger's syndrome, autism, mental retardation). However well-intended, using euphemistic terms and diagnoses may obscure the potential severity of the child's difficulties and direct clinicians away from providing beneficial treatment for the child or adolescent (Freeman & Duff, 2005).

It is also clear that the personality disorders co-occur with both internalizing and externalizing disorders. The externalizing disorders are, of course, far more likely to attract the attention of family and school personnel who may be less concerned about the child at risk or the child in the midst of acting out and more concerned with the safety of siblings or other students. The "acting in" or internalizing child or adolescent may raise some concerns, but given that the disorder mostly impacts the child, less action is likely given the hierarchies that schools and family systems operate within. For example, the compliant, dependent, obsessive compulsive, hard-working, success-driven/demanding child may succeed at school and be seen by teachers as a hard worker and superior student as measured by academic success. The results of the personality style in this instance may serve to enhance a child's school performance. The child may be rewarded by certificates, plaques, public recognition, or admiration of other students and may receive the approval of teachers, school administrators, and parents. After all, who wants their child to be an academic failure? The teacher earns acknowledgment for having a "good student" who "does well" and "brings credit to the school." Parents may get a bumper sticker.

Avoidant children may be overlooked by teachers and clinicians inasmuch as they are reserved and compliant, do not typically call attention to themselves, and rarely cause trouble in class. The fact that they play by themselves and stay on the outskirts of work and play groups typically will not raise concern so long as they do well in school. Inasmuch as they may relate well to family and close relatives, the families may not see any problems other than the children are noted to be "kind of shy." Even in adults, avoidant disorders may receive little attention.

The borderline child or antisocial child, however, attracts the notice of school personnel who have set out, in a post-Columbine era, a zero tolerance for many behaviors. For example, a 5-year-old boy in kindergarten who kisses a little girl on the cheek was suspended by the school for sexual harassment. We might conclude that there is no shortage of concern for dangerous behaviors on the part of students in school, but an ongoing concern on the part of mental health professionals to identify and diagnose them accurately.

The editors believed that there were several elements that should be addressed in our discussions of the personality disorders. Based in part on prior work by Kernberg, Weiner, and Bardenstein (2000), these included:

- *Temperament:* Based on biogenetic factors that constitute a disposition that influences the child's interaction with his or her world by affecting the nature and the style of the child's approach to others.
- *Identity:* The internal mental construction that involves the child's developing a sense of selfhood over time and situations.
- *Gender:* Though a component of identity, gender often defines individuals and embodies specific behavioral expectation.
- *Neuropsychological deficits:* Deficits in cognitive functioning that involve the processes by which the child processes, organizes, and recalls information.
- *Affect:* The child's repertoire of emotional responses that are both automatic and learned.
- *Coping style:* The child's characteristic mode of adapting to internal and external stressors.
- *Environmental factors:* Includes the child's family system, school, religious training, and the stability of the system(s). These are related to the reactivity and reciprocal behavior of others.
- *Motivation:* Reflects the "why" of behavior. What internal/external needs are unmet that eventuate in the observed behavior?
- *Social facility:* The child's repertoire of social interaction skills that will assist the child in relating to, and coping with, others in their environment or family and social system.
- *Cognitive development:* The child's level of cognitive development.
- *Basic schema:* The "rules" that the child uses as templates for understanding their world.

Each of the authors of the syndrome-specific chapters has tried to focus on as many of these elements as possible given the state of the research literature. When evidence was lacking, we asked authors for their clinical speculation and surmise. In our summary chapter, we address what we know and what we do not know and have yet to learn. Personality disorders are an important clinical and social concern. Our belief is that an understanding of how these conditions develop over the course of childhood and adolescence will allow us to develop more effective treatment programs and, as importantly, prevention programs. This volume represents an initial step toward achieving these goals.

REFERENCES

Bleiberg, E. (2004). *Treating personality disorders in children and adolescents: A relational approach.* New York: Basic Books.

Flynn, D. (2004). *Severe emotional disturbance in children and adolescents: Psychotherapy in applied contexts.* New York: Brunner-Routledge.

Freeman, A., & Duff, J. (2005). Are euphemistic labels obscuring treatment for children with personality disorders. In R. Menutti, A. Freeman, & R. W. Christner (Eds.), *Cognitive behavioral interventions in educational setting.* New York: Routledge.

Kernberg, O. (1984). *Severe personality disorder: Psychotherapeutic strategies.* New Haven, CT: Yale University Press.

Kernberg, P. F., Weiner, A. S., & Bardenstein, K. K. (2000). *Personality disorders in children and adolescents.* New York: Guilford Press.

Contributors

Anne Marie Albano, PhD
Department of Child Psychiatry
Columbia University
New York, New York

Darlys J. Alford, PhD
Psychology Department
University of Southern Mississippi
Gulfport, Mississippi

Tony Attwood, PhD
Asperger's Syndrome Clinic
Petrie
Queensland
Australia

Emily Becker-Weidman, PhD
Department of Psychiatry and
   Behavioral Sciences
Northwestern University
Chicago, Illinois

Robert F. Bornstein, PhD
Derner Institute
Adelphi University
Garden City, New York

Elissa J. Brown, PhD
NYU Child Study Center
New York, New York

Jeffrey D. Burke, PhD
Department of Psychiatry
Western Psychiatric Institute
   and Clinic
Pittsburgh, Pennsylvania

Sharon L. Cohan, PhD
Department of Child Psychiatry
Columbia University
New York, New York

Patricia R. Cohen, PhD
College of Physicians and Surgeons
Mailman School of Public Health
Columbia University
New York, New York

Thomas N. Crawford, PhD
College of Physicians and Surgeons
Columbia University
New York, New York

Nicki R. Crick, PhD
Institute of Child Development
University of Minnesota
Minneapolis, Minnesota

Robert A. DiTomasso, PhD
Department of Psychology
Philadelphia College of
   Osteopathic Medicine
Philadelphia, Pennsylvania

Carla D'Olio, MS
Center for the Study and Treatment
    of Anxiety
Department of Psychiatry
University of Pennsylvania
Philadelphia, Pennsylvania

Martin E. Franklin, PhD
Center for the Study and Treatment
    of Anxiety
Department of Psychiatry
University of Pennsylvania
Philadelphia, Pennsylvania

Arthur Freeman, EdD
Department of Psychology
Governors State University
University Park, Illinois

Rebecca Frontera, MA
Adler School of Professional
    Psychology
Chicago, Illinois

Gina M. Fusco, PsyD
Department of Psychology
Philadelphia College of
    Osteopathic Medicine
Philadelphia, Pennsylvania

Kathryn Gipe, MS
Department of Psychology
Philadelphia College of
    Osteopathic Medicine
Philadelphia, Pennsylvania

James B. Hale, PhD
Department of Psychology
Philadelphia College of
    Osteopathic Medicine
Philadelphia, Pennsylvania

James Hambrick, MA
Department of
    Child Psychiatry
Columbia University
New York, New York

Georges Han, PhD
Institute of Child Development
University of Minnesota
Minneapolis, Minnesota

Peter Kane, PhD
Warren Wright Adolescent Center
Department of Psychiatry
    and Behavioral Sciences
Northwestern University
    Medical School
Chicago, Illinois

William J. Lyddon, PhD
Department of Psychology
University of Southern
    Mississippi
Hattiesburg, Mississippi

John R. Lutzker, PhD
The Marcus Institute
Atlanta, Georgia

Jeffrey J. Magnavita, PhD
Graduate Institute of
    Professional Psychology
University of Hartford
West Hartford, Connecticut

George McCloskey, PhD
Department of Psychology
Philadelphia College of
    Osteopathic Medicine
Philadelphia, Pennsylvania

Amy McLaughlin, MS
Department of Psychology
Philadelphia College of
   Osteopathic Medicine
Philadelphia, Pennsylvania

Carrie Champ Morera, MS
Department of Psychology
Philadelphia College of
   Osteopathic Medicine
Philadelphia, Pennsylvania

Dianna Murray-Close, PhD
Institute of Child Development
University of Minnesota
Minneapolis, Minnesota

Corey Nigro, PsyD
Sheridan Shores Care and
   Rehabilitation Center
Chicago, Illinois

Joel Paris, MD
Department of Psychiatry
McGill University
Montreal, Quebec, Canada

John C. Piacentini, PhD
Department of Psychiatry
   and Biobehavioral Sciences
University of California, Los Angeles
Los Angeles, California

Mark A. Reinecke, PhD
Division of Psychology
Department of Psychiatry
   and Behavioral Sciences
Northwestern University
Chicago, Illinois

Joanna A. Robin, PhD
Department of Child Psychiatry
Columbia University
New York, New York

Tammie Ronen, PhD
Bob Shapell School of Social Work
Tel Aviv University
Tel-Aviv, Israel

Cynthia Cupit Swenson, PhD
Family Services Research Center
Department of Psychiatry
   and Behavioral Sciences
Medical University of South Carolina
Charleston, South Carolina

Stephen M. Timchack, MS
Department of Psychology
Philadelphia College of
   Osteopathic Medicine
Philadelphia, Pennsylvania

Yuma I. Tomes, PhD
Department of Psychology
Philadelphia College of
   Osteopathic Medicine
Philadelphia, Pennsylvania

Kathleen Woods, PhD
Institute of Child Development
University of Minnesota
Minneapolis, Minnesota

PART ONE

CHAPTER 1

Introduction

ARTHUR FREEMAN, MARK A. REINECKE, and YUMA I. TOMES

PERSONALITY TRAITS are pervasive and enduring patterns of perceiving, relating to, thinking about, and behaving in the environment that are exhibited in a wide range of social and personal contexts (*Diagnostic and Statistical Manual of Mental Disorders*, fourth edition, text revision [*DSM-IV-TR*]; American Psychiatric Association, 2000). In addition, personality traits might reflect how one perceives, thinks about, or acts toward oneself. Many behaviors may be considered strange, unusual, or self-punishing by an objective observer, but it is only when such behaviors are inflexible and maladaptive and cause significant functional impairment or subjective distress that they constitute personality disorders.

Three questions present themselves: (1) At what point does the mental health community intervene to modify behavior? (2) At what point do we determine that the situation is more chronic than acute? (3) At what point do we consider a pattern of behavior to be maladaptive? The essential feature of a personality disorder is that it is an enduring pattern of inner experience and behavior that deviates markedly from the expectations of the individual's culture (or subculture) and is manifested in at least two of the following areas: cognition, affectivity, and interpersonal functioning, or impulse control (*DSM* Criterion A). This enduring pattern is inflexible and pervasive across a broad range of personal and social situations (Criterion B) and leads to clinically significant distress or impairment in social, occupational, or other important areas of functioning (Criterion C). The pattern is stable and of long duration, and its onset can be traced back at least to adolescence or early adulthood (Criterion D). The pattern is not better accounted for as a manifestation or consequence of another mental disorder (Criterion E) and is not due to the direct physiological effects of a substance (e.g., a drug of abuse, a medication, exposure to a toxin) or a general medical condition (e.g., head trauma; Criterion F). Specific diagnostic criteria are provided for each of the personality disorders included in *DSM-IV*. The items in the criteria sets for each of the specific personality disorders are listed in order of decreasing diagnostic importance as measured by relevant data on diagnostic efficiency (when available).

The diagnosis of a personality disorder requires an evaluation of the individual's long-term patterns of functioning, and the particular personality features must be evident by early adulthood. The personality traits that define these disorders must also be distinguished from characteristics that emerge in response to specific situational stressors or more transient mental states (e.g., mood or anxiety disorders, substance intoxication). The clinician should assess the stability of personality traits over time and across different situations. Assessment can also be complicated by the fact that the characteristics that define a personality disorder may not be considered problematic by the individual (i.e., the traits are often ego-syntonic).

Obviously, judgments about personality functioning must take into account the individual's ethnic, cultural, and social background. Especially when evaluating someone from a different background, it is useful for the clinician to obtain additional information from informants who are familiar with that background.

Clinicians, especially those working in inpatient (acute treatment) and residential (long-term treatment) settings, typically see children and adolescents who meet criteria for a personality disorder. However, it is not the case that when adolescents reach the age of majority (typically 18) they are rewarded with graduation from school, enrollment in the military, a new car, and the official designation of a personality disorder.

Rather than try to find euphemistic terms, titles, or diagnoses for what are clinical precursors and parallels to the adult disorders, this book explores the clinical reality of personality disorders in childhood. For some children and adolescents, the disorder may cause significant and severe discomfort and dysfunction. For others, the personality style is ego-syntonic and the distress comes from others (family, peers, school). For still other children and adolescents, the disorder is currently functional; for example, a compliant, dependent, obsessive-compulsive, hard-working, success-driven, and demanding child will succeed at school and be seen as a hard worker and a superior student who wins awards, certificates, and medals for his or her academic performance.

Kernberg, Weiner, and Bardenstein (2000), Bleiberg (2001), Freeman and Rigby (2003), and Freeman and Duff (2006) have raised the question: Are children who manifest certain traits displaying what may be precursors to later personality disorders, or can they be diagnosed as having a personality disorder during childhood or adolescence? Clinicians have responded to this question in various ways, ranging from the affirmative to the negative and with a host of ethical, legal, and conceptual issues evoked for support.

ARGUMENTS AGAINST DIAGNOSING PERSONALITY DISORDERS IN CHILDREN AND ADOLESCENTS

One argument against childhood or adolescent diagnosis is the desire that a child not be burdened by the diagnosis of a personality disorder until he or she has reached early adulthood (whenever that is). Maturation into adulthood at age 18 is a Western tenet that may not apply in other cultures or in some subgroups of Western culture. The right to vote, bear arms, and carry the diagnosis of a personality disorder should not be mandated by an arbitrary and culturally enforced entry point for adulthood. Most clinicians generally agree that personality pathology originates in childhood and adolescence, and most adults with a personality disorder readily identify childhood and adolescent manifestations of the disorder, so it is surprising that there is any hesitation regarding early diagnosis. Addressing a mental health disorder as early as possible should be given the utmost priority, as is true for any medical disorder.

Another argument against diagnosing personality disorders in childhood is that children's bodies and personalities are rapidly developing and in a constant state of flux (Bleiberg, 2001; Freeman & Duff, 2006; Freeman & Rigby, 2003). Therefore, an inaccurate view of the patient is obtained by using a single snapshot to diagnose such a serious mental health disorder. Our response is that any time clinicians assess a patient they will get only a glimpse or a small portion of the overall picture. With additional evaluation data, school reports, and reports of parents and other caretakers, friends, and siblings, the original snapshot is enhanced in an almost digital manner. Now much finer details are obvious, where before there was a broad and sweeping view. To avoid assumptions and unnecessary generalizations, it is vital to obtain as much information as possible and gain valid corroboration. Clinicians can observe or receive reports of how the child or adolescent is interacting in his or her current environment. Assumptions may be made about how patients function across the variety of contexts in which they live and work, but ultimately a comprehensive history is necessary to complete the picture. The fact is that behaviors will most likely change across different contexts, and overall patterns of behavior will also be modified. We further respond to this criticism by pointing out that all diagnoses are conditional and can and should be revised as more information is obtained and the picture becomes larger and clearer.

For those who point to the "illegality" of diagnosing children and adolescents with a personality disorder, we recommend reading more than the criteria sets. Alone, these advise that the problem should be manifest "beginning by early adulthood." This statement does not say that a disorder begins *in* early adulthood, but rather *by* early adulthood, thereby implying that it begins earlier. In point of fact, *DSM-IV-TR* (American Psychiatric Association, 2000, p. 687) states:

> Personality disorders may be applied to children or adolescents in those relatively unusual instances in which the individual's particular maladaptive personality traits appear to be pervasive, persistent, and unlikely to be limited to a particular developmental stage or an episode of an Axis I disorder. It should be recognized that the traits of a Personality Disorder that appear in childhood will often not persist unchanged into adult life. To diagnose a Personality Disorder in an individual under age 18 years, the features must have been present for at least 1 year. The one exception to this is Antisocial Personality Disorder, which cannot be diagnosed in individuals under age 18 years. Although, by definition, a Personality Disorder requires an onset no later than early adulthood, individuals may not come to clinical attention until relatively late in life.

The inherent problem with personality disorders is that they often become "carryover" diagnoses. This leads to another popular argument against diagnosing personality disorders in youth. The belief is that teachers, clinicians, and all those involved in the care of the youth will simply give up on him or her after learning of such a "terminal diagnosis." The argument asks, "How can you label a child like that? Don't you know that diagnosis is going to stick with the child for the rest of his or her life?" We readily admit that this is a possible scenario, however, we believe no more so than with any other diagnosis. It may, in fact, be far less damaging than being diagnosed as an adult with Bipolar Disorder, for which the patient will need to maintain a pharmacological regimen for a lifetime. The stabilization of symptoms such as impulsiveness, depression, and poor anger control will be beneficial, and in some cases necessary, for treatment to even begin. However, without recognition of the patient's core beliefs, attitudes, and pathology, stabilization and maintenance is all that may ever be gained.

Another popular argument against diagnosing personality disorders in youth is that teachers, clinicians, and others involved in the care of these youth will simply give up on them after learning of the "terminal diagnosis." Those who argue this point fear that the label of, for instance, Antisocial Personality Disorder will stick with the child for the rest of his or her life.

We readily admit that this is a possible scenario; however, such labeling occurs with many other diagnoses. We believe it is more important that diagnosis take place as early as possible so that symptoms such as impulsiveness, depression, and poor anger control can be stabilized and treatment can begin. If we wait until the child is an adult, the damage is done, and stabilization and maintenance via a lifetime pharmacological regimen may be all we can hope to gain.

ASSESSMENT

Any child or adolescent who warrants an Axis II diagnosis must receive a comprehensive assessment. The clinician must evaluate the child's behaviors, affect, and cognition across a variety of situations, as well as obtain a thorough family and developmental history. Every attempt should be made to contact current and previous teachers, family members, and primary care providers. This aids in the assessment of the chronicity and pervasiveness of the current issues (Freeman & Rigby, 2003).

Based on Freeman and Rigby (2003), we would pose the following assessment questions:

- Does the reported and/or observed behavior have a normal developmental explanation? For example, a dependent 3-year-old is normal. The same dependence in a 15-year-old is a basis for concern.
- Does the behavior change over time or setting? Is it cyclical, variable, and unpredictable, or is it constant, consistent, and pre-

dictable? By definition, personality disorders are pervasive and persistent and will not likely show great variability.

- Could the behavior be the result of discrepancies between the child's chronological age and his or her cognitive, emotional, social, or behavioral age? Again, the issue of developmental stages must be assessed.

- Does the child function similarly in different environments? For example, does the behavior relate to the child's placement at home or in school?

- Is the behavior culturally related? Are the observed behaviors, for example, difficulty in making and maintaining eye contact, culturally based?

- Who has made the referral, and why was it made at this point? Is it because the child is disturbed or disturbing to others, and why?

- Is there agreement between parents, or between parents and teachers, on the cause and purpose of and need for the referral? The issue of pervasiveness must be assessed.

- What are the expectations of the clinician in responding to the referral? For example, how does the child's behavior compare or contrast with the behavior of other children in the family or socioeconomic and sociocultural setting? How does the child's behavior compare or contrast with the behavior of other children in that age or social group?

- What is the history of the child's behavior in terms of length of existence; duration when stimulated; and ability of the child to control, contain, or withdraw from the behavior? History and context will illuminate the picture.

- Does the child see the behavior as something that he or she is interested in modifying? The ego-syntonic nature of the behavior is emblematic of personality disorders. In fact, with successful and highly driven children, their obsessive style is rewarded by both the school and the parents.

- What are the differing views of the child's behavior? Are the clinician's sources of data reliable? For example, what is the parent report of the child's behavior at home? How does the child relate to siblings, neighborhood friends, clubs, sports, organizations, church activities, adult relatives, pets, and self-care?

- Has there been recurrent physical, emotional, sexual, or verbal abuse? The parental view of discipline versus child abuse is a key element to be considered.

- Within societal norms, is the parental behavior inappropriately sexual or seductive? Is incest suspected?

- What is the parent's view of privacy for the child? How are boundaries established and maintained in the family? Are the parents inappropriately, unreasonably, or unjustifiably interfering with the child's relationships with other children?

- Within societal norms, are the parents inappropriately involved with the child's personal hygiene beyond the child's needs?

- What is the impetus for the current referral? Are the caregiver's intentions altruistic, or is he or she attempting to obtain disability, social security, custody, or some other accommodation? If so, is it a reasonable request?

- When assessing current behaviors, it is necessary to determine what function those same behaviors have served in the past. The twin questions of the value and the purpose of the behavior must be explored.

- How has the family thus far reacted? Are they embarrassed? Has psychological intervention been expected? Is it welcome? Is this part of the family norm? Are other family members also receiving psychological services?

- With adolescents, the history of dating and relationships should be explored.

- When assessing the constancy and consistency of the behavior, has it been determined if there were any unsettling events recently, such as moving, transferring to a new school, the death of a family member or friend? Have there been any recent family illnesses? A time line may be beneficial to assess for the compounding of multiple, back-to-back events.

- How is the child's or adolescent's perception of self different from his or her ideal self or the person that others would like him or her to be? For example, the obsessive-compulsive may feel constant pressure from the real or perceived influence of others to be perfect, as evidenced by the core belief "I must not err."
- Who does the child consider a support or a stable figure in his or her life?

DIAGNOSING PERSONALITY DISORDERS: A CULTURAL PERSPECTIVE

Freeman and Rigby (2003) express concern that diagnosing personality disorders in children and adolescents carries with it the potential for malpractice. Care must be taken to avoid inappropriate diagnosis applied to socially and culturally different groups. Behavior must deviate markedly from the expectations of the individual's culture. The *DSM-IV-TR* (American Psychiatric Association, 2000, p. 686) clearly states:

> Judgments about personality functioning must take into account the individual's ethnic, cultural and social background. Personality disorders should not be confused with problems following immigration or with the expression of habits, customs, or religious and political values professed by the individual's culture of origin.

It is important to obtain additional information from informants who are familiar with the patient's cultural background.

The prevalence of personality disorder diagnoses has increased over the years (Iwamasa, Larrabee, & Merritt, 2000). This increase has been seen across various ethnic and cultural groups. Freeman and Duff (2006) point to diagnoses of personality disorder used when the individual's behavior is at variance with the broader society, even though such behavior may be consonant with subgroup behaviors. Solomon (1992) discussed how applying clinical diagnoses to ethnic minorities may be detrimental because of cultural differences in the expression of symptomatology, the use of instruments and evaluations that are culturally questionable and possibly invalid and unreliable, clinician bias and prejudice, and institutional racism.

The need to examine the role of ethnicity in psychopathology in general, and in personality disorders specifically, is of particular importance given what Iwamasa and colleagues (Iwamasa, Larrabee, & Merritt, 2000) have called the "browning" of the United States. In 1993, the American Psychological Association adopted "Guidelines for Providers of Psychological Services to Ethnic, Linguistic, and Culturally Diverse Populations," signifying that professional mental health providers must provide effective assessment and treatment interventions to an increasingly diverse population.

CULTURE

Culture can be defined as the structure and practices that uphold a particular social order by legitimizing certain values, expectations, and patterns of behavior: the ideas of a given people at a given time (Tomes, 2004). Culture comprises traditional ideas and related values and is the product of learning and sharing transmitted from one generation to the next (Diller, 2004).

Race

Although many people use the words *race* and *ethnicity* interchangeably, they do so incorrectly. Wilkinson (1993, p. 16) defines race as "a category of persons who are related by a common heredity or ancestry and who are perceived and responded to in terms of external features or traits." Race is the biological makeup of a particular group, based on heredity and genes and not necessarily the environment.

ETHNICITY AND ETHNIC GROUPS

An ethnic group collectively shares a common history, culture, values, behaviors, and other characteristics (Tomes, 2004). Differences in affective, attitudinal, and behavioral patterns across cultures have been termed "ethnic patterns" (Canino & Spurlock, 2000). Hale-Benson (1982, p. 26) further defines ethnic groups as "people who have a common history and generally share a language, a religion, or a racial identity. Each ethnic group forms a subculture with its own attitudes and behaviors." It is within these subgroups that the norms and mores for acceptable behaviors are generated. These behaviors are modeled at home, in peer groups, in religious settings, and in educational settings. For example, the behaviors acceptable in one ethnic neighborhood may be considered anywhere from unacceptable to illegal in another neighborhood or by a different ethnic group inasmuch as the behaviors violate the expectations and norms of the latter group.

CULTURAL INFLUENCES

ETHNIC IDENTITY BEHAVIORS

As cultures reflect eclectic behavioral patterns, it is important for clinicians to acknowledge children's acquisition and maintenance of their ethnic group's patterns. A number of authors have explored the value of children's development based on their ethnicity (K. Clark, 1965; Goodman, 1964; McGoldrick, 1998; McGoldrick, Giordano, & Garcia-Preto, 2005; Porter, 1971). It has been postulated that children as young as 3 are aware of aspects of their ethnic identity (McGoldrick, 1998; McGoldrick et al., 2005; Porter, 1971). Ethnic development and identification continue in adolescence, through the adolescent's interactions with peer groups and by responding to peer perceptions (Canino & Spurlock, 2000). It is through their cognitive processing that children and adolescents give meaning to their personal and group identification with their culture and ethnicity. They make a determination on how to respond to the culture within the self ("Who am I as a . . . ?").

They must also respond to the multitude of others both within and outside of their group. Their reactions to ethnic stimuli may depend on certain cues and reinforcers emanating from their immediate family, their subgroup, or the larger society. These ethnic reactions may be affective, perceptual, behavioral, systemic, or cognitive. For some ethnic and culturally diverse children and adolescents, the style, manner, and content of the perceptions of individuals outside of their ethnic group is critically important, compared to other ethnic groups who place greater value on within-group or on intraethnic perception. According to research by Gibbs (1989), Black children and adolescents tend to use other Blacks as a comparison group rather than their White counterparts. When a child or adolescent is biracial, a different set of norms may arise as he or she affiliates with one race more than the other. This affiliation may be situational, with affective, perceptual, behavioral, or cognitive elements. An adolescent's ethnic identity behavior may be more salient depending on the situation. For instance, in some situations, an adolescent may respond differently depending on the status of the group and its cultural homogeneity or heterogeneity. Changes in a child's ethnic awareness may result from changes in cohort or generational groups, varying interactions among influential individuals, and normal developmental changes (Canino & Spurlock, 2000). For example, many third-generation Mexican American children may not know much of their cultural history or their language but may still identify with their ethnic group. Jewish children may have a Jewish identity but not practice or observe prescribed rituals or holidays. The term "fallen-away Catholic" describes someone who no longer attends church or no longer believes in Catholic doctrine or dogma but nevertheless identifies as Catholic.

CULTURAL DEVIANCE

In American culture and society, there is a consensus that the broad range of psychopathology exists within all ethnic and racial cultures, though the manifestations of these disorders are often characterized differently by the members of that culture or may appear with a different flavor to the clinician. The problem facing many societies is how to provide an appropriate diagnosis, particularly as it relates to the standards and expectations of the culture. For example, an American Indian adolescent who is spiritually connected to the earth may have daily conversations with trees and other inanimate objects. He may isolate himself to increase his connection to the earth; he may use natural substances to increase his sensitivity, or he may fast or appear to be self-punishing to increase his relationship with the spirits. By his culture's standards, he is practicing traditionally held beliefs. However, according to the majority view that prevails in the West, this adolescent may be diagnosed as having a severe disorder, which may include a personality disorder; he may be hospitalized and quickly medicated so as to not become more "disturbed" and to be able to "adjust" and behave more "normally."

Clearly, more than one type of deviance is likely to exist in any culture. As a result, a person may be singled out based on some uncharacteristic element that distinguishes him or her from same-age individuals. Children's temperament is a common focus of attention in American culture. It is not uncommon to see parents or guardians trying to quiet their infants and toddlers because of the setting or cultural expectations. In contrast, in some African tribes (e.g., in Zaire) infants are encouraged to cry and yell regardless of the environment to express their existence. As the culture or community evokes this display of emotion, children are further encouraged as they grow to always speak their mind.

How, then, does a psychologist determine what is due to a true (personality) disorder and what is a result of the person's honoring cultural norms? Expectations surrounding child development and rearing practices vary throughout the world. No one culture or ethnic group can lay claim to the best method to raise a child. Yet the expectation is that a child or adolescent will reflect universal cultural expectations, which initiates the controversy of appropriate diagnosing. Milestones such as vocal expressions, walking without assistance, independence, and mastery of fine and gross motor skills acquire different meanings in different cultures.

Cultural norms are additionally influenced by the level of acculturation of a given family, even if they are indigenous to the country of interest (Canino & Spurlock, 2000). As a result, language and communication are critical when assessing for any type of disorder. Further, children and adolescents must be assessed within the framework of their familial and cultural expectations and not just those of the majority culture. For example, whereas some Western cultures place high value on early accurate vocalizations, other cultures equally value solitude and a slightly slower pace of language development. Therefore, children coming from a less verbal background may present characteristics commonly associated with a personality disorder (silence and withdrawal), but in actuality they are reflecting cultural norms (e.g., deference to authority).

Non-majority group communication may also signal differences between specific groups and the majority culture. For example, Latino and Caribbean parents often teach their children to be physically and emotionally expressive. It is expected that these children be creative and excited regardless of the situation or conversation. As they attempt to relate to one another or others outside of their culture, they may violate the "close proximity" or "personal space" rules held by many Americans. On the other hand, Asian American children are less likely to be so expressive and may not even make eye contact while communicating with an older person or a person perceived as having higher status. Within American Indian culture, emphasis is customarily placed on nonverbal communication. Personal feelings such as anger and discontent are not openly expressed (Katz, 1981).

Similar to Latino and Caribbean children, African American youth are encouraged to be animated and vocal when expressing even mundane or common events or occurrences. During this display of exuberance, their voices may reach a high pitch, which is often confused with yelling or screaming by majority Western standards. As a result, when African American children enter into formal educational settings, there are usually several cultural barriers between the school system and the students. As African American children may have been taught to speak up, in terms of both content and volume, teachers may have difficulty when this behavior appears to be a challenge to their authority. The behavior may even be diagnosed as Attention-Deficit/Hyperactivity Disorder (ADHD), calling for treatment, often medication. In many cases, the disequilibrium that has prevailed is simply that of cultural imbalances between teachers' expectations and the child's culture.

LINGUISTICS AND LANGUAGE

Another aspect of culture is the linguistic skills used by members of various cultural and ethnic groups. Language not only offers a means of intra- and interpersonal communication among members of ethnic groups, but also allows a cognitive restructuring of the child's or adolescent's world (Hilliard, 1983). However, language can create a problem in assessing a child's or adolescent's ability or level of current functioning. For example, "Navajo children usually adopt a slow, methodical speech pattern. When the children pause, Anglo-American teachers often regard this as a signal that they have completed their sentence" (Canino & Spurlock, 2000, pp. 60–61). This pattern of speech can present similar problems in personality assessment. In the administration of tests such as the Minnesota Multiphasic Personality Inventory (MMPI) and the Thematic Apperception Test (TAT), individuals are encouraged to respond in a timely matter, and not doing so may adversely affect their overall score.

The use of words, phrases, or terms that may have particular meaning within a subgroup may become problematic when used in the larger community. This is true not only of slang, but of words and terms taken from a native language.

PSYCHOSOCIAL ENVIRONMENT

There are two environmental and functioning cultural factors that clinicians must consider when assessing children: (1) social support and (2) interpretation of social stressors. In the Latino culture, individuals such as the *compadre (godfather)*, the *comadre (godmother)*, and the priest are called upon when the parents are not able to adequately provide financially for their children (Paniagua, 2001). Similarly, when trials befall African Americans, research has supported that they are more likely to confer with a minister (usually of a nonaffiliated church) or a community leader for assistance (Boyd-Franklin, 1989). As a result, ministers and community leaders may become surrogate parents for the children, at times adopting a new mindset, as to how to teach children to deal with adversity. This aspect of community can be seen in the Asian American culture as well, where the extended family plays a significant role in providing financial assistance, child care, and support to new immigrants, extending to many other levels of community support.

As children and adolescents develop, they encounter more experiences with the real world. The clinician must ascertain the context and meaning of their perceptions and not dismiss the perceptions as reflective of racial discrimination or stress. It is important for the clinician to understand that these types of perceptions can be easily misdiagnosed as mental disorder symptoms. For example, a question on a measure of intelligence asks, "What is the thing to do when a child much smaller than you starts a fight?" Clearly, "everyone" knows that the correct (the 2-point answer) is "Walk away, don't fight, he's much smaller." Yet in many cultures, to allow an individual who is smaller and possibly weaker to take advantage of one is a signal that one is weak; the answer that may be most correct or useful in such cultures is "Punch him in the face and warn him to never try that again or he will get far greater punishment." This response is scored a zero for violating majority culture rules.

HEALTHY CULTURE

The residual effects of slavery and racism are felt today by many African Americans. These hideous crimes have left indelible scars on

African Americans and on the American culture. One significant cultural aspect that has emerged for African Americans in particular is the development of what might be termed *adaptive cultural paranoia* (Paniagua, 2005). The experience of being a member of a minority (so designated even when outnumbering the majority culture in particular settings) has led many African Americans to be suspicious not only of White Americans, but also of African Americans who have apparently embraced White culture. For example, an African American psychologist who holds a doctorate from a prestigious university was interviewing an African American adolescent. The adolescent began the interview by stating, "You dress and talk White." The psychologist responded that he "dressed and spoke well." The adolescent's remark could be misperceived as evidence of a suspicious and paranoid style, meeting some criteria for a personality disorder, rather than evidence of cultural difference.

ASSESSMENT

Due to cultural bias, personality disorders have the potential to be diagnosed more than any other disorders. For example, in many Eastern cultures parents choose whom their children should marry. The involvement parents have in this decision provides a striking contrast to how Western cultures view marriage partners. In most Western cultures, parents tend to offer counsel to their children, but recognize that the final decision rests with the individual. "The potential for bias may be greatest when the mental health professional comes from a different culture from the person being assessed" (Blum & Pfohl, 1998, p. 204).

SCREENERS

Diagnostically based interviews for assessing personality disorders in different cultural groups tend to yield fairly consistent information. The reliability of these instruments is complex and varies. According to Zimmerman (1994), interrater reliabilities are higher for joint compared to separate interviews, and interrater reliability of highly skilled versus newly trained interviewers are expected to differ. Because of this degree of reliability, clinicians have considerable power in interpreting the eligibility criteria of a child or adolescent being diagnosed as having a personality disorder.

When selecting an instrument for use in diagnosing children or adolescents with a personality disorder, an important factor is organization and format. In some instruments, questions may be grouped diagnostically (e.g., *DSM-IV-TR* and the Structured Clinical Interview for DSM Axis I Disorders [SCID-II]), by topic (e.g., interpersonal issues versus intrapersonal issues), or by a version or format (e.g., parent version, student version, teacher version). In this categorical system, the personality disorder criteria are assessing for manifestations of the given personality disorder. This arrangement helps to accurately estimate whether a particular behavior exemplifies a core characteristic of the target behavior (L. A. Clark & Harrison, 2001). However, this is a potential weakness in this approach, especially as it relates to culture. If a child or adolescent appears to be exhibiting more characteristics for the first two criteria, patterns of inner experience that deviate from cultural expectation or enduring inflexible patterns across broad personal and social experiences, the clinician may become less objective and be more likely to classify the child as having a personality disorder without additional probing. It is through probing and the use of corroborating information that the clinician may uncover cultural information that supports the child's responses to the interview format and not deviance from the beliefs of the dominant population.

ACCULTURATION

The family culture of the child or adolescent is often threatened by the child's level of acculturation to a new country, environment, or even social setting. Most clinicians acknowledge that transition for a child or adolescent is difficult, but they may fail to take the level of acculturation into consideration when diagnosing the individual. The process of acculturation may in itself be the focus of clinical attention. Paniagua (2001) suggests several acculturation scales that can be used to assess children and adolescents. The Brief Acculturation Scale is recommended for clinicians and others who would like to perform a quick assessment of acculturation in children.

This level of assessment also looks into intellectual functioning and psychopathologies among culturally diverse groups. The *DSM-IV* suggests using "psychological tests in which the person's relevant characteristics are represented in the standardization sample of the test or . . . employing an examiner familiar with the aspects of the individual ethnic or cultural background" (Paniagua, 2001, p. 16). This recommendation may be excellent for diagnosis of mental retardation and learning disabilities, but there is an inherent problem: Just because a clinician comes from a cultural background similar to that of the child or adolescent does not mean that he or she has a complete grasp of the individual's experiences. It is possible that a White clinician of low socioeconomic status (SES) working with a low-SES African American adolescent may have more in common than a high-SES African American clinician working with a low-SES African American child.

COGNITIVE STYLES

The work of Jean Piaget has been a universal hallmark for understanding cognitive development. He determined the maturational and biological factors in the development of cognition. Researchers such as Jensen (1980) strongly believe that biological aspects play significant roles in cognition, but new scholars are acknowledging the importance of culture in accounting for differences among groups. This new approach looks at the relationship between one's culture and the kinds of cognitive skills one develops (Hale-Benson, 1982). For example, African Americans, in general, tend to be a verbal and loquacious ethnic group that has a history of oral tradition and passing down of stories. These verbal exchanges provide evidence for children who have a field-dependent/global cognitive style because they too are more likely to discuss material in order to comprehend information better in multiple contexts.

OVERDIAGNOSIS

The fear of overdiagnosing a particular pathology is real for many culturally diverse children and adolescents. The prevalence of ADHD can be seen throughout America's school landscape, and the epidemic appears to be worsening as teachers come into contact with multiple ethnic groups and cultures. One reason for overdiagnosis is that some of the assessment instruments used to determine pathology with a culturally diverse group were normed primarily on Anglo-Americans and so lack cross-cultural validity. Another reason for overdiagnosing is a lack of cultural awareness. Clinicians who are unfamiliar with the practices and beliefs of their multicultural clients my incorrectly diagnosis and report psychopathology.

PROJECTIVE TECHNIQUES

Projective measures have been used since the early 1930s to diagnose psychopathology among members of the majority culture (Abel, 1948). Time has revealed that these measures present inaccurate data for less well-known groups, such as minority populations. Tests such as the TAT and the Rorschach Inkblot Test provide valid information relevant to the dominant White majority but do little to account for cultural representation and individual adaptations (Abel, 1948). Further, the problem of interpretation is compounded, as demonstrated in the United States by the large number of immigrants (children included) who must adapt to an unfamiliar role in life. Biases enter as clinicians use their own frame of reference as a rubric to make judgments regarding the dysfunction and pathology of children and adolescents.

Attempts to make the tests relevant are often unsuccessful. An example is Thompson's (1950) modification of the TAT. Thompson had each of the TAT plates redone with African American figures. The effect was limited use inasmuch as the examiners at the time were primarily White. Thompson's TAT plates would be rejected today because the 1950 figures appear to be inaccurate and even insulting stereotypes.

REDUCING CULTURAL BIAS

The *DSM-IV-TR* (American Psychiatric Association, 2000) made efforts to reduce cultural bias. The first step called for examining individuals in the context of their cultural background. It is important for the clinician to consider the environment in which the child is being reared, the child's family constellation, the child's significant relationships, and cultural norms outside of the majority culture. For example, in the criteria for Schizotypal Personality Disorder, "odd" is used to describe various behaviors. The ensuing question should be, "Is the odd behavior consistent or inconsistent with cultural norms and expectations?" If the behavior reflects traditional elements common to the child's culture, then the child cannot be diagnosed with this personality disorder.

The second safeguard included in the *DSM-IV* deals with the magnitude of difficulty the disorder places on the child or adolescent. The disorder has to lead "to clinically significant distress or impairment in social, occupational, or other important areas of functioning" (American Psychiatric Association, 1994, p. 630).

Although there is no fairy-tale, culture-free assessment, clinicians should make a concerted effort to employ the least biased assessment strategies. Paniagua (2001) suggests that clinicians select and use strategies appropriate to the individual client's culture and ethnicity. For example, when assessing a person for Dependent Personality Disorder, the clinician should not rely solely on standardized tests (e.g., MMPI). The results of such tests can be enhanced with an assessment strategy in which the adolescent records actual behavior indicative of dependence on another person. The additional information would help to tease out what may be cultural norms rather than dependence. Overall, diagnostic instruments minimally, at best, recognize how cultural factors can influence the expression and definition of Schizophrenia and affective and personality disorders.

CONCLUSIONS

Determining the presence of a personality disorder in a child or adolescent is a daunting task. It is even more difficult when the child or adolescent is from a population different from the population the measure was normed on or when the race of the clinician may bias the diagnosis. As Paniagua (2001, p. 30) states, "Because all behaviors are learned in a cultural context and presented in a cultural context, accurate assessment, meaningful understanding, and appropriate intervention must attend to the cultural context." It is important for clinicians to incorporate some understanding of acculturation and enculturation processes in our thinking, as it can only benefit the children and adolescents being served.

Protocols and research on each of the personality disorders in children and adolescents must be developed. We must develop new and more effective diagnostic tools and sharpen our experience with existing tools. We have to evaluate best practices for treatment: What works best, with whom, in what time frame, and under what circumstances? We have to be able to determine ideal goals for treatment. We have to be ready to pay the price in staff time, clinician effort, and economic cost to treat these children.

Choosing to ignore the reality of personality disorders among children and adolescents, to downplay the problem, or to search for euphemistic terms all deny the severity and impact of these disorders on the present and future life experiences of children. The sooner we can accept the reality of personality disorders in children and adolescents, the sooner we will focus our efforts on appropriate assessment, conceptualization, diagnosis, and treatment. Finally, to recognize the reality of personality disorders can, ideally, relieve the suffering of these children.

REFERENCES

Abel, T. M. (1948). The Rorschach test in the study of culture. *Rorschach Research Exchange, 12,* 19–93.

American Psychiatric Association. (1994). *Diagnostic and statistical manual of mental disorders* (4th ed.). Washington, DC: Author.

American Psychiatric Association. (2000). *Diagnostic and statistical manual of mental disorders* (4th ed., text rev.). Washington, DC: Author.

American Psychological Association. (1993). Guidelines for providers of psychological services to ethnic, linguistic, and culturally diverse populations. *American Psychologist, 48,* 45–48.

Bleiberg, E. (2001). *Treating personality disorders in children and adolescents: A relational approach.* New York: Guilford Press.

Blum, N., & Pfohl, B. (1998). Personality disorders. In J. Williams & K. Ell (Eds.), *Advances in mental health research* (pp. 203–216). Washington, DC: National Association of Social Workers Press.

Boyd-Franklin, N. (1989). *Black family therapy: A multisystems approach.* New York: Guilford Press.

Canino, I., & Spurlock, J. (2000). *Culturally diverse children and adolescents: Assessment, diagnosis, and treatment* (2nd ed.). New York: Guilford Press.

Clark, K. (1965). *Dark ghetto: Dilemmas of social power.* New York: Harper & Row.

Clark, L. A., & Harrison, J. A. (2001). Assessment instruments. In W. J. Livesley (Ed.), *Handbook of personality disorders* (pp. 277–306). New York: Guilford Press.

Diller, J. V. (2004). *Cultural diversity.* Belmont, CA: Brooks/Cole.

Freeman, A. (2004). Cognitive-behavioral treatment of personality disorders in childhood and adolescence. In R. Leahy (Ed.), *Contemporary cognitive therapy: Theory, research, and practice.* New York: Guilford Press.

Freeman, A., & Duff, J. M. (2006). Personality disorders among children and adolescents: Are euphemistic labels hindering time-sensitive interventions? In R. Menutti, A. Freeman, and R. W. Christner (Eds.), *Cognitive behavioral interventions in educational settings* (pp. 221–238). New York: Routledge.

Freeman, A., & Rigby, A. (2003). Personality disorders among children and adolescents: Is it an unlikely diagnosis? In M. A. Reinecke, F. M. Dattilio, & A. Freeman (Eds.), *Cognitive therapy with children and adolescents: A casebook for clinical practice* (2nd ed., 434–464). New York: Guilford Press.

Gibbs, J. T. (1989). Biracial adolescents. In J. T. Gibbs, L. N. Huang, & Associates (Eds.), *Children of color: Psychological interventions with minority youth* (pp. 322–350). San Francisco: Jossey-Bass.

Goodman, M. E. (1964). *Race awareness in young children* (Rev. ed.). New York: Collier.

Hale-Benson, J. E. (1982). *Black children* (Rev. ed.). Baltimore: Brigham Young University Press.

Hilliard, A. G. (1983). Psychological factors associated with language in the education of the African-American child. *Journal of Negro Education, 52,* 24–34.

Iwamasa, G. Y., Larrabee, A. L., & Merritt, R. D. (2000). Are personality disorder criteria ethnically biased? A card-sort analysis. *Cultural Diversity and Ethnic Minority Psychology, 6*(3), 284–296.

Jensen, A. R. (1980). *Bias in mental testing.* New York: Free Press.

Katz, P. (1981). Psychotherapy with native adolescents. *Canadian Journal of Psychiatry, 26,* 455–459.

Kernberg, P. F., Weiner, A. S., & Bardenstein, K. K. (2000). *Personality disorders in children and adolescents.* New York: Basic Books.

McGoldrick, M. (1998). *Revising family therapy through: Race, culture, and gender in clinical practice.* New York: Guilford Press.

McGoldrick, M., Giordano, J., & Garcia-Preto, N. (Eds.). (2005). *Ethnicity and family therapy.* (3rd ed.). New York: Guilford Press.

Paniagua, F. A. (2001). *Diagnosis in a multicultural context.* Thousand Oaks, CA: Sage.

Paniagua, F. A. (2005). *Assessing and treating culturally diverse clients* (3rd ed.). Thousand Oaks, CA: Sage.

Porter, J. D. (1971). *Black child, White child: The development of racial attitudes.* Cambridge, MA: Harvard University Press.

Solomon, I. (1992). *The encyclopedia of evolving techniques in psychodynamic therapy.* Lanham, MD: Aronson.

Thompson, R. (1950). *The Thompson modification of the Thematic Apperception Test.* Boston: Harvard University Press.

Tomes, Y. I. (2004). Cognitive style, achievement, and ethnicity: A study in higher education. *Dissertation Abstracts International 66*(01). (UMI No. 3161498).

Wilkinson, D. (1993). Family ethnicity in America. In H. P. McAdoo (Ed.), *Family ethnicity: Strength in diversity* (pp. 15–59). Newbury Park, CA: Sage.

Zimmerman, M. (1994). Diagnosing personality disorders: A review of issues and research methods. *Archives of General Psychiatry, 51,* 225–245.

CHAPTER 2

The Role of Developmental Components in Treating Children with Personality Disorders

TAMMIE RONEN

CHILDREN ARE constantly changing. These changes involve all areas of the child's life: physical growth, age, cognitions, emotions, and social functioning. These changes also mean that the view of the child and his or her problems varies as the child develops; often, what is considered to be a problem one day will not be considered a problem the next, and vice versa. Consequently, during childhood, assessment as well as treatment and evaluation should include developmental components as a basic consideration in making decisions about the need to treat the child and in planning and conducting that treatment.

Effective interventions with children should directly relate child disturbances to developmental considerations. Only through knowledge of normal developmental processes can one begin to understand deviations in development and their importance for assessment and intervention (Forehand & Weirson, 1993; Ronen, 1997, 2003). Children's personality disorders, like other kinds of disorders, cannot be assessed or treated without considering the child's developmental stage. What might be considered signals for personality disorders at one stage could just be part and parcel of normal childhood behavior at another stage of development.

The purpose of the present chapter is to enhance the reader's sensitivity to the importance of developmental components as a backdrop to understanding personality disorders and to explicate the need to include these components in therapeutic decision making, from initial assessment all the way through to a successful outcome. To furnish developmental information, this chapter first focuses on what development is and what developmental considerations need to be taken into account, and then pinpoints how assessment and treatment are influenced by specific developmental components.

DEVELOPMENT VERSUS GROWTH

To thoroughly understand development, a differentiation must be made between heredity, growth, and development.

Heredity is the human being's inherent nature or internal components. The overall genetic endowment defines, within broad limits, an individual's basic overall potential and predisposition.

Growth refers to actual physiological, biological, and motoric changes that unfold in the human being from birth until maturity. Two issues relating to growth should be emphasized. First, growth varies from individual to individual; second, critical or sensitive periods emerge throughout development that will or will not meet the individual's unique needs and thus enable optimal growth. A critical period implies a time of ideal receptivity or greatest ease in acquiring or modifying a particular function.

Development refers to the changing structure of behavior over the life span, indicating not only changing degrees of organismic complexity but also changes in the biological and psychological substructures emerging and unfolding in social surroundings (Shapiro, 1995). In this chapter, I mainly emphasize cognitive development: changes in the complexity of functioning or degree of performance skills over the course of physical growth (Sahler & McAnarney, 1981).

It is important to emphasize that analogues exist between physical growth and development. Change does not occur in one realm but throughout the entire organism; therefore, we expect reciprocal influences between various realms.

Developmental components thus constitute crucial features for any professional attempting to assess, treat, and evaluate children. These constantly changing components include age, cognitive stage, acquisition of language, ability to process information, and emotional and social skills. Each of these components, as well as gender considerations, is described with an emphasis on how each should affect therapy.

AGE AS AN IMPORTANT
DEVELOPMENTAL COMPONENT

Age criteria are often crucial in determining when a behavior previously considered normal becomes maladaptive. One can expect discrepancies between a child's chronological, emotional, cognitive, and behavioral ages (Sahler & McAnarney, 1981). Such incongruities create a challenge for the therapist attempting to assess and diagnose an individual child. The therapist must address the child's age in terms of the normal behaviors characterizing other children of the same age, culture, and environment (Mash & Terdal, 1988).

To include age criteria in child assessment, the therapist should ask himself or herself the following questions: How old is the child? Is the behavior presented by the child normal for that chronological age? What are the chances that the problem will disappear as the child grows older?

RELEVANCE OF AGE TO CHILD THERAPY

Children develop different roles at each childhood age and stage, requiring a specific treatment plan best suited to facilitate the new roles (Forehand & Weirson, 1993). For example, when children are young and dependent on their caregiver, therapy usually has primary prevention aims (i.e., preventing future risk and reducing the incidence of disorder; Graham, 1994) and takes the form of counseling and supervising parents in educating and rearing their children. As children start school, therapy should be directed to the child within his or her natural environment (parents, teachers, and friends) and toward educational-therapeutic assignments (i.e., secondary prevention, which prevents existing problems from worsening and reduces the duration of the disorder; Graham, 1994). As children enter adolescence, therapy should be directed toward the child himself or herself and focus on tertiary prevention (i.e., therapy aims to solve an already existing problem, prevent future risks, and impart skills for decreasing its frequency).

Understanding the child's behavior at different age levels is critical not only in assessing the need for treatment and selecting the setting for intervention, but also during the intervention itself. Age should be a primary consideration in identifying the best techniques for a specific child. Dush, Hirt, and Schroeder (1989) found a positive relationship between age and treatment outcome, with older children benefiting more from cognitive treatments. The best results were found for adolescents (age 13 to 18 years), and good outcomes were also shown for preadolescents (age 11 to 13), but less success was demonstrated with younger children (age 5 to 11; Durlak, Fuhrman, & Lampman, 1991).

These outcomes suggest that different techniques in cognitive therapy be considered for children of different ages. Young children need simple, concrete instructions and can participate in behavioral techniques or cognitive techniques that are based on simple instructions (such as self-talk). Older children can benefit more from cognitive therapy and techniques such as changing automatic thoughts, rational analysis, and cognitive restructuring.

COGNITIVE STAGE AS AN IMPORTANT DEVELOPMENTAL COMPONENT

The most important feature relating to childhood development with implications for treatment consists of the child's cognitive developmental stage. This concept has been attributed to Piaget, the most well-known theorist of cognitive development in children. According to Piaget (1969, 1977), human beings develop cognitive structures and the ability to perform (Campbell, 2005; Campbell & Christopher, 1996). Development accrues as cognitive structures naturally change in the course of growth.

Piaget (1969, 1977) explained development in a way that avoided both "preformation" (the doctrine of innate ideas) and environmental determinism (Campbell, 2005). He defined cognitive development as a function of several factors: neurological maturation, adequate social environment, experience, and constant internal cognitive organization (Sahler & McAnarney, 1981).

Piaget felt that the most critical factor in child development is interaction with peers, because it elicits conflicts that turn into argument and debate. According to this view, heredity sets broad limits on intellectual functioning; experience modifies or reorganizes these reflexes into purposeful mental and physical activities to the extent permitted by the individual's current level of physiological maturation.

Piaget viewed development as a very complex organism's continual struggle to adapt to a very complex environment (Piaget & Inhelder, 1969). His theory focuses on two major principles: the tendency for all species to organize their activities, and the tendency for all species to adapt (Sahler & McAnarney, 1981). He claimed that as development proceeds, these structures accommodate to the environment. Movement to a higher level of development depends on "reflecting abstraction," which means coming to know properties of one's own actions, or coming to know the ways one's actions are coordinated.

The traditional theory of cognitive development described four developmental stages (Piaget, 1924): the sensorimotor stage (infants and very young children), the preoperational stage (school years), the concrete operational stage (the years leading to puberty), and the formal operational stage (preadolescence and adolescence). Each stage is characterized by different motoric, cognitive, and language skills, which result in different abilities to understand complex concepts.

Sensorimotor Stage

The first stage lasts from birth to approximately 2 years old. The infant's initial schemes are simple reflexes. At this stage, infants are limited to "thinking in action." They use senses to gain information and increase motor capabilities to seek new experiences. Their knowledge of the world is limited to physical interactions with people and objects. The sensorimotor stage ends with the development of language, an understanding of object permanency, and the ability to imitate someone else's action on the basis of memory alone. Children need to complete this stage to develop more sophisticated cognitive skills through physical interactions and procedures.

Preoperational Stage

This stage spans age 2 years to 6 years. The child begins to use symbols to represent the world cognitively, thus starting to use mental imagery and language. The child acquires the ability to anticipate— to think about some possibilities before acting on them. In this stage, the semiotic function appears, enabling a mental symbol, word, or object to stand for or represent something that is not present (Ginsburg & Opper, 1979). In this stage, language is at the preconcept level, and play is of a pretend nature. Children start to reason with the aid of memories from past events. Such reasoning permits guesses about future events. The child can solve problems through intuition but cannot explain his or her reasoning. Instead, the child applies transduction, that is, reasoning from one particular to another. For example, on a cloudy day, a child may reason that because the sun is not out, it is not daytime.

CONCRETE OPERATIONAL STAGE

This stage lasts between 6 and 12 years of age. In the concrete operational stage, in contrast with the sensorimotor, the child already possesses cognitive representations rather than only overt actions. Children at this stage can perform mental operations on the bits of knowledge that they possess. They can add, subtract, and count in order and in reverse. Logical structures like groupings become available, and children can create seriations by putting things in sequence. Children understand conservation of numbers, liquid, length, mass, and weight, and they can work out story problems based on fact. They can also take another person's point of view and see things from more than one perspective. Nevertheless, children are limited in their ability to generate possibilities systematically or to test hypotheses that require monitoring of multiple possibilities. Their ability to classify is limited to concrete objects. They can see and reason with concrete knowledge, but they cannot see the abstract side of things and develop all possible outcomes.

FORMAL OPERATIONS

This stage spans from 12 years of age to adolescence. Formal operations, as the final period in Piaget's stage hierarchy, has a starting point but no end point. The formal operational child is no longer limited to dealing largely with what is in front of him or her: concrete, tangible, real objects or materials (Vasta, Haith, & Miller, 1995). The child now has the capacity for logical thinking and use of abstract, idealistic, and logical concepts. This period includes all of the higher level abstract operations that do not require concrete objects or materials. At this stage, the child can perform hypothetical-deductive reasoning, raising a hypothesis and using deductive reasoning and guesses to solve problems (Piaget, 1977). The development of formal operations also enables understanding of moral, political, and philosophical ideas. Weiner and Elkind (1972, p. 171) state, "Adolescence is the era in which an individual becomes able to think abstractly and to deal with concepts like liberty and justice, to grasp metaphors and smile."

Recent developmental and cognitive theories have voiced opposition to Piaget's general and rigid view of children's cognitive development, claiming that his theory is epistemologically weak, philosophically naive, and empirically wrong. Some oppose the rigid classification of stages that do not take into account individual differences in development (Case, 1992). They suggest that children are capable of understanding complex concepts at earlier ages than Piaget proposed. In addition, critics claim that developmental processes do not end at the end of adolescence; people continue to develop their cognitive abilities throughout life.

RELEVANCE OF COGNITIVE DEVELOPMENT TO CHILD THERAPY

Whether therapists accept the very rigid cognitive stages described by Piaget (1924) or follow the more flexible view of the post-Piagetian theorists (e.g., Meadows, 1993), they cannot disconnect children's ability to participate in cognitive-behavioral therapy (CBT) from children's cognitive developmental level. Cognitive-behavioral therapy necessitates the ability to develop an understanding of the world and the ability to understand reasoning processes, whether formal or everyday (Siegal, 1997). Children also must be capable of analogical thinking and of causal reasoning to understand the connections between cognitions and behaviors (Goncalves, 1994).

Cognitive stages influence children's understanding, actions, and responses toward themselves and their environment (Davies, 1999); therefore, these stages are crucial for the understanding of childhood disorders (Crick & Dodge, 1994). Cognitive development plays an integral role in decision making about children's therapy throughout the entire course of intervention (Mash & Barkley, 1996; Mash & Dozois, 1996; Ronen, 2003, 2005).

Cognitive development mediates the way the child constructs and construes the view of the self, the world, and the problem. Hence, to assess the disorder and suggest a prognosis, one must understand the child's world, cognitive capabilities, cognitive skills, experiential knowledge, and attentional abilities (Crick & Dodge, 1994).

There is general agreement about the need for a good match between the child's stage and the selected intervention's level of complexity (Bierman & Furman, 1984; Knell, 1993; Ronen, 1997). For example, in the sensorimotor stage (birth to 2 years), it is impossible to treat children directly. They have not yet mastered language, concentration skills, or the ability to cooperate with the therapeutic process. Therapy should instead target the child's environment. In the preoperational stage, as children develop and acquire basic communication skills, they can now become involved in therapy themselves, provided that the therapist remembers to use symbolic language and concrete concepts and to appeal to the child's illogical, subjective way of thinking. Experiential therapy using drawing, painting, music, and dancing may best suit the child's ability to learn and gain new skills. During the concrete operational stage in the school years, verbal therapy can be applied if based on the child's day-to-day life and experiences rather than on universal concepts, notions, and rational arguments. In the abstract or formal operational stage (from age 12), the child may view verbal therapy as an interesting challenge, whereas nonverbal therapy may even be insulting to the young person who wishes to be treated as an adult (Ronen, 1992).

Understanding cognitive development can influence the content of intervention as well. During infancy, the developmental task consists of shifting from dependence on the caregiver to increased independence and self-regulation. It follows that problems in gaining initial achievements in autonomy at this stage usually derive from dependency issues and parenting style in educating the child. The major developmental task of early childhood is to begin mastery of academic and social situations. Hence, interventions at this age should involve parents' and teachers' supervision in how to use behavioral principles with children, as well as social skills training and group intervention. From middle childhood to early adolescence the main task consists of individual identity development and acquiring self-control. Thus, therapy should be based on training in social skills and self-control methods (i.e., self-talk, self-reinforcement). The task of individuation from the family and moving toward independence in middle adolescence requires interventions based on problem-solving skills and self-control training.

After utilizing cognitive developmental components to assess the problem, to make a decision about who should be treated (setting), and to select the contents that should be the focus of therapy, therapists should next consider how cognitive development influences the kinds of skills that a child needs to acquire and the best ways to teach these skills. Cognitive stage-dependent problems help determine the kind of strategies and techniques to be employed with children. For example, younger children exhibit a limited appreciation of time; distant goals and long-term benefits will seem incomprehensible, whereas short-term gratification and displeasure will be vivid, shaping the design of treatment objectives. Older children have already acquired abstract thinking; they can work on changing automatic thoughts into mediated ones and can practice this skill. In contrast, young children do not yet understand the concept of automatic thoughts, necessitating more concrete means to help them change their automatic unmediated thoughts into mediated ones.

LANGUAGE AS AN IMPORTANT DEVELOPMENTAL COMPONENT

Language develops as part of general cognitive development. However, because of the role language plays in the child's and family's life, it deserves separate consideration.

Building on Vygotzky's (1962) and Luria's (1961) theories about how language evolves, Mischel (1974) described children's ability to shift from being directed by adult external control to individual internal control as a matter of internalizing self-talk. Children move from talking aloud to internal self-talk, which actually constitutes a state of self-control that enables them to use cognitive thinking, stop automatic negative thoughts, and start using mediated dialogue (Meichenbaum, 1979; Meichenbaum & Goodman, 1971; Ronen, 1997).

A basic component of self-control is self-talk. Often, children who lack communication skills develop a range of disorders because they have difficulties using self-talk, and they act before thinking. The ability to use language as a self-control mechanism starts with experiencing adults' attempts to utilize language to instruct the child in what to do and adults' demonstrations of the role of instruction and self-talk in everyday life. Children then learn to imitate adults and talk to themselves (Ronen, 1997). Self-talk is a necessary skill for cognitive-behavioral therapy and a basic component for delaying gratification, coping with temptation, and mediating and controlling behavior (Meichenbaum & Goodman, 1971; Mischel, 1974; Ronen, 1997).

Relevance of Language Development to Child Therapy

The development of language is crucial for therapists to consider. First, the therapist needs to be aware of the child's stage of language development in order to conduct an effective assessment. Second, the therapist should consider language to design good communication with the child during assessment and therapy. Third, language ability can strongly impact decision making concerning the best mode of therapy for the child.

Children's ability to conduct conversation is crucial for therapy. Before the child acquires proper language, assessment can be based only on nonverbal, indirect methods. For this young age, therapists should employ unmediated therapeutic modes such as painting, free association, and storytelling, which all depend on the therapist's individual interpretation of the child's responses. Although the reliability or validity of these interpretations cannot be substantiated, the need to conduct a deeper inquiry into the child's personal attributions and thinking processes should be an important principle during assessment. Standard testing procedures, unfortunately, rarely incorporate the children's own explanations regarding their specific responses to test questions.

Awareness of idiosyncrasies in language and age-appropriate difficulties in communication should always be maintained during child assessment procedures. In therapy it is important to use the language that is familiar to the child and examples relating to the child's culture, hobbies, and interest.

THE CHILD'S ABILITY TO PROCESS INFORMATION AS AN IMPORTANT DEVELOPMENTAL COMPONENT

Information processing is another important cognitive developmental feature that impacts children's ability to benefit from therapy and that necessitates therapeutic decision making regarding how to apply therapy.

The traditional model of information processing has generally replaced Piaget's cognitive developmental stages as the mainstay of cognitive developmental theory. The basic information processing models are mediational, proposing that miniature prototypes of stimuli and responses operate inside the organism (Mahoney, 1991). Such models conceive human cognition as a system that involves three main parts: input, processing, and output.

The main goal in studying the processing of information in the human brain is to understand the process that occurs internally before the person takes action and to specify the underlying psychological processes and development that individuals undergo. The focus is on thinking styles and processes (Kail, 1992; Kail & Park, 1992). Within the cognitive domain, information processing constitutes one of the chief skills with implications for child therapy. Research has highlighted that the way children process information critically impacts not only how they behave but also how they think and feel; therefore, children's information processing must be a main feature in intervention design (Crick & Dodge, 1994).

According to Dodge's (Crick & Dodge, 1994; Dodge & Pettit, 2003) model of social information processing, children engage in four main steps before enacting competent social behavior. The first two steps are the encoding of situational cues and then representation and interpretation of those cues. Children focus on and encode particular cues in the social situation and then, based on these cues, construct an interpretation of the situation. The next two steps entail a mental search for possible responses to the situation and the selection of a response. Children access possible responses to the situation from long-term memory, evaluate those responses, and then select the most favorable one for enactment. The four-step model presumes that children possess limited capabilities and past experiences while facing a social situation (Crick & Dodge, 1994).

RELEVANCE OF INFORMATION PROCESSING TO CHILD THERAPY

To enhance their comprehension of children's normal behavior and maladjustment, cognitive-behavioral therapists should have knowledge of how children process information at various ages. Considering the importance of thinking style and information processing, the therapist should look for and assess the existence of those skills and try to impart them to the child if they are lacking.

The way the child processes information will help the therapist decide what the focus of therapy should be. If a child lacks the skills for encoding information, this should be at the center of therapy. If a child has no problem encoding information but distorts interpretation of this information (e.g., attributes solely hostile intentions to peers), then therapy should address this problem.

Thus, understanding how children process information can help the therapist in making decisions about how to apply cognitive therapy, what stages the therapist needs to focus on, and in what way the disorder may be influenced by the child's ability to process the information.

GENDER AS AN IMPORTANT DEVELOPMENTAL COMPONENT

Although gender is inborn rather than associated with a particular stage of development and does not change over time, it is a particularly important issue to consider during childhood. The reason is that boys and girls develop differently. These gender distinctions are evident not only in the speed of development (girls mature earlier) but also in the signs of development, the frequency of disorders, and the way disorders are manifested.

Gender differences may be explained by social norms or a variation in maturation processes. On the one hand, girls as a group mature more quickly than boys, so one can expect fewer disorders with an important developmental component among them. On the other hand, role taking influences girls by allowing them to talk more freely about anxieties and fears than do boys, so that reports of anxiety are usually higher among girls (Kazdin, 2000; Ronen, in press).

Basic cognitive and social learning research findings suggest that biological elements (genes and hormones) set the process of sex differentiation into motion but that environmental conditions, information processing models, and parental influences maintain this process (Vasta et al., 1995). The development of sexual identity among children emerges in three stages: First, children develop gender identity (categorizing themselves as male or female); second, gender stability emerges (awareness that usually boys grow up to be men and girls grow up to be women); third, gender consistency is attained (recognizing one's gender group and understanding the implications; Kohlberg, 1968).

Gender influences development and has an impact on behavioral dysfunction by influencing social expectations. For example, in general, patterns of play and social relations are different among boys and girls (Raviv, Keinan, Abazon, & Raviv, 1990). Girls are tied more to one or two significant friends of their own age and sex, whereas boys play in large same-sex groups. Girls find it more difficult to make new friends than do boys. Thus, sex mediates social relationships and to some degree predicts social adjustment to new environments (Raviv et al., 1990) and contributes to assessment and intervention processes.

RELEVANCE OF GENDER TO CHILD THERAPY

The assessment process and decision making about the best form of treatment should take gender issues into account not only with respect to children's sex differences but to the parents' and therapist's sex and their combinations (mother with son, mother with daughter, father with son, female therapist with male child, etc.).

Moreover, the treatment itself should be influenced by gender-related considerations. Women, for instance, generally have a greater willingness to seek and receive help than do men, and girls, like women, can more easily accept help in times of crisis (Nadler, 1986). In addition, girls' greater expressiveness and ability to share their feelings with others may have important ramifications in the planning of treatments for both sexes. Boys are more likely to enjoy computer games and could more easily cooperate with exposure treatments, paradoxical techniques, and gradual assignment techniques. Over the past decade, cognitive therapy has begun to pinpoint not only the "overcoming" techniques but also the "living with" techniques that foster the acceptance of negative emotions (Rosenbaum, 1993). Experiential techniques (accepting emotions, living with fears, self-talk, and imagination; see Rosenbaum, 1993) might be easier to design for girls, who are less afraid of being thought weak and "feeling bad" (Nadler, 1986).

The cognitive approach to gender-role development focuses not so much on the sociobiological differences between the genders as on the kind of gender schemata each child develops. The role of the cognitive therapist is to discover the gender schemata of the child and help him or her to develop healthy and functional gender schemata.

EMOTIONAL SKILLS AS AN IMPORTANT DEVELOPMENTAL COMPONENT

In his early work on cognitive therapy for depression, Beck (1963) emphasized the role of emotion as an outcome of thinking processes and pointed to the need to change one's emotions by learning to identify and change automatic thoughts into controlled thoughts. Negative emotions have been conceived as the outcome of negative automatic thoughts, which need to be changed in order to achieve behavior change.

In the past few years there has been a dramatic increase in interest in the role of emotion for therapy in general, and for cognitive-behavioral therapy in particular, bringing the issues of emotions into clear focus in therapy. Emotions are no longer considered to be a "by-product" or "outcome," but rather are a necessary and integral human function. Feelings are both the cause and the outcome of cognitions (Mahoney, 1991). Affect is thus a core constituent of the human self, establishing the link between self and environment and organizing self-experiences (Greenberg & Safran, 1987).

In the course of development, children gradually learn to *express* emotions verbally. Expressing emotion is one of the first stages in emotional development and can be expected among children at the age of a few weeks. Once a child can express the basic emotions (happiness, anger, fear, sadness), it is easier to progress to the next step of identifying emotion (Vasta et al., 1995). Children at 1 year of age can already *identify* various emotions. Children who are trained by their parents or immediate environment to identify and express emotion can move on to the next stage in emotional development. Later on, they can *accept* their own emotions and those of others. Gradually, by the age of 11 years, children are already more likely to *attribute* emotional arousal to internal causes than to external events, and then they start understanding emotion (Shirk & Russell, 1996; Thompson, 1989). Only once they *understand* emotion can they learn to *control* it.

In the course of development, children are increasingly able to demonstrate signs of emotions, talk about emotions, show an improved comprehension of emotional terms, understand situations that elicit emotions, induce emotions in themselves and others, understand emotional cues, and integrate successive or simultaneous emotions (Terwogt & Olthof, 1989).

The emergence of emotional expression is primarily guided by biological processes, but subsequently is tied to cognitive learning and influenced by the social environment (i.e., learned through modeling and reinforcement processes). Like other modes of development (age, gender development, and cognitive development), emotions also develop in stages, from diffuse, intense emotional states in infancy, to a rudimentary awareness and discernment of some affects, to a capacity to regulate some of one's own emotions, and gradually to a more mature differentiation between subtleties in affective experience and an increased level of control.

RELEVANCE OF EMOTIONAL DEVELOPMENT TO CHILD THERAPY

Studies have illuminated how emotions that emerge early begin to grow in sophistication and scope throughout the childhood years, contributing to knowledge about others and oneself (Thompson, 1989). Helping the child understand emotions is a vital part of cognitive therapy, which involves identifying internal cues, differentiating between thoughts and emotions, and learning how emotions elicit behavior.

Children are frequently referred for psychotherapy because of problems with emotions, and many childhood disorders can be viewed as involving difficulties with the experience, expression, or regulation of emotions (Shirk & Russell, 1996). To help children cope with, experience, and be able to express emotions, therapists need to understand the role of emotion in behavior in general and its role in the acquisition, maintenance, and change processes.

Determining the child's affective stage of development is a prerequisite for any efficient treatment. Children may be located at an early developmental stage, when they can already express and identify emotions. But, because of a lack of familial support or due to an inconsistent child-rearing and education style, they may not yet have gained the ability to understand emotion. Knowledge about the child's emotional development thus plays a vital role in applying therapy with the child. The child's emotional stage significantly shapes decision making about the kind of therapy the child needs and about the most favorable means to achieve the therapeutic goals.

Cognitive-behavioral therapy is targeted toward the self-control of emotions, whether to suppress or express them. Controlling and regulating emotions enables flexibility in social behavior, in communication, and in achieving the appropriate response to specific situations (Terwogt & Olthof, 1989). Control of emotion cannot be learned by means of trial and error but requires modeling, reinforcing, and mirroring. To control emotions, children need knowledge of when and how to control. Young children are rigid in the extent of control they apply, often demonstrating overcontrol or undercontrol in emotional functioning. Reinforcement, cognitions, and knowledge obtained throughout the childhood years influence the process of appraising, dealing with, and regulating emotions.

SOCIAL SKILLS AS AN IMPORTANT DEVELOPMENTAL COMPONENT

Social and emotional components are not separate entities but are interlinked. Schaffer (1996) emphasized that social development is an outcome of early attachment, awareness of the self (self-awareness, self-concept, self-esteem, and self-emotion), and socialization with parents, siblings, and environment. Social development therefore encompasses the acquisition of skills relating to *behaviors* (participating in the environment and learning social competencies), skills relating to *thoughts* (accepting and understanding social norms and rules and thinking it is important to be a part of society, comprehending what another person may be feeling or thinking), and skills relating to *emotions* (the wish to be a part of society, the feeling of belonging, feelings of empathy). Social experiences and social interactions critically influence the child's ability to become an integral part of society and to develop self-concept, self-identity, and self-control (Ronen, 2003).

Social development is an outcome of the child's process of learning how to be social, how to take others' perspectives into account, and how to acquire social skills and prosocial behaviors and values. Experience encompasses a chief part of this process. New circumstances and developmental changes contribute to the need to develop social abilities (Davies, 1999).

Just as for cognitive development and emotional development, social development is directly associated with children's ability to process information. It is also linked to cognitive and emotional development. Children must be able to understand social roles and to comprehend how their behavior affects their friends' responses, and vice versa. A deficiency in the cognitive skills of reasoning and understanding may impede social relationships (Davies, 1999).

RELEVANCE OF SOCIAL DEVELOPMENT TO CHILD THERAPY

Loneliness and social rejection in childhood are main predictors of problems in adjustment during adulthood. Assessing the child's social interactions, social support systems, and social skills can be crucial for the child's ability to adapt, adjust, and develop a healthy life. The child therapist should therefore be able to assess the child's social development in order to learn about the child's emotional stages and health.

As stated before, children develop different social roles at each childhood stage (Forehand & Weirson, 1993). The therapist should identify the child's social roles and social developmental stage to understand and clarify assessment of the child's disorder as well as to select the focus of therapy. By identifying the kinds of social skills the child possesses, the kinds of skills the child lacks, and the kinds of skills the child needs to acquire, the therapist can design a specific treatment plan best suited to facilitating the new social roles.

THE ROLE OF FAMILY ENVIRONMENT

When a child undergoes therapy, the parents must be involved. Cognitive-behavioral therapy has always focused on treating children within their natural environment (Bandura, 1969). Parents play a vital role in the development, continuation, and solution of their children's disorders. The interpersonal role of the child's pathology is inseparable from the familial influence that helped elicit this pathology. Research has underscored this link between parents' problems and those of their children (Kazdin, 1998). This link can be seen not only in terms of the parents' history of problems and frequency of disorders, but also in terms of belief systems and behavioral development. Research outcomes, for example, have presented a correlation between parents' self-control and children's self-control and also between parents' lack of self-control and children's high frequency of disorders.

Parents are not only responsible for the child's learning and normal development but are also important change agents for the child, facilitating the child's ability for change (Patterson, 1982; Webster-Stratton, 1993). Among all their other roles, parents act as role models and direct trainers, which have significant implications for children's skill acquisition (Patterson, 1982; Webster-Stratton, 1993).

CONCLUSIONS

The present chapter focuses on the role of developmental components in children's disorders. For the purpose of this chapter, we separated each of the components; however, in reality, they all interlink and interconnect, and that interplay among the components influences how disorders develop and how they can best be treated.

Developmental components can explain normal behavior as well as deviant behavior. They can also point to the optimal way for therapy to be applied as well as foster effective predictions about children's prognosis.

REFERENCES

Bandura, A. (1969). *Principles of behavior modification*. New York: Holt, Rinehart & Winston.

Beck, A. T. (1963). Thinking and depression. *Archives of General Psychiatry, 9,* 324–333.

Bierman, K. L., & Furman, W. (1984). The effects of social skills training and peer involvement on the social adjustment of preadolescents. *Child Development, 55,* 151–162.

Campbell, R. L. (2005). *Jean Piaget's genetic epistemology: Appreciation and critique.* Retrieved October 22, 2005, from http://hubcap.clemson.edu/-campber/index.html.

Campbell, R. L., & Christopher, J. C. (1996). Moral development theory: A critique of its Kantian presuppositions. *Developmental Review, 16,* 1048.

Case, R. (1992). *The mind's staircase: Exploring the conceptual underpinnings of children's thought and knowledge.* Hillsdale, NJ: Erlbaum.

Crick, N. R., & Dodge, K. A. (1994). A review and reformulation of social information-processing mechanisms in children's social adjustment. *Psychological Bulletin, 115,* 74–101.

Davies, D. (1999). *Child development: A practitioner's guide.* New York: Guilford Press.

Dodge, K. A., & Pettit, G. (2003). A biopsychosocial model of the development of chronic conduct problems in adolescence. *Developmental Psychology, 39,* 1–41.

Durlak, J. A., Fuhrman, T., & Lampman, C. (1991). Effectiveness of cognitive-behavior therapy for maladaptive children: A meta-analysis. *Psychological Bulletin, 110,* 204–214.

Dush, D. M., Hirt, M. L., & Schroeder, H. E. (1989). Self-statement modification in the treatment of child behavior disorders: A meta-analysis. *Psychological Bulletin, 106,* 97–106.

Forehand, R., & Weirson, M. (1993). The role of developmental factors in planning behavioral intervention for children: Disruptive behavior as an example. *Behavior Therapy, 24,* 117–141.

Ginsburg, H., & Opper, S. (1979). *Piaget's theory of intellectual development* (2nd ed.). Englewood Cliffs, NJ: Prentice-Hall.

Goncalves, O. F. (1994). Cognitive narrative psychotherapy: The hermeneutic construction of alternative meanings. In M. J. Mahoney (Ed.), *Cognitive and constructive psychotherapies: Theory, research and practice* (pp. 139–162). New York: Springer.

Graham, P. (1994). Prevention. In M. Rutter, E. Taylor, & L. Hersov (Eds.), *Child and adolescent psychiatry: Modern approaches* (3rd ed., pp. 815–828). Oxford, England: Blackwell.

Greenberg, L. S., & Safran, J. D. (1987). *Emotion in psychotherapy.* New York: Guilford Press.

Kail, R. (1992). Evidence for global developmental change is intact. *Journal of Experimental Child Psychology, 54,* 308–314.

Kail, R., & Park, Y. (1992). Global developmental change in processing time. *Merrill-Palmer Quarterly, 38,* 525–541.

Kazdin, A. E. (1998). Psychosocial treatments for conduct disorder in children. In D. E. Nathan & J. M. Gorman (Eds.), *A guide to treatments that work* (pp. 65–89). New York: Oxford University Press.

Kazdin, A. E. (2000). *Psychotherapy for children and adolescents: Directions for research and practice.* New York: Oxford University Press.

Knell, S. M. (1993). *Cognitive behavioral play therapy.* Northvale, NJ: Aronson.

Kohlberg, L. (1968). Early education: A cognitive developmental view. *Child Development, 39,* 1013–1062.

Luria, A. R. (1961). *The role of speech in the regulation of normal behaviors.* New York: Liveright.

Mahoney, M. J. (1991). *Human change processes.* New York: Basic Books.

Mash, E. J., & Barkley, R. A. (Eds.). (1996). *Child psychopathology.* New York: Guilford Press.

Mash, E. J., & Dozois, D. J. A. (1996). Child psychopathology: A developmental-systems perspective. In E. J. Mash & R. A. Barkley (Eds.), *Child psychopathology* (pp. 3–60). New York: Guilford Press.

Mash, E. J., & Terdal, L. G. (1988). Behavioral assessment of child and family disturbance. In E. J. Mash & L. G. Terdal (Eds.), *Behavioral assessment of childhood disorders* (2nd ed., pp. 3–65). New York: Guilford Press.

Meadows, S. (1993). *The child as thinker: The development and acquisition of cognition in childhood.* London: Routledge.

Meichenbaum, D. H. (1979). Teaching children self-control. In B. Lahey & A. Kazdin (Eds.), *Advances in clinical child psychology* (Vol. 2, pp. 1–30). New York: Plenum Press.

Meichenbaum, D. H., & Goodman, J. (1971). Training impulsive children to talk to themselves: A means of developing self-control. *Journal of Abnormal Psychology, 77,* 115–126.

Mischel, W. (1974). Processes in delay of gratifications. In L. Berkowitz (Ed.), *Advances in experimental and social psychology.* New York: Academic Press.

Nadler, A. (1986). Self-esteem and the seeking and receiving of help: Theoretical and empirical perspectives. *Experimental Personality Research, 14,* 115–163.

Patterson, G. R. (1982). *Coercive family process: A social learning approach.* Eugene, OR: Castalia.

Piaget, J. (1924). *The language and thought of the child.* London: Routledge & Kegan Paul.

Piaget, J. (1969). *The child's conception of time* (A. J. Pomerans, Trans.). London: Routledge & Kegan Paul.

Piaget, J. (1977). *The development of thought: Equilibrium of cognitive structures.* New York: Viking.

Piaget, J., & Inhelder, B. (1969). *The psychology of the child*. New York: Basic Books.

Raviv, A., Keinan, G., Abazon, Y., & Raviv, A. (1990). Moving as a stressful life event for adolescents. *Journal of Community Psychology, 18,* 130–140.

Ronen, T. (1992). Cognitive therapy with young children. *Child Psychiatry and Human Development, 23,* 19–30.

Ronen, T. (1997). *Cognitive developmental therapy with children*. Chichester, England: Wiley.

Ronen, T. (2003). *Cognitive constructivist psychotherapy with children and adolescents*. New York: Kluwer/Plenum Press.

Ronen, T. (2005). Skills directed therapy (SDT) with aggressive children. *Socialmedicink Tidskrift [Journal of Social Medicine, Sweden], 5,* 383–392.

Ronen, T. (in press). Cognitive development. In B. Thyer (Ed.), *Human behavior in the social environment*. Hoboken, NJ: Wiley.

Rosenbaum, M. (1993). The three functions of self-control behavior: Redressive, reformative, and experiential. *Journal of Work and Stress, 7,* 33–46.

Sahler, O. J. Z., & McAnarney, E. R. (1981). *The child from three to eight*. St Louis, MO: Mosby.

Schaffer, H. R. (1996). *Social development*. Oxford, England: Blackwell.

Shapiro, T. (1995). Developmental issues in psychotherapy research. *Journal of Abnormal Child Psychology, 23,* 31–44.

Shirk, S. R., & Russell, R. L. (1996). *Change process in child psychotherapy*. New York: Guilford Press.

Siegal, M. (1997). *Knowing children: Experiments in conversation and cognition* (2nd ed.). London: Psychological Press.

Terwogt, M. M., & Olthof, T. (1989). Awareness and self-regulation of emotion in young children. In C. Saarni & P. L. Harris (Eds.), *Children's understanding of emotion* (pp. 209–237). New York: Cambridge University Press.

Thompson, R. A. (1989). Causal attributions and children's emotional understanding. In C. Saarni & P. L. Harris (Eds.), *Children's understanding of emotion* (pp. 117–150). New York: Cambridge University Press.

Vasta, R., Haith, M. M., & Miller, S. A. (1995). *Child psychology: The modern science.* New York: Wiley.

Vygotsky, L. S. (1962). *Thought and language.* New York: Wiley.

Webster-Stratton, C. (1993). Strategies for helping early school-aged children with oppositional defiant and conduct disorders: The importance of home-school partnerships. *School Psychology Review, 22,* 437–457.

Weiner, I. B., & Elkind, D. (1972). *Child development: A core approach.* New York: Wiley.

CHAPTER 3

Temperament and Personality Disorders in Childhood and Adolescence

JOEL PARIS

TEMPERAMENT, PERSONALITY traits, and personality disorders have a hierarchical relationship (Rutter, 1987). Temperament consists of inborn predispositions affecting cognition, affect, and behavior. Personality traits are enduring dispositions that reflect an amalgam of temperament and experience. Personality disorders describe the dysfunctional effects of personality trait profiles. Thus, temperament is the genetic-biological bedrock on which personality disorders are built. However, it has been difficult in practice to separate temperament from traits. The reason is that one cannot easily determine the extent to which personality characteristics are inborn or learned; in young children, measures of temperament already reflect interactions between genes and environment. For this reason, although child researchers tend to describe temperament and adult researchers tend to describe traits, they may be measuring the same construct (Shiner, 2005).

A vast literature in trait psychology has led to a consensus about the underlying structure of personality. Most data support some version of the five-factor model (FFM; Costa & Widiger, 2001), which describes variations on five broad trait dimensions: neuroticism, extraversion, openness, agreeableness, and conscientiousness. Four of these factors (excluding openness) have been reproduced consistently by several other trait measures (Livesley, Jang, & Vernon, 1998). These basic dimensions of personality can be identified early in life and remain stable across the life cycle (Costa & Widiger, 2001; Shiner, 2005). Direct observation of temperamental variation in children (Rothbart, 2004) has yielded a model that resembles the FFM. In adults, traits and disorders have a continuous relationship with no sharp cutoff point (Livesley et al., 1998). For this reason, some researchers have suggested that the FFM might provide a better basis than the current Axis II categories for classifying personality disorders (Widiger, Simonsen, Krueger, Livesley, & Verheul, 2005).

Kagan (2005) has criticized the approach of trait psychology to the identification of personality dimensions due to its reliance on self-report. In Kagan's view, personality dimensions should be defined on the basis of biological markers and experimental observations. The problem is that we have few data on which to build such a schema. Livesley (2005), acknowledges that the broad factor-analytically derived traits have no specific biological correlates, but argues that personality has a hierarchical structure, in which genetic and biological influences act on the level of narrower traits or facets, whereas higher order dimensions are closer to observable behavioral patterns.

The Temperament and Character Inventory (TCI), developed by Cloninger, Svrakic, and Pryzbeck (1993), is somewhat different from the FFM. Confusingly, the TCI purports to be a measure of "temperament" rather than of personality traits. (A literature search using the key word "temperament" will elicit many articles using the TCI as a research tool.) However, there is no evidence that these temperament dimensions (harm avoidance, reward dependence, novelty seeking, persistence) are more related to inborn dispositions than other personality trait measures.

One reason for the popularity of the TCI is the claim that each dimension has a specific relationship to genetic, neurochemical, and neurophysiological systems. However, these hypotheses have not been supported by evidence, and the TCI dimensions do not appear to have biological coherence (Livesley, 2005; Paris, 2005a, 2005b).

To be sure that a personality characteristic is truly the result of temperament, one needs to measure it early in life, preferably in infants. In a well-known study, Chess and Thomas (1984) assessed temperament in a cohort of newborns who were then followed longitudinally into young adulthood. A number of temperament factors were described, falling into three broad dimensions: "easy," "difficult," and "slow to warm up." On follow-up, only difficult children were at greater risk for developing adult psychopathology (Chess & Thomas, 1990).

Rothbart (2004), a leading temperament researcher, has described the basic dimensions of variation in children in a schema containing three broad factors: extraversion (including impulsivity), negative affectivity, and effortful control. Although Rothbart uses a different terminology, these factors correspond to three of the five FFM dimensions. Thus, children vary on the extent to which behavior is directed outward to other people (extraversion), how easily they become upset (negative affectivity or neuroticism), and how much control they assert over their own behavior (effortful control or conscientiousness).

The FFM dimension of agreeableness is absent from this schema but may be more difficult to assess in infants.

In general, temperament is broadly continuous with adult personality (Caspi, Harrington, et al., 2003). However, because many temperament characteristics do not become stable until about age 2 to 3 (Rothbart & Bates, 1998), measures in infancy may not be as predictive as observations made later on in development. Moreover, only a few longitudinal studies of children varying in temperament characteristics early in life have been conducted.

Early temperament characteristics reflect genetic influences. Behavior genetic research shows that genes are as important for personality as for physical characteristics (Plomin, Asbury, & Dunn, 2001; Plomin, Defries, McClearn, & Rutter, 2001). Thus, if temperament is inborn, it should be heritable (even if intrauterine factors also play a role). A large body of research based on twin and adoption methods demonstrates that genetic factors account for between 40% and 50% of the variance on almost all personality traits in adults (Jang, 2005). In principle, this level of heritability should be associated with biological markers. However, there are no consistent findings yet linking personality and neurobiology.

Developmental psychologists also need to establish whether early temperamental patterns are associated with specific vulnerabilities to psychopathology (Kagan & Zentner, 1996). Some of the best-known research addressing this issue comes from a large-scale birth cohort study conducted in Dunedin, New Zealand. Caspi, Moffitt, Newman, and Silva (1996) showed that a 90-minute interview at age 3 determining extremes of temperament (overly aggressive or overly shy) could predict whether subjects were more likely to show antisocial or depressive symptoms, respectively, at age 18.

This research group has also examined relationships between specific allelic variations and behavioral outcomes in this cohort. Caspi et al. (2002) reported an association between a polymorphism in the gene affecting monoamine oxidase and antisocial behavior. Although this genetic marker predicted antisocial outcomes only in subjects also exposed to environmental adversities, the enzyme regulates the activity of neurotransmitters, so that genetic variations could affect thresholds for behavioral activation. Similarly, Caspi, Sugden, et al. (2003) examined the relationship between allelic variations affecting the serotonergic system and the development of depression and found a positive correlation.

Some markers reflect abnormal physiology. For example, Kagan and Snidman (1995) noted that their cohort with behavioral inhibition had unusually high heart rates. Another approach involves neuropsychological measures reflecting differences in brain wiring and/or neurotransmission. Deficits in executive functioning are seen in both Attention-Deficit/Hyperactivity Disorder and Conduct Disorder, conditions that, when they appear in combination, produce an increased risk for adult antisocial personality (Weiss & Hechtman, 1992). Finally, although few brain imaging studies have been carried out thus far in children, we might use functional magnetic resonance imaging, a relatively nonintrusive procedure that can be made into a game.

TEMPERAMENT AND THE ENVIRONMENT

Behavioral genetic research has yielded a major surprise for developmental psychologists, who always assumed that parenting is the main environmental factor in personality. In research using twins (Jang, 2005), one can measure the source of environmental variance affecting personality in regression models, separating variance into "shared" and "unshared" components, depending on whether children brought up in the same family are similar in personality traits.

The consistent finding is that environmental variance is entirely unshared; that is, it is unique to each child rather than explained by a common family environment. This observation has led some observers (Harris, 1998; Paris, 2000) to question whether the influence of parenting on child development has been exaggerated. However, the precise nature of unshared environmental factors remains to be determined

(Plomin, Asbury, et al., 2001). They might be attributable to influences outside the family, to differential parenting experiences, or to gene-environment interactions.

In practice, one cannot separate the effects of genes from environment. Gene-environment correlations fall into three categories (Plomin, DeFries, et al., 2001). They can be passive, in that parents tend to create family environments that reflect genotypes they share with their children. They can be evocative, in that children elicit responses from others, both positive and negative, depending on their temperament qualities. Or they can be active, in that children seek (or create) environments that fit their temperament.

An example of these relationships emerged from a study that attempted to separate temperament and environmental influences on development in a long-term follow-up of adolescent twins (Reiss, Neiderhiser, Hetherington, & Plomin, 2000). Path analysis demonstrated that when children were treated differently by parents, siblings, and peers, all these effects were strongly driven by temperament factors.

In summary, the influence of heritable temperament differences on personality and psychopathology can best be understood in the context of a stress-diathesis model describing interactions between genes and environment (Paris, 1999). Twin research shows that a wide range of psychological symptoms and mental disorders in adults are influenced by genetic factors, but that life events must also play a role. For example, in the Dunedin study (Caspi et al., 1996) genetic variations were significant predictors of outcome only in interaction with environmental stressors (Caspi, Harrington, et al., 2003; Caspi, Roberts, & Shiner, 2005).

TEMPERAMENT AND THE DEVELOPMENT OF PERSONALITY DISORDERS

We know from a vast literature on resilience that most children, even when exposed to highly adverse experiences, do not develop mental disorders (see reviews in Clarke & Clarke, 2003; Paris, 2000). This is, paradoxically, the strongest evidence for temperament factors in the development of mental disorders. Because adversity alone is insufficient to cause disorder, some children may have a temperament associated with greater sensitivity to the environment.

Even normal traits, when they fall within a high range, may be associated with greater vulnerability to disorder. For example, in the FFM, the most important dimension for psychopathological risk is neuroticism. It makes less difference if a child is extraverted or introverted, as there are social niches that fit both extremes of temperament. On the other hand, a combination of high neuroticism and extraversion may be associated with greater risk for psychopathology.

In general, psychiatric patients have high levels of neuroticism, a trait dimension that is particularly elevated in patients with Borderline Personality Disorder as well as with other Axis II disorders (Zweig-Frank & Paris, 1995). When emotions are easily activated, internalizing symptoms may develop. In individuals who are also low in conscientiousness and agreeableness, dysphoric emotions may lead to impulsive actions that produce a full picture of personality disorder.

Temperament also influences the environment of the child through gene-environment correlations. Just as resilient children find ways to protect themselves against adversity, vulnerable children create environmental circumstances that amplify and exaggerate their negative temperament characteristics. This process can create a vicious cycle that is difficult to escape.

On theoretical grounds, any mental disorder that begins early in life and is chronic over time should have an important genetic-temperament component (Paris, 1999). Thus, we would expect personality disorders, which begin in childhood and adolescence and continue for many years thereafter, to be strongly rooted in abnormalities of temperament. There is indeed some evidence that these variations predict abnormal personality.

The best research concerns antisocial behavior. The classic work of Robins (1966) established that Conduct Disorder in childhood is an essential precursor of Antisocial Personality Disorder in adulthood. As noted, Caspi et al. (1996) were able to predict antisocial outcomes from behavioral observations in 3-year-old children. In a longitudinal study, it was found that unusually high levels of aggressiveness in middle childhood predicted antisocial behavior (Tremblay, Pihl, Vitaro, & Dobkin, 1994) as well as drug abuse (Masse & Tremblay, 1996) in adolescence.

Some of these pathways differ depending on whether temperament vulnerabilities are seen early in development or later on. In general, the earlier pathology begins, the more likely it is to be temperamentally based, whereas disorders that begin later in life are more likely to be shaped by the environment (Paris, 1999). In this context, Moffitt (1993) made an important distinction between "life-course-persistent" and "adolescence-limited" antisocial behavior. The persistent form of Conduct Disorder that has an early onset tends to continue into adulthood, whereas cases with an adolescent onset are often associated with remission by young adulthood. Zoccolillo, Pickles, Quinton, and Rutter (1992) also found that an early onset and severe presentation of Conduct Disorder is associated with persistent antisocial symptoms in early adulthood. The implication is that Conduct Disorder prior to puberty is more strongly rooted in temperament, consistent with behavioral genetic evidence for the heritability of antisocial behavior (Cadoret, Yates, Troughton, Woodworth, & Stewart, 1995).

Antisocial personality has clearly been shown to have an important temperament component, but we lack parallel research on the other categories of personality disorder listed on Axis II of the *Diagnostic and Statistical Manual of Mental Disorders,* fourth edition, text revision (American Psychiatric Association, 2000). Many of these categories do not describe overt behaviors that can be readily assessed in children. For example, we know little about the temperamental precursors of Borderline Personality Disorder, which is a condition of clinical importance.

Two strategies have been used to examine the relationship between early temperament and personality disorder. One is to follow community or high-risk samples to determine whether childhood temperament predicts continued personality disturbance in adolescence and young adults. A second is to identify children who have symptoms similar to those of adult patients with personality disorders.

Beginning with the first strategy, a variety of evidence points to temperament abnormalities during childhood that precede specific categories of personality disorder. Thus, children who later develop Cluster A disorders on Axis II tend to show schizoid traits during childhood (Wolff, Townshend, McGuire, & Weeks, 1991). Children who later develop Cluster C disorders tend to have anxiety-related temperament characteristics in childhood (Paris, 1998). In this group, the research of Kagan (1994) on behavioral inhibition in infancy is relevant. A group of unusually shy children were followed into early adolescence, and some of them continued to be pathologically shy. But this cohort would have to be followed up for a longer time to determine the risk for Avoidant Personality Disorder.

In the Cluster B disorders, we have few data on histrionic or narcissistic personality. But it would be surprising if histrionic patients had not been highly extraverted as children, as that trait is such an important feature of the adult disorder (Paris, 2003). In one study on the childhood precursors of Narcissistic Personality Disorder (Guilé, 1996), a group of children were identified on the basis of traits and behaviors similar to those seen in adults with NPD. It would be instructive if this cohort could be followed into adulthood.

In the case of Borderline Personality Disorder (BPD), although the research base in adults is large, we still know too little about the origins of the disorder in childhood. The problem in identifying precursors of BPD is that most patients come to clinical attention only during adolescence, so that information about their earlier development is entirely retrospective. Although cases can show typical symptoms early in adolescence (Paris, 2005a), the BPD diagnosis before puberty remains controversial (Kernberg, Weiner, & Bardenstein, 2000).

Nonetheless, the main reason to believe that patients with BPD have an abnormal temperament in childhood is the heritable component in adult BPD (Torgersen et al., 2000), with biological correlates linked more strongly to personality traits than to BPD itself (Paris, 2003). Thus, we might be more likely to find problematic traits than diagnosable mental disorders in children who later develop BPD.

The nature of these traits remains a matter of controversy. Some have emphasized emotional dysregulation (Linehan, 1993); others have focused on impulsivity (Links, Heslegrave, & van Reekum, 1999). The most comprehensive view is that the dimensions underlying adult BPD consist of a combination of affective instability and impulsivity (Siever & Davis, 1991). These traits would correspond, respectively, to internalizing and externalizing symptoms described in children (Achenbach & McConaughy, 1997). It has been shown that adolescents with this combination are more likely to develop BPD (Crawford, Cohen, & Brook, 2001a, 2001b).

Although we do not know whether externalizing and internalizing symptoms are seen in children who later develop BPD, this clinical picture should, in principle, be observable during childhood. It would present as a combination of anxiety/depression with impulsive behavior patterns (Paris, 2000). This presentation would contrast with the primarily impulsive pattern seen in conduct-disordered children, who are not necessarily anxious or depressed.

To test this hypothesis, we need a large-scale longitudinal follow-up to do for BPD what the studies of Robins (1966, 1978), Tremblay et al. (1994), and Caspi et al. (2002) have done for precursors of antisocial personality. This would require a research design in which prospective follow-up begins very early in life. But the practical problems in developing such a study are formidable. Even in the Albany-Saratoga study, a large-scale project that examined the precursors of personality disorders (Johnson, Cohen, Brown, Smailes, & Bernstein, 1999;

Johnson, Cohen, Skodol, et al., 1999), follow-up began in middle childhood, and there was no formal measure of temperament.

CHILDHOOD SYMPTOMS THAT RESEMBLE ADULT PERSONALITY DISORDERS

Another approach to the relationship between temperament and personality disorder is to study children who have symptoms similar to adults with Axis II diagnoses. In most ways, Conduct Disorder and Antisocial Personality Disorder describe the same condition at different ages. Similarly, if behaviorally inhibited children were to develop avoidant personality as adults, symptoms would not have changed greatly.

However, the precursors of BPD present a more difficult problem, because one sees symptoms in adults (such as chronic suicidality) that are very uncommon in children.

Our research group (Guzder, Paris, Zelkowitz, & Feldman, 1999; Paris, Zelkowitz, Guzder, Joseph, & Feldman, 1999; Zelkowitz, Guzder, & Paris, 2001) studied a group of children with borderline pathology of childhood (BPC), a clinical picture marked, like BPD, by a mixture of affective, impulsive, and micropsychotic symptoms. Similar cohorts of children have been studied by other groups but labeled differently: by Cohen, Paul, and Volkmar (1987), as "multiple complex developmental disorder," and by Kumra et al. (1998) as "multidimensionally impaired syndrome." The clinical presentation of BPC, with severe dysfunction and multiple symptoms, points to temperament abnormalities.

The patients in the study were compared to a group of other severely ill children of school age attending a child day care center. The findings were that borderline children have risk factors similar to those of adults with BPD: histories of trauma, family histories of substance abuse and criminality, as well as abnormal executive function on neuropsychological testing (Paris, 2000; Zelkowitz et al., 2001). However, a follow-up of the BPC cohort showed that although most remained dysfunctional, they did not develop BPD, at least by midadolescence (Zelkowitz, Guzder, Feldman, & Paris, 2005). And one would not have expected a different result, given that most adult BPD patients are female, whereas most child psychiatry patients (including the cohort we studied) are male.

TEMPERAMENT AND PERSONALITY DISORDERS IN ADOLESCENCE

Why do personality disorders begin their clinical presentation only in the adolescent years? Although this is not always the case for Antisocial Personality Disorder (Moffitt, 1993), BPD almost always presents for the first time in adolescence (Zanarini, Frankenburg, Khera, & Bleichmar, 2001).

Evidently children can have temperament qualities that fall within a normal range and only later develop disorders. The biological, psychological, and social stresses of the adolescent years have led to the concept of a normative "adolescent turmoil," but this phenomenon is far from universal, even in North America (Offer & Offer, 1975). Moreover, cross-cultural studies suggest that disorders of impulsivity such as antisocial personality are rare in some societies (Compton et al., 1991).

One possibility is that adolescents are particularly affected by rapid social change, and that personality disorders of the impulsive type are becoming more common in modern (or modernizing) societies (Paris, 2004). Adolescents in traditional societies may exhibit impulsivity, but this is tempered by their society's predictable structure that provides clear social roles; in contrast, modern societies expect adolescents to develop their own identities and their own social niches. Even if personality and temperament show only minor variations from one society to another (Eysenck, 1982; McCrae & Terracciano, 2005), personality disorders could be more sensitive to social risks.

The effects of temperament always develop in a social context. Thus, we cannot understand the impact of an impulsive temperament without considering whether social circumstances allow it to be expressed through behavior. Similarly, we cannot understand the impact of an anxious temperament without considering whether this disposition runs counter to, or is supported by, social expectations. Even a withdrawn or schizoid temperament may be functional under some social conditions. As Beck and Freeman (2002) have pointed out, personality traits have evolved (and remained) in the population because they are functional; they become dysfunctional only when they are discordant with environmental conditions.

IMPLICATIONS OF TEMPERAMENT FOR TREATMENT

Seeing temperament as a risk factor for personality disorders has clinical implications for the treatment of children and their families. First, understanding temperament variations helps to make clinicians less judgmental. Characteristics such as neuroticism and impulsivity need not necessarily be dysfunctional (Beck & Freeman, 2002), yet in patients with personality disorders these traits are applied in inflexible ways that fail to take context into account. Changing behavior often means finding ways to make better use of an individual's temperament rather than trying to change it.

Second, it can be helpful to understand that temperament never exists in a vacuum, but can be associated with problematic responses to environmental stressors. When children and their parents are aware of temperament vulnerabilities, they are in a better position to recognize what kinds of events are most likely to press buttons and what kinds of behaviors are likely to ensue and to learn alternative and healthier ways to deal with stressors.

REFERENCES

Achenbach, T. M., & McConaughy, S. H. (1997). *Empirically based assessment of child and adolescent psychopathology: Practical applications* (2nd ed.). Thousand Oaks, CA: Sage.

American Psychiatric Association. (2000). *Diagnostic and statistical manual of mental disorders* (4th ed., text rev.). Washington, DC: American Psychiatric Press.

Beck, A. T., & Freeman, A. (2002). *Cognitive therapy of personality disorders* (2nd ed.). New York, Guilford Press.

Cadoret, R. J., Yates, W. R., Troughton, E., Woodworth, G., & Stewart, M. A. (1995). Genetic environmental interaction in the genesis of aggressivity and conduct disorders. *Archives of General Psychiatry, 52,* 916–924.

Caspi, A., Harrington, H., Milne, B., Amell, J. W., Theodore, R. F., & Moffitt, T. E. (2003). Children's behavioral styles at age 3 are linked to their adult personality traits at age 26. *Journal of Personality, 71,* 495–513.

Caspi, A., McClay, J., Moffitt, T. E., Mill, J., Martin, J., Craig, I. W., et al. (2002). Role of genotype in the cycle of violence in maltreated children. *Science, 297,* 851–854.

Caspi, A., Moffitt, T. E., Newman, D. L., & Silva, P. A. (1996). Behavioral observations at age 3 predict adult psychiatric disorders: Longitudinal evidence from a birth cohort. *Archives of General Psychiatry, 53,* 1033–1039.

Caspi, A., Roberts, B. W., & Shiner, R. L. (2005). Personality development: Stability and change. *Annual Review of Psychology, 56,* 453–484.

Caspi, A., Sugden, K., Moffitt, T. E., Taylor, A., Craig, I. W., Harrington, H., et al. (2003). Influence of life stress on depression: Moderation by a polymorphism in the 5-HTT gene. *Science, 301,* 386–389.

Chess, S., & Thomas, A. (1984). *Origins and evolution of behavior disorders: From infancy to adult life.* New York: Brunner/Mazel.

Chess, S., & Thomas, A. (1990). The New York Longitudinal Study: The young adult periods. *Canadian Journal of Psychiatry, 35,* 557–561.

Clarke, A., & Clarke, A. (2003). *Human resilience: A fifty year quest.* Philadelphia: Jessica Kingsley.

Cloninger, C. R., Svrakic, D. M., & Pryzbeck, T. R. (1993). A psychobiological model of temperament and character. *Archives of General Psychiatry, 50,* 975–990.

Cohen, D. J., Paul, R., & Volkmar, F. (1987). Issues in the classification of pervasive developmental disorders and associated conditions. In D. J. Cohen & A. M. Donnelean (Eds.), *Handbook of autism and pervasive developmental disorders* (pp. 20–39). New York: Wiley.

Compton, W. M., III, Helzer, J. E., Hwu, H. G., Yeh, E. K., McEvoy, L., Tipp, J. E., et al. (1991). New methods in cross-cultural psychiatry: Psychiatric illness in Taiwan and the United States. *American Journal of Psychiatry, 148,* 1697–1704.

Costa, P. T., & Widiger, T. A. (Eds.). (2001). *Personality disorders and the five factor model of personality* (2nd ed.). Washington, DC: American Psychological Association.

Crawford, T. N., Cohen, P., & Brook, J. S. (2001a). Dramatic-erratic personality disorder symptoms: Pt. I. Continuity from early adolescence to adulthood. *Journal of Personality Disorders, 15,* 319–335.

Crawford, T. N., Cohen, P., & Brook, J. S. (2001b). Dramatic-erratic personality disorder symptoms: Pt. II. Developmental pathways from early adolescence to adulthood. *Journal of Personality Disorders, 15,* 336–350.

Eysenck, H. J. (1982). Culture and personality abnormalities. In I. Al-Issa (Ed.), *Culture and psychopathology* (pp. 277–308). Baltimore: University Park Press.

Guilé, J. M. (1996). Identifying narcissistic personality disorders in preadolescents. *Canadian Journal of Psychiatry, 41,* 343–349.

Guzder, J., Paris, J., Zelkowitz, P., & Feldman, R. (1999). Psychological risk factors for borderline pathology in school-aged children. *Journal of the American Academy of Child and Adolescent Psychiatry, 38,* 206–212.

Harris, J. R. (1998). *The nurture assumption.* New York: Free Press.

Jang, K. L. (2005). *The behavioral genetics of psychopathology: A clinical guide.* Mahwah, NJ: Erlbaum.

Johnson, J. G., Cohen, P., Brown, J., Smailes, E. M., & Bernstein, D. P. (1999). Childhood maltreatment increases risk for personality disorders during early adulthood. *Archives of General Psychiatry, 56,* 600–606.

Johnson, J. G., Cohen, P., Skodol, A. E., Oldham, J. M., Kasen, S., & Brook, J. S. (1999). Personality disorders in adolescence and risk of major mental disorders and suicidality during adulthood. *Archives of General Psychiatry, 56,* 805–811.

Kagan, J. (1994). *Galen's prophecy.* New York: Basic Books.

Kagan, J. (2005). Temperament and personality. In M. Rosenbluth, S. H. Kennedy, & M. R. Bagby (Eds.), *Depression and personality: Conceptual and clinical challenges* (pp. 3–18). Washington, DC: American Psychiatric Press.

Kagan, J., & Snidman, N. (1995). *The long shadow of temperament.* Cambridge, MA: Belknap Press/Harvard University Press.

Kagan, J., & Zentner, M. (1996). Early childhood predictors of adult psychopathology. *Harvard Review of Psychiatry, 3,* 341–350.

Kernberg, P. F., Weiner, A. S., & Bardenstein, K. K. (2000). *Personality disorders in children and adolescents.* New York: Basic Books.

Kumra, S., Jacobsen, L. K., Lenane, M., Zahn, T. P., Wiggs, E., Alaghband-Rad, J., et al. (1998). Multidimensionally impaired disorder: Is it a variant of very early-onset schizophrenia? *Journal of the American Academy of Child and Adolescent Psychiatry, 37,* 91–99.

Linehan, M. M. (1993). *Dialectical behavioral therapy of borderline personality disorder.* New York: Guilford Press.

Links, P. S., Heslegrave, R., & van Reekum, R. (1999). Impulsivity: Core aspect of borderline personality disorder. *Journal of Personality Disorders,* 131–139.

Livesley, W. J. (2005). Behavioral and molecular genetic contributions to a dimensional classification of personality disorder. *Journal of Personality Disorders, 19,* 131–155.

Livesley, W. J., Jang, K. L., & Vernon, P. A. (1998). Phenotypic and genetic structure of traits delineating personality disorder. *Archives of General Psychiatry, 55,* 941–948.

Masse, L. C., & Tremblay, R. E. (1996). Behavior of boys in kindergarten and the onset of substance use during adolescence. *Journal of Personality Disorders, 54*, 62–68.

McCrae, R. R., & Terracciano, A. (2005). Personality profiles of cultures project: Universal features of personality traits from the observer's perspective: Data from 50 cultures. *Journal of Personality and Social Psychology, 88*, 547–561.

Moffitt, T. E. (1993). "Life-course persistent" and "adolescence-limited" antisocial behavior: A developmental taxonomy. *Psychological Review, 100*, 674–701.

Offer, D., & Offer, J. (1975). Three developmental routes through normal male adolescence. *Adolescent Psychiatry, 4*, 121–141.

Paris, J. (1998). Anxious traits, anxious attachment, and anxious cluster personality disorders. *Harvard Review of Psychiatry, 6*, 142–148.

Paris, J. (1999). *Nature and nurture in psychiatry.* Washington, DC: American Psychiatric Press.

Paris, J. (2000). *Myths of childhood.* Philadelphia: Brunner/Mazel.

Paris, J. (2003). *Personality disorders over time.* Washington, DC: American Psychiatric Press.

Paris, J. (2004). Sociocultural factors in the treatment of personality disorders. In J. Magnavita (Ed.), *Handbook of personality disorders: Theory and practice* (pp. 135–147). Hoboken, NJ: Wiley.

Paris, J. (2005a). Diagnosing borderline personality disorder in adolescence. *Adolescent Psychiatry, 29*, 237–247.

Paris, J. (2005b). Neurobiological dimensional models of personality disorders: A review of the models of Cloninger, Depue, and Siever. *Journal of Personality Disorders, 19*, 156–170.

Paris, J., Zelkowitz, P., Guzder, J., Joseph, S., & Feldman, R. (1999). Neuropsychological factors associated with borderline pathology in children. *Journal of the American Academy of Child and Adolescent Psychiatry, 38*, 770–774.

Plomin, R., Asbury, K., & Dunn, J. (2001). Why are children in the same family so different? Nonshared environment a decade later. *Canadian Journal of Psychiatry, 46,* 225–233.

Plomin, R., DeFries, J. C., McClearn, G. E., & Rutter, M. (2001). *Behavioral genetics* (4th ed.). New York: Freeman.

Reiss, D., Neiderhiser, J. M., Hetherington, E. M., & Plomin, R. (2000). *The relationship code: Deciphering genetic and social influences on adolescent development.* Cambridge, MA: Harvard University Press.

Robins, L. N. (1966). *Deviant children grown up.* Baltimore: Williams & Wilkins.

Robins, L. N. (1978). Sturdy childhood predictors of adult outcome. *Psychological Medicine, 8,* 611–622.

Rothbart, M. K. (2004). Temperament and the pursuit of an integrated developmental psychology. *Merrill-Palmer Quarterly, 50,* 492–505.

Rothbart, M. K., & Bates, J. E. (1998). Temperament. In W. Damon (Series Ed.) & N. Eisenberg (Vol. Ed.), *Handbook of child psychology* (5th ed., Vol. 3, pp. 25–104). New York: Wiley.

Rutter, M. (1987). Temperament, personality, and personality disorder. *British Journal of Psychiatry, 150,* 443–458.

Shiner, R. (2005). A developmental perspective on personality disorders: Lessons from research on normal personality development in childhood and adolescence. *Journal of Personality Disorders, 19,* 202–210.

Siever, L., & Davis, K. L. (1991). A psychobiological perspective on the personality disorders. *American Journal of Psychiatry, 148,* 1647–1658.

Torgersen, S., Lygren, S., Oien, P. A., Skre, I., Onstad, S., Edvardsen, J., et al. (2000). A twin study of personality disorders. *Comprehensive Psychiatry, 41,* 416–425.

Tremblay, R. E., Pihl, R. O., Vitaro, F., & Dobkin, P. L. (1994). Predicting early onset of male antisocial behavior from preschool behavior. *Archives of General Psychiatry, 51,* 732–739.

Weiss, G., & Hechtman, L. (1992). *Hyperactive children grown up* (2nd ed.). New York: Guilford Press.

Widiger, T. A., Simonsen, E., Krueger, R., Livesley, W. J., & Verheul, R. (2005). Personality disorder research agenda for the DSM-V. *Journal of Personality Disorders, 19*, 315–338.

Wolff, S., Townshend, R., McGuire, R. J., & Weeks, D. J. (1991). "Schizoid" personality in childhood and adult life: Pt. II. Adult adjustment and the continuity with schizotypal personality disorder. *British Journal of Psychiatry, 159*, 620–629.

Zanarini, M. C., Frankenburg, F. R., Khera, G. S., & Bleichmar, J. (2001). Treatment histories of borderline inpatients. *Comprehensive Psychiatry, 42*, 144–150.

Zelkowitz, P., Guzder, J., Feldman, R., & Paris, J. (2005, April). *Outcome of borderline pathology of childhood.* Paper presented to the Canadian Academy of Child and Adolescent Psychiatry.

Zelkowitz, P., Guzder, J., & Paris, J. (2001). Diatheses and stressors in borderline pathology of childhood: The role of neuropsychological risk and trauma. *Journal of the American Academy of Child and Adolescent Psychiatry, 40*, 100–105.

Zoccolillo, M., Pickles, A., Quinton, D., & Rutter, M. (1992). The outcome of childhood conduct disorder: Implications for defining adult personality disorder and conduct disorder. *Psychological Medicine, 22*, 971–986.

Zweig-Frank, H., & Paris, J. (1995). The five factor model of personality in borderline personality disorder. *Canadian Journal of Psychiatry, 40*, 523–526.

CHAPTER 4

The Behavioral Model of
Personality Disorders

ROBERT A. DITOMASSO, JAMES B. HALE,
and STEPHEN M. TIMCHACK

IN THIS chapter, our major thesis is that the behavioral models of learning, both operant and respondent, and their inherent principles, constructs, and processes can be useful in explaining and predicting the onset, development, and maintenance of clusters of psychopathological behaviors in children that may ultimately constitute specific criteria for one or more personality disorders. Personality disorders are characterized by three common factors: repetitive nonadaptive behavior patterns, inflexibility, and self-defeating behaviors (Millon, Grossman, Millon, Meagher, & Ramnath, 2004). We posit that the persistence, consistency, rigidity, inflexibility, and repetitiveness of these specific behaviors are primarily influenced by the presence of unique environmental stimuli, direct and vicarious learning influences, and environmental contingencies that constitute, shape, and maintain the unique learning histories of a particular child. We present a behavioral model of personality development by reviewing the critical role of learning in human behavior, the importance of behavioral principles in shaping and maintaining personality characteristics, and the value of the behavioral model in explaining and predicting personality dysfunction. Regardless of orientation, our position is that the behavioral model, as the foundation for evidence-based practice, provides the most sound technology for providing effective intervention. As knowledge of learning theory and principles (Hergenhahn & Olson, 2005) is the key to eliminating maladaptive learned habits (Wolpe, 1990), we must first examine the basic definition of learning.

LEARNING AND PERSONALITY: UNDERSTANDING COMPLEX BEHAVIOR

"Learning" may be defined as a relatively permanent change in behavior that results from the experience of the individual (Hergenhahn & Olson, 2005). Additionally, learning should not be considered a function of native or instinctual factors or temporary states such as alertness, fatigue, or drug states. The environment of an individual is thus viewed as the primary mechanism through which behavior is acquired, sustained, and generalized. In some instances, of course, behavior is a function of central nervous system development or dysfunction, and there is little reason to expect that learning processes may be the primary causative agent for explaining behaviors. Yet even in such instances, learning principles are inextricably intertwined with these individual differences, affecting response to environmental stimuli and operant strength. Regardless of a child's individual personality traits that may appear pathological, the environment governs these enduring behavior patterns, with contingent consequences determining the strength of operant behaviors and the pervasiveness of maladaptive behavior patterns. As a result, personality can be conceived of as learned behavioral repertoires (Staats, 1993), which allows us to target specific behaviors for intervention. Additionally, B. Skinner (1957) suggested that verbal behavior, likened to a verbal manifestation of personality, is developed, shaped, and maintained by a selection of consequences mediated through a social community. Hayes, Strosahl, and Wilson (2003) suggest that most forms of psychopathology and human suffering are verbal behavior gone awry. Behavior therapy, then, is about strengthening adaptive behavior repertoires, those benefiting the individual, and eliminating maladaptive ones, those that reduce the likelihood of personal goal attainment. Therefore, focusing on the environment not only helps identify specific maladaptive behaviors and repertoires, but it also allows for recognition of the interventions most likely to foster an individual's attainment of adaptive behavior (Gettinger & Stoiber, 2006), practices commonly associated with effective evidence-based programs (Kazdin & Weisz, 2003).

The question of personality, let alone personality disorders, is predicated on the viewpoint one takes in defining what constitutes personality. In defining "personality," Millon et al. (2004, p. 2) note the following: "Today, personality is seen as a complex pattern of deeply embedded psychological characteristics that are expressed automatically in almost every area of psychological functioning." From a behavioral perspective, personality is a constellation of observable behaviors that characterize a person's predictable interactions with the environment, the most powerful determinant of individual child behavior (Hunter, 2003). Overt behavior is emphasized because it is often the reason for identification or intervention, it is amenable to environmental manipulation or control, and it allows for documentation of intervention efficacy (Kazdin, 2001). The overt behaviors displayed by individuals with personality disorders actually constitute a number of stable habits that explain the consistency of behavior across a variety of situations.

This notion has led some, like the late Joseph Wolpe (1990), to suggest that personality is actually the totality of habits composing a person's behavioral repertoire. Personality is evidenced by generalized patterns of behavior across environments; individuals modify behavioral repertoires according to different aspects of discriminative stimuli. For example, tantrum behavior is resistant to extinction across environments because it is a product of both the child and the parent being reinforced for their respective maladaptive behaviors. Most people recognize that the child tantrums because the parent contingently provides reinforcement for the inappropriate behavior; yet the tantrum behavior is also a powerful aversive stimulus for the parent, who is negatively reinforced when the behavior stops. Therefore, the behavior is often generalized in other adult-child relationships in schools and other settings where adult authority figures are attempting to exert behavioral control over the child. As the child possesses a strong operant behavior that is naturally aversive to most individuals, the generalization of the tantrum behavior becomes likely.

When given consistent environmental stimuli and contingencies, the likelihood of a particular behavior pattern, whether adaptive or maladaptive, is quite strong for previously learned behavior or habits, which leads some observers to assume that these habits reflect an individual's personality traits. However, when given an unstructured or ambiguous situation, the discriminative stimuli are less clear and hold diffuse stimulus control. Therefore, the operant displayed may or may not reflect the individual's personality; rather a newly adapted form of generalized and discriminated responding can occur, thereby creating a topographically different, but functionally equivalent, behavior chain that ultimately adds to the individual's personality repertoire. When a maladaptive behavioral repertoire follows and is not modified according to subsequent environmental stimuli, the individual may experience aversive contingencies of increasing magnitude until the behavior chain is broken. It is in these cases that personality disorders are readily observed, as the individual demonstrates persistent maladaptive responses to increasingly obvious negative contingencies (Millon et al., 2004).

Although these behavior chains may be difficult to reverse because extensive practice and consistent reinforcement has made them habitual (Kaplan, 1995), they are clearly maladaptive and warrant intensive behavioral intervention. Because these behavior chains are often complex and difficult to alter, there is sufficient evidence to believe that a functional analysis of the controlling environmental variables will reveal some casual relations and improve the efficacy of interventions. For example, to explain the complexity of the environment and its specific and subtle control over behavior, B. Skinner (1957) proposed the notion of abstraction, which describes any stimulus that appears in various combinations or extensions or shares properties with other similar stimuli that ultimately generate a class of behavior. This process serves to diffuse stimulus control and creates opportunities for discrimination, generalization, and differential reinforcement, and can possibly lead to intervention difficulties such as facing behavior that is resistant to extinction.

When considering repertoires of behavior that constitute personality disorders, the clinician working with children, or adults for that matter, of such complex and strong learning histories, complicated environments, and myriad other maintaining variables may be better served by understanding and appreciating the subtleties involved in maintaining such behaviors. Psychopathology of all types has been traditionally approached by behaviorists with specific interest in identifying common functional dimensions that emerge from the application of psychological principles to a functional analysis of major problem domains (Hayes, Barnes-Holmes, & Roche, 2001).

This focus on observable behavior and the influence of environmental variables avoids putative causes or internal inferences to explain the behavior of children. Rather than focusing on some presumed underlying cause to explain behavior, the behavioral model places emphasis on the behavior itself, which is seen as the problem. The behavior of an individual in and of itself has particular significance.

Among the myriad behaviors that children learn over the course of their development, there are good habits as well as problematic ones. Adaptive behaviors in children are those that facilitate their successful navigation through situations and can be classified as promoting their well-being. They allow the individual to *adapt* to environmental stimuli and contingencies, modifying behavior to reap the rewards offered while simultaneously avoiding punishers. However, children may also learn maladaptive behaviors that ultimately undermine their attainment of adaptive objectives. One of the implicit assumptions of behavior analysis is described by Durand (1990, p. 6):

> Such behavior problems are not abnormalities. Instead, these responses are reasonable behavioral adaptations necessitated by the abilities of our students and the limitations of their environments. Therefore, we have looked to the environment and its effect on the behaviors of our consumers.

Some problematic behaviors have been strengthened by inconsistent or unpredictable consequences, resulting in maladaptive behavior that B. Skinner (1957) described as "superstitious" behavior. Superstitious behavior is manifested in stereotypic, maladaptive response chains that interfere with rule generation and efficient learning (Pisacreta, 1998). Some behaviors provide attainment of short-term contingencies or goals, but the long-term consequences may be quite costly. A major problem is that in most instances, maladaptive responses are essentially incompatible with adaptive responses. As a result, the maladaptive response precludes the emission or elicitation of an adaptive response, with the individual never having the opportunity to obtain the typical positive reinforcers most achieve for the adaptive response patterns. Instead, these individuals maintain maladaptive patterns because they are periodically reinforced for them, typically on a variable ratio schedule, which allows the maladaptive operants to persist with great strength.

Suppressing maladaptive behaviors through punishment (either positive or negative) is often not enough; our interventions also require differential reinforcement of adaptive replacement behaviors. Otherwise, variable ratio schedule reinforcement of a child's psychopathological behaviors will make them highly resistant to treatment and can ultimately lead to a personality disorder. In the treatment literature, this process is generally referred to as differential reinforcement of incompatible (DRI), alternative, or other behavior. Preferably, a DRI procedure is employed to reduce or eliminate the problem behavior because the reinforced replacement behavior is physically or topographically incompatible with the aberrant one (Deitz & Repp, 1983).

CLINICAL IMPLICATIONS

Why do some children learn, and sometimes overlearn, maladaptive habits, while others do not? This is a critical question. To account for the chronic maladaptive behaviors observed in some children, an understanding of reinforcement history is necessary. Cooper, Heron, and Heward (1987) define an individual's history of reinforcement (i.e., learning history) as a unique and cumulative set of experiences that ultimately determine whether a response is likely to be emitted under certain stimulus conditions. Each individual possesses a unique learning history through which behaviors are acquired and linked together. Early behaviorists considered learning history a critical factor in producing a specific outcome in a child. Controlling outcomes is simply a matter of manipulating contingencies in a systematic manner. Over the course of a child's development, it is not difficult to imagine how individual differences in parenting style and related family factors may provide, in part, the foundation for a child's future behavior (Turner & Sanders, 2006). Learning history may provide a blueprint for explicating the psycho-architecture on which childhood psychopathology and later personality problems are built (e.g., Kazdin & Weisz, 2003). If a child's unique learning history provides the blueprint for problematic behaviors, then significant figures in the child's life are, in part, responsible for the construction of problematic behavior patterns. Learning history provides the groundwork on which all future behaviors are built. We may thus expect to find some consistencies in behavioral patterns over the lifetime of a child.

When considering the development of personality disorders, the notion that the child gives birth to the adolescent and ultimately the adult probably never rings more true. There are a variety of potential mechanisms working in concert to produce what we observe as behavioral manifestations of personality disorders. These mechanisms include a variety of factors: positive reinforcement, negative reinforcement, extinction, punishment, and shaping. The complex interaction of these parsimonious principles, while seemingly straightforward in and of themselves, actually form the foundation for enduring patterns of behavior, either adaptive or maladaptive, depending on the individual's learning history. In the operant paradigm, numerous discriminative stimuli of differing positive and negative valences co-occur in the environment, yielding predictable behavioral outcomes. A reinforcer is any event whose contingent application following a specific behavior strengthens the likelihood that a behavior will occur in the future. A negative reinforcer is one whose contingent removal strengthens the likelihood of a future response. There are basically three classes of reinforcers, material, social, and activity, all of which have the capacity to influence behavior. Extinction refers to the withholding of a positive reinforcer following the occurrence of a behavior, which decreases the future occurrence of the behavior. Punishment refers to the contingent application of negative or undesired stimuli following the occurrence of a behavior. These four forces that govern behavior are easily depicted in Table 4.1. However, it is essential to understand that the effect of a reinforcing or punishing stimulus is not due to the perceived quality of the stimulus itself (e.g., M & M candies are not necessarily a positive reinforcer to all children; likewise, a harsh scolding may not necessarily serve as a punisher—although one may certainly believe these are effective strategies). Rather, this relationship must be discovered functionally, and individually, through reinforcer sampling procedures.

In this section we describe the processes through which a child may learn a specific behavior characteristic of personality problems. Take

Table 4.1

Environmental Manipulation

		Provide	Withdraw
	Positive consequence	Positive reinforcement	Negative punishment
		(Example: Praise)	(Example: Time-out)
Contingency	Negative consequence	Positive punishment	Negative reinforcement
		(Example: Yelling)	(Example: Tantrum stops after parent reinforces child's demands)

the example of a child who exhibits extreme dependency as a primary characteristic of concern. Most children are expected to exhibit a certain amount of dependent behavior. At an early stage of development, to do otherwise would be not only extremely unusual but also maladaptive. Like other behaviors, dependency at a given stage of development thus would be considered quite normal and adaptive. The existence of a particular behavior or pattern of behaviors may therefore be evaluated differently depending on when in time and for how long it is exhibited and persists. How much dependent behavior is too much also depends on the extent to which the dependency interferes with the functioning of the child. Initially, parents foster attachment by displaying consistent and contingent reinforcement for dependent behaviors, yet if the behavior pattern persists without modification beyond early childhood, the dependent behavior subsequently becomes overlearned to the extent that it may interfere with the performance of autonomous behavior when independence is developmentally appropriate. From a developmental standpoint, the failure to acquire autonomous behaviors may undermine the child's ability to attain developmentally appropriate behaviors. Others have used terminology such as "self-efficacy" or "self-confidence" or "independence" to describe learning outcomes related to autonomy, but it is clear that typical development requires extinction of dependent behaviors, and differential reinforcement of autonomous ones, if the child is to develop these attributes. In a normative sense, it is the outliers in the normal population who exhibit high levels of maladaptive behaviors that may become targets for reduction and low levels of adaptive behaviors that may need to be increased. How might we account for the observed individual differences in maladaptive behaviors in children?

To account for individual differences in behavior across children necessitates a thorough understanding of differences in the learning histories of the children. Learning histories are unique to each person and represent outcomes stemming from the systematic, consistent, and specific application or withdrawal of contingent reinforcers. The schedule of reinforcement will determine the strength of the behavior displayed or likelihood of extinction should reinforcement be withheld. Significant others in the environment of the child may deliver the necessary conditions that strengthen certain behaviors and weaken others. Ferster, Culbertson, and Boren (1975) describe each person's behavior as a function of environmental forces that alter behavior while the behavior also alters the action of the environment.

The behavioral model posits the existence of contingencies that have selectively rewarded dependent behaviors and perhaps extinguished any signs of independent behaviors in a child who becomes overly dependent. This outcome may represent the manner in which behaviors become part of the behavioral repertoire of a child. A child who has been shaped in this manner may be expected to generalize the dependency to other situations, people, and settings. In these other settings, individuals who display behaviors similar to those who initially reinforced dependent behavior are easily recognized and sought after, as these individuals display the discriminative stimuli, or abstractions thereof, which elicit the dependent maladaptive behaviors. Dependent deference to these individuals increases the probability that dependence will be reinforced on at least a variable ratio schedule. Repeated experiences with these individuals, otherwise known as practice, may serve to increase the habit strength of the maladaptive behavior in question. The contingent delivery of aversive stimuli that result from maladaptive behavior by significant others not only reduces the likelihood of the child displaying adaptive behaviors such as independence but may also result in repetition of the maladaptive behaviors performed. The pattern becomes more ritualized and strengthened across environments, so that when an adaptive behavior occurs at a very low level, there is less likelihood of the behavior being reinforced. In this sense, the behavior may become so overlearned that it is consistently demonstrated again and again. Because engaging in one maladaptive behavior may be incompatible with the emission of an adaptive behavior, the likelihood of adaptive behaviors occurring is further decreased.

The behavioral model proposes that children, like adults, are highly susceptible to the influence of contingencies, especially tangible and social reinforcers (Kazdin & Weisz, 2003). Mallot, Tillema, and Glenn (1978) describe an innate biological endowment that enables some stimuli to be rewarding whereas others remain punishing. Because the behavior of the child also impacts the environment, it is likely that the child elicits certain types of responses from important figures in the environment that may serve to sustain the behaviors. It is also likely that certain figures in the child's environment may come to serve as discriminative stimuli for the occurrence of the behavior in question. Over time, certain behaviors such as dependency may be selectively reinforced and learned to the exclusion of other, more adaptive behavior. With extinction of adaptive responding, and dependent maladaptive behaviors maintained on a variable ratio schedule of reinforcement, the likelihood of behavior change becomes improbable. Without intervention, these maladaptive habits continue despite even differential reinforcement of low rates or levels of responding, because the dependent child seeks the discriminative stimuli—the individuals and situations—that are most likely to reinforce and maintain the maladaptive behavioral repertoire.

The next question is why certain behaviors that constitute a personality disorder may co-occur. This is an interesting problem. A cluster of behaviors that consistently occur in a group of children who share a common diagnosis suggests a number of possibilities. The behavioral model proposes that these co-occurring behaviors are subject to laws of learning. Regardless of the behavior, they are similarly influenced by contingencies operating in the child's environment. This phenomenon may mean that because these behaviors co-occur, there is more opportunity for these clusters of behaviors to be jointly reinforced. One behavior may serve as a discriminative stimulus for the next, similar to the explanation of how complex behavior chains such as language are developed. Certain behavior chains within a given diagnostic category may therefore have more opportunity to be jointly reinforced than behavior chains occurring in another diagnostic category. Generally speaking, the fact that certain behaviors are more likely to occur together means that they may represent different aspects or facets of behavior domains. If certain behavior chains are more likely to receive concomitant reinforcement, they are more likely to be generalized across situations and environments than other behavior chains. As a result, these chains become more stable and consistent in their simultaneous manifestation, leading others to consider them comorbid disorders. As these comorbid disorders share substantial variance and are not easily discriminated at the disorder level (Lilienfeld, Waldman, & Israel, 1994), examining them in the context of discrete behavior chains is not only worthwhile diagnostically, but critical for intervention as well.

Of course, not all children who share a common diagnosis exhibit all of the behaviors listed as part of the formal criteria. Not all individuals who share a similar label are uniformly the same. The issue here is how to account for the occurrence of this phenomenon. As discussed earlier, to truly understand the development and persistence of behavior requires an appreciation of the unique learning history of a given individual. Two children who exhibit behaviors characteristic of being overly dependent may overlap on some behavioral criteria and not on others. The reason for this difference appears to lie in their learning histories. Given differences in family environments it is extremely unlikely that the exact same behaviors would be learned across all instances. Subtle differences in behaviors and schedules of reinforcement may be enough to account for this observation.

Borderline Personality Disorder is an excellent example of how different discriminative stimuli, contingency management, and schedules of reinforcement result in maladaptive behaviors that are similar to yet different from those found in other disorders (e.g., dependent behaviors, antisocial behaviors). A child may have developed the dependent behavior patterns described previously, only to have that established pattern disrupted by unpredictable negative punishment or withdrawal of reinforcement for the dependent behaviors. Predictably, the child then displayed an extinction burst (initial increased responding when contingent reinforcement is removed) in an attempt to maintain previously acquired operants. In the child with borderline features, this extinction burst includes defiance and verbal and/or physical aggressiveness, or perhaps withdrawal of affiliative or affectionate behaviors. But instead of having that extinction burst gradually eliminated through differential reinforcement of adaptive prosocial responding, the child is reinforced for these behaviors on a variable ratio or interval schedule, thereby maintaining the love-hate relationships these individuals often display.

Where do the volatile and paranoid behaviors come from? One need only look to respondent principles of experimental neurosis and operant principles of superstitious behavior to find the answer. Because of behavioral instability, a parent, friend, or partner who interacts with an individual with borderline behaviors may display inconsistent behaviors themselves. These behaviors serve as unpredictable discriminative stimuli for the person with borderline behaviors, as ambiguous stimuli can elicit or inhibit subsequent behaviors, leading to experimental neuroses (see Wolpe & Plaud, 1997). A child who cannot discriminate between parental expressions of acceptance and criticism is likely to develop considerable anxiety in performance situations, and this anxiety could unpredictably lead to dependent or disruptive behavior in an individual with borderline features. When poorly discriminated stimuli either elicit or inhibit subsequent behaviors, labile behavior is more likely to result. In addition, differential reinforcement and punishment of the individual's behavior in these situations is likely to occur in an unpredictable or random fashion, which leads to superstitious behavior (Heltzer & Vyse, 1994). These behaviors may be even more resistant to intervention if second-order response-independent contingencies are displayed, where high rates and durations of superstitious behavior are maintained in these conditions (e.g., Ninness & Ninness, 1999). These distorted, inconsistent, and apparently unpredictable behavioral patterns or repertoires may lead some clinicians to conclude that the borderline individual is suspicious or paranoid. Even the impulsivity inherent in borderline criteria can be explained by escape behavior resulting from increased sensitivity to external stimuli and loss of reinforcement (Bjork, Dougherty, Huang, & Scurlock, 1998).

Although we have used the term "behavior" to describe a generic and global set of observable responses that are presumed to reflect a child's level of personality functioning, the subtle and complex individual differences that constitute a child's learning history are so important to discuss and, to be true to the behavioral paradigm, require a considerable functional analysis, as this will serve as such a valuable key to intervention. Stimuli can either elicit behaviors or serve as consequences for behaviors, suggesting the need for integration of respondent and operant conditioning principles (Reidel, Heiby, & Kopetskie, 2001). Moreover, when discussing the determinants of personality development and dysfunction in children or adults, the traditional explanatory nomenclature consists of trait theory, developmental theories, or theories involving physiological discussions of temperament. Yet these do not serve us with the necessary causal relations that lead to efficacious functional interventions. Behaviorism and its scientific and applied offspring, including applied behavior analysis, experimental analysis of behavior, and behavior therapy, have done little in the way of providing a comprehensive analysis of personality development, let alone the development of personality disorders in children. This may be due to the absence of a unified approach across psychological orientations, where competing paradigms for explaining functional relationships of disordered personality behaviors fail to recognize other psychology perspectives (e.g., Staats, 1999). Regardless, much work is needed to understand the functional determinants of these maladaptive behaviors so that the experimental manipulation of these behaviors can follow. This information can help clinicians overcome their propensity to ignore or minimize environmental determinants of maladaptive behaviors in this population and recognize the utility of behavior therapy in helping these individuals overcome their personality disorder behavior.

Most clinicians understand and accept that behavior therapy is very effective at helping individuals eliminate certain maladaptive behaviors from their repertories. Individuals with anxiety, phobic, obsessive-compulsive, or autistic disorders are often cited as the few populations that can be helped through the highly effective procedures of behavior therapy (see Kazdin & Weisz, 2003), yet few realize the potential of extended applications of behavior therapy for individuals with personality disorders. Behaviorists, in part, may be to blame. In an attempt to quantify and objectify every instance of human interaction and avoid mentalistic explanations and explanatory fictions, behaviorists may have limited the technology and science of human behavior to particular clinical populations. Some disorders easily lend themselves to a functional analysis and quantifiable occurrence of responses, but other disorders, including those of personality, require a more sophisticated analysis. However, this does not negate the use of the basic principles of behavior when considering more complex disorders, including personality disorders.

As early as 1934, B. Skinner began considering a functional analysis of one of the most complex human behaviors: language. In infancy, children learn that sounds and gestures serve communicative intent by effecting behavior in the listener. Sounds and gestures gradually become associated and strengthened with certain utterances after repeated exposure to sound-behavior relationships result in reinforcing effects. Sounds, gestures, and utterances are eventually shaped into single-syllable words through continued stimulus pairing and then into practical and meaningful words. Through associative learning, words are paired with other words that represent external overt behaviors, allowing for more complex behavior chains that are subject to the laws of reinforcement. In fact, this aspect of language is now the focus of the field of linguistics and is called pragmatics, or the *function* of language.

As mentioned previously, the unique, subtle, and complex histories of learning by reinforcement and punishment are in part responsible for the total of an individual's habits: his or her personality. A behavioral analysis of personality is not entirely implausible when considering some of B. Skinner's original work. One of his landmark publications, *Verbal Behavior* (B. Skinner, 1957), provides a complete analysis of how language is learned, generalized, maintained, and converted into private verbal behavior, or what we commonly call thought (see Hayes, Barnes-Holmes, & Roche, 2001; Hayes, Strosahl, & Wilson, 2003).

Clinicians not trained in behavioral therapy are likely to believe that personality, and especially the development of personality disorders in children, are the result and function of qualities of temperament, including sociability, frustration tolerance, impulsivity, anxiety tolerance, and behavioral inhibition. Although these intrinsic or phylogenetic variables may be considered biological constraints on learning, thereby limiting the efficacy of behavioral applications, they simply classify and label theoretical reasons for behavior. Even if one acknowledges the relevance of these purported intrinsic constructs, it is essential to recognize that environmental contingencies determine the manifestation of these characteristics, their frequency, strength, severity, duration, and maintenance. Furthermore, classification and theoretical explanation are not the same as functional explanation. Although it is important to classify psychopathology, including personality disorders, for communicative ease when describing individual behavioral repertoires, the current diagnostic nomenclature provides little in the area of functional explanation or intervention.

Functional explanation of the development of personality disorders in children includes an in-depth analysis of their acquired chains of verbal behavior (language repertoires) and other operant and respondent chains (response classes). These behaviors are often given labels such as anxious, dependent, withdrawn, depressed, obsessive, aloof, inattentive, gregarious, aggressive, destructive, and cruel. One phenomenon that seems to transcend all child development is that infants often display behavior that is in their own self-interest. Behaviorally, there is a plausible explanation for their "selfish" behaviors, for the survival of infants is tenuous and dependent on others for both primary and secondary reinforcers. These behaviors are appropriate, but the concomitant behaviors of these adaptive responses can be strengthened and generalized by the environment and ultimately overlearned as adaptive or maladaptive responses.

Whereas other nomenclatures often rely on global characteristics that seem intransient, functional analysis provides us with the necessary explanatory guidance for subsequent intervention development and experimental manipulation of contingencies (O'Neill et al., 1997). For example, young children may grab toys from others or take over playground equipment. These kinds of behavior are typical and generally do not alarm most parents. When a child takes a toy from another child, or pushes another child off a swing or slide, that behavior could be described as curious, immature, inexperienced, selfish, rude, or aggressive, depending on the learning history of the labeler. Labels may be vague, suggesting that the child is "being a brat," or parents may defend their child by saying "he doesn't know any better." Nevertheless, the labeling of the child's behavior, especially offenses against another child, is paired over time with parental behaviors that can be described as visceral, even phylogenetically mediated emotional responses. The parent-mediated consequence for the child further develops the behavior chain. Often, parents will quickly snatch the toy back, verbally chastise the child, slap the child's hand, and deliver the toy to its rightful owner. To the offending child this is seen as punishment, yet to the parent this type of response is a corrective contingency. Parents typically overlook the child's desire or motivation to possess the toy. Although the child's behavior was corrected, the establishing operation, currently termed the motivational operation, for possessing the toy remains constant. The parent may not realize that punishment only suppresses the inappropriate behavior, failing to recognize that differential reinforcement of other, alternative, or incompatible behavior(s) must also occur if the maladaptive behavior is to be replaced. This failure to overlook the establishing operation of the behavior often demands that the child perform different behaviors to satisfy the desire for a particular reinforcer. As a result, there are multiple contingencies at work that mandate generalization of behaviors that vary according to different discriminative stimuli. Consequently, the child learns different responses in order to master the necessary contingency, and these behaviors may be considered maladaptive. Further functional analysis can then be used to explain the likelihood of future occurrences of specific selfish behaviors or functionally equivalent behaviors that are topographically different.

Functional analysis allows for direct examination of the antecedent and consequent events that maintain the target behaviors identified for change, thereby providing the impetus for experimental manipulation of either for subsequent behavior change (Schloss & Smith, 1994). Some might call children who display maladaptive behavior "devious" or "manipulative opportunists" who are "aggressive and oppositional"; yet when we examine the function of the behavior, the strength and quality of the learning history, the availability of competing behaviors, the current contingencies in place, and the differential reinforcement paradigms, we are more likely to view the child as an individual who is responding to and operating in accordance with environmental contingencies—and not as an individual with disordered personality. Once these antecedent and consequent events are identified, experimental manipulation is necessary to reduce maladaptive target behaviors, simultaneously increasing competing adaptive responses. For instance, for a selfish child, sharing and turn-taking behaviors can be reinforced, as they directly compete with the behaviors. It is difficult, but not impossible, for a child to be aggressive while sharing with other children, and careful behavioral monitoring of overt aggressive and prosocial behaviors is critical for determining positive behavioral change (McMahon & Frick, 2005). As stimulus control is established, the maladaptive behavioral repertoires that some may define as personality disorders can gradually be eliminated through extinction (and in some cases positive punishment), with alternative behaviors concomitantly reinforced to ensure that the problematic behaviors are not just suppressed, but are indeed replaced with adaptive ones. In this way, the science of behavior therapy is clearly demonstrated, and effective interventions are documented to ensure behavior change. Without this level of analysis, the maintenance of enduring, stable, and pervasive personality problems is likely. Overall, understanding the multiple sources of control for complex personality behavior, including the speaker-listener environment, the varying and specific properties of stimulus control, learning histories, levels of reinforcer satiation and deprivation, available and varying types of establishing operations, and extinction cues, is necessary in conceptualizing and providing a functional relationship between the environment and behavior manifestations that may be called personality disorders.

Behavior therapy is based on an experimental analysis of individual behavior, governed by single-subject methodological approaches to examine individual behavior change. These objective methods ensure that intervention approaches are developed, monitored, evaluated, and recycled to ensure objectivity in problem identification, problem analysis, intervention development and implementation, and intervention evaluation stages of problem solving, thereby ensuring ecological validity and treatment efficacy (e.g., C. Skinner, 2002). The focus of intervention is on objective, measurable, target behaviors, with contingencies used to effect behavior change. Single-subject approaches require careful contingency management, which must be individualized to address behavioral variability commonly associated with individualized reinforcer or punisher strength (Powell, 1987). This focus allows clinicians to examine apparently overwhelming and pervasive problem behaviors, breaking these complex rule-governed behaviors and behavior chains into subcomponents that are more amenable to behavior change. Advances in functional analytic techniques have allowed for more accurate clinical judgments and effective behavior therapy strategies, but limitations still must be acknowledged (Bellack & Hersen, 1998). Regardless, as the problematic behavioral complex is analyzed and deconstructed, by focusing on one instead of many target behaviors simultaneously, meaningful change becomes apparent, which can serve to document behavior change not only for the clinician, but for the individual as well. As a result, behavioral approaches provide us with not only the functional determinants of behavior, but the technology necessary to effectively reduce, and ultimately eliminate, the maladaptive behavior patterns that could be considered personality disorders.

CONCLUSIONS

Although many of these ideas are rooted in traditional behaviorism, it is important to realize that unification of multiple behavioral approaches should be accomplished to meet the needs of individuals with personality disorders (Staats, 1998). In this chapter, the primary focus has been on stimuli, overt behaviors, and consequences that lead to adaptive and maladaptive behavioral repertoires, with a notable dearth of mentalistic inferences inherent in more theoretical perspectives on personality disorders. To be sure, it can be difficult to apply traditional behavioral approaches to personality disorders (e.g., Nelson-Gray & Farmer, 1998). The organism plays some role in the development and maintenance of adaptive and maladaptive behavior repertoires (e.g., Goldfried & Sprafkin, 1976), suggesting that further examination of positions presented throughout this book is necessary to truly meet the needs of children and adolescents with behaviors characteristic of personality disorders. However, the position presented here is designed to overcome the tendency of those who operate from mentalistic perspectives when accounting for maladaptive behaviors and to promote a functional and objective science of behavior (B. Skinner, 1953).

We have argued that this behavioral perspective not only helps pinpoint problem behaviors, but also forms the basis for understanding and manipulating the overt determinants of these behaviors, with the result being reinforcement of adaptive replacement behaviors and subsequent extinction of maladaptive ones (O'Neill et al., 1997; Schloss & Smith, 1994)—which should be the goal regardless of one's orientation (Kaplan, 1995). A mentalistic approach requires theory-driven formulations and interventions, which is much less useful than data-based decision making using single-subject experimental designs (Kohlenberg & Tsai, 1991) in meeting the needs of individuals with maladaptive behavior characteristic of personality disorders.

REFERENCES

Bellack, A. S., & Hersen, M. (1998). *Behavioral assessment: A practical handbook* (4th ed.). Boston: Allyn & Bacon.

Bjork, J. M., Dougherty, D. M., Huang, D., & Scurlock, C. (1998). Self-reported impulsivity is correlated with laboratory-measured escape behavior. *Journal of General Psychology, 125,* 165–174.

Cooper, J. O., Heron, T. E., & Heward, W. L. (1987). *Applied behavior analysis.* Upper Saddle River, NJ: Prentice-Hall.

Deitz, D. E. D., & Repp, A. C. (1983). Reducing behavior through reinforcement. *Exceptional Education Quarterly, 3,* 34–46.

Durand, V. M. (1990). *Severe behavior problems: A functional communication training approach.* New York: Guilford Press.

Ferster, C. B., Culbertson, S., & Boren, M. C. (1975). *Behavior principles* (2nd ed.). Englewood Cliffs, NJ: Prentice-Hall.

Gettinger, M., & Stoiber, K. C. (2006). Functional assessment, collaboration, and evidence-based treatment: Analysis of a team approach for addressing challenging behaviors in young children. *Journal of School Psychology, 44*(3), 231–252.

Goldfried, M. R., & Sprafkin, J. N. (1976). *Behavioral personality assessment.* Morristown, NJ: General Learning Press.

Hayes, S. C., Barnes-Holmes, D., & Roche, B. (2001). *Relational frame theory: A post-Skinnerian account of human language and cognition.* New York: Kluwer Academic/Plenum Press.

Hayes, S. C., Strosahl, K. D., & Wilson, K. G. (2003). *Acceptance and commitment therapy: An experiential approach to behavior change.* New York: Guilford Press.

Heltzer, R. A., & Vyse, S. A. (1994). Intermittent consequences and problem-solving: The experimental control of "superstitious" beliefs. *Psychological Record, 44,* 155–165.

Hergenhahn, B. R., & Olson, M. H. (2005). *Introduction to theories of learning* (7th ed.). Upper Saddle River, NJ: Pearson Prentice-Hall.

Hunter, L. (2003). School psychology: A public health framework III: Managing disruptive behaviors in schools—The value of a public health and evidence-based perspective. *Journal of School Psychology, 41*(1), 39–59.

Kaplan, J. S. (1995). *Beyond behavior modification: A cognitive-behavioral approach to behavior management in the school* (3rd ed.). Austin, TX: ProEd.

Kazdin, A. E. (2001). *Behavior modification in applied settings* (6th ed.). Belmont, CA: Wadsworth.

Kazdin, A. E., & Weisz, J. R. (2003). *Evidence-based psychotherapies for children and adolescents.* New York: Guilford Press.

Kohlenberg, R. J., & Tsai, M. (1991). *Functional analytic psychotherapy: A guide for creating intense and curative therapeutic relationships.* New York: Plenum Press.

Lilienfeld, S. O., Waldman, I. D., & Israel, A. C. (1994). A critical examination of the use of the term and concept of comorbidity in psychopathology research. *Clinical Psychology: Science and Practice, 1,* 71–83.

Mallot, R. W., Tillema, M., & Glenn, S. (1978). *Behavior analysis and behavior modification: An introduction.* Kalamazoo, MI: Behaviordelia.

McMahon, R. J., & Frick, P. J. (2005). Evidence-based assessment of conduct problems in children and adolescents. *Journal of Clinical Child and Adolescent Psychology, 34*(3), 477–505.

Millon, T., Grossman, S., Millon, C., Meagher, S., & Ramnath, R. (2004). *Personality disorders in modern life* (2nd ed.). Hoboken, NJ: Wiley.

Nelson-Gray, R. O., & Farmer, R. F. (1998). Behavioral assessment of personality disorders. *Behavior Research and Therapy, 37,* 347–368.

Ninness, H. A. C., & Ninness, S. K. (1999). Contingencies of superstition: Self-generated rules and responding during second-order response-independent schedules. *Psychological Record, 49,* 221–243.

O'Neill, R. E., Horner, R. H., Albin, R. W., Sprague, J. R., Storey, K., & Newton, J. S. (1997). *Functional assessment and program development for problem behavior: A practical handbook.* Pacific Grove, OR: Brooks/Cole.

Pisacreta, R. (1998). Superstitious behavior and response stereotypy prevent the emergence of efficient rule governed behavior in humans. *Psychological Record, 48,* 251–274.

Powell, D. A. (1987). Cognitive and affective components of reinforcement. *American Psychologist, 42,* 409–410.

Reidel, H. P. R., Heiby, E. M., & Kopetskie, S. (2001). Psychological behaviorism theory of bipolar disorder. *Psychological Record, 51,* 507–532.

Schloss, P. J., & Smith, M. A. (1994). *Applied behavior analysis in the classroom.* Boston: Allyn & Bacon.

Skinner, B. F. (1953). *Science and human behavior.* New York: Free Press.

Skinner, B. F. (1957). *Verbal behavior.* Acton, MA: Copley.

Skinner, C. H. (2002). Inquiry and critical thinking in school-based problem solving: Behavioral psychology in the schools. *Inquiry: Critical Thinking across the Disciplines, 21,* 5–7.

Staats, A. W. (1993). Personality theory, abnormal psychology, and psychological measurement: A psychological behaviorism. *Behavior Modification, 17,* 8–42.

Staats, A. W. (1998). Unifying psychology: A scientific or non-scientific task. *Journal of Theoretical and Philosophical Psychology, 18,* 70–79.

Staats, A. W. (1999). Unifying psychology requires new infrastructure, theory, method and research agenda. *Review of General Psychology, 3,* 3–13.

Turner, K. M., & Sanders, M. R. (2006). Dissemination of evidence-based parenting and family support strategies: Learning from the triple P—Positive Parenting Program system approach. *Aggression and Violent Behavior, 11*(2), 176–193.

Wolpe, J. (1990). *The practice of behavior therapy* (4th ed.). New York: Pergamon Press.

Wolpe, J., & Plaud, J. J. (1997). Pavlov's contributions to behavior therapy. *American Psychologist, 52,* 966–972.

CHAPTER 5

Personality Disorders: A Cognitive Developmental Perspective

WILLIAM J. LYDDON and DARLYS J. ALFORD

INCREASINGLY OVER the years in our clinical work and supervision, we have become impressed by the way many of the clinical problems that clients bring into counseling make a lot of sense once they are situated in the context of both (a) the client's developmental history and (b) the unique way that he or she makes meaning out of that history. In other words, there often seems to be an inevitable developmental logic to many of the problems that clients bring to therapy, and even the most disturbed behavior often makes sense when seen through the lens of the client's developmental experiences (Ivey, 1989, 1991; Lyddon &

Sherry, 2001; Mahoney, 1991). In fact, we would go as far as to suggest that in *most* instances, rather than being irrational, meaningless, or nonsensical, client symptoms and problems can be viewed as strategies that were reasonably adaptive and functional in their original developmental contexts (Ecker & Hulley, 1996). However, in the context of current relationships and current developmental life challenges, these strategies no longer serve the client well and thus are no longer adaptive for the client.

Attachment theory (Bowlby, 1969) is a cognitive developmental theory that resonates well for researchers and therapists who take a developmental approach to their work (Lyddon & Alford, 1993; Lyddon & Sherry, 2001; Sherry, Lyddon, & Henson, in press). In fact, attachment theory has become a significant conceptual framework for understanding (a) the more or less adaptive and maladaptive ways persons negotiate various developmental life challenges as well as (b) many of the problems and issues that clients bring to the counseling arena (Guidano, 1991; Liotti, 1991; Liotti & Pasquini, 2000; Lopez, 1995; Lyddon, 1995; Paris, 1998). In recent years, it has been suggested that attachment concepts may be especially relevant to understanding the core features and unique symptom structure of personality disorders (Bender, Farber, & Geller, 2001; Lyddon & Sherry, 2001). As a result, the purpose of this chapter is to provide a cognitive developmental conceptualization of personality disorders in terms of attachment theory. Toward this end, we first provide an overview of some of the assumptions of attachment theory as it relates to personality development in general. Next we examine Bowlby's (1969, 1973, 1980) theory of attachment more closely as a precursor to a review of recent developments in the attachment literature. Third, using Bartholomew's (1990) four-dimensional model of attachment, each of the major types of personality disorders is (a) conceptualized as a particular attachment experience outcome and (b) described in terms of typical antecedent childhood attachment experiences, working models of self and others, and prototypical "feedforward" (Mahoney, 1991) cognitions that are associated with the personality disorder type. Last, the influence of attachment variables on personality development is situated in a broader context of developmental factors and influences with a particular focus on childhood and adolescence.

ATTACHMENT THEORY AND PERSONALITY DEVELOPMENT: SOME BASIC ASSUMPTIONS

There are at least three important assumptions associated with attachment theory as it relates to personality development. What follows is a brief overview of these broad assumptions.

ASSUMPTION 1

Central to an attachment theory conceptualization of personality and personality development is the idea that formative experiences with primary caregivers not only provide the foundation for a person's basic sense of self, but also influence the strategies and capacities he or she possesses to navigate various life span developmental challenges. In particular, experiences with caregivers are believed to influence the development of the following:

- One's basic sense of *self.* Generally speaking, this encompasses a person's fundamental sense of personal worth, value, and efficacy. In attachment terms, these constructs are generally encompassed by the notion of *internal working models of self* (Bowlby, 1973).

- One's basic sense of *others* and the *world.* This dimension refers to a person's view of the predictability, responsiveness, and reliability of others in his or her social world and, in a general sense, the person's evaluation of the degree to which the world is a safe place and others can be trusted. In attachment terms, these aspects of the self are generally referred to as a person's *internal working models of others* (Bowlby, 1973).

- One's capacity for maintaining healthy *self-other* boundaries. This generally refers to a person's ability to maintain a coherent sense of self in the context of interpersonal relationships.

Hypothesized to be indicative of one's relational working models, or *interpersonal schemas* (Safran & Segal, 1990), the capacity to maintain healthy self-other boundaries not only involves the ability to appropriately connect with others interpersonally, but also entails the ability to not lose one's sense of self in those relationships.

- One's ability to successfully regulate *emotional experience.* An important feature of attachment theory concerns the emotion regulation strategies that a person has developed over the life course and incorporated as part of his or her coping repertoire. Thus, in addition to the development of working models of self, other, and interpersonal interactions, attachment theory is also a theory about how individual differences in emotional regulation emerge as the outcome of different attachment experiences. Such affect-laden behavioral patterns become internalized as cognitive-emotional structures (working models) that are believed to influence one's strategies for coping with stressful situations and experiences. Recent neuroscience research suggests that these structures may have a physiological basis. For example, Schore (1994, 2001) indicates that brain development, especially in the orbitofrontal cortex, occurs during a sensitive period of social interaction between infant and caregiver and provides the basis for the infant's capacity for emotional self-regulation. Through repeated "state sharing" and "affect synchrony" (Stern, 1985), the various nonverbal and prelinguistic dialogues between infant and caregiver that are patterned in sequences of distress call (infant) and comforting (caregiver) become scripted in brain structures in such a way that the child repeats the sequences in similar (prelinguistic) dialogues with the self when the caregiver is not present. It is interesting to note that problems of emotional regulation are perhaps the most common problems clients bring to therapy—problems associated with either the underregulation or the overregulation of emotion (Greenberg & Paivio, 1997).

ASSUMPTION 2

Working models of self and others and the emotion regulation strategies forged in the context of early attachment relationships are thought to eventually generalize to a broader base of expectations about others and the world and have been shown to be remarkably stable over time. There are several developmental studies that lend support to this assumption, and a recent compilation of the results of the major longitudinal studies in this area provide compelling evidence for the stability of attachment patterns over time (Grossman, Grossman, & Waters, 2005). However, it is very important to note that from an attachment theory perspective, specific attitudes and feelings about self and others that persist into later periods of life, including adulthood, are not the exclusive result of working models developed in early attachment relationships. Attachment theorists identify at least two primary sources of continuity that explain the stability of one's sense of self and others over time. First, working models persist when they encounter attachment strains of a quality and intensity consistent with the child's early attachment experiences. Thus, one important source of continuity of working models of attachment is what Bowlby (1973) originally referred to as *environmental pressures* that reinforce and perpetuate the working models:

> Environmental pressures are due largely to the fact that the family environment in which a child lives and grows tends to remain relatively unchanged. This means that whatever family pressures led the development of a child to take the pathway he is now on are likely to persist and so to maintain development on that same pathway. (p. 368)

Thus, patterns of insecure attachment, for example, may be viewed as strategies employed by the child over time to cope with the relatively unchanging environmental pressures of a difficult social and interpersonal world.

A second source of continuity of attachment patterns is the way internal working models become self-confirmatory over time through the operation of assimilative, feedforward cognitive mechanisms (Mahoney, 1991). Feedforward processes actively anticipate and selectively attend to information so as to assimilate it into already held beliefs. Such mechanisms fit new experiences into existing cognitive constructions, making such constructions relatively impervious to new information. As Bowlby (1973, pp. 368–369) pointed out:

> Structural features of personality once developed, have their own means of self-regulation that tend also to maintain the current direction of development. For example, present cognitive or behavioral structures determine what is perceived and what is ignored, how a situation is construed, and what plan of action is likely to be constructed to deal with it. Current structures, moreover, determine what sorts of person and situation are sought after and what sorts are shunned. In this way an individual comes to influence the selection of his or her own environment, and the wheel comes full circle.

Bowlby was emphasizing what are now commonly referred to as the self-organizing and self-maintaining features of the human cognitive system—that is, the general tendency of the cognitive system to preserve and defend status quo structures and belief systems (Guidano, 1991; Mahoney, 1991), even when such structures are challenged by inconsistent and/or potentially disconfirming information.

Assumption 3

From an attachment theory perspective, different developmental trajectories produce different personality outcomes. Central to attachment theory is the notion that different attachment experiences facilitate the construction of different working models, which, in turn, tend to be related to qualitatively different personality outcomes. Generally speaking, from an attachment theory conceptualization, personality outcomes tend to fall into two broad categories: the *secure personality* and the *insecure personality*. The secure personality is characterized by a self-system that is relatively open to new information (or feedback).

Furthermore, the working models of secure individuals tend to exhibit a relative balance between feedforward (assimilative) and feedback (accommodative) processes. As a result, the secure personality is relatively flexible and can accommodate new learning and change. By way of contrast, the insecure personality tends to be relatively closed to new information. This seems to be because the working models of the insecure system tend to operate primarily in an assimilative mode and have often foreclosed around a few salient constructs or themes, such as dependence, mistrust, or personal worthlessness. In other words, insecure self-systems tend to be dominated by feedforward processes and as a result are not as open to feedback and new information. Insecure working models tend to assimilate new information under existing guidelines or rules, selectively attending to information that confirms the rules and filtering out information that disconfirms them. Working models of insecure attachment may therefore be viewed as highly developed feedforward strategies that are self perpetuating and relatively inflexible to new learning and change (Liotti, 1991; Lyddon & Alford, 1993; Lyddon & Sherry, 2001).

At their extreme, insecure working models of attachment are at the core of many client problems that involve prolonged and patterned difficulties in interpersonal relationships and emotion regulation. More often than not, such features are also a central feature of problematic developmental personality styles, commonly referred to as personality disorders (Ivey, 1991; Lyddon & Sherry, 2001). Regarding the issue of interpersonal difficulties, Widiger and Frances (1985, p. 620) point out:

> An interpersonal nosology is particularly relevant to personality disorders. Each personality disorder has a characteristic and dysfunctional interpersonal style that is often a central feature of the disorder. There is also some empirical support for the hypothesis that a personality disorder is essentially a disorder of interpersonal relatedness.

Regarding the issue of emotion regulation, Cole, Michel, and Teti (1994, p. 76) suggest that successful affect regulation involves the ability to respond to the ongoing demands of experience with the range of emotions in a manner that is socially tolerable and sufficiently flexible to permit spontaneous reactions as well as the ability to delay spontaneous reactions as needed.

By way of contrast, an inability to regulate affective experience is a significant characteristic of individuals diagnosed with personality disorders (Safran & Greenberg, 1991). Such persons frequently exhibit a low level of awareness of the emotional states of both themselves and others, which contributes significantly to their ongoing difficulties in interpersonal relationships (Cole et al., 1994; Fonagy, 1998).

BEGINNINGS OF ATTACHMENT THEORY

Attachment theory is based on the research and writing of John Bowlby (1969, 1973, 1980). In reaction to psychoanalytic theory, which emphasized children's fantasy life, Bowlby argued that significant real-life events and environmental influences should be the focus of study (Ainsworth & Bowlby, 1991). Based on his clinical observations, Bowlby found that a history of mother-child separations were more common among adolescents who engaged in stealing than those who did not. As a result, he suggested that early patterns of emotional bonding between caretakers and infants serve to later regulate behavior and emotion. According to Bowlby (1969, 1973), there are several inborn, biologically based components that are involved in directing an infant's attachment behaviors: built-in tendencies (a) to orient toward certain types of stimuli resulting in increased attention to the primary caregiver; (b) to attend to perceptual attributes of the primary attachment figure so as to discriminate from other figures; and (c) to prefer familiar figures, all of which serve to increase approach behaviors toward the primary caregiver. For example, the child's expressions of distress are designed to arouse discomfort in the caregiver, who should experience relief by quieting the child and meeting the child's needs. The infant eventually smiles at the caregiver in an effort to communicate a sense of safety and security. Because crying and smiling are recognized and understood universally as fundamental expressions of emotion (Ekman & Friesen, 1972), they become significant features of the child-caregiver patterns of communication and attachment. It is important to note that the goal directed partnership between the child and the caregiver is characterized by *both* behavioral and emotional interactions. Essentially, the caregiver and child are developing interactive emotion-regulation patterns, with each having a unique part to play. As noted earlier, these patterns of emotional regulation eventually become internalized in the child. In secure attachments, emotional self regulation becomes the normative outcome, whereas problems with emotion regulation are characteristic of children who have experienced insecure attachment relationships.

Initial empirical support for attachment theory is most associated with the work of Mary Ainsworth and her colleagues and a laboratory procedure known as the "Strange Situation" (Ainsworth & Bell, 1969; Ainsworth, Blehar, Waters, & Wall, 1978; Ainsworth & Wittig, 1969; Bell & Ainsworth, 1972). In the procedure a 1-year-old child's reactions to the primary caregiver's presence, departure, and return were systematically observed. In one variation of the protocol, a stranger also enters the room while the caregiver is absent to further examine the child's behavioral and emotional reactions. In all of the situations the child is evaluated according to the degree to which he or she (a) maintains proximity to the caregiver, (b) protests separation, (c) reestablishes proximity at the return of the caregiver, and (d) demonstrates pleasure at reunion. From these observations four patterns of attachment were identified (Ainsworth et al., 1978).

Securely attached infants explore their environment while looking back at the caregiver intermittently (Ainsworth, 1985). Though they show distress on separation from the caregiver, they seek proximity to their caregiver in response to distressing stimuli, and are easily comforted at reunion, as indicated by smiles, vocalization, waving, and eye contact. Securely attached children seem to experience the caregiver as responsive and available. The infant appears to operate around the caregiver as though the caregiver is a "secure base" (Bowlby, 1988) to return to when exploration of the environment provokes discomfort or anxiety.

Anxious-resistant (or *ambivalent*) children usually do not explore the environment; instead, they tend to cling to caregivers (Ainsworth, 1985). These children display great agitation upon separation, but at reunion they seek contact while at the same time resisting comforting by arching away from caregivers. The caregiver seems to be perceived by the child as inconsistently available or unresponsive when needed. As a result, during times of distress the child appears anxious and am-bivalent as to whether his or her attempts to attract attention and comfort will be met.

Avoidantly attached children display a pervasive indifference before and after separation with the caregiver (Ainsworth, 1985). These children do not appear distressed when separated from the caregiver and avoid proximity when the caregiver returns, usually exhibited by the children's flat facial expressions of affect and/or preoccupation with inanimate objects. This pattern of attachment is typified by the absence of proximity-seeking behaviors. It is presumed that in these cases the infant's prior attempts at proximity seeking have been either rebuffed or rejected; thus, the child has learned to make no further attempts to seek comfort.

It is important to note that in several studies involving the Strange Situation, there were some children who could not decisively be categorized into the three attachment groups. As a result, Main, Kaplan, and Cassidy (1985) later proposed a fourth category, *disorganized attachment*, to describe children who seemed to display a pronounced mixture of avoidant and ambivalent patterns.

According to Bowlby (1969), the child's ongoing experience of responsive behavior on the part of the caregiver and important others that promote comfort and security frame the quality and type of attachment the infant will develop toward the caregiver. The more secure the attachment, the more successful the child's adjustment and healthy exploration of the environment. These differential patterns of proximity seeking and responding by the caregiver provide the child with expectations that, over time, become internalized into cognitive representations (working models) of self and others. As previously noted, the child's working model of self is an evolving schema that summarizes the child's view of self in the attachment relationship and includes beliefs about worthiness and competence as an individual. Working models of others, on the other hand, are based primarily on the expectations established by the primary caregiver's responsiveness and gradually generalize to a broader base of expectations about others in the world.

TEMPERAMENT AND ATTACHMENT

Although caregiver parenting style is believed to play a significant role in the development of children's working models of self and other, it is important to note that infant temperament *and* caregiver characteristics (e.g., sensitivity) may either augment or erode the bonding process between child and caregiver (Mangelsdorf, McHale, & Diener, 2000; Martinez-Fuentes, Brito de la Nuez, & Perez-Lopez, 2000; Park, 2001). For example, infant level of emotionality is one temperament variable that has been shown to influence early bonding interactions and outcomes. Grossman, Grossman, and Schwann (1986) observed that infants with avoidant attachment patterns generally lacked emotional expressiveness. When separated from the caregiver, these avoidant infants typically displayed blunted or restricted affect and were less likely to communicate distress to the caregiver when they were upset. These researchers have suggested that poor quality of emotional interactions (or lack of emotional connection) may frustrate the caregiver and result in a reduction of soothing behaviors. Results from a longitudinal study of internationally adopted children who were followed from infancy to age 7 showed that infants with difficult temperament combined with disorganized attachment to predict poor ego control and lower levels of cognitive development at 7 years of age (Stams, Juffer, & van IJszendoorn, 2002). By way of contrast, adaptive emotional coping skills, positive peer relationships, and higher levels of cognitive development at age 7 were associated with secure attachment and more manageable temperament in infancy. Similarly, Park (2001) conducted interviews with mothers and completed observations of 47 mother-infant dyads and found that securely attached infants demonstrated more compliance, enjoyed physical contact, and displayed fewer fussy and difficult behaviors toward their caregivers at home when compared to their insecure counterparts.

The quality of the *interaction* between caregiver qualities and infant temperament may also have emotional consequences for both the adult and the infant. For example, Mayseiess and Scher (2002) found that caregivers who interacted with babies who had difficult temperaments (i.e., frequent crying, moaning, and reluctance to be soothed with contact or desired objects) have been found to exhibit higher levels of separation anxiety during brief separations than caregivers of children with easy temperament. These researchers concluded that more maladaptive child-caregiver interactions produced more insecure attachments in childhood. Similar findings have been reported by Denham and Moser (1994) and Belsky (1996).

Taken together, studies of temperament emphasize that the quality of the attachment relationship is a function of the infant's behaviors and how well these behaviors fit the personality characteristics of the caregiver. Some caregivers are better able to accommodate children with difficult temperament. By way of contrast, a parent who requires a great deal of positive feedback from external sources is likely to experience frustration or rejection from an infant who has very little emotional expressiveness. Once a parent begins to interpret the child's lack of emotional reaction as negative, it is often more difficult for the parent to maintain consistent approach behaviors toward the child. In the long term, a disappointed parent may feel that attempts to interact with the child are likely to be without pleasure and thus may decrease contact even when the child does express distress. Similarly, parents who have a low tolerance for social contact or intimacy may view the child's expressions of distress or desire for attention as aversive and avoid emotional interaction with the child. These mismatches between infant temperament and caregiver personality are more likely to lead the child to develop an insecure attachment style and concomitant negative working models of self and other.

MODELS OF ADOLESCENT
AND ADULT ATTACHMENT

Since the groundbreaking research of Ainsworth and colleagues, interest in the study of adolescent and adult attachment has increased dramatically (Bartholomew & Horowitz, 1991; Collins & Read, 1990; Griffin & Bartholomew, 1994; Hazen & Shaver, 1990). One model of adolescent and adult attachment that has generated considerable research attention is associated with the work of Bartholomew (1990). Bartholomew drew on Bowlby's (1973) notion of working models of self and others and proposed a four-dimensional system based on the intersection of positive and negative working models of self and others. The resulting four dimensions of attachment are (1) *secure*—positive self, positive other; (2) *preoccupied*—positive self, negative other; (3) *dismissing*—positive self, negative other; and (4) *fearful*—negative self, negative other (see Figure 5.1). According to Bartholomew (1990), secure persons possess a sense of self-worth and generally expect that others are trustworthy, available, and responsive. Those characterized by negative working models of self and positive working models of other (preoccupied attachment) maintain a sense of personal unworthiness while trying to meet the expectations of others, who are viewed as more worthy. Individuals who view themselves in positive ways while maintaining a model of others that is negative tend to dismiss others as unreliable and not trustworthy while at the same time elevating their own needs and concerns as more important and legitimate. Those whose working models of self and others are both negative (fearful category) expect that others will be rejecting and untrustworthy and tend to believe that they actually deserve the poor treatment of others. Bartholomew (1990, p. 162) cautioned that the

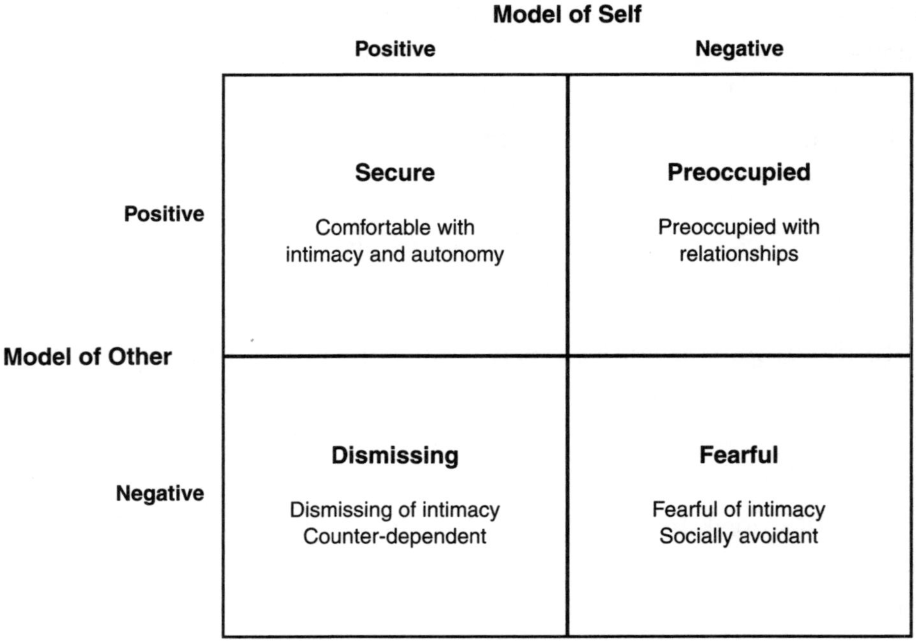

Model of Self

	Positive	Negative
Positive	**Secure** Comfortable with intimacy and autonomy	**Preoccupied** Preoccupied with relationships
Negative	**Dismissing** Dismissing of intimacy Counter-dependent	**Fearful** Fearful of intimacy Socially avoidant

Model of Other

Figure 5.1　The Four-Dimensional Model of Attachment

four categories of attachment were not generated on the assumption that "all individuals are expected to exhibit a single attachment style." Rather, the four attachment dimensions provide a prototype for differentiating the working models conceptually and identifying behaviors and feelings associated with these different cognitive schemas. According to Bartholomew, it is appropriate to view attachment as multidimensional, recognizing that some individuals may exhibit one or more dimensions predominantly.

ATTACHMENT AND PERSONALITY DYSFUNCTION

From an attachment theory perspective, we view personality disorders as the cognitive developmental outcome of insecure working models of self and others that have become self-confirmatory and dominated by feedforward processes. As a result, such working models are relatively inflexible, rigid, and closed to new information. Similarly, the emotional repertoires that are embedded in these working models are also problematic in that they are often inflexible and limit one's adaptive functioning in social, occupational, and relational situations. The four-dimensional model developed by Bartholomew and Horowitz (1991) is useful in understanding the working models and organizational features of thinking-feeling associated with those diagnosed with personality disorders.

The 10 personality disorders listed in the fourth edition of the *Diagnostic and Statistical Manual of Mental Disorders* (*DSM-IV*; American Psychiatric Association, 1994)—dependent, obsessive-compulsive, histrionic, avoidant, paranoid, antisocial, narcissistic, schizotypal, schizoid, and borderline—are described in a way that provides an excellent starting point for understanding the tendency of clients to repeat their developmental past in the present. However, as an atheoretical diagnostic guide, the *DSM-IV* does not provide much information on problem development or problem solution. When considering the role of individual differences in insecure attachment on the etiology of personality disorders, a viable cognitive developmental framework emerges. In the following section, we draw from the work of Lyddon and Sherry (2001) and others to illustrate hypothesized associations between the three insecure attachment dimensions (preoccupied, fearful, and dismissing) and the 10 personality disorders in terms of their developmental antecedents, working models of self and others, and core, feedforward beliefs. Toward this end, prototypical personality disorders associated with the primary insecure attachment dimensions are described, followed by an illustration of personality disorders that tend to reflect a combination of two or more insecure attachment dimensions.

PREOCCUPIED ATTACHMENT DIMENSION

Preoccupied individuals maintain a sense of personal unworthiness and a positive view of others. These patterns are descriptive of Dependent, Obsessive-Compulsive, and Histrionic Personality Disorders. People with a dependent personality style lack assertive communication skills and self-confidence. With other persons they often exhibit clinging, compliant, placating, and self-sacrificing behaviors. A common thread in family histories of those diagnosed with Dependent Personality Disorder is overprotection and a general message from caregivers that they are not capable of doing things by themselves (Bornstein, 1992). From an attachment theory perspective, the working model of self is one of inadequacy, and the model of others includes the theme that others are in one's life to take care of one. The range of affective expressions is usually limited to confusion, fear, or anxiety about inadequate performance, often coupled with the suppression of anger or other emotions that might threaten disapproval from those who are the target of the dependency. Core, feedforward beliefs include the following: "I can't survive without constant contact with someone who can take care of me"; "I am unable to function without continual help from others who are more capable than I" (Sperry & Mosak, 1996).

Those diagnosed with Obsessive-Compulsive Personality Disorder often exhibit patterns characteristic of workaholics and perfectionists. Family histories often include parental overinvolvement and demands for high achievement, with caregiver attention and approval conditionally based on these achievement standards (Ivey, 1991). Control is a central theme and extends to interpersonal, affective, and cognitive aspects of the disorder. For example, rules and orderliness are believed to bring about perfection, and this often leads to inflexibility and a sense of righteousness or superiority over those who don't follow the rules (Ingram, 1982). Demonstrations of spontaneous affection or emotionality may be seen as out of control. Behaviors associated with this disorder are similar to Type A personality traits that include hostility, competitiveness, and time urgency. Underlying efforts toward perfectionism is a constant fear of being discovered as inadequate, with no chances of reaching perfection. A person exhibiting Obsessive-Compulsive Personality Disorder exemplifies a preoccupied attachment (negative view of self and positive view of others), particularly in their ongoing fear of being discovered by others as inadequate and their constant strivings to be better than others (who might, in fact, be more "perfect"). A predominant feedforward message of the obsessive-compulsive self system is "Always be prepared for the unpredictable demands of life" (Sperry & Mosak, 1996).

Histrionic Personality Disorder is also characterized by a negative view of self and a positive view of others and is evidenced by the person's constant efforts to be the center of attention. Emotions are often displayed as a means to attract others' attention and may be very dramatic, though unrelated to any real experience of emotion. Others, in fact, typically see these "drama queen" performances as insincere and manipulative. These excessive appeals for attention are often the result of parenting styles that were either enmeshed or engulfing. The child basically learns from the parent, "If you do what I want, I will give you my attention" (Lyddon & Sherry, 2001, p. 409). Interestingly, histrionic individuals are often quite fearful or incapable of maintaining intimacy in relationships. The idea that the working model of others is positive can be seen in the high degree of suggestibility: opinions and feelings are easily influenced by others and by current fads (American Psychiatric Association, 1994, p. 655). Furthermore, the numerous ways the person seeks outside definition of the self through clothing, attention seeking, and suggestibility demonstrate the negative working model of self. All of these features tend to be captured by the dominant feedforward belief "I need the attention of others in order to feel important and worthwhile."

FEARFUL ATTACHMENT DIMENSION

The prototype of fearful attachment, Paranoid Personality Disorder, clearly demonstrates a strong mistrust of others and lack of confidence in self (negative working models of self *and* others). Persons diagnosed with this disorder are often viewed as hypervigilant, resistant to external influences, and chronically tense (American Psychiatric Association, 1994). They often show very restricted affect, probably in an effort to control outward expression of emotions and to prevent any revealing of vulnerability. Interpersonal relationships are difficult because of the person's distrustfulness, secrecy, and tendency to blame others. This insecure personality style is commonly associated with either a family history of outright rejection and persecution or experience with caregivers who utilize a vigilant and critical approach to parenting (Thompson-Pope & Turkat, 1993). In essence, the child comes to believe that he or she is defective in some way and that others are looking to discover these flaws. Beliefs about the harmful intentions of others often contribute to the paranoid person's increased social isolation; this makes it even more difficult for his or her core beliefs about self and others to change.

Dismissing Attachment Dimension

Those diagnosed with Schizoid Personality Disorder are prototypical of dismissing attachment (positive working model of self and a negative model of others). They have minimal interest in other people and are often aloof and indifferent. Family histories of such persons involve experiences with caregivers who are rigid, emotionally unresponsive, and undersocialized in interpersonal skills (Thompson-Pope & Turkat, 1993). This family environment conveys the message:

> "Who are you, what do you want?" These interactions lead to a view of the self that reinforces this difference from others while it decreases their immediate need for interaction with others. This rigid, unresponsive developmental history helps to create the belief "Others are indifferent and the world is difficult, so why try to establish relationships?" These individuals are not bothered by their lack of interpersonal relationships and therefore can be conceptualized with positive self view. (Lyddon & Sherry, 2001, p. 410)

Combined Attachment Dimensions

As Lyddon and Sherry (2001) note, certain personality disorders seem to reflect the combination of different attachment dimensions. For example, Avoidant Personality Disorder seems to incorporate both preoccupied and fearful attachment dimensions. The view of self is clearly negative, but the working model of others appears to fluctuate between positive and negative. For example, the essential feature of Avoidant Personality Disorder is a pervasive pattern of social inhibition and feelings of inadequacy. Such shyness seems to be based on the desire to be liked and accepted by others, but is also maintained by a fear of rejection and abandonment. This dilemma is captured by the feedforward belief "Life is unfair, people reject and criticize me, but I want someone to like me. Therefore, be vigilant, demand reassurance, and, if all else fails, fantasize and daydream" (Sperry & Mosak, 1996, p. 310).

Another example of combined attachment styles is Narcissistic Personality Disorder. Without a doubt, the dominant feature of this personality style is a negative and disdainful working model of others and a general presentation of self as superior. However, those diagnosed with the disorder often are thin-skinned and possess a fragile view of the self (Lyddon & Sherry, 2001). Although these individuals behave outwardly as possessing zealous confidence, this often is a mask for the intense insecurity they sometimes feel. As a consequence, their working models of self tend to vacillate between positive and negative self appraisals. In essence, the feedforward belief "I am special, unique, and entitled to special considerations" (positive self appraisal) comes in conflict with their more tacit sense of inadequacy. Rather than mitigating the narcissism, this conflict is most often dealt with through even more defensive and zealous claims of confidence and special privilege.

In the preceding we have attempted to provide an illustrative sample of personality disorders that may be understood in the context of prototypical and combined attachment dimensions. For additional elaborations and examples of the relationships among attachment dimensions, working models of self and others, and feedforward beliefs associated with all of the personality disorders, refer to Table 5.1 (also see Lyddon & Sherry, 2001; Sherry, in press; Sherry et al., in press).

Table 5.1

Relations among Attachment Dimensions, Personality Styles, Working
Models of Self and Others, and Feedforward Beliefs

Attachment Dimension	Personality Style	Model of Self	Model of Others	Feedforward Belief
Preoccupied	Dependent	Inadequate, fragile	Others need to take care of me	"I am a weak, fragile person and cannot survive without others."
	Obsessive-compulsive	Extremely reliable	Others expect me to be perfect	"I always have to be prepared to demonstrate my competency."
	Histrionic	Insignificant and unimportant	Others are a valuable source of attention	"I need the attention of others to feel important and worthwhile."
Preoccupied and fearful	Avoidant	Inadequate and frightened of rejection	Others are to be avoided	"Even though people reject me, I want someone to like me."
Fearful	Paranoid	Special, unique, and different	Others cannot be trusted	"I feel safer being alone because others cannot be trusted."
Fearful and dismissing	Antisocial	Unlovable (sense of self as entitled often develops as a defense)	Others will never love or care for me	"I need to be tough and powerful so I will not be hurt."
	Narcissistic	Extremely fragile but masked by overzealous confidence	Others expect greatness from me	"I am special, unique, and entitled to special considerations."
	Schizotypal	*Self-less,* non-existent	Others do not have good intentions	"I am a strange bird."
Dismissing	Schizoid	Positive, unaffected	Others are emotionally unresponsive	"The world is unresponsive, so don't even bother to establish relationships."
Disorganized attachment	Borderline	Positive and negative	Positive and negative	"If things don't go my way, I can't tolerate it. Others are great; no they're not."

ATTACHMENTS BEYOND INFANCY: IMPLICATIONS
FOR CHILDREN AND ADOLESCENTS

The continuity of attachment patterns from early childhood to middle childhood and adolescence is a well-established phenomenon (Grossman, Grossman, & Waters, 2005). For example, Grossman, Grossman, and Kindler (2005) present support for continuity of attachment patterns in their findings from the Bielefeld project, a longitudinal study of 46 middle-class German families assessing attachment patterns of individuals from birth to adulthood. The study was conducted from 1976 to 2000 and included data collection during infancy, childhood, adolescence, and young adulthood. The conclusion drawn from the study was that attachment patterns associated with romantic partners in young adulthood were consistent with childhood response strategies during emotional stress for secure and preoccupied typologies. Similar conclusions about the influence of early attachment relationships and adult romantic relationships was reported by Waters, Merrick, Treboux, Crowell, and Albershiem (2003) in a 20-year longitudinal study. Additional empirical support for the continuity of attachment patterns comes from the Berkeley Longitudinal Study (Main, Hesse, & Kaplan, 2005), in which assessments of 42 participants at infancy, 6 years, and 19 years were reported. Main et al. found that attachment at 1 year predicted a secure response pattern on the Separation Anxiety Test (Slough & Greenberg, 1990) at 6 years of age, and securely responding children at 6 years of age were assessed to be secure-autonomous at 19 years as assessed by the Adult Attachment Interview (Main et al., 1985). In sum, the findings of all of these ambitious longitudinal studies lend strong support to Bowlby's theory that infant-caregiver interaction is a core developmental component with behavioral influences that extend far beyond infancy.

As we have suggested, the significant role of individual differences in early attachment experiences looms large as one explanatory variable for both functional and dysfunctional personality outcomes beyond infancy. Formative experiences with primary caregivers provide the foundation for one's working models of self and others as well as one's emotion regulation strategies. Once established, these models and strategies have a way of perpetuating themselves through childhood and into adolescence and beyond. One reason for this continuity is the anticipatory, feedforward beliefs that serve to maintain the coherence and stability of the human cognitive system—even when those beliefs are not functional. Another reason for this continuity is the fact that the familial context that contributed to the development of the working models also extends into time and tends to be relatively unchanging, thus perpetuating the models that have already been established. In the case of secure attachment, these sources of continuity tend to be facilitative of positive growth and optimal development. Unfortunately, in the case of insecure attachment, the developmental trajectory tends to result in problematic outcomes: low self esteem, problematic interpersonal relationship with others, and emotion regulation difficulties. However, this is not the whole story. Attachment beyond early childhood can dramatically influence established working models—and these attachments may be both healthy and risky for *both* securely and insecurely attached children. This view is perhaps best exemplified by the social development model (SDS; Catalano, Kosterman, Hawkins, Newcomb, & Abbott, 1996).

According to the SDS, there are three essential factors and processes that influence human development: *bonding, opportunities,* and *rewards* (Catalano, Kosterman, Hawkins, Newcomb, & Abbott, 1996). Each of these factors and processes can dramatically alter the trajectory of one's development in either a positive (prosocial) or risky (antisocial) direction. The point here is that one's working models of self and others are always open to renegotiation and change, depending on the influence of subsequent attachment (bonds), the variety of opportunities for such engagements and bonds, and their consequences. As Abreu and Newcomb (2001, p. 95) point out:

Bonding can occur to either prosocial (e.g., school, church, healthy family) or antisocial (deviant peers, gangs, dropouts) groups or institutions. Opportunities represent occasions in which to engage in either prosocial (e.g., homework, exercise, volunteer) or antisocial (e.g., drugs, violence, delinquency) activities. Rewards are the reinforcers (e.g., praise, friendship, money, pleasure) that result from engaging in specific behaviors and that maintain those behaviors that are either prosocial or antisocial.

For example, children experience various significant caregiver-child attachments with teachers, siblings, extended family members, and friends as they begin to explore the world farther and farther from home. Exposure to different social environments may challenge the insecure working models of self and others—especially as avenues for new and potentially more positive engagements with others become available. Regarding the school environment, it is interesting to note that children are likely to engage in increased social comparison as soon as they enter school. There is evidence to show, for example, that as children evaluate themselves in various areas, self-esteem drops during their first few years of grade school (March, Craven, & Debus, 1998; Wigfield et al., 1997). However, from fourth to sixth grade, self-esteem rises for the majority of youngsters, who report positive feelings about their peer relationships and athletic capabilities (Twenge & Campbell, 2001; Zimmerman, Copeland, Shope, & Dielman, 1997). In addition, significant advances take place in both cognitive and emotional development during middle childhood (Berk, 2004). In particular, rapid gains in emotional self-regulation are evident, and there is an observable mastery of adaptive strategies for regulating emotions in most children by the age of 10 (Kliewer, Fearnow, & Miller, 1996).

While it is likely that individual differences in attachment may moderate these documented observations of change in self esteem and emotion regulation during middle childhood, the primary implication of these data is that views of self and emotional coping are flexible and can be altered by changing contexts and challenges. For teachers and counselors working in the schools, interventions designed to improve social skills and social problem solving are likely to have a positive influence on helping children weather various challenges to their self-esteem and emerging capabilities for emotional self-regulation. It is likely that such interventions will, in turn, lead to more positive social feedback that can alter negative working models of self and others. In particular, early intervention in what are likely to become more rigid and maladaptive cognitive emotional patterns can certainly set the stage for healthier adjustment during the unique challenges of adolescence.

The emergence of hypothetico-deductive reasoning and propositional thought (Inhelder & Piaget, 1955/1958) during adolescence opens the door to new learning if the young person is not already too rigid in his or her thinking and emotional regulation. As adolescents are afforded more and more freedom to spend time away from home, travel, and expand social contacts, opportunities for exploration and self change increase. Adolescence is also thought of as a time for identity development and consolidation (Erikson, 1968). From an attachment theory perspective, children who were securely attached in a family structure where exploration of the environment was encouraged by a supportive caregiver are likely to welcome the challenges and novel experiences of adolescence. They are likely to establish secure relationships with peers, particularly a best friend or a romantic partner who can lend support during stress and emotional disruption. For those who are insecurely attached, exploration and experimentation with new relationships may be overwhelming or avoided. It is also likely that the extreme rigidity of thinking and feeling that sets those with personality disorders apart is going to be particularly evident during adolescence and may serve to mitigate the development of higher level cognitive abilities.

CONCLUSIONS

In 1983, Guidano and Liotti, in their now classic work, *Cognitive Processes and Emotional Disorders*, highlighted the significance of dysfunctional patterns of attachment in the etiology of several clinical disorders: depression, Agoraphobia and related multiple phobias, Obsessive-Compulsive Disorder, and eating disorders. Although their work was based largely on developmentally focused case studies, it provided an important conceptual foundation for the emerging field of developmental psychopathology and opened the door to over 20 years of research designed to examine the role of dysfunctional patterns of attachment on the development and maintenance of a wide range of Axis I clinical disorders. As data from contemporary case studies and clinical research continue to highlight the developmental antecedents of Axis II personality disorders, attachment theory has also become a viable conceptual framework for understanding the etiology and maintenance of this diagnostic spectrum (Bender et al., 2001; Laporte & Guttman, 1996; Liotti & Pasquini, 2000; Lyddon & Sherry, 2001; Paris, 1998; Sabo, 1997; Sherry et al., in press).

In this chapter, we have described how differences in (a) the type and quality of bonding experiences with caregivers, (b) the interaction of infant and caregiver temperament, (c) internal cognitive representations of self and other, and (d) learned emotion regulation strategies often lead to qualitatively different personality outcomes in childhood, adolescence, and beyond. In the case of personality dysfunction, we have suggested that Bartholomew's (1990) four-dimensional model of attachment may be a particularly useful framework for distinguishing personality disorder typologies in terms of differences in attachment experiences, working models of self and others, and prototypical feedforward cognitions that are often at the core of each typology.

REFERENCES

Abreu, J. M., & Newcomb, M. D. (2001). Promoting healthy lifestyles among adolescents. In C. J. Juntunen & D. R. Atkinson (Eds.), *Counseling across the lifespan* (pp. 93–111). Thousand Oaks, CA: Sage.

Ainsworth, M. D. S. (1985). Patterns of infant-mother attachment: Pt. II. Attachment across the life span. *Bulletin of the New York Academy of Medicine, 61,* 771–812.

Ainsworth, M. D. S., & Bell, S. M. (1969). Some contemporary patterns of mother-infant interaction in the feeding situation. In A. Ambrose (Ed.), *Stimulation in early infancy* (pp. 113–170). San Diego, CA: Academic Press.

Ainsworth, M. D. S., Blehar, M. C., Waters, E., & Wall, S. (1978). *Patterns of attachment: A psychological study of the Strange Situation.* Hillsdale, NJ: Erlbaum.

Ainsworth, M. D. S., & Bowlby, J. (1991). An ethological approach to personality development. *American Psychologist, 46,* 333–341.

Ainsworth, M. D. S., & Wittig, B. A. (1969). Attachment and the exploratory behavior of 1-year-olds in a Strange Situation. In B. M. Foss (Ed.), *Determinants of infant behavior* (Vol. 4, pp. 113–136). London: Methuen.

American Psychiatric Association. (1994). *Diagnostic and statistical manual of mental disorders* (4th ed.). Washington, DC: Author.

Bartholomew, K. (1990). Avoidance of intimacy: An attachment perspective. *Journal of Social and Personal Relationships, 7,* 147–178.

Bartholomew, K., & Horowitz, L. M. (1991). Attachment styles among young adults: A test of a four-category model. *Journal of Personality and Social Psychology, 61,* 226–244.

Bell, S. M., & Ainsworth, M. D. S. (1972). Infant crying and maternal responsiveness. *Child Development, 43,* 1171–1190.

Belsky, J. (1996). Parent, infant, and social-contextual antecedents of father-son attachment security. *Developmental Psychology, 32,* 905–913.

Bender, D. S., Farber, B. A., & Geller, J. D. (2001). Cluster B personality traits and attachment. *Journal of the Academy of Psychoanalysis, 29,* 479–483.

Berk, L. E. (2004). *Development through the lifespan* (3rd ed.). New York: Allyn & Bacon.

Bornstein, R. F. (1992). The dependent personality: Developmental, social, and clinical perspectives. *Psychological Bulletin, 112,* 3–23.

Bowlby, J. (1969). *Attachment and loss: Vol. 1. Attachment.* New York: Basic Books.

Bowlby, J. (1973). *Attachment and loss: Vol. 2. Separation: Anxiety and anger.* New York: Basic Books.

Bowlby, J. (1980). *Attachment and loss: Vol. 3. Loss: Sadness and depression.* New York: Basic Books.

Bowlby, J. (1988). *Clinical applications of attachment theory: A secure base.* London: Routledge.

Catalano, R. F., Kosterman, R., Hawkins, J. D., Newcomb, M. D., & Abbott, R. D. (1996). Modeling the etiology of adolescent substance use: A test of the social development model. *Journal of Drug Issues, 26,* 429–455.

Cole, P. M., Michel, M. K., & Teti, L. O. (1994). The development of emotion regulation and dysregulation: A clinical perspective. *Monographs for the Society for Research in Child Development, 59,* 73–100.

Collins, N. L., & Read, S. J. (1990). Adult attachment, working models, and relationship quality in dating couples. *Journal of Social and Personal Relationships, 58,* 451–466.

Denham, S. A., & Moser, M. H. (1994). Mothers' attachment to infants: Relations with infant temperament, stress, and responsive maternal behavior. *Early Child Development and Care, 98,* 1–6.

Ecker, B., & Hulley, L. (1996). *Depth-oriented brief therapy.* San Francisco: Jossey-Bass.

Ekman, P., & Friesen, W. (1972). Constants across culture in the face of emotion. *Journal of Personality and Social Psychology, 17,* 124–129.

Erikson, E. H. (1968). *Identity, youth, and crisis.* New York: Norton.

Fonagy, P. (1998). An attachment theory approach to treatment of the difficult patient. *Bulletin of the Menninger Clinic, 62,* 147–169.

Greenberg, L. S., & Paivio, S. C. (1997). *Working with emotions in psychotherapy.* New York: Guilford Press.

Griffin, D., & Bartholomew, K. (1994). Models of the self and other: Fundamental dimensions underlying measures of adult attachment. *Journal of Personality and Social Psychology, 67*, 430–445.

Grossman, K., Grossman, K. E., & Kindler, H. (2005). Early care and the roots of attachment and partnership representations: The Bielefeld and Regensburg longitudinal studies. In K. E. Grossman, K. Grossman, & E. Waters (Eds.), *Attachment from infancy to adulthood: The major longitudinal studies* (pp. 98–136). New York: Guilford Press.

Grossman, K. E., Grossman, K., & Schwann, A. (1986). Capturing the wider view of attachment: A re-analysis of Ainsworth's Strange Situation. In C. Elzard & P. Read (Eds.), *Measuring emotions in infants and children* (pp. 124–171). New York: Cambridge University Press.

Grossman, K., Grossman, K. E., & Waters, E. (Eds.). (2005). *Attachment from infancy to adulthood: The major longitudinal studies.* New York: Guilford Press.

Guidano, V. F. (1991). *The self in process: Toward a post-rationalist cognitive therapy.* New York: Guilford Press.

Guidano, V. F., & Liotti, G. (1983). *Cognitive processes and emotional disorders.* New York: Guilford Press.

Hazen, C., & Shaver, P. R. (1990). Love and work: An attachment-theoretical perspective. *Journal of Personality and Social Psychology, 59*, 270–280.

Ingram, D. H. (1982). Compulsive personality disorder. *American Journal of Psychoanalysis, 42*, 189–198.

Inhelder, B., & Piaget, J. (1958). *The growth of logical thinking from childhood to adolescence: An essay on the construction of formal operational structure.* New York: Basic Books. (Original work published 1955)

Ivey, A. E. (1989). Mental health counseling. *Journal of Mental Health Counseling, 11*, 26–35.

Ivey, A. E. (1991). *Developmental strategies for helpers: Individual, family, and network interventions.* Belmont, CA: Brooks/Cole.

Kliewer, L. M., Fearnow, M. D., & Miller, P. A. (1996). Coping social-ization in middle childhood: Tests of maternal and parental influ-ences. *Child Development, 67,* 2339–2357.

Laporte, L., & Guttman, H. (1996). Traumatic childhood experiences as risk factors for borderline and other personality disorders. *Journal of Personality Disorders, 10,* 247–259.

Liotti, G. (1991). Patterns of attachment and the assessment of inter-personal schemata: Understanding and changing difficult patient-therapist relationships in cognitive psychotherapy. *Journal of Cognitive Psychotherapy: An International Quarterly, 5,* 105–144.

Liotti, G., & Pasquini, P. (2000). Predictive factors for borderline per-sonality disorder: Patients' early traumatic experiences and losses suffered by the attachment figure. *Acta Psychiatrica Scandinavica, 102,* 282–289.

Lopez, F. G. (1995). Contemporary attachment theory: An introduction with implications for counseling psychology. *Counseling Psycholo-gist, 23,* 395–415.

Lyddon, W. J. (1995). Attachment theory: A metaperspective for coun-seling psychology. *Counseling Psychologist, 23,* 479–483.

Lyddon, W. J., & Alford, D. J. (1993). Constructivist-assessment: A developmental-epistemic perspective. In G. J. Neimeyer (Ed.), *Constructivist assessment: A casebook* (pp. 31–57). Newbury Park, CA: Sage.

Lyddon, W. J., & Sherry, A. (2001). Developmental personality styles: An attachment theory conceptualization of personality disorders. *Journal of Counseling and Development, 79,* 405–414.

Mahoney, M. J. (1991). *Human change processes.* New York: Basic Books.

Main, M., Hesse, E., & Kaplan, N. (2005). Predictability of attachment behavior and representational processes at 1, 6, and 19 years of age: The Berkeley Longitudinal Study. In K. E. Grossman & K. Gross-man (Eds.), *Attachment from infancy to adulthood: The major longitudi-nal studies* (pp. 245–304). New York: Guilford Press.

Main, M., Kaplan, N., & Cassidy, J. (1985). Security in infancy, childhood, and adulthood: A move to the level of representation. *Monographs for the Society of Research in Child Development, 50,* 66–104.

Mangelsdorf, S. C., McHale, J. L., & Diener, M. (2000). Infant attachment: Contributions of infant temperament and maternal characteristics. *Infant Behavior and Development, 23,* 175–196.

March, H. W., Craven, R., & Debus, R. (1998). Structure, stability, and development of young children's self-concepts: A multicohort-multioccasion study. *Child Development, 69,* 1030–1053.

Martinez-Fuentes, M. T., Brito de la Nuez, A. G., & Perez-Lopez, J. (2000). Infant temperament and maternal personality as precursors of attachment security. *Annario de Psicologia, 31,* 25–42.

Mayseiess, O., & Scher, A. (2000). Mothers' attachment concerns regarding spouse and infant's temperament as modulators of maternal separation anxiety. *Journal of Child Psychology and Psychiatry, 41,* 917–925.

Paris, J. (1998). Does childhood trauma cause personality disorders in adults? *Canadian Journal of Psychiatry, 43,* 148–153.

Park, K. J. (2001). Attachment security of 12-month-old Korean infants: Relations with maternal sensitivity and infants' temperament. *Child Development and Care, 167,* 27–38.

Sabo, A. N. (1997). Etiological significance of associations between childhood trauma and borderline personality disorder: Conceptual and clinical implications. *Journal of Personality Disorders, 11,* 50–70.

Safran, J. D., & Greenberg, L. S. (1991). Emotion in human functioning: Theory and therapeutic implications. In J. D. Safran & L. S. Greenberg (Eds.), *Emotion, psychotherapy, and change* (pp. 3–18). New York: Guilford Press.

Safran, J. D., & Segal, Z. V. (1990). *Interpersonal processes in cognitive therapy.* New York: Basic Books.

Schore, A. N. (1994). *Affect regulation and the origin of the self: The neurobiology of emotional development.* Hillsdale, NJ: Erlbaum.

Schore, A. N. (2001). Effects of a secure attachment relationship on right brain development, affect regulation, and infant mental health. *Infant Mental Health Journal, 22,* 7–66.

Sherry, A. (in press). An attachment theory approach to the short-term treatment of a woman with borderline personality disorder and co-morbid diagnoses. *Clinical Case Studies.*

Sherry, A., Lyddon, W. J., & Henson, R. (in press). Adult attachment and developmental personality styles: An empirical study. *Journal of Counseling and Development.*

Slough, N. M., & Greenberg, M. T. (1990). Five-year-olds' representations of separation from parents: Responses from the perspective of self and others. *New Directions in Child Development, 48,* 67–84.

Sperry, L., & Mosak, H. H. (1996). Personality disorders. In L. Sperry & J. Carlson (Eds.), *Psychopathology and psychotherapy* (pp. 279–335). Washington, DC: Accelerated Development.

Stams, G. J., Juffer, F., & van IJszendoorn, M. H. (2002). Maternal sensitivity, infant attachment, and temperament in early childhood predict adjustment in middle childhood: The case of adopted children and their biologically unrelated parents. *Developmental Psychology, 38,* 806–821.

Stern, D. N. (1985). *The interpersonal world of the infant.* New York: Basic Books.

Thompson-Pope, S. K., & Turkat, I. D. (1993). Schizotypal, schizoid, paranoid, and avoidant personality disorders. In P. B. Sutker & H. E. Adams (Eds.), *Comprehensive handbook of psychopathology* (pp. 411–434). New York: Plenum Press.

Twenge, J. M., & Campbell, W. K. (2001). Age and birth cohort differences in self esteem: A cross-temporal meta-analysis. *Personality and Social Psychology Review, 5,* 321–244.

Waters, E., Merrick, S., Treboux, J., Crowell, J., & Albersheim, L. (2003). Attachment security in infancy and early adulthood: A twenty year longitudinal study. In M. E. Hertzig & E. A. Farber (Eds.), *Annual progress in child psychiatry and child development* (pp. 63–72). New York: Brunner-Routledge.

Widiger, T. A., & Frances, A. (1985). Axis II personality disorders: Diagnostic and treatment issues. *Hospital and Community Psychiatry, 36*, 619–627.

Wigfield, A., Eccles, J. S., Yoon, K. S., Harold, R. D., Arbreton, A. J., Freeman-Doan, C., et al. (1997). Changes in children's competence beliefs and subjective task values across the elementary school years: A 3-year study. *Journal of Educational Psychology, 89*, 451–469.

Zimmerman, M. A., Copeland, I. A., Shope, J. T., & Dielman, T. E. (1997). A longitudinal study of self-esteem: Implications for adolescent development. *Journal of Youth and Adolescence, 26*, 117–141.

CHAPTER 6

A Systemic Family Perspective on Child and Adolescent Personality Disorders

JEFFREY J. MAGNAVITA

MOST METAL health clinicians who have seen children in various clinical settings can clearly remember a particular child or adolescent who presented a significant treatment challenge. These children and adolescents often respond so poorly to first-line treatment interventions that the clinician is left feeling frustrated and inadequate and without a clear conceptualization of what went awry in the treatment. Often clinicians are left wondering if the personality system of the patient was dysfunctioning and creating havoc within him or her in terms of emotional regulation, self-esteem, and impulse control, as well as in those around him or her, in family disturbances and school and community disruption. These children and adolescents often present with clinical syndromes such as oppositional defiance, Conduct Disorder, attention deficit, learning disabilities, psychotic reactions, affective disorders, and the like. What often becomes evident is that something more is dysfunctioning, beyond the child's intrapsychic system alone. Interactions and relationships with family members, peers, neighbors, and school authorities seem to be fraught with difficulty and recurrent patterns of maladaptation.

The child and adolescent personality is clearly embedded in relational process of interpersonal, family, and social structures (Magnavita & MacFarlane, 2004). From our earliest period of development we are dependent on the relational system in which we are conceived and born. Personality functioning cannot be isolated from the relational system and studied independently without a loss of critical information regarding structure, function, and process. All human behavior is holonic, or characterized by part-whole relationships; parts cannot be isolated without understanding how they operate in the whole system. A theoretical model is the most powerful tool that clinicians and researchers have to recognize patterns, make inferences, and test these hypotheses. Clinicians do so by intervening, observing the reaction, and then altering their approach when necessary. A unified systemic perspective based on the centrality of the family and relational systems offers an overarching framework with which to understand the complex phenomenon of child and adolescent personality dysfunction and disorder.

CONVERGENCE IN CLINICAL SCIENCE WITH APPLICATION TO PERSONALITY DISORDERS

There has been a convergence of trends in clinical science, such as neuroscience, developmental psychopathology, relational and cognitive science, and psychotherapeutics, which has provided an explosion in the field of personology and personality disorders (Magnavita, 2002, 2006; Millon, 2000). The identification, classification, and discoveries concerning the etiology of personality disorders in adults has spawned a new era of interest that has resulted in advances in strategies and the development of specialized treatment (Magnavita, 2004a). More recently theorists, clinicians, and researchers are beginning to explore the precursors of adult personality disorders (PDs) as they emerge in children and adolescent populations, as well as how PDs manifest in children and adolescents, as this book attests. This represents an important stage in applying clinical science to issues of child and adolescent PDs.

Although the diagnosis of child and adolescent personality disorders is controversial, there appears to be an increased need for clinicians who see disturbed child and adolescent patients to be able to better classify, diagnose, and effectively treat them, and their families, as well as the sociocultural systems in which they are embedded when there are signs of chronic personality dysfunction that can become a personality disorder. This chapter presents a unified framework for navigating the total ecological system of these children and adolescents so that clinicians can better focus their treatment, provide psychoeducation to parents and family members, and, most important, intervene early enough, in a focal way, to prevent the development and crystallization of adult personality disorders. Converging evidence and empirical findings are presented to support this systemically and family-based unified theoretical framework.

HISTORICAL BACKGROUND, CONCEPTUAL ISSUES, AND DEFINITIONS OF PERSONALITY DISORDERS

Personality has been an area of intense fascination dating back to the early Egyptians and the Greeks, who offered a theory of the four humors or temperaments (choleric, melancholic, sanguine, and phlegmatic; Alexander & Selesnick, 1966). Contemporary personality, or personology, as coined by Henry Murray (1938), began to emerge as a field of interest in the late nineteenth century, when descriptive psychiatry began classifying mental disorders. During this period the term *moral insanity* was applied to those who displayed impulsive and self-damaging acts but whose reason was unimpaired. Psychoanalytic theory gave rise to the first metapsychology of character that evolved over the twentieth century, resulting in the description of various character types, such as phallic- narcissistic, passive, obsessional, and hysterical. Later, in the 1980s, with the development of a formal and more clearly elaborated diagnostic system for classifying mental disorders, personality was placed on a separate Axis II from clinical syndromes, which were recorded on Axis I (American Psychiatric Association, 1980). Identifying personality disorders on a separate axis and providing atheoretical, objective descriptors that could be used by researchers and clinicians led to a renewal of interest in the study and treatment of disorders of personality. This, combined with what appeared to be an increasing number of individuals with personality dysfunction seen in clinical practice, led to what Sperry (1995) described as a paradigmatic shift, leading to three significant developments: (1) theoretical convergence/technical blending, (2) psychopharmacotherapeutic and psychotherapeutic integration, and (3) multimodal treatment combinations. These developments as well as others are highlighted in this chapter and are consistent with the assumptions of the unified systemically based framework presented.

The next wave in the evolution of personology and the science of personality disorders is to develop clinically pragmatic and empirically sound methods for identifying personality dysfunction in childhood and adolescence and to clarify under what circumstances dysfunction should be classified as a personality disorder and when it represents a precursor to personality disorder. A relational diagnostic and treatment model allows for a unique type of identification (Kaslow, 1996; MacFarlane, 2004; Magnavita, 2000). It emphasizes the contextual nature in which personality dysfunction in children and adolescents emerges, enabling clinicians to select and develop the most effective treatment interventions so that the developmental trajectory might be altered. Of primary concern is preventing childhood and adolescent personality dysfunction, as well as prodromal manifestations of personality disorder, from becoming crystallized and entrenched and transmitted to the next generation; this is termed "the multigenerational transmission process." There is converging evidence that personality dysfunction is transmitted through a complex interaction of genes, familial influence, and societal forces.

CONCEPTUAL ISSUES

The formal classification of personality disorders in adults is a relatively recent (past 25 years) endeavor for clinical scientists and theorists, and there remain many problematic issues with using the predominant categorical model of the *Diagnostic and Statistical Manual of Mental Disorders [DSM-IV]*; American Psychiatric Association, 2000). The *categorical* model basically arranges personality disorders in separate categories that are either present or absent depending on the number of diagnostic criteria met. One problem that has been well documented is the high number of individuals who receive multiple personality disorder diagnoses, which suggests problems with overlap among the 10 personality disorders. This indicates that there is a lack of conceptual clarity in the categories, and an effort is under way to revise these (Cohen, 2005). Other systems of classification have been developed and offer advantages as well as disadvantages. These include *factor-dimensional* (normal and abnormal personality consists of five factors, which are disturbed on a continuum; Costa & McCrae, 1992), *prototypical* (a combination of categorical and dimensional features; Millon & Davis, 1996; Shedler & Westen, 2004), *structural dynamic* (based on integrity of the structure, that is, normal, neurotic, borderline, psychotic—mixed with various personality types—dependent, obsessive etc.; Kernberg, 1984; McWilliams, 1994), and *relational* (interpersonal and triadic—larger systems; Bowen, 1976; Sullivan, 1953). Each system of classification has merit, but no one system alone captures the complexity of the personality. When some of these systems of classification and diagnostic models are applied to children and adolescent personality variation there are likely to be many challenges. Some of these systems were developed in clinical settings based on adult psychopathology; others were primarily based on studies of college students; still others do not pay attention to the importance of the context in which PDs emerge, which is especially critical when focusing on child and adolescent forms.

There is far less evidence about whether applying the construct of personality disorder to children and adolescent populations is warranted. The *DSM* allows for the diagnosis of children and adolescents but only in cases where the disorder has been clearly extant for at least a year, with the exception of Antisocial Personality Disorder, which cannot be diagnosed until 18 years. There are those who feel that labeling adults with personality disorders is unnecessary and stigmatizing "and eschew the construct" (Jordan, 2004, p. 120). However, many believe that the construct has utility for adults. Relative to children and adolescents, until very recently little in the way of theoretical or empirical findings has been available to guide the clinician, and clinical judgment needs to be exercised when considering applying these diagnoses. Kernberg, Weiner, and Bardenstein (2000, p. 6) write, "One reason for this reluctance is that all professionals who deal with children have reservations about labeling them with a diagnosis that implies severity and nonmalleability." Even if personality is relatively fixed in adulthood, as some believe, there is little evidence to suggest that personality is stable in children and adolescents. Thus, it is best to identify and intensively treat these dysfunctional systems as early as possible.

How Does Personality Disorder Manifest in Adults, Adolescents, and Children?

In adults personality dysfunction becomes problematic and warrants a diagnosis of personality disorder when there "is an enduring pattern of inner experience and behavior that deviates markedly from the expectations of the individual's culture, is pervasive and inflexible, has an onset in adolescence or early adulthood, is stable over time, and leads to impairment" (American Psychiatric Association, 1994, p. 629). Personality disorders can be diagnosed in children and adolescents "in those relatively unusual instances in which the individual's particular maladaptive personality traits appear to be pervasive, persistent, and unlikely to be limited to a particular developmental stage or an episode of an Axis I disorder" (p. 631). Conceptualizing and diagnosing personality disorders in children and adolescents is an area that remains conceptually murky, and few available guidelines exist for the clinician and researcher (see Bleiberg, 2004). In one of the few volumes on the topic of personality disorders in children and adolescents, Kernberg et al. (2000) state that very little attention has been given to these conditions, even though it is estimated that approximately 10% of the general population qualify for a PD diagnosis as adults (Merikangas & Weissman, 1986). Therefore, there exist a relatively high percentage of children whose developmental trajectory will result in a personality disorder diagnosis in adulthood. Referring to the empirical literature, Kernberg et al. (2000, p. 4) write, "Most epidemiological studies of mental disorders in children and adolescents typically do not search for the presence of a PD." With children and adolescents there is a great deal of clinical and anecdotal evidence that their personality systems do dysfunction and can represent a chronic course. The most recent "findings from the CIC [Children in the Community] Study make it clear that PD symptom constellations identified in adulthood have their origins in childhood and can be reliably assessed in combined youth and parent reports" (Cohen, Crawford, Johnson, & Kasen, 2005, p. 481). A robust finding has been established between childhood Conduct Disorder and adult Antisocial PD (Lahey, Loeber, Burke, & Applegate, 2005), and early behavior problems are related to adult psychopathology (McGue & Iacono, 2005).

Contemporary Conceptualizations and Paradigms

Personality disorders are a process, not a state—a process that evolves over time through the interaction of temperament, environmental, familial, and sociocultural factors and forces. Adolescents and especially children are unlikely to display fixed patterns of behavior in the absence of familial and environmental contingencies and the processes that maintain them. According to developmental psychopathologists, there are problems with the disorder construct for children (Cummings, Davies, & Campbell, 2000, pp. 344–345):

> The disorder concept implies relatively fixed assumptions about likely etiology and developmental course. In contrast, consistent with a developmental psychopathology perspective, when children's problems are seen as part of a continuum, a different set of assumptions about the etiology and developmental course may apply (e.g., multidetermined and not necessarily likely to persist). Issues of assessment also are intertwined with the classification of children's problems. Placing children into categories of disorders and/or describing their behavior along dimensions of symptom clusters obviously means that children's behavior needs to be measured in some way.

And yet the authors also note the need to classify and diagnose: "Almost all clinicians use some system to classify children's problems, because it provides a shorthand way of communicating with other professionals, and most mental health facilities require that a diagnosis be assigned" (p. 343).

The early Greeks were indeed prescient in their identification of four factors that determine personality, even if they were incorrect in their belief about the way humors influence personality. It has been repeatedly demonstrated by various models that there are three to five primary factors that can account for most personality variations. However, reducing personality to three to five superordinate factors does not adequately account for the uniqueness of personality: No two personalities are ever alike, even in identical twins! One way personality disorders may be contextualized is as a process of dysfunctioning personality or, as previously described, a *dysfunctioning personologic system*, which includes the multiple levels in which the individual is embedded, from the micro-level to the macro-level. The human personality system may be best characterized as holonic. A *holon* is a term coined by Koestler (1978) to describe an individual as both "an independent and self-determining system as well as a dependent part of a larger structure" (Laveman, 1997, p. 58). There is increasing empirical evidence to support this viewpoint. In a review of the literature, Cummings et al. (2000, p. 254) report, "Children repeatedly exposed to intense marital conflict are more emotionally (e.g., angry, distressed) and behaviorally (aggressive, prone to mediate in parental disputes) reactive to these events and report cognitive reactions indicative of greater threat and self-blame. Heightened reactivity to conflict, in turn, has been related to increased risk for adjustment problems in children." The problems associated with labeling a child or an adolescent with what might be construed as a lifelong stigma need to be considered. The construct personality dysfunction is holistically embedded in the systemic framework presented in this chapter, and refers to a system that is not adaptively functioning or is manifesting "bionegativity" (Angyal, 1982) or a "harmful dysfunction" (Wakefield, 1999). Thus, in large part, PDs and early-stage adult versions in children and adolescents are contextual.

Etiological Factors and Empirical Findings

There has been accumulating empirical and clinical evidence concerning the etiological factors involved in the development of personality disorders in adults. There is little question that the etiology of personality disorders is multifactorial and complex, probably with multiple developmental pathways, with roots in childhood experience and temperament predispositions. "The broad categories include: (1) genetic predisposition, (2) attachment experience, (3) traumatic events, (4) family constellation, and (5) sociocultural and political forces" (Magnavita, 2004a, p. 16). "The higher-order genetic factors that undergird abnormal personality variation are important organizing influences, but they are not sufficient to account for the richness of etiological factors that impact on observed personality variation" (Krueger, 2005, p. 246). Personality disorders likely have multiple pathways with no single cause. A recent landmark longitudinal study that followed a large random sample of 800 youths, tracking developmental trajectory, found that

> low family SES, family welfare support, single parent, parental conflict, paternal and maternal sociopathy, and parental illness and death were each independently related to later PD symptoms. Parenting and parent-child relationships—including low closeness to mother, low closeness to father, power assertive punishment, maternal control through guilt, having been the result of an unwanted pregnancy—were predictive of later PD symptoms. (Cohen et al., 2005, p. 471)

With regard to the child cohort, the results show that "childhood characteristics including behavior problems, social isolation, and poor health at mean age 6 also predicted young adult PD symptoms assessed some 16 years later" (p. 471). Focusing on the adolescent cohort, "low social competence, introversion, low self-esteem, not being attractive, high emotionality, and abrasiveness predicted elevated symptoms, including those score two SD's above the mean" (p. 471). The most powerful long-term predictors included early onset of "PD, disruptive disorder, and depressive symptoms" (p. 471). Although childhood abuse elevates the odds of developing a personality disorder, other factors seem more robust, especially maladaptive parenting. The researchers termed this the "maltreatment effect" (p. 471). What is evident from this and other studies is that the relational matrix is the crucible for development of personality disorders, and empirical evidence has provided strong converging evidence that "childhood abuse—physical, sexual and verbal—and neglect emerged as related to personality disorders" (Clark, 2005, p. 525). The family system remains the main relational system responsible for the socialization and rearing of children.

A Paradigmatic Shift: Toward Unified Clinical Science

There has been an emerging movement toward unification of clinical science and the main subdisciplines, personality theory, psychopathology, and psychotherapy, as well as related disciplines such as neuroscience, developmental and relational science, anthropology, and sociology (Magnavita, 2004b). Unified clinical science is benefiting from collaborative interdisciplinary models that utilize new tools such as videotape technology, PET scans, and electrophysiological devices to investigate the mind and relationships (Gopnik, Meltzoff, & Kuhl, 2001; Magnavita, 2002). The identification and treatment of children and adolescents with personality dysfunction require a unified approach that considers all elements responsible for shaping, maintaining, and ultimately providing effective treatment and prevention, so that these systems do not become entrenched or consolidated and lead to lifelong disturbances.

A systemic theory perspective provides a basic framework for unifying these three aspects of clinical science. According to Sroufe, Egeland, Carlson, and Collins (2005, p. 29):

> In general terms, systems imply the mutual definition and interdependence of parts and wholes. Dynamic, living systems consist of mutually influencing constituents interacting over time. Only in functioning does the whole (or a part) have meaning. Such relationships between constituents and whole tend to be maintained even as parts (and the whole) change. In terms of human relationship systems, this is what accounts for continuity across generations. . . . In systems viewpoints new, nonobvious forms of increasing complexity "emerge" from the co-actions of existing parts and/or in the face of new environmental demands.

They describe three principles: (1) The unity of development is the person adapting to his or her context; (2) "Development is characterized by emerging complexity or self-organization. New more complex behavior emerges from what was present previously, and new structures show emergent properties not specified in the constituent parts"; and (3) "At first, there is a mass of undifferentiated units (e.g., cells that are virtually all the same). Then, these form general structures. Later, these structures become more refined and specialized as they are organized into systems. . . . The same principles of integration, self-organization, and differentiation govern abnormal development as well as normal development" (pp. 30–31).

PERSONALITY SYSTEMATIC FRAMEWORK

Personality is not a fixed entity but a system of interrelated domains from the biopsychosocial sphere that are in constant feedback circuits. The personality systematic framework is a component systems model based on the interrelated domains of human functioning from the microsystem to the macrosystem; it can be conceptualized as nested structures (Bronfenbrenner, 1979). Laveman (1997, p. 61) describes the holonic nature of this perspective: "Since the premise that *parts are embedded within wholes producing part/wholes* is true for every level of existence, there is no limit to how far up or down the hierarchy we can go." A personality systemic framework is based on contextualism and is consistent with recent advances in developmental psychopathology (Cummings et al., 2000). "Contextualism conceptualizes development as the ongoing interplay between an active, changing organism in a dynamic, changing context" (p. 24). The authors offer a theoretical framework based on Bronfenbrenner's ecological perspective, congruent with the one presented in this chapter, which they articulate this way:

> Contextualism regards development as embedded in series of nested, interconnected wholes or networks of activity at multiple levels of analysis, including the intraindividual subsystem (e.g., interplay between specific dimensions within a domain such as affect or cognition), the intraindividual system (e.g., interplay between biology, cognition), the interpersonal (e.g., family or peer relationship quality), and ecological or sociocultural system (e.g., community, subculture, culture). Thus, development regulates and is regulated by multiple factors, events, and processes at several levels that unfold over time. (p. 24)

In a landmark volume, *From Neurons to Neighborhoods: The Science of Early Childhood Development*, the National Research Council and Institute of Medicine, Shonkoff, and Phillips (2000, pp. 23–24) used a similar framework to describe human development:

> Virtually all contemporary researchers agree that the development of children is a highly complex process that is influenced by the interplay of

nature and nurture. The influence of nurture consists of the multiple nested contexts in which children are reared, which include their home, extended family, child care settings, community, and society, each of which is embedded in the values, beliefs, and practices of a given culture. The influence of nature is deeply affected by these environments and, in turn, shapes how children respond to their experiences.

Based on an extensive review of the clinical and empirical literature we can divide the total ecological system of human functioning into four interrelated levels, moving from microscopic to macroscopic perspectives (Magnavita, 2004c, 2005a, 2005b).

MICRO-LEVEL STRUCTURES AND PROCESS

The Intrapsychic-Biological Matrix

The intrapsychic-biological matrix basically subsumes the processes and structures that occur within an individual (intraindividual). These include neurobiological processes-structures, affective-defensive functions, cognitive schemata, and temperament predispositions. The process by which this matrix operates can be simplified using a triangular representation. At the lower corner of the triangle the *cognitive-affective schemata* are located. *Anxiety* is on the upper right-hand corner, and on the upper left side is *defense*. These three corners of the triangle all work in synchrony. The lower the level of differentiation, the more diffusion is evident in the way the subsystem functions. The following are the three basic subcomponents of this triangle:

1. *Emotion-Affect and Cognitive Schemata.* Emotion refers to the physiological experience of the basic bodily felt sensations, which include joy, love, anger, grief, sadness, guilt, and shame. There are various lists of the primary emotions that offer somewhat different emphasis (Ekman & Davidson, 1994). In addition, emotional experience must be labeled using the lexicon of emotion before it can be communicated. This has been termed "emotional intelligence"

(Salovey & Mayer, 1990) and popularized by Goleman (1995). Emotional responses are evolutionarily adapted to aid in survival by activating the system and alerting the organism to what is important in the environment to attend to. "Emotion is primary in organizing attachment behaviors and how self and other are experienced in intimate relationship" (Johnson & Whiffen, 1999, p. 367). Cognition refers here to the thoughts and beliefs that an individual uses to form templates or schematic representations for self and others, such as "I am evil or bad" and thus "deserve to be mistreated by others." Emotion and cognition are inextricably interrelated. In a bidirectional process, cognitions activate emotional experience and emotions can elicit cognitions.

2. *Anxiety* is the fuel of much symptom disturbance, clinical syndromes, physical illness, and social disruption. Chronic anxiety is like driving your car with the brakes on; it leads to undue system stress or burnout of component parts-systems. Chronic anxiety, which results from a dysfunctional intrapsychic-biological matrix, can get channeled into various zones. First, defensive operations can become predominant. Individuals can become so overly defended or constricted that they are emotionally unresponsive and detached, or so emotionally dysregulated that their lives are ruled by emotional storms.

3. *Defensive Operations.* Defenses are mechanisms by which we manage and contain the affect that is aroused by life's challenges and the demands of survival. Anxiety can be an adaptive reaction, designed to alert the individual to danger so that immediate appraisal can occur and then a flight-or-fight response can be quickly selected. Defenses are incorporated when there is too much anxiety or when emotion is too powerful for the system to experience and process. Defenses change over the course of development, and there is strong empirical evidence to show that various defenses are more commonly incorporated during different stages of development (Cramer, 1987, 1995, 1997, 1998; Cramer & Gaul, 1988). For example, if a patient is described as

"stamping his or her feet, throwing things, becoming obstinate and growling," it makes a difference if we are describing a 3-year-old or a 23-year-old. Over 100 defenses have been identified and organized into the following categories: *psychotic* (e.g., delusion, hallucination, confabulation), *primitive/immature* (e.g., grandiosity, projection, acting-out), *neurotic* (e.g., displacement, intellectualization, avoidance), and *mature* (e.g., humor, suppression, anticipation; see Blackman, 2004; Vaillant, 1992). Constellations of defenses are as unique as a thumbprint; no two people have the same, even if they have been diagnosed with the same personality disorder. At the risk of oversimplification, defenses in children and adolescents, as with adults, can be said to be either directed inward, as in the inhibited constricted individuals (best described as Cluster C disorders—avoidant, dependent, obsessive-compulsive), or outward (Cluster B disorders—histrionic, antisocial, borderline, and narcissistic), whereas the odd or eccentric presentation (Cluster A—schizoid, schizotypal, and paranoid) are more likely to incorporate defenses that primarily compromise cognitive and perceptual functions.

In most adults this system operates effortlessly on a moment-to-moment basis. When emotion is stimulated by life events, there is some increase in anxiety, and defenses are used adaptively to maintain system integrity. When emotion is experienced at a high level and balanced with rational thought, we describe these individuals as having high emotional intelligence. They are capable of emotional regulation, are aware of the meanings and experience of shifting affective-emotional states, and understand the link to experiences and cognitions and beliefs, past, present, and future. Regulatory functions are an essential process of this subsystem. "Reaction and regulation can be seen in all aspects of life, from the capacity to work harder when one is rested better to the capacity to fight diseases better when one is able to both turn on and off the immune system more efficiently" (National Research Council and Institute of Medicine et al., 2000, p. 94). And, as we shall see shortly, "Regulation in early development is deeply embedded in the child's relations to others" (p. 94). In children and adolescents the system is much more fluid. In young children states of emotional dysregulation, perceptual distortion, and use of primitive defenses are part of the developmental trajectory. Problems ensue when the child or adolescent does not differentiate and integrate higher levels of adaptive capacity. Over time a system that is not evolving, reorganizing, and restructuring itself is generally in serious distress. Developmental progression, although occurring at various rates, can become problematic when fixated. This process of shaping the personality is facilitated by interpersonal and family functions-process-structures that promote emotional, social, and intellectual growth and maturity (Greenspan, 1997; Siegel, 1999). Personality is an emergent phenomenon seen at birth in temperament predispositions, which can dramatically differ from child to child, even within the same family constellation. Any parent who has had more than one child can attest to the temperament differences and their impact on parental responsiveness. As the temperament and attachment experiences unfold and shape one another, the child begins to incorporate models of relationships, emotional regulation, and self-concept by modeling, experience, conditioning, and child-rearing practices. As the developmental process unfolds, we witness the continued shaping of the personality by the unique process, which characterizes each family as well as extrafamilial experiences, such as provided by school, church, and community. Over time, personality seems to shift from temperament predispositions to something inherently different, encompassing the internalized schemata, emotional regulatory capacities and unique defensive structure, and more. The other becomes internalized in various schematic representations, and these are recapitulated. "The individual and his or her environment do not form separate entities. The individual is an active, intentional part of the environment with which he or she interacts" (Magnusson, 1995, p. 34).

When the intrapsychic system is exposed to various traumata, developmental insufficiencies, neurobiological insult, or other bionegativity, the system may show signs of dysfunctioning. We will discuss the traumatic influences later in this chapter. A combination of dysfunctional cognitive schemata and a low capacity to tolerate emotional experience often results in increasing levels of anxiety when life events are stressful. As the anxiety is activated defenses are brought into operation in an attempt to regulate the system. The defenses themselves may then cause difficulty, especially if they are lower level or more primitive ones; in children they may be developmentally appropriate, whereas later they might be assessed immature. For example, a temper tantrum in our 3-year-old might have features similar to a tantrum in the 23-year-old. In the later case, the regressive defenses are more likely to be problematic and represent a harmful dysfunction. Chronic dysfunction in this level of the system may add to developmental disruption in children and adolescents, as they are ill prepared to navigate successive stages of development, which are more complex and demand higher levels of emotional maturity and more flexible and varied defensive operations.

Suggestions for Pattern Recognition and Subsystem Navigation

- Catalogue the defenses of all the members of a system you are seeing by observing their static state defenses (low anxiety) and higher state defenses (higher anxiety). If individuals shift rapidly to lower levels, the system is fragile. If, on the other hand, they can withstand some anxiety, the system is more stable.
- Assess whether defenses are developmentally appropriate and educate parents about developmental appropriateness where possible.
- Identify cognitive and relational schema that maintain a coherent sense of self and restructure when maladaptive.
- Notice how anxiety is experienced and channeled: Does it go into symptoms, clinical syndromes, behavioral disorder, relational disturbances, and somatic disturbance, or is it expressed in character or personality, for example, grandiosity, passivity, lack of empathy?
- Investigate system vulnerabilities such as temperament, neurobiological, and intrapsychic.

- Assess capacity for affective regulation. Is affect directed inward (such as in internalizing conditions, avoidant, dependent, or obsessive-compulsive), or is affect spilling out (borderline conditions, histrionic, antisocial), or does affect derail cognition (schizotypal, schizoid, and paranoid conditions)?

MACRO-LEVEL STRUCTURE AND PROCESS

Interpersonal-Dyadic Matrix

The interpersonal-dyadic matrix primarily accounts for processes that occur between two people in regulating the tension between intimacy and separateness. "Relationship difficulties are among the most common reasons individuals consult mental health professionals" (Whisman & Snyder, 1999, p. 345). According to Berscheid (1999, pp. 261–262), we are witnessing "the greening of a new science of interpersonal relationships": "We are born into relationships with other humans, we live our lives in relationships with others, and when we die, the effects of our relationships survive in the lives of the living, reverberating throughout the tissue of their relationships." The primary attachment system is the maternal-infant dyad, which is the foundational dyad that begins to shape the emergent self from the genetic and temperament substrate. Attachment systems develop in the rich nutrient of attunement, regulation, and repair, and then become a robust predictor of adult interpersonal styles (Schore, 2003b). The interpersonal matrix offers a window into the rich tapestry of attachment experiences that are re-created in relationships with others and in therapeutic relationships. *Attachment leads to capacity for intimacy.* Attachment experiences build the capacity and interest in developing intimacy as development progresses. "Intimacy is not only important to family relationships, it is the necessary, albeit not sufficient, ingredient for human survival" (L'Abate, 1986, p. 227). "In the process of relating to another over time, we weave the fabric of separateness and togetherness into the complex tapestry of intimacy" (Butz, Chamberlain, & McCown, 1997, p. 74). This level can also be depicted by a triangular configuration, which captures the processes of dyadic interpersonal relationships. The lower corner represents past relationships; in the upper-right corner are the relational schemas and attachment systems that are used to guide current relationships; in the upper-left corner are expected relationships (e.g., the therapeutic relationship). All relationships are based on our internalized relational schemata based on attachment experiences and family and extrafamilial relationships. The three basic components are the following:

1. *Past relationships.* Our experience with our formative relationships shapes our internal relational schemata. Beginning with our earliest attachment experiences we build an internal representation of self and others. If development unfolds without insult and family relationships are conducive to growth, personality will unlikely severely dysfunction unless there are significant genetic vulnerabilities that even a functional family can't mediate. If, however, there are traumatic experiences or losses or parental neglect, the personality of the child or adolescent will show signs of problematic behavior and maladjustment, which can further activate a cascading sequence of rebounding social, neurobiological, and emotional circuits. Based on an extensive review and integration of findings of clinical science, Schore (2003a, p. 184) writes, "The neurobiological literature underscores a central finding of developmental science—that the maturation of the infant's brain is experience-dependent and that these experiences are embedded in the attachment relationship."

2. *Current relationships.* Our current relational capacities are based on overall system integrity. The capacity to form and maintain intimate relationships is highly influenced by our level of self-other differentiation and ability to modulate the ebb and flow of intimacy and autonomy needs. Too low a level of self-other differentiation leads to fused or enmeshed relationships. As

children progress they increasingly separate from attachment figures and seek out similar relationships with others, whether functional or not (Drapeau & Perry, 2004). Our current relationships are an excellent window into recurrent patterns. For example, "In couple therapy, the therapist's direct access to exchanges between partners affords a unique opportunity for linking enduring relationship themes to current relationship events" (Snyder, 1999, p. 356).

3. *Expected relationships.* Whenever we enter into a new relationship we bring with us all our past relational expectancies and experience, which we maintain at both conscious and unconscious levels of awareness. A major portion of therapeutic action occurs in this sphere. The patient expects a certain way of being treated, and when this is explored or experienced differently, changes in internal schemata occur. Therapists witness and experience how each child or adolescent approaches us relationally and the expectancies in how they believe we will respond, consistent with his or her internal schematic representations. When dysfunctional, these are restructured, using various methods and relational ingredients.

We both shape and mutually influence our interpersonal relationships in a complex array of communicative processes and patterns. Affective processes are a convergent force in the relational system, and personality has been conceptualized as an "affect-processing system" (Block, 2002). As we will discuss later, even infants can recognize and discriminate facial representations of affect. Our defensive organization and personality style exert an influence on those we select as friends, partners, and workmates. One of the most fundamental developmental tasks is the development of the capacity for forming intimate relationships with others. Prager (1995, p. 5) writes, "Intimate interactions and intimate relationships exert their effects on individual well-being in part by responding to the needs, concerns, and stresses that arise with

each stage of development." There are three components of intimacy, summarized by Prager:

> (1) the cognitive component, which is perspective taking, or the ability to
> see the world through the eyes of another; (2) the affective component,
> which is empathy or the ability to experience vicariously the emotions
> and experiences of another; and (3) the behavioral component, which in-
> volves trustworthy behavior, sensitivity and responsiveness, and effec-
> tive communication. (p. 59)

Clinicians and relational researchers (Berscheid, 1999) gather data
by observing interpersonal relationships and then looking for patterns that will explain what is transpiring. Relationships between
domains are being elucidated. For example, neuroscientific findings
suggest that in highly emotional situations the amygdala is activated
and the prefrontal cortex involved in problem solving is inhibited.
Berscheid reports that these "neuropsychological findings are not
only consistent with clinical observations by therapists that quarrel-
ing couples sometimes seem to be behaving without the full benefit
of prefrontal cortex, but they are consistent with many previous
findings by relationship researchers as well" (p. 263). Based on the
data gathered and patterns identified, suggestions about how to intervene are formulated and tested.

Suggestions for Pattern Recognition and Navigating Subsystem

- Observe the dyadic process between family members and assess
  level of self-other differentiation (e.g., look for fused or enmeshed
  relationships).
- Identify repetitive or recurrent interpersonal patterns and explore multigenerational connections (e.g., history of trauma, neglect, conflicted parenting).
- Explore the themes of the recurrent patterns and assist in finding
  more adaptive and functional patterns (e.g., improved communication, enhanced differentiation).

INCREASINGLY MACRO-LEVEL STRUCTURE AND PROCESS

Relational-Triadic Matrix

The relational-triadic matrix depicts what transpires in unstable dyads (Bowen, 1978): "It is the instability of dyads that produces relationship triangles" (Guerin, Fogarty, Fay, & Kautto, 1996, p. 8). Again we can depict the processes using a triangular configuration. At the bottom of the triangle is a third (triangulated) person; the top two corners represent two people in a dyad. An unstable dyad is one in which each member is relatively undifferentiated, which refers to both emotional differentiation, or what has been termed emotional intelligence, as well as self-other differentiation, which refers to appropriate boundaries. Because this type of dyad does not effectively maintain intimacy and closeness in a regulated way—it tends to try to fuse or is overly distant, or fluctuates wildly between the two poles—it tends to spill emotions into third parties in an attempt to stabilize the dyad. "When individuals are caught in triangles, their freedom of movement is severely circumscribed," and "a person emotionally trapped in a triangle is likely, by virtue of being trapped, to suffer some loss of function" (Guerin et al., 1996, pp. 24, 31). In threesomes, as opposed to triangles, there is a lack of emotional reactivity. Triangles are in effect defenses, which can serve to allow a relationship to continue without change. For example, an ongoing affair might keep the couple from having to address issues vital to their marriage; a triangulated child might keep parents from addressing their differences in attitudes toward child rearing. The three basic components of this triangle are the following:

1. *Person 1* is any individual who is in a dyadic relationship in which there exists a low level of emotional differentiation and self-other differentiation, so that the individual might be prone to emotional leakage, without owning his or her behavior directly.

2. *Person 2* is an individual in relationship with person 1 who also tends to have a low level of emotional differentiation and self-other differentiation.

3. *Person 3* is usually a vulnerable third person who is caught in the relational transaction of the dyad. This person may absorb the anxiety from the dyad and usually becomes symptomatic because the anxiety is more than his or her intrapsychic-biological matrix can metabolize.

Triangular configurations are ubiquitous in human relationships. It is common to have a threesome shift and be unstable. Anyone who has witnessed three children playing will observe how at one moment two members move closer and the third is pushed out, and then the tension becomes high and the dyad shifts and the outside person is in the dyad and another is out. This is a normal developmental experience, which allows children to experiment with closeness-intimacy and self-other issues. However, when these triangular configurations become fixed in adulthood, and the third person is symptomatic, the triadic-relational subsystem is dysfunctioning. An example is a preadolescent male whose parents are divorcing and who is conflicted between his loyalties to both parents but becomes the carrier of the father's anger and becomes overly anxious and symptomatic. Guerin et al. (1996, p. 52) give a clear example of this process:

> Take Jane F. and her 6-year-old daughter, Jennifer, as an example. The relationship between them exists in what we might call relationship space. The relationship space between the two is a channel within which there is an invisible flow of the emotional energy coming from each person. If Jane, for example, is anxious about her relationship with her husband, Peter, Jennifer may pick up her mother's anxiety, without necessarily knowing what it is about. The absorption of Jane's anxiety will trigger an emotional reaction in Jennifer, which she may convert into symptomatic behavior [refer to intrapsychic-biological matrix]—for example, the child becomes whiny and demanding. Jane may complain to Peter about the child, and he may join her in disciplining Jennifer. Thus Peter and Jane both become focused on Jennifer and avoid their own relationship and its conflict. This is the point at which emotions activate a triangle. The process appears natural and automatic, but we can track it. The therapist watches one person's emotional arousal (as tension, anxiety, internal conflict, or something similar) feed into the dyad that cannot tolerate that level of emotionality. It is then the triangle is activated.

Unlike the intrapsychic-biological matrix, where anxiety is transmitted to defenses or symptoms, this matrix transmits anxiety to another person, whose vulnerability or diathesis will determine how the anxiety will be managed (e.g., acting out versus turning in).

Suggestions for Pattern Recognition and Navigating the System

- Consider a symptomatic child or adolescent a possible navigational waypoint to a highly conflicted dyad. These conflicted dyads can exist across generational boundaries (e.g., between grandmother and adult child).

- When there are chronic symptoms of personality dysfunction in a child or adolescent, evaluate the family to determine if there is evidence of a dysfunctional personologic system (see following section).

- Therapeutic methods, which encourage self-focus, reduce triangulation, as blaming feeds reactivity (Guerin et al., 1996, p. 44).

- Where possible, increase tension in the dyad and reduce tension in the third party.

- Observe that fixed triangles are more pathogenic of personality dysfunction. "Overt conflicts that shift around from relationship to relationship usually characterize a relatively fluid triangle" (Guerin et al., 1996, p. 62).

- Observe that there is always a dialectic process between the comfort of stability and the need for change that allows adaptation (Guerin et al., 1996).

THE MESOSYSTEM LEVEL OF STRUCTURE AND PROCESS

Sociocultural-Familial Matrix

The sociocultural-family matrix is the macrosystem in which the individual, couples, families and groups, and culture operate and have mutual influence. "The defining features of the human species—such as using language and passing on inventions and adaptations to subsequent generations—are our cultural heritage" (Rogoff, 2003, p. 64). Cultural values and "memes," which are social units transmitted like genes, only socially (Dawkins, 1976), have a powerful impact on the components and processes identified as occurring at other levels of the personality system. Prager (1995, p. 237) writes, "Cultural values with respect to intimacy likely affect the importance individual dyad members place on intimacy in their families." The value placed on intimacy varies from culture to culture. "Especially apparent is the interplay between partners' personality characteristics, such as private self-consciousness, need strengths, relationship beliefs, and intimate relationships" (p. 238). Culture also confers identity and so is linked to all four levels of the human personality system. Prager (1995, p. 81) describes what she terms the cultural community:

> A community involves generations that move through it, with customary ways of handling the transitions of generations. To continue to function, a community also adapts with changing times, experimenting with and resisting new ideas in ways that maintain core values while learning from changes that are desired or required.

Cultural and societal bionegativity and dysfunction, such as poverty, racism, genocide, lack of medical care, and inequalities, have a strong and determining effect on family adaptation. When society and government cannot meet basic needs, higher order needs cannot be attended to (Erikson, 1968). In a recent edition of *Scientific American*, Sapolsky (2005) makes a cogent case that poverty is a major psychosocial stressor, which has a harmful influence on health. The results of the CIC study also identify poverty as being a risk factor for personality disorder (Cohen et al., 2005). Three aspects of the sociocultural-familial matrix, which can be depicted as a triangular configuration, include the following:

1. *Individual Personality System.* The individual personality system is essentially the operations, which have been defined as the

intrapsychic-biological triangle, and represent the unique personality configuration of the person.

2. *Family System.* This represents the family and extended family in which the individual operates and is related. The family is the basic unit of socialization of society (Ackerman, 1966).

3. *Sociocultural System.* These are the institutions, cultural processes, and social forces that are part of the total ecological system. Human functioning is characterized by the development of cultural systems in which we operate and evolve.

Sociocultural systems exert tremendous influence on both the individual and the family personality system. Human beings are embedded in a complex interrelationship whereby we are influenced by culture and mutually shape and alter culture. The rise of culture in hominid evolution was based in part on an increasing capacity to communicate both verbal and nonverbal information to coordinate group activity and increase the chances for survival.

Family structure and process exert potent influence on the development of personality dysfunction. For example, in a summary of the literature on the impact of divorce on children, Rutter and Rutter (1993) suggest that the experience of a discordant nondivorced family as well as divorced families are more likely to result in "conduct-disorder type—with aggression, poor impulse control, noncompliance and disturbed peer relationships, rather than depression." The "clear inference is that the main risk factor stems from discord and disturbed parenting that sometimes accompanies divorce rather than from the loss *per se*" (p. 134). A substantial amount of literature has been accumulated concerning factors related to Conduct Disorder, which is a type of chronic personality dysfunction. Cultural factors can amplify the conditions that lead to dysfunctioning families. This was demonstrated in one study of African American children in disadvantaged neighborhoods. Disadvantage amplified the relationships among "harsh-inconsistent parenting, low levels of nurturant-involved parenting, and deviance-prone attitudes and behavior among older siblings [which] contributed uniquely to younger siblings' conduct problems" (Brody et al., 2003, p. 218).

Suggestions for Pattern Recognition and Navigating the Subsystem

- Look for obvious signs of dysfunction that is affecting family cohesion, stability, and functions, such as poverty, discrimination, genocide, and cultural expectations. Address these whenever possible.

- Familiarize yourself with the cultural, ethnic, social, political, and economic forces that represent the ecological system of the family and individuals being assessed and treated.

- Educate families about the impact of contemporary popular culture and some of the toxic effects, such as excessive television viewing by children and adolescents and Internet addiction.

STRUCTURE, FUNCTION, AND PROCESS IN A UNIFIED FRAMEWORK

A unified systemic framework for depicting human functioning and dysfunction is based on developments and advances in our understanding of how complex systems are structured and function. The human personality system is a self-organizing one that seeks to adapt to the ecological demands that act as constraints. The total relational matrix of the individual is constantly changing and evolving, attempting to flexibly adapt to environmental, social, cultural, and family demands. Ackerman (1966, p. 61) describes the interplay of individual, family, and society:

> The organization of society and the patterning of the family are interdependent and interpenetrating. Society shapes the functions of the family to its own historically emerging goals. The family molds the kind of persons that are required to express these goals. The members themselves, as far as they are able, fit the family entity to their respective individualized needs. In circular fashion, the pattern of the family then exerts an influence on the evolving trends of the wider community.

The personality system goes through phases of stability, and then, due to small or larger perturbations, reorganizes and reconfigures itself. The function of any complex system is self-maintenance, so that new demands, such as developmental challenges, external stressors, and internal stressors, will create disequilibrium. A flexible system can tolerate a certain level of disequilibrium without becoming extremely dysfunctional or chaotic; an inflexible one will become chaotic and may have difficulty reestablishing equilibrium. Development is characterized at every level with constant fluctuations and restructuring of the system.

> A central tenet of dynamic systems theory holds that at particular critical moments, a flow of energy allows the components of a self-organizing system to become increasingly interconnected, and in this manner organismic form is constructed in developmental processes. As the patterns of relations among the components of a self-organizing system become increasingly interconnected and well ordered, it is more capable of maintaining coherence of organization in relation to variations in the environment. (Schore, 2003b, p. 266)

The lenses of developmental science and developmental psychopathology are critical to deciphering the etiological and ontological aspects of, as well as clinical implications of, child and adolescent personality dysfunction. A major report by the National Research Council and Institute of Medicine et al. (2000) entitled *From Neurons to Neighborhoods* was based on a massive review of the extant empirical findings and theoretical constructs. The report highlighted the 10 underlying developmental principles, which are consistent with the systemic framework presented in this chapter:

1. Human development is shaped by a dynamic and continuous interaction between biology and experience.
2. Culture influences every aspect of human development and is reflected in the childrearing beliefs and practices designed to promote healthy adaptation.

3. The growth of self-regulation is a cornerstone of early childhood development that cuts across all domains of behavior.

4. Children are active participants in their own development, reflecting the intrinsic human drive to explore and master one's environment.

5. Human relationships, and the effects of relationships on relationships, are the building blocks of healthy development.

6. The broad range of individual differences among young children often makes it difficult to distinguish normal variations and maturational delays from transient disorders and persistent impairments.

7. The development of children unfolds along individual pathways whose trajectories are characterized by continuities and discontinuities, as well as by a series of significant transitions.

8. Human development is shaped by the ongoing interplay among sources of vulnerability and sources of resilience.

9. The timing of early experiences can matter, but, more often than not, the developing child remains vulnerable to risks and open to protective influences throughout the early years of life and into childhood.

10. The course of development can be altered in early childhood by effective interventions that change the balance between risk and protection, thereby shifting the odds in favor of more adaptive outcomes (pp. 23–32).

THE CENTRALITY OF THE FAMILY SYSTEM

The family is the primary unit for shaping personality and thus is a critical component of a unified framework. Advances in our understanding of system theory (von Bertalanffy, 1968) provided the impetus for the development of the field of family therapy (Minuchin & Fishman, 1981). Much of what was groundbreaking has been absorbed into many aspects of clinical science, but recent advances in chaos and complexity theory have added to our understanding of how complex systems organize themselves and change.

Extensive research has documented the adverse impacts on young children of parental mental illness (particularly maternal depression), substance abuse, and recurrent violence. The prevalence of such problems is high, the extent to which they are overlooked problematic, and the relatively limited availability of specialized expertise to address them reflects an urgent unmet need. Although these conditions are more common among families living in poverty, they are found in all social classes. Moreover, significant dysfunctions frequently cluster together—that is, maternal depression and substance abuse often go hand in hand; family and community violence may often affect the same child. (National Research Council and Institute of Medicine et al., 2000, p. 390)

To conceptualize the familial influence on the development of personality dysfunction, we can consider the systems in which personality disorder arises, which are presented in the following section.

Dysfunctional Personologic Systems

An alternative way to conceptualize personality disorder is as part of a dysfunctional system. In this way personality functioning can be seen as contextualized in a complex system, which, under certain circumstances, can lead to what Wakefield, in his critique of the *DSM*, defines as a "harmful dysfunction" (1992): "where dysfunctions are failures of internal mechanisms to perform naturally selected functions" (1999, p. 374). This view is also supported by the findings: "The stability of personality is, to some degree, an aspect of the stability of the environment (Shoda, Mischel, & Wright, 1993), so some flexibility can be expected in a changed environment" (Klein, 1999, p. 424). In a review of the CIC study, Clark (2005, p. 525) writes that one "robust" finding is "that much personality disorder does resolve with time," which runs "counter to prevailing belief." Recently reported longitudinal findings also suggest that for a significant subset of individuals, personality disorders may diminish to subdiagnostic thresholds naturally over time. As has been suggested and supported by Cummings et al. (2000, p. 344), individually oriented "classification systems run the risk of focusing too much attention on the overt manifestations of children's unhappiness and distress, thereby overlooking salient aspects of the child's environment." Various types of family systems that are seen in clinical settings seem to produce a greater share of individuals who will suffer with personality dysfunction. Paris (2001, p. 233) summarizes the adversities that can occur: "(1) dysfunctional families (the effects of parental psychopathology, family breakdown, or pathogenic parenting practices), (2) traumatic experiences (e.g., childhood sexual abuse or physical abuse), and (3) social stressors." A typology of these systems was developed (Magnavita, 2000) as a guide to advance the field of relational science and relational diagnosis (Kaslow, 1996). Butz et al. (1997) describe the central feature of rigid or chaotically enmeshed families as communicating in a perseverative way, eventually becoming fixed on a single theme. These systems represent families who, over generations, continue to show signs of dysfunction, which are transmitted by various forms to the next generation. They are defined as follows:

- A dysfunctional family system in which a preponderance of individuals have personality pathology, often observable over generations.
- A lineage of certain types of personality pathology associated with central family themes, dynamics, and triangles (Magnavita, 2000, p. 49).

Features of Dysfunctional Personologic Systems

Dysfunctional personologic systems display a number of features observed in clinical practice and reviews of the literature. They include, but are not limited to, the following:

- Impermeable external boundaries that separate the family system from others.
- Poor boundaries among family members.
- Disturbed levels of communication and overreliance on primitive defenses.
- Reversal of the parent-child relationship.
- Need for family to revolve around a narcissistic parent.

- Poor emotional differentiation and regulation.
- Emotional malnourishment.
- Financial instability.
- Multigenerational transmission process (Magnavita, 2000, p. 54).

Types of Dysfunctional Personologic Systems

There are various types of dysfunctional personologic systems that have been presented in previous volumes (Magnavita, 2000, pp. 439–441; 2005a).

Addictive Dysfunctional Personologic System This system revolves around addictive process. There is an assumption that without substances, survival is threatened. Codependency is a substitute for intimacy. A positive feedback loop (as the substance use creates more chaos, substance abuse increases) produces marginally functioning systems; members may gravitate toward substances as a way to buttress fragile defense mechanisms. Research has shown that "the strong association between substance abuse, conduct disorder, and antisocial PD is well established" (Cohen et al., 2005, p. 477). There is some evidence that Antisocial Personality Disorder is both familially and genetically predisposed (Langbehn & Cadoret, 2001). Conduct Disorder is a significant predictor of adult Antisocial PD (Lahey et al., 2005).

> We have investigated mental health outcomes associated with adolescent substance use, sexuality, and trouble with police in a sample of 1,252 adolescents and found that adolescent behavior, especially when expressed early, is associated with substantial increases in the risk of nicotine dependence, alcohol abuse or dependence, major depressive disorder, and antisocial personality disorder diagnosis in early adulthood. These findings support the general nature of risk for common mental disorders and underscore the prognostic significance of early adolescent behavior problems. (McGue & Iacono, 2005, p. 1123)

Narcissistic Dysfunctional Personologic System This system's major theme is false protection and avoidance of the vulnerable self. Donaldson-

Pressman and Pressman (1994) described these families in their book *The Narcissistic Family: Diagnosis and Treatment,* which provides useful reading for many patients. In these families, public images must be maintained. Children's achievement that reflects favorably on the parents often becomes the substitute for core affirmation and validation. Men with Narcissistic Personality Disorder have a higher risk of battering (O'Leary, 1999).

Covertly Narcissistic Dysfunctional Personologic System   Another system identified by Donaldson-Pressman and Pressman (1994) is the covertly narcissistic family. This system, more subtle than the previous type, creates chronic feelings of not being understood, validated, or affirmed. There is pressure to compensate for self-deficits in members, particularly parents. Affirmation is provided for emotional caretaking, often taken on by children. This reversal is often seen in parent-child interactions and, although subtle, is nonetheless pervasive and limits full development of the child. The child is covertly made responsible for the emotional regulation of the parent. The research on child development indicates that emotional regulation is a critical aspect of normal development. "Emotional security is the goal-state of homeostatic apparatus encompassing not only emotions but also behavior, thoughts, and physiological responses. Hence, it extends beyond conscious thoughts and feelings and subsumes both present and past situational influences" (Cummings et al., 2000, p. 339). Research has shown that "maternal inconsistency significantly predicted offspring with borderline PD, and maternal overinvolvement predicted offspring histrionic PD" (Cohen et al., 2005, p. 476).

Psychotic Dysfunctional Personologic System   The theme of this system is adaptation to chaos. Family members struggle with feelings of insecurity and fragmentation. Research has demonstrated a relationship among psychiatric disorders and marital dissatisfaction (Whisman & Snyder, 1999). When marital tension is high, this negatively impacts personality development of the children. Autonomy is severely threatened and may be seen in fused relationships and, in some cases, shared psychotic behavior. Although there may be various types of physical, sexual, and emotional abuse forced on the children, often in addition to neglect, the primary reason for the abuse and neglect is the untreated severe psychiatric disorder in the parent or parents. The most common attachment type for children in these systems is a chaotic one, which may lead to adult dissociative disorders and odd or eccentric Cluster A personality disorders. Research has shown that "parental psychiatric disorder also predicted offspring PD in early adulthood but not independently of maladaptive parental behaviors" (Cohen et al., 2005, p. 471).

Developmentally Arrested Dysfunctional Personologic System   The theme of this system is inability to tolerate individuation. Separation is viewed as dangerous to family survival and cohesion. The relational dynamic is differentiation versus fusion. It should be noted that this system may be culturally determined and therefore, under some circumstances, functional. If, however, there is evidence of personality dysfunction over the generations, one should evaluate carefully the adaptive capacity of the system.

Physically or Sexually Traumatizing Dysfunctional Personologic System
The theme of this system is accommodation to chronic abuse patterns. Family members are viewed as objects to be dominated by the powerful members. Relational themes are "use and abuse" dynamics. Violence, sexual and emotional abuse, as well as neglect can co-occur and predominate in family communication patterns. There is some empirical support for this family typology from the Minnesota Study of Risk and Adaptation from Birth to Adulthood (Sroufe et al., 2005). In a review of videotaped mother-child interactions, the researches found evidence of "patterns of sexualized care" (p. 115). Research has shown that a history of sexual abuse significantly increases the odds of being diagnosed as an adult with a Cluster A personality disorder (Cohen, Brown, & Smailes, 2001). The interrelationship between abuse and personality disorder is well documented. Men who batter their partner often have comorbid personality disorders, with "three major types of profiles: narcissistic/antisocial, schizoidal/borderline, and dependent/compulsive"

(O'Leary, 1999, p. 400). Only 12% of batterers were found to be free of psychopathology.

Depressogenic Dysfunctional Personologic System   Insufficient emotional resources typify this system. There is typically a history of an untreated affective disorder, influencing parental style, attachment systems, and marital function. "Maternal depression may actually serve as a highly stressful or traumatic experience for infants and children" (Cozolino, 2002, p. 260). Summarizing the literature, Miller et al. (2000, p. 539) wrote, "Families with a depressed member have significant levels of family dysfunction or marital discord." Concluding their own research, they state:

> The results of this study indicated that the personality features of the hospitalized depressed patients and the level of psychiatric symptoms in their partners were the variables most associated with levels of family functioning. These results indicate that families in which the depressed patient has significant Axis II pathology and the nonpatient partner has significant psychological distress are most likely to have poorer family functioning. (p. 544)

In depressed systems, the quality of attachments does not provide a solid base for security and emotional growth (Diamond, Diamond, & Liddle, 2000). The dominant fear is that there are not enough resources to meet members' needs. Family development is stunted because of the chronic emotional insufficiency. There is accruing empirical evidence that depression is transmitted via the multigenerational transmission process. Summarizing the work of Cummings and Cicchetti (1990), Cummings et al. (2000, p. 337) write, "Disturbances in attachment have long been implicated theoretically and empirically in the development, maintenance, and intergenerational transmission of depression in families."

Chronic Medically Ill Dysfunctional Personologic System   The theme in this system is the domination of family functions by the business of medical illness. The chronic stress of coping may lead to emotional strain, which, if left unattended, can alter the manner in which the system adapts and functions.

Paranoid Dysfunctional Personologic System   The theme in this system is an "us versus them" dichotomy. Family members feel compelled to protect themselves from intrusion from outsiders or from extended family members. Cohesion is maintained through a sharing of this paranoid view. Clinicians must be alert to the possibility that the social milieu may engender this reaction, as in cases of ethnic or racial subjugation or covert discrimination.

Somatic Dysfunctional Personologic System   The theme of this system is the substitution of somatic for emotional expression. The only "valid" and safe form of affective communication and nurturing is through somatic language and expression. There is usually an extreme demand placed on primary care providers by these systems. "Among the most challenging patients presenting in medical contexts are those with somatoform symptoms" (Watson & McDaniel, 2000, p. 1068).

Families that manifest these dysfunctional personologic features and themes are vulnerable and should be the focus of intensive intervention. The basic assessment for any family can be enhanced using a family genogram (McGoldrick & Gerson, 1985), which is an essential tool for determining whether a family qualifies as a dysfunctional personologic system. Although there is a dearth of empirical findings and longitudinal studies, clinical evidence from converging sources implicate families with chronic dysfunction as a major developmental pathway to personality disorders in adults, requiring early identification of at-risk children and adolescents.

DEVELOPMENTAL SCIENCE, PSYCHOPATHOLOGY, AND RELATIONAL SCIENCE

Any theory that attempts to capture the complexity of personality and the conditions and pathways that lead to dysfunction must take into account developmental processes. Human development proceeds through stages whereby the individual becomes increasingly differentiated, structures and processes are formed, and integration occurs at a greater level of complexity, known as the orthogenetic principle (Werner, 1957). Werner (1948, p. 41) wrote:

> The development of biological forms is expressed by an increasing differentiation and increasing subordination or hierarchization of parts. Hierarchization means that for any organic structure the organization of the differentiated parts is a closed totality, an ordering and grouping of parts in terms of the whole organism.

Optimal personality development cannot occur in situations in which familial and social dysfunction is chronic and pervasive. The results of a major longitudinal study have just been published (Livesley, 2005), which, according to Cohen et al. (2005, p. 469), are "unique in being able to address questions about developmental trajectories of adolescent PDs." "These studies also stress that personality abnormality can, and should, be addressed more often in childhood" (Tyrer, 2005, p. 575; Westen, Dutra, & Shedler, 2005).

We can naturally divide personality development into three separate stages.

The Child Personality System

The child personality system begins before the child is conceived. The family expectations, whether the child is wanted, the mother's emotional state, stress, and so forth can affect stress hormones in the mother, which can impact the fetus, especially at vulnerable developmental points. After birth infants become increasingly attuned to the relational and environmental context in which they exist. Emotional development is primed at birth. According to findings from developmental science:

> Within the first 9 months, before babies can walk or talk or even crawl, they can tell the difference between expressions of happiness and sadness and anger, and even can recognize that a happy-looking face, a face with a smile and crinkly eyes, goes with the chirp of a happy tone of voice. (Gopnik et al., 2001, p. 28)

The way the child understands the people around him or her "is part of becoming a particular sort of person" and a characteristic of the emergent self (p. 24). These leading developmental scientists write:

> The new idea about attachment, or bonding, is that babies and young children develop "internalized working models" that are systematic pictures of how people relate to one another—theories of love. Of course, these models are heavily influenced by children's observations of the people around them (Doane & Diamond, 1994). And also, these models, like scientific theories, influence the ways children interpret new observations. If you see that the people you rely on for warmth and comfort turn away from you when you're in distress that may influence your expectations about how other people will act and your interpretations of what they actually do. But rather than being fixed, these internalized working models are actually flexible. Like scientific theories they can be changed with enough evidence. (p. 49)

The child's temperament, attachment system, and family system are intricately involved in shaping the child's personality system. Kagan and Snidman (2004, p. 24) state, "Family socialization styles and values operate first. Parents who encourage boldness and sociability and gently discourage timidity motivate their high-reactive children toward a less inhibited profile."

> We believe that these considerations that apply to the development of the body and the brain apply to the human personality. Because of emergent complexity and the phenomenon of differentiation, early distortions may have a profound, far-reaching implication, even though they cannot be said to specify or by themselves directly cause later forms. (Sroufe et al., 2005, p. 31)

In an examination of a variety of variables affecting infant development, Sroufe et al. found:

> Factors and processes contributing to care-giving quality are complex. However, our data suggest that maltreatment or grossly inadequate care-giving evolves from the interaction of psychological characteristics of

vulnerable, at-risk mothers in the context of environmental stress and lack of support. Isolation in the midst of challenging life events, as well as a history of unresolved, harsh care-giving experiences may all contribute to feelings of powerlessness, suspicion and fear, and the inability to control hostile impulses that influence care-giving ability. (p. 94)

The Adolescent Personality System

There are new demands on the adolescent personality that increase the tendency to become chaotic. Adolescence is a critical time for the development of identity, during which a shift occurs from the familial system to the peer system; it is also a period of experimentation with adult behaviors. The adolescent is also increasing his or her capacity to develop intimate relationships with extrafamilial members. "A second striking feature of our data is the age-at-onset effect: adolescent problem behavior before age 15 is associated with a substantially increased risk of adult disorders. This effect is particularly salient when the multiple problem behaviors are aggregated" (McGue & Iacono, 2005, p. 1123).

The Young Adult Personality System

The young adult personality system has to master a number of issues to be able to function adaptively within the constraints of society. Selection of partner, career choice, and starting a family are developmental choices for most young adults and fraught with difficulties when there is little support from family or social systems to achieve these milestones.

TRAUMA AND PERSONALITY DEVELOPMENT

The study of traumatology has advanced greatly since the beginning of the twentieth century. The impact of trauma on personality development has been described in various literatures in clinical science, ranging from psychodynamics to neuroscience (Schore, 2003a, 2003b). There is also accumulating empirical evidence from longitudinal studies that trauma in overt forms as well as the ongoing trauma of parental conflict is highly implicated in many adult personality disorders.

APPLICATION AND UTILITY OF MODEL FOR IDENTIFICATION, PREVENTION, AND TREATMENT OF CHILD AND ADOLESCENT PERSONALITY DYSFUNCTION

The most essential requirement of a unified system is to be able to identify children and adolescents in states of chronic personality dysfunction, which, if left untreated, will develop into adult forms of personality disorder. Individuals, families, couples, as well as children and adolescents need to be identified and engaged in treatment where possible. "Findings from the CIC Study make it clear that PD symptom constellations identified in adulthood have their origins in childhood and can be reliably assessed in combined youth and parent reports" (Cohen et al., 2005, p. 481). Greenberg (2002, p. 155) describes a holistic system approach thus:

> Each therapeutic approach probably affects the system at a chosen level—cognitive, emotional, behavioral, or interactions—and any specific effect at one level of the system probably reverberates through the highly interconnected levels of the system and produces comparable change in the whole person.

A systemic framework allows the clinician to intervene at a variety of levels within the relational system. Again, Greenberg (2002, p. 155) describes a systemic framework: "With a complex system view . . . it is clear that intervention can and should occur at different levels at different times or with different components of the system." Millon et al. (1999, p. 37). describes this trend as psychosynergy: "Synergism represents the conjoining of normally separate venues, creating thereby a process of interrelatedness, and producing effects that successfully 'work together.'" Working with the entire system allows the clinician to combine modalities and approaches using the systemic framework as the guiding light. Cummings et al. (2000, pp. 30, 116–117) describe the importance of maintaining a holonic perspective for researchers, equally important to clinicians:

> Components of any whole that is studied are themselves wholes. For example, while parent-child attachment is a component of the "whole" of the family system, it is also a whole that warrants study in itself. This hierarchical, nested structure of part-whole relations can be further extended in both directions toward the more specific (e.g., components of attachment such as appraisals of parents and emotional reactivity) and more general (e.g., family system as a part nested in the larger whole, of the community or neighborhood). Since an element is itself a whole, floating holism asserts that the elements and the whole may both be appropriate areas of inquiry depending on the goals of the researcher [and clinician].

Practical Guidelines for Intervention

- Maximize and attend to developmental transitions. These are periods that, when navigated successfully, strengthen the system but can also result in the system becoming stuck in more chronic patterns.
- Where possible, identify personality disorders in parents and primary attachment figures and attempt to engage them or refer them for treatment. Personality disordered parents are the carriers of the multigenerational transmission process.
- Initiate intervention at any point in the system that the system will tolerate and accept and then build alliance. The development of a compassionate and caring alliance will engender trust.
- Use an intermittent model and allow people to access services when they see problems brewing.
- When the system is unable to provide sufficient attachments for the children take a long-term perspective and work with the caregivers on supportive long-term or intermittent treatment.
- Utilize a multidisciplinary approach where possible.

- Maintain hope. Every step forward may result in backward movement, but overall most systems can change dramatically and the rest can take baby steps or be maintained in the least virulent form.

- Become trained in multiple modalities of treatment and work with others who provide treatment modalities and services that you are not able to offer.

- Offer psychoeducation to parents and other professionals so that they can identify and refer.

CONCLUSIONS

As advanced by developmental psychopathologists and supported by the author:

> There is a particularly urgent need for theory in the case of research guided by the developmental psychopathology perspective given the fact that this approach fosters mulitdomain, multimethod, and multidisciplinary studies of child development; that is, the complexity of results and findings that inevitably emerge from such sophisticated and diverse approaches to a phenomenon has the inherent potential to be overwhelming to researchers and must always be a paramount and ultimate goal and concern while pursuing at the same time the highest standards of empirical research. (Cummings et al., 2000, p. 337)

Personality dysfunction in children and adolescents is a major issue for mental health clinicians. Longitudinal studies are beginning to shed light on the developmental trajectory of personality dysfunction. The presence of personality dysfunction and disorder in children is best characterized as an emergent phenomenon of a complex interrelated system and is thus contextual. A systemically based family perspective offers a unified framework with hopes of eventually stopping or at least slowing down the multigenerational transmission process of personality disorders.

REFERENCES

Ackerman, N. W. (1966). *Treating the troubled family.* New York: Basic Books.

Alexander, F. G., & Selesnick, S. T. (1966). *The history of psychiatry: An evaluation of psychiatric thought and practice from prehistoric times to present.* New York: Harper & Row.

American Psychiatric Association. (1980). *Diagnostic and statistical manual of mental disorders* (3rd ed.). Washington, DC: Author.

American Psychiatric Association. (1994). *Diagnostic and statistical manual of mental disorders* (4th ed.). Washington, DC: Author.

American Psychiatric Association. (2000). *Diagnostic and statistical manual of mental disorders* (4th ed., text rev.). Washington, DC: Author.

Angyal, A. (1982). *Neurosis and treatment: A holistic theory.* New York: Da Capo Press.

Berscheid, E. (1999). The greening of relational science. *American Psychologist, 54*(4), 260–266.

Blackman, J. S. (2004). *101 defenses: How the mind shields itself.* New York: Brunner-Routledge.

Bleiberg, E. (2004). Treatment of dramatic personality disorders in children and adolescents. In J. J. Magnavita (Ed.), *Handbook of personality disorders: Theory and practice* (pp. 467–497). Hoboken, NJ: Wiley.

Block, J. (2002). *Personality as an affect-processing system: Toward an integrative theory.* Mahwah, NJ: Erlbaum.

Bowen, M. (1976). Theory and practice of family therapy. In P. J. Guerin Jr. (Ed.), *Family therapy: Theory and practice* (pp. 42–90). New York: Gardner Press.

Bowen, M. (1978). *Family therapy in clinical practice.* New York: Aronson.

Brody, G. H., McBride Murry, V., Ge, X., Kim, S. Y., Simons, R. L., Gibbons, F. X., et al. (2003). Neighborhood disadvantage moderates associations of parenting and older sibling problem attitudes and behavior with conduct disorders in African American children. *Journal of Consulting and Clinical Psychology, 71*(2), 211–222.

Bronfenbrenner, U. (1979). *The ecology of human development: Experiments by nature and design.* Cambridge, MA: Harvard University Press.

Butz, M. R., Chamberlain, L. L., & McCown, W. G. (1997). *Strange attractors: Chaos, complexity, and the art of family therapy.* New York: Wiley.

Clark, L. A. (2005). Stability and change in personality pathology: Revelations of three longitudinal studies. *Journal of Personality Disorders, 19*(5), 524–532.

Cohen, P. (2005). Response to comments on our review of the Children in the Community study of personality disorders in a general population of youth. *Journal of Personality Disorders, 19*(5), 594–596.

Cohen, P., Brown, J., & Smailes, E. (2001). Child abuse and neglect and the development of mental disorders in the general population. *Developmental Psychopathology, 13,* 981–999.

Cohen, P., Crawford, T. N., Johnson, J. G., & Kasen, S. (2005). The Children in the Community study of developmental course of personality disorder. *Journal of Personality Disorders, 19*(5), 466–486.

Costa, P. T., & McCrae, R. R. (1992). The five-factor model of personality and its relevance to personality disorders. *Journal of Personality Disorders, 6,* 343–359.

Cozolino, L. (2002). *The neuroscience of psychotherapy: Building and rebuilding the human brain.* New York: Norton.

Cramer, P. (1987). The development of defense mechanisms. *Journal of Personality, 59*(1), 39–55.

Cramer, P. (1995). Identity, narcissism, and defense mechanisms in late adolescence. *Journal of Research in Personality, 29,* 341–361.

Cramer, P. (1997). Identity, personality, and defense mechanisms: An observer-based study. *Journal of Research in Personality, 31,* 58–77.

Cramer, P. (1998). Defensiveness and defense mechanisms. *Journal of Personality, 66*(6), 879–894.

Cramer, P., & Gaul, R. (1988). The effects of success and failure on children's use of defense mechanisms. *Journal of Personality, 56*(4), 729–742.

Cummings, E. M., & Cicchetti, D. (1990). Towards a transactional model of relations between attachment and depression. In M. Greenberg, D. Cicchetti, & E. M. Cummings (Eds.), *Attachment in the preschool years: Theory, research, and intervention* (pp. 339–372). Chicago: University of Chicago Press.

Cummings, E. M., Davies, P. T., & Campbell, S. B. (2000). *Developmental psychopathology and family process: Theory, research, and clinical implications.* New York: Guilford Press.

Dawkins, R. (1976). *The selfish gene.* New York: Oxford University Press.

Diamond, G. M., Diamond, G. S., & Liddle, H. A. (2000). The therapist-parent alliance in family-based therapy for adolescents. *Journal of Clinical Psychology/In Session: Psychotherapy in Practice, 56,* 1037–1050.

Doane, J. A., & Diamond, D. (1994). *Affect and attachment in the family.* New York: Basic Books.

Donaldson-Pressman, S., & Pressman, R. M. (1994). *The narcissistic family: Diagnosis and treatment.* New York: Maxwell Macmillan International.

Drapeau, M., & Perry, J. C. (2004). Childhood trauma and adult interpersonal functioning. *Child Abuse and Neglect, 28.*

Ekman, P., & Davidson, R. J. (Eds.). (1994). *The nature of emotions: Fundamental questions,* New York: Oxford Press.

Erikson, E. (1968). *Identity, youth and crisis.* New York: Norton.

Goleman, D. (1995). *Emotional intelligence.* New York: Bantam Books.

Gopnik, A., Meltzoff, A. N., & Kuhl, P. K. (2001). *The scientist in the crib: What early learning tells us about the mind.* New York: Perennial.

Greenberg, L. S. (2002). Integrating an emotion-focused approach to treatment into psychotherapy integration. *Journal of Psychotherapy Integration, 12*(2), 154–189.

Greenspan, S. I. (1997). *The growth of the mind and the endangered growth of intelligence.* Reading, MA: Perseus Books.

Guerin, P. J., Fogarty, T. F., Fay, L. F., & Kautto, J. G. (1996). *Working with relational triangles: The one-two-three of psychotherapy.* New York: Guilford Press.

Johnson, S. M., & Whiffen, V. E. (1999). Made to measure: Adapting emotionally focused couple therapy to partners' attachment styles. *Clinical Psychology: Science and Practice, 6*(4), 366–381.

Jordan, J. V. (2004). Personality disorder or relational disconnection. In J. J. Magnavita (Ed.), *Handbook of personality disorders: Theory and practice* (pp. 120–134). Hoboken, NJ: Wiley.

Kagan, J., & Snidman, N. (2004). *The long shadow of temperament.* Cambridge, MA: Belknap Press of Harvard University Press.

Kaslow, F. W. (Ed.). (1996). *Handbook of relational diagnosis and dysfunctional family patterns.* New York: Wiley.

Kernberg, O. F. (1984). *Object relations theory and clinical psychoanalysis.* New York: Aronson.

Kernberg, P. F., Weiner, A. S., & Bardenstein, K. K. (2000). *Personality disorders in children and adolescents.* New York: Basic Books.

Klein, D. F. (1999). Harmful dysfunction, disorder, disease, illness, and evolution. *Journal of Abnormal Psychology, 108*(3), 421–429.

Koestler, A. (1978). *Janus: A summing up.* New York: Vintage Books.

Krueger, R. F. (2005). Continuity of Axes I and II: Toward a unified model of personality, personality disorders, and clinical disorders. *Journal of Personality Disorders, 19*(3), 233–261.

L'Abate, L. (1986). *Systemic family therapy.* New York: Brunner/Mazel.

Lahey, B. B., Loeber, R., Burke, J. D., & Applegate, B. (2005). Predicting future antisocial personality disorder in males from a clinical assessment in childhood. *Journal of Consulting and Clinical Psychology, 73*(3), 389–399.

Langbehn, D. R., & Cadoret, R. J. (2001). The adult antisocial syndrome with and without antecedent conduct disorder: Comparisons from an adoption study. *Comprehensive Psychiatry, 42,* 272–282.

Laveman, L. (1997). The macrosystemic model of psychotherapy: Autonomy and attachment in family systems. *Journal of Psychotherapy Integration, 7*(1), 55–74.

Livesley, W. J. (2005). Introduction to the special issue on longitudinal studies. *Journal of Personality Disorder, 19*(5), 463–465.

MacFarlane, M. M. (2004). *Family treatment of personality disorders: Advances in clinical practice.* New York: Haworth Press.

Magnavita, J. J. (2000). *Relational therapy for personality disorders.* Hoboken, NJ: Wiley.

Magnavita, J. J. (2002). *Theories of personality: Contemporary approaches to the science of personality.* Hoboken, NJ: Wiley.

Magnavita, J. J. (2004a). Classification, prevalence, and etiology of personality disorders: Related issues and controversy. In J. J. Magnavita (Ed.), *Handbook of personality disorders: Theory and practice* (pp. 3–23). Hoboken, NJ: Wiley.

Magnavita, J. J. (2004b). The relevance of theory in treating personality dysfunction. In J. J. Magnavita (Ed.), *Handbook of personality disorders: Theory and practice* (pp. 56–77). Hoboken, NJ: Wiley.

Magnavita, J. J. (2004c). Toward a unified model of treatment for personality dysfunction. In J. J. Magnavita (Ed.), *Handbook of personality disorders: Theory and practice* (pp. 528–553). Hoboken, NJ: Wiley.

Magnavita, J. J. (2005a). *Personality-guided relational therapy: A unified approach.* Washington, DC: American Psychological Association.

Magnavita, J. J. (2005b). Systems theory foundation of personality, psychopathology, and psychotherapy. In S. Strack (Ed.), *Handbook of personology and psychopathology* (pp. 140–163). Hoboken, NJ: Wiley.

Magnavita, J. J. (2006). In search of the unifying principles of psychotherapy: Conceptual, empirical, and clinical convergence. *American Psychologist, 61*(8), 882–892.

Magnavita, J. J., & MacFarlane, M. M. (2004). Family treatment of personality disorders: Historical overview and current perspectives. In M. M. MacFarlane (Ed.), *Family treatment of personality disorders: Advances in clinical practice.* New York: Haworth Press.

Magnusson, D. (1995). Individual development: A holistic, integrated model. In P. Mohen, G. H. Elder Jr., & K. Luscher (Eds.), *Examining lives in context: Perspectives on the ecology of human development* (pp. 19–60). Washington, DC: American Psychological Association.

McGoldrick, M., & Gerson, R. (1985). *Genograms in family assessment.* New York: Norton Press.

McGue, M., & Iacono, W. G. (2005). The association of early adolescent problem behavior with adult psychopathology. *American Journal of Psychiatry, 162*(6), 1118–1124.

McWilliams, N. (1994). *Psychoanalytic diagnosis: Understanding personality structure in clinical practice.* New York: Guilford Press.

Merikangas, K., & Weissman, M. (1986). Epidemiology of DSM-III Axis II personality disorders. In A. Frances & R. Hales (Eds.), *APA annual review* (Vol. 5, pp. 258–278). Washington, DC: American Psychiatric Press.

Miller, I. W., McDermut, W., Gordon, K. C., Keitner, G. I., Ryan, C. E., & Norman, W. (2000). Personality and family functioning in families of depressed patients. *Journal of Abnormal Psychology, 109*(3), 539–545.

Millon, T. (with Grossman, S., Meagher, S., Millon, C., & Everly, G.). (1999). *Personality-guided therapy.* New York: Wiley.

Millon, T. (2000). Toward a new model of integrative psychotherapy: Psychosynergy. *Journal of Psychotherapy Integration, 10*(1), 37–53.

Millon, T., & Davis, R. D. (1996). *Disorders of personality: DSM-IV and beyond.* New York: Wiley.

Minuchin, S., & Fishman, H. C. (1981). *Family therapy techniques.* Cambridge, MA: Harvard University Press.

Murray, H. A. (1938). *Explorations in personality.* New York: Oxford University Press.

National Research Council and Institute of Medicine, Shonkoff, J. P., & Phillips, D. A. (Eds.). (2000). *From neurons to neighborhoods: The science of early childhood development* (Committee on Integrating the Science of Early Childhood Development, Board on Children, Youth, and Families, Commission on Behavioral and Social Sciences and Education). Washington, DC: National Academy Press.

O'Leary, K. D. (1999). Developmental and affective issues in assessing and treating partner aggression. *Clinical Psychology: Science and Practice, 6*(4), 400–414.

Paris, J. (2001). Psychosocial adversity. In W. J. Livesley (Ed.), *Handbook of personality disorders: Theory, research, and treatment* (pp. 231–241). New York: Guilford Press.

Prager, K. J. (1995). *The psychology of intimacy.* New York: Guilford Press.

Rogoff, B. (2003). *The cultural nature of human development.* New York: Oxford University Press.

Rutter, M., & Rutter, M. (1993). *Developing minds: Challenge and continuity across the life span.* New York: Basic Books.

Salovey, P., & Mayer, J. D. (1990). Emotional intelligence. *Imagination, Cognition, and Personality, 9*, 185–211.

Sapolsky, R. (2005). Sick of poverty. *Scientific American, 293*(6), 94–99.

Schore, A. N. (2003a). *Affect regulation and disorders of the self.* New York: Norton.

Schore, A. N. (2003b). *Affect regulation and the repair of the self.* New York: Norton.

Shedler, J., & Westen, D. (2004). Dimensions of personality pathology: An alternative to the five-factor model. *Journal of Psychiatry, 167*(10), 1743–1754.

Shoda, Y., Mischel, W., & Wright, J. C. (1993). The role of situational demands and cognitive competencies in behavior organization and personality coherence. *Journal of Personality and Social Psychology, 65,* 1023–1035.

Siegal, D. J. (1999). *The developing mind: Toward a neurobiology of interpersonal experience.* New York: Guilford Press.

Snyder, D. K. (1999). Affective reconstruction in the context of a pluralistic approach to couple therapy. *Clinical Psychology: Science and Practice, 6*(4), 349–365.

Sperry, L. (1995). *Handbook and diagnosis and treatment of DSM-IV personality disorders.* New York: Brunner/Mazel.

Sroufe, L. A., Egeland, B., Carlson, E. A., & Collins, W. A. (2005). *The development of the person: The Minnesota Study of Risk and Adaptation from Birth to Adulthood.* New York: Guilford Press.

Sullivan, H. S. (1953). *The interpersonal theory of psychiatry.* New York: Norton.

Tyrer, P. (2005). Temporal change: The third dimension of personality disorder. *Journal of Personality Disorders, 19*(5), 573–580.

Vaillant, G. E. (Ed.). (1992). *Ego mechanisms of defense: A guide for clinicians and researchers.* Washington, DC: American Psychiatric Press.

von Bertalanffy, L. (1968). *General system theory: Foundations, development and applications.* New York: Braziller.

Wakefield, J. C. (1992). Disorder as harmful dysfunction: A conceptual critique of DSM-III-R's definition of mental disorder. *Psychological Review, 99,* 232–247.

Wakefield, J. C. (1999). Evolutionary versus prototype analysis of the concept of disorder. *Journal of Abnormal Psychology, 108*(3), 374–399.

Watson, W. H., & McDaniel, S. H. (2000). Relational therapy in medical settings: Working with somatizing patients and their families, *Journal of Clinical Psychology/In Session: Psychotherapy in Practice, 56*(8), 1065–1082.

Werner, H. (1948). *The comparative psychology of mental development.* New York: International University Press.

Werner, H. (1957). The concept of development from a comparative and organismic point of view. In D. B. Harris (Ed.), *The concept of development* (pp. 125–148). Minneapolis: University of Minnesota Press.

Westen, D., Dutra, L., & Shedler, J. (2005). Assessing adolescent personality pathology. *British Journal of Psychiatry, 186,* 277–238.

Whisman, M. A., & Snyder, D. K. (1999). Affective and developmental considerations in couple therapy: Introduction to the special series. *Clinical Psychology: Science and Practice, 6*(4), 345–347.

CHAPTER 7

Assessment of Personality Disorders in Childhood

GEORGE McCLOSKEY, PETER KANE, CARRIE CHAMP MORERA,
KATHRYN GIPE, and AMY McLAUGHLIN

ASSESSMENT PLAYS a central role in all aspects of clinical work with children and adolescents exhibiting disordered behavior and thought patterns. Assessment provides the basis for the initial diagnosis of a personality disorder; it can also guide the development of a treatment plan and be utilized to monitor intervention efforts over time. Assessment procedures initially can be used to establish the behavior and thought patterns exhibited by a child or adolescent and the degree to which these patterns are judged to be adaptive or maladaptive. In the case of personality disorder, assessment procedures are used to render judgments as to whether the observed behaviors and reported thought patterns reflect significant and enduring adjustment problems. When considering the treatment needs of a child or adolescent identified as having a personality disorder, assessment results provide the basis for assigning administrative classification status to enable access to services or for referring the child or adolescent to an appropriate treatment provider. Once a personality disorder has been identified, assessment can provide a framework for developing a treatment plan and for helping parents and teachers understand and deal with the child's or adolescent's problem behaviors and disordered thought processes. As treatment progresses, assessment procedures can enable clinicians to gauge the effectiveness of treatment efforts.

Although the diagnosis and treatment of personality disorders has traditionally been restricted to the age of 18 and beyond, the most prominent classification system used by clinicians, the *Diagnostic and Statistical Manual of Mental Disorders* (*DSM-IV*; American Psychiatric Association, 2000, p. 687), has offered some guidelines for making a diagnosis of personality disorder in childhood and adolescence:

> Personality disorder categories may be applied to children or adolescents in those relatively unusual instances in which the individual's particular maladaptive personality traits appear to be pervasive, persistent, and unlikely to be limited to a particular developmental stage or an episode of an Axis I disorder. It should be recognized that the traits of a Personality Disorder that appear in childhood will often not persist unchanged into adult life. To diagnose a Personality Disorder in a person under 18, the features must have been present for at least 1 year.

Although this *DSM-IV* statement indicates that personality disorder diagnosis in children and adolescents should be a "relatively unusual instance," research summarized in the chapters that follow offer evidence suggesting that such diagnoses are warranted in a greater number of instances than currently acknowledged. Like the diagnoses themselves, the assessment of personality disorders in children and adolescents is an emerging field that has not been extensively discussed or researched in the professional literature. In fact, there are no generally accepted procedures for assessing or diagnosing Axis II phenomena in children and adolescents (Westen, Dutra, & Shedler, 2005). Thus, there is a need to develop valid and reliable methods that ensure ethical and humane treatment of children and adolescents.

WHAT IS PERSONALITY ASSESSMENT?

The meaning of the term "assessment" varies widely in the professional psychology literature, especially as it is applied to the areas of personality and personality disorders. Definitions of personality assessment range from very broad conceptions, such as that of Wiggins (2003), to very specific delineations, such as that of Hilsenroth and Segal (2004). In his extensive overview of the field entitled *Paradigms of Personality Assessment*, Wiggins defined personality assessment as a process that involves collecting and evaluating various sources of information about an individual to serve purposes such as selection, placement, diagnosis, and case formulation. Within this broad framework, the specific methods of assessment can include psychological tests, interviews, and biographical material. In contrast, Hilsenroth and Segal have a much narrower perspective on what constitutes personality assessment, as evidenced by their selection of content for *Personality Assessment*, volume 2 of their *Comprehensive Handbook of Psychological Assessment*. In this reference work, personality assessment refers to specific tests of personality divided into two broad categories: objective assessments and projective assessments. Within this framework, objective assessments include objective tests designed to assess personality constructs or psychiatric disorders as well as structured and semistructured interview techniques because of their standardized approach to the collection and evaluation of information. The definition of projective assessments within this framework is somewhat less specific, but the unifying dimension is the fact that in the range of projective techniques discussed, each provides a structure of similar conditions for the collection, evaluation, and interpretation of samples of behavior.

As Wiggins (2003) noted, personality conceptualizations lack scientific value unless they can be operationalized and translated into concrete measurement procedures. For the purposes of clinical practice, there must be a formal framework and set of procedures for rendering judgments about the adequacy of these operationalized measurement procedures. A professionally sanctioned framework and set of procedures for this purpose are set forth in *The Standards for Educational and Psychological Testing*, jointly developed by the American Educational Research Association (AERA), the American Psychological Association (APA), and the National Council of Measurement in Education (NCME; 1999). The standards specifically address issues such as standardization procedures and the establishment of reliability and validity, and set forth guidelines for acceptable procedures and methods for demonstrating the psychometric adequacy of an assessment procedure. Because consideration of the adequacy of the broad range of assessment approaches discussed by Wiggins is beyond the scope of this chapter, the emphasis here is placed on discussing the psychometric considerations for the development and use of personality disorder assessments in the context of the definition utilized by Hilsenroth and Segal (2004), specifying personality assessments as objective tests (including structured and semistructured interviews) and projective techniques. Because this chapter deals with the assessment of children's and adolescents' personalities, another important form of assessment is included in the objective test category: rating scales based on the reports of others such as parents, caregivers, and teachers. For the purposes of this chapter, the term "test" often is used when making global statements that are meant to refer to all forms of personality assessment encompassed by the Hilsenroth and Segal definition. When self-report and rating scales are referred to as a single group, they are referred to as "self- and other-report measures" or simply as "objective tests." Readers interested in considering the nature of assessment techniques from a broader perspective than the one pre-sented here are referred to Wiggins's (2003) *Paradigms of Personality Assessment* as a potential starting point.

PSYCHOMETRIC CONSIDERATIONS IN DEVELOPMENT AND USE OF PERSONALITY TESTS

Personality assessment methods vary widely in the theoretical orien-tations of the proponents of the methods and the manner in which theoretical conceptions are operationalized to form test instruments. Regardless of the theoretical orientation of the test authors or the spe-cific format of a test, certain basic psychometric qualities must be demonstrated for clinicians to engage in professionally sound use of a test. The following sections discuss these basic psychometric proper-ties under the headings of "Standardization," "Reliability," and "Va-lidity." Standardization refers to the processes involved in test development and construction, including item development, adminis-tration, and scoring procedures, and score interpretation frameworks. Reliability refers to the consistency and stability of results obtained from a test. Validity refers to the evidence provided to demonstrate that the test measures what it is intended to measure and that the test can be used for its stated purposes. Although these features are dis-cussed separately, they are inextricably interwoven elements. When done correctly, the test construction process itself is a form of valida-tion of the test, and although it is theoretically possible for a test to be valid without being reliable, sound assessment instruments must demonstrate an adequate degree of reliability before they can be validly used to assist in rendering professional judgments.

STANDARDIZATION

During the development phase, selection of test content is determined by the specific theoretical orientation of the test authors. Despite statements by some test authors who claim an atheoretical stance, all tests have a theoretical basis. What varies is not the degree to which a test is based on theory, but rather the degree to which the test authors consciously acknowledge the theoretical underpinnings of the test's content. Although theory and the intended purposes of the test drive the generation of test content, in the final analysis these aspects of test construction become issues of validity. Beyond the rationale for content selection, standardization of a test involves how ideas are turned into a concrete, operationalized measure, that is, how ideas about test content are translated into test items, how test items are administered and scored, and how frames of reference (usually in the form of test norms) are specified for score interpretation. Care must be taken to ensure that the test is constructed in a manner that enables consistent administration and scoring through the use of well-designed, easily used materials and item formats that are consistent with the instrument's intended assessment purposes.

RELIABILITY

Reliability, defined in relation to personality tests, refers to the consistency of personality test results. The more reliable a test, the more likely it is that an examinee will receive the same, or nearly the same, score on repeated administrations of the test. A personality test attempts to ascertain personality characteristics of an individual through the person's responses to test items, or the responses provided by others who know the person. In the case of objective tests, item responses reflect judgments based on the recollections of and reflection on selected perceptions, thoughts, feelings, and actions that have occurred, or were thought to have occurred, over a specified, or nonspecified, period of time. Objective test reliability, therefore, indicates the consistency of the test respondent's perceptions. In the case of projective tests, item responses are thought to be meaningful representations that are interpreted by the examiner as reflecting ways that the person tends to perceive, think, feel, and act. Projective test reliability, therefore, indicates the consistency of the meaningful representations provided by the respondent, as well as the consistency of the interpretations ascribed to those representations through the judgments of the examiner.

Realizing that reliability is a function of respondent judgments or respondent productions and examiner judgments, it should be apparent that several factors greatly influence the reliability of a test, including characteristics of the test, characteristics of the examiners who give the tests, and characteristics of the respondents who take the test. Methodologically, there are two basic approaches used for establishing the reliability of a test: test-retest methods and internal consistency methods. A third method, interrater reliability, can be used to describe the consistency of examiners in their application of test scoring criteria.

Characteristics of Tests

Consistency of test results can be greatly influenced by several factors related to test construction. These include the development of test administration directions, item formatting, and item scoring rules. For both objective and projective tests, development of test administration directions must be done carefully to ensure that all examiners and respondents, to the greatest extent possible, have the same understanding of the nature of the task and how it is to be accomplished. Statements to examiners must clearly specify what is said to examinees and how tasks or examples are to be explained. Statements made to examinees by examiners must be worded as clearly as possible so that there is no confusion about what is expected in terms of performance. Poorly specified examiner instructions and examinee directions increase the possibility that examiners will alter the manner in which they communicate the nature of the task, and consequently examinees might perform the tasks differently from one time to the next.

The way test items are formatted and presented also can affect examinee performance. In the case of objective tests, the wording of items should receive careful editorial and professional content review to ensure that they are easy to read and understand. Complex grammatical constructions and double negatives should be avoided. For example, the statement "I get so angry that I can't control it" is much preferred to the statement "I don't get so angry that I can't control it"; the first statement is much more likely to be understood and completed in a manner consistent with the examinee's intended response. Care must also be taken in the selection of response option descriptions when using multipoint scales. The more clearly defined each response option, the greater the likelihood that an examinee will respond consistently to the item on more than one occasion. When options are not clearly defined, examinees must rely on their own perceptual judgments to make distinctions between options, thereby increasing the likelihood that an examinee will interpret the options in an unpredictably different manner if the test is taken more than once.

Layout and design of the test form must be well thought out. Test forms that tightly pack questions into a small space and use very small type run the risk of examinees skipping items or misaligning responses with items. Forms that employ multiple columns on a single page also must be carefully designed to avoid confusion regarding where responses should be recorded. For projective tests, formatting of test items typically is not a concern. Sentence completion tests tend to be unambiguous and well structured in terms of format. Tasks such as the Rorschach and the Thematic Apperception Test use a separate card for each item. Graphic measures have no items to format.

Characteristics of Examiners

The way an examiner engages in test administration and scoring can greatly affect the consistency of test results. Just as great care must be taken to develop well-standardized examiner administration instructions and examinee directions, equal care must be taken by the examiner to ensure that instructions and directions are delivered in a manner that does not lead to inconsistent performance. Strict adherence to standardized instructions and directions is critical in all but the most unusual of circumstances. Skipping, shortening, and rewording directions can reduce the likelihood that items will be completed in a consistent manner. Examiner interactions also can affect a respondent's performance. A proper professional demeanor during presentation of instructions and directions communicates a no-nonsense attitude toward the test situation and maximizes the likelihood that the examinee will approach the test in an equally serious manner.

The greatest threat to reliability from the perspective of the examiner, and perhaps from all perspectives, is a lack of adherence to the standardized application of item scoring rules. This threat is especially evident in the case of projective tests, where complicated scoring systems must be learned and applied with fidelity to ensure reliable results. With the exception of the electronic scan forms used with some objective tests, the need to perform simple calculation and clerical tasks to obtain raw scores and norm-based conversion scores is present to some degree with each administration of a personality test. Basic calculation and clerical scoring errors are a major source of test unreliability, and one that is often not reflected in the quantified estimates of test reliability reported in test manuals, as the cases used in reliability studies typically are thoroughly checked multiple times for possible scoring errors.

Characteristics of Respondents

No matter how well constructed a test or how competent and thorough the examiners who administer it, estimates of a test's reliability will never reflect perfect consistency. The unattainable nature of perfect consistency is due in large part to the third source of influence on a test's reliability: the respondents who take the test. Even when respondents are determined to perform in a consistent manner, two characteristics of human nature stand in the way of perfect consistency: All humans make mistakes at one time or other, and all humans perceive, think, feel, and act somewhat differently at any given moment, even in the presence of the same stimuli. Respondent tendencies toward inconsistency affect objective test performance as much as they affect projective test performance. In the case of objective tests, biological variations in human capacities assure that some test respondents will not be attending in the same way to all of the directions every time they take a test; nor will some attend to or process equally effectively every item on the test. Such lapses of attention and processing effort result in inconsistent response patterns across multiple test administrations. Some respondents will not perceive the task demands in quite the same way when taking the test more than once, thereby altering their performance across administrations. Some respondents will find it difficult to consistently interpret the difference between response multipoint options no matter how clear the differentiation between them seems to be, changing from one to another across administrations (e.g., shifting from "Nearly all the time" to "Sometimes"); some will find it difficult to consistently interpret the difference between dichotomous choices such as "true" and "false" when considering statements about how they perceive, think, feel, and act.

This last difficulty might seem exceptionally capricious as there are only two choices to consider, but in actuality, difficulty with dichotomous response options is perhaps the most understandable. If faced with a true-false choice, how should a reasonable adolescent respond to the following statement: "My parents control my life"? What if, as the adolescent reflects on the events of the past 6 months, he or she feels that sometimes the parents exerted an unreasonable amount of influence, but at other times they were exceptionally open to letting the adolescent do as he or she chose? How then, should the question be answered: true or false? One can easily imagine a scenario in which, having just been confronted about staying out too late the night before, an adolescent respondent chooses "true" even though at that same moment he or she has recollected many times when the parents did not exert such control. The next time the adolescent takes the test, no such negative event has recently occurred. Now, without the sting of a recent curtailment and feeling pretty good about the parents, the adolescent gives more weight to all the instances in which they allowed choice and responds with "false." Although respondents are directed to consider their perceptions, thoughts, feelings, and actions across an extended period of time, it is difficult even for a well-trained respondent, let alone an average child or adolescent, to engage in objective recollection that equally weights all salient past circumstances (and only salient circumstances) to arrive at a quantitative estimate of frequency of occurrence for a specific statement.

The previous discussion focused on respondents' self-reports about their own perceptions, thoughts, feelings, and actions, yet the issues raised apply equally to the ratings provided by others who are familiar with the perceptions, thoughts, feelings, and actions of the client, such as family members (especially parents) and teachers. Ratings from these individuals are often used when attempting to ascertain the personality characteristics of children and adolescents. They also are sometimes used with adults when the client is not viewed as a credible source of self-report information. Rating scales of this type can help to ensure a more accurate portrayal of a child's or adolescent's personality, but as tests themselves, their reliability also must be demonstrated.

The issue of capacity for balanced recollection of past experiences brings to light another respondent factor that can affect response consistency: the age of the respondent. Inspection of test-retest and internal consistency reliability data reported in various objective personality test manuals shows a consistent pattern whereby reliability estimates increase incrementally with the age of respondents. In contrast to the progression seen in personality test manuals, test-retest and internal consistency data provided in intelligence and achievement test manuals do not show a similar pattern of progression, as reliability estimates remain highly similar across the age range from 8 to 90 for tasks of similar content. Although it could be hypothesized that the reason for the reliability differences is that adult personality tests are better constructed, such a hypothesis seems highly unlikely in light of the fact that professional reviews provide evidence to support the premise that most tests of child and adolescent personality are as well-constructed as adult measures. A more likely explanation for the reliability progression effect is that self-report measures of personality place specific cognitive processing demands on respondents, and these processing demands are much more sensitive to the maturation of neural capacities than other types of tests. Self-report assessments of personality typically are not standardized with samples younger than age 8. Reaching 8 years of age, however, does not mean that children now have the same capacity as an adult, or even an adolescent, to respond in a consistent manner to questions that require them to reflect on and render judgments about their own perceptions, thoughts, feelings, and actions in an objective manner. Such capability likely develops slowly over time, consistent with the maturation of specific areas of the prefrontal cortex that play a large role in the development of self-reflection and judgment capabilities.

The developmental trend observed with objective tests often is not present in the reliability data reported for projective tests of personality. In the case of projective tests, although the developmental nature of the respondent's productions is apparent (Leichtman, 2004), 3-week retest studies of projective test administrations to children have reported reliability estimates consistent with those obtained for adult samples (Weiner, 2004). These results are understandable because in the case of objective tests, the perceptions of the respondents directly produce the data that are the basis of reliability estimates. Conversely, in the case of projective tests, the productions of the respondent are scored by examiners, and these scores, produced by the examiners and not by the respondents, are the data that are the basis of reliability estimates. Recognizing the developmental nature of respondent projective test productions, test developers provide scoring systems that control for identifiable developmental variations in response. Illustrative of the nature of controlling for developmental influences in projective test scoring systems, consider the fact that a specific drawing of a person, or a specific Rorschach response, would not be scored the same way or receive the same quantitative scores when produced by an 8-year-old child and a 45-year-old adult. Although these developmental scoring systems control for developmental variation across time, they do not necessarily control for how a respondent chooses to express perceptions, thoughts, feelings, and tendencies to act through the production of a response to the ambiguous stimuli of a projective test. Variation in respondent productions from one administration to another, therefore, remains a potential source of inconsistency in reliability measurement. Objective tests are at greater risk of the influence of inconsistent responding due to developmental status of the respondent, and projective tests are more vulnerable to threats to reliability from the combined sources of respondent production inconsistency and examiner scoring inconsistency. The fact that projective tests scores are found to be as reliable as most other forms of measurement (Meyer, 2004) is a credit to test developers who place great effort on standardizing projective test administration and scoring to the highest standards possible.

Test-Retest Reliability

For both objective and projective tests, test-retest reliability methodology provides a way to quantify the degree of consistency demonstrated by a group of respondents who take the test more than once. The degree of consistency between two administrations of the same test to the same group of respondents is typically quantified in the form of a correlation coefficient. Correlation coefficients can range from −1.0 to +1.0, with positive correlation values indicating that the two sets of scores are positively correlated and negative values indicating that the two sets of scores are negatively correlated. Positive correlations are desired, and the closer to a value of +1.0, the greater the consistency between the two sets of scores.

Correlation coefficients generally are an effective means of quantifying the degree of consistency between two sets of test scores; however, they can underestimate the degree of consistency of test performance. This is especially true when the range of possible scores is highly restricted, such as a scale with a score range of 5 or fewer possible points. In these cases, the use of the percentage of agreement of test scores can be a better indicator of consistency of test scores. In many cases, these agreement percentages can be evaluated using the *kappa* statistic to test for the extent to which agreement percentages are an improvement over what would be expected by chance. In an example provided by McCloskey (1990), a correlation coefficient of .59 was obtained from a data set comparison in which 82% of the respondents provided identical responses on the first and second administration of the test. A second data set yielded a correlation coefficient of .84 with 76% of the respondents providing identical responses on the first and second administration. In addition, the respondents of the second data set that did not demonstrate identical performance on the two administrations showed a greater range of variation from first to second administration than the respondents of the first data set. Both data sets were based on the same number of respondents (163), and the possible response score range for both tests was 5 points. A major difference between the two samples was that the scores of the respondents of the first group distributed across a range of only 3 of the 5 possible points, whereas the scores of the respondents in the second data set were distributed across the entire 5-point range. The restricted range of the first data set actually reflected a greater degree of consistency in responses, and yet the correlation coefficient of the first group (.59) was significantly lower than that obtained from the second group (.84). Percentage of agreement statistics might be much more effective in portraying the consistency of scores for less psychometrically sophisticated measures that often utilize restricted score ranges, such as basic clinical outcome measures.

This highlights the effect of restriction of score range on estimates of test-retest reliability. The time interval between the first and second administration of a test also can have an impact on consistency of measurement under certain conditions. If the trait being assessed is thought to be stable over long periods of time (e.g., tendencies to act aggressively toward others), then the time period between administrations is not of great concern, and longer time intervals during a test-retest study should not impact significantly the consistency of scores from one administration to the next. If the variable being measured is susceptible to change over a short period of time (e.g., anger state), then the time interval can have a very significant impact on score consistency between first and second administrations of the test. Test-retest studies are typically completed using time intervals ranging from several days to a few months. Studies that use longer time intervals actually are not measuring consistency of performance in the strict sense of test-retest reliability, but rather are attempting to measure the stability of the personality characteristics over time.

Sources that impact test-retest reliability include test, examiner, and respondent characteristics, although the degree of influence of each varies depending on whether the measure is an objective or a projective test. Test-retest estimates of reliability for objective tests tend to be influenced by item and respondent characteristics much more than examiner characteristics, as many objective tests are scored by computer. Although computerized scoring does not completely eliminate examiner sources of unreliability, they do greatly reduce their possible influence. Test-retest reliability estimates for projective tests tend to be equally influenced by item, examiner, and respondent characteristics. Examiner characteristics are more pronounced for projective tests than for objective tests due to the complex nature of the scoring systems that are employed by these tests. Additional methods, discussed later in this section, can be used to address specifically the issue of examiner scoring consistency, which is an especially important issue in the case of projective tests.

Scale Internal Consistency

Internal consistency methodology provides estimates of the extent to which responses to the items of a test, or subsections of the test, are consistent with each other. Such estimates can be calculated on the entire contents of a personality test, but they typically are calculated on subsets of items, usually referred to as scales, which often are further divided into subsets of subsets, referred to as subscales. The scale and subscale composition of a test represents the operationally defined structural relationships of the personality constructs the test is intended to measure. For example, an objective test of internalizing disorders might be composed of two scales labeled Depression and Anxiety. These two scales might be further divided into three subscale measures representing cognitive, affective, and physiological components, for a total of six subscales. Each of these six subscales, as well as the two scales, would likely be analyzed for internal consistency. The most common type of internal consistency analysis yields a correlation coefficient, called "coefficient alpha," which represents an averaging of the relationship of every item on the scale or subscale with every other item on the scale or subscale. These estimates can range from 0.00 to 1.00, with larger values indicating greater consistency among the items. A reasonable degree of consistency is desirable, as it indicates that an examinee is providing responses that conceptually go together to represent a pattern of perception, thought, feeling, or action. For example, if an objective test subscale composed of 10 items thought to measure borderline personality characteristics produced a coefficient alpha estimate of 0.20, this value suggests that a majority of examinees did not respond consistently to the 10 items. The lack of consistency could be due to some aspect of the items' or response options' wording or scoring, or due to a lack of conceptual coherence among the perceptions, thoughts, feelings, or actions represented by the items. Either of these sources would suggest that some aspect of test construction was not conducted adequately enough to produce a consistent measure.

In the case of projective tests, examiner scores for a number of features of an examinee's production might be aggregated to produce an index score. If the internal consistency estimate for the aggregation of these scoring features was 0.20, this value would suggest that a majority of the examiners did not assign scores of the same or similar magnitude to each of the features. The lack of consistency could be due to a lack of clarity in the scoring directions, inability of the various examiners to objectively judge the features, inconsistency in the way respondents produce the features, or a lack of conceptual fit of these features as a group to represent a measurable construct. Any of these sources would suggest that some aspect of test construction was not completed adequately enough to produce a consistent measure.

The premise underlying construction of scales that use multiple items to assess psychological constructs is that each item, while representative of the construct overall, also represents a unique aspect of the construct that is not necessarily captured by any other item on the scale. Complex constructs require several items for assessment because few persons are likely to demonstrate all of the characteristics that are representative of the construct, but are likely to manifest a greater number of all of the possible characteristics. This premise is somewhat counter to the idea of internal consistency in that if the items of a scale were completely internally consistent, that would mean that examinees were responding in the same way to every item of the scale; every person would either be a pure representation of the construct or not. If that were the case, there would be no need to include multiple items on the scale, as a single item would suffice for accurate measurement. Because pure typing of this kind is not an accurate characterization of how persons manifest psychological constructs, extremely high internal consistency estimates are not really desirable in a personality test. Moderate values in the high .70s to high .80s are certainly adequate to indicate a sufficiently high degree of internal consistency.

Final judgments of the reliability of the test should be made only after considering additional sources of information about measurement consistency, including test-retest reliability and, if dictated by the type of test, interrater reliability.

Interrater Reliability

When examiner judgments play a critical role in the scoring of a test, as is the case for virtually all projective personality tests, it is necessary to ascertain the degree of consistency of scores provided by examiners. The methods used to quantify examiner scoring consistency are referred to as interrater reliability analyses. These analyses are typically conducted using correlation methods similar to those described for test-retest reliability. Instead of correlating the scores of examinees across two administrations of the same test, interrater reliability analyses correlate the scores assigned by two or more examiners to the test responses of a group of examinees. Interrater agreement is most affected by two factors: the scoring system applied to obtain scores (a test characteristic) and the professional skill and judgment of the examiners. Because the same set of responses or productions are scored by multiple examinees, respondent characteristics do not have any effect on the consistency of the scores derived from them.

As has already been discussed in detail, the development of well-conceived, well-standardized scoring systems is central to reliable assessment. When a highly capable group of examiners cannot demonstrate consistent scoring, it is highly likely that there are flaws in the scoring system that need to be addressed to improve test reliability. Conversely, when a group of novice examiners can produce highly consistent results, it is highly likely that the scoring system is very robust and is likely to demonstrate a high degree of consistency for examiners with varying degrees of expertise.

In cases where a novice group of examiners fails to produce consistent scoring results, it is difficult to know whether the poor agreement was due to examiner inexperience or poor scoring guidelines. Because these two sources of variability are always potentially present to some degree, it is important that reliability analyses address the effect of examiner expertise on test reliability. This can be done by reporting separate studies done with novice and with experienced examiners, or by including examiner experience as a moderating variable in the analysis of reliability data.

VALIDITY

Although test validity has been a central concept in test development since its inception, the concept has undergone a substantial transformation in recent decades (Goodwin, 2002; Goodwin & Leech, 2003).

The current *Standards for Educational and Psychological Testing* issued in 1999 define validity and the process of validating a test:

> Validity refers to the degree to which evidence and theory support the interpretations of test scores entailed by proposed uses of tests. Validity is, therefore, the most fundamental consideration in developing and evaluating tests. The process of validation involves accumulating evidence to provide a sound scientific basis for the proposed score interpretations. It is the interpretations of test scores required by proposed uses that are evaluated, not the test itself. When test scores are used or interpreted in more than one way, each interpretation must be validated. (AERA, APA, & NCME, 1999, p. 9)

The validity of a personality test relates to the adequacy of the evidence gathered in support of the intended professional uses of the test. Tests that lack validity are considered poor sources of information about respondents, as they are thought to provide little in the way of an accurate characterization of personality traits and little in the way of useful information that can be used to help make professional decisions about a client's situation. Conversely, a valid test is one that has demonstrated evidence of the test's effectiveness in accurately characterizing personality traits and in providing valuable information that enhances clinical decision making.

The process of validating a personality test involves gathering evidence to support its effectiveness. Test authors and publishers summarize the evidence they have collected to support a test's validity in one or more chapters in the test manual. These findings typically are presented using a traditional, but now outdated, format that has utilized three distinct headings—content validity, criterion-related validity, and construct validity—and treats these three areas as if they are distinct types of validity. Content validity traditionally has referred to the adequacy of the content of the test to represent the constructs that are thought to be measured by the test. Criterion-related validity has referred to the comparison of test results with other measures of the same construct or with predicted outcomes. Construct validity has referred to the extent to which the test measures the trait or construct that it purports to measure.

Acknowledging the substantial overlap of these three traditional validity types and their lack of fit to present-day conceptions of validity, the *Standards for Educational and Psychological Testing* presented a reconceptualization of validity, distinguishing among the kinds of information that should be gathered to demonstrate the validity of a test rather than separate "types" of validity. This reconceptualization indicates that evidence for validity can be obtained through examination of five specific sources: (1) evidence based on test content, (2) evidence based on response processes, (3) evidence based on internal structure, (4) evidence based on relations to other variables, and (5) evidence based on the consequences of testing. The standards also made it clear that "validity" is a global term that defines the sum of all efforts made to demonstrate evidence of the effectiveness of test scores and their interpretation in serving the intended purposes of the test:

> These sources of evidence may illuminate different aspects of validity, but they do not represent distinct types of validity. Validity is a unitary concept. It is the degree to which all of the accumulated evidence supports the intended interpretation of test scores for the intended purposes. (AERA, APA, & NCME, 1999, p. 11)

Although the tripartite organizational structure of validity was replaced with the concept of examining sources of evidence, it is important to note that, in the vast majority of test manuals, test validity chapters continue to be divided into separate sections that address content, criterion-related, and construct validity, even for tests developed after 1999. Goodwin (2002; Goodwin & Leech, 2003) has noted the significant lag between the issuance of the new standards and the adoption of these standards in measurement textbooks and test manuals, and has provided a helpful framework for translating the older validity concepts into the new evidence-based framework. The following sections address the issue of the validity of personality tests using the five areas of evidence stated in the new *Standards* document.

Evidence Based on Test Content

Test content evidence relates to the rationale for item construction and selection during the test development process. The development of a personality test should involve generation of a blueprint to guide content selection and overall structural organization of the test. Logical arguments, expert reviews, and empirical analyses of content domains and items and item tryout data can be presented in the test manual to offer evidence of the adequacy of test construction efforts in this early stage of development. This source also includes evidence from empirical analyses of item data to detect possible sources of bias (e.g., gender, culture, age) that could influence the valid use of the test for specific groups of respondents. In many ways, this source coincides with various aspects of the older concepts of content validity and construct validity.

This source is where examiners would expect to find information about the underlying structure of a test. For example, do the content divisions of an objective test follow a *DSM-IV* categorization, or the structure of some theory of personality, or both? What is the underlying rationale for the constellation of the scored variables of the Rorschach? Also covered would be the extent to which the items placed on specific subscales seem to fit. For example, what evidence is offered to support the 10 items selected for placement on a subscale thought to assess Avoidant Personality Disorder? Evidence could be provided to support the contention that use of a specific Rorschach stimulus card does not produce gender or ethnic bias in estimates of performance on specific Rorschach score variables.

Evidence Based on Response Processes

Evidence based on response processes refers to examination of evidence indicating that the types of tasks or item responses required of examinees are an effective means for assessing the test content. This source has traditionally been addressed in sections on construct validity and includes the rationale for translating the content into items or tasks, justification for the methods used to administer the items or tasks, and a rationale for the development of a system for scoring items. Questions investigated and reported on in the case of an objective test might include the following: Can a paper-and-pencil test adequately reflect in a meaningful way a respondent's perceptions, thoughts, feelings, and actions in reference to one or more personality traits that the test is attempting to measure? Does the test have a way to demonstrate that respondents are answering questions in a truthful manner? Evidence related to adequacy of scoring systems, a major concern of projective tests, would also be addressed in this section. For example, what evidence is provided to support the scoring process, scoring criteria, and score values applied to responses to sentence completion items or human figure drawings? For objective tests, evidence could be offered to justify the use of dichotomous (true-false or yes-no) scoring options over multipoint rating options, or vice versa.

Evidence Based on Internal Structure

This evidence addresses the extent to which the structure of the test's content matches the theorized or empirically demonstrated structure of the construct or constructs that the test is supposed to be measuring. Evidence supporting internal structure has traditionally been the central focus of construct validity discussions. Empirical approaches for providing evidence can include item intercorrelations, such as those conducted to demonstrate internal consistency reliability, as these analyses demonstrate the extent to which items placed on a scale or subscale yield similar response patterns. Factor analysis currently is the preferred method of most test developers to provide empirical support for proposed scale and subscale divisions within a test (Nunnally & Bernstein, 1994). The popularity of this technique has generated an almost monolithic approach to evaluating evidence of internal structure, such that tests that do not show strong factor structures are suspect in terms of adequacy for clinical purposes. In actuality, a highly discrete factor structure can sometimes indicate that too much attention has been paid to placing items onto scales to produce the intended factor structure, and too little attention has been paid to the meaningfulness of the item content and the clinical utility of the scores that relatively "pure" factors yield (Nunnally & Bernstein, 1994; Thorndike, 1997). Evidence to support internal structure might address the appropriateness of dividing an objective test's scale content into separate subscales to assess Avoidant, Borderline, Obsessive-Compulsive, Schizotypal, and Paranoid Personality Disorder characteristics instead of providing only a single Personality Disorder Scale.

Evidence Based on Relations to Other Variables

This source offers evidence of the extent to which test results relate to the results obtained with other tests or to other criteria, such as observable behaviors and clinical diagnoses. This source coincides with traditional presentations of criterion-related validity, including concurrent and predictive validity evidence, and construct validity evidence typically involving convergent and discriminant analyses of score relationships. Most important, this source provides support for the intended clinical uses of the test.

The most common types of data analyses traditionally reported in personality test manuals to demonstrate criterion-related and construct validity involve correlational studies, especially comparisons of the test with other measures thought to be measuring the same, or different, personality traits or constructs. Also frequently reported are studies that compare test scores for sample groups, for example, test scores for a sample of nonreferred children or adolescents compared with the test scores of children or adolescents already diagnosed with one or more personality disorders. Less frequently reported are experimental design studies, such as intervention studies that use test scores as criteria of pre- and postintervention status. For example, if an intervention known to have great success with adolescent clients is utilized, and the test is thought to be a valid measure of change in perceptions, thoughts, feelings, or actions that are known to change from exposure to the intervention, then postintervention test scores should show changes in the expected direction when compared with preintervention test scores.

Evidence Related to the Consequences of Testing

This source is intended to address the consequences that derive from the use of a test. These consequences might be anticipated or unanticipated during the inception of the test, and might be positive or negative in nature. Specification of this source as a basis for judging the validity of a test has generated a great deal of controversy (Linn, 1997; Popham, 1997; Shepard, 1997). Despite its controversial nature, this source was added in the 1999 *Standards*. Because of its relatively new status as a source of evidence for the validity of a test, it has received little consideration in the validity chapters of personality test manuals. This new area of consideration could attempt to address questions such as the following: Is the use of personality tests with children and adolescents for the purpose of diagnosing personality disorders a good or bad professional practice? Does the use of personality test results help children get the professional assistance and community support they might need so that their lives can improve, or does it mark them permanently as defective and reduce their chances of leading meaningful, fulfilling lives? If a personality test demonstrates evidence of the ability to identify, or help to identify, treatment goals, are the goals derived in this manner ones that really should be the focus of treatment and that will ultimately benefit the child or adolescent? If a personality test demonstrates sensitivity to changes in perceptions, thoughts, feeling, or actions over time such that it is used to monitor progress in treatment, is the test really monitoring the important aspects of changes that should be occurring if the child or adolescent is to truly benefit in the long term from the treatment? These are difficult questions that must be posed and discussed in open, objective forums.

Test Validation and the Five Sources of Evidence

Although all of these sources can be used to develop an argument to support the validity of a test, it is not necessary for every test to provide information for all five of these sources. In some cases, one source might be much more important for establishing the validity of a test than the others. Judging the validity of a test can be a complicated matter, which can be made easier by maintaining focus on the most important aspect of validity: demonstrating evidence that the test can be used effectively and with good benefit for the purposes for which it is being used.

It is critical to appreciate that some potential uses of a test might not be anticipated by the test developers. In these cases, studies external to the test development process must be conducted to provide evidence to support the new use of the test. The fact that this new use was not stated as one of the original uses of the test is less important than whether substantial evidence has been provided to support the new, unanticipated use of the test. Having more than 20 years of experience in the field of test development, the first author is frequently asked a single question pertaining to various tests: "Is test X a valid test?" The response provided is always the same: "That depends. For what purpose is test X being used?" Validity cannot be established independent of the intended uses of a test.

In the case of personality tests used with children and adolescents suspected of demonstrating personality disorders, the most likely uses of the test would be to assist with diagnosis of psychological problems, to plan for treatment, and to monitor the effects of treatment. To be judged valid for the purpose of diagnosis of personality disorders, the test would need to show evidence that test score interpretation effectively identifies personality disorders or provides incremental improvement in rendering personality disorder diagnoses over the use of other techniques employed without the test. Relative to treatment planning, test developers would need to provide evidence that interpretation of test performance can be effectively used to plan treatment in a manner that is equal to or improves such planning over techniques that do not include the use of test results. For the purposes of monitoring effects of treatment, test developers would need to demonstrate that the test is sensitive to changes in children's or adolescents' perceptions, thoughts, feelings, or actions thought to be representative of the personality traits that the test is intended to measure. Finally, the issue of evidence of the consequences of the use of the test would need to be addressed in the test manual and discussed openly in the professional literature. The outcome of such discussions should be evidence of the final form mentioned in the *Standards:* that of evidence based on the consequences of testing. Hopefully, such evidence would support the contention that the test is a useful tool that can be put to good use for the benefit of the children and adolescents with whom it might be used.

OVERVIEW OF THE ASSESSMENT OF CHILD AND ADOLESCENT PERSONALITY DISORDERS

This chapter has focused on the characteristics necessary for a standardized test of personality or personality disorders to be considered a reliable and valid assessment tool. As noted earlier, however, tests are only one of several assessment methods that can and should be used when attempting to identify children and adolescents who meet criteria for personality disorders. Consistent with the general best practices for the assessment of behavior problems exhibited by children, assessment related specifically to the diagnosis and treatment of a personality disorder in children should involve a multisource, multimethod approach that includes interviews with the child or adolescent and parents and caregivers, administration of one or more developmentally appropriate self-report measures, and collection of collateral information from as many sources as possible. This section discusses the role of each of these assessment methods in the overall assessment process.

COLLECTION OF COLLATERAL INFORMATION AND RECORDS REVIEW

Gathering information from collateral sources is the cornerstone of assessment of childhood and adolescent personality disorders. Input from the child's or adolescent's parents or primary caregivers is considered essential for valid diagnosis. Parents typically have the greatest degree of familiarity with the child's or adolescent's thought and behavior patterns across the longest period of time, at least in the case of intact, stable families. In cases where family structure or function has been disrupted significantly (divorce, death of a parent, abandonment, adoption, foster care arrangements, etc.), input from primary caregivers is critical, although the accuracy and reliability of the information provided in these circumstances might be less than desired. Whenever possible, it is prudent to gather information from more than one parent or guardian. Data from multiple family members increases the likelihood that the family input is reliable and valid. To assist in determining whether disordered thought and behavior patterns are persistent across settings and situations, input is often requested from classroom teachers and other school staff who interact frequently with the child or adolescent. Educational policies and practices also enable more effective collection and review of historical records than is the case with adult clients. These records can be extremely helpful in determining the extent to which disordered thought and behavior patterns represent long-standing concerns or merely transient occurrences.

A primary technique for the collection of information from collateral sources for childhood and adolescent behavior problems is the completion of behavior rating scales by parents or other caregivers and teachers. The two most commonly used scales for this purpose are the Behavior Assessment System for Children—Second Edition (BASC-II; C. R. Reynolds & Kamphaus, 2004) and the Achenbach System of Empirically Based Assessment (Achenbach & Rescorla, 2004) Child Behavior Checklist (CBCL) and Teacher Report Form (TRF). These scales have demonstrated their utility in the assessment of behavioral and emotional problems, including psychiatric disorders such as depression, anxiety, and Conduct Disorder, although they originally were not designed to provide rater information about the occurrence of thoughts and behaviors associated with specific personality disorders as described in the *DSM-IV*.

Despite the widespread use of these measures for assessment of Axis I emotional and behavioral problems, their utility in assessing personality psychopathology is virtually unknown. A review of the CBCL suggests that although the items were selected to assess for Axis I syndromes and problems, many items may be useful in identifying specific enduring and maladaptive personality traits of children and adolescents. For example, items such as "Fears he or she might think or do something bad," "Shy or timid," and "Self-conscious or easily embarrassed" may be potential indicators of extreme shyness or avoidant personality characteristics. Additionally, items such as "Acts too young for his or her age" and "Clings to adults or is too dependent" may be indicators of dependent personality traits, and "Whining" or "Strange behaviors," "Would rather be alone than with others," "Strange ideas," and "Withdrawn, doesn't get involved with others" may be indicators of schizoid personality traits.

Although there may be correspondence between numerous items on the Achenbach measures and other child and adolescent rating scales and personality problems, it is unclear if Axis II phenomena can be identified by the CBCL and TRF. Searches of the literature for research using the CBCL, TRF, or BASC in assessment of personality disorders revealed only one study. Bradley, Conklin, and Westen (2005) used the CBCL, as completed by clinicians, to help validate empirically derived subgroups of adolescent females meeting criteria for Borderline Personality Disorder (BPD). They derived and labeled four subgroups of BPD girls based on their Q-sort methodology: high-functioning internalizing, depressive internalizing, histrionic, and angry externalizing. In support of their hypotheses, Bradley et al. found that additional validation analyses showed that the depressive internalizing group had higher scores on the Internalizing scale of the CBCL than the other groups, whereas the angry externalizing group had the highest scores on the Externalizing scale. Thus, results from the CBCL provided some validation for Bradley et al.'s method of establishing subgroups of girls with BDP. This suggests that the broad-band scales of the CBCL may be meaningful dimensions on which to begin to identify more enduring personality dimensions of psychopathology. However, it is noteworthy that Bradley et al. used clinician ratings rather than parent ratings. Thus, the empirical evidence to date is weak regarding the use of popular parent and teacher rating scales of child psychopathology. Clearly, more research is needed in this area and should be a high priority for researchers studying Axis II problems in youth.

The Adolescent Psychopathology Scale (APS; W. M. Reynolds, 1998) is the only self-report measure that can be used with adolescents that, in part, was specifically designed to address personality disorders as defined in the *DSM-IV*. The APS provides numerous content scales that assess the symptoms of many of the psychological disorders described in *DSM-IV*, including specific scales that assess the severity of symptoms related to five of the *DSM-IV* personality disorders (Avoidant, Obsessive-Compulsive, Borderline, Schizotypal, and Paranoid). The validity data reported in the APS technical manual appear sound, and the instrument shows great promise for clinical and research use in relation to the five personality disorders it assesses. It is important to note that although objective test self-report methodology appears to be a valid technique for obtaining information about psychological functioning from adolescents and older children (W. M. Reynolds, 1993), the specific application of the method to the diagnosis of personality disorders is not well established yet. Clinicians should gauge carefully the reliability of self-reports provided by adolescent respondents who do exhibit certain personality disorders.

INTERVIEW TECHNIQUES

A number of researchers have suggested that clinical interviews are the principal method of assessment of personality disorders in general clinical practice (Watkins, Campbell, Nieberding, & Hallmark, 1995; Westen, 1997; Widiger & Samuel, 2005). Although unstructured interviews can be useful in obtaining information about patients in a nonthreatening manner, several drawbacks have been reported with their application. Problems with unstructured interviews include potentially failing to incorporate discussion of all of the necessary diagnostic criteria (Blashfield & Herkov, 1996; Zimmerman & Mattia, 1999), exaggerating similarities among nonidentical stimuli by overlooking within-group variability, discounting disconfirming evidence, focusing on stereotypic examples of the category (Cantor & Genero, 1986), diagnosing disorders hierarchically, and failing to assess for additional symptoms once a particular disorder has been identified (Alder, Drake, & Teague, 1990; Herkov & Blashfield, 1995). Idiosyncratic interests of the clinician can also influence the diagnosis assigned to a client (Gunderson, 1992; Mellsop, Varghese, Joshua, & Hicks, 1982). In addition to methodological pitfalls, the few studies that have been conducted to assess the reliability of unstructured interviews for personality disorder diagnosis have not been encouraging (Blashfield & Herkov, 1996; Zimmerman & Mattia, 1999).

Semistructured interviews have been developed to address the shortcomings of unstructured interview techniques and have been researched more widely in terms of their applicability to the diagnosis of personality disorders. The design of semistructured interviews ensures that a systematic and comprehensive consideration of all personality disorders occurs (Widiger & Samuel, 2005). Although it is typically assumed that interviewees will respond in an open and reliable manner to interview questions, this assumption of openness may be unwarranted in the case of children and adolescents who exhibit certain personality disorders. In addition, some researchers have found the reliability and validity of child interviews to be severely lacking in many instances and questionable to some degree even in the best of conditions (Myers & Winters, 2002). As noted earlier, the reliability of an assessment procedure is not simply a function of the development of the assessment method, but is also a function of the interaction between the assessment method and the individual being assessed. As self-informants, children and adolescents are much less reliable than adults, and the younger the child, the less reliable the information obtained (McCloskey, 1990). Although it is important to interview a child or adolescent suspected of having a personality disorder, clinicians must be careful to obtain information from multiple collateral sources to verify the accuracy or substantiate the plausibility of statements made by the child or adolescent.

One less structured interview for children and adolescents is the Personality Assessment Interview (PAI; Selzer, Kernberg, Fibel, Cheruliez, & Mortati, 1987). The PAI is a 45-minute interview with a psychoanalytic orientation designed to assess children's and adolescents, self- and object representations, affect, thinking, capacity for reflection, and empathy with the interviewer (Kernberg, Weiner, & Bardenstein, 2000). This measure was adapted from Kernberg's (1988) structural interview designed to assess basic structural constellations of personality—neurotic, borderline, and psychotic—and is discussed by Kernberg et al. Information gathered from the PAI is then used to help make determinations about personality structure and possible Axis II diagnoses.

However, this interview technique appears limited in several important ways. First, although the interview is theoretically derived, its empirical properties are unknown. No research is available to assess either the validity or reliability of this measure. Consequently, it is unclear exactly what constructs, and how reliably, the interview assesses. Second, the operationalization of the theoretical constructs the PAI is believed to measure seems incomplete. Constructs such as object representations and self-representations are highly abstract ideas about mental operations but are not well articulated into observable and measurable phenomena. Third, the lack of standardization makes this measure particularly vulnerable to a variety of methodological problems described previously, including exaggeration similarities by overlooking within-group variability, discounting disconfirming evidence, focusing on stereotypic examples of categories, and a potential focus on idiosyncratic interests of the clinician. Fourth, it is unclear how information gathered from this measure maps onto personality disorder constructs as defined by the *DSM-IV*. Kernberg et al. (2000) discuss the results of the PAI in terms of personality "organization" types but fail to articulate how these translate into Axis II diagnoses.

A more reliable and valid approach to interviewing may be the use of structured and semistructured interviews. Currently, the only structured or semistructured direct interviews developed for use with children and adolescents as the primary informants are the Diagnostic Interview Schedule for Children, Version 2.3 (Shaffer et al., 1996), and the Diagnostic Interview for Children and Adolescents (Reich, 1998), and these do not directly address issues related specifically to childhood personality disorders. The Structured Clinical Interview for *DSM-IV* Personality Disorders (SCID-II; First, Gibbon, Spitzer, Williams, & Benjamin, 1997), often used in the assessment of adults, has demonstrated some promise in the assessment of adolescent personality disorders. In their research involving evidence-based assessment of personality disorders, Widiger and Samuel (2005) point out that the SCID-II stipulates that clinicians need to verify the presence of diagnostic criteria over a 5-year time span. When assessing a very young adult using the SCID-II, all or part of the 5-year period prior to the interview could encompass the adolescent years. In an effort to examine the association between childhood psychopathology and young adult personality disorders, the SCID-II was utilized 8 to 10 years after initially assessing study participants (Kasen, Cohen, Skodol, Johnson, & Brook, 1999). At the outset of the Children in the Community study (CIC), a longitudinal study of risk factors for child psychopathology begun in the 1970s, participants were 1 to 10 years old. The first follow-up session took place 8 years after the inception of the study. The SCID-II was used during the first and all subsequent follow-up sessions. Items drawn from the SCID-II were used to help make *DSM-III-R* diagnoses of Avoidant, Borderline, Dependent, Histrionic, Narcissistic, Obsessive-Compulsive, Paranoid, Passive-Aggressive, Schizoid, and Schizotypal Personality Disorders in youth. SCID-II data were combined with interview and questionnaire data collected from children and their mothers to make Axis II diagnoses. Thus, the SCID-II was not used alone.

However, the diagnostic procedures in this study, including the SCID-II, appear to demonstrate validity as evidenced by several follow-up studies of the sample. Bernstein et al. (1993) found that diagnoses of personality disorders among children and adolescents were associated with multiple indicators of distress and impairment, including poorer quality peer and romantic relationships, greater school and work performance and behavioral problems, increased likelihood of contact with police, and greater Axis I psychopathology. Additionally, Cohen et al. (2005) showed that Cluster A odd/eccentric personality disorders diagnosed in adolescence were subsequently predictive of poorer adjustment during the transition to adulthood, as indicated by fewer years of postsecondary education or training and earlier parenthood.

Thus, available evidence suggests that the SCID-II may be a valid and important interview used in the diagnosis of Axis II phenomena in children and adolescents. However, the evidence also suggests that there may be some limitations to the SCID-II. Foremost is the seeming lack of stability of diagnoses in the CIC sample. As Bernstein et al. (1993) noted, fewer than half of the subjects given an Axis II diagnosis at Time 2 received any Axis II diagnosis at Time 3, just 2 years later. Additionally, the prevalence of moderate to severe personality disorders peaked at age 12 for boys and age 13 for girls. In contrast to theoretical increases in personality disorders as development proceeds, diagnoses declined from peaks in early adolescence through the teen years. Taken together, these findings may indicate shortcomings of the SCID-II, or other measures, as diagnostic tools. Additionally, it seems that diagnoses made at least in part by the SCID-II may show short-term instability as well as declining courses during adolescence.

PERSONALITY TESTS

Objective self-report measures and projective methods can be applied to gather information directly from children and adolescents. The two most widely used adult self-report measures, the Minnesota Multiphasic Personality Inventory II and the Millon Clinical Multiaxial Inventory III, also have corresponding adolescent versions: the Minnesota Multiphasic Personality Inventory—Adolescent (MMPI-A; Butcher et al., 1992) and the Millon Adolescent Clinical Inventory (MACI; Millon, Millon, Davis, & Grossman, 1997). Although the MMPI-A does not contain scales that directly correspond to the *DSM-IV* personality disorder classifications, it does provide five Personality Psychopathology scales (Aggressiveness, Psychoticism, Disconstraint, Negative Emotionality/Neuroticism, Introversion/Low Positive Emotionality) and other content scales that address perceptions, thoughts, feelings, and behaviors characteristic of adolescents exhibiting personality disorders. The MACI also does not have specific scales corresponding to *DSM-IV* personality disorder classifications, providing instead multiple content scale configurations and several sets of content scales assessing personality patterns, such as Borderline Tendency, Self-Demeaning, Oppositional, Conforming, Egotistic, Unruly, and Forceful. Each of these content scales comprises multiple subscales; for example, the Borderline Tendency scale includes three subscales: Temperamentally Labile, Cognitively Capricious, and Uncertain Self-Image. As their names imply, he MMPI-A and the MACI assess only the personality characteristics of adolescents ages 12 to 18. Although the MMPI does not have a scale that is designed to assess preadolescent children, the MACI does have a children's counterpart, the Millon Pre-Adolescent Clinical Inventory (M-PACI, Tringone, Millon, & Kamp, 2007). The M-PACI is designed for use with children ages 9 to 12, but the content scales are of a more general nature and are not directly tied to personality disorder classifications. The two scales most frequently used to assess general behavior problems in children—the BASC-II and the CBCL—have child and adolescent self-report versions, but the structures of these self-report measures correspond closely to those of the parent and teacher versions and therefore do not contain scales that align with any of the *DSM-IV* personality disorder classifications.

Various projective techniques have been used to assess multiple aspects of child and adolescent personality and psychopathology (Knoff, 1986). These include the Rorschach Inkblot Test, the Thematic Apperception Test (Murray, 1943), projective drawing tests such as the Draw-A-Person test (Machover, 1949), and the Sentence Completion Test for Children and Youth (Westenberg, Treffers, & Drewes, 1998). However, the reliability and validity of projective measures for assessing personality psychopathology remain questionable. Additionally, as is the case with self-report measures, the use of projective techniques in the diagnosis of personality disorders in children and adolescents has not yet been well established in the professional literature.

Q-SORT

Westen's work on personality assessment and diagnosis of Axis II problems in adolescents stands in contrast to the limited methods and literature surrounding numerous other personality measures. Shedler and Westen (1998) have attempted to develop an alternative approach to assessing Axis II disorders. Their method, the Shedler-Westen Assessment Procedure (SWAP), has undergone three revisions. The first version, the SWAP-167, was a 167-item version, which was tested on the Axis II Cluster B disorders (Shedler & Westen, 1998). The SWAP-200 was normed on a sample of 530 personality disordered patients. The current version, the SWAP-II, is normed on a sample of 1,201 patients with mild to severe personality pathology. An adolescent version of the SWAP-200 was also developed, the SWAP-200-A, and was normed on 294 adolescents exhibiting a range of personality pathology (Westen, Shedler, Durrett, Glass, & Martens, 2003). The current version, the SWAP-II-A is being normed on 950 adolescents with mild to severe personality pathology (Westen, Shedler, & Bradley, 2005).

The SWAP uses the Q-sort method of personality assessment. It consists of 200 items derived from various sources, including the personality disorder diagnostic criteria from the text and appendixes of the *DSM-III-R* and *DSM-IV*; selected items from Axis I that could reflect personality pathology; a substantial number of descriptors of personality derived from the literature on personality and personality disorders written over the past 50 years; research on coping and defensive processes; research on interpersonal pathology of personality disordered patients; research on typical personality traits and development; and extensive pilot interviews. The items developed for the SWAP-II-A also took into consideration research on adolescent development, personality, and psychopathology. To provide a comprehensive profile of a patient's strengths in addition to pathology, many of the items are designed to assess aspects of personality pathology that are not severe enough to warrant an Axis II diagnosis, as well as aspects of healthy functioning (Westen et al., 2005).

The Q-sort method utilizes a set of statements that describe different aspects of personality and psychological functioning, each printed on a separate index card (Westen & Shedler, 1999). A clinician or interviewer who knows the patient well must sort the cards into categories based on the degree to which they accurately describe the patient. The SWAP-II requires clinicians to sort the 200 statements into eight categories, ranging from 0 (irrelevant or inapplicable) to 7 (highly descriptive). The statements are intended to provide a standard vocabulary to assist clinicians in expressing their observations and inferences in a way that can be quantified, compared with descriptions of other clinicians, and analyzed statistically. The authors note that there are two major ways that the SWAP procedure differs from Axis II criteria. The first is that items were developed to operationalize psychological constructs, such as defensive processes, that were excluded from the *DSM-IV* because of concern that these processes could not be measured reliably. Second, the range of items is expanded to include aspects of functioning that could be clinically important but that Axis II does not address, such as motives, conflicts among motives, affect regulation strategies, milder aspects of personality pathology, and areas of positive adaptive functioning (Westen & Shedler, 1999). When using the SWAP-II method it is also important to note that the clinician does not decide how many items to put in each category; instead, the items must be arranged into a fixed distribution with a specified number of statements in each category. This procedure was used for its psychometric advantages, such as minimizing measurement error (Westen et al., 2005). The fixed distribution was modeled after the right half of a normal, bell-shaped curve distribution (Westen & Shedler, 1999). Thus, many items will receive low values (0, 1, and 2), but only a few will receive values of 7. There is an electronic version of the SWAP-II Q-sort that can be utilized.

The SWAP-II (for adults) and the SWAP-II-A (for adolescents) were recently used in two large studies funded by the National Institute of Mental Health that were conducted as part of the revision of Axis II (Westen et al., 2005); analysis of the collected data is currently under way. The first study utilized a large number of doctoral-level clinicians across North America to provide quantified data on a patient in their care. The data collected will be analyzed to identify the most characteristic as well as the most distinctive features of each disorder. Q factor analysis and latent class analysis will be used to empirically identify diagnostic groupings irrespective of current *DSM-IV* criteria. The data can also be analyzed to identify the underlying trait structure for each personality disorder while retaining the *DSM-IV* personality disorder constructs. Finally, the data can be used to identify the trait structure of personality pathology independent of current diagnoses.

In another recent study by Shedler, Westen, and Bradley (2006), a random national sample of 291 psychiatrists and clinical psychologists described a randomly selected patient in their care. Clinician-provided diagnostic data were used to generate categorical and dimensional *DSM-IV* diagnoses (number of symptoms present per disorder). Clinicians also utilized one of two prototype matching systems to provide a diagnosis for the selected patient. Analysis of the results found that prototype diagnosis yielded reduced comorbidity relative to *DSM-IV* diagnosis; produced similar estimates of validity in predicting criterion variables, such as adaptive functioning, treatment response, and etiology; and was better than *DSM-IV* diagnosis in ratings of clinical utility and ease of use. Based on their results, the authors concluded that adding a personality health prototype further increases accuracy of prediction. The study found evidence that a simple prototype matching procedure provides a viable alternative for improving diagnosis of personality disorders in clinical practice. Shedler et al. concluded that a prototype diagnosis is easy to use, minimizes artifactual comorbidity, is compatible with naturally occurring cognitive processes, and translates readily into both categorical and dimensional diagnosis. Although the SWAP-II-A is still in the early stage of development, it shows great promise for significantly enhancing or reshaping current assessment practices related to personality disorders.

CONCLUSIONS

The assessment of children and adolescents for the purpose of establishing a diagnosis of personality disorder is a relatively new practice, despite ample research and long-standing clinical beliefs regarding the significance of children's personality attributes for psychopathology. That aside, there are a number of published studies that suggest that maladaptive, inflexible, and enduring psychological problems of children and adolescents can be assessed and are a legitimate area of study. A number of studies suggest that Borderline, Schizoid, and Avoidant Personality Disorders, as well as others, can be assessed during childhood and adolescence and, as expected, are related to poorer quality development.

Despite these successes, the current state of the literature on assessment of Axis II phenomena in children can best be described as lacking For the most part, current assessment practices involving personality tests are downward extensions of the techniques used with adults. As Bradley et al. (2005) note, at least for Borderline Personality Disorder, numerous studies have used adult criteria to diagnose adolescents with apparent success. Assessments based on adult criteria have appropriately identified adolescents with significant psychopathology as well as impairments and have been validated against other assessment methods. However, the question still remains whether these are the optimal criteria for diagnosis. This is not a problem limited to research on BPD. Evidence for the optimal diagnostic criteria for virtually all Axis II disorders, and even Axis I conditions such as Bipolar Disorder and Major Depression, is unclear.

Perhaps the existing literature in this regard is a good start. But it seems that one of the most important goals for future research in child personality psychopathology is to refine and establish key diagnostic criteria.

An additional limitation is the paucity of research establishing standard measures of Axis I psychopathology, such as the CBC and TRF, as measures of Axis II problems. However, many items included in these measures to identify major Axis I problems also may be useful in identifying maladaptive and persistent traits. A review of the Achenbach scales reveals many items that may tap a range of personality disorders, including Schizoid, Borderline, and Avoidant. Popularly used scales such as the CBCL, TRF, and BASC may have utility in assessing personality problems. However, the literature is quite limited in demonstrating the empirical value in this approach. Virtually no studies have been identified that have tested the reliability and validity of major Axis I rating scales in assessing personality disorders in children and adolescents. And the literature on other measures, such as personality tests, projective tests, and interviews, is quite restricted as well. Thus, a major goal for the field should be rigorous examination of existing measures to determine their validity and reliability in assessment.

A greater focus on children is also needed. Much of the existing literature is based on adolescents. Consequently, there is a greater array of measures and a more developed evidence base for assessing personality problems among teenagers. Some of this literature has been innovative, particularly the work of Westen and colleagues, and initial work on validating both diagnostic criteria and measures has been promising. It is not surprising that more work has been done on adolescent samples given the tendency among researchers to extend methods from the adult literature to younger age groups. However, the focus on teenagers has resulted in an even more limited scope on children. Although some literature suggests that assessment of children is possible (Kasen et al., 1999), more research is needed.

REFERENCES

Achenbach, T. M., & Rescorla, L. A. (2004). The Achenbach system of empirically based assessment (ASEBA) for ages 1.5 to 18 years. In M. E. Maruish (Ed.), *The use of psychological testing for treatment planning and outcomes assessment: Vol. 2. Instruments for children and adolescents* (pp. 179–213). Mahwah, NJ: Erlbaum.

Alder, D., Drake, R., & Teague, G. (1990). Clinicians' practices in personality assessment: Does gender influence the use of *DSM-III* Axis II? *Comprehensive Psychiatry, 31,* 125–133.

American Educational Research Association, American Psychological Association, & National Council on Measurement in Education. (1999). *Standards for educational and psychological testing.* Washington, DC: Author.

American Psychiatric Association. (2000). *Diagnostic and statistical manual of mental disorders* (4th ed., text rev.). Washington, DC: Author.

Bernstein, D. P., Cohen, P., Velez, C. N., Schwab-Stone, M., Siever, L. J., & Shinsato, L. (1993). The prevalence and stability of the *DSM-III-R* personality disorders in a community-based survey of adolescents. *American Journal of Psychiatry, 150,* 1237–1243.

Blashfield, R. K., & Herkov, M. J. (1996). Investigating clinician adherence to diagnosis by criteria: A replication of Morey and Ochoa (1989). *Journal of Personality Disorders, 10,* 219–228.

Bradley, R., Conklin, C. Z., & Westen, D. (2005). The borderline personality diagnosis in adolescents: Gender differences and subtypes. *Journal of Child Psychology and Psychiatry, 46,* 1006–1019.

Butcher, J. N., Williams, C. L., Graham, J. R., Archer, R. P., Tellegen, A., Ben-Porath, Y. S., et al. (1992). *The Minnesota Multiphasic Personality Inventory—Adolescent (MMPI-A): Manual for administration and scoring.* Minneapolis: University of Minnesota Press.

Cantor, N., & Genero, N. (1986). Psychiatric diagnosis and natural categorization: A close analogy. In T. Millon & G. Klerman (Eds.),

Contemporary directions in psychopathology (pp. 233–256). New York: Guilford Press.

Cohen, P., Chen, H., Kasen, S., Johnson, J. G., Crawford, T., & Gordon, K. (2005). Adolescent Cluster A personality disorder symptoms, role assumption in the transition to adulthood, and resolution or persistence of symptoms. *Development and Psychopathology, 17,* 549–568.

First, M. B., Gibbon, M., Spitzer, R. L., Williams, J. B. W., & Benjamin, L. S. (1997). *Structured Clinical Interview for* DSM-IV *Axis II personality disorders (SCID-II).* Washington, DC: American Psychiatric Press.

Goodwin, L. D. (2002). Changing conceptions of measurement validity: An update on the new standards. *Journal of Nursing Education, 41,* 100–106.

Goodwin, L. D., & Leech, N. L. (2003). The meaning of validity in the new standards for educational and psychological testing: Implications for measurement courses. *Measurement and Evaluation in Counseling and Development, 36*(3), 181–191.

Gunderson, J. G. (1992). Diagnostic controversies. In A. Tasman & M. B. Ribba (Eds.), *Review of psychiatry* (Vol. 11, pp. 9–24). Washington, DC: American Psychiatric Press.

Herkov, M. J., & Blashfield, R. K. (1995). Clinicians' diagnoses of personality disorder: Evidence of a hierarchical structure. *Journal of Personality Assessment, 65,* 313–321.

Hilsenroth, M. L., & Segal, D. L. (Eds.). (2004). *Comprehensive handbook of psychological assessment: Vol. 2. Personality assessment.* Hoboken, NJ: Wiley.

Kasen, S., Cohen, P., Skodol, A. E., Johnson, J. G., & Brook, J. (1999). Influence of child and adolescent psychiatric disorders on young adult personality disorder. *American Journal of Psychiatry, 156*(10), 1529–1535.

Kernberg, P. F. (1988). Children with borderline personality organization. In C. J. Kestenbaum & D. T. Williams (Eds.), *Handbook of clinical assessment of children and adolescents* (pp. 604–625). New York: New York University Press.

Kernberg, P. F., Weiner, A. S., & Bardenstein, K. K. (2000). *Personality disorders in children and adolescents.* New York: Basic Books.

Knoff, H. M. (Ed.). (1986). *The assessment of child and adolescent personality.* New York: Guilford Press.

Leichtman, M. (2004). Projective tests: The nature of the task. In M. L. Hilsenroth & D. L. Segal (Eds.), *Comprehensive handbook of psychological assessment: Vol. 2. Personality assessment* (pp. 297–314). Hoboken, NJ: Wiley.

Linn, R. L. (1997). Evaluating the validity of assessments: The consequences of use. *Educational Measurement: Issues and Practice, 16*(2), 14–16.

Machover, K. (1949). *Personality projection in the drawings of the human figure.* Springfield, IL: Charles C Thomas.

McCloskey, G. (1990, Fall). Selecting and using early childhood rating scales. *Topics in Early Childhood Special Education, 10*(3).

Mellsop, G., Varghese, F. T. N., Joshua, S., & Hicks, A. (1982). The reliability of Axis II of *DSM-III. American Journal of Psychiatry, 139,* 1360–1361.

Meyer, G. J. (2004). The reliability and validity of the Rorschach and Thematic Apperception Test (TAT) compared to other psychological and medical procedures: An analysis of systematically gathered evidence. In M. L. Hilsenroth & D. L. Segal (Eds.), *Comprehensive handbook of psychological assessment: Vol. 2. Personality assessment* (pp. 315–342). Hoboken, NJ: Wiley.

Millon, T., Millon, C., Davis, R., & Grossman, S. (1997). *The Millon Adolescent Clinical Inventory (MACI).* Minneapolis, MN: National Computer Systems.

Murray, H. A. (1943). *The Thematic Apperception Test: Manual.* Cambridge, MA: Harvard University Press.

Myers, K., & Winters, N. (2002). Ten-year review of rating scales: Pt. I. Overview of scale functioning, psychometric properties, and selection. *Journal of the American Academy of Child and Adolescent Psychiatry, 41*, 114–122.

Nunnally, J. C., & Bernstein, I. H. (1994). *Psychometric theory* (3rd ed.). New York: McGraw-Hill.

Popham, W. J. (1997). Consequential validity: Right concern—Wrong concept. *Educational Measurement: Issues and Practice, 16*(2), 9–13.

Reich, W. (1998). *The Diagnostic Interview for Children and Adolescents (DICA): DSM-IV version.* St. Louis, MO: Washington University School of Medicine.

Reynolds, C. R., & Kamphaus, R. W. (2004). *Behavior assessment system for children: Manual* (2nd ed.). Circle Pines, MN: American Guidance Service.

Reynolds, W. M. (1993). Self-report methodology. In T. H. Ollendick & M. Hersen (Eds.), *Handbook of child and adolescent assessment* (pp. 98–123). New York: Pergamon Press.

Reynolds, W. M. (1998). *Adolescent Psychopathology Scale: Psychometric and technical manual.* Odessa, FL: Psychological Assessment Resources.

Selzer, M. A., Kernberg, P. F., Fibel, B., Cheruliez, T., & Mortati, S. (1987). The Personality Assessment Interview: Preliminary evidence. *Psychiatry, 50*, 142–153.

Shaffer, D., Fisher, P., Dulcan, M. K., Davies, M., Piacentini, J., Schwab-Stone, M. E., et al. (1996). The NIMH Diagnostic Interview Schedule for Children (DISC 2.3). *Journal of the American Academy of Child and Adolescent Psychiatry, 35*, 878–888.

Shedler, J., & Westen, D. (1998). Refining the measurement of Axis II: A Q-sort procedure for assessing personality pathology. *Assessment, 5*, 333–353.

Shedler, J., Westen, D., & Bradley, R. (2006). A prototype approach to personality disorder diagnosis. *American Journal of Psychiatry, 163*, 846–856.

Shepard, L. A. (1997). The centrality of test use and consequences for test validity. *Educational Measurement: Issues and Practices, 16*(2), 5–8, 13, 24.

Thorndike, R. M. (1997). *Measurement and evaluation in psychology and education* (6th ed.). Upper Saddle River, NJ: Merrill.

Tringone, R., Millon, T., & Kamp, J. (2007). Clinical utility of two child-oriented inventories: The Millon pre-adolescent clinical inventory and the Millon adolescent clinical inventory. In S. Smith & L. Handler (Eds.), *The clinical assessment of children and adolescents: A practitioners handbook* (pp. 267–287). Mahwah, NJ: Erlbaum.

Watkins, C. E., Campbell, V. L., Nieberding, R., & Hallmark, R. (1995). Contemporary practice of psychological assessment by clinical psychologists. *Professional Psychology: Research and Practice, 26,* 54–60.

Weiner, I. B. (2004). Rorschach assessment: Current status. In M. L. Hilsenroth & D. L. Segal (Eds.), *Comprehensive handbook of psychological assessment: Vol. 2. Personality assessment* (pp. 343–355). Hoboken, NJ: Wiley.

Westen, D. (1997). Divergences between clinical and research methods for assessing personality disorders: Implications for research and the evolution of Axis II. *American Journal of Psychiatry, 154*(7), 895–902.

Westen, D., Dutra, L., & Shedler, J. (2005). Assessing adolescent personality pathology. *British Journal of Psychiatry, 186,* 227–238.

Westen, D., & Shedler, J. (1999). Revising and assessing Axis II: Pt. I. Developing a clinically and empirically valid assessment method. *American Journal of Psychiatry, 156,* 258–272.

Westen, D., Shedler, J., & Bradley, R. (2005). *A practice research network approach to the classification of personality pathology in adults and adolescents: "Virtual field trials."* Unpublished paper.

Westen, D., Shedler, J., Durrett, C., Glass, S., & Martens, A. (2003). Personality diagnosis in adolescence: *DSM-IV* Axis II diagnoses and an empirically derived alternative. *American Journal of Psychiatry, 160,* 952–966.

Westenberg, P. M., Treffers, P. D. A., & Drewes, M. J. (1998). A new version of the WUSCT: The sentence completion test for children and youths (SCT-Y). In J. Loevinger (Ed.), *Technical foundations for measuring ego development* (pp. 81–89). Mahwah, NJ: Erlbaum.

Widiger, T. A., & Samuel, D. B. (2005). Evidence-based assessment of personality disorders. *Psychological Assessment, 17*(3), 278–287.

Wiggins, J. S. (2003). *Paradigms of personality assessment.* New York: Guilford Press.

Zimmerman, M., & Mattia, J. (1999). The reliability and validity of a screening questionnaire for 12 *DSM-IV* Axis I disorders in psychiatric outpatients. *Journal of Clinical Psychiatry, 60*(10), 677–684.

CHAPTER 8

Issues of Maltreatment and Abuse

CYNTHIA CUPIT SWENSON, ELISSA J. BROWN,
and JOHN R. LUTZKER

CHILD ABUSE and neglect is a major public health problem that impacts millions of children and families annually. The impact may come in many forms. Of particular concern and pertinent to this chapter are the potential health and mental health outcomes. Some children will not experience mental health difficulties from being the victims of child maltreatment. For others, mental health symptomatology will be short term and may dissipate without formal intervention. Most disconcerting are those children for whom abuse and neglect experiences in childhood set patterns of behavior and coping that, though initially adaptive, become disruptive to the management of behavior, emotions, and relationships and can persist throughout the life course. For these youth, formal intervention may be helpful or even required. With regard to health, the stress and potential trauma from child maltreatment can impact biological systems and set a trajectory for poor health. The interaction of mental health and physical health problems related to abuse and neglect can impact individuals in such a way that lives are shortened and abusive and neglectful behavior is carried on through future generations.

In this chapter, we examine the role of abuse and neglect in negative life outcomes. First, we consider the short- and long-term effects of maltreatment. We then examine the scope of the problem of abuse and neglect. Last, we discuss clinical and treatment issues, including a review of the treatment research and indications for intensive or restrictive treatments.

THE EFFECTS OF CHILD ABUSE AND NEGLECT

At present, a causal link has not been established between child maltreatment and poor mental and physical health outcomes. However, a sizable body of literature has established a correlation between the two. At this time, the most definitive statement that can be made about the effects of child maltreatment is that when children experience these events, the impact depends on a variety of factors related to the child's abuse or neglect experience, cultural and community context, family, and individual characteristics. Such factors may potentiate a negative or a buffering effect. Emerging research includes studies of these potential mediating and moderating factors.

FACTORS THAT INFLUENCE ABUSE AND NEGLECT IMPACT

Risk Factors

Factors that exacerbate the effects of abuse and neglect include children's trauma history and other individual characteristics, family and caregiver functioning, and social ecology. Certain assault and offender characteristics increase the risk of negative mental health outcomes (Kendall-Tackett, Williams, & Finkelhor, 1993). Use of threats, force, weapons, and penetration in sexual abuse increase the likelihood of mental health problems such as Posttraumatic Stress Disorder (PTSD). Additionally, the closeness of the relationship between the victim and the offender is associated with symptom severity (Beitchman et al., 1992). Greater frequency and longer duration of maltreatment also are associated with increased psychiatric symptomatology (E. J. Brown & Kolko, 1999; Kendall-Tackett et al., 1993).

Exposure to multiple incidents of maltreatment and other forms of trauma increase survivors' vulnerability for the development of mental health problems. Experiencing more than one type of maltreatment is associated with more substance abuse, severe suicidal behavior, and emotional problems (G. R. Brown & Anderson, 1991; Chaffin & Hanson, 2000; Saunders, 2003). As the number and type of traumatic events accumulate, the outcomes appear to worsen. Among children who experienced both physical and sexual abuse, the rates of PTSD ranged from 71% to 82% (Kiser, Heston, Millsap, & Pruitt, 1991). Retrospective studies of adults (e.g., Koenen et al., 2002; Tanskanen et al., 2004) found that the number of traumatic experiences was associated with symptom severity of depression, PTSD, and externalizing symptoms (Banyard, Williams, & Siegel, 2001; E. J. Brown & Kolko, 1999). The earlier in childhood the physical abuse first occurs, the more severe the internalizing and externalizing symptoms in adolescence (Keiley, Howe, Dodge, Bates, & Pettit, 2001). Chronicity of physical punishment during childhood also has been associated with delinquent behavior, symptoms of depression, suicidal thoughts, and alcohol abuse later in life (Straus & Kantor, 1994). More frequent and diverse types of maltreatment are related to greater economic costs for mental health and medical services (Walker et al., 1999).

In addition to trauma history, other factors specific to individual children may put them at risk for psychiatric symptomatology. Girls may be at greater risk for internalizing symptoms, such as depression, whereas boys may be at greater risk for externalizing behavior problems, such as aggression (Swenson & Chaffin, 2006). Children with developmental disabilities may be more vulnerable to maltreatment (Sullivan & Knudson, 2000).

With regard to family factors, greater family conflict, maternal stress, and poor conflict management among family members is associated with severity of functional impairment among abused children (E. J. Brown & Kolko, 1999; Finkelhor & Berliner, 1995). Low family cohesion and high family conflict are common risk factors for aggression and substance abuse problems (McCord, 1983). A multivariate study found that family system stress (e.g., low educational attainment among caregivers, low socioeconomic status) is associated with caregivers' substance abuse and domestic violence, which in turn are associated with maltreatment severity (E. J. Brown, Swenson, Saunders, Kilpatrick, & Chaplin, 2006). Finally, witnessing sibling violence has been associated with self-reported violence in college students (Gully, Dengerink, & Pepping, 1981).

Protective Factors

A supportive stance by family members and other caregivers may serve as a buffer to negative mental health correlates of child maltreatment. In particular, support from nonabusing parents has been found to be a critical component of children's recovery from sexual abuse (see Elliott & Carnes, 2001, for a review). For both child and adult survivors of sexual abuse, a positive reaction from the first person told in childhood disclosure was associated with more positive mental health outcomes (Bal, De Bourdeaudhuij, Crombez, & Van Oost, 2005; Jonzon & Lindblad, 2005; Roesler, 1994). In general, appraisal support (i.e., having someone to talk to) relates to more positive mental health among adults who were sexually abused as children (Hyman, Gold, & Cott, 2003). In contrast, children who are blamed by others for the maltreatment tend to blame themselves and, perhaps as a result, have higher PTSD symptoms (Chaffin, Wherry, & Dykman, 1997).

Short-Term Effects of Maltreatment

For the purposes of this chapter, short-term effects are defined as those clinical correlates of child maltreatment that are assessed while the survivor is still in childhood (up to age 18). Thus, studies reviewed are those in which children are the participants. Retrospective studies of adult reports of effects of abuse they endured during childhood are not included in this section.

Physical Abuse and Neglect

Multiple developmental correlates have been associated with the occurrence of child physical abuse (CPA) and neglect (Gaudin, 1999; Kolko & Swenson, 2002). These effects broadly include (a) behavioral and emotional difficulties, (b) social and relationship difficulties, and (c) cognitive and neuropsychological impairment.

One of the most robust findings in the scientific literature is that physically abused children tend to exhibit aggression (Conaway & Hansen, 1989). Teachers and parents of physically abused children rate them as more aggressive and oppositional than their nonabused peers (Cummings, Hennessy, Rabideau, & Cicchetti, 1994; Dodge, Pettit, & Bates, 1997). The aggression is directed not only toward other children, but is also toward adults (Hoffman-Plotkin & Twentyman, 1984; Shields & Cicchetti, 2001).

When children experience traumatic events, the consequences are often characterized by internalizing problems, such as anxiety or depression. As CPA is a potentially traumatizing event, research has investigated the presence of PTSD among these children. Findings indicate that the majority of children do not show PTSD following CPA; rates range from 0% to 50% (Deblinger, McLeer, Atkins, Ralphe, & Foa, 1989; Pelcovitz et al., 1994). Child physical abuse has also been associated with depression, Overanxious Disorder, Generalized Anxiety Disorder, and Agoraphobia (Flisher et al., 1997; Kaplan et al., 1998). When CPA is combined with other risk factors, it contributes to longer term disorders such as dysthymia and Conduct Disorder (Kaplan et al., 1998).

Physically abused children experience more relationship difficulties than their peers, which may be due to deficits in social competence. For example, physically abused preschoolers have been shown to initiate fewer positive interactions with peers and adults and avoid peers more often (George & Main, 1979; Howes & Espinosa, 1985). Parents of physically abused children perceive them to be less socially skilled and mature than their nonabused peers (Hoffman-Plotkin & Twentyman, 1984; Kravic, 1987).

With regard to relationships with adults, abused children frequently have insecure attachments to their caregivers, which may result in difficulties sustaining interpersonal relationships later in life. Maltreatment of very young children is associated with insecure attachment. When children have an anxious attachment to key adults in their life, they are expected to develop poor relationship skills and demonstrate aggressive behavior in established relationships. Indeed, nonsecure attachment in infancy has been shown to relate to poorer social competence and increased aggression during the school years (Lamb & Nash, 1989; Mueller & Silverman, 1989). In late adolescence and early adulthood, insecure attachment relates to difficulty managing conflict and low confidence in regulating negative mood (Creasey, Kershaw, & Boston, 1999).

Compared to their nonabused peers, abused children are more likely to show skill deficits in receptive language (McFayden & Kitson, 1996), expressive language, reading ability (Burke, Crenshaw, Green, Schlosser, & Strocchia-Rivera, 1989), initiation of tasks (Allen & Tarnowski, 1989), comprehension and abstraction (Allen & Tarnowski, 1989), auditory attention, and verbal fluency (Tarter, Hegedus, Winsten, & Alterman, 1984). They tend to perform lower on math and reading than nonabused peers and are 2.5 times more likely to repeat a grade in school (Eckenrode, Laird, & Doris, 1993).

Recent research on the effects of trauma on emotion processing and brain functioning suggests that the stress of maltreatment results in adverse brain development. In preliminary studies, maltreated children have demonstrated neurotransmitter and neuroendocrine dysregulation as well as volumetric brain differences associated with PTSD and other psychiatric disturbances. Compared to overanxious nonmaltreated children and healthy children, maltreated children with PTSD excreted greater concentrations of baseline urinary norepinephrine and dopamine. They also showed greater concentrations of urinary free cortisol than healthy children and greater concentrations of urinary epinephrine than overanxious nonmaltreated children (De Bellis, Baum, et al., 1999). In animal models, activation of these systems is shown to produce anxious and hypervigilant behavior. Typically, acute environmental stress leads to elevation of serum cortisol, which has been found to have harmful effects on brain development, but chronic stress can lead to cortisol reduction.

Children with PTSD also showed smaller intracranial and cerebral volumes than control participants (De Bellis, Keshavan, et al., 1999). A cross-sectional investigation of brain development in medically healthy youth with chronic PTSD due to maltreatment and nontraumatized healthy control subjects demonstrated that maltreated children and adolescents with PTSD had smaller structural measures of intracranial volumes, cerebral volumes, and midsagittal corpus callosum areas and larger lateral ventricles than did controls. Intracranial volumes correlated positively with the age of onset of abuse and negatively with abuse duration and PTSD symptoms. The positive correlation of intracranial volumes with age of onset of PTSD trauma suggests that traumatic stress is associated with disproportionately negative consequences if it occurs during early childhood.

Sexual Abuse

Similar to physical abuse, a wide range of outcomes is associated with child sexual abuse (CSA). Importantly, no specific behavioral profile of sexually abused children exists to date. In fact, sexually abused youth may not show social or emotional symptoms at the time they are assessed. As shown in a review by Kendall-Tackett and colleagues (1993), one-fourth to one-half of sexually abused children were asymptomatic at the time of assessment. That said, Bal et al. (2005)

found that about half of sexually abused youth continue to experience clinically significant trauma symptoms 6 months following disclosure. For some children, symptoms may be gradual or delayed. As indicated earlier, the range of outcomes is likely due to differences in context, frequency, duration, and intensity of abuse. The effects related to CSA broadly include (a) behavioral and emotional difficulties, (b) social and relationship difficulties, and (c) cognitive difficulties.

Sexually abused youth show more symptoms of depression and anxiety than nonabused youth (Boney-McCoy & Finkelhor, 1995; Mannarino & Cohen, 1996a). Regardless of whether the comparison group is a clinical or a nonclinical sample, sexually abused youth report higher levels of PTSD symptoms (Boney-McCoy & Finkelhor, 1995). According to their caregivers, sexually abused youth have more behavioral problems than nonabused youth (Mannarino & Cohen, 1996a, 1996b). For roughly one-third of CSA survivors, behavior problems may be sexual in nature (Friedrich, 1993). Sexually abused children are reported to show more sexual behavior than clinical comparisons of neglected or physically abused youth (Friedrich, Jaworski, Huxsahl, & Bengston, 1997; Kendall-Tackett et al., 1993).

In general, the symptoms sexually abused children experience appear to differ according to developmental level. For example, preschoolers are more likely to show anxiety symptoms, nightmares, PTSD, internalizing and externalizing behaviors, and sexual acting-out. School-age children are more likely to experience fears, aggression, and school problems. Adolescents are more prone to depression, suicidal or self-injurious behavior, running away, somatic complaints, substance abuse, and illegal acts (Kendall-Tackett et al., 1993).

Similar to findings in the physical abuse literature, sexually abused youth are less socially competent than their nonabused peers (Mannarino & Cohen, 1996a). Difficulties in peer relations may be due in part to the tendency to have reduced trust of others (Mannarino, Cohen, & Berman, 1994).

Cognitive factors that relate to sexual abuse are in the areas of school achievement and cognitive distortions. At least one study has found deficits in school achievement among sexually abused youth (Rust & Troupe, 1991). The greater issue related to cognitive factors is that sexually abused youth tend to view themselves as different from peers and are more likely to inflict self-blame for negative events in their lives (Mannarino et al., 1994). Interestingly, the self-blame generally is not applied to the sexual abuse event, as offenders are more likely to be held responsible for the abuse (Hunter, Goodwin, & Wilson, 1992).

LONG-TERM EFFECTS OF CHILD ABUSE AND NEGLECT

For the purposes of this chapter, long-term effects are defined as the clinical correlates of child maltreatment found in adult survivors. Thus, studies reviewed are those in which adults are the participants. Retrospective and prospective studies of adult reports of effects of abuse they endured during childhood are included.

Methods for Studying Long-Term Consequences of Maltreatment

There are two methods available for the investigation of the consequences of experiencing childhood maltreatment on adult functioning. The first, and more methodologically rigorous, is prospective, longitudinal studies (Kazdin, 1992). In prospective studies, participants are assessed repeatedly over time, ideally during childhood, adolescence, and adulthood. To examine the consequences of abuse and neglect, assessments include measures of maltreatment exposure and biopsychosocial functioning. Youth who reported maltreatment are compared to demographically similar youth who denied having been maltreated (i.e., controls) on measures of emotional, behavioral, social, and cognitive functioning. Given the base rates (i.e., occurrence) of various forms of maltreatment (see epidemiology section), extremely large sample sizes are required to ensure that enough maltreated children are identified and followed over time. As a result of the number of participants included, prospective research is expensive and time-consuming.

The less expensive method of assessing correlates of maltreatment is cross-sectional, retrospective research. In retrospective studies, participants are assessed at one time point for a history of particular events and current functioning. Cross-sectional, retrospective research allows for the study of correlational, not causal, relations. To investigate the association between maltreatment and biopsychosocial limitations, adults complete measures of child abuse and neglect history and current emotional, behavior, social, and cognitive problems. Cross-sectional, retrospective studies are less burdensome to participants and investigators than prospective studies. Nevertheless, causal relations cannot be evaluated in retrospective research.

The following is a review of the prospective and retrospective studies designed to examine relations between childhood maltreatment and adult psychopathology.

Physical Abuse and Neglect

The long-term effects of CPA and neglect on adults fall broadly into three categories: aggression, substance abuse, and emotional problems. Aggression is expressed toward peers, family members, and dating partners. In retrospective studies, several populations that have engaged in violent crime indicate a childhood history of physical abuse. Convicted male felons, especially those with a history of sexual offending, reported higher rates of CPA than noninstitutionalized males (Sack & Mason, 1980). In a prospective study, CPA was linked with violent crimes such as assault and rape (McCord, 1983). Male and female outpatients who were assessed to be homicidal also showed higher rates of CPA (Rosenbaum & Bennett, 1986). Even among female college students, CPA has been linked to aggression (Briere & Runtz, 1990).

Childhood physical abuse has been identified as a risk factor for physical abuse toward one's own children. Among adults who were physically abused in childhood, approximately one-third abuse their own children, a phenomenon that has been termed "intergenerational transmission" (Kaufman & Zigler, 1987).

A third type of aggression that has been found among adults who experienced CPA is violence toward dating partners. Laner and

Thompson (1982) found that college students with a CPA history endorsed higher rates of dating violence than those who had not been abused. In fact, in one study 75% of abusive persons used the same form of violence on dating partners that they had experienced or observed in childhood (Bernard & Bernard, 1984). Child physical abuse has been found to predict both received and inflicted dating violence for women but not for men (L. L. Marshall & Rose, 1990; Sigelman, Berry, & Wiles, 1984). To carry violence into adult dating relations, individuals do not need to directly experience violence, but may have higher rates of observing physical assault in their family of origin (Bernard & Bernard, 1984). In fact, experiencing CPA and observing marital violence is associated with higher rates of dating violence in male and female college students (Riggs, O'Leary, & Breslin, 1990).

The relationship between maltreatment and substance use has been shown in several studies. Longitudinal studies show an association between CPA and alcohol use (Schuck & Widom, 2003). Adults who use substances report a higher incidence of CPA than the general population, but not higher than those who were neglected (McCord, 1983). Not only is CPA associated with substance use, but it also is associated with more lifetime treatment and a more severe course of substance abuse later in adulthood (Westermeyer, Wahmanholm, & Thuras, 2001).

Physical abuse in childhood has been found to relate to a host of emotional difficulties in adulthood. Somatization, anxiety, depression, hostility, paranoid ideation, psychosis, and dissociation have been reported in female inpatient and community samples with histories of CPA. Similarly, CPA is associated with self-injurious and suicidal behaviors in male and female outpatients. Among college students, CPA by mothers relates to dissociation (Briere & Runtz, 1988; Trickett, Noll, Reiffman, & Putnam, 2001) and increased suicidal ideation among females (Briere & Runtz, 1988).

Sexual Abuse

The long-term effects of CSA on adults fall broadly into five categories: traumatic sexualization, parenting problems, health problems, substance abuse, and emotional problems. Traumatic sexualization refers to sexual difficulties or maladaptive sexual behavior that has a relationship to sexual abuse in childhood. Adults who experienced CSA are more likely to engage in greater sexual activity and sexual risk-taking behaviors (Fergusson, Horwood, & Lynskey, 1997). In fact, prostitution is more common among adults who have experienced CSA (Simons & Whitbeck, 1991; Widom & Kuhns, 1996). Interestingly, CSA also is linked to greater sexual problems in adulthood, such as lack of sexual responsiveness and satisfaction, and sexual dysfunction (Grauerholz, 2000).

Parenting problems related to CSA have mainly been examined among female caregivers. Mothers who experienced CSA show a higher reliance on negative parenting techniques, such as physical discipline, and have less emotional control in interactions with their children (DiLillo, Tremblay, & Peterson, 2000). Even in the absence of CPA, a history of CSA is related to increased use of physical discipline (Banyard, 1997). Additionally, mothers who experienced CSA have been found to be 70% more likely to engage in neglect (Cash & Wilke, 2003) and have higher rates of permissive parenting (Ruscio, 2001).

A history of CSA has been associated with a number of health problems. Women who experienced CSA are more likely to experience adult reproductive and sexual health problems such as sexually transmitted diseases, spontaneous miscarriages, infertility, and painful intercourse (Golding, 1996). Childhood sexual abuse is associated with chronic headaches (Domino & Haber, 1987; Golding, 1999), abdominal pain (Biggs, Aziz, Tomenson, & Creed, 2003), and more frequent emergency room visits (Walker et al., 1999). More recently, a small positive relationship has been shown between CSA and HIV risk (Arriola, Louden, Doldren, & Fortenberry, 2005).

The relationship between maltreatment and substance abuse is well established in clinical and community samples (Wilsnack, Wilsnack, & Hiller-Sturmhofel, 1994). In fact, Kendler and colleagues (2000) report from their twin study that CSA is causally related to an increased risk for substance abuse disorders. Having a history of CSA is more predictive of alcohol problems than of other mental health problems (Wilsnack & Wilsnack, 1995). The prevalence of CSA among female problem drinkers is twice that of nonproblem drinkers (Wilsnack, Klassen, Brett, & Wilsnack, 1991). When the history includes CSA and CPA, the risk for substance abuse doubles (Najavits, Weiss, & Shaw, 1997).

Childhood sexual abuse has been linked to a variety of emotional problems in adulthood. In a prospective study, Sparato and colleagues (Sparato, Mullen, Burgess, Wells, & Moss, 2004) found higher rates of personality disorders, anxiety disorders, and major affective disorders in sexually abused men and women than in the general Australian population. A history of CSA has been consistently linked to high levels of depression and depressive symptomatology (Mullen, Martin, Anderson, & Romans, 1996), anxiety and PTSD (Polusny & Follette, 1996), and dissociative disorders such as memory impairment and detachment or numbing during times of stress (Polusny & Follette, 1996). In a cohort of adult male and female HMO members, a history of suicide attempts was more than twice as likely for those with a history of CSA when compared to nonabused adults. Adults with a CSA history also express less satisfaction in relationships, more isolation, and greater marital dissolution (Fleming et al., 1997). The combination of CSA, maternal depression, and partner violence may result in a greater likelihood of negative parental perception and higher punitive discipline toward one's own children (Schuetze & Eiden, 2005).

Cumulative Impact of Maltreatment and Other Adverse Events

Emerging research has begun to investigate the cumulative impact of maltreatment and other forms of trauma on children. In a study of children's exposure to traumatic events, including maltreatment, Costello, Erkanli, Fairbank, and Angold (2002) found that 25% of a general population sample endorsed exposure to trauma. Of the child trauma survivors, 18% reported exposure to two and 10% reported exposure to three or more traumatic events. Vulnerability factors (e.g., parental psychopathology, poor communication among family members, poverty) incrementally increased the likelihood of trauma exposure, from 13% with no vulnerability factors to 57% at 10 or more. Parental psychopathology and family relationship problems, common among maltreated children, were the strongest predictors of trauma exposure.

The cumulative effect of experiencing abuse and other adverse events has been examined across retrospective studies (Chapman et al., 2004; Felitti et al., 1998), referred to as Adverse Childhood Experiences (ACES) studies, involving a sample size of over 13,000 adults. The results show that cumulative events relate to a host of physical and mental health problems. Persons who experienced four or more ACES had 4- to 12-fold increased health risks for alcoholism, drug abuse, depression, and suicide attempts. In addition, multiply exposed adults had a 4-fold increase in smoking, poor self-rated health, 50 or more sexual partners, and sexually transmitted diseases, and a 1.4- to 1.6- fold increase in physical inactivity and severe obesity. Women reporting five or more ACES had a 5-fold increased risk for lifetime history of depression and a 6-fold increased risk for recent depression. Adverse childhood experiences in any category increased the risk of attempted suicide 2- to 5-fold. The number of ACES showed a graded relationship with ischemic heart disease, cancer, chronic lung disease, skeletal fractures, and liver disease. In addition, persons with multiple ACES were more likely to have multiple health risk factors later in life.

EPIDEMIOLOGY AND ETIOLOGY

PHYSICAL ABUSE

National surveys have been conducted by various investigators to determine the scope of CPA and other forms of maltreatment (Finkelhor & Dziuba-Leatherman, 1994; Gallup, 1995; Gelles & Straus, 1987; National Center for Child Abuse and Neglect, 1981, 1988, 1996, 2004; Wolfner & Gelles, 1993). The National Center for Child Abuse and Neglect (NCCAN; 1981, 1988, 1996, 2004) conducted a series of National

Incidence Studies of Child Abuse and Neglect using reporting practices of professionals. The most recent study yielded a CPA incidence rate of approximately 2.3/1,000 children. Finkelhor and Dziuba-Leatherman (1994), in their National Youth Victimization Prevention Study, found that 5.2% of a nationally representative sample of 2,000 children (ages 10 to 16) reported having been assaulted by a family member during the previous year, approximately 20% of whom were assaulted by a parent (resulting in a rate of 0.9%). Other studies have yielded much higher incidence rates of CPA. The 1995 Gallup poll estimated the rate of CPA to be 49/1,000 children, more than five times the NCCAN report. Even more startling is the finding in both the First and Second National Family Violence Surveys (Gelles & Straus, 1987; Wolfner & Gelles, 1993) that abusive physical punishment in reaction to parent-child conflict occurred with about 10% of children in any given year. In the only prospective, longitudinal study conducted to date, Chaffin, Kelleher, and Hollenberg (1996) analyzed data from Waves 1 and 2 of the National Institute for Mental Health's Epidemiologic Catchment Area survey and found that .9% of caregivers who did not report CPA at Wave 1 endorsed CPA at the Wave 2 assessment.

SEXUAL ABUSE

The national incidence rate of CSA in the third National Incidence Study of Child Abuse and Neglect was 1.2 per 1,000 children (NCCAN, 2004). Retrospective investigations conducted with adults to assess the prevalence of CSA suggest significantly higher rates. Telephone and mail surveys on a national probability sample indicated that approximately 30% of women and 15% of men reported a contact sexual offense by age 18 (Finkelhor, 1994).

NEGLECT

Neglect is the most common form of child maltreatment. According to national data for 2002 (U.S. Department of Health and Human Services [USDHHS], 2004) a rate of 7.2 victims per 1,000 children in the United States experienced neglect. In the longitudinal study conducted by Chaffin and colleagues (1996), 1.2% of caregivers who did not report neglect at Wave 1 endorsed at least one neglectful act at Wave 2.

REVICTIMIZATION

The likelihood of revictimization is highest if the initial allegation is physical abuse or physical neglect (versus sexual abuse). Physical abuse tends to be a chronic rather than an acute experience. The likelihood of recurrence appears to be highest during the first 6 months following initial Child Protective Services contact (English, Marshall, Brummel, & Orme, 1999; D. Marshall & English, 1999). The rates of resubstantiation within 6, 12, and 18 months are 6%, 9%, and 11%, respectively. Rates of reoccurrence for neglect are even higher than those for physical abuse (D. Marshall & English, 1999; Zuravin & DePanfilis, 1996). D. Marshall and English reported a 53% higher chance of multiple recurrent referrals when physical neglect is the primary allegation. Similarly, the USDHHS (2004) reported a 27% chance of reoccurring maltreatment for children who had been neglected.

CORRELATES OF CHILD ABUSE AND NEGLECT

The body of research on correlates of abuse and neglect indicates that such maltreatment is related to multiple etiological factors across multiple systems. There is a great deal of overlap in factors related to physical abuse and neglect. Factors related to sexual abuse, on the other hand, differ from those for physical abuse and neglect. The etiology may lie primarily within the individual abuser (e.g., a chronic child molester planning access to a child unbeknown to his or her family), or family risk factors may be involved (e.g., a mother with a substance abuse lifestyle and multiple male partners who are high and have unlimited access to the children).

The factors that indicate risk for the occurrence or recurrence of abuse will differ by family. For example, abuse or neglect risk may be high in one family due to parental substance abuse and child noncompliance and high in a different family due to domestic violence, parental depression, and child problems at school. Risk factors for child maltreatment are generally related to any combination of *child, parent, family, or community.*

Physical Abuse and Neglect

Child Factors

Child factors that correlate with abuse risk include age, development, and behavioral difficulties. Some of the child problems noted earlier under short-term effects may be due to physical abuse, but these factors may also increase the risk of violent physical punishment. Children who are younger, who have developmental delays, or who have other special needs such as chronic medical conditions are at higher risk of abuse and neglect than are children without delays (Ammerman, 1990; Ammerman, Hersen, Van Hasselt, McGonigle, & Lubetsky, 1989; Sullivan & Knutson, 2000; Swenson & Chaffin, 2006). With regard to child behavior, noncompliant children are at higher risk for being abused (Belsky, 1993).

Parent Factors

No single trait or profile pinpoints an individual as likely to physically abuse his or her child, but a number of parental factors correlate with abuse risk. These broadly defined characteristics include a history of childhood abuse, cognitive factors, affect regulation problems, behavioral problems, and psychiatric disorders. Roughly one-third of adults who were physically abused as children go on to abuse their own children (Kaufman & Zigler, 1987). Not only does this experience transmit the teaching of physical force as a way to parent; adults who were physically abused as children are also at risk of multiple mental health problems that may interfere with their capacity to parent in a more positive way.

With regard to cognitive factors, parent attributional biases affect discipline of children. Abusive parents view their children in a more negative light (Azar & Siegel, 1990) and may distort beliefs about the motives of their child's behavior (e.g., "He left that toy out just to ruin my day") or the child's responsibility for the parent's welfare (Azar, 1997). Parents may also have unrealistic expectations for their child's behavior. When these are not met, the parent experiences frustration, which may result in the use of force toward the child (Azar, Robinson, Hekimian, & Twentyman, 1984). Physically abusive parents are also more likely to support the use of harsh punishment (Simons, Whitbeck, Conger, & Chyi-In, 1991).

Use of threats and difficulty regulating emotions such as irritability, sadness, anxiety, explosiveness, hostility, and anger have been associated with harsh parenting (Caspi & Elder, 1988; Simons et al., 1991). Abusive parents have been shown to perceive their lives as more stressful than nonabusive parents (Milner, 1998) and tend to use heightened emotion-focused coping, becoming reactive to stress (Cantos, Neale, & O'Leary, 1997). Behavioral problems such as low impulse control may result in negative comments, threats, and physical force toward a child (Caselles & Milner, 2000). Adults who physically abuse their children have been shown to exhibit deficits in positive parenting such as attention, positive affect and social behavior, physical affection, and problem solving skills (Azar et al., 1984; Kavanagh, Youngblade, Reid, & Fagot, 1988).

Psychiatric disorders such as depression (Whipple & Webster-Stratton, 1991), PTSD (Famularo, Kinscherff, & Fenton, 1992), and substance abuse (Kelleher, Chaffin, Hollenberg, & Fischer, 1994) correlate with risk of physical abuse and neglect. These disorders may make parenting and general problem solving difficult and hamper an individual's capacity to regulate emotions.

Parental substance abuse in particular is a factor that places parents at significant risk of neglecting their children. Over half of neglecting parents meet criteria for a lifetime substance abuse disorder (Chaffin et al., 1996). Substance abuse has been identified in up to

79% of child protection cases and is the deciding factor in the majority of cases in which children are taken into custody and placed out of the home (Besinger, Garland, Litrownik, & Landsverk, 1999). Substance abuse is associated with severe disciplinary practices (Hien & Honeyman, 2000) and high child abuse potential ratings (Fuller & Wells, 2003), particularly for women who experience high levels of environmental stress (Nair, Schuler, Black, Kettinger, & Harrington, 2003). Moreover, many of the environmental factors associated with a substance-abusing lifestyle place children at increased risk of neglect (Chasnoff & Lowder, 1999). Mothers who are addicted to substances are at risk of neglecting their children when engaged in drug-seeking behaviors (NCCAN, 2003) and using their limited resources to obtain substances rather than to care for their children (Young, Gardner, & Dennis, 1998). When mothers are under the influence of substances, they are less likely to supervise (Wallace, 1996) or provide a safe environment for their children (Shepard & Raschick, 1999). Compared with other women who enter substance abuse treatment, those with co-occurring issues of child maltreatment tend to have more children, to have experienced homelessness, and to be unemployed (USDHHS, 1999).

Family Factors

Three categories of family factors correlate with physical abuse risk: volatile home environment, limited psychosocial resources, and general family stressors. A growing body of research has documented the relationship between domestic violence and CPA. Partner hostility is common in volatile families (Fantuzzo et al., 1991), and family interactions may be characterized by verbal abuse (Claussen & Crittenden, 1991).

The potential for physical abuse has been associated with low levels of family cohesion and expressiveness (Mollerstrom, Patchner, & Milner, 1992). Physically abusive parents are often described as isolated (Milner & Dopke, 1997), as they have limited contact with friends and have been shown to be generally dissatisfied with social supports

(Crittenden, 1985). When resources are available, they tend to not use them (Corse, Schmid, & Trickett, 1990).

Heightened family stressors such as family disruption and moves are common among families where physical abuse occurs (Emery & Laumann-Billings, 1998). Other life stressors such as limited financial resources and poverty are predictors of physical abuse risk (Whipple & Webster-Stratton, 1991).

Family poverty is one of the most powerful risk factors for neglect. Families living below the poverty line are 22 times more likely to have a report of maltreatment, predominantly neglect (Sedlak & Broadhurst, 1996).

Community Factors

Studies examining community factors that relate to child abuse and neglect risk are limited, but existing research has identified three primary factors: economic disadvantage, instability and isolation, and neighborhood burden. Communities with economic disadvantage have higher rates of child maltreatment than more advantaged communities (Coulton, Korbin, Su, & Chow, 1995). In addition, disadvantaged communities are characterized by high resident turnover, instability, vacant structures, and low organization (Bursik & Grasmich, 1993; Zuravin, 1989), which limit the psychosocial support available to families. Neighborhoods that have greater child care needs have higher rates of abuse (Coulton, Korbin, & Su, 1999).

SEXUAL ABUSE

Child Factors

Several child factors increase the risk that a child will be vulnerable to sexual abuse. Although sexual abuse happens to boys, female children are at higher risk (Fleming, Mullen, & Bammer, 1997). Children who have previously been sexually abused are at increased risk for subsequent abuse and greater abuse impact (Boney-

McCoy & Finkelhor, 1995). It is unclear whether the risk for subsequent abuse is due to living in a high-risk environment or to individual child factors such as expectations of sexual behavior in relationships.

Abuser Factors

Being male is the most robust factor associated with risk of sexual abuse of a child (Silovsky, Niec, & Hecht, 2000). Age is also a risk factor for committing sexual abuse. The most common age for committing abuse is 13 to 16 years (Caldwell, 2002), though most boys in this age range do not sexually abuse children.

When the abuser is in a parental role, he is often a stepfather or father surrogate (Finkelhor & Baron, 1986; Radhakrishna, Bou-Saada, Hunter, Catellier, & Kotch, 2001). Experiencing sexual abuse as a child may increase an adult's or adolescent's risk for engaging in future sexually abusive behavior, but the intergenerational transmission appears to be much less prevalent than it is for physical child abuse (Chaffin, Letourneau, & Silovsky, 2002). Factors such as paraphilias, sexual attraction to children, antisocial or psychopathic traits, and loneliness may play a role in the etiology of sexually abusive behavior among adults, and factors such as sexual curiosity and general delinquent tendencies may play a role in the etiology of sexual abuse by adolescents (Chaffin et al., 2002).

Family Factors

Virtually no characteristics identified in epidemiologic research have a sufficiently robust association with sexual abuse to identify a typical family description (Finkelhor, 1993). What is more clear is the role that the family's reaction to disclosure of the abuse can play in a child's subsequent well-being (see Elliott & Carnes, 2001, for a review).

Community Factors

Few studies have addressed the relationship of community factors to CSA. Though there is insufficient evidence to relate socioeconomic factors to sexual abuse, the cultural norms of a community can play an important role in protecting children. Unwanted sexual experiences in early adolescence, such as peer sexual assaults, may be associated with low monitoring by parents or neighborhood adults in the child's environment (Small & Kerns, 1993).

TREATMENT ISSUES

Child maltreatment is an experience, not a diagnosis, making the selection of a treatment modality less clear. In fact, as reviewed previously, maltreated children vary in the severity and nature of their mental health sequelae. Thus, assessment and intervention approaches have been developed to address children's symptoms of PTSD, separation and generalized anxiety, depression, disruptive behavior disorders, and social skills deficits. Therapeutic approaches also need to address the ecological factors that maintain the maltreatment, including caregiver, family, community, and cultural characteristics. Typically, families who come under the supervision of child protection are required to complete a host of services. It is not uncommon for families to be required to pursue services that may involve as many as 10 different providers (e.g., individual child, parenting, anger management, substance abuse, domestic violence group). Families who are already excessively stressed may simply be unable to meet the treatment requirements that allow them to keep their children in their home. As such, the way treatment is delivered and the demands made on stressed families may place them in a no-win situation. Further, many of the treatments provided have no support for their efficacy or effectiveness.

In recent years, the evidence-based movement has begun to grow in the child welfare area. What follows is a review of the treatment outcome literature for maltreatment, highlighting the value of complex psychosocial interventions and supplemental pharmacological treatment. We mainly cover treatments that have been evaluated through rigorous scientific methods.

PSYCHOSOCIAL INTERVENTIONS FOR MALTREATMENT

Sexual Abuse

The majority of the treatment studies conducted to date have been of cognitive-behavioral therapy (CBT) for victims of CSA. In the first study of a standard treatment protocol for CSA-related PTSD, Deblinger and colleagues (Deblinger, McLeer, & Henry, 1990) found significant reductions in PTSD, general anxiety, and depression for 19 girls receiving 12 sessions of CBT. Because it was preliminary research, there was no control group; participants ranged in age from 3 to 16. Using a multiple baseline design across time and focusing on a narrower age bracket (only preschoolers), Stauffer and Deblinger (1996) investigated the efficacy of concurrent CBT for 19 preschool CSA victims and their nonoffending mothers. No significant changes were evidenced from baseline to pretreatment, whereas significant prepost gains were evidenced on measures of parental psychopathology, parenting practices, and children's sexual behavior problems. These gains were maintained at the 3-month follow-up assessment. Farrell, Haims, and Davies (1998) also conducted a multiple baseline design investigation of CBT for CSA victims with PTSD. The three (of four) children with clinically significant symptoms at baseline reported decreases in PTSD, depression, and anxiety symptoms during treatment.

In the only quasi-experimental design with a wait-list control group, McGain and McKinzey (1995) evaluated treatment with 30 school-age girls who had experienced CSA within the past year. After treatment, about one-third of the 15 participating girls were exhibiting behavioral problems, whereas more than two-thirds of the 15 controls continued to exhibit behavior problems. Conclusions are limited because the treatment was not standardized, assignment to group was not randomized, and investigators did not conduct a time-by-treatment interaction analysis.

Many of the limitations of the aforementioned studies have been addressed by a number of randomized clinical trials (RCTs). Berliner and Saunders (1996) compared CBT (parallel groups for children and caregivers) with and without gradual exposure. There were no significant differences between the groups on the degree of reduction in fear, anxiety, depression, behavior problems, and inappropriate sexual behaviors. Berliner and Saunders attributed their findings to the lack of clinically significant symptom levels at pretreatment; perhaps exposure therapy is more important for children with more severe symptomatology.

In another investigation of school-age victims of CSA, Celano, Hazzard, Webb, and McCall (1996) compared structured (designed to address maladaptive abuse-related cognitions) to unstructured, supportive individual psychotherapy conducted with school-age children and their caregivers. The participants were primarily from low-income, African American families and none had received treatment prior to the study. There were no significant differences across treatment conditions on measures of children's symptoms, but the structured psychotherapy was associated with significant increases in caregivers' support of their children and decreases in caregivers' self-blame and expectations of undue negative consequences of the abuse on their children.

Cohen and Mannarino (1998) conducted an RCT of CSA-related PTSD in 8- to 14-year-olds and found that, among treatment completers, trauma-focused cognitive-behavioral therapy (TF-CBT) was superior to nondirective supportive therapy (NST). The TF-CBT group continued to report significantly greater improvement than those in the NST group on measures of anxiety, depression, sexually inappropriate behaviors, and dissociation 6 months following termination and on measures of PTSD and dissociation 12 months following termination (Cohen, Mannarino, & Knudsen, 2005). In a parallel study, Cohen and Mannarino (1996b) found that TF-CBT was superior to NST in improving PTSD symptoms and internalizing and externalizing behavior problems in preschoolers. These differences were maintained at a 1-year follow-up (Cohen & Mannarino, 1997). In an examination of mediators of outcome, Cohen and Mannarino (1996a) found that care-givers' response to the abuse was predictive of improvements in chil-dren's social competence and behavior problems, revealing the potential importance of caregiver participation in treatment.

Extending Cohen and Mannarino's (1996a) mediational study high-lighting the impact of caregivers, investigators have evaluated the rel-ative importance of caregiver involvement in treatment. Deblinger, Lippmann, and Steer (1996) demonstrated that TF-CBT was superior to treatment-as-usual in improving PTSD symptoms, depression, and behavior problems in sexually abused children and parenting prac-tices. Deblinger et al.'s design, in which parents and/or children par-ticipated in treatment, indicated that reductions in children's PTSD symptoms were evidenced only when the children were randomly as-signed to CBT in which they directly participated, and reductions in children's depression and externalizing behavior problems were evi-denced only when their parents directly participated. Similarly, King et al. (2000) compared TF-CBT provided to sexually abused children alone or to children and parents, to a wait-list control condition and found both TF-CBT conditions to be superior to the control in improv-ing PTSD and anxiety at posttreatment. At the 3-month posttreatment follow-up, TF-CBT for parents and children was superior to TF-CBT for children only in improving anxiety symptoms.

Criticisms of the aforementioned research (e.g., sample size) were addressed by the first multisite RCT for traumatized children (Cohen, Deblinger, Mannarino, & Steer, 2004). The investigators demonstrated the superiority of TF-CBT over child-centered therapy (CCT) in de-creasing the likelihood of meeting criteria for PTSD and improving symptoms in each of the three PTSD symptom clusters in sexually abused children. The children receiving TF-CBT also exhibited greater reductions in depression and anxiety symptoms, behavior problems, and abuse-related attributions than the children receiving CCT. Compared to the caregivers attending CCT, those attending TF-CBT showed greater improvements in depression, emotional distress related to the child's abuse, support of the child, and positive parenting practices.

Physical Abuse

The majority of treatment outcome studies for CPA do not target (a) children's symptoms, (b) caregivers' recidivism, and (c) factors such as cognitive processing and parenting practices associated with children's symptoms and caregivers' recidivism. The few treatment outcome studies that evaluated interventions with CPA victims have been limited to preschoolers and consist either of specific interventions that address only one area, such as social skills (Fantuzzo, Bulotsky-Shearer, & McWayne, 2006), or broad interventions focusing on cognitive and social development, such as day treatment programs (Culp, Little, Letts, & Lawrence, 1991; Culp, Richardson, & Heide, 1987; Gabel, Swanson, & Shindledecker, 1990). In a small pilot study of 16-week cognitive-behavioral group therapy with school-age physically abused children, Swenson and Brown (1999) found reductions on self-report measures of PTSD, general anxiety, depression, and anger symptoms. There was no improvement on social competence and externalizing behaviors, potentially highlighting the need to include caregivers in treatment (Deblinger et al., 1996; Webster-Stratton & Hammond, 1997).

There is preliminary evidence that caregiver correlates of CPA (e.g., parenting practices, social support, self-report of child abuse potential) are responsive to parent training programs (Borrego, Urquiza, Rasmussen, & Zebell, 1999; Brunk, Henggeler, & Whelan, 1987; Urquiza & McNeil, 1996; Wolfe, Edwards, Manion, & Koverola, 1988). That said, emerging literature suggests that multisystemic interventions are more efficacious in the prevention and treatment of child psychopathology than approaches that target only the caregivers (Kazdin, 1997; Webster-Stratton & Hammond, 1997). In a randomized clinical trial of the Parents and Children Series, Webster-Stratton and Hammond compared parent training only, child treatment only, combined parent training and child treatment, and a wait-list control group. Treated parents showed more positive interactions with their children than untreated parents, and treated children showed more improvements in problem solving and conflict management skills than untreated children. At the 1-year follow-up assessment, families in the combined condition were significantly more improved than those in the single-participant conditions.

Kolko (1996b) conducted the first randomized clinical trial with physically maltreating caregivers and their maltreated school-age children, aimed at reducing high-risk parental behaviors and minimizing the adverse impact of abuse on children. Kolko (1996b) compared CBT conducted with physically abusive caregivers and their abused children (i.e., separate but parallel protocols), family therapy, and routine community services. Caregivers in the CBT and family therapy conditions exhibited more improvement than those receiving routine community services on parental distress, abuse risk, and family cohesion and conflict. Children in the CBT and family therapy conditions evidenced greater decreases in anxiety, depression, behavior problems, and child-to-parent aggression than those in the routine community services condition. Weekly monitoring data indicated that CBT was more efficacious than family therapy in decreasing caregivers' anger and use of physical discipline (Kolko, 1996a). Although this study represents a critical step in the literature, not all families had been indicated for physical abuse, resulting in a relatively less severe group of abusers.

Parent-child interaction therapy (PCIT) has been adapted for physically abusive parents and their children, particularly families with younger children (Urquiza & McNeil, 1996). This therapy involves training parents in specific behavioral parenting techniques using live coaching of skills in dyadic parent-child sessions. These parenting techniques include relationship enhancement skills, such as use of labeled praise and reflection, as well as consistent use of a specific time-out protocol for compliance training. Results from a controlled trial show that physically abusive families receiving PCIT had considerably fewer future physical abuse referrals than families receiving a group-based parent education program without live behavioral coaching of skills (Chaffin et al., 2004).

Multisystemic therapy (MST) is an intensive family- and community-based treatment program that includes home-based delivery of services and applies empirically validated interventions to all systems. To date, two randomized controlled trials have evaluated the efficacy and effectiveness of MST with abused children and their families. The first RCT with maltreating parents showed that MST was more effective than parent training for alleviating family difficulties (Brunk et al., 1987). The second RCT is a recently completed 5-year study funded by the National Institute for Mental Health comparing MST with parent training plus standard mental health services (Swenson, 2000). This project targeted physically abused adolescents ages 10 to 17 and their families and was implemented through a county mental health center (Charleston/Dorchester Mental Health Center in Charleston, South Carolina). Short-term results indicate promise for reducing out-of-home placements, reducing adolescent depression, increasing youth perceptions of safety, and increasing parental nonphysical discipline (Swenson, 2005). Importantly, this study led to adaptations in the standard MST model that was developed for delinquent youth and their families. Beyond standard MST treatments, these adaptations generally involve protocols for safety, use of functional analysis to manage abuse risk, treatment for PTSD, anger management, parental substance abuse, family communication and problem solving, collaborative work with child protection, and psychiatric care. In addition, all families are asked to complete a process involving clarification or parental acceptance of responsibility for the abuse or neglect to address the maladaptive abuse-specific cognitions experienced by abuse victims (Kolko & Swenson, 2002; Lipovsky, Swenson, Ralston, & Saunders, 1998; Swenson & Kolko, 2000). Preliminary research on the clarification process reveals that greater adherence to the procedure is associated with decreases in caregiver stress and substance use and child psychopathology (Swenson, Randall, Henggeler, &

Ward, 2000). The adapted MST model is referred to as MST for child abuse and neglect.

Presently, a newly developed model called Building Stronger Families (Swenson & Schaeffer, 2006) is being piloted in New Britain, Connecticut, via a collaboration of the Connecticut Department of Children and Families, the Annie E. Casey Foundation, the Medical University of South Carolina, and Johns Hopkins University. The model features an integration of MST for child abuse and neglect (Swenson, Saldana, Joyner, & Henggeler, 2006) and reinforcement-based therapy (Jones, Wong, Tuten, & Stitzer, 2005), and is applied to cases involving co-occurring CPA and/or neglect and parental substance abuse. Building Stronger Families uses a home-based model of service delivery and is short term (6 to 8 months), intensive (multiple contacts per week), and predicated on therapists having small caseloads (a maximum of 4 families each), strong supervisory support, and weekly expert consultation in Building Stronger Families interventions.

Neglect

The ecobehavioral model was first described with Project 12-Ways (Lutzker, Frame, & Rice, 1982) for multiproblem families involved in the Child Protective Services system for neglect, physical abuse, or both. The model was used in university-based trials in rural Illinois beginning in 1979 (Lutzker & Rice, 1984). Project 12-Ways defines intervention targets encompassing family social ecology (i.e., environment, parenting, interface with the health care system), defines goals and intervention activities in behavioral terms, and uses a behavioral case conceptualization in intervention techniques. Specific behavioral interventions are used and measurement of progress against criteria is tracked across time. All services are provided in the home (i.e., the family's social ecology) to enhance generalization of skills and increase the attendance of the participants (Lutzker, Bigelow, Doctor, Gershater, & Greene, 1998). Originally, 12 services were provided, with selection depending on initial behavioral assessment: parent training, stress reduction, basic skills training for children, money management training, social support, home safety, behavior management, health and nutrition, problem solving, marital counseling, alcohol abuse referral, and single-mother services (Lutzker & Rice, 1984). Families served by Project 12-Ways were less likely to be re-reported for child maltreatment or have children removed than comparison families (Lutzker & Rice, 1987; Wesch & Lutzker, 1991). Gershater-Molko, Lutzker, and Wesch (2002) described highly successful and significant survival rates for families who received Project SafeCare, a systematic replication of the 12-Ways model. The SafeCare model is being tested statewide in Oklahoma and replicated in Georgia.

In sum, cognitive-behavioral approaches to the treatment of PTSD, anxiety, depression, and externalizing behavior problems have been efficacious with children exposed to various forms of maltreatment. Comprehensive models that include single providers who use empirically supported treatment strategies are showing promise for reducing out-of-home placements and actual reabuse and changing key risk factors within the youth's ecology. These conclusions are strengthened by the fact that the more recent studies used larger sample sizes and rigorous design, administered assessments to children and their caregivers, examined psychiatric symptoms and social competence, and monitored treatment integrity and parental satisfaction.

PHARMACOLOGICAL INTERVENTIONS FOR MALTREATMENT

Pharmacology cannot treat an event, such as child maltreatment. Instead, the role of pharmacological interventions has been to supplement the psychosocial interventions, often by treating the symptoms (e.g., sleep disturbance) that impede the success of psychotherapy. Early studies of the efficacy of psychopharmacological interventions focused on the treatment of nightmares and other reexperiencing symptoms that are particularly troubling for children with PTSD. An open study by Famularo, Kinscherff, and Fenton (1988) looked at the use of propanolol in the treatment of acute PTSD in 11 children ages 6 to 12 years using an ABA design. Starting dosage of propanolol was

0.8 mg/kg/d in three divided doses. The dose was gradually increased over a 2-week period to a maximum of 2.5 mg/kg/d. The medication was given for 4 weeks and then tapered over the fifth week. No other medications were used. Children received concomitant psychotherapy. Blood pressure and pulse were monitored twice weekly. The PTSD inventory was completed during treatment and 3 weeks after the medication was discontinued. There was a significant prepost improvement on PTSD severity. Adverse effects included sedation and mildly lowered blood pressure and pulse, but no child required discontinuation of medicine due to side effects. The tendency toward relapse after medication discontinuation suggested that propanolol was beneficial in the treatment of acute PTSD only during its use.

Given the side effects of propanolol, later research on the treatment of reexperiencing symptoms in children evaluated alternative medications. Looff, Grimley, Kuller, Martin, and Shonfield (1995) reported results of the treatment of 12 girls and 16 boys (ages 8 to 17) with a diagnosis of PTSD with carbamazepine during hospitalization in a state hospital. The 28 participants had histories of chronic sexual abuse and symptoms of intrusive thoughts, flashbacks, hypnogogic phenomena, and nightmares. More than half of the subjects had comorbid conditions. The initial starting dosage of carbamazepine was 100 mg bid and was titrated up every 4 to 7 days. Carbamazepine was dosed (300 to 1,200 mg/day) to a serum level of 10.0 to 11.5 mcg/ml. There were no adverse drug reactions. Four of the patients with comorbid ADHD also had methylphenidate or clonidine added. Four depressed patients were also treated with antidepressants (selective serotonin reuptake inhibitors or a tricyclic). Twenty-two out of the 28 patients became asymptomatic, and the remaining six were significantly improved (with rare abuse-related nightmares).

In a similar examination of an alternative medication for children's nightmares, Horrigan and colleagues (Horrigan, Barnhill, & Jarrett, 1996) described the use of clonidine and guanfacine in the treatment of nightmares in a 7-year-old girl diagnosed with chronic PTSD. The patient had a history of physical abuse and exposure to domestic violence. She had remained symptomatic following 3 months of psychotherapy, at which point clonidine 0.05 mg qhs was introduced. This medication was initially helpful in reducing the nightmares; however, breakthrough nightmares began after 3 weeks. A change to guanfacine 0.5 mg qhs was made due to its longer half-life relative to clonidine. The nightmares resolved and remained suppressed for the subsequent 7 weeks. The medication was well tolerated and there were no adverse effects reported.

Although Horrigan and colleagues (Horrigan et al., 1996) found clonidine problematic in the treatment of nightmares, Harmon and Riggs (1996) reported success with clonidine for symptoms of aggression, hyperarousal, and sleep disturbances. The investigators conducted an open trial of clonidine in seven preschool children diagnosed with PTSD resulting from severe maltreatment. The children ranged in age from 3 to 6 years and were receiving psychosocial treatment at a day hospital. Medication was provided for those children whose symptoms of hyperarousal, impulsivity, and aggression remained severe after 1 month in the day hospital. Children were physically healthy with no neurological impairments. Starting dosage of clonidine was 0.05 mg qam. and if well tolerated a second dose was added of 0.05 mg qhs. The average range of dose was 0.1 mg qhs to 0.05 mg bid and 0.1 mg qhs. Two of the children were also being treated with imipramine for depression. One boy with severe PTSD was already on clonidine at the time of admission. The clonidine patch was utilized in all seven subjects in an effort to avoid the initial sedating effects and was found to be well tolerated, with less sedation and greater compliance with treatment. Target symptoms, assessed weekly, were rated as moderately to greatly improved with clonidine treatment by both teachers and physicians. This study did not use standardized symptom-assessment scales, and results were based on subjective clinical impressions. Nevertheless, clonidine was deemed to be effective in reducing symptoms of aggression, hyperarousal, and sleep disturbances in children with PTSD. In addition, the parents and clinicians were of the opinion that the medication was necessary to enable the child to benefit from psychosocial treatments.

Instead of focusing on a single PTSD symptom cluster, recent studies of psychopharmacological interventions have evaluated the efficacy of medications for all three clusters of PTSD symptoms. Seedat, Lockhat, Kaminer, Zungu-Dirwayi, and Stein (2001) conducted a 12-week open trial on the use of citalopram in adolescents with PTSD. The authors hypothesized that Saris may relieve intrusive, avoidant, and hyperarousal symptoms, as well as treat comorbid conditions. Based on support for this hypothesis from research on adults, Seedat's group conducted a trial of citalopram with eight adolescents (mean age = 14.8 years). Participants were diagnosed with moderate to severe PTSD. Comorbid anxiety or mood disorders were permitted as long as they did not precede the PTSD diagnosis. Six of the adolescents met criteria for mild Major Depression and one for Panic Disorder. They were given 20 mg of citalopram and administered a diagnostic measure of PTSD every 2 weeks over a period of 12 weeks. Seven of the adolescents completed the study and all seven responded to citalopram, rated by clinicians as "much improved" or "very much improved" on PTSD. There was a 38% reduction in PTSD symptoms. Five of the six with Major Depression no longer met criteria for this disorder at the end of study, although they continued to have depressive symptoms.

Seedat et al. (2002) continued their examination of citalopram in another open trial comparing response to treatment in children, adolescents, and adults with PTSD. The authors conducted an 8-week trial that compared 24 children and adolescents whose ages ranged from 10 to 18 (mean = 14.3 years) to 14 adults whose ages ranged from 20 to 52 (mean = 33.5 years). The sample from the 2001 study was included in the group of children and adolescents. Biweekly assessments included an age-appropriate diagnostic interview and PTSD symptoms scales. Mean duration of PTSD symptoms was 10.96 months in children and 38.4 months in adults. Participants who met criteria for Bipolar Disorder, a psychotic disorder, substance abuse, or an organic disorder in the preceding 6 months were excluded. Comorbid mood and anxious disorders were excluded only if they preceded the diagnosis of PTSD. Twelve children and 6 adults met criteria for a depressive disorder. One adolescent met criteria for Panic Disorder. Patients previously treated with citalopram were excluded. There was a 2-week washout period for all participants. Concomitant pharmacotherapy or psychotherapy was not permitted during this trial; however, supportive counseling was provided by the treating clinician. Participants were prescribed 20 mg to 40 mg of citalopram daily. Mean dose of citalopram in adults was 27.9 mg versus 20 mg in children and adolescents. In the child and adolescent group, 16 were responders, 5 were minimally improved, and 3 were minimally worse on the PTSD symptom measure, with a 54% reduction in PTSD severity. In the adult group, 9 were classified as responders, 4 were minimally improved, and 1 minimally worse, with a 39% reduction in PTSD severity. There were no significant differences between the two age groups, except for greater improvement on hyperarousal cluster symptoms in children and adolescents at week 8.

In sum, pharmacological interventions have been shown to be a helpful adjunct to psychotherapy for treating symptoms that impede treatment progress. In particular, studies show success for reducing internalizing symptoms such as depression and PTSD.

Treatment for Adult Survivors of Childhood Abuse

Like the treatment outcome literature conducted on children with maltreatment-related mental health problems, the studies of adult survivors tend to focus on sexual abuse. A number of open trials have been conducted to examine the impact of cognitive-behavioral, experiential, psychodynamic, and supportive psychotherapies conducted in individual (Price, Hilsenroth, Callahan, Petretic-Jackson, & Bonge, 2004; Price, Hilsenroth, Petretic-Jackson, & Bonge, 2001) and group (Callahan, Price, & Hilsenroth, 2004; Kessler, White, & Nelson, 2003) formats. Most of these studies found significant improvements in survivors' PTSD, anxiety, depression, and interpersonal functioning. The participants in studies that included follow-up assessments reported maintaining gains at posttreatment. Limitations include no control group or comparison condition, lack of random assignment, and inclusion of evaluators who were not blind to treatment condition.

In the only study of residential treatment, adult survivors of childhood physical, sexual, and/or emotional abuse participated in a specialized, comprehensive psychoeducational inpatient program in an open trial (Wright, Woo, Muller, Fernandes, & Kraftcheck, 2003). The 6-week program included community meetings and groups on education about trauma responses, skill-building, and affective expression. As with the outpatient programs, participants reported significant decreases in PTSD at posttreatment and maintained these treatment gains at 1-year follow-up.

Emerging RCTs have addressed the limitations of the aforementioned open trials. Zlotnick and Pearlstein (1997) randomly assigned childhood sexual abuse survivors to a psychoeducation and skills group or to a wait-list control condition. They found significantly more improvement in PTSD and dissociative symptoms for the treatment participants than those in the wait-list condition. In their RCT, Cloitre, Koenen, Cohen, and Han (2002) compared CBT to a minimal attention wait-list condition. Therapy consisted of two phases: (1) skill building for affect and interpersonal regulation and (2) conducting a modified trauma narrative. Participants in the CBT condition reported significantly greater improvements in PTSD symptoms, affect dysregulation, and interpersonal deficits. Gains were maintained 3 and 9 months post-termination. In an examination of mediators and moderators of outcome, Cloitre, Chase Stovall-McClough, Miranda, and Chemtob (2004) found that therapeutic alliance levels and affection regulation abilities were predictive of improvement.

OTHER CLINICAL ISSUES

The experience of abuse or neglect presents special clinical issues that require therapist attention to facilitate treatment. These include safety, crisis stabilization, trust, and including family in interventions. In addition, when Child Protective Services is involved with a family, it is essential for therapists to work cooperatively with the caseworker and the courts.

SAFETY

For children experiencing anxiety due to the abuse or neglect, safety must be assured before the emotional effects of the abuse can be addressed. Therapists can address safety in a number of ways. First, if the child is living with the person who abused him or her and child protection has determined that the environment is safe, the therapist, family, and caseworker work together to establish a concrete, attainable safety plan. This plan should be reviewed on a regular basis and revised as necessary. If the child is living in an environment in which he or she is afraid of harm, regardless of whether the setting is home, shelter, or foster home, the caseworker will need to be informed and an immediate plan to create safety should be developed. In some cases, children come into individual treatment with an understanding from the offending parent that they are not supposed to talk about the abuse. It is standard for the therapist to have the parent or a family member give the child permission to talk about the situation to the therapist. The discussion to arrange this "permission giving" should be out of the vision and hearing range of the child.

CRISIS STABILIZATION

At the onset of treatment, children and their parents should be informed of the limits of confidentiality. New abuse incidents and suicidal or homicidal ideation or intent are not kept confidential. For sexually abused children, the distinction is made between confidential or private and secret (Swenson & Hanson, 1998). Because the abuser may have told the child that the incident was a secret, the therapist must explain that treatment is private, not secret; children are allowed to discuss the content of treatment with anyone they wish. The rules for therapists' confidentiality must be explained in detail, including to whom and when confidentiality is broken. If the child is suicidal or homicidal, this crisis should be managed and stabilized prior to any work on abuse-related anxiety, such as a trauma narrative.

TRUST

Therapists should not assume that children, especially maltreated children, will automatically trust them. Children should be treated with formal clinical boundaries that may adjust as the therapeutic alliance develops. No matter how young the child and how tactile the therapeutic approach, therapists should ask children before engaging in touching. If the child is a young sexually abused child who attempts to touch the therapist inappropriately, the therapist should stop the child and explain the rules for touching. Children who have been normalized to sexual abuse must learn new interpersonal rules. In addition, put-downs of the parent or the person who abused the child should be avoided to prevent the child from being placed in a loyalty conflict. Finally, when asking children to process traumatic memories, therapists must take care to do so in a way that is developmentally appropriate for the child and at a pace comfortable for the child.

SPLITTING, THERAPEUTIC ALLIANCE, WORKING WITH
THE FAMILY, AND CULTURAL ISSUES

Although the treatment outcome literature provides important guidance for the selection and implementation of mental health treatment for maltreated children, there are clinical challenges in conducting this work that warrant specific attention. We have argued for the involvement of children and caregivers in multisystemic approaches to treatment. In these approaches, there are multiple clients: each child, each caregiver, each dyad, and the family unit. A therapeutic alliance needs to be formed with all clients. To accomplish this, ground rules about information sharing and expectations of treatment participants need to be discussed at the initiation of treatment. Development of a therapeutic alliance with maltreating caregivers may be particularly challenging. Therapists have to address their own feelings about the abusive or neglectful caregiver, which can be more difficult over time as the therapist becomes closer to the maltreated child. The therapist-caregiver relationship is more complicated if the caregiver has been mandated to treatment. The caregiver may see that therapist as an extension of Child Protective Services and thus be unwilling to disclose information that he or she believes may be incriminating, though it may help the therapeutic process. Therapists must distinguish themselves from Child Protective Services while minimizing criticism of Child Protective Services that the caregiver may repeat to caseworkers.

These complicated relationships must be put into a cultural context. Abuse-specific CBT has been found to be feasible, acceptable, and efficacious with multicultural families (E. J. Brown, 2006). Nevertheless, culturally specific characteristics may impact our engagement with families and implementation of treatment components. For example, adaptations for Latino children and their caregivers may include direct discussion of cultural values about the purpose and process of therapy, inviting the entire family to a session (to show respect), engagement with the elder male (to address *respeto* and traditional gender roles), and allowing for less stringent boundaries and more disclosure by the therapist (to respect *personalismo;* Bernal, Bonilla, & Bellido, 1995; de Arellano et al., 2005). The abuse-specific CBT concepts can be presented using metaphors in the form of *dichos* (i.e., idioms) and other techniques consistent with cultural values (e.g., de Arellano et al. suggest presenting parent training in the context of *respeto*). Cognitive restructuring may warrant inviting a perceived expert (e.g., clergyman) to counter negative, irrational thoughts (e.g., shame at the loss of virginity as a result of CSA).

WORKING WITH CHILD PROTECTION AND THE COURTS

The role of Child Protective Services (CPS) is to take reports of suspected maltreatment, conduct an investigation, develop a safety plan, decide whether to take the child into protective custody, assist the child and family in connecting with treatment, monitor safety, and determine when to reunite the family, close the case, or recommend termination of parental rights. Therapists can be helpful to CPS workers in assuring that decision making is based on clinical information and family progress. As soon as the therapist obtains a release or exchange of information signed by the legal guardian, an initial contact to CPS should occur. Through this contact, therapists can determine CPS's goals and form a collaborative relationship to advocate for the family. The family and protective services should have shared goals. If not, the therapist can facilitate improvements in the relationship between the family and CPS to guide them toward shared goals. Together, the therapist and parent can give direct input into the family's safety plan. The therapist should listen to the family's complaints but never engage in negative judgments about CPS; all discussion of the adversarial relationship should be focused on a solution. Likewise, at no time should the therapist engage in "parent bashing" with the CPS worker. Therapists can help CPS workers remain focused. That is, conversations can focus on strengths the parent has, what the parent is currently doing well, and goals that continue to be the focus of treatment. A collaborative relationship with CPS can accomplish multiple goals, including meeting concrete needs of the family (e.g., purchasing clothing, paying bills) and working out details regarding the court process in a nonadversarial way. When children remain in the home, therapists can keep the CPS worker informed of treatment progress and concerns about child or family safety.

Involvement with the courts can include informal consulting or advocacy or can be more formal, such as serving as a fact or expert witness. In a consulting capacity and as an advocate for the child and family, therapists can be invaluable in helping to set up a family court treatment plan. Working closely with CPS legal council and the family's attorney, the therapist can offer recommendations for the treatment plan regarding who needs treatment, the nature of that treatment, the risk, and parent-child visitation. Such negotiations can save the court time and money. Rather than arguing each side in a hearing, both sides can go before the judge with consistent recommendations. Doing so reduces the adversarial nature of the process for parents.

Often, therapists will be asked to testify in family court. This experience can be intimidating, especially for new therapists. However, court testimony provides an opportunity for the therapist to teach the judge, family, and CPS about the needs of the family and what it will take to reduce the risk for reabuse. Therapists may also serve as an expert witness to offer the court scientific information regarding child maltreatment issues and child and adult disorders. The reader is referred to two excellent books by Brodsky (1991) and Stern (1997) that prepare professionals to serve as expert witnesses.

INDICATION AND IMPACT OF INTENSIVE OR RESTRICTIVE TREATMENTS

INDICATIONS

There is limited research to guide the use of restrictive placements for abused and neglected children. Such children may be placed in restrictive settings, such as congregate care, for reasons that range from there being no other available placement to their having severe psychiatric difficulties that are unmanageable in less restrictive settings. The quality of treatment varies greatly across institutions. In some cases, treatment is time-contingent; that is, the program is considered to be a 1-year program and the child stays until the program is over. In other cases, clear goals are set and discharge is based on progress. In addition, available services (e.g., family therapy) vary across programs. A common problem involves children being placed in institutions that are physically distant from their family. The distance creates a hardship on the family with regard to visitation and participating in the treatment, especially for families who cannot afford a trip to the institution. Furthermore, the child's time spent in an institution does nothing to change the family's ecology, which may have been reinforcing or maintaining behavioral difficulties.

Given the variable characteristics of institutions and the tendency for children in institutions to interact with other troubled children, congregate care should be reserved for extreme behavioral or psychiatric difficulties that absolutely cannot be managed within a home environment (e.g., regularly attempts suicide). Confinement should be conducted for a limited time based on specific goals, and the youth should be provided with intensive, targeted, evidence-based treatments to work toward these goals. The family also should undergo intensive treatment to help them manage the child and make changes in the ecology that will support adaptive behavior.

In recent years, multidimensional treatment foster care (MTFC; Chamberlain & Smith, 2005) has been developed and tested across several rigorous clinical trials. Consistent positive outcomes with regard to reduced days in placement and reductions in violent behavior (Eddy, Whaley, & Chamberlain, 2004; Leve & Chamberlain, 2005; Leve, Chamberlain, & Reid, 2005) have garnered MTFC a place in the prestigious Blueprints (Elliott, 1998) for Violence Prevention. Outcomes from MTFC lend support to the notion that when children require placement, mental health and behavioral outcomes depend on quality of placement and content of treatment provided in placement (Handwerk, Field, & Friman, 2000).

WHEN PLACEMENTS ARE IATROGENIC

There are serious potential risks to institutional placement and foster care. Children may be reabused in the very settings that are designed to protect them (USDHHS, 2005), a phenomenon known in the adult literature as "sanctuary trauma" (Cusack, Frueh, Hiers, Suffoletta-Maierle, & Bennett, 2003). A second risk to children in congregate care is that they may decline behaviorally due to deviant peer associations. A strong predictor of delinquency is spending time with delinquent peers (Dishion, McCord, & Poulin, 1999). Recent research shows that adolescents who engage in antisocial behavior may actually increase antisocial behavior when they participate in treatments that provide heavy association with deviant peers, such as group therapy (Arnold & Hughes, 1999; Dishion et al., 1999). Congregate care provides a dose of negative peer association 24 hours a day, 7 days a week. When congregate care of any type is considered as a placement for an abused or neglected child, great care should be taken to monitor the quality and training of the staff, as well as the associations the child is making with peers. Great efforts should be made to provide high-quality, evidence-based services such as MTFC.

CONCLUSIONS

Maltreatment places children at risk of a trajectory that includes enduring patterns of maladaptive coping in adulthood. Whether mental and physical health difficulties will occur appears related to multiple factors, and these should be considered when treating children or adults who have been maltreated. At the least, care must be taken to assure that treatment is not iatrogenic and that it does not solely focus on the child but addresses the broader ecology where risk factors exist. In addition, the importance of applying evidence-based strategies cannot be overstated.

A number of lessons can be taken from the child maltreatment literature:

- There are many types of mental health problems associated with child maltreatment.
- For those impacted in childhood, the effects of child maltreatment may follow youth into adulthood and, for some families, follow on through the generations.
- Experiences early in life do not have uniform consequences for mental health outcomes in later life; the influences of early life vary depending on what happens in subsequent stages of life.
- More maltreatment is worse.
- Factors that increase the likelihood of a negative outcome are clear.
- Factors that buffer from a negative outcome are clear.

- The power of family, friends, and social supports must not be underestimated.
- Treatment must include determining how to keep children safe without taking them away from their family, home, neighborhood, school, and peers.
- Treatment must involve linking children and their families with support in their natural environment.
- We must provide treatments that have research support indicating that they are safe and effective. Some practices are based on clinical lore and tradition rather than scientific outcome research, and some run counter to research evidence. Outcomes from randomized controlled trials are the gold standard.
- We must understand and respect the family's strengths and highlight those strengths in treatment.
- We must not make negative assumptions about families from cultural and socioeconomic backgrounds different from our own.
- We must invite an understanding of cultural differences to help us understand how best to work together.
- We must understand the etiology of a given family's situation.
- We must stop separating substance abuse from child abuse; indeed, they commonly co-occur, and both are our responsibility to treat.
- We must assure that the way we provide treatment is not exacerbating the problem and contributing to treatment failure.
- We must assure that we are not asking families to do more than they can actually do and that the family is kept separate if they are unsuccessful in meeting demands.
- We must understand the great importance of the CPS caseworker to treatment. As such, we must strive to work in partnerships in the best interest of families.
- We must be available to communities to help broadly address risk factors for maltreatment.

- We must strive to help create safe communities so that the ACES do not accumulate.
- We must work toward the safety of children. Out-of-home placements do not guarantee safety.
- Safety may require much more intensive work on our part and much broader interventions.

The challenges that lie in helping children and adults overcome the impact of maltreatment are vast. Many of the tools required to be successful in this endeavor are available. We need only use science as our guide.

REFERENCES

Allen, D. M., & Tarnowski, K. J. (1989). Depressive characteristics of physically abused children. *Journal of Abnormal Child Psychology, 17,* 1–11.

Ammerman, R. T. (1990). Etiological models of child maltreatment. *Behavior Modification, 14,* 230–254.

Ammerman, R. T., Hersen, M., Van Hasselt, V. B., McGonigle, J. J., & Lubetsky, M. (1989). Abuse and neglect in psychiatrically hospitalized multihandicapped children. *Child Abuse and Neglect, 13,* 335–343.

Arnold, M. E., & Hughes, J. N. (1999). First do no harm: Adverse effects of grouping deviant youth for skills training. *Journal of School Psychology, 37,* 99–115.

Arriola, K. R. J., Louden, T., Doldren, M. A., & Fortenberry, R. M. (2005). A meta-analysis of the relationship of child sexual abuse to HIV risk behavior among women. *Child Abuse and Neglect, 29,* 725–746.

Azar, S. T. (1997). A cognitive behavioral approach to understanding and treating parents who physically abuse their children. In D. Wolfe, R. J. McMahon, & R. D. Peters (Eds.), *Child abuse: Vol. 4. New directions in prevention and treatment across the lifespan* (pp. 79–101). Thousand Oaks, CA: Sage.

Azar, S. T., Robinson, D. R., Hekimian, E., & Twentyman, C. T. (1984). Unrealistic expectations and problem-solving ability in maltreating and comparison mothers. *Journal of Consulting and Clinical Psychology, 52,* 687–691.

Azar, S. T., & Siegel, B. R. (1990). Behavioral treatment of child abuse: A developmental perspective. *Behavior Modification, 14,* 279–300.

Bal, S., De Bourdeaudhuij, I., Crombez, G., & Van Oost, P. (2005). Predictors of trauma symptomatology in sexually abused adolescents: A 6-month follow-up study. *Journal of Interpersonal Violence, 20,* 1390–1405.

Banyard, V. L. (1997). The impact of childhood sexual abuse and family functioning on four dimensions of women's later parenting. *Child Abuse and Neglect, 21,* 1095–1107.

Banyard, V. L., Williams, L. M., & Siegel, J. A. (2001). The long-term mental health consequences of child sexual abuse: An exploratory study of the impact of multiple traumas on a sample of women. *Journal of Traumatic Stress, 14,* 697–715.

Beitchman, J. H., Zucker, K. J., Hood, J. E., daCosta, G. A., Akman, D., & Cassavia, E. (1992). A review of the long-term effects of child sexual abuse. *Child Abuse and Neglect, 16,* 101–118.

Belsky, J. (1993). Etiology of child maltreatment: A developmental-ecological analysis. *Psychological Bulletin, 114,* 413–434.

Berliner, L., & Saunders, B. E. (1996). Treating fear and anxiety in sexually abused children: Results of a controlled 2-year follow-up study. *Child Maltreatment, 1,* 294–309.

Bernal, G., Bonilla, J., & Bellido, C. (1995). Ecological validity and cultural sensitivity for outcome research: Issues for the cultural adaptations and development of psychosocial treatment with Hispanics. *Journal of Abnormal Child Psychology, 23,* 67–82.

Bernard, J. L., & Bernard, M. L. (1984). The abusive male seeking treatment: Jekyll and Hyde. *Journal of Applied Family and Child Studies, 33,* 543–547.

Besinger, B. A., Garland, A. F., Litrownik, A. J., & Landsverk, J. A. (1999). Caregiver substance abuse among maltreated children placed in out-of-home care. *Child Welfare League of America, 78,* 221–239.

Biggs, A., Aziz, Q., Tomenson, B., & Creed, F. (2003). Do childhood adversity and recent social stress predict health care use in patients presenting with upper abdominal or chest pain? *Psychosomatic Medicine, 65,* 1020–1028.

Boney-McCoy, S., & Finkelhor, D. (1995). Prior victimization: A risk factor for child sexual abuse and for PTSD-related symptomatology among sexually abused youth. *Child Abuse and Neglect, 19,* 1401–1421.

Borrego, J., Urquiza, A. J., Rasmussen, R. A., & Zebell, N. (1999). Parent-child interaction therapy with a family at high risk for physical abuse. *Child Maltreatment, 4,* 331–342.

Briere, J., & Runtz, M. (1988). Symptomatology associated with childhood sexual victimization in a nonclinical sample. *Child Abuse and Neglect, 12,* 51–59.

Briere, J., & Runtz, M. (1990). Differential adult symptomatology associated with three types of child abuse histories. *Child Abuse and Neglect, 14,* 357–364.

Brodsky, S. (1991). Advocacy: 1. The "bought expert" accusation. In S. Brodsky (Ed.), *Testifying in court: Guidelines and maxims for the expert witness* (pp. 5–7). Washington, DC: American Psychological Association.

Brown, E. J. (2006, April). *The systematic study of cultural adaptations.* Paper presented as part of a Symposium titled Guidelines for Culturally Competent Trauma-Informed Interventions for Children at the annual meeting of the National Child Traumatic Stress Network, Chicago.

Brown, E. J., & Kolko, D. J. (1999). Child victims' attributions about being physically abused: An examination of factors associated with symptom severity. *Journal of Abnormal Child Psychology, 27,* 311–322.

Brown, E. J., Swenson, C. C., Saunders, B. E., Kilpatrick, D. G., & Chaplin, W. F. (2006). *Community and family characteristics associated with adolescent physical abuse.* Manuscript in preparation.

Brown, G. R., & Anderson, B. (1991). Psychiatric morbidity in adult in-patients with childhood histories of sexual and physical abuse. *American Journal of Psychiatry, 148*, 55–61.

Brunk, M., Henggeler, S. W., & Whelan, J. P. (1987). Comparison of multisystemic therapy and parent training in the brief treatment of child abuse and neglect. *Journal of Consulting and Clinical Psychology, 55*, 171–178.

Burke, A. E., Crenshaw, D. A., Green, J., Schlosser, M. A., & Strocchia-Rivera, L. (1989). Influence of verbal ability on the expression of aggression in physically abused children. *Journal of the American Academy of Child Psychiatry, 28*, 215–218.

Bursik, R. J., & Grasmich, H. G. (1993). *Neighborhood and crime.* New York: Lexington Books.

Caldwell, M. F. (2002). What we do not know about juvenile sexual re-offense risk. *Child Maltreatment: Journal of the American Professional Society on the Abuse of Children, 7*, 291–302.

Callahan, K., Price, J., & Hilsenroth, M. (2004). A review of interpersonal-psychodynamic group psychotherapy outcomes for adult survivors of childhood sexual abuse. *International Journal of Group Psychotherapy, 54*, 491–519.

Cantos, A. L., Neale, J. M., & O'Leary, K. D. (1997). Assessment of coping strategies of child abusing mothers. *Child Abuse and Neglect, 21*, 631–636.

Caselles, C. E., & Milner, J. S. (2000). Evaluation of child transgressions, disciplinary choices, and expected child compliance in a no-cry and a crying infant condition in physically abusive and comparison mothers. *Child Abuse and Neglect, 24*, 477–491.

Cash, S. J., & Wilke, D. J. (2003). An ecological model of maternal substance abuse and child neglect: Issues, analyses, and recommendations. *American Journal of Orthopsychiatry, 73*, 392–404.

Caspi, A., & Elder, G. H. (1988). Emergent family patterns: The intergenerational construction of problem behavior and relationships. In

R. A. Hinde & J. Stevenson-Hinde (Eds.), *Relationships with families: Mutual influences* (pp. 218–240). Oxford, England: Clarendon Press.

Celano, M., Hazzard, A., Webb, C., & McCall, C. (1996). Treatment of traumagenic beliefs among sexually abused girls and their mothers: An evaluation study. *Journal of Abnormal Child Psychology, 24,* 1–17.

Chaffin, M., & Hanson, R. F. (2000). The multiply traumatized child. In R. M. Reece (Ed.), *The treatment of child abuse* (pp. 271–288). Baltimore: Johns Hopkins University Press.

Chaffin, M., Kelleher, K., & Hollenberg, J. (1996). Onset of physical abuse and neglect: Psychiatric, substance abuse, and social risk factors from prospective community data. *Child Abuse and Neglect, 20,* 191–203.

Chaffin, M., Letourneau, E., & Silovsky, J. F. (2002). Adults, adolescents, and children who sexually abuse children: A developmental perspective. In J. E. B. Meyers, L. Berliner, J. Briere, C. T. Hendrix, C. Jenny, & T. A. Reid (Eds.), *The APSAC handbook on child maltreatment* (2nd ed., pp. 205–232). Thousand Oaks, CA: Sage.

Chaffin, M., Silovsky, J. F., Funderburk, B., Valle, L. A., Brestan, E. V., Balachova, T., et al. (2004). Parent-child interaction therapy with physically abusive parents: Efficacy for reducing future abuse reports. *Journal of Consulting and Clinical Psychology, 72,* 500–510.

Chaffin, M., Wherry, J., & Dykman, R. (1997). School age children's coping with sexual abuse: Abuse stresses and symptoms associated with four coping strategies. *Child Abuse and Neglect, 21,* 227–240.

Chamberlain, P., & Smith, D. (2005). Multidimensional treatment foster care: A community solution for boys and girls referred from juvenile justice. In E. D. Hibbs & P. S. Jensen (Eds.), *Psychosocial treatments for child and adolescent disorders: Empirically based strategies for clinical practice* (2nd ed., pp. 557–573). Washington, DC: American Psychological Association.

Chapman, D., Whitfield, C., Felitti, V., Dube, S., Edwards, V., & Anda, R. (2004). Adverse childhood experiences and the risk of depressive disorders in adulthood. *Journal of Affective Disorders, 82,* 217–225.

Chasnoff, I. J., & Lowder, L. A. (1999). Parental alcohol and drug use and risk for child maltreatment: A timely approach to intervention. In H. Dubowitz (Ed.), *Neglected children: Research, practice, and policy* (pp. 132–155). Thousand Oaks, CA: Sage.

Claussen, A. H., & Crittenden, P. M. (1991). Physical and psychological maltreatment: Relations among types of maltreatment. *Child Abuse and Neglect, 15,* 5–8.

Cloitre, M., Chase Stovall-McClough, K., Miranda, R., & Chemtob, C. (2004). Therapeutic alliance, negative mood regulation, and treatment outcome in child abuse-related posttraumatic stress disorder. *Journal of Consulting and Clinical Psychology, 72,* 411–416.

Cloitre, M., Koenen, K., Cohen, L., & Han, H. (2002). Skills training in affective and interpersonal regulation followed by exposure: A phase-based treatment for PTSD related to childhood abuse. *Journal of Consulting and Clinical Psychology, 70,* 1067–1074.

Cohen, J. A., Deblinger, E., Mannarino, A. P., & Steer, R. A. (2004). A multisite, randomized controlled trial for children with sexual abuse-related PTSD symptoms. *Journal of the American Academy of Child and Adolescent Psychiatry, 43,* 393–402.

Cohen, J. A., & Mannarino, A. P. (1996a). Factors that mediate treatment outcome of sexually abused preschool children. *Journal of the American Academy of Child and Adolescent Psychiatry, 35,* 1402–1410.

Cohen, J. A., & Mannarino, A. P. (1996b). A treatment outcome study for sexually abused preschool children: Initial findings. *Journal of the American Academy of Child and Adolescent Psychiatry, 35,* 42–50.

Cohen, J. A., & Mannarino, A. P. (1997). A treatment study for sexually abused preschool children: Outcomes during a 1-year follow-up. *Journal of the American Academy of Child and Adolescent Psychiatry, 36,* 1228–1235.

Cohen, J. A., & Mannarino, A. P. (1998). Interventions for sexually abused children: Initial treatment outcome findings. *Child Maltreatment, 3*(1), 17–26.

Cohen, J. A., Mannarino, A. P., & Knudsen, K. (2005). Treating sexually abused children: 1 year follow-up of a randomized controlled trial. *Child Abuse and Neglect, 29*(2), 135–145.

Conaway, L. P., & Hansen, D. J. (1989). Social behavior of physically abused and neglected children: A critical review. *Clinical Psychology Review, 9,* 627–652.

Corse, S. J., Schmid, K., & Trickett, P. K. (1990). Social network characteristics of mothers in abusing and nonabusing families and their relationships to parenting beliefs. *Journal of Community Psychology, 18,* 44–59.

Costello, E., Erkanli, A., Fairbank, J., & Angold, A. (2002). The prevalence of potentially traumatic events in childhood and adolescence. *Journal of Traumatic Stress, 15,* 99–112.

Coulton, C. J., Korbin, J. E., & Su, M. (1999). Neighborhoods and child maltreatment: A multi-level study. *Child Abuse and Neglect, 23,* 1019–1040.

Coulton, C. J., Korbin, J. E., Su, M., & Chow J. (1995). Community level factors and child maltreatment rates. *Child Development, 66,* 1262–1276.

Creasey, G., Kershaw, K., & Boston, A. (1999). Conflict management with friends and romantic partners: The role of attachment and negative mood regulation expectancies. *Journal of Youth and Adolescence, 28,* 523–543.

Crittenden, P. M. (1985). Social networks, quality of childrearing, and child development. *Child Development, 56,* 1299–1313.

Culp, R. E., Little, V., Letts, D., & Lawrence, H. (1991). Maltreated children's self-concept: Effects of a comprehensive treatment program. *American Journal of Orthopsychiatry, 61,* 114–121.

Culp, R. E., Richardson, M. T., & Heide, J. S. (1987). Differential developmental progress of maltreated children in day treatment. *Social Work, 32,* 497–499.

Cummings, E. M., Hennessy, K. D., Rabideau, G. J., & Cicchetti, D. (1994). Responses of physically abused boys to interadult anger involving their mothers. *Development and Psychopathology, 6,* 31–41.

Cusack, K. J., Frueh, B. C., Hiers, T., Suffoletta-Maierle, S., & Bennett, S. (2003). Trauma within the psychiatric setting: A preliminary empirical report. *Administration and Policy in Mental Health, 30,* 453–460.

de Arellano, M., Waldrop, A., Deblinger, E., Cohen, J., Danielson, C., & Mannarino, A. (2005). Community outreach program for child victims of traumatic events: A community-based project for underserved populations. *Behavior Modification, 29,* 130–155.

De Bellis, M. D., Baum, A. S., Birmaher, B., Keshavan, M. S., Eccard, C. H., Boring, A. M., et al. (1999). Developmental traumatology: Pt. I. Biological stress systems. *Biological Psychiatry, 45,* 1259–1270.

De Bellis, M. D., Keshavan, M. S., Clark, D. B., Casey, B. J., Giedd, J. N., Boring, A. M., et al. (1999). Developmental traumatology: Pt. II. Brain development. *Biological Psychiatry, 45,* 1271–1284.

Deblinger, E., Lippmann, J., & Steer, R. (1996). Sexually abused children suffering posttraumatic stress symptoms: Initial treatment outcome findings. *Child Maltreatment, 1,* 310–321.

Deblinger, E., McLeer, S. V., Atkins, M. S., Ralphe, D., & Foa, E. (1989). Post-traumatic stress in sexually abused, physically abused, and nonabused children. *Child Abuse and Neglect, 13,* 403–408.

Deblinger, E., McLeer, S. V., & Henry, D. (1990). Cognitive behavioral treatment for sexually abused children suffering post-traumatic stress: Preliminary findings. *Journal of the American Academy of Child and Adolescent Psychiatry, 29,* 747–752.

DiLillo, D., Tremblay, G. C., & Peterson, L. (2000). Linking childhood sexual abuse and abusive parenting: The mediating role of maternal anger. *Child Abuse and Neglect, 24,* 767–779.

Dishion, T. J., McCord, J., & Poulin, F. (1999). When interventions harm: Peer groups and problem behavior. *American Psychologist, 54,* 755–764.

Dodge, K. A., Pettit, G. S., & Bates, J. E. (1997). How the experience of early physical abuse leads children to become chronically aggressive. In D. Cicchetti & S. L. Toth (Eds.), *Rochester Symposium on*

Developmental Psychopathology: Vol. 8. Developmental perspectives on trauma: Theory, research and intervention (pp. 263–288). Rochester, NY: University of Rochester Press.

Domino, J. V., & Haber, D. (1987). Prior physical abuse in women with chronic headache: Clinical correlates. *Headache: Journal of Head and Face Pain, 27,* 310–314.

Eckenrode, J., Laird, M., & Doris, J. (1993). School performance and disciplinary problems among abused and neglected children. *Developmental Psychology, 29,* 53–62.

Eddy, J. M., Whaley, R. B., & Chamberlain, P. (2004). The prevention of violent behavior by chronic and serious male juvenile offenders: A 2-year follow-up of a randomized clinical trial. *Journal of Emotional and Behavioral Disorders, 12,* 2–8.

Elliott, A. N., & Carnes, C. N. (2001). Reactions of nonoffending parents to the sexual abuse of their child: A review of the literature. *Child Maltreatment, 6,* 314–331.

Elliott, D. S. (Series Ed.). (1998). Blueprints for violence prevention (University of Colorado, Center for the Study and Prevention of Violence). Boulder, CO: Blueprints Publications.

Emery, R. E., & Laumann-Billings, L. (1998). An overview of the nature, causes, and consequences of abusive family relationships. *American Psychologist, 53,* 121–135.

English, D. J., Marshall, D. B., Brummel, S., & Orme, M. (1999). Characteristics of repeated referrals to Child Protective Services in Washington State. *Child Maltreatment, 4,* 297–307.

Famularo, R., Kinscherff, R., & Fenton, T. (1988). Propanolol treatment for childhood posttraumatic stress disorder, acute type. *American Journal of Disorders in Children, 142,* 1244–1247.

Famularo, R., Kinscherff, R., & Fenton, T. (1992). Psychiatric diagnoses of abusive mothers. *Journal of Nervous and Mental Diseases, 180,* 658–661.

Fantuzzo, J. W., Bulotsky-Shearer, R., & McWayne, C. M. (2006). The pursuit of wellness for victims of child maltreatment: A model for targeting relevant competencies, contexts, and contributors. In J. R. Lutzker (Ed.), *Preventing violence: Research and evidence-based intervention strategies* (pp. 69–91). Washington, DC: American Psychological Association.

Fantuzzo, J. W., DePaola, L. M., Lambert, L., Martino, T., Anderson, G., & Sutton, S. (1991). Effects of interparental violence on the psychological adjustment and competencies of young children. *Journal of Consulting and Clinical Psychology, 59,* 258–265.

Farrell, S. P., Haims, A. A., & Davies, D. (1998). Cognitive behavioral interventions for sexually abused children exhibiting PTSD symptomatology. *Behavior Therapy, 29,* 241–255.

Felitti, V. J., Anda, R. F., Nordenberg, D., Williamson, D. F., Spitz, A. M., Edwards, V., et al. (1998). Relationship of childhood abuse and household dysfunction to many of the leading causes of death in adults: The Adverse Childhood Experiences (ACE) Study. *American Journal of Preventive Medicine, 14,* 245–258.

Fergusson, D. M., Horwood, L. J., & Lynskey, M. T. (1997). Childhood sexual abuse, adolescent sexual behaviors and sexual revictimization. *Child Abuse and Neglect, 21,* 789–803.

Finkelhor, D. (1993). Epidemiological factors in the clinical identification of child sexual abuse. *Child Abuse and Neglect, 17,* 67–70.

Finkelhor, D. (1994). Current information on the scope and nature of child sexual abuse. *Future of Children, 4,* 31–53.

Finkelhor, D., & Baron, L. (1986). Risk factors for child sexual abuse. *Journal of Interpersonal Violence, 1,* 43–71.

Finkelhor, D., & Berliner, L. (1995). Research on the treatment of sexually abused children: A review and recommendations. *Journal of the American Academy of Child and Adolescent Psychiatry, 34,* 1408–1423.

Finkelhor, D., & Dziuba-Leatherman, J. (1994). Children as victims of violence: A national survey. *Pediatrics, 94,* 413–420.

Fleming, J., Mullen, P., & Bammer, G. (1997). A study of potential risk factors for sexual abuse in childhood. *Child Abuse and Neglect, 21,* 49–58.

Flisher, A. J., Kramer, R. A., Hoven, C. W., Greenwald, S. M. A., Bird, H. R., Canino, G., et al. (1997). Psychosocial characteristics of physically abused children and adolescents. *Journal of the American Academy of Child and Adolescent Psychiatry, 36,* 123–131.

Friedrich, W. N. (1993). Sexual victimization and sexual behavior in children: A review of recent literature. *Child Abuse and Neglect, 17,* 59–66.

Friedrich, W. N., Jaworski, T. M., Huxsahl, J. E., & Bengston, B. S. (1997). Dissociative and sexual behaviors in children and adolescents with sexual abuse and psychiatric histories. *Journal of Interpersonal Violence, 12,* 155–171.

Fuller, T. L., & Wells, S. J. (2003). Predicting maltreatment recurrence among CPS cases with alcohol and other drug involvement. *Children and Youth Services Review, 25,* 553–569.

Gabel, S., Swanson, A. J., & Shindledecker, R. (1990). Aggressive children in a day treatment program: Changed outcome and possible explanations. *Child Abuse and Neglect, 14,* 515–523.

The Gallup Organization. (1995). *Gallup nationwide poll.* Washington, DC: U.S. Government Printing Office.

Gaudin, J. M. (1999). Child neglect: Short-term and long-term outcomes. In H. Dubowitz (Ed.), *Neglected children: Research, practice, and policy* (pp. 89–108). Thousand Oaks, CA: Sage.

Gelles, R. J., & Straus, M. A. (1987). Is violence toward children increasing? A comparison of 1975 and 1985 national survey rates. *Journal of Interpersonal Violence, 2,* 212–222.

George, C., & Main, M. (1979). Social interactions of young abused children: Approach, avoidance, and aggression. *Child Development, 50,* 306–318.

Gershater-Molko, R., Lutzker, J. R., & Wesch, D. (2002). Using recidivism data to evaluate Project SafeCare: Teaching bonding, safety, and health care skills to parents. *Child Maltreatment, 7,* 277–285.

Golding, J. (1996). Sexual assault history and women's reproductive and sexual health. *Psychology of Women Quarterly, 20,* 101–121.

Golding, J. (1999). Sexual assault history and long-term physical health problems: Evidence from clinical and population epidemiology. *Current Directions in Psychological Science, 8,* 191–194.

Grauerholz, L. (2000). An ecological approach to understanding sexual revictimization: Linking personal, interpersonal, and sociocultural factors and processes. *Child Maltreatment, 5,* 5–17.

Gully, K. J., Dengerink, H. A., & Pepping, M. (1981). Research note: Sibling contribution to violent behavior. *Journal of Marriage and the Family, 4,* 333–337.

Handwerk, M. L., Field, C. E., & Friman, P. C. (2000). The iatrogenic effects of group intervention for antisocial youth: Premature extrapolations? *Journal of Behavioral Education, 10,* 223–238.

Harmon, R., & Riggs, P. (1996). Clonidine for posttraumatic stress disorder in preschool children. *Journal of the American Academy of Child and Adolescent Psychiatry, 35,* 1247–1249.

Hien, D., & Honeyman, T. (2000). A closer look at the drug abuse-maternal aggression link. *Journal of Interpersonal Violence, 15,* 503–522.

Hoffman-Plotkin, D., & Twentyman, C. T. (1984). A multimodal assessment of behavioral and cognitive deficits in abused and neglected preschoolers. *Child Development, 55,* 794–802.

Horrigan, J., Barnhill, L., & Jarrett, L. (1996). The suppression of nightmares with guanfacine. *Journal of Clinical Psychiatry, 57*(5), 38–44.

Howes, C., & Espinosa, M. P. (1985). The consequences of child abuse for the formation of relationships with peers. *Child Abuse and Neglect, 9,* 397–404.

Hunter, J. A., Goodwin, D. W., & Wilson, R. J. (1992). Attributions of blame in child sexual abuse victims: An analysis of age and gender influences. *Journal of Child Sexual Abuse, 1,* 75–89.

Hyman, S. M., Gold, S. N., & Cott, M. A. (2003). Forms of social support that moderate PTSD in childhood sexual abuse survivors. *Journal of Family Violence, 18,* 295–300.

Jones, H. E., Wong, C. J., Tuten, M., & Stitzer, M. L. (2005). Reinforcement based therapy: 12-month evaluation of an outpatient drug-free treatment for heroin abusers. *Drug and Alcohol Dependence, 79,* 119–128.

Jonzon, E., & Lindblad, F. (2005). Adult female victims of child sexual abuse: Multitype maltreatment and disclosure characteristics related to subjective health. *Journal of Interpersonal Violence, 20,* 651–666.

Kaplan, S., Pelcovitz, D., Salzinger, S., Weiner, M., Mandel, F. S., Lesser, M. L., et al. (1998). Adolescent physical abuse: Risk for adolescent psychiatric disorders. *American Journal of Psychiatry, 155,* 954–959.

Kaufman, J., & Zigler, E. (1987). Do abused children become abusive parents? *American Journal of Orthopsychiatry, 57,* 186–192.

Kavanagh, K. A., Youngblade, L., Reid, J. B., & Fagot, B. I. (1988). Interactions between children and abusive versus control parents. *Journal of Clinical Child Psychology, 17,* 137–142.

Kazdin, A. E. (Ed.). (1992). *Methodological issues and strategies in clinical research.* Washington, DC: American Psychological Association.

Kazdin, A. E. (1997). Parent management training: Evidence, outcomes, and issues. *Journal of the American Academy of Child and Adolescent Psychiatry, 36,* 1349–1356.

Keiley, M. K., Howe, T. R., Dodge, K. A., Bates, J. E., & Pettit, G. S. (2001). The timing of child physical maltreatment: A cross-domain growth analysis of impact on adolescent externalizing and internalizing problems. *Development and Psychopathology, 13,* 891–912.

Kelleher, K., Chaffin, M., Hollenberg, J., & Fischer, E. (1994). Alcohol and drug disorders among physically abusive and neglectful parents in a community-based sample. *American Journal of Public Health, 84,* 1586–1590.

Kendall-Tackett, K. A., Williams, L. M., & Finkelhor, D. (1993). Impact of sexual abuse on children: A review and synthesis of recent empirical studies. *Psychological Bulletin, 113,* 164–180.

Kendler, K. S., Bulik, C. M., Silberg, J., Hettema, J. M., Myers, J., & Prescott, C. A. (2000). Childhood sexual abuse and adult psychiatric and substance use disorders in women: An epidemiological and cotwin control analysis. *Archives of General Psychiatry, 57,* 953–959.

Kessler, M., White, M., & Nelson, B. (2003). Group treatments for women sexually abused as children: A review of the literature and recommendations for future outcome research. *Child Abuse and Neglect, 27,* 1045–1061.

King, N. J., Tonge, B. J., Mullen, P., Myerson, N., Heyne, D., Rollings, S., et al. (2000). Treating sexually abused children with post traumatic stress symptoms: A randomized trial. *Journal of the American Academy of Child and Adolescent Psychiatry, 39,* 1347–1355.

Kiser, L. J., Heston, J., Millsap, P. A., & Pruitt, D. B. (1991). Physical and sexual abuse in childhood: Relationship with post-traumatic stress disorder. *Journal of the American Academy of Child and Adolescent Child Psychiatry, 30,* 776–783.

Koenen, K. C., Harley, R., Lyons, M. J., Wolfe, J., Simpson, J. C., Goldberg, J., et al. (2002). A twin registry study of familial and individual risk factors for trauma exposure and posttraumatic stress disorder. *Journal of Nervous and Mental Disease, 190,* 209–218.

Kolko, D. J. (1996a). Clinical monitoring of treatment course in child physical abuse: Psychometric characteristics and treatment comparisons. *Child Abuse and Neglect, 20,* 23–43.

Kolko, D. J. (1996b). Individual cognitive behavioral treatment and family therapy for physically abused children and their offending parents: A comparison of clinical outcomes. *Child Maltreatment, 1,* 322–342.

Kolko, D. J., & Swenson, C. C. (2002). *Assessing and treating physically abused children and their families: A cognitive-behavioral approach.* Thousand Oaks, CA: Sage.

Kravic, J. N. (1987). Behavior problems and social competence of clinic-referred abused children. *Journal of Family Violence, 2,* 111–120.

Lamb, M. E., & Nash, A. (1989). Infant-mother attachment, sociability, and peer competence. In T. J. Berndt & G. W. Ladd (Eds.). *Peer relationships in child development* (pp. 219–245). New York: Wiley.

Laner, M. R., & Thompson, J. (1982). Abuse and aggression in courting couples. *Deviant Behavior, 3,* 229–244.

Leve, L., & Chamberlain, P. (2005). Association with delinquent peers: Intervention effects for youth in the juvenile justice system. *Journal of Abnormal Child Psychology, 33,* 339–347.

Leve, L., Chamberlain, P., & Reid, J. B. (2005). Intervention outcomes for girls referred from juvenile justice: Effects on delinquency. *Journal of Consulting and Clinical Psychology, 73,* 1181–1185.

Lipovsky, J. A., Swenson, C. C., Ralston, M. E., & Saunders, B. E. (1998). The abuse clarification process in the treatment of intrafamilial child abuse. *Child Abuse and Neglect, 22,* 729–741.

Looff, D., Grimley, P., Kuller, F., Martin, A., & Shonfield, L. (1995). Carbamazepine for PTSD. *Journal of the American Academy of Child and Adolescent Psychiatry, 34*(6), 703–704.

Lutzker, J. R., Bigelow, K. M., Doctor, R. M., Gershater, R. M., & Greene, B. F. (1998). An ecobehavioral model for the prevention and treatment of child physical abuse: History and application. In J. R. Lutzker (Ed.), *Handbook of child abuse and neglect research and treatment* (pp. 239–266). New York: Plenum Press.

Lutzker, J. R., Frame, J. R., & Rice, J. M. (1982). Project 12-Ways: An ecobehavioral approach to the treatment and prevention of child abuse and neglect. *Education and Treatment of Children, 5,* 141–155.

Lutzker, J. R., & Rice, J. M. (1984). Project 12-Ways: Measuring outcome of a large in-home service for treatment and prevention of child abuse and neglect. *Child Abuse and Neglect, 8,* 519–524.

Lutzker, J. R., & Rice, J. M. (1987). Using recidivism data to evaluate Project 12-Ways: An ecobehavioral approach to the treatment and prevention of child abuse and neglect. *Journal of Family Violence, 2,* 283–289.

Mannarino, A. P., & Cohen, J. A. (1996a). Abuse-related attributions and perceptions, general attributions, and locus of control in sexually abused girls. *Journal of Interpersonal Violence, 12,* 155–171.

Mannarino, A. P., & Cohen, J. A. (1996b). Family-related variables and psychological symptom formation in sexually abused girls. *Journal of Child Sexual Abuse, 5*(1), 105–120.

Mannarino, A. P., Cohen, J. A., & Berman, S. R. (1994). The relationship between preabuse factors and psychological symptomatology in sexually abused girls. *Child Abuse and Neglect, 18,* 63–71.

Marshall, D., & English, D. (1999). Survival analysis of risk factors for recidivism in child abuse and neglect. *Child Maltreatment, 4,* 287–296.

Marshall, L. L., & Rose, P. (1990). Premarital violence: The impact of family origin violence, stress, and reciprocity. *Violence and Victims, 5,* 51–64.

McCord, J. (1983). A forty year perspective on effects of child abuse and neglect. *Child Abuse and Neglect, 7,* 265–270.

McFayden, R. G., & Kitson, W. J. H. (1996). Language comprehension and expression among adolescents who have experienced childhood physical abuse. *Journal of Child Psychology and Psychiatry and Allied Disciplines, 37,* 551–562.

McGain, B., & McKinzey, R. K. (1995). The efficacy of group treatment in sexually abused girls. *Child Abuse and Neglect, 19,* 1157–1169.

Milner, J. S. (1998). Individual and family characteristics associated with intrafamilial child physical and sexual abuse. In P. K. Trickett & C. J. Schellenbach (Eds.), *Violence against children in the family and community* (pp. 141–170). Washington, DC: American Psychological Association.

Milner, J. S., & Dopke, C. (1997). Child physical abuse: Review of offender characteristics. In D. Wolfe & R. J. McMahon (Eds.), *Child abuse: New directions in prevention and treatment across the lifespan* (pp. 27–54). Thousand Oaks, CA: Sage.

Mollerstrom, W. W., Patchner, M. M., & Milner, J. S. (1992). Family functioning and child abuse potential. *Journal of Clinical Psychology, 48*, 445–454.

Mueller, E., & Silverman, N. (1989). Peer relations in maltreated children. In D. Cicchetti & V. Carlson (Eds.), *Child maltreatment: Theory and research on the causes and consequences of child abuse and neglect* (pp. 529–578). New York: Cambridge University Press.

Mullen, P., Martin, J., Anderson, J., & Romans, S. (1996). The long-term impact of the physical, emotional, and sexual abuse of children: A community study. *Child Abuse and Neglect, 20,* 7–21.

Nair, P., Schuler, M. E., Black, M. M., Kettinger, L., & Harrington, D. (2003). Cumulative environmental risk in substance abusing women: Early intervention, parenting stress, child abuse potential, and child development. *Child Abuse and Neglect, 27,* 997–1017.

Najavits, L. M., Weiss, R. D., & Shaw, S. R. (1997). The link between substance abuse and posttraumatic stress disorder in women: A research review. *American Journal on Addictions, 6,* 271–283.

National Center for Child Abuse and Neglect, Department of Health and Human Services, Office of Human Development Services. (1981). *Study findings: Study of national incidence and prevalence of child abuse and neglect.* Washington, DC: U.S. Government Printing Office.

National Center for Child Abuse and Neglect, Department of Health and Human Services, Office of Human Development Services. (1988). *Study findings: Study of national incidence and prevalence of child abuse and neglect.* Washington, DC: U.S. Government Printing Office.

National Center for Child Abuse and Neglect, Department of Health and Human Services, Office of Human Development Services. (1996). *Study findings: Study of national incidence and prevalence of child abuse and neglect.* Washington, DC: U.S. Government Printing Office.

National Center for Child Abuse and Neglect, Department of Health and Human Services, Office of Human Development Services. (2004). *Study findings: Study of national incidence and prevalence of child abuse and neglect.* Washington, DC: U.S. Government Printing Office.

National Clearinghouse on Child Abuse and Neglect. (2003, December). *Substance abuse and child maltreatment.* Washington, DC: U.S. Department of Health and Human Services.

Pelcovitz, D., Kaplan, S., Goldenberg, B., Mandel, F., Lehane, J., & Guarrera, J. (1994). Post-traumatic stress disorder in physically abused adolescents. *Journal of the American Academy of Child and Adolescent Psychiatry, 33,* 305–312.

Polusny, M., & Follette, V. (1996). Remembering childhood sexual abuse: A national survey of psychologists' clinical practices, beliefs, and personal experiences. *Professional Psychology: Research and Practice, 27,* 41–52.

Price, J., Hilsenroth, M., Callahan, K., Petretic-Jackson, P., & Bonge, D. (2004). A pilot study of psychodynamic psychotherapy for adult survivors of childhood sexual abuse. *Clinical Psychology and Psychotherapy, 11,* 378–391.

Price, J., Hilsenroth, M., Petretic-Jackson, P., & Bonge, D. (2001). A review of individual psychotherapy outcomes for adult survivors of childhood sexual abuse. *Clinical Psychology Review, 21,* 1095–1121.

Radhakrishna, A., Bou-Saada, I. E., Hunter, W. M., Catellier, D. J., & Kotch, J. B. (2001). Are father surrogates a risk factor for child maltreatment? *Child Maltreatment, 6,* 281–289.

Riggs, D. O., O'Leary, K. D., & Breslin, F. C. (1990). Multiple correlates of physical aggression in dating couples. *Journal of Interpersonal Violence, 5,* 61–73.

Roesler, T. A. (1994). Reactions to disclosure of childhood sexual abuse: The effect on adult symptoms. *Journal of Nervous and Mental Diseases, 182,* 618–624.

Rosenbaum, M., & Bennett, B. (1986). Homicide and depression. *American Journal of Psychiatry, 143,* 367–370.

Ruscio, A. M. (2001). Predicting the child-rearing practices of mothers sexually abused in childhood. *Child Abuse and Neglect, 25,* 369–387.

Rust, J. O., & Troupe, P. A. (1991). Relationships of treatment of child sexual abuse with school achievement and concept. *Journal of Early Adolescence, 11,* 410–429.

Sack, W. H., & Mason, R. (1980). Child abuse and conviction of sexual crimes: A preliminary finding. *Law and Human Behavior, 4,* 211–215.

Saunders, B. E. (2003). Understanding children exposed to violence: Toward an integration of overlapping fields. *Journal of Interpersonal Violence, 18,* 356–376.

Schuck, A. M., & Widom, C. S. (2003). Childhood victimization and alcohol symptoms in women: An examination of protective factors. *Journal of Studies on Alcohol, 64,* 247–256.

Schuetze, P., & Eiden, R. D. (2005). The relationship between sexual abuse during childhood and parenting outcomes: Modeling direct and indirect pathways. *Child Abuse and Neglect, 29,* 645–659.

Sedlak, A. J., & Broadhurst, D. D. (1996). *Third National Incidence Study of Child Abuse and Neglect: Final report.* Washington, DC: U.S. Department of Health and Human Services.

Seedat, S., Lockhat, R., Kaminer, D., Zungu-Dirwayi, N., & Stein, D. (2001). An open trial of citalopram in adolescents with post-traumatic stress disorder. *International Clinical Psychopharmacology, 16,* 21–25.

Seedat, S., Stein, D. J., Ziervogel, C., Middleton, T., Kaminer, D., Emsley, R. A., et al. (2002). Comparison of response to a selective serotonin reuptake inhibitor in children, adolescents and adults with posttraumatic stress disorder. *Journal of Child and Adolescent Psychopharmacology, 12,* 37–46.

Shepard, M., & Raschick, M. (1999). How child welfare workers assess and intervene around issues of domestic violence. *Child Maltreatment, 4,* 148–156.

Shields, A., & Cicchetti, D. (2001). Parental maltreatment and emotion dysregulation as risk factors for bullying and victimization in middle childhood. *Journal of Clinical Child Psychology, 30,* 349–363.

Sigelman, C. K., Berry, C. J., & Wiles, K. A. (1984). Violence in college students' dating relationships. *Journal of Applied Social Psychology, 14,* 530–548.

Silovsky, J. F., Niec, L., & Hecht, D. (2000, January). Clinical presentation and treatment outcome of preschool children with sexual behavior problems. In E. J. Brown (Chair), *Children with sexual behavior problems: Treatment outcome and service delivery.* Paper presented at the San Diego Conference on Responding to Child Maltreatment, San Diego, CA.

Simons, R. L., & Whitbeck, L. B. (1991). Sexual abuse as a precursor to prostitution and victimization among adolescent and adult homeless women. *Journal of Family Issues, 12*(3), 361–379.

Simons, R. L., Whitbeck, L. B., Conger, R. D., & Chyi-In, W. (1991). Intergenerational transmission of harsh parenting. *Developmental Psychology, 27,* 159–171.

Small, S. A., & Kerns, D. (1993). Unwanted sexual activity among peers during early and middle adolescence: Incidence and risk factors. *Journal of Marriage and the Family, 55,* 941–952.

Sparato, J., Mullen, P. E., Burgess, P. M., Wells, D. L., & Moss, S. A. (2004). Impact of child sexual abuse on mental health: Prospective study in males and females. *British Journal of Psychiatry, 184,* 416–421.

Stauffer, L. B., & Deblinger, E. (1996). Cognitive behavioral groups for nonoffending mothers and their young sexually abused children: A preliminary treatment outcome study. *Child Maltreatment, 1,* 65–76.

Stern, P. (1997). *Preparing and presenting expert testimony in child abuse litigation: A guide for expert witnesses and attorneys.* New York: Sage.

Straus, M. A., & Kantor, G. K. (1994). Corporal punishment of adolescents by parents: A risk factor in the epidemiology of depression, suicide, alcohol abuse, child abuse, and wife beating. *Adolescence, 29,* 543–561.

Sullivan, P. M., & Knutson, J. F. (2000). Maltreatment and disabilities: A population-based epidemiological study. *Child Abuse and Neglect, 24,* 1257–1273.

Swenson, C. C. (2000, October). *Community-based treatment of child physical abuse: Costs and outcomes.* In M. Rowland (Chair), MST Research, University Affiliated Projects. Symposium conducted at the First International MST Conference, Savannah, GA.

Swenson, C. C. (2005, April). *Treatment for families experiencing child physical abuse.* Workshop presented to the Foster Care Assessment Program of the Children's Hospital, Seattle, WA.

Swenson, C. C., & Brown, E. J. (1999). Cognitive-behavioral group treatment for physically abused children. *Cognitive and Behavioral Practice, 6,* 212–220.

Swenson, C. C., & Chaffin, M. (2006). Beyond psychotherapy: Treating abused children by changing their social ecology. *Aggression and Violent Behavior, 11,* 120–137.

Swenson, C. C., & Hanson, R. F. (1998). Sexual abuse of children: Assessment, research, and treatment. In J.R. Lutzker (Ed.), *Handbook of child abuse research and treatment* (pp. 475–499). New York: Plenum Press.

Swenson, C. C., & Kolko, D. J. (2000). Long-term management of the developmental consequences of child physical abuse. In R.M. Reece (Ed.), *The treatment of child abuse* (pp. 135–154). Baltimore, MD: Johns Hopkins University Press.

Swenson, C. C., Randall, J., Henggeler, S. W., & Ward, D. (2000). Outcomes and costs of an interagency partnership to serve maltreated children in state custody. *Children's Services: Social Policy, Research, and Practice, 3,* 191–209.

Swenson, C. C., Saldana, L., Joyner, C. D., & Henggeler, S. W. (2006). Ecological treatment for parent to child violence: Interventions for children exposed to violence. In A. F. Lieberman & R. DeMartino (Eds.), *Interventions for children exposed to violence* (pp. 155–185). New Brunswick, NJ: Johnson & Johnson Pediatric Institute.

Swenson, C. C., & Schaeffer, C. (2006, June). *Building stronger families: Ecological treatment for co-occurring parental substance abuse and child maltreatment.* Workshop presented at the annual colloquium of the American Professional Society on the Abuse of Children, Nashville, TN.

Tanskanen, A., Hintikka, J., Honkalampi, K., Haatainen, K., Koivumaa-Honkanen, H., & Viinamaki, H. (2004). Impact of multiple traumatic experiences on the persistence of depressive symptoms: A population based study. *Nordic Journal of Psychiatry, 58,* 459–464.

Tarter, R. E., Hegedus, A. M., Winsten, N. E., & Alterman, A. I. (1984). Neuropsychological, personality, and familial characteristics of physically abused delinquents. *Journal of the American Academy of Child Psychiatry, 23,* 668–674.

Trickett, P., Noll, J. G., Reiffman, A., & Putnam, F. W. (2001). Variants of intrafamilial sexual abuse experience: Implications for short- and long-term development. *Development and Psychopathology, 13,* 1001–1019.

Urquiza, A. J., & McNeil, C. B. (1996). Parent-child interaction therapy: An intensive dyadic intervention for physically abusive families. *Child Maltreatment, 1,* 132–141.

U.S. Department of Health and Human Services. (1999). *Blending perspectives and building common ground: A report to Congress on substance abuse and child protection.* Washington, DC: U.S. Government Printing Office.

U.S. Department of Health and Human Services. (2004). *National Center on Child Abuse and Neglect, Child Maltreatment, 2002: Reports From the States for the National Child Abuse and Neglect Data Systems.* Washington, DC: U.S. Government Printing Office.

U.S. Department of Health and Human Services. (2005). *Child maltreatment 2003.* Washington, DC: Administration for Children and Families.

Walker, E. A., Unutzer, J., Rutter, C., Gelfand, A., Saunders, K., VonKorff, M., et al. (1999). Costs of health care use by women HMO members with a history of childhood abuse and neglect. *Archives of General Psychiatry, 56,* 609–613.

Wallace, H. (1996). *Family violence: Legal, medical, and social perspectives.* Needham Heights, MA: Allyn & Bacon.

Webster-Stratton, C., & Hammond, M. (1997). Treating children with early-onset conduct problems: A comparison of child and parent training interventions. *Journal of Consulting and Clinical Psychology, 65,* 93–109.

Wesch, D., & Lutzker, J. R. (1991). A comprehensive 5-year evaluation of Project 12-Ways: An ecobehavioral program for treating and preventing child abuse and neglect. *Journal of Family Violence, 6,* 17–35.

Westermeyer, J., Wahmanholm, K., & Thuras, P. (2001). Effects of childhood physical abuse on course and severity of substance abuse. *American Journal on Addiction, 10,* 101–110.

Whipple, E. E., & Webster-Stratton, C. (1991). The role of parental stress in physically abusive families. *Child Abuse and Neglect, 15,* 279–291.

Widom, C. S., & Kuhns, J. B. (1996). Childhood victimization and subsequent risk for promiscuity, prostitution, and teenage pregnancy: A prospective study. *American Journal of Public Health, 86,* 1607–1612.

Wilsnack, S. C., Klassen, A. D., Brett, E., & Wilsnack, R. W. (1991). Predicting onset and chronicity of women's problem drinking: A 5-year longitudinal analysis. *American Journal of Public Health, 81,* 305–318.

Wilsnack, S. C., & Wilsnack, R. W. (1995). Drinking and problem drinking in U.S. women: Patterns and recent trends. In M. Galanter (Ed.), *Recent developments in alcoholism: Vol. 12. Alcoholism and women* (pp. 29–60). New York: Plenum Press.

Wilsnack, S. C., Wilsnack, R. W., & Hiller-Sturmhofel, S. (1994). How women drink: Epidemiology of women's drinking and problem drinking. *Alcohol Health and Research World, 18,* 173–181.

Wolfe, D. A., Edwards, B., Manion, I., & Koverola, C. (1988). Early intervention for parents at risk for child abuse and neglect: A preliminary report. *Journal of Consulting and Clinical Psychology, 56,* 40–47.

Wolfner, G. D., & Gelles, R. J. (1993). A profile of violence toward children: A national study. *Child Abuse and Neglect, 17,* 197–212.

Wright, D., Woo, W., Muller, R., Fernandes, C., & Kraftcheck, E. (2003). An investigation of trauma-centered inpatient treatment for adult survivors of abuse. *Child Abuse and Neglect, 27,* 393–406.

Young, N. K., Gardner, S. L., & Dennis, K. (1998). *Responding to alcohol and other drug problems in child welfare: Weaving together practice and policy.* Washington, DC: Office of Juvenile Justice and Delinquency Prevention.

Zlotnick, C., & Pearlstein, T. (1997). Posttraumatic stress disorder (PTSD), PTSD comorbidity, and childhood abuse among incarcerated women. *Journal of Nervous and Mental Diseases, 185,* 761–763.

Zuravin, S. (1989). The ecology of child abuse and neglect: Review of the literature and presentation of data. *Violence and Victims, 4,* 101–120.

Zuravin, S., & DePanfilis, D. (1996). *Child maltreatment recurrences among families served by Child Protective Services* (Final report to the National Center on Child Abuse and Neglect). Washington, DC: U.S. Government Printing Office.

PART TWO

CHAPTER 9

Asperger's Disorder: Exploring the Schizoid Spectrum

TONY ATTWOOD

THE FOURTH edition, text revision of the *Diagnostic and Statistical Manual of Mental Disorders* (*DSM-IV-TR*; American Psychiatric Association, 2000, p. 639) groups the diagnoses of Schizoid, Schizotypal, and Paranoid Personality Disorders together in Cluster A, based on descriptive similarities of the symptom clusters, labeling them "eccentric." The specific characteristics that place these groups together are behavioral styles, social and interpersonal relatedness skills, and interactive deficits. These patterns, often observable from early childhood, place these children outside of typical childhood social and work groups, often making them objects of ridicule from other children and a target for the avoidance or discomfort of adults. Terms and descriptors such as "eccentric," "weird," "unusual," "strange," "creepy," or "odd" are often attached to these children's behavior, demeanor, or, more globally, to the children themselves.

Individuals with a Paranoid Personality Disorder (PPD) demonstrate a chronic and pervasive pattern of distrust, hostility, resentment, and consequent anger. They perceive the motives of others to be malevolent and so respond in what is best termed a self-protective manner. They do this by constantly scanning for any possibilities of potential attack or assault so that they are primed for an immediate response. They perceive themselves as righteous (and often isolated) protectors of their person and space, and others as potentially (or actively) abusive and discriminatory. Their style is to be in a constantly defensive mode (Beck et al., 2004).

Individuals with a Schizoid Personality Disorder (SPD) are socially detached, but experience little anxiety from their initially self-imposed isolation. Their preference for being alone might manifest either as an aloofness that separates them from others or as a remoteness that excludes others from their personal sphere (Millon & Everly, 1985). The descriptors of eccentricity are also used to describe the interpersonal style of the child with SPD. In cultures where shared space, collaborative effort, and teamwork are frequently appreciated, respected, and prized, the child with SPD stands out in sharp relief. Noticeable by their isolative style, these children consequently have few opportunities to develop and hone the skills of social relatedness. Although the child may not see this disorder as negative, and although it may not be perceived at all by family members, who simply label the child "shy," the child with SPD may come into conflict in the school community.

Individuals who are diagnosed with a Schizotypal Personality Disorder are as socially uncomfortable as the previous two groups and show, in addition, cognitive and perceptual distortions and eccentricities of behavior (*DSM-IV*; American Psychiatric Association, 1994, p. 629). They may exhibit perceptual distortions that may approach delusions and perceptual experiences that have a hallucinatory quality. What ties these groups together is their isolation and avoidance of others.

Wolff (1991a, 1991b), Wolff, Townshend, McGuire, and Weeks (1991), and Wolff (1998), describe a "schizoid spectrum" that includes autism, Asperger's syndrome, and childhood Schizoid Personality Disorder. In Wolff's view, all of these disorders have in common impaired social relationships and developmental delays and abnormalities. In addressing the assessment, understanding, and treatment of children who exhibit these socially avoidant behaviors, I have chosen to follow Wolff's schizoid spectrum as a model for understanding both the etiology and patterns of behavior in children and later as adults. In this chapter, which describes the observed and typical styles of the Cluster A groups, I describe the eccentric, socially isolated, and possibly bizarre behavior of these children as seen through the lens of the developmental issues of the child with Asperger's syndrome.

We currently use the diagnostic term Asperger's Disorder based on the descriptions of Hans Asperger (1944/1991), a Viennese pediatrician who, in the late 1930s, noticed that some of the children referred to his clinic had very similar personality characteristics and behavior. He suggested a new diagnostic term, *Autistische Psychopathen im Kindesalter*, to describe this phenomenon. A modern translation of the original German psychological term for "psychopathy" into current clinical terminology is "personality disorder"—that is, a description of someone's personality rather than a mental illness, such as Schizophrenia.

Asperger noted that children with, to use his original term, autistic personality disorder had an unusual profile of abilities that included a conspicuous delay in social maturity and social reasoning, and that some aspects of their social abilities were quite unusual at any stage of development. The children had difficulty making friends, and they were often teased and tormented by other children. There were impairments in language abilities, especially the conversational or pragmatic

302   PERSONALITY DISORDERS IN CHILDHOOD AND ADOLESCENCE

aspects of language. The children's use of language was pedantic, and some children had an unusual prosody that affected the tone, pitch, and rhythm of their speech. The grammar and vocabulary may have been relatively advanced, but at the end of the conversation one had the impression of an inability on the part of the child to have the typical conversation that would be expected with a child of that age. Asperger also observed and described significant impairments in the communication and control of emotions and a tendency to intellectualize feelings. Empathy was not as mature as one would expect, considering the children's intellectual abilities. The children also had an egocentric or idiosyncratic preoccupation with a specific topic or interest that would dominate their thoughts and time. Some of the children had difficulty maintaining attention in class, and although some showed academic excellence in areas such as reading, spelling, and mathematics, others had specific learning problems that required remedial education programs. Asperger noted that the children often needed more assistance from their mother with self-help and organizational skills than one would expect. He described conspicuous clumsiness in terms of gait and coordination. He also noted that some children were extremely sensitive to particular sounds, aromas, textures, and touch. These characteristics form the basis of the current diagnostic criteria for Asperger's Disorder.

Asperger found that these characteristics could be identified in some children as young as 2 to 3 years, although in other children, the characteristics became conspicuous only when the child started school and was expected to be able to intuitively socialize with same-age peers. He also noticed that some of the parents, especially the fathers, of such children appeared to share some of the personality characteristics of their child. He suggested that the condition was probably due to genetic or neurological, rather than psychological or environmental, factors. In his initial and subsequent publications and in a recent analysis of his patient records for children he saw over 3 decades, it is apparent that he considered autistic personality disorder to be part of a natural continuum of abilities that merges into the normal range (Asperger, 1944/1991, 1952, 1979; Hippler & Klicpera, 2004).

He conceptualized the disorder as a lifelong and stable personality type and did not observe the disintegration and fragmentation that occurs in Schizophrenia. He also noted that some of the children had specific talents that could lead to successful employment, and some could develop lifelong relationships.

PATHWAYS TO A DIAGNOSIS

The primary diagnostic pathway commences when an experienced teacher observes a child who is very unusual in terms of his or her ability to understand social situations and conventions. The child is obviously not intellectually impaired, but appears to lack the social understanding of his or her peers. When on the playground, the child may actively avoid social play with peers or be socially naive, intrusive, or dominating. In class, the teacher recognizes that the child does not seem to notice or understand the nonverbal signals that convey such messages as "Not now" or "I am starting to feel annoyed." The child can become notorious for interrupting or not responding to the social context in ways that would be expected of a child of that age and intellectual ability. The child is also recognized as immature in the ability to manage emotions and to express empathy. The teacher may also notice that the child becomes extremely anxious or agitated if routines are changed or if he or she cannot solve a problem. The child may have an unusual learning style, with remarkable knowledge in an area of interest to the child, such as dinosaurs, but significant learning or attention problems for academic skills. The teacher may also notice problems with motor coordination, such as in handwriting, running, and catching a ball. The child may cover his or her ears in response to sounds that are not perceived as unpleasant by other children.

Another pathway, the diagnosis of classic autism in early childhood, was first described by Lorna Wing, a British child psychiatrist. She used the eponymous diagnostic term Asperger's Disorder in 1981 to describe a specific area of the autism spectrum or continuum. She observed that some children who had clear signs of severe autism in infancy and early childhood could achieve remarkable progress and move along the autism continuum as a result of early diagnosis and intensive and effective early intervention programs (Wing, 1981). The previously socially aloof and silent child now wanted to play with other children and could talk using complex sentences, such that the child's profile of abilities more closely resembled Hans Asperger's clinical descriptions. Peter Szatmari (2000), a Canadian child psychiatrist, has suggested that those children with autism who develop functional language in early childhood eventually join the developmental trajectory and have a profile of abilities typical of a child with Asperger's Disorder. Thus, at one point in a child's early development, autism is the correct diagnosis, but a distinct subgroup of children with autism can show a remarkable improvement in language, play, and motivation to socialize with their peers between the ages of 4 and 6 years. The developmental trajectory for such children has changed, and their profile of abilities in the elementary school years is consistent with the characteristics of Asperger's Disorder (Attwood, 1998; Dissanayake, 2004; C. Gillberg, 1998; Wing, 1981).

A third diagnostic pathway is when a child's developmental history includes another disorder. Clinicians have recognized for some time that children with Asperger's Disorder can also have signs of Attention-Deficit/Hyperactivity Disorder, which has been confirmed by several research studies and case descriptions (Ehlers & Gillberg, 1993; Fein, Dixon, Paul, & Levin, 2005; Ghaziuddin, Wieder-Mikhail, & Ghaziuddin, 1998; Klin & Volkmar, 1997; Perry, 1998; Tani et al., 2006). The two diagnoses are not mutually exclusive.

We also know that young children with Asperger's Disorder are prone to develop mood disorders (Attwood, 2003), and some children seem to be almost constantly anxious, which might indicate Generalized Anxiety Disorder. Some children with Asperger's Disorder use their intellect rather than intuition to succeed in some social situations; as a result, they may be in an almost constant state of alertness and anxiety, leading to the risk of mental and physical exhaustion, one of the contributory factors for the development of a clinical depression. A referral to a clinical psychologist, psychiatrist, or mental health service for children with a mood disorder may lead to an additional diagnosis of Asperger's Disorder when a detailed and comprehensive developmental history is completed (Towbin, Pradella, Gorrindo, Pine, & Leibenluft, 2005).

Serious eating disorders such as Anorexia Nervosa can be associated with Asperger's Disorder; approximately 18% to 23% of adolescent girls with Anorexia Nervosa also have signs of Asperger's Disorder (C. Gillberg & Billstedt, 2000; C. Gillberg & Rastam, 1992; I. C. Gillberg, Gillberg, Rastam, & Johansson, 1996; Rastam, Gillberg, & Wentz, 2003; Wentz et al., 2005; Wentz Nilsson, Gillberg, Gillberg, & Rastam, 1999). Thus, the diagnosis of an eating disorder could be the starting point for a diagnostic assessment for Asperger's Disorder.

In his original publication, translated from German into English by Uta Frith in 1991, Hans Asperger (1944/1991) described a subgroup of children with a tendency to have conduct problems, leading to their being suspended from school. Sometimes children with Asperger's Disorder perceive themselves as more adult than child. Young children with the disorder may act in the classroom as though they were an adult, correcting and disciplining the other children. In situations of conflict, they are less likely to refer to an adult to act as an adjudicator and are liable to take the law into their own hands, especially when bullied, teased, or tormented. Conflict and confrontation with adults can be made worse by noncompliance, negativism, and difficulty in perceiving the differences in social status or hierarchy, resulting in a failure to respect authority or maturity. The child may not accept a particular school rule if it appears to be illogical, and may pursue a point or argument as a matter of principle. This can lead to a history of significant conflict with teachers and school authorities, which can be another pathway to a diagnosis of Asperger's Disorder.

QUESTIONNAIRES AND RATING SCALES
FOR ASPERGER'S DISORDER

When a school or therapist identifies a developmental history and profile of abilities that could indicate a diagnosis of Asperger's Disorder, the next stage is usually the completion of a questionnaire or rating scale to substantiate a referral to a specialist. We currently have seven screening questionnaires that can be used with children and adolescents. A recent review of assessment scales and questionnaires for Asperger's Disorder concluded that there are problems with validity, reliability, specificity, and sensitivity with all the instruments (Howlin, 2000). There is as yet no questionnaire or rating scale of first choice. The following are the questionnaires and scales for children and adolescents in alphabetical order:

Asperger Disorder Diagnostic Interview (ASDI; C. Gillberg, Gillberg, Rastam, & Wentz, 2001)

Asperger Disorder Diagnostic Scale (ASDS; Myles, Bock, & Simpson, 2001)

Australian Scale for Asperger's Disorder (ASAS; Garnett & Attwood, 1998)

Autism Spectrum Screening Questionnaire (ASSQ; Ehlers, Gillberg, & Wing, 1999)

Childhood Asperger's Screening Test (CAST; Scott, Baron-Cohen, Bolton, & Brayne, 2002; Williams et al., 2005)

Gilliam Asperger's Disorder Scale (GADS; Gilliam, 2002)

Krug Asperger's Disorder Index (KADI; Krug & Arick, 2002)

A recent review of the ASDS, ASSQ, CAST, GADS, and KADI suggests that these rating scales all had significant psychometric weaknesses, particularly in the use of normative samples; the KADI showed the strongest psychometric properties and the ASDS had the weakest (Campbell, 2005).

There are two diagnostic tests that have been designed for children with autism: the Autism Diagnostic Interview-Revised (Lord, Rutter, & Le Couteur, 1994) and the Autism Diagnostic Observation Schedule—Generic (Lord et al., 2000). However, because they were primarily designed for the diagnosis of autism, these instruments are not sensitive to the more subtle characteristics of Asperger's Disorder (C. Gillberg, 2002; Klin, Sparrow, Marans, Carter, & Volkmar, 2000).

THE DIAGNOSTIC CRITERIA

The inclusion of Asperger's Disorder in the *DSM-IV* in 1994 was welcomed by clinicians as a wise decision, as was the decision to move the Pervasive Developmental Disorders, including autism and Asperger's Disorder, from Axis II (for long-term, stable disorders with a relatively poor prognosis for improvement) to Axis I (which implies that individuals can improve with early intervention and treatment). However, there are problems with the diagnostic criteria in *DSM-IV* and *DSM-IV-TR*, especially the differential criteria in the manual that distinguish between autism and Asperger's Disorder (Table 9.1).

LANGUAGE DELAY

Speech and language pathologists have criticized the following *DSM-IV-TR* (American Psychiatric Association, 2000, p. 84) criterion for Asperger's Disorder: "There is no clinically significant general delay in language, for example, single words used by age 2 years, communicative phrases used by age 3 years." In other words, if there have been signs of early language delay, then the diagnosis should not be Asperger's Disorder, but autism, even if all the other criteria, developmental history (apart from language acquisition), and current profile of abilities are met for Asperger's Disorder. Diane Twatchman-Cullen (1998), a speech and language pathologist with considerable experience

Table 9.1

Diagnostic Criteria for Asperger's Disorder

According to *DSM-IV-TR*

A. Qualitative impairment in social interaction, as manifested by at least two of the following:
   1. marked impairment in the use of multiple nonverbal behaviors such as eye-to-eye gaze, facial expression, body postures, and gestures to regulate social interaction
   2. failure to develop peer relationships appropriate to developmental level
   3. a lack of spontaneous seeking to share enjoyment, interests, or achievements with other people (e.g., by a lack of showing, bringing, or pointing out objects of interest to other people)
   4. lack of social or emotional reciprocity

B. Restricted repetitive and stereotyped patterns of behavior, interests, and activities, as manifested by at least one of the following:
   1. encompassing preoccupation with one or more stereotyped and restricted patterns of interest that is abnormal either in intensity or focus
   2. apparently inflexible adherence to specific, non-functional routines or rituals
   3. stereotyped and repetitive motor mannerisms (e.g., hand or finger flapping or twisting, or complex whole-body movements)
   4. persistent preoccupation with parts of objects

C. The disturbance causes clinically significant impairment in social, occupational, or other important areas of functioning.

D. There is no clinically significant general delay in language (e.g., single words used by age 2, communicative phrases used by age 3).

E. There is no clinically significant delay in cognitive development or in the development of age-appropriate self-help skills, adaptive behavior (other than in social interaction), and curiosity about the environment in childhood.

F. Criteria are not met for another specific Pervasive Developmental Disorder or Schizophrenia.

---

in autism spectrum disorders, has criticized this exclusion criterion on the grounds that the term *clinically significant* is neither scientific nor precise but left to the judgment of clinicians without an operational definition. A further criticism is that research on the stages of early language acquisition has established that single words emerge around the child's first birthday, communicative phrases at about 18 months, and short sentences around 2 years. In fact, the *DSM-IV-TR* criteria describe a child who actually has a significant language delay. In my opinion, and that of many clinicians, early language delay is not an exclusion criterion for Asperger's Disorder and may actually be an inclusion criterion. The focus during the diagnostic assessment should be on current language use (the pragmatic aspects of language) rather than the history of language development.

SELF-HELP SKILLS AND ADAPTIVE BEHAVIOR

The *DSM-IV-TR* (American Psychiatric Association, 2000, p. 84) criteria refer to children with Asperger's Disorder as having "no clinically significant delay in cognitive development, in the development of age-appropriate self-help skills, adaptive behavior (other than in social interactions), and curiosity about the environment in childhood." Clinical experience and research indicate that parents, especially mothers, of children and adolescents with Asperger's Disorder often have to provide verbal reminders and advice regarding self-help and daily living skills. This can range from help with problems with dexterity affecting activities such as using cutlery, to reminders regarding personal hygiene and dress sense, to encouragement with planning and time management skills. When parents complete a standardized assessment of self-care skills and adaptive functioning, such abilities in children with Asperger's Disorder are below the level expected for their age and intellectual ability (Smyrnios, 2002). Clinicians have also recognized significant problems with adaptive behavior, especially with regard to anger management, anxiety, and depression (Attwood, 2003).

THE INCLUSION OF OTHER IMPORTANT OR TRANSITORY CHARACTERISTICS

The diagnostic criteria of the *DSM-IV-TR* do not include a description of the unusual characteristics in the pragmatic aspects of language originally described by Asperger and portrayed in the clinical literature, namely, the pedantic use of language and unusual prosody. The *DSM-IV* criteria also fail to make adequate reference to problems with sensory perception and integration, especially auditory sensitivity and hypersensitivity to light intensity, tactile experiences, and aromas.

These aspects of Asperger's Disorder can have a profound effect on the person's quality of life. The criteria also exclude reference to motor clumsiness, which was described by Asperger and has been substantiated in the research literature (D. Green et al., 2002).

The diagnostic criteria in the *DSM-IV-TR* can also be criticized for emphasizing characteristics that can be rare or transitory. The criteria refer to "stereotyped and repetitive motor mannerisms (e.g., hand or finger flapping or twisting, or complex whole-body movements)" (American Psychiatric Association, 2000, p. 84), yet clinical experience indicates that many children with Asperger's Disorder never display such characteristics. Among those who do, research indicates that these characteristics have disappeared by the age of 9 (Church, Alisanski, & Amanullah, 2000).

THE GILLBERG AND GILLBERG DIAGNOSTIC CRITERIA

The diagnostic criteria of choice for many clinicians, especially in Europe and Australia, are those of C. Gillberg and Gillberg (1989), which represent more accurately the original descriptions of Asperger and the profile of abilities of children referred for a diagnostic assessment for Asperger's Disorder (Table 9.2). According to the Gillbergs' criteria, the prevalence rate for Asperger's Disorder is between 36 and 48 per 10,000 children, or between 1 in 250 or 200 children (Ehlers & Gillberg, 1993; Kadesjo, Gillberg, & Hagberg, 1999).

GENDER ISSUES

Clinical experience suggests that girls with Asperger's Disorder may be more difficult to recognize and diagnose than boys, due to coping and camouflaging mechanisms that are rarely used by boys. One mechanism used by girls is learning how to act in a social setting, as described by Liane Holliday Willey (1999) in her autobiography, *Pretending to Be Normal*. The child appears able to engage in a reciprocal conversation and use appropriate affect and gestures during the inter-

Table 9.2

The Gillberg Diagnostic Criteria for Asperger's Disorder

1. *Social impairment (extreme egocentricity; at least two of the following):*
   - Difficulties interacting with peers
   - Indifference to peer contacts
   - Difficulties interpreting social cues
   - Socially and emotionally inappropriate behavior

2. *Narrow interest (at least one of the following):*
   - Exclusion of other activities
   - Repetitive adherence
   - More rote than meaning

3. *Compulsive need for introducing routines and interests (at least one of the following):*
   - Which affect the individual's every aspect of everyday life
   - Which affect others

4. *Speech and language peculiarities (at least three of the following):*
   - Delayed speech development
   - Superficially perfect expressive language
   - Formal pedantic language
   - Odd prosody, peculiar voice characteristics
   - Impairment of comprehension including misinterpretations of literal/implied meanings

5. *Nonverbal communication problems (at least one of the following):*
   - Limited use of gestures
   - Clumsy/gauche body language
   - Inappropriate facial expression or limited facial expression
   - Peculiar, stiff gaze

6. *Motor clumsiness*
   - Poor performance in neurodevelopmental test

action. However, further investigation and observation at school may determine that the child adopts a social role and script, basing her persona on the characteristics of someone who is socially skilled in the situation and using intellectual abilities rather than intuition to determine what to say or do.

Girls with Asperger's Disorder can develop the ability to disappear in a large group, deliberately being on the periphery of social interaction. Some girls use strategies to avoid active participation in class proceedings, such as being well-behaved and polite, thus being left alone by teachers and peers; some use tactics to passively avoid cooperation and social inclusion at school and at home. Girls with

312 PERSONALITY DISORDERS IN CHILDHOOD AND ADOLESCENCE

Asperger's Disorder are less likely to be "bitchy" or inconsistent in friendships in comparison to other girls. They are more likely than boys to develop a close friendship with someone who demonstrates a maternal attachment to this socially naive and immature, but "safe," girl. These characteristics reduce the likelihood of being identified as having one of the main diagnostic criteria for Asperger's Disorder, namely, a failure to develop peer relationships. With girls, it is not a failure but a qualitative difference in this ability.

COMPENSATORY AND ADJUSTMENT STRATEGIES TO BEING DIFFERENT

By definition, a child with Asperger's Disorder is different from other children. Based on my extensive clinical experience I have identified four compensatory or adjustment strategies used by these children. The strategy used by a particular child will depend on his or her personality, experiences, and circumstances. Those children who tend to internalize thoughts and feelings may develop signs of self-blame and depression, or alternatively use imagination and a fantasy life to create another world in which they are more successful. Those children who tend to externalize thoughts and feelings can either become arrogant and blame others for their difficulties, or view others not as the cause but as the solution to their problems and develop an ability to imitate other children or characters. Thus, some psychological reactions can be constructive, whereas others can lead to significant psychological problems.

A REACTIVE DEPRESSION

Social ability and friendship skills are highly valued by peers and adults, and not being successful in these areas can lead some children with Asperger's Disorder to internalize their thoughts and feelings and become overly apologetic, self-critical, and increasingly socially withdrawn. Children as young as 7 may develop a clinical depression as a result of insight into being different and perceiving themselves as socially defective. There can be changes in sleep patterns and appetite and a negative attitude that pervades all aspects of life. In extreme cases, children may talk of suicide and even make impulsive or planned suicide attempts.

ESCAPE INTO IMAGINATION

A more constructive internalization of thoughts and feelings of being socially defective can be to escape into imagination. Children with Asperger's Disorder can develop vivid and complex imaginary worlds, sometimes with make-believe friends. In their imaginary worlds with imaginary friends, these children are understood and successful socially and academically. Another advantage is that the responses of the imaginary friends are under the child's control and the friends are instantly available. Imaginary friends can prevent the child from feeling lonely. Having an imaginary friend is typical of the play of many young children and is not necessarily of clinical significance. However, the child with Asperger's Disorder may have only imaginary friends, and the intensity and duration of the imaginary interactions can be qualitatively unusual.

An interest in other cultures and worlds can explain the development of a special interest in geography, astronomy, and science fiction, such that the child discovers a place where his or her knowledge and abilities are recognized and valued. Sometimes the degree of imaginative thought can lead to an interest in fiction, both as a reader and an author. Some children with Asperger's Disorder, especially girls, can develop the ability to use imaginary friends, characters, and worlds to write quite remarkable fiction.

Under conditions of extreme stress or loneliness, their propensity to escape into an imaginary world and imaginary friends can lead to internal fantasies becoming their reality. They may be perceived as developing delusions and being out of touch with reality (Adamo, 2004). This could result in a referral for a diagnostic assessment for Schizophrenia.

DENIAL AND ARROGANCE

An alternative to internalizing negative thoughts and feelings is to externalize the cause of and solution to feeling different. In this case, the child may overcompensate for feeling defective in social situations by denying that there is any problem or may become arrogant and determine that the fault or problem is in other people. These children consider themselves to be above the rules that they find so difficult to understand. They may go into "God mode," believing that they are an omnipotent person who never makes a mistake and whose intelligence must be worshipped. Such children deny that they have any difficulties making friends or reading social situations or others' thoughts and intentions. They believe that they do not need any special programs or to be treated differently from other children. They vehemently do not want to be referred to a psychologist or psychiatrist and are convinced that they are not mad or stupid.

Nevertheless, these children do know, but will not publicly acknowledge, that they have limited social competence, and they are desperate to conceal any difficulties in order to not appear stupid. A lack of ability in social play with peers and in interactions with adults can result in the development of behaviors to achieve dominance and control in a social context; these include the use of intimidation and an arrogant and inflexible attitude. Other children and parents are likely to capitulate to avoid yet another confrontation. The child can become intoxicated by such power and dominance, which may lead to conduct problems.

Unfortunately, arrogance can further alienate the child from natural friendships, and refusal to enter programs to improve social understanding can increase the gap between the child's social abilities and that of his or her peers. We can understand why the child would develop these compensatory and adjustment strategies. But the long-term consequences of these compensatory mechanisms can have a significant effect on friendships and prospects for relationships and employment as an adult.

IMITATION

An intelligent and constructive compensatory mechanism used by some children is to observe and absorb the personae of those who are socially successful. Such children initially remain on the periphery of social play, watching and noting what to do. They may then reenact the activities they have observed in their own solitary play, using dolls, figures, or imaginary friends at home. They are rehearsing, practicing the script and their role, to achieve fluency and confidence before attempting to be included in real social situations. Some children can be remarkably astute in their observational abilities, copying gestures, tone of voice, and mannerisms. They are developing a natural ability to act.

Becoming an expert mimic can have other advantages. The child may become popular for imitating the voice and persona of a teacher or a character from television. The adolescent with Asperger's Disorder may apply knowledge acquired in drama classes to everyday situations, determining who would be successful in a given situation and adopting the persona of that person. The child or adult may remember the words and body postures of someone in a similar situation in real life or in a television program or film. He or she then reenacts the scene using borrowed dialogue and body language. There is a veneer of social success, but on closer examination the apparent social competence is not spontaneous or original but artificial and contrived. However, practice and success may improve the person's acting abilities such that acting becomes a possible career option.

There are also disadvantages to imitation. The child may choose to observe and imitate popular but notorious models, for example, the school bad guys. This group may accept the adolescent with Asperger's Disorder who wears the group's uniform, speaks their language, and knows their gestures and moral code; but this in turn may alienate the adolescent from more appropriate models. The group will probably recognize that the person is a fake, desperate to be accepted, who is probably not aware that he or she is being covertly ridiculed and set up. Another disadvantage is that some psychologists and psychiatrists may fail to recognize that imitation is a constructive adaptation to having Asperger's Disorder and may diagnose the person as having signs of Multiple Personality Disorder.

STRATEGIES FOR CHANGE

TEACHING FRIENDSHIP SKILLS

One of the essential characteristics of Asperger's Disorder is a qualitative impairment in social interaction, which can be further described as a lack of social or emotional reciprocity and failure to develop peer relationships appropriate to developmental level. To date we do not have standardized tests of social interaction and social reasoning for typical children that can be used to produce a "social quotient" for a child with Asperger's Disorder. The interpretation of aspects of social skills and social understanding such as reciprocity and peer relationships is currently a subjective clinical judgment. The clinician therefore needs to have considerable experience in the social development of typical children to act as a comparison for the child who is referred for a diagnostic assessment for Asperger's Disorder.

I have noted that the child with Asperger's Disorder usually has a concept of friendship that is immature and at least 2 years behind that of his or her age peers (Attwood, 2003; Botroff, Bartak, Langford, Page, & Tonge, 1995). The child with Asperger's Disorder typically has fewer friends and plays with other children less often and for a shorter duration in comparison to peers (Bauminger & Kasari, 2000; Bauminger & Shulman, 2003; Bauminger, Shulman, & Agam, 2003). This can also occur during adolescence. There are many advantages in having friends. The research evidence suggests that children without friends may be at risk for later difficulties and delay in social and emotional development, low self-esteem, and the development of anxiety and depression as an adult (Hay, Payne, & Chadwick, 2004). Having friends can be a preventive measure for mood disorders.

ACTIVELY ENCOURAGING FRIENDSHIPS

In typical children, the acquisition of friendship skills is based on an innate ability that develops throughout childhood in association with progressive changes in cognitive ability and is modified and matured through social experiences. Unfortunately, children with Asperger's Disorder are not able to rely on intuitive abilities in social settings and must rely on their cognitive abilities and experiences. Children and adults with Asperger's Disorder have difficulty in social situations that have not been rehearsed or prepared for. Thus, it is essential that such children receive tuition and guided practice in the ability to make and keep friends and that their friendship experiences are constructive and encouraging (Attwood, 2000).

Parents can try to facilitate social play at home with siblings and other children invited for a play date, but they will have difficulty providing the range of experiences and degree of supervision and tuition required for a child with Asperger's Disorder. The optimum environment to develop reciprocal play with peers is at school. Educational services will need to be aware of the importance of a social curriculum as well as an educational curriculum for a child with Asperger's Disorder. The social curriculum must have an emphasis on friendship skills and include appropriate staff training and relevant resources. The following suggestions are designed for implementation by teachers and parents for each of the developmental stages of friendship that occur in typical children that can be applied to children with Asperger's Disorder.

SOCIAL STORIES™

A successful strategy to learn the relevant social cues, thoughts, feelings, and social behavior script is to write Social Stories™, which were originally developed by Carol Gray (1998), a teacher specializing in children with Asperger's Disorder. Preparing Social Stories™ also enables other people (adults and peers) to understand the perspective of the child with Asperger's Disorder and why his or her social behavior can appear confused, anxious, aggressive, or disobedient. Gray (2004) has recently revised the criteria and guidelines for writing a Social Story™; the following is a brief summary of the guidelines.

A Social Story™ describes a situation, skill, or concept in terms of relevant social cues, perspectives, and common responses in a specifically defined style and format. The intention is to share accurate social and emotional information in a reassuring and informative manner that is easily understood by the child (or adult) with Asperger's Disorder. The first Social Story™, and at least 50% of subsequent Social Stories™, should describe, affirm, and consolidate existing abilities and knowledge and what the child does well; this way, the child will not associate the Social Story™ only with ignorance or failure. Social Stories™ can also record achievements in using new knowledge and strategies. It is important that Social Stories™ are viewed as a means of recording social knowledge and social success.

Gray's (1998, 2004) original work on Social Stories™ has now been examined by several independent research studies and found to be remarkably effective in improving social understanding and social behavior in children with autism and Asperger's Disorder (Hagiwara & Myles, 1999; Ivey, Heflin, & Alberto, 2004; Lorimer, 2002; Norris & Dattilo, 1999; Rogers & Myles, 2001; Rowe, 1999; Santosi, Powell Smith, & Kincaid, 2004; Scattone, Wilczynski, Edwards, & Rabian, 2002; Smith, 2001; Swaggart et al., 1995; Thiemann & Goldstein, 2001).

IMPROVE THEORY OF MIND ABILITIES

The psychological term "theory of mind" (ToM) refers to the ability to recognize and understand the thoughts, beliefs, desires, and intentions of other people in order to make sense of their behavior and predict what they are going to do next. It has also been described as mind reading, and a deficiency in this ability has been described as mind blindness (Baron-Cohen, 1995) or, colloquially, a difficulty in putting oneself in another person's shoes. A synonymous term is "empathy" (Gillberg, 2002). The child or adolescent with Asperger's Disorder does not recognize or understand the cues that indicate the thoughts or feelings of the other person at a level expected for someone of that age.

Several studies have examined whether ToM abilities can be improved using training programs specifically designed to improve social cognition. The programs have used social skills training with a group format (Ozonoff & Miller, 1995), simple computer programs (Swettenham, Baron-Cohen, Gomez, & Walsh, 1996), and a teaching manual and workbook (Hadwin, Baron-Cohen, Howlin, & Hill, 1996). Pre- and posttreatment assessment using the standard measures of ToM abilities has confirmed that the programs improve the ability to pass ToM tasks. However, these studies have not found a generalization effect to tasks not included in the training program.

Comic Strip Conversations

Comic strip conversations can be used to improve ToM abilities using simple drawings such as stick figures, thought and speech bubbles, and text in different colors to illustrate the sequence of actions, emotions, and thoughts in a specific social situation (Gray, 1994). Children are familiar with thought bubbles from reading comics and cartoons. We know that children as young as 3 to 4 years understand that thought bubbles represent what someone is thinking (Wellman, Hollander, & Schult, 1996). Recent studies examining whether thought bubbles can be used to acquire ToM abilities in children with autism found some success with this method (Kerr & Durkin, 2004; Rajendran & Mitchelle, 2000; Wellman et al., 2002).

Using comic strip conversations, the child recreates a recent social exchange by drawing the scene. In the process, the child has a visual "conversation" with the adult (a therapist or teacher) about what the characters are thinking or feeling, or said, did, or could do. Color can be used to identify the emotional tone or motivation, and a color chart can be used to associate a specific color or depth of color with a specific emotion. For example, the child may use a red crayon to indicate that the words spoken by the other child were in an angry tone of voice. This provides an opportunity to learn the child's perception of the event and to correct any misinterpretations. One of the advantages of this approach is that the child and adult are not looking at each other; their joint focus is on the evolving drawing in front of them. I make regular use of comic strip conversations in my clinical treatment of mood disorders in children with Asperger's Disorder. Such children often communicate their thoughts and feelings more eloquently using drawings rather than speech.

Computer Programs

A remarkable encyclopedia of emotions entitled *Mind Reading: The Interactive Guide to Emotions* Baron-Cohen (2004) is now available on DVD. Simon Baron-Cohen and colleagues (2004) at the University of Cambridge identified 412 human emotions (excluding synonyms). They examined the age at which children understand the meaning of each emotion and developed a taxonomy that assigned all the distinct emotions to one of 24 groups. A multimedia company then developed interactive software for children and adults to learn what someone may be thinking or feeling. On the DVD, actors demonstrate facial expressions, body language, and speech qualities associated with a specific emotion. The DVD also includes audio recordings that illustrate aspects of prosody and stories that illustrate the circumstances and contexts for each emotion. There is an emotions library, a learning center, and a games zone.

Emotion Management

We recognize an association between Asperger's Disorder and the development of an additional or secondary mood disorder, especially depression, or an anxiety disorder. Studies suggest that around 65% of adolescents with Asperger's Disorder have a mood disorder. The most common disorder is an anxiety disorder (Ghaziuddin et al., 1998; Gillot, Furniss, & Walter, 2001; J. Green, Gilchrist, Burton, &

Cox, 2000; Kim, Szatmari, Bryson, Streiner, & Wilson, 2000; Konstantareas, 2005; Russell & Sofronoff, 2004; Tantam, 2000; Tonge, Brereton, Gray, & Einfeld, 1999). The rate of comorbid depression is also high (Clarke, Baxter, Perry, & Prasher, 1999; Gillot et al., 2001; J. Green et al., 2000; Kim et al., 2000; Konstantareas, 2005). Research has indicated a greater probability than in the general population among individuals with Asperger's Disorder of developing Bipolar Disorder (DeLong & Dwyer, 1988; Frazier, Doyle, Chiu, & Coyle, 2002), and there is research evidence to suggest an association with Delusional Disorder (Kurita, 1999), paranoia (Blackshaw, Kinderman, Hare, & Hatton, 2001), and Conduct Disorder (J. Green et al., 2000; Tantam, 2000).

Studies conducted on the family histories of children with Asperger's Disorder and autism have identified a higher than expected incidence of mood disorders in family members (Bolton, Pickles, Murphy, & Rutter, 1998; DeLong, 1994; Ghaziuddin & Greden, 1998; Lainhart & Folstein, 1994; Micali, Chakrabarti, & Fombonne, 2004; Piven & Palmer, 1999). A child with Asperger's Disorder could have a genetic predisposition to strong emotions. This would be one of several factors that explain problems with the intensity and management of emotions that are characteristic of this disorder.

When one considers the inevitable difficulties these children and adolescents have with regard to social reasoning, empathy, conversation skills, a different learning style, and heightened sensory perception, they are clearly prone to considerable stress, anxiety, frustration, and emotional exhaustion. They are also prone to being rejected by peers and frequently being teased and bullied, which can lead to low self-esteem and feelings of depression. During adolescence, they may become increasingly aware of their lack of social success and have greater insight into being different from other people—another factor in the development of a reactive depression. There may be genetic and environmental factors that explain the higher incidence of mood disorders.

Studies of executive function and Asperger's Disorder suggest characteristics of being disinhibited and impulsive, with a relative lack of insight that affects general functioning (Eisenmajer et al., 1996; Nyden, Gillberg, Hjelmquist, & Heiman, 1999; Ozonoff, South, & Miller, 2000; Pennington & Ozonoff, 1996). Impaired executive function can also affect the cognitive control of emotions. Parents and teachers often report that these children have a tendency to react to emotional situations without thinking. An impulsive retaliation can cause the child with Asperger's Disorder to be diagnosed as having Conduct Disorder or a problem with anger management.

Research using neuroimaging technology has also identified structural and functional abnormalities of the amygdala, a part of the limbic system associated with the recognition and regulation of emotions (Adolphs, Sears, & Piven, 2001; Baron Cohen et al., 1999; Critchley et al., 2000; Fine, Lumsden, & Blair, 2001), including anger, anxiety, and sadness. Thus we also have neuroimaging evidence that suggests there will be problems with the perception and regulation of emotions.

COGNITIVE-BEHAVIOR THERAPY

When a secondary mood disorder is diagnosed in a child with Asperger's Disorder, the clinical psychologist or psychiatrist needs to know how to modify psychological treatments for mood disorders to accommodate the unusual cognitive profile of people with Asperger's Disorder. The primary psychological treatment for mood disorders is cognitive-behavior therapy (CBT), which focuses on the maturity, complexity, subtlety, and vocabulary of emotions, and dysfunctional or illogical thinking and incorrect assumptions. Thus, it has direct applicability to children and adolescents with Asperger's Disorder who have impaired or delayed ToM abilities and difficulty understanding, expressing, and managing emotions. We now have published case studies and objective scientific evidence that CBT does significantly reduce mood disorders in children and adolescents with Asperger's

Disorder (Bauminger, 2002; Fitzpatrick, 2004; Hare, 1997; Reaven & Hepburn, 2003; Sofronoff, Attwood, & Hinton, 2005).

Cognitive-behavior therapy proceeds in several stages, the first being an assessment of the nature and degree of the mood disorder using self-report scales and a clinical interview. The next stage is affective education to improve the child's understanding of emotions. Discussion and activities examine the connections among thoughts, emotions, and behavior and identify the way the child conceptualizes emotions and perceives various situations. The more the child understands emotions, the more he or she is able to express and control them appropriately. The third stage of CBT is cognitive restructuring to correct distorted conceptualizations and dysfunctional beliefs and to constructively manage emotions. The last stage is a schedule of activities to practice new cognitive skills to manage emotions in real-life situations.

AFFECTIVE EDUCATION

In the affective education stage of CBT the child learns about the advantages and disadvantages of emotions and how to identify different levels of expression in words and actions. For children, this can be undertaken as a science project. A basic principle is to explore one emotion at a time, starting with a positive emotion before moving on to an emotion of clinical concern. Another important aspect of affective education in CBT is to enable the child to discover the salient cues that indicate a particular level of emotion in terms of his or her body sensations, behavior, and thoughts. These sensations can act as early warning signs of an impending escalation of emotion. In part, affective education aims to improve the function of the amygdala in informing the frontal lobes of the brain about increasing stress levels and emotional arousal.

During CBT for emotion management it is important to ensure that the child and the therapist agree on the definitions of words and gestures. Any semantic confusion should be clarified. My clinical experience has indicated that some children and adolescents with Asperger's Disorder tend to use extreme statements when agitated. Affective education increases the person's vocabulary of emotional expression to ensure precision and accuracy in verbal expression, thereby avoiding extreme expressions. There is a new affective education resource kit specifically designed for children and adolescents with Asperger's Disorder, the CAT-kit (Callesen, Moller-Nielsen, & Attwood, 2005). Further information is available at www.cat-kit.com.

COGNITIVE RESTRUCTURING

Children with Asperger's Disorder sometimes make false assumptions about their circumstances and the intentions of others due to impaired or delayed ToM abilities. They also have a tendency to make literal interpretations, and a casual comment may be taken out of context or to the extreme. The cognitive restructuring component of CBT enables these children to correct the thinking that creates emotions such as anxiety and anger or feelings of low self-esteem. The therapist helps the children change their thoughts, emotions, and behavior using reasoning and logic. Cognitive-behavior therapy also encourages children to be more confident and optimistic.

AN EMOTION REPAIR TOOLBOX

Another aspect of cognitive restructuring is increasing the range of constructive responses to a particular situation. Unfortunately, children and adolescents with Asperger's Disorder usually have a limited range of responses to situations that elicit anxiety or anger. I recently developed the concept of an emotion repair toolbox, which has proved to be a successful strategy for cognitive restructuring in the treatment of anxiety and anger in children with Asperger's Disorder (Sofronoff et al., 2005). The idea is to identify different types of tools to fix the problems associated with negative emotions, especially anxiety, anger, and sadness. The range of tools can be divided into those that quickly and constructively release or slowly reduce emotional energy, and those that improve thinking. The therapist works with the child and the family to identify different tools that help fix the feeling, as well as some tools that can make the emotions or consequences worse. During a brainstorming session they draw a toolbox and depict and write descriptions of different types of tools and activities that can encourage constructive emotion repair.

PRACTICING COGNITIVE-BEHAVIORAL STRATEGIES

Once the child or adolescent with Asperger's Disorder has improved his or her intellectual understanding of emotions and identified strategies (or tools) to manage emotions, the next stage of CBT is to start practicing the strategies in a graduated sequence of assignments. The therapist can model and the child can practice appropriate thinking and actions in role-play activities in which the therapist or child vocalizes his or her thoughts to monitor cognitive processes. A form of graduated practice is used, starting with situations associated with a relatively mild level of distress or agitation. A list of situations that precipitate specific emotions is created, each situation written on a small card. The child uses a graphic thermometer or measuring instrument to determine the hierarchy or rank order of situations. The most distressing are placed at the upper level of the thermometer. As the therapy progresses, the child works through the hierarchy to manage more intense emotions.

PSYCHOTHERAPY

Traditional psychoanalytical psychotherapy has very little to offer a child or adolescent with Asperger's Disorder (Jacobsen, 2003, 2004). Although there are published case studies that have used traditional and modified psychoanalytical psychotherapy (Adamo, 2004; Alvarez & Reid, 1999; Pozzi, 2003; Rhode & Klauber, 2004; Youell, 1999), the detailed psychoanalysis of the mother and infant relationship in these case studies may be irrelevant to understanding the mind of a child with Asperger's Disorder, and may lead to the mother developing considerable guilt and the child being very confused. Asperger's Disorder is not caused by the inability of a child's mother to love and relate to her son or daughter.

The methods of analysis used in traditional psychoanalytical therapy are based on a conceptualization of the development of typical children, but children with Asperger's Disorder perceive and experience a very different world from their peers. In psychoanalytical therapies, the pretend play of the child is analyzed to explore his or her inner thoughts. The imaginative play of children with Asperger's Disorder is often an accurate reenactment of a scene from a favorite story and is not necessarily a metaphor for their life. When using projective testing, the child with Asperger's Disorder is more likely to provide factual information than projections of the self. The child is simply describing what he or she sees.

Children and adolescents with Asperger's Disorder can benefit from psychotherapy, but the therapy must be based on a comprehensive understanding of the nature of Asperger's Disorder, especially the ability of the child to understand and express thoughts and feelings and the concept of self in terms of self-image, self-esteem, and self-acceptance, based on the typical life experiences of a child with Asperger's Disorder. This will require the psychotherapist to know the latest cognitive psychology research on Asperger's Disorder, particularly the studies on ToM and executive function; to have read the life experiences described in the autobiographies; and to be prepared to make appropriate modifications to conventional psychotherapies.

The theory of personal constructs, originally developed by George Kelly in the 1950s, has a logical theoretical framework and is a practical approach to psychotherapy that is well suited to the mindset of people with Asperger's Disorder (Hare, Jones, & Paine, 1999). Personal construct psychology (PCP) is based on the principle that people develop their own unique models of reality (Fransella, 2005). This approach is especially applicable to adolescents with Asperger's Disorder. The repertory grid technique of PCP uses a measuring system and mathematical formula that provides a visual representation of self-characterization and the way the person construes his or her world and relates to others. It also provides directions for change in self-understanding and personal qualities.

I have noted that adolescents with Asperger's Disorder tend to have immature constructs and that some constructs are common. For example, these adolescents typically place a high value on intellectual ability. Thus, being called stupid is a particularly hurtful insult as the adolescent with Asperger's Disorder clearly admires people with high intellect. Intellectual arrogance can also develop as part of the personality profile of children and adolescents with Asperger's Disorder. This discovery has been valuable. Telling a typical child that something he or she did made someone delighted or proud is an effective reward or motivator. That altruistic desire to please people can be less of a motivation for children with Asperger's Disorder. I usually prefer to appeal to the intellectual vanity of such children and commend them for their intelligence, how smart they are, rather than commenting on how pleased I am.

IMPEDIMENTS TO TREATMENT

The development of rapport between client and therapist is essential. Children and adolescents with Asperger's Disorder sometimes instantly, and permanently, like or dislike other people, especially professionals. Identifying a psychotherapist who is likely to be accepted requires careful consideration. The psychotherapist will need an understanding of the language profile associated with Asperger's Disorder, including difficulties with the pragmatic aspects of language, especially conversational turn-taking and knowing when and how to interrupt, and the tendency to make literal interpretations and be pedantic. The child or adolescent with Asperger's Disorder will require more time to cognitively process explanations and will benefit from a clear, structured, and systematic approach with shorter but more frequent therapy sessions. It will also help to have the main points from each session typed and made available to the child and his or her parents and to review those points at the start of the subsequent session. The psychotherapist will need to explain the nature and boundaries of a therapeutic relationship and reinforce that he or she is helping in a professional capacity, not as a personal friend (Hare & Paine, 1997).

EVALUATING OUTCOMES

Standard assessment measures can be used to evaluate outcomes with regard to the treatment of a secondary mood disorder, but we do not currently have instruments to accurately measure the profile of abilities associated with Asperger's Disorder to determine whether programs to improve maturity in friendship skills, ToM abilities, or self-understanding and self-esteem are successful. Over the next decade, I suspect that we will design and evaluate appropriate instrumentation, but at present we can only use subjective judgments of improved well-being and quality of life.

CONCLUSIONS

Asperger's Disorder is a relatively recently defined disorder of children and adults, and we clearly need research on further defining the nature of the differences between such children and their typical peers. The current diagnostic criteria are very much a work in progress and need to be revised to be consistent with research studies and clinical experience. We also need to encourage clinicians to specialize in Asperger's Disorder so that they can modify existing therapies to accommodate the unusual profile of abilities and developmental history of these children, and possibly develop completely new strategies and effective therapies based on careful observation of and discussion with the children.

One way of conceptualizing Asperger's Disorder is to consider it a description of someone who perceives and thinks about the world differently from other people. When explaining the disorder to children, I say that the child's brain is wired differently but not necessarily defectively. The child's profile of abilities can include conspicuous abilities in areas such as science, problem solving, and imagination. An area to consider in the future is how to actively encourage the talents of children with Asperger's Disorder for the benefit of the child and society.

Further work needs to be done to examine the relationship and correspondence between Asperger's syndrome and the Cluster A disorders in children.

REFERENCES

Adamo, S. (2004). An adolescent and his imaginary companions: From quasi-delusional constructs to creative imagination. *Journal of Child Psychotherapy, 30,* 275–295.

Adolphs, R., Sears, L., & Piven, J. (2001). Abnormal processing of social information from faces in autism. *Journal of Cognitive Neuroscience, 13,* 232, 196–240.

Alvarez, A., & Reid, S. (Eds.). (1999). *Autism and personality: Findings from the Tavistock Autism Workshop.* London: Routledge.

American Psychiatric Association. (1994). *Diagnostic and statistical manual of mental disorders* (4th ed.). Washington, DC: Author.

American Psychiatric Association. (2000). *Diagnostic and statistical manual of mental disorders* (4th ed., text rev.). Washington, DC: Author.

Asperger, H. (1952). *Heilpadagogik: Einfuhrung in die Psychopathologie des Kindes fur Arzte, Leher, Psychologen und Fursorgerinnen.* Wien, Austria: Springer.

Asperger, H. (1979). Problems of infantile autism. *Communication: Journal of the National Autistic Society, London, 13,* 45–52.

Asperger, H. (1991). Autistic psychopathy in childhood. In U. Frith (Ed. & Trans.), *Autism and Asperger's syndrome* (pp. 37–92). Cambridge, England: Cambridge University Press. (Original work published 1944)

Attwood, T. (1998). *Asperger's syndrome: A guide for parents and professionals.* London: Jessica Kingsley.

Attwood, T. (2000). Strategies for improving the social integration of children with Asperger syndrome. *Autism, 4,* 85–100.

Attwood, T. (2003). Frameworks for behavioral interventions. *Child and Adolescent Psychiatric Clinics, 12,* 65–86.

Baron-Cohen, S. (1995). *Mind blindness: An essay on autism and theory of mind.* Cambridge, MA: MIT Press.

Baron-Cohen, S. (2004) *Mind Reading: The interactive guide to emotions* [DVD]. London: Jessica Kingsley.

Baron-Cohen, S., Ring, H. A., Wheelwright, S., Bullmore, E. T., Brammer, M. J., Simmons, A., et al. (1999). Social intelligence in the normal autistic brain: An fMRI study. *European Journal of Neuroscience, 11,* 1891–1898.

Bauminger, N. (2002). The facilitation of social-emotional understanding and social interaction in high functioning children with autism: Intervention outcomes. *Journal of Autism and Developmental Disorders, 32,* 283–297.

Bauminger, N., & Kasari, C. (2000). Loneliness and friendship in high functioning children with autism. *Child Development, 71,* 447–456.

Bauminger, N., & Shulman, C. (2003). The development and maintenance of friendship in high-functioning children with autism. *Autism, 7,* 81–97.

Bauminger, N., Shulman, C., & Agam, G. (2003). Peer interaction and loneliness in high-functioning children with autism. *Journal of Autism and Developmental Disorders, 33,* 489–506.

Beck, A. T., Freeman, A., Davis, D. D., Pretzer, J., Fleming, B., & Beck, J. (2004). *Cognitive therapy of personality disorders* (2nd ed.). New York: Guilford Press.

Blackshaw, A. J., Kinderman, P., Hare, D. J., & Hatton, C. (2001). Theory of mind, causal attribution and paranoia in Asperger syndrome. *Autism, 5,* 147–163.

Bolton, P., Pickles, A., Murphy, M., & Rutter, M. (1998). Autism, affective and other psychiatric disorders: Patterns of familial aggregation. *Psychological Medicine, 28,* 385–395.

Botroff, V., Bartak, L., Langford, P., Page, M., & Tonge, B. (1995, February). *Social cognitive skills and implications for social skills training in adolescents with autism.* Paper presented at the Australian Autism Conference, Flinders University, Adelaide, Australia.

Callesen, K., Moller-Nielsen, A., & Attwood, T. (2005). *The CAT-kit: Cognitive Affective Training.* Jystrup, Denmark. Available for order from www.cat-kit.com.

Campbell, J. (2005). Diagnostic assessment of Asperger's disorder: A review of five third-party rating scales. *Journal of Autism and Developmental Disorders, 35,* 25–35.

Church, C., Alisanski, S., & Amanullah, S. (2000). The social, behavioral and academic experiences of children with Asperger disorder. *Focus on Autism and Other Developmental Disabilities, 15,* 12–20.

Clarke, D., Baxter, M., Perry, D., & Prasher, V. (1999). Affective and psychotic disorders in adults with autism: Seven case reports. *Autism, 3,* 149–164.

Critchley, H. D., Daly, E. M., Bullmore, E. T., Williams, S. C. R., Van Amelsvoort, T., Robertson, D. M., et al. (2000). The functional neuroanatomy of social behavior. *Brain, 123,* 2203–2212.

DeLong, G. (1994). Children with autistic spectrum disorder and a family history of affective disorder. *Developmental Medicine and Child Neurology, 36,* 647–688.

DeLong, G., & Dwyer, J. (1988). Correlation of family history with specific autistic subgroups: Asperger's syndrome and bipolar affective disease. *Journal of Autism and Developmental Disorders, 18,* 593–600.

Dissanayake, C. (2004). Change in behavioral symptoms in children with high functioning autism and Asperger syndrome: Evidence for one disorder? *Australian Journal of Early Childhood, 29,* 48–57.

Ehlers, S., & Gillberg, C. (1993). The epidemiology of Asperger's syndrome: A total population study. *Journal of Child Psychology and Psychiatry, 34,* 1327–1350.

Ehlers, S., Gillberg, C., & Wing, L. (1999). A screening questionnaire for Asperger syndrome and other high-functioning autism spectrum disorders in school age children. *Journal of Autism and Developmental Disorders, 29,* 129–141.

Eisenmajer, R., Prior, M., Leekham, S., Wing, L., Gould, J., Welham, M., et al. (1996). Comparison of clinical symptoms in autism and Asperger's disorder. *Journal of the American Academy of Child and Adolescent Psychiatry, 35,* 1523–1531.

Fein, D., Dixon, P., Paul, J., & Levin, H. (2005). Brief report: Pervasive developmental disorder can evolve into ADHD—Case illustrations. *Journal of Autism and Developmental Disorders, 35,* 525–534.

Fine, C., Lumsden, J., & Blair, R. J. R. (2001). Dissociation between theory of mind and executive functions in a patient with early left amygdala damage. *Brain Journal of Neurology, 124,* 287–298.

Fitzpatrick, E. (2004). The use of cognitive behavioral strategies in the management of anger in a child with an autistic disorder: An evaluation. *Good Autism Practice, 5,* 3–17.

Fransella, F. (Ed.). (2005). *The essential practitioner's handbook of personal construct psychology.* Chichester, West Sussex, England: Wiley.

Frazier, J., Doyle, R., Chiu, S., & Coyle, J. (2002). Treating a child with Asperger's disorder and comorbid bipolar disorder. *American Journal of Psychiatry, 159,* 13–21.

Garnett, M., & Attwood, T. (1998). The Australian Scale for Asperger's Syndrome. In T. Attwood (Ed.), *Asperger's syndrome: A guide for parents and professionals* (pp. 16–19). London: Jessica Kingsley.

Ghaziuddin, M., & Greden, J. (1998). Depression in children with autism/pervasive developmental disorders: A case-control family history study. *Journal of Autism and Developmental Disorders, 28,* 111–115.

Ghaziuddin, M., Wieder-Mikhail, W., & Ghaziuddin, N. (1998). Comorbidity of Asperger syndrome: A preliminary report. *Journal of Intellectual Disability Research, 42,* 279–283.

Gillberg, C. (1998). Asperger syndrome and high functioning autism. *British Journal of Psychiatry, 171,* 200–209.

Gillberg, C. (2002). *A guide to Asperger syndrome.* Cambridge, England: Cambridge University Press.

Gillberg, C., & Billstedt, E. (2000). Autism and Asperger syndrome: Coexistence with other clinical disorders. *Acta Psychiatrica Scandinavica, 102,* 321–330.

Gillberg, C., & Gillberg, I. C. (1989). Asperger syndrome: Some epidemiological considerations—A research note. *Journal of Child Psychology and Psychiatry, 30,* 631–638.

Gillberg, C., Gillberg, I. C., Rastam, M., & Wentz, E. (2001). The Asperger Syndrome (and High-Functioning Autism) Diagnostic Interview (ASDI): A preliminary study of a new structured clinical interview. *Autism, 5,* 57–66.

Gillberg, C., & Rastam, M. (1992). Do some cases of anorexia nervosa reflect underlying autistic like conditions? *Behavioral Neurology, 5,* 27–32.

Gillberg, I. C., Gillberg, C., Rastam, M., & Johansson, M. (1996). The cognitive profile of anorexia nervosa: A comparative study including a community based sample. *Comprehensive Psychiatry, 37,* 23–30.

Gilliam, J. (2002). *GADS examiner's manual.* Austin, TX: ProEd.

Gillot, A., Furniss, F., & Walter, A. (2001). Anxiety in high-functioning children with autism. *Autism, 5,* 277–286.

Gray, C. (1994). *Comic strip conversations.* Arlington, TX: Future Education.

Gray, C. (1998). Social Stories and comic strip conversations with students with Asperger syndrome and high-functioning autism. In E. Schopler, G. Mesibov, & L. J. Kunce (Eds.), *Asperger's syndrome or high-functioning autism?* (pp. 167–198). New York: Plenum Press.

Gray, C. (2004). Social Stories 10.0. *Jenison Autism Journal, 15,* 2–21.

Green, D., Baird, G., Barnett, A., Henderson, L., Huber, J., & Henderson, S. (2002). The severity and nature of motor impairment in Asperger's syndrome: A comparison with specific developmental disorder of motor function. *Journal of Child Psychology and Psychiatry, 43,* 655–668.

Green, J., Gilchrist, A., Burton, D., & Cox, A. (2000). Social and psychiatric functioning in adolescents with Asperger syndrome compared with conduct disorder. *Journal of Autism and Developmental Disorders, 30,* 279–293.

Hadwin, J., Baron-Cohen, S., Howlin, P., & Hill, K. (1996). Can we teach children with autism to understand emotions, belief, or pretence? *Development and Psychopathology, 8,* 345–365.

Hagiwara, T., & Myles, B. S. (1999). A multimedia social story intervention: Teaching skills to children with autism. *Focus on Autism and Other Developmental Disabilities, 14,* 82–95.

Hare, D. J. (1997). The use of cognitive-behavioral therapy with people with Asperger syndrome: A case study. *Autism, 1,* 215–225.

Hare, D. J., Jones, J., & Paine, C. (1999). Approaching reality: The use of personal construct assessment in working with people with Asperger syndrome. *Autism, 3,* 165–176.

Hare, D. J., & Paine, C. (1997). Developing cognitive behavioral treatments for people with Asperger's syndrome. *Clinical Psychology Forum, 110,* 5–8.

Hay, D., Payne, A., & Chadwick, A. (2004). Peer relations in childhood. *Journal of Child Psychology and Psychiatry, 45,* 84–108.

Hippler, K., & Klicpera, C. (2004). A retrospective analysis of the clinical case records of "autistic psychopaths" diagnosed by Hans Asperger and his team at the University Children's Hospital, Vienna. In U. Frith & E. Hill (Eds.), *Autism: Mind and brain* (pp. 21–42). Oxford: Oxford University Press.

Howlin, P. (2000). Assessment instruments for Asperger syndrome. *Child Psychology and Psychiatry Review, 5,* 120–129.

Ivey, M., Heflin, L., & Alberto, P. (2004). The use of Social Stories to promote independent behaviors in novel events for children with PDD-NOS. *Focus on Autism and Other Developmental Disabilities, 19,* 164–176.

Jacobsen, P. (2003). *Asperger syndrome and psychotherapy: Understanding Asperger perspectives.* London: Jessica Kingsley.

Jacobsen, P. (2004). A brief overview of the principles of psychotherapy with Asperger's syndrome. *Clinical Child Psychology and Psychiatry, 9,* 567–578.

Kadesjo, B., Gillberg, C., & Hagberg, B. (1999). Autism and Asperger syndrome in 7-year-old children: A total population study. *Journal of Autism and Developmental Disorders, 29,* 327–331.

Kerr, S., & Durkin, K. (2004). Understanding of thought bubbles as mental representations in children with autism: Implications for theory of mind. *Journal of Autism and Developmental Disorders, 34,* 637–647.

Kim, J. A., Szatmari, P., Bryson, S. E., Streiner, D. L., & Wilson, F. (2000). The prevalence of anxiety and mood problems among children with autism and Asperger syndrome. *Autism, 4,* 117–132.

Klin, A., Sparrow, S., Marans, W., Carter, A., & Volkmar, F. (2000). Assessment issues in children and adolescents with Asperger syndrome. In A. Klin, F. Volkmar, & S. Sparrow (Eds.), *Asperger syndrome* (pp. 309–339). New York: Guilford Press.

Klin, A., & Volkmar, F. (1997). Asperger's syndrome. In D. J. Cohen & F. Volkmar (Eds.), *Handbook of autism and pervasive developmental disorders* (pp. 94–122). New York: Guilford Press.

Konstantareas, M. (2005). Anxiety and depression in children and adolescents with Asperger syndrome. In K. Stoddart (Ed.), *Children, youth, and adults with Asperger syndrome: Integrating multiple perspectives* (pp. 47–59). London: Jessica Kingsley.

Krug, D., & Arick, J. (2002). *Krug Asperger's Disorder Index.* Austin, TX: ProEd.

Kurita, H. (1999). Brief report: Delusional disorder in a male adolescent with high-functioning PDDNOS. *Journal of Autism and Developmental Disorders, 29,* 419–423.

Lainhart, J., & Folstein, S. (1994). Affective disorders in people with autism: A review of published cases. *Journal of Autism and Developmental Disorders, 24,* 587–601.

Lord, C., Risi, S., Lambrecht, L., Cook, E., Leventhal, B., DiLavore, P., et al. (2000). The Autism Diagnostic Observation Schedule—Generic: A standard measure of social and communication deficits associated with the spectrum of autism. *Journal of Autism and Developmental Disorders, 30,* 205–223.

Lord, C., Rutter, M., & Le Couteur, A. (1994). Autism Diagnostic Interview-Revised: A revised version of a diagnostic interview for caregivers of individuals with possible pervasive developmental disorders. *Journal of Autism and Developmental Disorders, 24,* 659–685.

Lorimer, P. A. (2002). The use of Social Stories as a preventative behavioral intervention in a home setting with a child with autism. *Journal of Positive Behavior Interventions, 4,* 53–60.

Micali, N., Chakrabarti, S., & Fombonne, E. (2004). The broad autism phenotype: Findings from an epidemiological survey. *Autism, 8,* 21–37.

Millon, T., & Everly, G. S. (1985). *Personality and its disorders: A biosocial learning approach.* New York: Wiley.

Myles, B. S., Bock, S. J., & Simpson, R. L. (2001). *Asperger Syndrome Diagnostic Scale examiner's manual.* Austin, TX: ProEd.

Norris, C., & Dattilo, J. (1999). Evaluating effects of a social story intervention on a young girl with autism. *Focus on Autism and Other Developmental Disabilities, 14,* 180–186.

Nyden, A., Gillberg, C., Hjelmquist, E., & Heiman, M. (1999). Executive function/attention deficits in boys with Asperger syndrome, attention disorder and reading/writing disorder. *Autism, 3,* 213–228.

Ozonoff, S., & Miller, J. (1995). Teaching theory of mind: A new approach to social skills training for individuals with autism. *Journal of Autism and Developmental Disorders, 25,* 415–433.

Ozonoff, S., South, M., & Miller, J. (2000). DSM-IV-TR defined Asperger syndrome: Cognitive, behavioral and early history differentiation from high-functioning autism. *Autism, 4,* 29–46.

Pennington, B. F., & Ozonoff, S. (1996). Executive functions and developmental psychopathology. *Journal of Child Psychology and Psychiatry Annual Research Review, 37,* 51–87.

Perry, R. (1998). Misdiagnosed ADD/ADHD: Re-diagnosed PDD. *Journal of the American Academy of Child and Adolescent Psychiatry, 37,* 113–114.

Piven, J., & Palmer, P. (1999). Psychological disorder and the broad autism phenotype: Evidence from a family study of multiple-incidence autism families. *American Journal of Psychiatry, 156,* 557–563.

Pozzi, M. (2003). The use of observation in the psychoanalytic treatment of a 12-year-old boy with Asperger's syndrome. *International Journal of Psychoanalysis, 84,* 1333–1349.

Rajendran, G., & Mitchelle, P. (2000). Computer mediated interaction in Asperger's syndrome: The bubble dialogue program. *Computers and Education, 35,* 189–207.

Rastam, M., Gillberg, C., & Wentz, E. (2003). Outcome of teenage onset anorexia nervosa in a Swedish community based sample. *European Journal of Child and Adolescent Psychiatry, 12*(Suppl. 1), 178–190.

Reaven, J., & Hepburn, S. (2003). Cognitive-behavioral treatment of obsessive-compulsive disorder in a child with Asperger syndrome. *Autism, 7,* 145–164.

Rhode, M., & Klauber, T. (2004). *The many faces of Asperger's syndrome.* London: Karnac Books.

Rogers, M. F., & Myles, B. S. (2001). Using Social Stories and comic strip conversations to interpret social situations for an adolescent with Asperger's syndrome. *Intervention in School and Clinic, 38,* 310–313.

Rowe, C. (1999). Do Social Stories benefit children with autism in mainstream primary school? *British Journal of Special Education, 26,* 12–14.

Russell, E., & Sofronoff, K. (2004). Anxiety and social worries in children with Asperger syndrome. *Australian and New Zealand Journal of Psychiatry, 39,* 633–638.

Santosi, F., Powell Smith, K., & Kincaid, D. (2004). A research synthesis of social story interventions for children with autism spectrum disorders. *Focus on Autism and Other Developmental Disabilities, 19,* 194–204.

Scattone, D., Wilczynski, S. M., Edwards, R. P., & Rabian, B. (2002). Decreasing disruptive behaviors of children with autism using social stories. *Journal of Autism and Developmental Disorders, 32,* 535–543.

Scott, F. J., Baron-Cohen, S., Bolton, P., & Brayne, C. (2002). The CAST (Childhood Asperger Syndrome Test): Preliminary development of a UK screen for mainstream primary-school-age children. *Autism, 6,* 9–31.

Smith, C. (2001). Using social stories with children with autistic spectrum disorders: An evaluation. *Good Autism Practice, 2,* 16–23.

Smyrnios, S. (2002). *Adaptive behavior, executive functions and theory of mind in children with Asperger's syndrome.* Unpublished master's thesis, Victoria University of Technology, Melbourne, Australia.

Sofronoff, K., Attwood, T., & Hinton, S. (2005). A randomized controlled trial of a CBT intervention for anxiety in children with Asperger syndrome. *Journal of Child Psychology and Psychiatry, 46,* 1152–1160.

Swaggart, B. L., Gagnon, E., Bock, S. J., Earles, T. L., Quinn, C., Myles, B. S., et al. (1995). Using Social Stories to teach social and behavioral skills to children with autism. *Focus on Autistic Behavior, 10,* 1–16.

Swettenham, J., Baron-Cohen, S., Gomez, J. C., & Walsh, S. (1996). What's inside a person's head? Conceiving of the mind as a camera helps children with autism develop an alternative theory of mind. *Cognitive Neuropsychiatry, 1,* 73–88.

Szatmari, P. (2000). Perspectives on the classification of Asperger syndrome. In A. Klin, F. Volkmar, & S. Sparrow (Eds.), *Asperger syndrome* (pp. 403–417). New York: Guilford Press.

Tani, P., Lindberg, N., Appelberg, B., Nieminen-von Wendt, T., von Wendt, L., & Porkka Heiskanen, T. (2006). Childhood inattention and hyperactivity symptoms self-reported by adults with Asperger syndrome. *Psychopathology, 39,* 49–54.

Tantam, D. (2000). Psychological disorder in adolescents and adults with Asperger disorder. *Autism, 4,* 47–62.

Thiemann, K. S., & Goldstein, H. (2001). Social Stories, written text cues and video feedback: Effects on social communication of children with autism. *Journal of Applied Behavior Analysis, 34,* 425–446.

Tonge, B., Brereton, A., Gray, K., & Einfeld, S. (1999). Behavioral and emotional disturbance in high-functioning autism and Asperger syndrome. *Autism, 3,* 117–130.

Towbin, K., Pradella, A., Gorrindo, T., Pine, D., & Leibenluft, E. (2005). Autism spectrum traits in children with mood and anxiety disorders. *Journal of Child and Adolescent Psychopharmacology, 15,* 452–464.

Twatchman-Cullen, D. (1998). Language and communication in high-functioning autism and Asperger syndrome. In E. Schopler, G. Mesibov, & L. Kunce (Eds.), *Asperger syndrome or high-functioning autism* (pp. 119–225). New York: Plenum Press.

Wellman, H. M., Baron-Cohen, S., Caswell, R., Gomez, J. C., Swettenham, J., Toye, E., et al. (2002). Thought-bubbles help children with autism acquire an alternative theory of mind. *Autism, 6,* 343–363.

Wellman, H. M., Hollander, M., & Schult, C. (1996). Young children's understanding of thought bubbles and of thoughts. *Child Development, 67,* 768–788.

Wentz, E., Lacey, J., Waller, G., Rastam, M., Turk, J., & Gillberg, C. (2005). Childhood onset neuropsychiatric disorders in adult eating disorder patients: A pilot study. *European Journal of Child and Adolescent Psychiatry, 14*, 431–437.

Wentz Nilsson, E., Gillberg, C., Gillberg, I. C., & Rastam, M. (1999). Ten year follow-up of adolescent onset anorexia nervosa: Personality disorders. *Journal of the American Academy of Child and Adolescent Psychiatry, 38*, 1389–1395.

Willey, L. H. (1999). *Pretending to be normal: Living with Asperger's syndrome.* London: Jessica Kingsley.

Williams, J., Scott, F., Stott, C., Allison, C., Bolton, P., Baron-Cohen, S., et al. (2005). The CAST (Childhood Asperger Syndrome Test): Test accuracy. *Autism, 9*, 45–68.

Wing, L. (1981). Asperger's syndrome: A clinical account. *Psychological Medicine, 11*, 115–130.

Youell, B. (1999). Matthew: From numbers to numeracy—From knowledge to knowing in a 10-year-old boy with Asperger's syndrome. In A. Alvarez & S. Reid (Eds.), *Autism and personality: Findings from the Tavistock Autism Workshop* (pp. 186–202). London: Routledge.

Wolff, S. (1991a, November). Schizoid personality in childhood and adult life: Pt. I. The vagaries of labeling. *British Journal of Psychiatry, 159*, 615–620.

Wolff, S. (1991b, November). Schizoid personality in childhood and adult life: Pt. III. The childhood picture. *British Journal of Psychiatry, 159*, 629–634.

Wolff, S. (1998). The links with aspergers syndrome, schizophrenic spectrum disorders, and elective mutism. In E. Schopler, G. B. Mesibov, & L. J. Kunce (Eds.), *Asperger syndrome of high functioning autism* (pp. 123–142). New York: Plenum Press.

Wolff, S., Townshend, R. M., McGuire, R. J., & Weeks, D. J., (1991, November). "Schizoid" personality in childhood and adult life: Pt. II. Adult adjustment and the continuity with schizotypal personality disorder. *British Journal of Psychiatry, 159*, 620–629.

CHAPTER 10

The Development of Borderline Personality Disorder: Current Progress and Future Directions

NICKI R. CRICK, KATHLEEN WOODS,
DIANNA MURRAY-CLOSE, and GEORGES HAN

BORDERLINE PERSONALITY Disorder (BPD) is a persistent and enduring psychiatric condition involving compromised cognitive, emotional, and behavioral functioning. Individuals with BPD exhibit affective instability, enmeshed interpersonal relationships, high impulsivity, paranoid thoughts, and suicidal ideation or behaviors (Crick, Murray-Close, & Woods, 2005; Paris, 2005). This disorder is a particularly devastating form of psychiatric illness because it is associated with persistent maladaptive functioning in a variety of domains, including poor relationships with others, substance abuse, and suicide (Hobson, Patrick, Crandell, Garcia-Perez, & Lee, 2005; Paris, 2005; Solof, Lis, Kelly, Cornelius, & Ulrich, 1994). However, despite the deleterious outcomes associated with BPD, limited research addresses the developmental etiology of this pathology (Crick et al., 2005; Geiger & Crick, 2001; Paris, 2003). The purpose of the present chapter is to explore how developmental theory and research may inform our understanding of the development and treatment of borderline personality features in childhood and adolescence.

To date, the vast majority of research regarding BPD has focused on this disorder in adulthood. This approach reflects, at least in part, the belief that stable personality disorders do not emerge until late adolescence or early adulthood (see Crick et al., 2005). Consistent with this perspective, the diagnosis of BPD in childhood or adolescence is discouraged by the fourth edition, text revision of the *Diagnostic and Statistical Manual of Mental Disorders* (*DSM-IV-TR*; American Psychiatric Association, 2000). Given the dearth of BPD research including child and adolescent participants, we briefly review what is known about BPD in adulthood and then discuss how this information can be used in conjunction with what we know about developmental psychopathology to better understand of the development of this personality disorder in younger samples.

Although there are a variety of measures of borderline pathology in adulthood (e.g., Personality Assessment Inventory, or PAI; Morey, 1991), BPD is most frequently identified using criteria set forth by the *DSM-IV-TR*. According to this approach, individuals are diagnosed with BPD when they exhibit five out of the nine following symptoms: affective instability; inappropriate, intense anger; chronic feelings of emptiness; recurrent suicidal thoughts or behavior; impulsivity; intense or unstable interpersonal relationships; efforts to avoid abandonment; identity disturbance; and paranoia or dissociative symptoms (American Psychiatric Association, 2000). Research indicates that the prevalence rate of BPD is approximately 1% in community samples (Samuels et al., 2002). Despite the relatively low prevalence rate in the general population, BPD is frequently seen in clinical settings. In fact, BPD is the most common Axis II disorder in clinical samples (Trull, Stepp, & Durrett, 2003). Consistent with this, one study found that 15% to 20% of inpatients suffered from BPD (Skodol et al., 2002). Moreover, more women than men exhibit BPD, with estimates indicating that approximately 70% to 80% of adults with BPD are female (Gunderson, Zanarini, & Kiesel, 1991; Skodol et al., 2002; Swartz, Blazer, George, & Winfield, 1990; Torgersen, Kringlen, & Cramer, 2001). To our knowledge very few, if any, studies have yet explored the prevalence rates of BPD among various racial and/or ethnic groups.

Researchers have identified a number of potential biological and social contributors to the emergence of BPD in adulthood. First, BPD may have some etiological underpinnings in genetic factors. Consistent with this view, evidence indicates that adult BPD is highly heritable (.69 in one twin study; Torgersen et al., 2000). However, the genetic influences on BPD may be mediated by personality traits that place individuals at risk for borderline pathology (e.g., impulsivity; Siever, Torgersen, Gunderson, Livesley, & Kendler, 2002). In other words, it has been proposed that various genetically influenced traits may be associated with increased risk for a BPD diagnosis among adults. For example, both affective instability and impulsivity have been identified as important traits in popular adult models of personality (e.g., the five-factor model; McCrae & Costa, 1999) and are moderately heritable (Coccaro, Bergeman, & McClearn, 1993; Livesley, Jang, & Vernon, 1998; Torgersen et al., 2000). In addition to a focus on genetically influenced personality traits, some researchers have explored the association between physiological factors and BPD. For example, a number of studies have explored the relation between serotonergic activity and BPD (see Hansenne et al., 2002). Overall, this research indicates that individuals may exhibit biological vulnerabilities to borderline pathology.

Researchers have also identified the role of social stress and social experiences in the development of BPD in adulthood. For example, evidence indicates that borderline pathology is related to experiences of childhood abuse and neglect (Herman, Perry, & van der Kolk, 1989; Paris, Zweig-Frank, & Guzder, 1994; Zanarini, 2000). In addition, parental variables are related to BPD. For example, a child's quality of attachment with a primary caregiver predicts BPD in young adulthood (Nickell, Waudby, & Trull, 2002). The overall family context or dynamic also may play an important role. Bradley, Jenei, and Westen (2005) found significant, independent contributions of abuse, family environment (e.g., warmth, stability), and parental psychopathology in the prediction of BPD symptoms. They also found that family environment served as a partial mediator between abuse and BPD symptoms. The results of this work indicate that there are likely a number of biological and social risk factors involved in the development of BPD.

These biological and social factors may also interact in their prediction of BPD. This approach is consistent with a diathesis-stress model in which biological predispositions toward BPD are more likely to be expressed when the individual has also encountered stress (i.e., social risk factors). For example, it has been proposed that deficits in aspects of neuropsychological functioning serve as a biological risk factor for BPD. However, this risk factor may more frequently result in a BPD diagnosis when the individual encounters social experiences such as abuse or violence (Zelkowitz, Paris, Guzder, & Feldman, 2001). Children demonstrating higher levels of borderline pathology have also been found to be exposed to higher levels of parental dysfunction (e.g., divorce, criminality, substance abuse), which might reflect a combination of both genetic and environmental forms of risk factors (e.g., Guzder, Paris, Zelkowitz, & Feldman, 1999; Guzder, Paris, Zelkowitz, & Marchessault, 1996).

Although diagnosis of BPD is discouraged prior to adulthood, it is likely that there are developmental precursors to the adult diagnosis of such pathology (i.e., BPD does not just appear at age 18) and that these developmental precursors reflect stable patterns of cognition, emotion, and behavior that are significant in their own right. Denying the possibility of the emergence of borderline personality features prior to adulthood limits our ability to study developmental precursors to such pathology and to intervene when these stable patterns begin to emerge. Thus, we argue that it is critical for researchers to attend to the development of BPD. The purpose of the present chapter is to use a developmentally-based approach to identify features that may reflect emerging borderline pathology in childhood and adolescence and to discuss how such an approach might inform intervention and prevention with these samples.

We believe that the relevant population for examination of the development of BPD includes both normative and clinical samples. Indeed, although the majority of research with adults involves a categorical diagnosis of BPD as set forth by the *DSM-IV-TR* and tends to focus on clinical samples, we posit that the study of borderline personality in childhood and adolescence should incorporate a dimensional approach and include community samples (Crick et al., 2005). This perspective is informed by a developmental psychopathology approach in which maladaptive functioning is viewed as the failure to negotiate developmentally appropriate tasks (Sroufe & Rutter, 1984). Because personality is still forming in childhood and adolescence, identification of a broad range of borderline symptoms in normative samples will allow researchers to assess trajectories toward or away from BPD over time (Crick et al., 2005). Moreover, given research evidence that boys are overrepresented in treatment facilities (e.g., Guzder et al., 1996), it is imperative that normative samples in childhood be included in relevant studies to gain an accurate understanding of potential gender differences in borderline pathology. Inclusion of clinical samples, in turn, will allow for more detailed and powerful predictions of extreme forms of borderline pathology. Thus, in the present chapter, we discuss the ways research and intervention regarding BPD can be applied to both clinical and community samples of children and adolescents.

Although a substantial number of studies address BPD in adulthood, less is known about the development of this disorder during childhood and adolescence. For example, there is very little information on the prevalence rate in these developmental periods. In one study, 10% of boys and 18% of girls in a French high school were identified as exhibiting BPD (Chabrol, Montovany, Chouicha, Callahan, & Mullet, 2001). However, this relatively high estimate may reflect turbulence due to the many emotional, cognitive, biological, and social changes that occur during the adolescent period (Trull, Stepp, et al., 2003). In addition, it is unclear when gender differences in BPD emerge. In one study using a dimensional assessment of borderline pathology in childhood, elementary school girls were more likely than boys to report experiencing borderline symptoms (Crick et al., 2005). Clearly, more studies are needed before firm conclusions can be drawn regarding prevalence rates and gender differences (if any) in borderline pathology in childhood and adolescence. Particularly needed are prospective, long-term studies that begin in childhood and follow participants through adolescence and adulthood.

Finally, researchers should attend to biological and social influences on BPD in childhood and adolescence. For example, given the relative emphasis on the role of social experiences (e.g., abuse, attachment) that occur in childhood, prospective longitudinal work exploring these relations prior to adulthood is sorely needed. Moreover, because the substrates of personality may be present at birth (Hartup & van Lieshout, 1995), researchers may benefit from exploring how personality development relates to emerging borderline pathology (Mervielde, De Clercq, De Fruyt, & Van Leeuwen, 2005; Shiner, 2005). This is consistent with a developmental psychopathology perspective in which it is asserted that abnormal development is best understood within the context of the processes of normal development (Sroufe & Rutter, 1984). Overall, we believe that there is much to be gained from adopting a developmental perspective regarding the etiology and treatment of BPD.

DEVELOPMENTAL PERSPECTIVES

We propose that the understanding of developmental influences on BPD promises to enhance our ability to identify and treat individuals suffering from this devastating form of psychopathology. There are a number of different ways in which developmental processes may be reflected in BPD. First, risk factors for BPD may exist in childhood and reflect maladaptive negotiation of developmentally salient tasks (Geiger & Crick, 2001). Second, risk factors for BPD may be present in childhood and reflect patterns of personality development (Caspi & Shiner, 2006). Finally, BPD may exist in a rudimentary form among children but be expressed in developmentally congruent ways (Crick et al., 2005). Although each of these approaches reflects a unique perspective regarding the emergence of borderline pathology, all three suggest that researchers must attend to developmental considerations when evaluating and treating BPD.

RISK FACTORS FOR BORDERLINE PERSONALITY DISORDER REFLECT A FAILURE TO NEGOTIATE DEVELOPMENTALLY SALIENT TASKS

The first possibility regarding the development of BPD is that borderline pathology in adulthood may reflect a failure to negotiate developmentally salient challenges in childhood. This approach is consistent with a developmental psychopathology perspective whereby trajectories of adaptation reflect individuals' abilities to master important developmental tasks (Sroufe, 1997; Sroufe & Rutter, 1984). In other words, at each stage of development, children are faced with unique challenges. For example, an important task among young children is establishing a secure attachment relationship with their primary caregiver (Ainsworth, 1979), whereas adolescents face the challenge of forming intimate relationships with peers (Hartup, 1992). From the developmental psychopathology perspective, positive adaptation results from successful negotiation of these tasks across development, whereas psychopathology reflects an inability to utilize internal and external resources to negotiate these challenges. Thus, BPD may result from children's failure to manage developmentally salient challenges.

If BPD reflects a failure to negotiate important tasks in childhood, then the pathology exhibited by individuals with BPD should echo the themes of these developmental tasks. In a recent content analysis of symptoms assessed for diagnosis of personality disorders in the *DSM*, Geiger and Crick (2001) identified five factors that capture unique facets of BPD. These authors suggested that these factors reflect a failure to master developmentally salient challenges in childhood. Specifically, they proposed the following childhood indicators of BPD: (1) hostile, paranoid worldview; (2) intense, unstable, inappropriate emotion; (3) overly close relationships; (4) impulsivity; and (5) lack of sense of self.

Regarding the first childhood indicator, an important facet of BPD in adults is the tendency to adopt a hostile, paranoid worldview. In other words, adults with BPD tend to focus on negative cues and information in the environment and to be suspicious or paranoid (e.g., Morey, 1988a, 1988b). From the developmental psychopathology perspective, this hostile, paranoid worldview may result from a failure to develop the ability to accurately identify and interpret the behaviors of others during childhood (Geiger & Crick, 2001). Indeed, a number of studies have demonstrated that some children attribute hostile intentions to others in ambiguous situations (e.g., being knocked over by a peer; for a review, see Crick & Dodge, 1994), and that these children are at risk for the development of adjustment problems (e.g., aggressive behavior patterns; Crick & Dodge, 1994). Thus, the failure to negotiate the developmental task of adaptive social interactions with others (e.g., correctly identifying and interpreting the perspective of others) in childhood may serve as a risk factor for BPD.

The second proposed childhood indicator of BPD is intense, unstable, and inappropriate emotion. For example, individuals with BPD frequently experience exaggerated emotional reactions to interpersonal situations (Morey, 1991). A number of researchers have identified the development of emotion regulation skills as an important task in infancy (e.g., Mangelsdorf, Shapiro, & Marlzolf, 1995; Thompson, 1994), and evidence suggests that poor emotion regulation skills are associated with poor adjustment outcomes (Belsky, Friedman, & Hsieh, 2001). From a developmental psychopathology perspective, the emotional reactivity among individuals with BPD may reflect the failure to develop appropriate emotion regulation skills in childhood (Geiger & Crick, 2001).

The third proposed indicator of borderline features in childhood is overly close relationships (Geiger & Crick, 2001). Individuals with BPD tend to have relationships with others that are highly dependent and enmeshed (Block, Westen, Ludolph, Widon, & Jackson, 1991; Morey, 1991). Establishing appropriately intimate relationships (i.e., balancing autonomy and trust) has been identified as an important developmental task beginning in early childhood (Erikson, 1963). The overly dependent and enmeshed relationships characteristic of individuals with BPD may reflect failure to successfully negotiate this developmental challenge. For example, an inability to establish a secure attachment relationship with one's caregiver in infancy and the failure to engage in satisfying friendships in middle childhood may serve as a risk factor for the tendency to seek overly intimate and dependent relationships, which in turn is an important facet of BPD.

The fourth proposed childhood indicator of BPD is impulsivity; this includes the inability to inhibit excesses in behavior (e.g., lack of self-restraint) and the tendency to engage in aggressive outbursts (Geiger & Crick, 2001). Researchers have identified the capacity to control one's impulses as an important task during childhood (Bandura, 1986; Kopp, 1987; Mischel, 1986), and children who are unable to successfully negotiate this challenge are at heightened risk for aggressive and risk-taking behaviors (Coie & Dodge, 1998). Thus, the highly impulsive behaviors characteristic of individuals with BPD may reflect a failure to develop self-control abilities in childhood.

Finally, the fifth proposed childhood indicator of BPD is a lack of sense of self (Geiger & Crick, 2001). An important facet of BPD identified by the *DSM* criteria for diagnosis is identity disturbance (American Psychiatric Association, 2000). The lack of a coherent sense of self characteristic of patients with BPD, however, may reflect a failure in identity formation processes and self-understanding in childhood.

Coming to recognize the self as independent of others is a developmental task that begins early in infancy (Harter, 1983); during middle childhood and adolescence, individuals exhibit changes toward a more sophisticated understanding of the self (Damon & Hart, 1988). Failure to develop an appropriate sense of self during childhood may place individuals at risk for BPD. Consistent with this perspective, research indicates that adults with BPD have a compromised ability to report autobiographical memories (i.e., memories of one's own life; Jones et al., 1999), which is an important component of identity development. Overall, then, children's failure to negotiate important developmental tasks (e.g., identify formation) may place them at risk for BPD.

In a recent study examining four of the five factors proposed by Geiger and Crick (2001; hostile, paranoid worldview; intense, unstable, inappropriate emotion; overly close relationships, and impulsivity), Crick et al. (2005) followed a sample of 400 fourth-, fifth-, and sixth-graders for a year (three assessments were conducted: in fall and spring of the first academic year and in fall of the second academic year). Results of Linear Mixed Model analyses showed that all four factors tracked over time with levels of borderline pathology. Further, each of the four indicators uniquely predicted borderline personality features over time, above and beyond the longitudinal association between borderline features and the other three indicators. These findings provide initial evidence that, as proposed by Geiger and Crick, the failure to successfully negotiate important development tasks in childhood that are relevant to BPD places children at risk for borderline pathology.

RISK FACTORS FOR BORDERLINE PERSONALITY DISORDER REFLECT PATTERNS OF PERSONALITY DEVELOPMENT

A second perspective regarding the role of development in BPD is that children exhibit risk factors for the disorder that reflect patterns of personality development. Although related to the perspective of Geiger and Crick (2001), this approach emphasizes personality development rather than children's mastery of various specific developmental tasks. Caspi and Shiner (2006) have identified five processes whereby personality development may lead to psychopathology: (1) vulnerability association, (2) spectrum association, (3) resilience association, (4) maintenance association, and (5) scarring association.

The first proposed mechanism linking personality development and psychopathology is vulnerability association (Caspi & Shiner, 2006). This approach suggests that personality profiles place children at risk for psychopathology. Personality and temperament may create vulnerability to risk factors for psychopathology, including BPD, in a number of ways. First, children with particular temperaments may elicit environmental risk factors. For example, evidence indicates that children with difficult temperaments are at heightened risk for abuse by caregivers, which in turn increases their likelihood of developing BPD (Paris et al., 1994; Zanarini, 2000). Second, personality factors may affect individuals' construal of their environment. For example, an individual high in neuroticism may be at increased risk for interpreting stimuli in the environment in a hostile or paranoid way, which in turn is an important facet of BPD. Indeed, evidence indicates that heightened negative affect (i.e., depression) is related to a tendency to interpret the intentions of others in ambiguous provocation situations as hostile and mean (Quiggle, Panak, Garber, & Dodge, 1992). In a similar vein, the negative affect characteristic of neurotic individuals may place them at increased risk for developing a paranoid and hostile view of those around them. Finally, temperamental characteristics may affect children's tendency to select environments associated with risk for the development of BPD. For instance, children with a genetic propensity toward thrill seeking may select peers who are also thrill seekers, increasing their psychosocial risk over time (Plomin & Rutter, 1998). In this way, temperament factors may affect the number of environmental risk factors for BPD that a child encounters.

The second mechanism proposed to link personality development and psychopathology is spectrum association (Caspi & Shiner, 2006). From this perspective, BPD may reflect the extreme end of normative personality dimensions. Consistent with this approach, Trull, Widiger,

Lynam, and Costa (2003) argue that BPD may reflect a specific constellation of the Big Five personality factors. For example, researchers have demonstrated that there is a positive association between neuroticism and borderline symptoms (Clarkin, Hull, Cantor, & Sanderson, 1993). In one study, scores on the five-factor model (i.e., the Revised NEO Personality Inventory) predicted as much (and sometimes more) variance in factors associated with BPD (e.g., suicide attempts, level of functioning) as a measure designed to assess borderline pathology (i.e., Revised Diagnostic Interview for Borderlines; Morey & Zanarini, 2000). In a separate study, Trull, Widiger, and colleagues (2003) reported that an empirically derived five-factor borderline profile was as highly correlated with factors known to be related to BPD (e.g., history of abuse, dysfunction) as traditional measures of BPD. This research provides preliminary evidence consistent with the hypothesis that BPD may reflect extreme variation of normative personality characteristics.

The third mechanism that may link personality development and BPD is resilience association (Caspi & Shiner, 2006). From this perspective, some personality traits may serve as protective factors. In other words, personality profiles may reduce the likelihood of developing BPD under adverse conditions. For example, research indicates that the experience of abuse during childhood is related to the development of BPD (Paris et al., 1994; Zanarini, 2000). However, abused children with particular personality profiles may be less likely than their abused peers to develop BPD. Consistent with this hypothesis, in one study, children exposed to a number of risk factors who nevertheless exhibited positive outcomes in adulthood had unique personality profiles (e.g., easygoing, affectionate; Werner & Smith, 1992). A similar process may be evident among children at risk for BPD who nonetheless exhibit positive adaptation over development. However, the extent to which vulnerability association and resilience association represent similar developmental processes (e.g., high levels of neuroticism may serve as a vulnerability association, whereas low levels of neuroticism may serve as a resilience association) is unclear (Caspi & Shiner, 2006).

The fourth potential mechanism linking personality development and BPD is maintenance association. From this perspective, personality factors influence the onset, course, and prognosis of psychopathology (Caspi & Shiner, 2006). That is, certain personality profiles may make individuals more or less responsive to treatment of BPD. For example, BPD patients high in conscientiousness may be more likely to follow treatment regimens and take prescribed medication, thus improving their prognosis over time.

Finally, the fifth proposed mechanism that may link personality and BPD is scarring association (Caspi & Shiner, 2006). From this perspective, the experience of psychopathology may alter personality development. For example, a diagnosis of BPD may affect one's tendency to evaluate oneself negatively and to react with negative emotions to environmental stressors (i.e., to develop neuroticism). To date, little research has examined the potential scarring effect of psychopathology, but some researchers have argued that this effect may be more important in childhood than adulthood because personality is forming during this developmental period. Thus, this is an important avenue for future developmental work.

BORDERLINE PATHOLOGY EXISTS IN CHILDHOOD BUT IS EXPRESSED IN DEVELOPMENTALLY SALIENT WAYS

A final possibility is that borderline personality pathology exists in childhood but is manifested in developmentally salient ways. In other words, children may exhibit features of borderline pathology before reaching adulthood. From this perspective, instead of looking at risk factors for BPD in childhood, researchers may benefit from assessing behavioral and emotional features demonstrated in childhood that would be consistent with the development of the core deficits or problematic behaviors involved in borderline personality pathology. Consistent with this approach, Crick and colleagues (2005) developed a measure of borderline pathology for use with children in middle childhood, the Borderline Personality Features Scale for Children (BPFS-C). Specifically, these researchers adapted the Borderline Personality Disorder Scale from the PAI commonly used with adult samples (Morey, 1991). The BPFS-C includes age-appropriate items adapted from the original PAI to reflect (a) affective instability, (b) identity problems, (c) negative relationships, and (d) self-harm. Evidence indicates that this measure is a reliable and valid measure of borderline pathology during childhood (Crick et al., 2005). This work suggests that patterns of thinking, feeling, and behaving reflective of the core problems or deficits of BPD may be present in childhood.

It is important to note, however, that even this perspective does not suggest that BPD exists in childhood. Rather, because personality is still forming across childhood, the borderline pathology in younger samples may be less stable than among adults. Childhood borderline pathology may be best conceptualized as placing children on a developmental trajectory toward adult BPD in much the same way that Conduct Disorder in childhood is related to Antisocial Personality Disorder in adulthood. To date, the possibility that an emerging form of borderline pathology may place individuals at risk for adult BPD is largely unexplored and is an important direction for future research.

Moreover, we should not expect children with borderline pathology exhibit the exact same behaviors that adults with BPD do. Instead, the expression of borderline pathology may look quite different across development. Indeed, a number of researchers have identified the importance of heterotypic continuity in which behaviors reflecting the same underlying problems are manifested differently across time (e.g., Caspi, 1998). For example, the enmeshed relationships characteristic of borderline pathology may be expressed as overly exclusive friendships in middle childhood and as dependent romantic relationships in adulthood. Difficulties maintaining these relationships might also be demonstrated. Thus, researchers working with children would benefit from careful consideration of developmental tasks and processes in conceptualizing and assessing expressions of borderline symptoms across development.

ASSESSMENT OF BORDERLINE PERSONALITY

There are currently a number of issues that make the study of BPD in childhood and adolescence difficult. Perhaps most important, there are few valid and reliable instruments available to assess BPD prior to adulthood. The current conceptualization of personality disorders by many in the field (e.g., *DSM*) as being confined to adulthood is naturally associated with more assessment tools appropriate for adults. These tools include self-report inventories and semistructured interviews assessing various personality traits or maladaptive patterns of functioning (e.g., Minnesota Multiphasic Personality Inventory 2 [MMPI-2], DIPD-IV) as well as those that are more specific to borderline personality features (e.g., Diagnostic Interview for Borderline Personality Disorder; Clark & Harrison, 2001). However, aside from perhaps the MMPI-2, these measures are more likely to be used in a research setting than in a clinical setting, where the psychologist is more likely to rely on observations of the client's behavior and first-person accounts of life history and events to reveal such a pattern over the course of assessment and treatment (Zimmerman & Mattia, 1999).

Just as we advocate applying a developmental perspective to the conceptualization of BPD, we advocate for a similar approach to the assessment of its features. Thus, the tools used to assess BPD in adults may not be appropriate for assessment in children and adolescents. There are a variety of considerations that must be taken into account when assessing borderline features in this population. First, as previously discussed, there is likely to be heterotypic continuity in the way these features are manifested across development. Thus, the developmentally appropriate indicators of borderline pathology identified by Geiger and Crick (2001) discussed previously (e.g., development of hostile, paranoid worldview; development of overly close relationships; impulsivity) are likely to be informative in identifying what sorts of items are appropriate to include or look for in questionnaires, interviews, and behavioral observations.

Another, more obvious concern in assessing features of personality disorders among children and adolescents is their varying levels of skill in their ability to report on their own thoughts, behaviors, and emotions when directly asked. Therefore, as with the assessment of other forms of psychopathology, questionnaires and interviews may be supplemented with other measures, such as behavioral observations, projective assessment, and parent reports of children's current behaviors and history (P. Kernberg, Weiner, & Bardenstein, 2000). For example, P. Kernberg et al. indicated that many of the items of a widely used parent-report measure, Achenbach's Child Behavior Checklist, would be appropriate to use to assess the constellations of symptoms that define each of the different personality disorders. According to these authors, items reflective of borderline personality features include the following: argues a lot, complains of loneliness, and deliberately harms self or attempts suicide. P. Kernberg et al. also suggested that aspects of personality (e.g., cognition, affect, self-representation, empathy) that are often assessed in interviews with older adolescents and adults may be assessed in younger, school-age children via observations of play.

We would like to provide a brief example of how these issues may be addressed in the development of tools to assess borderline features in children in adolescents. In our own quest for a developmentally appropriate self-report measure of borderline personality features, we began by examining various adult instruments, particularly the PAI (Morey, 1991). This instrument, designed for individuals age 18 and older, consists of a number of subscales, one of which assesses borderline pathology (the BOR subscale). The BOR assesses pathology in four domains: affective instability, identity problems, negative relationships, and self-harm. The PAI has demonstrated reliability and validity and has been shown to be particularly useful for the assessment of psychopathology (including borderline personality) in nonclinical populations (e.g., Kurtz, Morey, & Tomarken, 1993; Morey, 1991). In consultation with the author of the PAI, Crick adapted the items of the BOR so that they addressed the same underlying constructs (e.g., affective instability), but assessed them in an age-appropriate manner (i.e., consistent with children's social, emotional, cognitive, and behavioral experiences and abilities). The resulting instrument, the Borderline Features Scale for Children (BPFS-C), is appropriate for use with children as young as 9 years.

Results provided construct validity for the BPFS-C as a developmentally appropriate tool for the assessment of borderline personality features in childhood. We advocate for similar approaches to the development of additional questionnaires and interviews to assess this constellation of symptoms in children and adolescents for use in both research and clinical settings.

DIAGNOSTIC ISSUES

A number of significant limitations are apparent in existing studies that hamper our understanding of borderline pathology and its diagnosis. For example, despite evidence indicating that borderline personality pathology is relatively frequent in community samples (Gunderson & Zanarini, 1987), the majority of studies have been conducted with clinical samples (Trull, 1995). As a result, we know relatively little about borderline personality features as they exist in normative populations. This limitation is particularly significant when considering issues of development and etiology because clinical samples are unlikely to be representative of the relevant populations. For example, clinical samples are more likely to suffer from comorbid disorders, to experience difficulties that are relatively extreme in nature, and to have been the recipients of past treatment (Trull, 1995).

Overreliance on clinical samples has been particularly misleading in investigations of borderline personality pathology among children and adolescents (e.g., Guzder et al., 1996) because boys are far more likely than girls to appear in treatment facilities during childhood and thus are significantly more likely to be selected as research participants. For example, in one study of children recruited through day treatment centers (see Paris, 2003), girls composed less than 20% of the sample. The composition of this sample and others like it contrasts sharply with adult studies of gender differences that demonstrate that BPD is more prevalent among females than males (e.g., Block et al., 1991). One interpretation of these findings is that many existing studies of borderline personality pathology during childhood are most revealing for the gender that is less likely to suffer from the disorder. Biases such as these have led some researchers to conclude that "mental health care professionals are missing troubled girls" (Paris, 2003, p. 40; see also Crick & Zahn-Waxler, 2003).

We propose that the preliminary state of research on developmental precursors strongly suggests that a focus on the entire range of borderline symptoms using dimensional assessments of a normative sample (as opposed to a narrow focus on clinically relevant symptoms and categorical measures) will be most productive in initial studies. This approach avoids the biases inherent in using clinical samples cited previously, many of which are particularly problematic for understanding etiology. Further, this strategy will allow us to identify children who may not currently exhibit clinically diagnosable levels of borderline pathology but who nonetheless are at significant risk for the development of clinical levels in the future. Clearly, this information is important for the development of programs that are effective for preventing borderline pathology.

CLINICAL VIGNETTE: TOO CLOSE FOR COMFORT—DEVON

To illustrate some of the ways that borderline pathology may be exhibited in childhood, we provide the clinical case of Devon. In particular, we highlight how the childhood indicators proposed by Geiger and Crick (2001; e.g., hostile, paranoid worldview) are apparent in Devon's cognitive, emotional, and behavioral functioning as well as in her relationships with others.

DEVELOPMENTAL HISTORY

Devon was born 4 years after her parents' marriage. Her mother, Violet, had a stormy relationship with her mother-in-law, who provided child care for Devon and her older brother, Brandon, until they were old enough to enter school. Because Brandon was 2 years her senior, Devon spent 2 years in her maternal grandmother's care without him as a buffer. The battle for loyalty and changing allegiances between Violet and her mother-in-law made it difficult for Devon to trust adults and created doubt about the "rightness" of her own feelings and reactions to others. Her parents engaged in frequent verbal fights, mostly regarding money and her father's alcohol abuse. When her father drank, he became verbally and physically abusive to Violet and the children. In the school setting, however, Devon demonstrated advanced academic skills early on. She responded favorably to the positive praise she got from her teachers for her abilities, which seemed to contribute to her motivation to do well; however, academic setbacks, no matter how small (e.g., receiving a B on a spelling test), often left her feeling discouraged and mistrustful of the teacher she viewed as responsible for the setback. Devon seemed to also have difficulties with peer relations. She made friends easily and quickly felt close to them, but she was unable to keep friends for any length of time.

Despite performing well academically, starting at age 10, Devon began to miss school regularly, pleading with her mother to care for the aches and pains that prevented her from sleeping. At the beginning, the mother took time off from work to take care of her daughter. After a while, the mother suspected that the child's symptoms were psychosomatic in nature rather than physical illness per se. At this point, the mother sought help with a local therapist recommended by the school counselor.

CHILDHOOD INDICATORS OF BORDERLINE PERSONALITY FEATURES

Hostile, Paranoid Worldview

As mentioned, Devon had a history of difficulty in maintaining close friendships throughout her childhood. She often would initially be an enthusiastic and attractive playmate and friend and seemed very much to want to be involved with other children. However, she was also very sensitive in her interactions with others and reacted quite strongly when she perceived she was left out or slighted in some way, even if this was not the intention of her friends. Losing at games was difficult for her, and she seemed to take it as a personal offense if her friend would beat her. Her emotional reactions were very strong to these situations, and she was quick to seek the assistance of the teacher to indicate that her friends were being mean. Her erratic behavior was often met with confusion from her peers and her teachers.

By the time Devon entered junior high school, she had become a tall, beautiful young woman; however, her beauty sometimes elicited unwanted attention. After an unhealthy relationship and bad breakup with her most recent boyfriend, she started to become paranoid when any male classmates or friends approached her socially. Devon started to dress differently, wearing mostly baggy clothes to hide her body. She eventually started to starve herself in a desperate attempt to remain more childlike so as not to attract sexual attention from the opposite sex.

Intense, Unstable, Inappropriate Emotion

During that same period, Devon felt a lack of motivation to do the things she used to enjoy and often felt uncontrollably sad, to the point where she would burst into tears in the middle of class and have to excuse herself. Her English teacher noted that her essay assignments began to enumerate themes of darkness, frustration, and alienation. Devon continued to struggle with her dieting and felt uneasy in front of her family during meal times.

Overly Close Relationships

Because her mother was a busy professional working in the finance industry, Devon relied heavily on her brother for a sense of connectedness. Brandon obliged with her demanding nature but also openly expressed his frustrations with his sister's developmentally inappropriate clinging behaviors. One minute she would beg him to spend time with her, and the next she would treat him like a stranger and tell him to leave her alone and never speak with her again. Brandon suspected that there were deeper troubles but felt that it was his responsibility to show love to his sister as much as he could. He also felt a need to compensate for the amount of family chaos that was occurring in the home and thus was rather protective of his younger sister.

Devon also had difficulty letting peers penetrate bonds she had with her friends. She felt extreme jealousy whenever she returned to school on a Monday and found out that two of her friends had spent time together without her over the weekend, despite the fact that they may not have intentionally left her out. She would punish her friends for situations like this by giving them the cold shoulder for a few days or trying to get other friends to not like the girls she felt slighted by.

Impulsivity

When Brandon was unable to spend extra time with her after school, Devon would act out in fits of screaming, kicking, trashing her room, and writing her brother nasty text messages on her cell phone. These outbursts of anger put a strain on their relationship, and Brandon continued to be perplexed by his sister's emotional roller-coaster rides. To make up for her misbehaviors, Devon would spend inappropriate amounts of money and shower her brother with gifts at random times. If Brandon refused to accept the gifts, Devon would become depressed and question his acceptance of her kindness.

Lack of Sense of Self

Devon became accustomed to depending on her brother and did little on her own. She felt unhappy most of the time and had trouble recalling important life events when questioned by others. Instead, to fill in the blanks, she designed intricate fantasy worlds and lives that she would live out to drown her edginess. When asked by her therapist what she thought her primary problem was, Devon responded, "People are rotten to me. I try so hard to take care of my family and my friends and to do what makes them happy, and in the end they only care about themselves." After additional clinical interviews and further probing of her family history, the therapist in charge of Devon's care discussed her borderline features with her parents and recommended adolescent dialectical behavior therapy.

INTERVENTION: GOALS, STRATEGIES, OUTCOME ASSESSMENT, AND POSSIBLE IMPEDIMENTS

SPECIFIC TREATMENT STRATEGIES AND TECHNIQUES

Historically, psychoanalytically oriented therapies were the most commonly utilized treatments for personality disorders, approaches that aimed to modify behaviors that cause intra- and interpersonal harm (Bateman & Holmes, 1995). However, it is not until recent times that empirical studies have been systematically conducted to evaluate the efficacy and specificity of different approaches to treating BPD. Further, given that BPD is most commonly diagnosed among adults, it is not surprising that much of the work on development and empirical validation of treatment strategies for the disorder has been based on work with adults. Thus, we begin with a brief description of current treatment strategies currently used with this age group. Consistent with our overall approach in this chapter, we employ a developmental perspective in considering the necessary elements for treatment of children and adolescents with emerging borderline features. Finally, we examine existing treatment models for children and adolescents as well as our own thoughts on future directions in treatment of this population.

Individual, Group, and Family Therapies

The complexity of BPD is naturally associated with great complexity in developing effective treatment strategies. As Hurt, Clarkin, Munroe-Blum, and Marziali (1992, p. 200) stated, the "heterogeneity among individuals with the disorder makes it difficult to develop a unified treatment strategy." Current strategies employed for adults have drawn from a variety of theoretical backgrounds, including psychodynamic/psychoanalytic, cognitive-behavioral, and behavioral theories. One of the most effective and commonly used strategies is dialectical behavior therapy (DBT), which was developed by Marsha Linehan (1987). As described by Linehan and Heard (1992, p. 249), this form of therapy "is based on a dialectical world view, a biosocial (behavioral) theory, and a theoretical framework for understanding therapy-interfering behaviors." The therapy has five targets or goals: (1) eliminating suicidal behaviors; (2) eliminating therapy-interfering behaviors (e.g., tardiness for appointments, power struggles); (3) eliminating behaviors that are life-interfering or contribute to escape (e.g., impulsivity, substance abuse); (4) addressing posttraumatic stress; and (5) developing self-respect. Such goals are addressed through a combination of individual and group therapy. In addition, clinicians administering DBT receive consultation and support from their own peers, given the challenges of working with these clients and the need for clinicians to monitor their own behaviors that might interfere with therapy.

Given the level of pathology, stress, and dysfunctional interpersonal behaviors that often occur in the families of people diagnosed with BPD, some have suggested incorporating the family in treatment (e.g., Clarkin, Marziali, & Munroe-Blum, 1991; Hoffman et al., 2005). One model of family therapy developed by Hoffman, Fruzzetti, and Swenson (1999) is Dialectical Behavior Therapy—Family Skills Training, which is based on Linehan's DBT approach. This involves providing psychoeducation to the family, increasing mutual validation among family members, and improving the emotion regulation and interpersonal skills of all family members. This method is designed to be used to supplement individual DBT and improve the family environment. Hoffman et al. (2005) have also developed a program (Family Connections) that is based on a family education model in trained family members of those diagnosed with BPD lead groups for other family members. These groups do not include the patient with BPD. In addition to focusing on some of the family skills mentioned above, these groups also target the emotional well-being of family members and provide interpersonal support for these family members.

A cognitive approach introduced by Beck and Freeman (1990) focuses on maladaptive cognitive schemas regarding the world (e.g., as dangerous and malevolent) and the self (e.g., as vulnerable, powerless, and unacceptable). More psychodynamically or psychoanalytically based treatments, such as that developed by O. Kernberg, Selzer, Koenigsberg, Carr, and Applebaum (1989), as well as relation management psychotherapy (e.g., Dawson, 1988) involve the use of the client-therapist relationship as a means of addressing difficulties those with BPD have integrating various aspects of the self or their identity, which contributes to problems with affect, behavior, and interpersonal interactions. Although their primary theoretical influences are different, some of these forms of treatment share various treatment methods (e.g., contracting, including individual and group work; for a more thorough review of similarities and differences of some of these forms of treatment, see Hurt et al., 1992).

Psychopharmacological Approaches

There is no specific form of medication developed to treat BPD per se; instead, several types of medication may be used to treat individual features or symptoms of severe BPD. For example, one major goal of psychopharmacological treatment of BPD is the prevention of self-injurious behavior or manifestations of other types of aggression. Furthermore, it is important to be mindful that the use of medication with each individual client is a clinical trial, as individual reactions may vary greatly; thus, clients with BPD treated with medication need to be monitored regularly by their psychiatrist and health provider.

To treat the cognitive symptoms of BPD (e.g., paranoia, suspiciousness, ideas of reference, and dissociative episodes), the recommended class of medication is the atypical antipsychotics. Medications that fall under this classification include olanzapine, quetiapine, and risperidone. In an 8-week open-label trial of olanzapine ($N = 11$), clients treated with this medication evidenced reduction in symptoms of depression, interpersonal sensitivity, anger, and psychoticism (Schulz, Camlin, Berry, & Jesberger, 1999). A more recent investigation of only female participants ($N = 28$) who were in a 6-month double-blind placebo-controlled trial of olanzapine found that those treated with this medication manifested significant reduction in anger, hostility, paranoia, anxiety, and interpersonal sensitivity (Zanarini & Frankenburg, 2001).

Selective serotonin reuptake inhibitors are also often used to treat symptoms of affective instability such as anger, irritability, anxiety, and depression in clients with BPD. In an open trial of venlafaxine, this medication was shown to reduce somatic complaints and self-injurious behavior in individuals with BPD (Markovitz & Wagner, 1995). Occasionally, anticonvulsants may be used to treat symptoms of impulsive aggression in clients with BPD. To date however, there have been few empirical studies documenting the use of pharmacological treatment of personality disorders in children and adolescents.

Hospitalization

Hospitalization has been shown to sometimes play an important role in the management of episodes of acute crisis in adults with BPD. Usually, this involves short-term stays with a clinical focus on relieving intense acute symptoms such as suicidality. This crisis management approach is not able to target more complicated therapeutic goals such as personality restructuring. Overall, the BPD treatment literature suggests a limited use of full hospitalization and emphasizes partial hospitalization (Bateman & Fonagy, 2003) and outpatient treatment as important pragmatic treatment alternatives. The use of such strategies with children and adolescents has not been empirically documented, however.

DEVELOPMENTAL CONSIDERATIONS

Because we believe that a developmental psychopathology perspective is important in understanding the emergence of borderline personality features in children and adolescents, we propose that it is also important to keep this perspective in mind when considering the best methods to employ in the treatment of children and adolescents. That is, it is important to consider what developmental tasks children and adolescents are likely to be negotiating and understand how these processes influence and are influenced by various treatment approaches. In addition, as with child and adolescent therapy in general, it is important to ensure that the chosen treatment methods are commensurate with the child's or adolescent's current developmental stage.

Children's cognitive abilities are likely to be relatively concrete, which may limit more abstract, introspective thinking until early to middle adolescence (see DeHart, Sroufe, & Cooper, 2000). More abstract thinking is likely necessary to engage in some of the aspects of treatment employed with adults. Dialectical principles of acceptance and change or a direct focus on maladaptive cognitions, for example, are less likely to be understood by children; however, it may be possible to more indirectly influence cognitive schemas and behavior through the pattern of client-therapist interactions in conversation, play, modeling and behavioral shaping. Subsequently, a greater emphasis could be placed on directly addressing maladaptive cognitions as a child's cognitive capabilities increase in complexity.

It is also important to realize that the developmental tasks (e.g., emotion regulation, impulse control, sense of self, autonomy) that are most salient at particular ages are likely to influence the goals we set in therapy in addressing the emergence of borderline personality features, as well as when we deem it necessary and appropriate to intervene. Across the course of middle childhood and into adolescence, children begin to develop the abilities necessary to engage in more complex cognitions (e.g., theory of mind) and emotional reasoning (e.g., empathy, moral development; see DeHart, Sroufe, & Cooper, 2000) that would allow them to think about and engage in effective discourse on the thoughts and feelings of themselves and others.

Some of the early relationships (e.g., dysfunctional attachment histories, invalidating family interactions) and traumatic events (e.g., abuse, neglect) that are believed to contribute to the problematic pattern of behavior and interpersonal interactions characteristic of adults with BPD are likely to be the environment in which children with borderline personality features are currently functioning (e.g., Bradley et al., 2005; Nickell et al., 2002). Thus, it may be important to incorporate family therapy or more direction on parent-child interaction into the treatment of children and adolescents with borderline personality features. Moreover, it is important to keep in mind that the environments in which children and adolescents are operating (e.g., the child in the family, student at school, beginning romantic relationships) are somewhat different from the contexts in which adults typically operate (e.g., as parents and spouses in families, as employees or employers in the workplace, more experience in romantic relationships); this will need to be considered in how therapy addresses borderline personality features for different developmental stages.

CURRENT MODELS FOR TREATMENT OF CHILDREN AND ADOLESCENTS

Models for treatment of children and adolescents demonstrating borderline personality features are not as prevalent as adult models. One example, however, is a model proposed by Bleiberg (2004). This model has been proposed for the treatment of dramatic personality disorders (e.g., antisocial, narcissistic, histrionic, and borderline) in children and adolescents. It integrates individual therapy, family therapy, and psychopharmacotherapy. Bleiberg indicates that his model of treatment is based on mentalization, which he defines as "the biologically prepared capacity to interpret, represent, and to respond to human behavior (that of self and others) in human, meaningful terms" (p. 468). Bleiberg explains that maladaptive early relationships inhibit the development of healthy mentalization, which he asserts contributes to such developmental achievements as self-agency, an autobiographical narrative, social reciprocity and empathy, self-regulation, and capacity to symbolize and play.

Given this framework, the following is a brief summary of the components of Bleiberg's (2004) treatment model. The beginning of treatment involves creating a "representational mismatch" (Horowitz, 1987, as cited by Bleiberg, 2004) for the child in which the child's current expectations for interpersonal relations are challenged by those interactions occurring in the context of the therapy. Part of this involves shifting the focus from the problematic behaviors of the child to the relationships and the associated internal states the child is experiencing. Thus, the therapist works to include the parents as participants in this process. In the early stages of the treatment, the therapist can decide whether he or she would like to simultaneously conduct the individual and family treatment or would like a separate clinician to do the individual treatment. Bleiberg indicated that adolescents often prefer a separate clinician for the individual treatment. In the early stages of therapy, Bleiberg's model includes a variety of techniques (e.g., play, humor, psychoeducation) to address the following areas: enhancing mentalization, strengthening impulse control and enhancing self-regulation, and creating awareness of others' mental states. In the middle and late stages of this model, the therapist works to use the therapeutic connection with the child to help him or her move to a more integrated, continuous sense of self.

Family work includes working with parents to develop more adaptive parenting strategies, enhance their own mentalization, and work to understand how stressors in their lives influence the parent-child interactions (Bleiberg, 2004). Finally, Bleiberg discusses the fact that medication can be used as an adjunct to therapy to address "dysregulations of arousal, cognition, affect, and impulse that promote the inhibition of mentalization" (p. 471). In all, this model is lengthy and quite time-intensive; Bleiberg reports that two or more sessions per week will likely be needed for 1 to 3 years.

Another model that has been recently developed and focuses on treating adolescents who meet BPD criteria and have co-occurring substance abuse problems is integrative borderline adolescent family therapy (I-BAFT; Santisteban, Muir, Mena, & Mitrani, 2003). Santisteban et al. have incorporated important developmental characteristics of adolescence (e.g., cognitive sophistication, greater strides toward independence within the family, concerns with future goals, beginning romantic relationships) in their model, which is based on the notion that

> maladaptive family interactions, some of which are the result of the adolescent borderline behavior and some of which have always existed in the family, begin to interact with the adolescent's vulnerability to emotion

dysregulation in such a way that the family becomes the fertile ground in which the borderline behaviors, including drug abuse, blossom fully. (p. 256)

This model is composed of three treatment components (i.e., individual therapy, family therapy, and skills training), which draw on the already established family interventions and DBT (Linehan, 1993, as cited by Santisteban et al., 2003).

More specifically, in the individual therapy component, goals include establishing strong engagement between therapist and adolescent, helping the adolescent to establish healthy goals in a variety of life domains, monitoring self-destructive behaviors, aiding in the generalizability of the newly learned life skills to the adolescent's everyday life, and preparing the adolescent for difficulties in the family session and training him or her to contribute to change in this system. The family therapy component aims to help family members understand the adolescent's emotional and behavioral dysregulation as a vulnerability, help the family understand the interactional or systemic context of the problem, facilitate and improve communication among family members, develop effective parenting skills, encourage the broadening of the adolescent's supportive network to other responsible adults (e.g., extended family members, older siblings), and reduce negative family interactions. Finally, the skills component draws on Linehan's (1993, as cited by Santisteban et al., 2003) DBT program, with the following goals: increasing mindfulness, teaching interpersonal effectiveness, teaching greater emotion regulation for negative or aversive emotions, and increasing distress tolerance. In addition, Santisteban et al. (2003) added the goal of HIV risk reduction in their skills training component, given the potential for borderline adolescents to engage in risky sexual behavior.

Similar to Bleiberg's (2004) model, the I-BAFT model is likely to require more than one professional per case. That is, they suggest that a therapist conduct both the individual and family therapy sessions and that the adolescent also be involved with a skills trainer. If the adolescent requires psychopharmacological treatment as well, this will require contact with a psychiatrist. Also somewhat similar to the Bleiberg model, I-BAFT requires multiple sessions per week. However, I-BAFT is estimated to last 6 to 8 months, rather than the 1 to 3 years estimated for the Bleiberg model.

MECHANISMS OF CHANGE

In recent years, the mental health field has increasingly encouraged the identification of evidence-based explanations of treatment, in contrast to existing trademarked or credentialed treatments (Ablon, Levy, & Katzenstein, 2006). Although efficacy and effectiveness studies of treatments are necessary, their value for delineating the putative mechanisms of constructs proposed to be central to the clinical disorder of interest is notably limited. Many studies have reported both efficacy (e.g., Bateman & Fonagy, 1999; Linehan, 2000; Verheul et al., 2003) and effectiveness (e.g., Clarkin et al., 2001; Stevenson, Meares, & D'Angelo, 2005) data on the treatment of BPD. Further research investigating the mechanisms of change of different methods of treating BPD would likely lead to the development of innovative tailoring of treatment to better suit the needs of individual clients. In addition, in an effort to reduce the high cost of treating those with such a debilitating disorder, active components of a specific treatment could be intensified while allocating less time and fewer resources to nonspecific elements of treatment.

There are several approaches to the study of mechanisms of change in the treatment of Borderline Personality Disorder (e.g., Levy et al., 2006). First, one could use a dismantling strategy, whereby the proposed active ingredient is removed. Then the treatment can be evaluated comparing the original and dismantled versions. An example of this is removing the emotion regulation module from DBT and comparing the efficacy of this dismantled version with the original version of DBT. Another way of studying mechanisms of change is by creating an additive treatment where two or more separate therapy techniques are combined and then compared to the original techniques separately. For example, the therapeutic model proposed by Bleiberg (2004) may be combined with that proposed by Santisteban et al. (2003) and then compared to the two isolated therapies.

Future studies of mechanisms of change in treatments of BPD should include consideration of important predictors (e.g., developmental neurotraumatology), moderators (e.g., therapist characteristics, gender, age, race/ethnicity), and mediators (e.g., participant's self-esteem). In the future, uncovering mechanisms of change could bring about prescriptive benefits in helping to identify clients who would be more responsive to particular treatments (Clarkin & Levy, 2006).

RECOMMENDED FUTURE DIRECTIONS IN TREATMENT

It is encouraging to see the work of those such as Bleiberg (2004) and Santisteban et al. (2003) who are becoming attentive to the developmental processes contributing to the emergence of borderline personality features and examining developmentally appropriate ways to address this in childhood and adolescence. There are a number of ways in which both of these models seem to be commensurate with our own developmental perspective. One example of this is the focus on the salience of the parent-child relationship and inclusion of the family in treatment. In addition, both models focus on areas of functioning and development (e.g., emotions, cognitions, behavior, formation of integrated sense of self) that are rather consistent with those indicators that members of our research team (i.e., Geiger & Crick, 2001) identified in completing a content analysis of BPD symptoms based on a developmental psychopathology perspective. We recommend that future endeavors to address borderline features in children and adolescents use models that emphasize salient developmental tasks (e.g., Geiger & Crick, 2001; Ryan, 2005) to guide treatment design. Finally, it is recommended that more long-term, treatment outcome studies be conducted with samples of children and adolescents who have gone through these treatment models to assess their effectiveness.

Another issue that is important to address concerns the logistics of this type of treatment. As was pointed out, both the Bleiberg (2004) and I-BAFT (Santisteban et al., 2003) models are complex, time-intensive processes involving multiple care providers (e.g., multiple therapists, psychiatrists). It would likely be most beneficial for the families involved and the treating clinicians for services to be centralized in one clinic, both for the convenience of the families and for ease of communication among the treatment providers. In addition, it would be helpful for those working in this clinic to have a working knowledge of treating problems known to have a high incidence of comorbidity with BPD in childhood and adolescence (e.g., substance abuse, depression, anxiety).

POSSIBLE IMPEDIMENTS TO TREATMENT

There are a variety of possible impediments to treatment of borderline personality features in children and adolescents that must be considered when working with this population. One of the most basic impediments is a lack of willingness to identify these features or give the diagnosis to children or adolescents. As stated by Santisteban et al. (2003), such practices have likely contributed to the hindrance of the development of specific treatment methods with which to address these problems in the child and adolescent population. It is likely that such reluctance is related to concerns about stigma and the limitations of the current diagnostic system in labeling a constellation of developmental precursors to BPD. We understand the reluctance of clinicians to give a diagnosis that suggests a well-entrenched manner of behaving in and interacting with the world when various aspects of the child that contribute to and constitute his or her personality are likely still in the course of development. However, we do not currently have a diagnostic label for children and adolescents who fit the profile of developmental precursors we have discussed in this chapter, which is a significant impediment to accurately communicating the symptom picture for an individual demonstrating these difficulties. Moreover, without an accepted diagnostic label or code, insurance companies are not likely to cover treatment. Another impediment related to diagnosis is gender stereotyping. It has been proposed that gender impacts the susceptibility to and expression of the development of personality disorder features (P. Kernberg et al., 2000). Furthermore, some children exhibiting maladaptive personality features may go undiagnosed and end up not receiving appropriate treatment because their manifest behaviors are considered gender-typical.

Another possible impediment is how time-intensive and costly this type of treatment is likely to be. Both the child and adolescent models discussed here (i.e., Bleiberg, 2004; Santisteban et al., 2003) involve multiple practitioners working with each individual for multiple hours per week for anywhere from 8 months to 3 years. Because BPD can be considered a disorder that severely disrupts the individual's emotional, cognitive, and behavioral regulatory systems, progress in therapy is much slower than with other types of disorders, even with the most effective treatments (e.g., Linehan, 1993). On the other hand, BPD is associated with a variety of impulsive and self-injurious behaviors that could lead to a wide array of other costs to both the individual and society (e.g., chemical dependency treatment, hospitalizations) that could be incurred across the lifetime of an individual with BPD if not treated effectively. It will also be important that those intervening with this population receive specialized training in treating these problems in a developmentally appropriate manner to ensure the effectiveness of these treatments.

Finally, by definition, Borderline Personality Disorder involves "a pervasive pattern of instability in interpersonal relationships" (American Psychiatric Association, 2000, p. 706). Psychologists and other mental health professionals are not immune to the difficulties and stress in interpersonal interactions that come along with this syndrome. Helping individuals learn to manage such extreme emotional and behavioral dysregulation and the behaviors associated with such vulnerabilities (e.g., suicide attempts, substance abuse, risky sexual activity, cutting and other self-injurious behavior) can be extremely stressful for clinicians.

Moreover, the maladaptive pattern of behaviors that individuals with borderline personality features demonstrate (e.g., vacillating between aggrandizing and devaluing) may test even the most skilled of clinicians in terms of the appropriate manner with which to react in such interactions. At times, the individuals seeking therapy can inadvertently reinforce or intentionally provoke attending mental health care professionals to engage in ineffective behaviors. This is why it is often suggested that clinicians working with individuals with BPD get consistent consultation and support from their colleagues (e.g., Linehan, 1993). It is believed that the context of supportive supervision and consultation will diminish chaotic staff relations and help therapists to develop more realistic demands on themselves to promote positive change in their clients while maintaining a manageable and emotionally healthy work setting.

CONCLUSIONS

Clearly, a great deal of work lies ahead if we are to generate a comprehensive understanding of the individual (e.g., cognitive, biological, behavioral, and emotional) and contextual (e.g., familial, peer, ethnic, gender, and cultural) factors that significantly influence the development and maintenance of borderline personality pathology. A number of future directions for our collective research agenda seem warranted. First and foremost, it is imperative that we initiate studies with long-term, prospective designs, particularly those that begin in childhood, that focus on the study of theoretically and empirically relevant risk factors for the development of borderline pathology. It is only through these types of studies that we will be able to identify the developmental trajectories that are most likely to result in BPD and to develop prevention and intervention programs that are effective in alleviating this form of pathology.

As described previously, it also imperative that we focus on both normative and clinical samples so that we may develop theoretical models that capture development of the full range of borderline pathology. Another important avenue for future studies concerns the inclusion of ethnically and racially diverse samples, along with theoretically guided attention to the ways that borderline pathology may or may not manifest differently in these groups. For example, a particular criterion for diagnosing BPD or risk factors for such pathology may vary for various ethnic/racial groups such that it indicates pathology for some groups but not for others (e.g., extremely close relationships may be normative and considered appropriate for some cultures and may not be an appropriate indicator of borderline pathology).

An additional avenue for future research involves the use of established, reliable, and valid instruments to assess borderline pathology in children and adolescents. Given the lack of availability of these types of assessment tools for these young age groups, particularly those that yield dimensional evaluations of borderline pathology (for an exception, see Crick et al., 2005), it will be extremely important to develop new, scientifically viable instruments that are developmentally appropriate for use with a variety of age groups that range from early childhood to late adolescence and beyond (and/or a parallel set of measures that target particular age groups). Finally, given the complex nature of borderline pathology and the difficulties inherent in understanding the developmental precursors and trajectories of this disorder, it will be necessary to involve collaborators and consultants from diverse disciplines (e.g., clinical psychology, developmental psychology, psychiatry, developmental behavioral neuroscience, statistics) if we are to come to gain a better understanding of such a complex disorder.

REFERENCES

Ablon, J. S., Levy, R. A., & Katzenstein, T. (2006). Beyond brand names of psychotherapy: Identifying empirically supported change processes. *Psychotherapy: Theory, Research, Practice, Training, 43*(2), 216–231.

Ainsworth, M. D. S. (1979). Attachment as related to mother-infant interaction. In J. S. Rosenblatt, R. A. Hinde, C. Beer, & M. Busnel (Eds.), *Advances in the study of behavior* (Vol. 9). Orlando, FL: Academic Press.

American Psychiatric Association. (1994). *Diagnostic and statistical manual of mental disorders* (4th ed.). Washington, DC: Author.

American Psychiatric Association. (2000). *Diagnostic and statistical manual of mental disorders* (4th ed., text rev.). Washington, DC: Author.

Bandura, A. (1986). *Social foundation of thought and action: A social cognitive theory.* Englewood Cliffs, NJ: Prentice-Hall.

Bateman, A. W., & Fonagy, P. (1999). Effectiveness of partial hospitalization in the treatment of borderline personality disorder: A randomized controlled trial. *American Journal of Psychiatry, 156,* 1563–1569.

Bateman, A. W., & Fonagy, P. (2003). Health service utilization costs for borderline personality disorder patients treated with psychoanalytically oriented partial hospitalization versus general psychiatric care. *American Journal of Psychiatry, 160,* 169–171.

Bateman, A. W., & Holmes, J. (1995). *Introduction to psychoanalysis: Contemporary theory and practice.* London: Routledge.

Beck, A. T., & Freeman, A. (1990). *Cognitive therapy of personality disorders.* New York: Guilford Press.

Belsky, J., Friedman, S. L., & Hsieh, K. (2001). Testing a core emotion-regulation prediction: Does early attentional persistence moderate the effect of infant negative emotionality on later development? *Child Development, 72,* 123–133.

Bleiberg, E. (2004). Treatment of dramatic personality disorders in children and adolescents. In E. J. Magnavita (Ed.), *Handbook of personality disorders: Theory and practice* (pp. 467–497). Hoboken, NJ: Wiley.

Block, M. J., Westen, D., Ludolph, P., Widon, J., & Jackson, A. (1991). Distinguishing female borderline adolescents from normal and other disturbed female adolescents. *Psychiatry, 54,* 89–103.

Bradley, R., Jenei, J., & Westen, D. (2005). Etiology of borderline personality disorder: Disentangling the contributions of intercorrelated antecedents. *Journal of Nervous and Mental Diseases, 193,* 24–30.

Caspi, A. (1998). Personality development across the life course. In W. Damon (Series Ed.) & N. Eisenberg (Vol. Ed.), *Handbook of child psychol-*

ogy: Vol. 3. Social, emotional, and personality development (pp. 311–388). New York: Wiley.

Caspi, A., & Shiner, R. L. (2006). Personality development. In W. Damon & R. Lerner (Series Eds.) & N. Eisenberg (Vol. Ed.), *Handbook of child psychology, Vol. 3. Social, emotional, and personality development* (6th ed., pp. 300–365). Hoboken, NJ: Wiley.

Chabrol, H., Montovany, A., Chouicha, K., Callahan, S., & Mullet, E. (2001). Frequency of borderline personality disorder in a sample of French high school students. *Canadian Journal of Psychiatry, 46,* 847–849.

Clark, L. A., & Harrison, J. A. (2001). Assessment instruments. In W. J. Livesley (Ed.), *Handbook of personality disorders: Theory, research, and treatment* (pp. 277–306). New York: Guilford Press.

Clarkin, J. F., Foelsch, P. A., Levy, K. N., Hull, J. W., Delaney, J. C., & Kernberg, O. F. (2001). The development of a psychodynamic treatment for patients with borderline personality disorder: A preliminary study of behavioral change. *Journal of Personality Disorders, 15*(6), 487–495.

Clarkin, J. F., Hull, J. W., Cantor, J., & Sanderson, C. (1993). Borderline personality disorder and personality traits: A comparison of SCID-II BPD and NEO-PI. *Psychological Assessment, 5,* 472–476.

Clarkin, J. F., & Levy, K. N. (2006). Psychotherapy for patients with borderline personality disorder: Focusing on the mechanisms of change. *Journal of Clinical Psychology, 62*(4), 405–410.

Clarkin, J. F., Marziali, E., & Munroe-Blum, H. (1991). Group and family treatments for borderline personality disorder. *Hospital and Community Psychiatry, 42,* 1038–1042.

Coccaro, E. F., Bergeman, C. S., & McClearn, G. E. (1993). Heritability of irritable impulsiveness: A study of twins reared together and apart. *Psychiatry Research, 48,* 229–242.

Coie, J. D., & Dodge, K. A. (1998). Aggression and antisocial behavior. In W. Damon (Series Ed.) & N. Eisenberg (Vol. Ed.), *Handbook of child psychology: Vol. 3. Social, emotional, and personality development* (5th ed.). New York: Wiley.

Crick, N. R., & Dodge, K. A. (1994). A review and reformulation of social-information-processing mechanisms in children's social adjustment. *Psychological Bulletin, 115,* 74–101.

Crick, N. R., Murray-Close, D., & Woods, K. (2005). Borderline personality features in childhood: A short-term longitudinal study. *Development and Psychopathology, 17,* 1051–1070.

Crick, N. R., & Zahn-Waxler, C. (2003). The development of psychopathology in females and males: Current progress and future challenges. *Development and Psychopathology, 15,* 719–742.

Damon, W., & Hart, D. (1988). *Self-understanding in childhood and adolescence.* New York: Cambridge University Press.

Dawson, D. (1988). Treatment of the borderline patient: Relation management. *Canadian Journal of Psychiatry, 33,* 370–374.

DeHart, G., Sroufe, L. A., & Cooper, R. (2000). *Child development: Its nature and course* (4th Edition). New York: McGraw-Hill.

Erikson, E. H. (1963). *Childhood and society* (2nd ed.). New York: Norton.

Geiger, T., & Crick, N. R. (2001). A developmental psychopathology perspective on vulnerability to personality disorders. In R. E. Ingram & J. M. Price (Eds.), *Vulnerability to psychopathology: Risk across the lifespan* (pp. 55–102). New York: Guilford Press.

Gunderson, J. G., & Zanarini, M. C. (1987). Current overview of the borderline diagnosis. *Journal of Clinical Psychiatry, 48,* 5–11.

Gunderson, J. G., Zanarini, M. C., & Kiesel, C. L. (1991). Borderline personality disorder: A review of data on *DSM-III-R* descriptions. *Journal of Personality Disorders, 5,* 340–352.

Guzder, J., Paris, J., Zelkowitz, P., & Feldman, R. (1999). Psychological risk factors for borderline pathology in school-age children. *Journal of the American Academy of Child and Adolescent Psychiatry, 38,* 206–212.

Guzder, J., Paris, J., Zelkowitz, P., & Marchessault, K. (1996). Risk factors for borderline pathology in children. *Journal of the American Academy of Child and Adolescent Psychiatry, 35,* 26–33.

Hansenne, M., Pitchot, W., Pinto, E., Reggers, J., Scantamburlo, G., Fuchs, S., et al. (2002). 5-HT dysfunction in borderline personality disorder. *Psychological Medicine, 32,* 935–941.

Harter, S. (1983). Developmental perspectives on the self-system. In P. H. Mussen (Ed.), *Handbook of child psychology: Vol. 4. Socialization, personality, and social development* (pp. 275–385). New York: Wiley.

Hartup, W. W. (1992). Friendships and their developmental significance. In H. McGurk (Ed.), *Childhood and social development: Contemporary perspectives* (pp. 175–206). London: Erlbaum.

Hartup, W. W., & van Lieshout, C. F. M. (1995). Personality development in social context. *Annual Review of Psychology, 46,* 655–687.

Herman, J., Perry, C., & van der Kolk, B. (1989). Childhood trauma in borderline personality disorder. *American Journal of Psychiatry, 146,* 490–495.

Hobson, R. P., Patrick, M., Crandell, L., Garcia-Perez, R., & Lee, A. (2005). Personal relatedness and attachment in infants of mothers with borderline personality disorder. *Development and Psychopathology, 17,* 329–347.

Hoffman, P. D., Fruzzetti, A. E., Buteau, E., Neiditch, E. R., Penney, D., Bruce, M. L., et al. (2005). Family connections: A program for relatives of persons with borderline personality disorder. *Family Process, 44,* 217–225.

Hoffman, P. D., Fruzzetti, A., & Swenson, C. (1999). Dialectical behavior therapy—Family skills training. *Family Process, 38,* 399–414.

Hurt, S. W., Clarkin, J. F., Munroe-Blum, H., & Marziali, E. (1992). Borderline behavioral clusters and different treatment approaches. In J. F. Clarkin, E. Marziali, & H. Munroe-Blum (Eds.), *Borderline personality disorder: Clinical and empirical perspectives* (pp. 199–219). New York: Guilford Press.

Jones, B., Heard, H., Startup, M., Swales, M., Williams, J. M. G., & Jones, R. S. P. (1999). Autobiographical memory, dissociation, and parasuicide in borderline personality disorder. *Psychological Medicine, 29,* 1397–1404.

Kernberg, O., Selzer, M., Koenigsberg, H., Carr, A., & Applebaum, A. (1989). *Psychodynamic psychotherapy of borderline patients.* New York: Basic Books.

Kernberg, P., Weiner, A. S., & Bardenstein, K. K. (2000). *Personality disorders in children and adolescents.* New York: Basic Books.

Kopp, C. B. (1987). The growth of self-regulation: Caregivers and children. In N. Eisenberg (Ed.), *Contemporary topics in developmental psychology* (pp. 34–55). New York: Wiley.

Kurtz, J. E., Morey, L. C., & Tomarken, A. J. (1993). The concurrent validity of three self-report measures of borderline personality. *Journal of Psychopathology and Behavioral Assessment, 15,* 255–266.

Levy, K. N., Clarkin, J. F., Yeomans, F. E., Scott, L. N., Wasserman, R. H., & Kernberg, O. F. (2006). The mechanisms of change in the treatment of borderline personality disorder with transference focused psychotherapy. *Journal of Clinical Psychology, 62*(4), 481–501.

Linehan, M. M. (1987). Dialectical behavioral therapy: A cognitive behavioral approach to parasuicide. *Journal of Personality Disorders, 1,* 328–333.

Linehan, M. M. (1993). *Cognitive-behavioral treatment of borderline personality disorder.* New York: Guilford Press.

Linehan, M. M. (2000). The empirical basis of dialectical behavior therapy: Development of new treatments versus evaluation of existing treatments. *Clinical Psychology: Science and Practice, 7*(1), 113–119.

Linehan, M. M., & Heard, H. L. (1992). Dialectical behavioral therapy for borderline personality disorder. In J. F. Clarkin, E. Marziali, & H. Munroe-Blum (Eds.), *Borderline personality disorder: Clinical and empirical perspectives* (pp. 248–267). New York: Guilford Press.

Livesley, W. J., Jang, K. L., & Vernon, P. A. (1998). Phenotypic and genetic structure of traits delineating personality disorder. *Archives of General Psychiatry, 55,* 941–994.

Mangelsdorf, S. C., Shapiro, J. R., & Marzolf, D. (1995). Developmental and temperamental differences in emotion regulation in infancy. *Child Development, 66,* 1817–1828.

Markovitz, P. J., & Wagner, C. (1995). Venlafaxine in the treatment of borderline personality disorder. *Psychopharmacology Bulletin, 31,* 773–777.

McCrae, R. R., & Costa, P. T. (1999). A five-factor theory of personality. In L. A. Pervin & O. P. John (Eds.), *Handbook of personality* (2nd ed., pp. 139–153). New York: Guilford Press.

Mervielde, I., De Clercq, B., De Fruyt, F., & Van Leeuwen, K. (2005). Temperament, personality, and developmental psychopathology as childhood antecedents of personality disorders. *Journal of Personality Disorders, 19,* 171–201.

Mischel, W. (1986). *Introduction to personality* (4th ed.). New York: Holt, Rinehart, & Winston.

Morey, L. (1988a). The categorical representation of personality disorder: A cluster analysis of DSM-III-R personality features. *Journal of Abnormal Psychology, 97,* 314–321.

Morey, L. (1988b). Personality disorders in DSM-III and DSM-III-R: Convergence, coverage, and internal consistency. *American Journal of Psychiatry, 145,* 573–577.

Morey, L. (1991). *Personality Assessment Inventory.* Odessa, FL: Psychological Assessment Resources.

Morey, L. C., & Zanarini, M. C. (2000). Borderline personality: Traits and disorder. *Journal of Abnormal Psychology, 109,* 733–737.

Nickell, A. D., Waudby, C. J., & Trull, T. J. (2002). Attachment, parental bonding, and borderline personality disorder features in young adults. *Journal of Personality Disorders, 16,* 148–159.

Paris, J. (2003). *Personality disorders over time: Precursors, course, and outcome.* Arlington, VA: American Psychiatric Publishing.

Paris, J. (2005). Borderline personality disorder. *Canadian Medical Association Journal, 172,* 1579–1583.

Paris, J., Zweig-Frank, H., & Guzder, J. (1994). Psychological risk factors for borderline personality disorder in female patients. *Comprehensive Psychiatry, 35,* 301–305.

Plomin, R., & Rutter, M. (1998). Child development, molecular genetics, and what to do with genes once they are found. *Child Development, 69,* 1223–1242.

Quiggle, N. L., Garber, J., Panak, W. G., & Dodge, K. A. (1992). Social information processing in aggressive and depressed children. *Child Development, 63,* 1305–1320.

Ryan, R. M. (2005). The developmental line of autonomy in the etiology, dynamics, and treatment of borderline personality disorders. *Development and Psychopathology, 17,* 987–1006.

Samuels, J., Eaton, W. W., Beinvenue, J., Clayton, P., Brown, H., Costa, P. T., et al. (2002). Prevalence and correlates of personality disorders in a community sample. *British Journal of Psychiatry, 180,* 536–542.

Santisteban, D. A., Muir, J. A., Mena, M. P., & Mitrani, V. B. (2003). Integrative borderline adolescent family therapy: Meeting the challenges of treating adolescents with borderline personality disorder. *Psychotherapy: Theory, research, practice, and training, 40,* 251–264.

Schulz, S. C., Camlin, K., Berry, S., & Jesberger, J. (1999). Olanzapine safety and efficacy in patients with borderline personality disorder and comorbid dysthymia. *Biological Psychiatry, 46,* 1429–1435.

Shiner, R. L. (2005). A developmental perspective on personality disorders: Lessons from research on normal personality development in childhood and adolescence. *Journal of Personality Disorders, 19,* 202–210.

Siever, L. J., Torgersen, S., Gunderson, J. G., Livesley, W. J., & Kendler, K. S. (2002). The borderline diagnosis: Pt. III. Identifying endophenotypes for genetic studies. *Biological Psychiatry, 51,* 964–968.

Skodol, A. E., Gunderson, J. G., Pfohl, B., Widiger, T. A., Livesley, W. J., & Siever, L. J. (2002). The borderline diagnosis: Pt. I. Psychopathology, comorbidity, and personality structure. *Biological Psychiatry, 51,* 936–950.

Solof, P. H., Lis, J. A., Kelly, T., Cornelius, J., & Ulrich, R. (1994). Self-mutilation and suicidal behavior in borderline personality disorder. *Journal of Personality Disorders, 8,* 257–267.

Sroufe, L. A. (1997). Psychopathology as an outcome of development. *Development and Psychopathology, 9,* 251–268.

Sroufe, L. A., & Rutter, M. (1984). The domain of developmental psychopathology. *Child Development, 55,* 17–29.

Stevenson, J., Meares, R., & D'Angelo, R. (2005). Five-year outcome of outpatient psychotherapy with borderline patients. *Psychological Medicine, 35*(1), 79–87.

Swartz, M., Blazer, D., George, L., & Winfield, I. (1990). Estimating the prevalence of borderline personality disorder in the community. *Journal of Personality Disorders, 4,* 257–272.

Thompson, R. A. (1994). Emotion regulation: A theme in search of definition. *Monographs of the Society for Research in Child Development, 59,* 250–283.

Torgersen, S., Kringlen, E., & Cramer, V. (2001). The prevalence of personality disorders in a community sample. *Archives of General Psychiatry, 58,* 590–596.

Torgersen, S., Lygren, S., Oien, P. A., Skre, I., Onstad, S., Edvardsen, J., et al. (2000). A twin study of personality disorders. *Comprehensive Psychiatry, 41,* 416–425.

Trull, T. J. (1995). Borderline personality disorder features in nonclinical young adults: I. Identification and validation. *Psychological Assessment, 7,* 33–41.

Trull, T. J., Stepp, S. D., & Durrett, C. A. (2003). Research on borderline personality disorder: An update. *Current Opinion in Psychiatry, 16,* 77–82.

Trull, T. J., Widiger, T. A., Lynam, D. R., & Costa, Jr., P. T. (2003). Borderline personality disorder from the perspective of general personality functioning. *Journal of Abnormal Psychology, 112,* 193–202.

Verheul, R., van den Bosch, L. M., Koeter, M. W., de Ridder, M. A., Stijnen, T., & van den Brink, W. (2003). Dialectical behaviour therapy for women with borderline personality disorder: 12-month, randomised clinical trial in The Netherlands. *British Journal of Psychiatry, 182*(2), 135–140.

Werner, E. E., & Smith, R. S. (1992). *Overcoming the odds: High risk children from birth to adulthood.* Ithaca: Cornell University Press.

Zanarini, M. C. (2000). Childhood experience associated with the development of borderline personality disorder. *Psychiatric Clinics of North America, 23,* 89–101.

Zanarini, M. C., & Frankenburg, F. R. (2001). Olanzapine treatment of borderline patients: A double-blind, placebo-controlled study. *Journal of Clinical Psychiatry, 62*(11), 849–854.

Zelkowitz, P., Paris, J., Guzder, J., & Feldman, K. (2001). Diathesis and stressors in borderline pathology of childhood: The role of neuropsychological risk and trauma. *Journal of the American Academy of Child and Adolescent Psychiatry, 40,* 100–105.

Zimmerman, M., & Mattia, J. I. (1999). Differences between clinical and research practices in diagnosing borderline personality disorder. *American Journal of Psychiatry, 156,* 1570–1574.

CHAPTER 11

The Narcissistic Child: When a State Becomes a Trait

ARTHUR FREEMAN

RACHEL WAS always the star in every class play and dramatic effort. She had been entered in child beauty contests since she was 2 years old. At age 11 she described her future life as a movie star. She would, she stated, be a movie star today if her father was not so rigid about "his need" for her to focus on school. When Rachel was 14, a new child, Trudy, entered her class and did not pay homage to Rachel's beauty and talents. In fact, the new child even spoke of trying out for the school play. Rachel tried denigrating the new girl's lack of talent, unattractive looks, and weight. This was followed by Rachel trying to mobilize other children against Trudy. When this also failed, Rachel went to the teacher and demanded that Trudy not be allowed to try out for the play because she was "too new." When the teacher told Rachel that anyone could try out for the school play, Rachel became furious and began screaming insults at the teacher. This was followed by Rachel's mother coming to school and speaking to the school administration about the inappropriate way Rachel was being treated.

Alan, age 6, soon made his style known to the teacher in his first-grade class. Whenever he did not get what he wanted, whether his desired color for painting, having to wait in line for his turn, or sharing toys or equipment with other children, Alan would have a tantrum. This involved his throwing himself to the floor, screaming, and kicking. Other children were frightened of Alan, as he had, on many occasions, destroyed the work of other children. When his parents were called in for a parent-teacher conference regarding Alan's behavior, his mother pointedly said to the teacher that she was not sending Alan to school to be frustrated. She stated that both she and her husband had earned doctorates, and that Alan was a gifted child and should be allowed whatever he wanted. This was what he had experienced at home.

From the time that he could walk, Eric was told by his father that he would be a great ice hockey star. He learned to skate at about the time he learned to walk. He had an ice rink set up in his backyard along with a goal. As Eric came of age, he joined various age-appropriate youth hockey teams. Despite his early start, constant practice, and family support, he never became a first-string hockey player in high school, much less the varsity all-star his father had predicted (or that Eric assumed he would become). His academic work was mediocre, as all his efforts and attention were on his sport. He was acknowledged by coaches and college scouts to be a "good" player with "a lot of heart," but not one with a great future in hockey.

Eric claimed that his problem was that the coach was a failed professional hockey player and was jealous of Eric's superb skills and professional potential. The coach therefore played "lesser" players and did not give Eric the time on the ice that he deserved. Eric's fantasies of professional stardom were matched only by his father's view of what Eric should become. When he was scouted by college scouts, he was never given a tryout or an opportunity to show his skill. When Eric accosted one of the college scouts and demanded a visit to the college and a bid to play for the college team, the scout told Eric that he simply wasn't good enough for their NCAA team. When Eric protested that he was better than the players on the college team, the scout's response was that Eric was "a legend in his own mind."

All three of these children have passed the point of positive self-esteem and have passed into the realm of narcissism.

INTRODUCTION

The narcissistic style and personality have been discussed by every psychoanalytic writer. Millon, Davis, Millon, Escovar, and Meagher (2000, p. 283) state that the "psychoanalytic literature regarding narcissism is so voluminous that it resists summary" and that "the route from Freud's 1914 paper to contemporary conceptions is long and twisted, and space does not permit its review here." Given the long history of the disorder and the descriptions of such individuals throughout recorded history, it is interesting that the diagnosis did not enter the nosology of the *Diagnostic and Statistical Manual of Mental Disorders* until *DSM-III* (American Psychiatric Association, 1980). The 10th edition of the *International Classification of Diseases* (WHO, 1993) does not include this diagnosis. This raises questions of the cultural context and cultural expressions of this style. One might ask whether narcissism is more quintessentially a product of contemporary American culture, behavior, and interpersonal style. Is the premium placed by contemporary American culture on individualism, hedonism, self-gratification, and self-serving action a root of narcissism? Among the criticisms of America in many third world protests is what is termed American "arrogance," that is, the belief that what is American is good by definition, whether the American political system or the American fast food system.

We might question whether narcissism is a genetic predisposition designed for survival of the fittest and the best. For example, does the Alpha position in a pack imply narcissism, inasmuch as the Alpha is a very special individual? The Alpha animal in a group or pack gets more food, the choice of food, the choice of mates, control over others, the death or banishment of adversaries, and the choice of sleeping accommodations. Any challenge to the Alpha's position may be fought to the death. Synonyms or descriptors for narcissism or for the term narcissistic include selfish, self-loving, excessive admiration for self, lack of humility, an infantile developmental stage, erotic self-love, lack of empathy, uncaring of others, vain, self-absorbed, egotistical, and conceited.

THE MYTH OF NARCISSUS

In the Greek myth, Narcissus was the product of his mother's rape by the river god Cephisus. Narcissus was an incredibly beautiful baby who grew into an incredibly beautiful young man. Although many individuals, men and women, would fall in love with him, Narcissus did not reciprocate but kept his distance from everyone. When Echo, a wood nymph, saw him she immediately fell hopelessly in love with him. When he heard of Echo's love for him he told her that he would rather die than allow her to have any part of him. Rejected, Echo died. One day, thirsty from hunting, Narcissus found a calm and beautiful pool of water. As he leaned over to quench his thirst he saw his own image in the water and, like others, fell in love with this beautiful being. The harder he tried to embrace and kiss the beautiful creature he saw, the more frustrated and lovesick he became. He finally died and was changed into the beautiful flower, the narcissus, that grows at the water's edge.

The themes of the myth encapsulate the issues and problems of the narcissist. These individuals are oblivious to the needs and feelings of others, are hypervigilant and focused on their image, are selfish, surround themselves with those who reinforce their self-view of specialness, seem unable to see the impact of their actions on others, have poor understanding of self and motives, have fragile self-esteem that can be easily threatened, and may be willing to die rather than be less than the beautiful and special person that they believe themselves (and others should recognize them) to be.

THE DISORDER DEFINED

The *DSM-IV-TR* (American Psychiatric Association, 2000, p. 717) defines the state of narcissism as "a pervasive pattern of grandiosity (in fantasy or behavior), need for admiration, and lack of empathy, beginning *by* early adulthood and present in a variety of contexts, as indicated by five (or more) of the following":

1. Has a significantly higher than average sense of self-importance (e.g., expects to be recognized as superior based on achievements).
2. Is often occupied with fantasies of unlimited success, power, brilliance, beauty, or ideal love.
3. Believes that he or she is "special" and unique and can only be understood by, or should associate with, other special or high-status people (or institutions).
4. Expects high levels of admiration or adulation by others.
5. Has a sense of entitlement, that is, has expectations of especially favorable treatment or automatic compliance with his or her expectations.
6. Is interpersonally exploitative, that is, takes advantage of others to achieve his or her own ends.
7. Lacks empathy: does not seem to recognize or identify with the feelings and needs of others.
8. Is often envious of others or believes that others are envious of him or her.
9. As a consequence of the above, shows what are often interpreted to be arrogant, haughty behaviors, or attitudes.

The diagnosis of Narcissistic Personality Disorder was a new addition to *DSM-III* (American Psychiatric Association, 1980) and has been maintained in *DSM-III-R* (American Psychiatric Association, 1987), *DSM-IV* (American Psychiatric Association, 1994), and *DSM-IV-TR* (American Psychiatric Association, 2000). It is interesting that, in accord with the wording in *DSM-IV-TR*, the individual with a Narcissistic Personality Disorder *suffers* from a "pervasive pattern of grandiosity (in fantasy or behavior), lack of empathy, and hypersensitivity to the evaluation of others" (italics mine). Whether or not the individual "suffers" depends on how the narcissism is perceived by others and how it is perceived and used by the individual. The pattern of grandiosity occurs whether or not an objective evaluation of talent, accomplishment, physical prowess, intelligence, competence, physical attractiveness, sense of humor, or creativity is made. If the self-assessment is reinforced by others, narcissists have reason to maintain and support their self-view.

HISTORY OF THE DISORDER

Although theorists differ about the effect of developmental events that eventuate in narcissism or a narcissistic style, they agree on the clinical description of the narcissist. What can be agreed upon is that in the most usual circumstances, an infant is treated as a very special person. Infants are fed (either on a schedule or demand) and kept warm, comfortable, and clean. It would be reasonable to assume that the child might develop representations of being unconditionally loved, continually cared for, and being a special "gift" to the family. Most children therefore are raised to see themselves as important. Kernberg, Weiner, and Bardenstein (2000), and Bleiberg (2001) both describe the development of the broad range of personality disorders in children and adolescents. Freud's 1914 paper "On Narcissism: An Introduction" was among his most important early works in that it first introduced the basic concept of the ego-ideal and the self-observing rule-driven portion of the psyche that Freud was later to describe as the superego (Fonagy, Person, & Sandler, 1991; Erwin, 2002).

The early, self-involved behavior of the infant was seen by Freud to be a transitional state, eventually maturing into the ability to transfer this self-love into the ability to love others. The basic psychoanalytic model of narcissism posits a disruption in the maturation process that fixates the individual's ability to love at the level of self-love and, to a greater or lesser degree, creating difficulty in extending love to others. Fine (1979, p. 413) summarized the new points in Freud's paper on narcissism:

1. It describes libido as a quantitatively variable force, whose transformations explain the manifestations of psychosexuality.
2. It contains the first systematic description of object choice.
3. It establishes the various meanings of "narcissism," a most useful clinical concept.
4. It offers a new classification of human beings on a therapeutic basis: the division into narcissistic neurosis, in which the patient is unable to make a relationship to the therapist, and transference neurosis, in which he is able to form a relationship. The notion that human beings could be classified in accordance with their therapeutic reactions was an idea with extensive implications.
5. It introduces for the first time the concept of ego-ideal, which was later rechristened the superego, one of the best fruits of Freud's genius.

Ansbacher & Ansbacher, 1956 describe Alfred Adler's view in that he saw the child's need for affection as part of the general striving for superiority and perfection and as the forerunner of later social interest or social feeling. Adler, however, sees the affectional "drive" or tendencies as reciprocal: "As a rule, and with good reason, the satisfaction of the need for affection cannot be had for nothing (i.e., without giving something in return). Thus the need for affection becomes the lever of education" (Ansbacher & Ansbacher, 1956, p. 40). Further, "it is only after satisfaction has been denied to the out-going seeking of affection that the child turns upon himself in self-love" (p. 40). For Adler, the final goal had as its purpose the attainment of superiority. His description in many ways defines the narcissist. It involved "conquering all of the difficulties of life" and is "apperceived by the childish imagination and under the exigencies of hard reality, as victory over men, over difficult enterprises, over social or natural limitations. It appears in one's attitude toward others, toward one's vocation, toward the opposite sex" (pp. 95–96). Adler therefore saw narcissism as a failure to develop *social interest* and of taking a "backward" emphasis. The neurotic has likely "been a child to whom leaning on other people offered a possibility of success. Such a child experienced, developed, and secured for himself during several years of his life an enriched and elevated position by obtaining everything easily" (p. 241). The child develops what Adler called a "pampered lifestyle." The child who has not developed social interest "has pictured himself a world in which he is entitled to be first in everything" (p. 242). The key ingredient, according to Adler, is not simply the way the child is treated, but "is the child, and is very frequently found even where there is no evidence whatever of pampering by another person" (p. 242). A relevant and key Adlerian construct is that of *compensation,* wherein the child learns to compensate for feelings of inferiority by either seeking a superior position in life or, in the case of the narcissist, in fantasies.

The narcissistic child later becomes the "user" and "getter" who demands that his or her needs are met first and foremost, even to the point of avoiding meeting the needs of others. Ansbacher and Ansbacher (1956, p. 423) attribute addictive behaviors and cravings to "a superiority complex in the form of boastfulness, a malicious criminal tendency (and) a longing for power."

Federn (1952) differentiated between healthy and pathological narcissism. Healthy narcissism contributes to hope and ambition, which motivates the individual to grow and be creative. Pathological narcissism serves as a substitute for hope and ambition. The more it serves as a substitute, the more pathological it is. In healthy or normal narcissism, the boundaries of the ego are firm and resilient. In pathological narcissism, ego boundaries are unstable. Finally, the fantasies of the normal or healthy narcissism on both conscious and unconscious levels are more in accord with reality and are less infantile. The grandiose and magical elements that are the hallmark of narcissistic fantasies are related to how far the narcissistic style differs from normal.

Bacon and Gedo (1993) credit Sandor Ferenczi with first placing narcissism into a developmental framework.

Horney (1937, p. 163) also differentiates between healthy strivings for power and neurotic strivings:

> The feeling of power, for example, may in a normal person be born of the realization of his own superior strength, whether it be physical strength or ability, mental capacities, maturity or wisdom. Or his striving for power may be connected with some particular cause; family, political, or professional group, native land, a religious or scientific idea. The neurotic striving for power, however, is born out of anxiety, hatred and feelings of inferiority. To put it categorically, the normal striving for power is born of strength, the neurotic of weakness.

Though she rarely uses the term "narcissistic" in her discussion of the quest for power, prestige, and possession (chap. 10). Horney also describes the importance of culture in the search for power. She points out, "Neither Adler nor Freud has recognized the role that anxiety plays in bringing about such drives, nor has either of them seen the cultural implications in the forms in which they are expressed" (p. 187). She summarizes the aims and functions of the neurotic striving as follows (p. 186):

Aims	Reassurance Against	Hostility Appears in the Form Of
Power	Helplessness	A tendency to dominate
Prestige	Humiliation	A tendency to humiliate
Possession	Destitution	A tendency to deprive others

Like Adler, Horney (1937) sees the narcissistic striving and the resultant behavior as expressions of weakness and deprivation for which the self-glorying and self-righteousness of the narcissist are not functions of self-love, but rather self-hate. The narcissistic style "has nothing to do with any kind of self-love; it does not even contain any element of complacency or conceit, because contrary to appearances, there is never a real conviction of being right, but only a constant desperate need to appear justified" (p. 210).

Erikson (1968, p. 70) summarized Freud's view of self-esteem as:

> the residue of childish narcissism, that is, the child's natural self love; such infantile omnipotence as is corroborated by experience giving the child the feeling that he fulfills his own ego ideal; and the gratification of object libido, that is, the love for others.

Further, Erikson states, "But in a healthy residue of infantile narcissism, which is to survive, the maternal environment must create and sustain it with a love which assures the child that it is good to live in the social coordinates in which he happens to find himself" (p. 71). This awareness of the social context, which was Erikson's major modification of Freud's psychosexual development, becomes especially important to the child. The adolescent's development of self-esteem is dependent on "whether or not the adolescent can expect the opportunity to employ what he has learned in childhood and to acquire thereby a feeling of continued communal meaning" (p. 7).

The object relations theorists (Kernberg, 1976; Kohut, 1968, 1971) view narcissism as a paradoxical response to emotional deprivation during the early developmental stages. In effect, the exaggeration and overvaluation serve the *defensive* purpose of protecting the real self, which is threatened and weak. This idea is in accord with the Adlerian idea of "compensation" for perceived lesser status and/or inferiority.

Highly intelligent narcissists may, in fact, have good impulse control, social functioning, and the capacity for active and consistent work, which may allow them to achieve success. They "can be found as leaders in industrial organizations or academic institutions; they may also be outstanding performers in some artistic domain" (O. Kernberg, 1976, p. 229). This latter group can have "evidence" of their importance and success. Their difficulty will surface when they no longer have the accoutrements and trappings of success.

Discussing narcissism in adolescents, Masterson (1985, p. 39) states:

> The narcissistic, magical, and omnipotent fantasies erected by these patients to contend with these defects and to protect themselves from the painful memory traces of a traumatic infancy and childhood are of little help in coping with the realities of the adult world. . . . In spite of their unadaptive value, these fantasies are cherished by the patients who even live their lives around them, perhaps in an effort at belated mastery.
>
> Although there is an extensive literature of case reports on the treatment of narcissist individuals, all of which point to deprivation and abandonment as key features of their experience, there is little empirical research validating the notion that early deprivation will lead to an inflated sense of self even as a compensation. Studies of emotional deprivation have, in fact, presented evidence that emotional deprivation in infancy leads to apathy, withdrawal, poor social skills, and an avoidance of social interaction (or, more broadly, depression).

In discussing the etiology of a narcissistic personality, Millon and Everly (1985) and Millon et al. (2000) believe the initiation and development of the narcissistic personality is environmentally based, as "there is virtually no promising evidence to point to" (Millon & Everly, 1985, p. 76). They describe three "potent" factors: parental indulgence and overvaluation, learned exploitive behavior, and only-child status.

Ronningstam (2005) addresses the myth that narcissists cannot be treated and offers a dimensional model that helps to place the narcissist on a continuum from behavioral expressions that may be adaptive and functional to the disorder that usually comes to mind when hearing the term.

In terms of *parental indulgence,* the parents view the child as special, better, perhaps, than all others, even better than siblings and relatives. These children learn several things:

1. That they deserve to be treated with distinction without having to do anything to earn such treatment.
2. That they are special, superior people.
3. That they can expect compliance and even subservience from other not-so-special people.
4. That they can expect commendation and praise for virtually everything they do.
5. They believe that the world revolves around their whims and wishes.
6. They are egotistical in their perspectives.
7. They are narcissistic in their expressions of love and emotion. (Millon & Everly, 1985, pp. 75–76)

As these children move outside the favored position within the family, they have learned to expect to be treated in similar ways. After all, how else should they be treated? They quickly learn to manipulate others and situations so as to receive the special status that they have learned that they should get, regardless of their performance or ability. They learn the buttons to push and the idiosyncrasies of others. They then can manipulate and exploit others, all with the intent and expectation of getting the recognition that they "deserve." "Exploitation of others seems to be powerfully reinforcing and, therefore, difficult to bring to extinction" (Millon & Everly, 1985, p. 77).

Finally, there is "only child" status. This status may not be the sole province of only children. Children whose next sibling is several years younger may be treated as only children inasmuch as the child is, in effect, an only child for many years.

Personality disorders in children have been addressed from a cognitive-behavioral perspective (Freeman & Duff, 2006; Freeman

& Rigby, 2003). Cognitive-behavior therapy (CBT) is an active, directive, goal-oriented, solution-focused, structured, dynamic, psychoeducational, and often time-limited approach to psychotherapy. Originally evolving out of the behavior therapy tradition, CBT has become increasingly popular in recent decades.

Cognitive-behavioral therapists simultaneously focus on four levels: cognition, mood, environment, and behavior. Due to the inherent interplay of these levels, a change in one is assumed to effect changes in the others. Cognitive-behavior therapy works to bring about change in one's environment, cognition, and behavior directly, and affect indirectly. The emphasis is on helping individuals to detect and interpret internal and environmental cues. In essence, events alone are not inherently good or bad, right or wrong, fearful or calming; rather, one's interpretation of the event determines one's emotional reaction to it. How or why people perceive situations in varying manners, and the result of doing so, is the foundation of cognitive theory.

In every human action, reaction, and interaction, individuals are guided by the template of the personal, cultural, family, religious, gender-, and age-related schemas that they have developed over the years (Beck et al., 1990, 2004; Beck, Rush, Shaw, & Emery, 1979; Freeman, Pretzer, Fleming, & Simon, 1990, 2004). Schemas both direct behavior and affect in particular directions and help to give meaning to one's world. The schemas are involved in memory (what is selected for recall or what is "suppressed"), cognition (the abstraction and interpretation of information), affect (the generation of feelings), motivation (wishes and desires), action and control (self-monitoring, inhibition, or direction of action; Beck et al., 1990). By this selectivity, the schemas allow for more efficient information processing.

Understanding schemas, belief systems, and underlying attitudes is thus the essential ingredient in understanding the behavior of individuals, families, and groups. It will influence individuals in their role as a member of a family or group, and will then impact the behaviors of entire cultures. These societal influences generate both stereotyping and what are objectively acknowledged to be cultural descriptions of a group or subgroup. It is the development of specific schemas that can lead to the development of a personality disorder.

These schemas and the resultant behaviors begin to be established from the moment of birth. Some schemas are strongly and vigorously held; others are more transient and easily surrendered, disputed, or modified by the individual. The schemas that are strongly held often appear immutable (to both therapist and patient) and become how the patient is defined by self and others. A particular pattern of a schema about the need for perfection in thought and deed would likely result in a child perceiving the world in dichotomous terms. This would result in the child experiencing a constant demand on self and others for perfect performance, with consequent feelings of failure if performance is only 98%.

Schemas are not isolated, but are interlocking and appear in various constellations. For example, although most children have learned and would subscribe to the basic personal, religious, and cultural schema "Thou shalt not steal," they might take something belonging to another child. The rationale for the narcissistic child for stealing would probably be based on other parallel "rules," such as "I deserve it," "It is due to me," or "If anyone has something that I do not have, it is intolerable for me."

Schemas are in a constant state of change and evolution. From the child's earliest years, previously formed schemas are altered and new schemas are being developed to meet the increasingly complex demands of the world. Infants' perceptions of reality are governed by their limited interaction with their world; thus, the infant may initially perceive the world as the crib and the few caretakers that care for him or her. As infants develop additional skills of mobility and interaction, they perceive their world as significantly broader, both in size and complexity. During the exploratory period, children develop mobility and begin to examine their world more extensively. They can see that their world is indeed huge. With increased interaction with the world, the child begins to incorporate family and cultural schemas.

One way of conceptualizing the change process is to utilize the Piagetian concept of adaptation, with its two interrelated processes, assimilation and accommodation (Rosen, 1985). Assimilation involves the way individuals utilize their environment in terms of how they conceive the world. Environmental data and experience are only taken in by the individual as they can be utilized in terms of the individual's subjective experiences. The self-related schemas then become selective; individuals may ignore environmental stimuli that they are not able to integrate or synthesize. Accommodation involves the ability to modify a schema based on the subjective judgment that the schema no longer serves to organize and explain experiences adequately. The assimilative and accommodative processes are interactive and stand in opposition to each other. We then have an active and evolutionary process whereby all perceptions and cognitive structures are applied to new functions (assimilation), while new cognitive structures are developed to serve old functions in new situations (accommodation). Individuals who exhibit the greatest dysfunction persist in utilizing old structures without fitting them to the new circumstances in which they are involved, but using them *in toto*, without measuring for fit.

Schemas are often difficult to alter because they are composed of five factors in differing proportions. First is a strong affective component. A particular belief or belief system may engender a great deal of emotion and is emotionally bound to the individual's past experience. Second is the amount of the time that the schemas have been held. Schemas that are old, having been part of the personal history for many years, will be more powerful. Third is the individuals from whom the schemas were acquired. The more important (and credible) the source, the more powerful will be the schema. Fourth, the cognitive element of the schema accounts for the manner in which the schemas pervade the individual's thoughts and images. The schemas can be described in great detail and can also be deduced from behavior. Finally, there is the behavioral component of the schema, which involves the way the belief system governs the individual's responses to a particular stimulus or set of stimuli. In seeking to alter particular schemas that have endured for a long period of time, are strongly believed, and were learned from a significant and credible source, it would be necessary to help the patient examine the belief from as many different perspectives as possible. The goal of Adlerian psychotherapy, according to Ansbacher and Ansbacher (1956) is

> to get the patient to recognize the mistake in his lifestyle [schemas], as the therapist has understood it and then shared that percept with the patient. The goal, thereby, is to increase the patient's ability to cooperate [in the change process]. This is a process of a cognitive reorganization, and of belated maturation.

For some individuals, a particular set of core schemas are well-established in early to middle childhood. What differentiates the child who develops a schema that is held with moderate strength and amenable to change later on from the individual who develops a core belief that is powerful and apparently immutable? We would posit several possibilities: (a) In addition to the core belief, the child maintains an associated belief that he or she cannot change; (b) the belief system is powerfully reinforced by parents or significant others; (c) although the dysfunctional belief system is not especially reinforced, any attempt to believe the contrary may not be reinforced or may even be punished, for example, if parents implied, "You may be able to change, but we are not sure we would love you if you did change"; (d) the child is not explicitly told he or she lacks worth, but any attempt to assert worth would be ignored; and (e) the parents or significant others may offer direct instruction contrary to developing a positive image, for example, "It's not nice to brag" or "It's not nice to toot your own horn because people will think less of you."

Individuals tend to distort information in a direction that reinforces their views of self, world, and future. There are several cognitive distortions that are emblematic of the narcissistic individual. Arbitrary inference occurs when the person draws conclusions that are not consistent with objective evidence. A depressed person may make negative interpretations of events when neutral or positive ones would be more appropriate. Narcissistic children might conclude that others believe them to be special even if other children ignore or even shun them.

Personalization involves inappropriately attaching self-evaluative meanings to neutral situations. Overhearing children speaking of a talented child, narcissistic children conclude that the other children must be referring to them.

Selective abstraction occurs when a person overattends to schema-consistent information and underattends to information inconsistent with those assumptions. It is an instance of confirmatory bias in information processing. Narcissistic children continually seek information consistent with their positive (or grandiose) views of self, world, and future and do not seek, perceive, or see as valid information that contrasts with this view.

Overgeneralization involves applying conclusions appropriate to a specific instance to an entire class of experience based on perceived similarities. It is an instance of global reasoning. Having been successful at one task, narcissistic children conclude that they will be successful at all similar tasks.

Magnification and minimization occur when the person overattends to and exaggerates the importance of aspects of experience and discounts or underestimates the relevance of negative or nonconfirmatory experience.

Narcissistic persons are more likely to negatively interpret situations when their self-worth is on the line. Thus, when an event is most in need of critical analysis, the narcissist may be less likely to accommodate and more likely to attempt to assimilate the new situation into the existing repertoire of knowledge and responses. In the best of circumstances, this has adaptive purposes: A quick assessment of a strange situation, using old knowledge, may save one's life. Unfortunately, it becomes problematic when the assessment discounts essential information that would call for a different response.

DEVELOPMENTAL EXPERIENCE

The parent who accepts the young child's grandiose visions of self, experience, or future possibilities without offering realistic feedback and pointing out the child's limits and boundaries might very well reinforce this overinflated and potentially dysfunctional self-view. Schools may further contribute to the lack of limits by offering special treatment and extreme positive feedback to children who are seen as positively "special," that is, gifted in some way.

Hamner and Turner (1985) make three assumptions about the development of self-concept: first, that it is learned; second, that this learning occurs early in the socialization process; and third, that the self-concept is a powerful determinant of behavior. This view implies that inappropriate early socialization could result in the individual's learning an unrealistically high appraisal of his or her capabilities and developing a pathological level of narcissism. But it does not specify *what* socialization issues would produce this problem.

Theories regarding the development of the self-concept provide another perspective on narcissism. During normal development, a major part of the parental role is to help a child develop a positive self-image and a strong sense of self-concept or self-esteem (Hamner & Turner, 1985). This would ideally translate into a sense of personal efficacy, a feeling of satisfaction that is derived from successfully dealing with stressors and limitations imposed by one's environment and what may be termed "healthy or adaptive narcissism" that is, a positive sense of self that is developed by having a sensitivity, awareness, and acceptance of one's abilities and limitations with a concomitant striving to further develop one's abilities and reduce negative or limiting experiences or circumstances.

THE NARCISSISTIC FAMILY

Based on Freeman and Rigby (2003), we can identify a number of family and systemic factors that contribute to the development of a narcissistic character:

- Parents fail to teach the child frustration tolerance.
- Parents fail to teach the child the meaning and importance of boundaries and limits.
- Parents are overly permissive, imposing no consequences for inappropriate behavior.
- The parents' value system is skewed toward the child being special.
- Family narcissism is present and can be easily modeled and then reinforced. The parental style of manifesting self-esteem will often be reflected by the child. If a parent is narcissistic, he or she will model certain behaviors and a general style for the child.
- Parents neglect and/or reject the child, which leads to narcissistic overcompensation.
- Parentified children are put into positions and roles that exceed their age appropriateness.
- The only child or only grandchild is rewarded for little achievement.
- Parents act out their frustration at never having been able to achieve the goals that they (or their parents) had for them and that they will get vicariously through their child.
- Parents are unskilled in child rearing and allow their child everything that he or she requests or demands.

Donaldson-Pressman and Pressman (1994) add the element of skewed responsibility: The child becomes responsible for meeting the needs of the parents. This programs the child to not act on his or her own feelings or inclinations, but rather to be more reactive to what he or she perceives to be the expectations of others and to respond to them. The family may be overt or covert in their messages about the child's need to be special, not necessarily for the child's sake, but for the sake of the parents. The child becomes responsible for being the special child that the parents demand. The parents may then identify with the child and see the child as the carrier of the hopes, dreams, and expectations that the parents were unable themselves to meet, or use the child to aggrandize their own position.

THE EXPERIENCE OF NARCISSISM

The constant pursuit of reinforcement and acknowledgment of their special status requires considerable effort and often leaves narcissists feeling empty and depressed. When the desired (positive) reactions from others are received, this may give the narcissist a brief period of happiness but is usually followed by a let-down resulting from the cessation of the positive acknowledgment. This may then lead to a subsequent drive to reacquire the positive and accepting reaction.

Several elements may combine to establish and maintain the early exaggeration and overvaluation of self. Narcissistic individuals will often go to considerable lengths to maintain their high opinion of themselves. Maintaining physical health may become exaggerated into fad dieting or working out to maintain the illusion of strength, health, and beauty. Even at relatively young ages, girls will make use of makeup to garner comments on their appearance. As adolescents they may utilize reconstructive surgery to "correct" physical flaws to the point of body dysmorphia. Les, a 29-year-old male, described one of the most embarrassing experiences of his adolescence. His parents were, he stated, "perfect." Both had had extensive plastic surgery. His mother had her nose, hips, lips, breasts, and chin "remodeled." His father had hair implants, his nose reconstructed, and liposuction. They both vigorously insisted that Les have his nose "redone" when he turned 16. He dreaded his coming birthday. Despite his arguments and refusals, the surgery was scheduled and Les (once again) complied. About 2 months after the surgery, Les discovered that his parents had scheduled a family get-together so that the family could see Les's new nose. He was appalled as each relative inspected his nose.

The need for the child's academic success may result in a joyless, educationless school experience that centers on grades and recognition rather than on learning or enjoying the learning process. This may be strongly reinforced by family, peers, and teachers. The grades that they receive allow narcissists to maintain the ideal of grades being the sine qua non of schooling.

A common corollary to narcissists' belief in their specialness is that they deserve special treatment and must not be stopped or slowed from seeking pleasure, status, rewards, or notice. For these individuals the natural course of events involves self-aggrandizement, and any deterrent or obstacle to these goals is to be avoided or even destroyed. Narcissists believe it is unfair, persecutory, or wrong to stop their goal-driven behavior.

We might also look to the Bible and its instruction "Blessed are the meek: for they shall inherit the earth." Narcissists do not wait to inherit the earth. They believe that it is due to them now.

TREATMENT ISSUES

The issues in treatment revolve around not so much the events in the child's life, but what the child has learned from those early experiences that are coded as schema. The clinician must think in terms of the child's temperament, which is seen as the genotype. The genotype represents the genetic contribution to the child's development and behavioral style. The child's observable behavior and physical appearance is the phenotype. The cultural, family, and environmental context in which the child develops can be thought of as the sociotype. The interplay of these elements makes for the colors and shading of the disorder.

Several questions are raised regarding the treatment of the narcissistic child or adolescent. First, what will bring the narcissistic child into therapy? Second, and probably more important, what will keep the child in treatment? Third, what are the goals of therapy? Fourth, who will be involved in the therapy? Similar to their adult counterparts, the narcissistic child will likely be referred for treatment for a problem other than narcissism.

Like so many other child referrals, the child will need to have upset adults. These may be the parents or the school personnel, and they must be upset or concerned enough to consider the intervention of a therapist. These children may not be aware of the upset that they create in others or in systems, and may have little motivation to change their behavior, their view of the world, or their opinion of themselves or others with whom they interact. A more confused referral occurs when the school refers a child for treatment but the parents are either naive, ignorant, or simply resistant to the treatment referral. This is especially true when the child is satisfying the parents' narcissism ("We have this special child") or when the child's narcissistic behavior is consonant with the behavior and views of the parents. In fact, the parents may accept the referral to mollify the school, but will then sabotage treatment either overtly or covertly. A referral that relates to another problem may be "easier" for the parents to accept. For example, John, age 12, was referred by his parents for treatment of his anxiety. When interviewed, it became clear to the therapist that what made John anxious was when he was unable to be at the top of his class in every area. When he slipped to having the second highest average in any subject, he became agitated. His agitation was labeled by the school and his parents as anxiety. The therapist chose to maintain the label of anxiety so as to maintain the motivation of John and his parents for therapeutic intervention. In interviewing John's parents, it was clear that they derived great satisfaction and pleasure from John's school performance. A less than perfect score on an examination was met with stony silence at home and gentle but firm instructions to John to "try harder," "study harder," and to "keep his eye on the ball." The "ball" in this case was John's ultimately being accepted to an Ivy League university 6 years hence and then to a top-rated law school.

ASSESSMENT

The assessment must start with a clear, specific, and targeted referral. To assure a useful referral, it is essential to request behavioral examples of the problematic behavior rather than vague, amorphous statements, for example, "to be more cooperative." The assessment must include structured clinical interviews with the parent and significant others, a structured clinical interview with the child, and a family (especially sibling) history from an accurate reporter (or the best available). If possible, the clinician should have an opportunity to make behavioral observations at home. Also important are structured school behavior report forms, informal comments of classroom personnel, direct observation of the child, medical or psychological reports/archives, and formal psychological testing. One of the most valuable sources of data is the clinician's personal reactions to the child, family, and circumstance (the "reasonable person hypothesis").

Whose report or concern initiated the referral? Was it the parents', child self-report, school, or the criminal justice system? Are there problems with parents, with siblings? Are there family problems in general, school or academic problems, social problems with friends and peers, or are the problems intrapersonal issues?

The specific assessment for narcissism includes the following:

- Assessment of the individual's empathy skills via history and observation.
- Are empathy skills situational or contextual?
- What is his or her threshold for being empathic?
- What is the gain or value to the child to be empathic?
- Has there been a payoff for limiting or lack of empathy?
- Is empathy (or lack thereof) culturally related?
- Does the child understand the construct and purpose of empathy?
- Are empathy and morality connected by the individual?
- What empathy skill set is missing for the individual?
- How can the skills be taught or modeled by the therapist?
- Does the child understand the idea, purpose, and rationale for assuming the perspective of another?
- How will it profit the child to become aware of the needs, views, and feelings of another?
- Will the parents or caretakers cooperate with the therapeutic goals?
- How will it profit the parents for the child to be less narcissistic?

Narcissism occurs on a range, from mild to severe. A mild form may be interpreted as high self-esteem and be seen by parents and the school as a positive aspect of the child's personality. The moderate to severe manifestations are less easily excused or seen as positive. We might look at several different types of narcissist, each with its own style and impact on the personal style of the child. Another spectrum is the altruist-narcissist continuum. At one end is the altruist, whose major concern is for others, even to the extent of a loss of personal safety or recognition or profit. Conversely, the narcissist evidences a total self-concern with a concomitant lack of caring or empathy for others.

Probably the only place one can find a "pure" narcissist is in the pages of *DSM-IV-TR* (American Psychiatric Association, 2000). Clinical presentations generally include Axis I disorders (depression and anxiety) but also include mixed presentations of Axis II, Cluster B combinations of narcissistic/histrionic, narcissistic/antisocial, and narcissistic/borderline. We might also view narcissistic behavior in terms of several differing, though overlapping styles, each of which will require a different therapeutic approach:

- *Positive self-esteem:* In this expression, narcissistic children generally view themselves in positive ways. They can accept and state that they feel good about themselves, given the exigencies of developmental crises.

- *"Healthy" narcissism:* These children have attributes that they recognize as special or superior to their age-mates, family members, or schoolmates. They do not, however, flaunt their gifts.

- *"Group" narcissism:* The child's special status is conferred and maintained by membership in a group. The group might be a gang, religious group, family group, or school group or team. Without the group the status is lost and is not transferable.

- *"Helpful" narcissism:* These children are usually unaware that their "helpfulness" at guiding and correcting others is negatively perceived. They offer to help, even when their help is not sought or appreciated. They may correct peers or teachers.

- *"Real" narcissism:* These children believe that they are superior to others. This view may be justified and consensually validated. They are not, however, hesitant to point out their gifts to others.

- *"Compensated" narcissism:* These children feel so bad about themselves that they create a super-person to make up for their perceived lacks and failures.

- *"Oblivious" narcissism:* These children are unaware of their effect on others. They may be excluded from groups or social settings and have no idea why they are excluded.

- *"Hypervigilant" narcissism:* These children are constantly scanning for any tiny insult or denigration, and they fear being discovered to be less powerful or able than they see themselves. To not be powerful is to be vulnerable.

- *"Ruthless" narcissism:* These children gain satisfaction and enjoyment from the discomfort of others. They may often be the cause of the discomfort by teasing, insulting, or pointing out the flaws and foibles of others.

  —Is there a normal developmental explanation for the child's behavior?

  —Is the behavior variable or cyclical, or is it constant, consistent, and predictable?

  —Could it be a result of discrepancies or inconsistencies between the child's chronological age and cognitive, emotional, social, and/or behavioral ages?

  —Does the child function similarly in different environments and with different people?

  —Does the problem behavior relate to the child's environment or situation?

  —Is the observed behavior a result of the child's linguistic style, thinking style, or attitude?

  —Is the behavioral style culturally related?

DEVELOPING A THERAPEUTIC RELATIONSHIP

A key ingredient in the treatment of the narcissistic child or adolescent is the development of a therapeutic alliance or a treatment bond. Often thought of as synonymous, they are, in fact, quite different, with different goals and foci. The treatment bond involves the relationship between the therapist and the patient. The treatment alliance involves the treatment plan, treatment goals, and agreement to work on those agreed upon goals. The treatment bond may be far more difficult to establish and maintain with the narcissistic child or adolescent. The bond, generally, is far more useful in working with children. The alliance is a far better focus for work with adolescents. With narcissistic youth, however, there may be far greater interest in the treatment alliance. They may, in fact, be resistant to the emotional connection that is part of the treatment bond. In light of their difficulty in establishing and maintaining relationships and their tendency to push the bounds of acceptable behavior, the treatment alliance is, for them, a far safer treatment focus.

The alliance can be structured so that the focus and goals are in their informed and enlightened self-interest. This may help avoid the challenges and "contests" that are part of the treatment bond. A continual theme in treatment is for the therapist to keep focusing on what is in the best interest of an informed and enlightened patient. Simply put, the therapist keeps asking the questions, "How do you profit from this?" "How does this help *you*?" and "Why continue behavior that seems to keep getting you less of what you want rather than more?" In effect, the theme of the therapy is to use the narcissism rather than try to fight against it. This has the net result of using the child's pathology in the service of the therapy.

After the initial assessment, the building of a strong collaborative relationship that focuses on the alliance is essential because participation in psychotherapy requires that narcissistic youth be asked to do things that they have had great difficulty doing, have never had to do, or have never learned to do. These tasks include tolerating frustration, problem solving, socially appropriate behavior, and accepting the views of others in an empathic manner.

Collaboration can be difficult both because of the characteristics of the patient and the reactions the patient elicits from the therapist. Unless the therapist has a clear, strong, reasonable, and realistic idea and image of what the desired outcome will be, treatment *cannot* be successful or will succeed only by accident. The therapist must be able to collaborate with the patient to outline what the "finished product" will look like, act like, and sound like. The patient must agree as part of the working alliance.

The patient's narcissism, most naturally, will become a focus of therapy as it often impedes progress toward accomplishing more concrete goals. In practice, it may be far more realistic to work on changing specific behaviors and on helping the child be more moderate in his or her narcissism than to plan to change a lifelong narcissistic pattern. As noted earlier, insofar as possible, the therapist must work with, rather than against, the narcissistic pattern to minimize unproductive conflict and to engage the patient in therapy. The therapist who is not willing or able to tolerate the narcissistic patient's behavior and accommodate to it will have difficulty inducing the patient to persist in therapy. Conversely, the therapist who is unwilling to confront the child because the child is so easily offended, or is concerned about being the target of the child's tantrum, is likely to have no therapeutic impact. It is essential for the therapist to establish and maintain firm guidelines and limits for the child and the family early in therapy. This may be as straightforward as asking a child to not put muddy shoes on a couch in the office or to not steal toys from a playroom or magazines from the waiting room. The rules and limits should cover as many potentialities as possible, for example, frequency of phone calls, length of phone calls, types and frequency of discipline, agreement between parents on the use of discipline, how parents can offer mutual support in dealing with the child, attendance at support groups, and rules regarding the child's interaction with siblings. These rules need to be set without rancor toward or upset with the child's behavior.

The Narcissistic Injury

The parents must also be educated in the nature of the narcissistic injury. They need to be educated to the possibility of the child becoming very upset when the child's narcissistic striving is challenged or previously uninterrupted behavior is now challenged. Children may respond to the perceived loss or threat of loss of the narcissistic "prizes" with anger, frustration, or aggression. They may try to "heal" the injury or to recoup the perceived loss. They may even perceive the need to injure the perpetrator. They may escalate their demands, increase the frequency and volume of their protests, or threaten injury to themselves or others unless they are allowed to proceed as before. Interestingly, even small covert actions may be satisfying enough to heal the loss and injury. The parents will need education, support, and insight to effectively cope.

Treatment Planning

The treatment goals must meet a number of criteria. These include:

- The goals of the treatment must be realistic. Often, parents or therapists want to set goals that are idealistic, for example, to rid the child of his or her self-damaging narcissistic style forever. A far more realistic goal is to reduce the narcissism to manageable and more acceptable proportions.

- Treatment must be reasonable in terms of timing and frequency of sessions, attendance at sessions, and pacing of the sessions and the therapy more generally.

- The therapy goals must be hierarchical and sequential. The treatment plan must map goals so that the therapy can build on present skills and later acquired skills.

- Treatment goals must be proximal to improve the chance of the goals being reached. Distal goals can be reached when they are themselves more proximal and built on the skills and changes built previously.

- Vague goals lead to vague therapy, which leads to vague results. The better delineated the therapeutic goals, the better the chances for therapeutic success.

- The therapist must do a careful assessment of the emotional, behavioral, contextual, and cognitive repertoire of the child and the parents or caretakers. Once the baseline repertoire is established, the treatment map will dictate what additional skills need to be developed.

- The treatment goals must be agreed to by the child and the parents before treatment can proceed.

- The goals of treatment must be seen by the child and the parents as valuable. Of all the requirements of treatment, this is perhaps the most important. While perceived value is important for any treatment, it is especially important in the treatment of the narcissistic child. To have the child give up what has been so very rewarding for so long must require a value that can potentially equal or even exceed that of the more dysfunctional behavior.

- There must be a system put in place for contingency management. Parents, caretakers, school personnel, and clergy must all be in agreement in regard to the requirements and demands of the therapy. All must be informed and willing to set and maintain limits and to offer the child appropriate feedback on behavior and rewards that are reasonable and that would defuse or no longer fuel the narcissism.

- Finally, therapy may need to be ongoing for several years as the child goes through various developmental periods and developmental crises. Each developmental period will have a different impact on how the narcissism is expressed. This is especially true during adolescence, when narcissism is the norm for most youth.

THE THERAPEUTIC ALLIANCE

As noted earlier, the therapeutic bond is distinct from the therapeutic alliance: The therapeutic bond refers to the relationship between the child and the therapist; the therapeutic alliance refers to the treatment plan. There may, in fact, be an alliance without the bond when the therapy is structured to reach goals that, in the child's view, are in his or her enlightened self-interest (i.e., How can the child profit from the therapy?). Narcissistic children are suspicious of any relationship or involvement in which they are in a "one down" position. By definition, the patient-therapist relationship is exactly that. Trying to build a bond is likely to be negatively perceived by the child. Offering unconditional positive regard may feed into the narcissism, whereas certain behaviors cannot be accepted. Clearly, the bond alone is not sufficient for change. However, there must be a therapeutic connection that offers the child something that he or she values. "The child's affective orientation to therapy has an important bearing on the child's collaboration with the therapeutic task. Children who felt more positively toward *therapy* were more likely to talk about feelings than children who were more negative" (Shirk & Saiz, 1992).

The therapeutic alliance requires that there be an agreement or contract on the goals, tasks, and focus of therapy. There may be a number of signatories to the contract. The question that will need to be kept at the forefront of the therapy work is, What will the child perceive the therapy can offer in regard to his or her best interest? This might be read as the therapist and family system either allowing or feeding the child's narcissism. We would view it as limiting the narcissism so that it no longer creates the internal and external problems for the child. Given that the narcissism has reached the point of being so noticeable and problematic for the child in regard to peers, family, or school, it will not be totally removed. In fact, to set this as a goal of treatment will likely spell failure. Helping the child to be less noticeable and behave more in concert with the group will have the effect of the child being more acceptable within society.

THERAPY FORMATS

The child or adolescent can be seen alone. However, this one-to-one format may be counterproductive with narcissistic children. Their antennae may go up in this situation, and they may gird themselves for the power struggle that they so often anticipate and then generate. We would also recommend against the typical therapeutic hour. For the most part, children are not used to spending 45 to 60 minutes alone with an adult. As their anxiety increases, they will be more likely to fall back on the narcissistic struggle. We must ascertain whether the child has the motivation for treatment, whether the child's developmental stage will enable verbal therapy, and whether the child has the ability to sit still, listen, concentrate, focus, and integrate and generalize diverse pieces. The therapist must evaluate whether the child's verbal skills will enable him or her to use the therapy productively. We would recommend that the child or adolescent be seen for multiple half sessions of no more than 30 minutes. This will reduce the child's anxiety and will limit the full bloom of the narcissism.

Given the child's life context, we must involve the parents and caretakers in the treatment. We must then ascertain the parents' motivation for treatment. The therapist may, in fact, choose to see the parents alone for treatment, with only occasional child visits. Essentially, unless and until the parents gain the skills and support they need, they may be unable to impact the child's narcissistic behavior. To reach all members of the system, the therapist can alternate between seeing the child and seeing the parents. The parents can be seen for half the session and the child for the other half. On a periodic basis, depending on the content and course of therapy, family therapy sessions can be held. Or the therapist can alternate between seeing the child, seeing the parents, and family sessions.

Unless there is a compelling reason (i.e., abuse), there is usually little need to remove the child from danger in the home and arrange placement in an appropriate residential setting. This would be more likely with the aggressive narcissistic child.

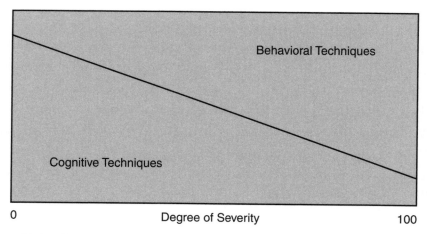

Figure 11.1 Relative Use of Cognitive/Affective Interventions and Contextual Behavioral Interventions

Therapeutic Interventions

A number of interventions are available. We can classify them into cognitive, behavioral, environmental/contextual, and affective interventions. The proportion of each class of intervention can be summarized in the following manner. The more severe and impairing the narcissistic behavior, the greater the proportion of environmental/contextual and behavioral techniques. The milder the narcissistic impairment, the greater the proportion of cognitive and affective interventions (Figure 11.1).

Cognitive and Affective Interventions

An initial intervention would be to help the child learn to monitor his or her internal dialogue and self-statements. Narcissistic children can learn to identify negative self-talk or self-talk that results in their getting into trouble with parents, peers, and school personnel. They can be taught the following techniques.

Self-Instructional Statements The child can be instructed on the development of basic self-instructional techniques. When in certain situations that had, in the past, triggered greater levels of narcissistic behavior, he or she can use the environmental stimuli to direct a series of statements, for example, "I may be smarter than these people, but it will not serve me well to rub their nose in it. Keep quiet!"; "The use of silence may even make me look even smarter or more talented"; "Challenging authority figures has in the past caused me more trouble than it is worth. I need to remove myself from conflict"; "If someone challenges me, even subtly, I can show myself to be above their petty challenges by smiling and not responding."

Building Adaptive Coping Statements and Adaptive Self-Talk The therapist can work with the child during the session to build a list of coping statements that are more adaptive than the statements the child presently uses. These adaptive coping statements can then be used as self-instructional statements. For example, if the child's attempt to cope is encapsulated in the statement "Any attempt to have me look like less than another person must be immediately struck down," or "It is most important to look good, even to strangers," a more adaptive coping statement might be "I generally need not care what others think of me. I know how good I really am," or "The opinion of others does not define me."

We have made the point earlier in this chapter that one of the major skill deficits of narcissistic children is problem solving. The therapy sessions for both the children and their parents should include problem-solving training (D'Zurilla & Nezu, 2006).

The therapist can help these children by expanding their emotional vocabulary—not just the words, but their repertoire of emotional response. Helping them move from the limited "defend and attack" mode to additional possible emotional reactions helps them become or appear more "normal." This includes developing empathic statements in appropriate situations.

Perhaps the greatest (and most challenging) work of therapy with narcissistic children is the development of empathy. This involves several steps. Children must first be instructed in what empathy is, when it is appropriate, the importance and value of empathy, how it is expressed (verbally and nonverbally), why it is expressed, why it would be in their best interest to include empathic responses as part of their repertoire of response, to whom it should be expressed, and how showing empathy is not always the same as being empathic. (This is, in fact, a skill that is taught in graduate courses in psychotherapy and counseling. The famous [or infamous] therapeutic intervention "Uh-huh" is taught as an indication to patients that the therapist has heard them, understands them, and is encouraging them to continue.) Simple statements such as "I'm sorry," "That is too bad," "It is unfortunate that that has happened to you," and "That must have really hurt" are easily learned and then attached to specific situations. Even if the child's internal language is still "Like I really care," "What is that to me?," or "The fact that you may suffer is of little interest to me," he or she can learn that empathic responses are generally useful to gain even more recognition as a "feeling" person. These initially externally motivated lessons are learned rather late in development; if frequently used they become more easily said and more appropriate. At that point they begin to approximate the more normal assessment of "Should I commiserate with this person, what should I say, and when would be a good time to say it?," which is the hallmark of the empathic individual and sounds very much like what we all do.

Behavioral and Environmental/Contextual Interventions

For many narcissistic children, behavioral/environmental interventions will be required. The major impediment to the use of these interventions is whether there will be consistency at home and at school to manage the child's behavior. It is beyond this chapter to explain and detail the myriad applications of behavioral work with these children. Relevant interventions include contingency management, modeling of more adaptive behavior by therapists and parents, the withdrawal of reinforcements of the narcissistic behavior that would lead to extinction, positive reinforcement of more prosocial actions, clear and frequent feedback on behavior, prompting when necessary, and task analysis, which can help the child feel a greater sense of mastery.

No one set of behavioral interventions is a better fit for the narcissistic child.

RESISTANCE AND SABOTAGE

As with any patient, resistance and sabotage are common phenomena. For narcissistic children and their narcissistic parents, these phenomena can be taken to new and incredible heights. The sabotage may take the form of the child, parents, school, or family not complying with treatment recommendations after they have made an agreement to do so. It may take the form of withdrawing the child from therapy, often precipitously. When parents and families are seen, one or both parents may monopolize the therapeutic effort so that little occurs in the therapy; the therapy stays focused on the parents and not the family system or interactions. Part of the sabotage may involve criticizing the child for bringing the family to a crisis point or criticizing the family therapy efforts as unnecessary, an imposition on time, energy, or finances, as not relevant to the family, or by hostile, challenging actions or fighting with the therapist, agency, or school.

The "forgetting" so typical of the passive-aggressive may be part of the narcissistic family. They may fail or forget to make necessary disclosures regarding previous treatment, family history, or behaviors.

Of course the ultimate sabotage is the refusal to pay for therapy. For example, one family argued that they should not have to pay. They were, they opined, "so interesting that the therapist could use their family as a case study or even as the focus of a book, which was more than enough compensation."

COUNTERTRANSFERENCE

Unless countertransference is under control, the therapist cannot effectively treat the narcissistic child. Narcissists generally can be labeled "the patients that we love to hate" (Freeman, 2006). They arouse in many therapists very negative reactions on many levels. If the therapist has been taught and has accepted that "the meek shall inherit the earth," then narcissists evoke great enmity. These are not the children with "broken wing syndrome" that the therapist is compelled to heal. When therapists gather to share war stories, narcissistic patients prompt stories that usually begin, "You won't believe this kid. He and his parents came into my office. . . ."

The therapist needs to be aware of several different types of countertransference. First is the countertransference *reaction*. The reaction is to something that occurs in the session and is brief and fleeting. The therapist may be momentarily stopped (or shocked) but moves on with no residue. Second is what we term countertransference *stress*. This involves a reaction that has a residue that may be remembered and mulled over by the therapist for a longer time. This is often accompanied by the thought, "I can't believe. . . ." Third is termed countertransference *structure*. This occurs when the therapist's reaction to the youth or patients becomes far more widespread. For example, when the therapist looks at his or her appointment book and sees that a particular patient is coming for therapy, there is a powerful positive or negative reaction. Fourth is the countertransference *neurosis*. This occurs when the boundaries of therapy are allowed by the therapist to slip, and unethical or illegal behavior ensues. Finally, we have what we term the *reasonable person hypothesis*. This involves a reaction to the patient that upon discussion with colleagues nets a similar reaction.

Case Illustration

Seth Smith* was an 8-year-old child of wealth and privilege. His family had recently moved into a city and Seth was placed in one of the few private schools there. On the 1st day he came into conflict with the other children, teachers, and school administrators. This came about as he spent considerable time each day criticizing the school and comparing it to his previous school. The present school was of a lower level, more poorly equipped, had lower standards for its teachers, allowed "just anybody" to attend, had poorly maintained athletic facilities, had inferior athletic teams, poor quality food at lunch, lower academic standards, less attractive school uniform dress requirements, and unattractive buildings. His comments were always couched with descriptions of his previous school, which, by comparison, was not just better, but "far superior." His constant comments brought him into physical conflict with classmates by the end of his 1st week. This eventuated in a flurry of calls between the school counselor and Seth's parents.

* Not the child's real name.

Mr. and Mrs. Smith came in to meet with the school counselor, Seth's teacher, a vice principal, and a consulting psychologist. The meeting time and length were negotiated a day earlier. The meeting was scheduled for an evening, necessitating the school personnel to return to the school. Mrs. Smith stated that neither she nor her husband could make the meeting at any of the day times offered by the school.

The parents started the meeting by asking for the credentials of each of the school personnel at the meeting and demanded to know why the consulting psychologist was there. Rather than allow a distraction and poor use of time to fight the battle of the credentials, the school staff each briefly reviewed their credentials. The teacher and the counselor had master's degrees, the vice principal a doctorate in developmental reading, and the psychologist a doctorate and state licensure as a clinical psychologist. These were all written down by Mrs. Smith.

Mr. Smith immediately began defending Seth, claiming that all that he had said was true, that they had moved because he accepted a promotion and was transferred, and that they brought with them brochures and material from the previous school. The parents made it clear that Seth was stating obvious "truths," and that it was the school's responsibility to defend Seth's freedom of speech.

The vice principal rose to the challenge that the Smiths set out. He stated that inasmuch as the Smiths found so much wrong with the school, the school was prepared to return their tuition and have Seth leave the school, effective immediately. The Smiths could then seek a place for Seth in another private school in the city, at a greater distance from his home. At this point, the Smiths seemed stunned. It was not the school's offer to have Seth leave the school that stunned them, but, as stated by Mr. Smith, "That means that he would have to attend an even worse private school, or a *public* school." It was then suggested that Seth attend a parochial school. The Smiths were Catholic, but quickly vetoed that possibility. "We do not think that either of those possibilities would be a solution for Seth." The teacher suggested that the Smiths home-school Seth, thus assuring that he would have the very best of everything. This was quickly vetoed, as both Mr. and Mrs. Smith were far too busy to do that.

The psychologist then offered the possibility of Seth continuing at the present school, but that he would have to make some accommodation, as would Mr. and Mrs. Smith. The recommendation was that Seth and his parents meet with the psychologist for several "consultation" sessions. When Mr. Smith asked, "You mean therapy?," the psychologist was very clear and stated that these sessions were not therapy, but consultation. Mrs. Smith then smiled and said, "No insult intended, doctor, but what credentials do you have to do this?" Rather than get into the credentials issue again, the psychologist chose to use their narcissism for possible gain. The Smiths were informed that the psychologist had published a number of books in psychology. Mrs. Smith asked, "You mean locally?" Trying to not rise to the implied challenge, the therapist answered that the books were published by several international publishers. They looked at each other and then agreed to meet with the psychologist.

Subsequent to the initial meeting, the psychologist met with all school personnel who interacted with Seth to get their informed view. With the parents' release of information, Seth's previous school faxed a copy of a psychological report done the previous year.

The initial consultation meeting was with Mr. and Mrs. Smith so that the purpose of the consultation, the ground rules of the consultation, the goals of the consultation, and the timing of the consultation were discussed. The psychologist had to walk a fine line between consulting with the Smiths about Seth and their interest in using the meetings to discuss the psychologist's work. Prior to the first consultation, they had searched the Internet for the psychologist's work. Finding that he was, indeed, a published author, but had also lectured internationally, they were willing to use his consultation services to help Seth.

The techniques that worked best with the Smiths were those that asked them to use their own experience. Both Mr. and Mrs. Smith were asked about their work and whether they found that the people who were in positions over them were in fact, incompetent, stupid, or disturbed. They both nodded assent. When asked if either of them had ever considered telling their supervisor or boss what they really thought of him or her, Mr. Smith's response was that though he had considered it, he did not do it because he would lose his job if he did.

"So what?" asked the psychologist. "Someone as well credentialed as you would have no problem getting an even better job."

"Yes, that's true. But I'll do that when I'm ready to leave, and not before. I'm not about to put my future in their hands."

After several more examples, the psychologist asked the Smiths to apply that to what Seth was doing at school. They once again tried to make it an issue of free speech. It was pointed out that Mr. Smith should have the same free speech at work, but then he would have to live with the consequences. It was then agreed that Mr. and Mrs. Smith would bring Seth to the next session.

Seth was seen for half of the next session. He was a bright, verbal, articulate, and pretentious child. He started by trying to regale the psychologist with the wonders of his previous school. When the psychologist interrupted with a question, "Do you enjoy being called names or seen as a jerk by the other kids?," Seth tried to continue his school description. The psychologist interrupted again and asked the same question.

Seth, exasperated, said, "Of course not. These Nanderthals are just jealous of me. That's why they pick on me."

"Wow," responded the psychologist. "That is quite a big word for someone your age."

"Yes. I'm pretty smart."

"Where on earth did you learn such a big word?"

"From my dad," Seth replied.

At this point, the psychologist told Seth that it was time for his parents to join them. When Mr. and Mrs. Smith came in, the psychologist asked Seth to repeat the big word. Seth proudly said, "Nanderthals." Mr. Smith corrected Seth and slowly said, "Seth, the word is *NE*anderthals." Seth was clearly upset and told his father with great emotion that the last time that Mr. Smith used that word he pronounced it as "Nanderthals."

Mr. Smith corrected Seth once again, which upset Seth even more. It seemed clear that being corrected was a supreme insult. His view of the children in his school was a mirror of his parents' view. Seth wanted to please them and, at the same time, show his mastery of language.

It became important to meet with the parents to help them to back off from fueling Seth's upset. If the Smiths could allow Seth to relate to his peers, they could all breathe more easily. In a meeting with just Mr. and Mrs. Smith it became clear that the promotion and geographical shift was not a choice that they made, but one the company required so that Mr. Smith's skills could be used to increase the productivity of the local plants. The next session was scheduled for Seth alone.

In the next session the therapist started by expressing great surprise that Seth was in the predicament that he was in with the other kids. Seth's response was to say that the other children were "just Neanderthals and that's the way Neanderthals act . . . like Neanderthals." It was important for Seth to prove to the psychologist that he knew and could pronounce the word. He even described what Neanderthals were.

The goal in meeting with Seth was to help him to use his considerable intelligence and his narcissism in the service of greater adaptation. To try to rid Seth of his narcissistic style would be difficult, if not impossible. The behavior was modeled and reinforced at home. The following is a shortened version of the themes of the therapy as explored through Socratic dialogue. The questions asked included:

- Your previous school was pretty neat, wasn't it?
- It was a whole lot better than where you go now, wasn't it?
- The kids at your new school don't even know what they are missing, do they?
- They are operating in the dark, aren't they?
- How can they find out what they are missing?
- Can you tell them?
- How can you tell them so that they won't be insulted and then get angry?
- Do you think that you can be the leader of the school that helps them to get better?
- What would you need to do differently? Do you think that you are able to do such a difficult thing?
- What would happen if you were to take this on? What would the result be?
- Would you be willing to have me serve as your consultant in this very difficult issue?

Seth continued for 3 months of "consultation," along with his parents. The parenting work focused on their stepping back and not feeding Seth negative statements and negative views and neither inspiring nor modeling negative behaviors. As Seth followed the consultant's recommendations, he was better able to interact with his peers. The use of self-instructions such as "Keep quiet, let them ask me what to do" served him well. Toward the end of the school year he had friends in school. They were, like Seth, a small and somewhat narcissistic group who saw themselves as being above the other students. Seth affiliated with the group's leader and was seen as being high in the pecking order. He did share his ideas to make the school a better place. Many of his ideas were implemented, and at the end of the year, Seth reported back to a joint consultation meeting with his mother and father that he now liked school, as he had helped to make it more like his old school.

Was Seth cured of his narcissism? No. It was reduced. He demonstrated greater empathy for his peers and they responded positively. He was more adaptive, more functional, and better integrated within the school. His parents continued to be supportive of his efforts and made great efforts to not share with Seth their view of the provincialism and limits of their new city. The pattern of these parents and of parents who are stylistically similar are discussed by Brown (2001).

CONCLUSIONS

The distance between positive self-esteem and narcissism may be very small. The narcissistic child comes by his or her style honestly, learning in the context of the family, modeling important, powerful, and credible others, and having the narcissistic style and behavior reinforced.

Narcissism is not a unitary phenomenon, but a collection of related behaviors and styles that are then seen to typify the child. When these styles or modes interfere with adaptation, a disorder emerges. Stemming from early interactions with family, the direction of the narcissism will reflect the culture, demands, expectations, and schematic modes of the family. When the behaviors are further reinforced by peers, teachers, school personnel, or relatives, these children may see little reason to modify, much less give up, their narcissism.

A far more reasonable approach is to help the children or adolescents be less obvious in their narcissistic expressions, be more adaptive, show greater flexibility and less compulsivity, and be willing to modulate their behavior, all in the service of getting more of what they want. In effect, the therapy must focus on using the narcissistic pathology in the service of the child's best interest.

REFERENCES

American Psychiatric Association. (1980). *Diagnostic and statistical manual of mental disorders* (3rd ed.). Washington, DC: Author.

American Psychiatric Association. (1987). *Diagnostic and statistical manual of mental disorders* (3rd ed., rev.). Washington, DC: Author.

American Psychiatric Association. (1994). *Diagnostic and statistical manual of mental disorders* (4th ed.). Washington, DC: Author.

American Psychiatric Association. (2000). *Diagnostic and statistical manual of mental disorders* (4th ed., text rev.). Washington, DC: Author.

Ansbacher, H. L., & Ansbacher, R. R. (1956). *The individual psychology of Alfred Adler.* New York: Harper & Row.

Bacon, K., & Gedo, J. E. (1993). Ferenczi's contributions to psychoanalysis: Essays in dialogue. In L. Aron & A. Harris (Eds.), *The legacy of Sándor Ferenczi* (pp. 121–139). Hillsdale, NJ: Analytic Press.

Beck, A. T., Freeman, A., Davis, D. D., Pretzer, J., Fleming, B., & Beck, J. (1990). *Cognitive therapy of personality disorders.* New York: Guilford Press.

Beck, A. T., Freeman, A., Davis, D. D., Pretzer, J., Fleming, B., & Beck, J. (2004). *Cognitive therapy of personality disorders* (2nd ed.). New York: Guilford Press.

Beck, A. T., Rush, A. J., Shaw, B. F., & Emery, G. (1979). *Cognitive therapy of depression.* New York: Guilford Press.

Bleiberg, E. (2001). *Treating personality disorders in children and adolescents: A relational approach.* New York: Guilford Press.

Brown, N. W. (2001). *Children of the self-absorbed.* Oakland, CA: New Harbinger Press.

Donaldson-Pressman, S., & Pressman, R. M. (1994). *The narcissistic family: Diagnosis and treatment.* San Francisco: Jossey-Bass.

D'Zurilla, T., & Nezu, A. M. (2006). *Problem-solving therapy: A positive approach to clinical intervention.* New York: Springer.

Erikson, E. H. (1968). *Identity: Youth and crisis.* New York: Norton.

Erwin, E. (Ed.). (2002). *The Freud Encylopedia: Theory, Therapy, and Culture* (pp. 355–359). New York: Routledge.

Federn, P. (1952). *Ego psychology and the psychoses*. New York: Basic Books.

Fine, R. (1979). *A history of psychoanalysis*. New York: Columbia University Press.

Fonagy, P., Person, E., & Sandler, J. (Eds.). (1991). *Freud's on narcissism*. New Haven: Yale University Press.

Freeman, A. (2006, June). *Cognitive behavioral treatment of the narcissistic personality: The patient that we love to hate*. Workshop presentation to the Lehigh Valley Psychological Association, Allentown, PA.

Freeman, A., & Duff, J. (2006). Treatment of children with narcissistic personality disorders. In R. Mennuti, A. Freeman, & R. Christner (Eds.), *Cognitive behavioral interventions in school settings* (pp. 221–238). New York: Routledge.

Freeman, A., Pretzer, J., Fleming, B. A., & Simon, K. M. (1990). *Clinical applications of cognitive therapy*. New York: Plenum.

Freeman, A., Pretzer, J., Fleming, B. A., & Simon, K. M. (2004). *Clinical applications of cognitive therapy* (2nd ed.). New York: Springer Publishing Company.

Freeman, A., & Rigby, A. (2003). Personality disorders among children and adolescents: Is it an unlikely diagnosis? In M. A. Reinecke, F. M. Dattilio, & A. Freeman (Eds.), *Cognitive therapy with children and adolescents* (2nd ed., pp. 434–464). New York: Guilford Press.

Hamner, T. J., & Turner, P. H. (1985). *Parenting in contempory society*. Englewood Cliffs, NJ: Prentice-Hall.

Horney, K. (1937). *The neurotic personality of our time*. New York: Norton.

ICD-10. (1993). Classification of Mental and Behavioral Diseases. Geneva, Switzerland: World Health Organization.

Kernberg, O. (1976). *Borderline conditions and pathological narcissism*. New York: Aronson.

Kernberg, P. F., Weiner, A. S., & Berdenstein, K. K. (2000). *Personality disorders in children and adolescents.* New York: Basic Books.

Kohut, H. (1968). The psychoanalytic treatment of narcissistic personality disorders. *The search for the self* (Vol. 1, pp. 477–509). New York: International Universities Press.

Kohut, H. (1971). *The analysis of the self: A systematic approach to the psychoanalytic treatment of narcissistic personality disorder.* New York: International Universities Press.

Masterson, J. F. (1985). *Treatment of the borderline adolescent: A developmental approach.* New York: Brunner/Mazel.

Millon, T., & Davis, R. D. (1996). An evolutionary theory of personality disorders. In M. F. Lenzenweger & J. F. Clarkin (Eds.), *Major theories of personality disorder* (pp. 221–346). New York: Guilford Press.

Millon, T., Davis, R., Millon, C., Escovar, L., & Meagher, S. (2000). *Personality disorders in modern life.* New York: Wiley.

Millon, T., & Everly, G. S. (1985). *Personality and its disorders: A biosocial learning approach.* New York: Wiley.

Ronningstam, E. F. (2005). *Identifying and understanding the narcissistic personality.* New York: Oxford University Press.

Rosen, H. (1985). *Piagetian dimensions of clinical relevance.* New York: Columbia University Press.

Shirk, S., & Saiz, C. (1992). Clinical, empirical, and developmental perspectives on the therapeutic relationship in child psychotherapy. *Development and Psychopathology, 4,* 713–728.

CHAPTER 12

Antisocial Personality Disorder

JEFFREY D. BURKE

ANTISOCIAL BEHAVIOR is by definition a primary concern of any society. Yet antisocial behavior has persistently defied efforts to categorize and explain it, perhaps because of its broad, varied, and pervasive nature. Numerous disciplines have concerned themselves with the study of the topic and with efforts to intervene and reduce the diverse and costly effects of these behaviors. As early as 1801, descriptions of antisocial behavior as a mental illness were put forward (Andrews, 1991), with the construct of *moral insanity* emerging several decades later. By the end of the nineteenth century, the classification of *psychopathic personality* was introduced (Zuckerman, 1999), with Cleckley (1941) providing an influential revision of the condition. In the third edition of the *Diagnostic and Statistical Manual of Mental Disorders* (*DSM-III*; American Psychiatric Association, 1980), an effort to introduce greater reliability to diagnostic definitions led to important modifications to the clinical conceptualization of antisocial behavior as a mental disorder. Presently, in the fourth edition, text revision of the *DSM* (*DSM-IV-TR*; American Psychiatric Association, 2000), persistent and enduring antisocial behavior is identified in adulthood with the diagnosis of Antisocial Personality Disorder (APD).

Antisocial Personality Disorder is part of a developmental hierarchy of disorders of antisocial behavior, with Oppositional Defiant Disorder (ODD) and Conduct Disorder (CD) describing earlier steps in a pathway of antisocial psychopathology. As such, in contrast to other Axis II disorders, there exists a large literature base with evidence for a model of APD in childhood and adolescence, as represented by ODD and CD. On the whole, the model is both useful and well-supported by empirical evidence. However, there are a number of controversial and unresolved issues that impact the description of the disorder and the identification of children and adolescents at risk for APD.

Although APD has been demonstrated to have adequate reliability (Mellsop, Varghese, Joshua, & Hicks, 1982; Widiger et al., 1996), it nevertheless has been subject to criticism due to the symptoms that have been included and those that have been left out (Hare, Hart, & Harpur, 1991). Of particular concern is the degree to which the exclusion of certain personality features may lead to fewer valid cases of APD being identified than should be. Furthermore, emerging evidence suggests that callous and unemotional (CU) traits may describe early childhood and adolescent antisocial personality, may identify those who will show more persistent and severe conduct problems, and may predict APD (Loeber, Burke, & Lahey, 2002). Nevertheless, these behaviors are not included among the symptoms of ODD or CD. Thus, questions about which antisocial individuals are and are not being identified by the diagnostic criteria remain over the span of development from childhood to adulthood.

Literature regarding the treatment of APD is sparse, but continued focus on treatment for ODD and CD has provided greater evidence regarding which components of treatment are effective and which are not. Given the explicit linkage between APD and CD, treatments for CD are pertinent to an understanding of treatments for APD, particularly when considering children and adolescents most at risk for the development of APD. The possibility that CU traits in childhood may be diagnostically and prognostically useful suggests that they are also potential intervention targets over and above the symptoms of ODD or CD, which are discussed in this chapter.

In this chapter, the term APD will be used specifically to refer to APD as defined by the *DSM-IV* (American Psychiatric Association, 1994) and distinguished from psychopathy (Hare et al., 1991) as well as Dissocial Personality Disorder as described in the tenth edition of the *International Classification of Diseases* (ICD-10; World Health Organization [WHO], 1992). It is often the case that APD and psychopathy are regarded as equivalent. In fact, large literature databases, such as PsycInfo (American Psychological Association, 2006), explicitly treat the two as synonymous. There are important differences between these constructs. These differences have had significant influence on the study of the development of APD from childhood through adolescence and on the development of intervention methods for the disorder and its childhood precursors. Conflating the terms makes it difficult to identify subsets of the literature necessary to explain the differences in the disorder and develop more comprehensive models. Before discussing alternative models and their implications for childhood etiology and treatment, it is necessary to describe the model currently in use in the *DSM-IV*.

ANTISOCIAL PERSONALITY DISORDER

As defined by the *DSM-IV*, APD is "a pervasive pattern of disregard for and violation of the rights of others" (American Psychiatric Association, 1994, p. 649). It reflects a pattern of antisocial behavior in adulthood that is pervasive and impairing to the individual as well as to those close to the individual and to society in general. It is presumed to be present from childhood. As such, there is a diagnostic requirement that antisocial behavior has been present since the age of 15 and that there is evidence of at least "some symptoms" of CD before 15.

PREVALENCE

According to the Epidemiologic Catchment Area Study, the lifetime prevalence of *DSM-III* APD is 4.5% for adult males (Robins, Tipp, & Przybeck, 1991). In a recent representative sample of the United States, the lifetime prevalence of APD among 15- to 54-year-olds was similarly found to be 5.8% for males (Kessler et al., 1994). A survey of a large representative sample in Edmonton, Canada, found lifetime prevalence rates for *DSM-III* APD of 8.7% for males and 0.9% for females in the 18 to 29 age range (M. C. Swanson, Bland, & Newman, 1994). Most studies find gender differences in the rate of APD, with males showing a far higher prevalence of APD than females (Kessler et al., 1994; Swanson et al., 1994). A disparity by gender is also seen in the increased prevalence of CD among boys relative to girls (Keenan, Loeber, & Green, 1999), although there is some evidence that the risks for developing APD among boys and girls with CD are approximately equal (Zoccolillo, Pickles, Quinton, & Rutter, 1992). These findings are consistent with evidence of a narrowing in the gender differences in rates of antisocial behavior as children age (for a review, see Silverthorn & Frick, 1999).

DISTINCTIONS BETWEEN ANTISOCIAL PERSONALITY DISORDER AND OTHER AXIS II DISORDERS

Antisocial Personality Disorder is distinguished from other personality disorders by a number of features. Most obvious among these is the fact that APD is intended to indicate a distinct quality, severity level, and type of harm to others (see Table 12.1, column 1, for the diagnostic criteria for APD). Although harm to others may occur as part

Table 12.1

Item Overlap between Antisocial Personality Disorder
and Psychopathy Checklist

Antisocial Personality Disorder	Psychopathy Checklist—R
Criterion C. History of Conduct Disorder	Early behavioral problems Juvenile delinquency
Failure to conform to social norms with respect to lawful behavior	Criminal versatility Revocation of conditional release
Deceitfulness	Pathological lying Conning/manipulative
Irritability and aggressiveness	Poor behavioral controls
Impulsivity or failure to plan ahead	Impulsivity Lack of realistic, long-term goals
Irresponsibility in work behavior or financial obligations	Irresponsibility
Reckless disregard for safety	
Lacks remorse	Lack of remorse or guilt
	Failure to accept responsibility
	Callous/lack of empathy
	Glibness/superficial charm
	Grandiose sense of self-worth
	Shallow affect
	Parasitic lifestyle
	Promiscuous sexual behavior
	Need for stimulation/proneness to boredom
	Many short-term marital relationships

of any number of other disorders, the persistence across time and pervasiveness across relationships, settings, and life events sets the harm associated with APD apart from that arising due to other disorders.

Apart from being specifically distinct from other Axis II disorders due to the content of the symptoms and features underlying the diagnosis, there are other distinctive aspects of APD. First is the specification that the individual must be at least 18 years old. Other personality disorders do not impose a minimum age to meet criteria. In the case of APD, however, antisocial behavior that is present from adolescence and continues into young adulthood suggests a noteworthy condition that persists through key developmental periods. Antisocial behavior by an adolescent in the context of the family, school, and community that continues as one moves into what should putatively be greater independence in young adulthood suggests that the individual is unresponsive to socializing factors or to the mechanisms by which society attempts to elicit prosocial behavior.

Antisocial Personality Disorder is also the only personality disorder diagnosis that requires the presence of an Axis I disorder; evidence of CD is required to have been present before the age of 15. As a result, to meet criteria for this personality disorder, a separate behavioral disorder must have previously been present. Is this requirement sensible? Two diagnostic details in particular support it. First, the presence of CD prior to age 15 would suggest that, if antisocial behavior is present in young adulthood, some type of antisocial behavior has been present over at least several years during an individual's development. Consistent with the diagnoses of personality disorders, this would illustrate that antisocial behavior has been a chronic and persistent facet of that person's functioning. Second, within the overall scheme of the *DSM*, it is sensible because CD is intended to be "symptomatic of an underlying dysfunction within the individual" (American Psychiatric Association, 1994, p. 88), despite the fact that the disorder is defined entirely by a circumscribed set of explicit behaviors. To the degree that this is accurate, CD behaviors would serve as a reliable marker for antisocial personality traits.

The decision to include a requirement of childhood conduct problems in the definition of APD was influenced by Robins's (1978, p. 611) conclusion that "adult antisocial behavior virtually *requires* childhood antisocial behavior." In four samples available at that time, she found that 65% to 82% of highly antisocial adults displayed high levels of antisocial behavior as children or adolescents. There is some evidence, from retrospective self-report data, that having a history of CD is distinct to the adult criteria for APD, in contrast to other personality disorders (Dowson, Sussams, Grounds, & Taylor, 2001).

There is also prospective empirical evidence to suggest that CD is a strong predictor of APD (Lahey, Loeber, Burke, & Applegate, 2005; Loeber et al., 2002). Insufficient evidence exists to say with any certainty how often APD arises without a history of CD or, if it does, whether it truly represents a distinct condition from APD with prior CD (Langbehn & Cadoret, 2001). It is possible to imagine an individual who lacks empathy, manipulates others, does not show remorse, and fails to plan ahead but who fails to meet criteria for CD due to an absence of aggression, property crimes, or status offenses in adolescence.

A DEVELOPMENTAL PATHWAY OF ANTISOCIAL PSYCHOPATHOLOGY

The relationship between ODD, CD, and APD is a hierarchical one, in which the early disruptive behavior problems reflected in ODD precede the development of CD, which reflects more severe, diverse, and harmful antisocial behavior arising typically in adolescence (see Table 12.2 for the *DSM-IV* diagnostic criteria for ODD and CD). Conduct Disorder precedes APD in young adulthood, as described earlier. Thus, APD represents the highest level of a developmental pathway of antisocial behavior in the *DSM-IV* (American Psychiatric Association, 1994).

The diagnostic criteria illustrate the explicit link between CD and APD and the underlying hypothesis that a developmental relationship exists between the disorders. Furthermore, there are specific definitional links between ODD and CD. Oppositional Defiant Disorder is not diagnosed in addition to CD; ODD symptoms are instead presumed to underlie CD symptoms. This yields an implicit link between ODD and APD because the presence of CD is both required for APD and presumptive evidence of ODD. On the other hand, progression along the pathway of ODD, CD, and APD is not inexorable, nor necessarily sequential. In fact, studies show that the majority of those with ODD do not go on to develop CD (Loeber, Burke, Lahey, Winters, & Zera, 2000; Rowe, Maughan, Pickles, Costello, & Angold, 2002), and

Table 12.2

DSM-IV Criteria for Oppositional Defiant Disorder and Conduct Disorder

Oppositional Defiant Disorder:

A. A pattern of negativistic, hostile, and defiant behavior lasting at least 6 months, during which four (or more) of the following are present:
   1. Often loses temper
   2. Often argues with adults
   3. Often actively defies or refuses to comply with adults' requests or rules
   4. Often deliberately annoys people
   5. Often blames others for his or her mistakes or misbehavior
   6. Is often touchy or easily annoyed by others
   7. Is often angry and resentful
   8. Is often spiteful or vindictive

Conduct Disorder:

A. Repetitive pattern of violating social norms and rights of others indicated by three of the following in last 12 months:
   1. Frequent bullying
   2. Often starts physical fights
   3. Using weapons
   4. Physical cruelty to people
   5. Physical cruelty to animals
   6. Theft with confrontation of victim
   7. Often out late without permission, starting < 13 years of age
   8. Often truant from school, starting < 13 years of age
   9. Vandalism
   10. Breaking and entering
   11. Frequent manipulative lying
   12. Covert stealing
   13. Forced sex
   14. Deliberate fire setting to cause harm
   15. Running away from home overnight

the majority of those with CD do not develop APD (Burke, Loeber, & Lahey, 2003). It is also frequently the case, evident from population-based samples, that CD develops in children who do not meet the criteria for ODD (Lahey, McBurnett, & Loeber, 2000; Rowe et al., 2002). As a result, it is not clear whether the diagnostic presumption of ODD given CD is well founded, and it may be of greater utility to allow for the diagnosis of both ODD and CD. The prohibition against assigning both diagnoses has also likely impeded the scientific inquiry into the developmental relationship between ODD and CD (Greene et al., 2002; Kuhne, Schachar, & Tannock, 1997). It is far more often the case that when disruptive behavior disorders are studied, researchers combine ODD and CD and often include Attention-Deficit/Hyperactivity Disorder (ADHD) in the same construct. The result is that information about differences between these disorders and between individuals with one versus another disorder is lost.

In terms of the focus of this chapter, the childhood expression of features of APD, this information is crucial. The explicit linkage between ODD, CD, and APD is intended to describe a persisting antisocial trait expressed over time. On the other hand, estimates are that only about one third of those with ODD will develop CD, and only about one third of those with CD will develop APD. If children with an antisocial personality trait are marked by behavioral disorders in childhood, they are hidden within a much larger group of children who will show disruptive behavior at one time yet will desist in a manner that would suggest something other than an enduring personality trait.

It is also clear that not all of those who show antisocial behavior in young adulthood meet criteria for APD. Many criminals and prisoners, for example, do not meet criteria for APD (Robins et al., 1991). The *DSM-IV* indicates that if the criteria for APD are not met, instrumental criminal behavior can be diagnostically described as Adult Antisocial Behavior, as one of the "Additional Conditions That May Be a Focus of Clinical Attention." On the other hand, there is no specification that a diagnosis of CD may *not* be given to a person over 18, so it is conceivable that a diagnosis of CD could be given to an adult who did not meet the criteria for APD. The same is true for ODD, so that antisocial behavior in young adulthood could be described on Axis II as APD, or on Axis I as CD or ODD, or with the code for Adult Antisocial Behavior. In practice, however, it is essentially never the case that adults are given a diagnosis of CD or ODD.

RESEARCH ON THE DEVELOPMENT TOWARD ANTISOCIAL
PERSONALITY DISORDER

Research on the developmental precursors of APD has been held back
by several limitations. First, the requirement within the definition of
APD of the presence of CD prior to adulthood (American Psychiatric
Association, 1994) makes it impossible to ascertain to what extent CD
is a precursor to APD, unless researchers employ a modified definition of APD that does not include this criterion. Several studies that
have used such a modified form of APD have shown that, although
CD is a very strong predictor of APD (Lahey et al., 2005; Loeber et al.,
2002), only about 30% to 40% of children with CD develop APD
(Robins, 1966; Robins et al., 1991). However, it remains far from clear
what the characteristics are that distinguish those children with CD
who developed APD from children with CD who did not develop
APD. A second limitation of studies is that a proportion of children
outgrow CD during childhood and adolescence rather than progressing on to APD, constituting false positives in the prediction of APD.
For that reason, precursors to APD may be best studied using data collected over a period after which some of the CD youth typically have
desisted from CD, which requires a longitudinal perspective and suitable proportions of children with CD.

Unfortunately, such suitable data sets are rare, so studies using
less than ideal methodologies, particularly retrospective analyses,
have been relied on for some evidence. Langbehn, Cadoret, Yates,
Troughton, and Stewart (1998), using retrospective data from men
and women, found that ODD symptoms distinctly predicted APD,
even after controlling for CD symptoms, and that ODD symptoms in
men may reflect a psychopathic component of adult antisocial behavior. However, this contrasts with analyses from a prospective study
of boys followed from childhood into young adulthood. Lahey and
colleagues (2005) found that childhood ODD no longer predicted
APD after controlling for CD, and Loeber and colleagues (2002)
found that ODD in adolescence was eliminated from a regression
model predicting APD.

Simonoff and colleagues (2004) reported distinct prediction of APD from adolescent hyperactivity over and above the prediction from CD symptoms, also using retrospective data. They found that criminality in adolescence was predictive of APD in young adulthood, which was in turn predictive of criminality after age 35. Nevertheless, the study design and methodology presented a number of challenges to a clear interpretation of the results, including nonstandard definitions and symptom counts for disorders, and particularly a failure to measure ODD, which has been demonstrated in a number of other studies to be crucial to understanding the development from ADHD to later CD (Lahey et al., 2000; Loeber, Green, Keenan, & Lahey, 1995). It is important that ODD be examined in the prediction from hyperactivity to later APD before any conclusions about significant risks for severe adult outcomes may be drawn regarding ADHD. One study using prospective data suggests that no significant direct relationship exists between ADHD and APD (Lahey et al., 2005).

THE EMERGENCE OF SYMPTOMS OVER TIME

Beyond the typical progression from ODD to CD to eventual symptoms of APD, there is some evidence to suggest that certain symptoms within the disorders precede other symptoms. Keenan and Wakschlag (2000) found that ODD and CD symptoms evident among preschoolers distinguished those children who would eventually be referred for services from more normative antisocial behavior among young children. Loeber, Burke, et al. (2000) found that the one symptom most predictive of progression from ODD to CD was persistent physical fighting, and that those boys who desisted from physical fighting over time had mothers who scored lower on measures of APD. Frick and colleagues (1993), in a meta-analysis, found that within the symptoms of ODD and CD, two dimensions of conduct problems could be distinguished: a dimension of overt versus covert behaviors and a dimension of destructive versus nondestructive behaviors. Within the four quadrants defined by these dimensions, ODD and CD symptoms clustered into subsets of oppositionality, status offenses, property crimes, and aggression. The authors further demonstrated that there was a developmental progression among these symptoms, with oppositional behaviors emerging first, followed by aggression, property crimes, and status offenses.

Loeber and colleagues (1993) developed a model of the symptoms of ODD and CD that is not bound to the diagnostic definitions of each disorder and focuses instead on the sequential nature of development of specific symptoms across the ODD and CD spectrums. Examination of the developmental sequences and the severity of individual symptoms of ODD and CD showed that some symptoms temporally preceded other symptoms, but not exclusively within the diagnoses of ODD and CD (Loeber, Green, Lahey, Christ, & Frick, 1992). Instead, an incremental, integrated three-level model of Disruptive Behavior Disorder was suggested, with modified ODD, intermediate CD, and advanced CD. Evidence of the validity of this model was presented by Lahey and Loeber (1994), Russo, Loeber, Lahey, and Keenan (1994), and Loeber, DeLamatre, Keenan, and Zhang (1998). In the model, the onset of intermediate CD symptoms (e.g., lying, truancy) occurs prior to the onset of advanced CD symptoms, including robbery, burglary, assault with a weapon, and rape (Loeber et al., 1992, 1993; Russo et al., 1994). Boys with advanced CD are very likely to have gone through earlier stages of less serious CD symptoms (e.g., truancy, frequent lying; Robins & Wish, 1977). Some APD symptoms, unlike those of ODD or CD, become more developmentally relevant from adulthood onward, such as irresponsibility in work behavior or financial obligations, or the former symptom of failure to sustain a monogamous relationship for a year. Typically, studies of ODD, CD, and APD have not sufficiently employed a developmental model integrating these disorders.

This succession of symptoms tends to persist over time. For example, evidence has been mounting regarding the continuity of delinquent behaviors (Blumstein, Cohen, Roth, & Visher, 1986; Loeber,

1982; Sampson & Laub, 1993) and aggression (Olweus, 1979). Moreover, Loeber (1988) proposed that instead of one disruptive symptom replacing another symptom, heterotypic continuity occurs, primarily in that new problem symptoms are added to existing ones, gradually leading to a diversification of problem behavior. What type of model can best fit both diversification and persistence of disruptive behaviors over time? An answer to that question is crucial for the prediction and early identification of those children and adolescents most at risk for APD.

PSYCHOPATHY

As noted, the characteristics of APD have been established for several decades, but scholars have continued to disagree about essential features, particularly about the exclusion of a number of items that emphasize personality traits (Hare et al., 1991; Widiger, 1992; Widiger & Corbitt, 1993), provoking the criticism that APD is "the most controversial of all the personality disorders" (Frances, 1980, p. 1053). Within the literature, two distinct conceptualizations have emerged from common early models of adult antisocial behavior. The model described in the *DSM-IV* (American Psychiatric Association, 1994, p. 649) focuses on "a pervasive pattern of disregard for, and violation of, the rights of others that begins in childhood or early adolescence and continues into adulthood." Originally, *DSM* conceptualizations of APD included a greater focus on aspects of antisocial personality, such as a lack of empathy, being glib or superficially charming, and displaying a grandiose sense of self-worth. In an effort to increase diagnostic consistency and reliability, APD was defined for the *DSM-III* (American Psychiatric Association, 1980) using criteria with a greater reliance on antisocial behaviors and less reliance on personality traits, a decision that did yield acceptable levels of reliability in general clinical practice (Mellsop et al., 1982). The diagnostic criteria for APD since that time have continued to be arguably skewed toward a single factor of irresponsible and antisocial behavior (Robins, 1966; Robins et al., 1991).

Psychopathy shares some characteristics with APD, but not all psychopaths are very aggressive and engage in chronic antisocial behavior (Connor, 2002). The most commonly used measure of psychopathy, the Psychopathy Checklist (PCL; Hare, 1991), assesses two factors, one reflective of personality features such as egocentricity, callousness, and manipulativeness, and a second of antisocial behavior such as impulsivity, irresponsibility, and antisocial behavior, more consistent with components of *DSM-IV* APD. See Table 12.1 for the overlap between the items of APD and psychopathy. Recently, researchers have begun exploring the possibility that the model of psychopathy items might be better described using more than two factors (e.g., Cooke & Michie, 2001).

In the *DSM-IV* field trials evaluating potential revisions to APD (Widiger et al., 1996), the reliability and concurrent validity of the *DSM-III-R* (American Psychiatric Association, 1987) were compared with the items of the PCL (Hare et al., 1991) and with the symptoms of Dissocial Personality Disorder in the *ICD-10* (WHO, 1992). The concerns about the reliability of the less discrete symptoms that assess personality features were not borne out. The authors found that the items of the PCL and the *ICD-10* were assessed as reliably as the symptoms of APD (Widiger et al., 1996).

Critics of the *DSM* APD model have raised concerns about threats to the clinical validity of the construct, given that personality traits had historically been included with greater prominence among past diagnostic criteria, and a concern that clinicians might continue to rely on those features for diagnosing APD regardless of their exclusion from the formal criteria (for a review, see Zuckerman, 1999). Hare and colleagues (1991) argued that the criteria for APD are both overly broad, because they may include criminals and antisocial individuals who are psychologically heterogeneous, and yet too narrow, because they may exclude some with a psychopathic personality who have not exhibited some of the specific antisocial behaviors listed for APD. These authors have argued that APD symptoms "represent a rather radical break with clinical tradition, clinical practice, with earlier versions of the *DSM* and with international diagnostic nomenclature" (p. 392).

The diagnostic criteria of the *ICD-10* (WHO, 1992) diagnosis of Dissocial Personality Disorder (DPD) incorporate personality features to a greater degree than the *DSM-IV* (American Psychiatric Association, 1994). Specific examples among the symptoms of DPD include "callous unconcern" for others, a low tolerance for frustration, an incapacity to maintain enduring relationships, and a marked disposition to blame others. The *DSM-IV* field trials found that the symptoms of DPD were assessed as reliably as those of APD and of psychopathy, and found no consistent advantage for any one of the three criteria sets in terms of concurrent validity when compared with other measures of antisocial personality, empathy, or Machiavellian personality (Widiger et al., 1996).

In addition to concerns about the historical definition of the disorder versus the manner in which the current diagnostic criteria might be employed by clinicians, critics of the *DSM* conceptualization of APD have raised concerns about its content and construct validity. Some argue that clinical conceptions of antisocial personality traits require inferences about the capacity for empathy, remorse, or guilt. Others have argued more specifically that behavioral symptoms of APD are secondary, or result from, underlying personality traits. McCord and McCord (1964, as cited by Cooke, Michie, Hart, & Clark, 2004) regarded it as a "mistake" to equate antisocial behavior with psychopathic personality disorder, suggesting that the use of behavioral referents to define the construct was inadequate. They argued that antisocial behavior is instead an effect of psychopathy, and as a result would not be accurately characterized as symptomatic. If antisocial behavior were in fact only one particular manifestation of an underlying antisocial personality disorder, relying on behavioral referents alone could potentially lead to the misidentification of a notable proportion of individuals. In turn, if antisocial behavior arises as a result of a variety of causes other than antisocial personality, individuals who did not actually have such an underlying pathology would be erroneously grouped with those who did.

Recent evidence has provided some limited support for the assertion that antisocial behavior is an outcome of psychopathic personality features. Cooke and colleagues (2004) found evidence that antisocial behaviors are distinct from psychopathic personality features, and that introducing measures of antisocial behavior into a model of psychopathic features led to a poorer model fit. They also found some evidence for a model in which the personality trait "arrogant and deceitful personality style" led to behaviors representing relationship lability, and in which a path from "impulsive and irresponsible behavioral style" to criminal behavior was mediated by early behavioral problems.

Both findings are consistent with the assertion that behavioral problems arise from personality features. On the other hand, regarding the latter finding, the degree to which impulsivity is a behavioral feature versus a personality trait is debatable, and it may be argued that the factor they describe as "impulsive and irresponsible behavioral style" is reflective more of impulsive behavior. The fact that a path from impulsive behavior to later criminal behavior is mediated in their model by the presence of early behavioral problems is reminiscent of the findings that the link between ADHD and later CD is explained by the early presence of ODD (Burke, Loeber, Lahey, & Rathouz, 2005; Lahey et al., 2000).

Whether the symptoms of APD sufficiently identify those individuals whom the disorder is intended to describe, or whether a set of individuals who should otherwise be regarded as meeting the criteria is being excluded, remains to be assessed. The temporal associations and temporal precedent between components of psychopathy and antisocial behavior remain to be investigated. Data sets with longitudinal measures of these features would be best suited to such analyses. In addition, analyses of a construct similar to psychopathy in children will also provide crucial information to inform the understanding of the developmental associations between personality features and behavior.

OTHER DEVELOPMENTAL ASPECTS OF ANTISOCIAL BEHAVIOR

In addition to the developmental hierarchy of ODD, CD, and APD, which describes a pathway of antisocial behavior from early in childhood to adulthood, there are a number of features that are associated with the development of antisocial behavior over the life course. Furthermore, the symptoms used to define ODD and CD do not include certain aspects of APD, particularly impulsivity and personality traits. Substance abuse is highly involved in the development of antisocial behavior. Negative affect is a component of ODD, and affective conditions are often comorbid with CD. Environmental aspects of the child's world also influence the development of antisocial behavior. These include parenting behaviors and styles and interactions with peers and teachers, among other figures of the environment. Not all antisocial behavior is preceded by these features, nor do these features necessarily result in antisocial behavior. A more comprehensive review of the literature regarding the many domains of risk factors and correlates of ODD and CD can be found in Burke, Loeber, and Birmaher (2002).

CALLOUS AND UNEMOTIONAL TRAITS IN CHILDHOOD

The exclusion of personality traits from the diagnostic criteria is much more evident among the symptoms of ODD and CD than APD. Oppositional Defiant Disorder includes items that may be seen to reflect negative affect or temperament, as well as behaviorally oriented items, and CD symptoms consist solely of behaviors. Although, as noted earlier, there is a presumption that the diagnosis of CD reflects an underlying condition, it is defined only by observable and discrete behaviors. Clearly, this has implications not only for the accuracy of the diagnosis, but also for prognosis and for intervention. It is unknown, for example, whether those who do not progress from CD to

APD could be more reliably identified by the absence of antisocial personality features.

During the past decade, increasing attention has been given to the examination of antisocial personality features present in childhood and adolescence. Lynam (1997) noted that prior attempts to reduce the heterogeneity among behavioral disorder symptoms have typically not yielded a great deal of success, likely due to the fact that prior attempts have focused primarily on subtyping the behavioral indicators (such as by type, pattern, sequence of onset, or developmental timing). He observed, on the other hand, that heterogeneity among adult chronic offenders had been more successfully resolved with the use of information about personality features. Using items from two existing measures for children, the Child Behavior Checklist (Achenbach & Edelbrock, 1983) and a version of the California Child Q-Set (Block & Block, 1980), Lynam created a measure of psychopathy in childhood that corresponds with the elements assessed by the PCL (Hare et al., 1991) for adults. Lynam found that children with psychopathy, whom he termed "fledgling psychopaths," showed higher levels of serious antisocial behavior than those without and that they had a more stable course of antisocial behavior.

Another line of research undertaken by Paul Frick and colleagues has investigated a construct associated with antisocial personality in children (Frick, O'Brien, Wootton, & McBurnett, 1994), referred to as callous and unemotional traits. Frick, Cornell, Bodin, and colleagues (2003) postulated that some CD cases score high on CU, and that the presence of such symptoms presages a higher continuity of CD and a higher probability of escalation from CD to APD, compared to CD cases with low levels of CU traits. Initial support for the role of CU in adolescence in the escalation from CD to APD has been reported by Loeber and colleagues (2002). There is also evidence that CU traits, in a nonreferred sample, predict higher rates of delinquent behaviors and instrumental aggression (Frick, Cornell, Barry, Bodin, & Dane, 2003). Similarly, Pardini, Obradovic, and Loeber (2006), in a longitudinal, community-based data set, found that interpersonal callousness predicted persistent delinquency, although they found this to be the case only among the oldest of three cohorts (13 years of age at the beginning of the study, in contrast to 7- and 10-year-old cohorts). Whether this reflects a developmental change in the influence of CU traits over time remains to be replicated in other studies.

It is also thought that CU is present early in the development of antisocial behavior and often precedes the development of CD. Barry and colleagues (2000) compared groups of children who had ADHD and an aggregated ODD/CD construct who were either high or low in CU. They found that those who were high in CU were low on anxiety symptoms and were less distressed by peer rejection and disciplinary confrontations than the group with low levels of CU. Frick, Cornell, Barry, and colleagues (2003) reported that children with higher CU showed a more severe and aggressive pattern of conduct problems than other antisocial youth. Kimonis, Frick, and Barry (2004) found that a group of CU boys showed CU traits before the onset of conduct problems.

Recent evidence suggests that there is continuity between measures of callousness (Burke, Loeber, & Lahey, in press) or psychopathy (Lynam, Caspi, Moffitt, Loeber, & Stouthamer-Loeber, in press) in childhood and psychopathy as measured by the PCL-R in young adulthood. In both papers, there was some evidence to suggest that the strength of the relationship was greater when factors of the PCL-R measuring antisocial behavioral, rather than antisocial personality features, were the predicted outcome. In a clinical sample, both callousness and CD together predicted the antisocial behavioral features of PCL-R Factor 2, and an interaction suggested that being elevated on either measure independently of the level of the other indicated an increased risk for elevated antisocial behavior in young adulthood (Burke et al., in press).

Both ODD and CU traits have been found to predict conduct problems. There is some evidence (Frick, Cornell, Bodin, et al., 2003) that CU traits are not related to emotional reactivity to provocation, which may be akin to the irritability component of ODD. It remains to be determined whether high levels of CU identify a distinct subset of children from those with ODD or CD, or whether CU represents an independent pathway to CD, and greater clarity is needed regarding how CU might relate to ODD as a whole, as well as at the symptom level.

How do CU traits and internalizing disorders, which are both associated with antisocial behavior, relate to one another? One hypothetical model proposes that CU traits predict antisocial outcomes and are integral to the development toward APD, but are independent from affective disorders. More specifically, it may be that CU traits, or antisocial personality features, predict antisocial behavior, but affective disorders result from antisocial behaviors. Support for this model comes from the findings of Barry and colleagues (2000), who demonstrated that CU traits did not predict affective disorders, but were close correlates of CD symptoms. Conduct Disorder symptoms may be linked to affective disorders only to the degree that they are causal of psychosocial problems, with ODD explaining the remainder of the CD-depression link (Burke et al., 2005). It is possible, though not demonstrated yet, that distinct classes of individuals could be identified by the presence of primarily behavioral features (ADHD, ODD behavioral symptoms, CU features) versus affective features (ODD negative emotional symptoms, symptoms of depression and anxiety). These groups would potentially differ in terms of adult outcomes of APD, depressive disorders, or suicidality.

Negative and Irritable Affect

New evidence is emerging that suggests that ODD symptoms may encompass two distinct dimensions, one of antisocial behavior in the form of authority conflict, and the other of irritable affect. The former includes symptoms of rule breaking and defiant behavior, and the latter symptoms reflecting irritability, and anger (Burke et al., 2005). Whether these factors are reliably identified as distinct in different samples and over time remains to be determined. However, if they are, it is possible that these features may help to improve the description of the early development of antisocial behavior and the role of negative affect in that development.

Several studies suggest that the symptoms associated with irritable affect are distinct from the authority conflict symptoms. For example, Waldman and Lilienfeld's (1991) analysis of the most defining symptoms of ODD singled out the affective symptoms. Also, Angold and Costello (1996) found that endorsement of several of the irritable affect symptoms of ODD was largely higher depending on whether they included child report as well as parent report.

Depression co-occurs with ODD and CD at greater-than-chance levels (Angold, Costello, & Erkanli, 1999; Maughan, Rowe, Messer, Goodman, & Meltzer, 2004), and their comorbidity may have specific implications for treatment (Reinecke, 1995). Studies have found that ODD symptoms may explain the comorbidities that have been historically evident between CD and depression (Burke et al., 2005; Maughan et al., 2004), and that poor psychosocial outcomes or stressful life events resulting from antisocial behavior may explain the remainder of the link between CD and depression (Burke et al., 2005). Rowe and colleagues (2002) found a very low rate of progression from ODD to CD among girls across the ages of 9 to 16, yet found substantial prediction from ODD to later affective disorders, as well as to persistent ODD. Among boys in the same study, they found significant prediction from ODD to CD, but not to later affective disorders. In the context of Zoccolillo and colleagues' (1992) finding of consistency between boys and girls on the progression from CD to APD, the divergence between genders on the progression from ODD to CD found by Rowe and colleagues (2002) is intriguing and is not inconsistent with the notion that ODD symptoms include both a behavioral component and an affective component and may represent a fork in the developmental pathway toward APD.

Like CD, APD is often comorbid with depression, which gives rise to particular concerns of suicidal behavior among a group prone to violent resolution of problems. It is possible that similar processes explain linkages between APD and depression. If so, this would suggest that an important component of intervention strategies should be targeted at coping constructively with the negative consequences of antisocial behavior. Additionally, studies of these issues may help to develop a more coherent conceptualization of antisocial personality features across developmental periods.

IMPULSIVITY

One of the explicit criteria of the diagnosis of APD is the presence of impulsivity. Not only is impulsivity regarded as a key indicator of an antisocial lifestyle, but it is also regarded as a mechanism in the expression of the antisocial behavioral features throughout the life course. Impulsivity is a primary diagnostic component of ADHD. Although often comorbid with CD, ADHD is diagnostically distinct from CD. Furthermore, as noted earlier, evidence has emerged over the past decade to illustrate that links between ADHD and later CD are largely explained by the presence of ODD (Burke et al., 2005; Lahey et al., 2000). The only study to find contrary findings using measures of ODD, CD, and ADHD during the past decade known to the author did find that ADHD predicted CD independently of ODD. However, that study also found that *ODD itself did not predict CD* (Mannuzza, Klein, Abikoff, & Moulton, 2004). This unusual absence of a relationship between ODD and CD is certainly intriguing, but makes it difficult to integrate those findings with other studies regarding the developmental pathways among ADHD, ODD, and CD.

The suggestion that antisocial behavior in the form of CD does not arise due to ADHD, in the absence of preexisting ODD, is consistent with the proposition that an antisocial trait or disposition may be evident from childhood (e.g., Lahey & Waldman, 2002; Moffitt, 1993). Loeber and colleagues (1995) suggested that the role of ADHD in the development of CD was to accelerate or enhance the development of antisocial behavior, but not to precipitate CD. Similarly, in a nonreferred group of grade school children, the presence of CU traits, but not impulsivity, predicted greater levels of antisocial behavior at 1-year

(Frick, Cornell, Barry, et al., 2003) and 3-year follow-ups (Frick, Stickle, Dandreaux, Farrell, & Kimonis, 2005).

In the latter study, interesting results were found regarding the role of impulsivity in the course of antisocial behavior over time. Frick and colleagues (2005) found that controlling for impulsivity did not alter trajectories of delinquent behavior shown by four groups of children defined by the presence or absence of CU and of conduct problems, but did alter the trajectories of conduct problems. However, controlling for impulsivity *reduced* the decline and stabilized the trajectories of conduct problems for all groups.

Thus, not only does it appear that impulsivity does not play a direct and necessary role in the development of antisocial behavior, but its role in hastening the course of conduct problems may be more complicated than previously believed. In general, it may be the case that a preexistent disposition toward antisocial behavior interacts with impulsivity by lessening the effectiveness of internal controls that might otherwise inhibit a child from acting on antisocial impulses. This model would accord with the fact that many children who are impulsive and hyperactive never engage in marked antisocial or harmful behavior.

The role of impulsivity should also be given greater scrutiny across the life course not only to help clarify findings such as those of Frick and colleagues (2005), but also because it is one element of the disruptive behavior disorders for which there is well-established pharmacological intervention. Although there has not been an accumulation of consistent evidence supportive of the use of medications to treat ODD or CD specifically (see later discussion), medications for ADHD have been found to help reduce problems with disruptive behavior disorders when they are comorbid with ADHD. As our understanding of the expression of ADHD among adults expands, and along with it the understanding of pharmacotherapy for ADHD in adulthood, it may be that evidence will be found for the use of these medications with adults who are impulsively antisocial. It should be noted that among the symptoms of APD are one of the hallmark features of ADHD (impulsivity or failure to plan ahead) and a former symptom of ADHD (reckless disregard for safety, from the *DSM-III-R*; American Psychiatric Association, 1987).

Evidence from the Study of Reactive and Proactive Aggression

Some evidence suggests that the type of aggression that children show may predict who progresses from early disruptive behavior to CD, and perhaps thus to APD. Oppositional Defiant Disorder may be associated more with reactive than with proactive aggression, whereas CD is typified more by proactive aggression. If this is the case, it may be informative to consider the evidence regarding correlates and outcomes of reactive and proactive aggression. Dodge, Lochman, Harnish, Bates, and Pettit (1997) found that reactive aggression was more typical of boys with CD and ADHD, whereas boys with CD alone more typically displayed proactive aggression. Unfortunately, data regarding ODD without CD were not presented in the study.

Compared to proactive aggression, reactive aggression has been shown to be more strongly associated with internalizing disorders (Connor, Steingard, Cunningham, Anderson, & Melloni, 2004; Vitaro, Gendreau, Tremblay, & Oligny, 1998) and poor social and classroom functioning (Poulin & Boivin, 2000; Vitaro et al., 1998; Waschbusch, Willoughby, & Pehlam, 1998). Waschbusch and colleagues found that reactive, compared to proactive, aggression was associated more strongly with poor functioning in early and middle childhood. Furthermore, ODD was associated with classroom behavior problems and peer adjustment problems over and above the effects of proactive and reactive aggression, whereas CD was not.

Substance Use

It is clear that conduct problems (Kuperman et al., 2001), aggression (Giancola & Parker, 2001; White, Loeber, Stouthamer-Loeber, & Farrington, 1999), and general childhood disruptive behavior (Dobkin,

Tremblay, Masse, & Vitaro, 1995) predict substance abuse in adolescence. There is also evidence that reciprocal influence between aggression and substance use may persist through adolescence (White et al., 1999), and that substance use predicts young adult delinquency (Brook, Whiteman, Finch, & Cohen, 1996). Barkley, Fischer, Smallish, and Fletcher (2004) found evidence to suggest that adolescent substance use may predict a drug-related factor of antisocial behavior distinctly from a predatory-overt factor in young adulthood. There is also evidence from prospective studies (Loeber et al., 2002; Myers, Stewart, & Brown, 1998) and retrospective studies (Ridenour et al., 2002) to suggest that those with CD who show higher levels of substance use are at increased risk of transition from CD to APD.

Environmental Features and the Development of Antisocial Behavior

It is clear that elements of the environment impinge upon and exacerbate children's antisocial behavior. A number of studies (Cadoret, Yates, Troughton, Woodworth, & Stewart, 1995; Caspi et al., 2002) have provided evidence for a stress-diathesis model of the emergence of antisocial behavior, in which environmental adversity acts on a genetic liability to elicit early conduct problems in children.

Interactions with parents or adult caregivers and with the environment determined by parents are primary experiences for all children. Parents typically have the earliest and most extensive contact with the child, and poor parenting behaviors have frequently been noted to be a risk for the emergence of behavioral problems (Wasserman, Miller, Pinner, & Jaramillo, 1996). Specific parenting behaviors have been linked to different types of antisocial behavior in children: physically aggressive punishment and child aggression, and low parental warmth/involvement and oppositional child behavior (Stormshak, Bierman, McMahon, & Lengua, 2000). On the other hand, positive parenting appears to protect children from antisocial outcomes (McCord, 1991; Werner, 2005) and to buffer children from the effects of negative macro-environmental conditions (Beyers, Bates, Pettit, & Dodge, 2003; Brody et al., 2001; Gutman, McLoyd, & Tokoyawa, 2005; McLoyd, 1998).

One model of the development of early antisocial behavioral problems is the transactional model described by Greene and colleagues (Greene, Ablon, & Goring, 2003; Greene & Doyle, 2000). They have described a transactional model of the development of ODD in which poor affect modulation or compromised self-regulation interacts with adult or environmental responses to yield the behaviors observed in ODD. The authors propose a role for cognitive deficits (such as those seen in ADHD) as a precursor to compromised self-regulation. Comorbid conditions, notably anxiety and to a lesser degree depression, are identified as potential influences on poor affect modulation. The transaction between child and adult is conceptualized in terms of compatibility. Parents with styles compatible with their children's behavior help the child to develop positive regulatory skills and reduce antisocial outcomes. Reciprocal and interactive processes, such as those that are part of the Greene model, are also found in the coercive model described by Patterson (Snyder & Patterson, 1995; Stoolmiller, Patterson, & Snyder, 1997), in which children's past displays of noxious antisocial behavior lead parents to respond to poor behavior with avoidant or timid parenting behaviors and ineffective disciplinary strategies.

A BROADER MODEL OF THE CHILDHOOD ETIOLOGY OF ANTISOCIAL PERSONALITY DISORDER

A more complex developmental model than that of ODD predicting CD and CD predicting APD may be hypothetically constructed using the findings described earlier (see Figure 12.1). Attention-Deficit/Hyperactivity Disorder appears to play a role in the development of ODD and to influence CD primarily through ODD. Within ODD, subsets of symptoms distinguished by their behavioral aspects (authority conflict) or their affective aspects (irritability) may be identified and may

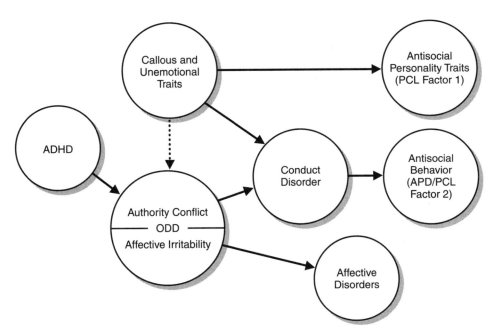

Figure 12.1 Developmental Model for Attention-Deficit/Hyperactivity Disorder Linked to Oppositional Defiant Disorder

explain recent findings of stronger links between ODD and depression than CD and depression. Callous and unemotional traits appear to be independent of the characteristics of ODD, yet also influence CD as well as antisocial behavior in general. Theoretically they are linked with adult psychopathy, although CU traits are but one subscale of items on a larger measure of psychopathy designed for use with children. Conduct Disorder is predictive of APD, but it is not known if CD would predict antisocial personality traits in adulthood if prior CU were controlled. Antisocial Personality Disorder and psychopathy in adulthood overlap, but the degree to which they do and the full nature of their similarities and dissimilarities remain to be described.

ASSESSMENT

One of the great difficulties of assessing APD, as with the assessment of most personality disorders, is that in typical clinical practice, one must rely heavily on self-report. For those with APD, self-report is subject to distortion due to a number of reasons. Among these are cognitive distortions, self-promotion, and minimization of criminal behavior, although some evidence suggests that no difference in reliability was found among those who endorse lying compared to those who do not (Cottler, Compton, Ridenour, Ben Abdallah, & Gallagher, 1998). Among forensic populations, greater access to reports from a variety of other observers and official records helps to improve the ability to identify symptoms of the disorder. Likewise, the assessment of CD (and similarly of ODD) is greatly improved by the availability of multiple informants. It had been believed that the utility of child report for ODD and CD symptoms was low. Some evidence did demonstrate that, independently, children's report of ODD predicted only school suspensions and not a number of other outcomes and tended to produce significantly lower prevalence estimates for oppositional behavior and conduct problems (Loeber, Green, Lahey, & Stouthamer-Loeber, 1991). However, it would be a mistake to extrapolate from these findings that children's reports do not have diagnostic utility. Recent evidence has suggested that child reports, in addition to reports from other informants, may provide novel, valid, and reliable diagnostic information for CD in children as young as 5 years (Arseneault, Kim-Cohen, Taylor, Caspi, & Moffitt, 2005) and for ODD symptoms in late childhood as well (Angold & Costello, 1996). There is also evidence that, among boys 12 years and under, using a broad range of self-reported delinquent acts in addition to children's report of CD symptoms improves the prediction of persistent CD (meeting criteria three or more times between 13 and 17) in adolescence (Burke, Loeber, Mutchka, & Lahey, 2002). After accounting for other covariates, child self-report of delinquent behaviors and of CD remained significant predictors of later persistent CD, whereas parent-reported CD did not.

When assessing childhood antisocial disorders, it is important to be mindful that different reporters (most commonly teachers and parents, as well as children) often have access to different types of information and provide very different reports of ODD and CD symptoms (e.g., Jensen et al., 1999). Often, antisocial behavior by a child occurs in settings outside the home and outside the awareness of the parent (Hart, Lahey, Loeber, & Hanson, 1994; Loeber, Green, Lahey, & Stouthamer-Loeber, 1989). Rather than automatically accepting as valid one informant's report and rejecting a discrepant report from another, Jensen and colleagues suggest a set of guidelines for making decisions about how to integrate multiple and differing reports from different informants. Among these was a recommendation to take into account the degree to which a given type of informant has the opportunity to observe or come to know about a given symptom (such as a parent being more likely than a teacher to describe a child's sibling interactions or sleeping difficulties). Furthermore, the authors suggested that external validators, such as indicators of impairment or enrollment into a treatment program, may be taken into account when making diagnostic decisions. For APD features in childhood, such external validators might include police contacts or adjudications for delinquency, school disciplinary referrals, or evidence of peer rejection associated with aggressive or bullying behavior or affiliation with delinquent peers. That said, many such conditions that co-occur with antisocial behavior or personality traits also occur independently of them, so such external validators must support other diagnostic material, not supplant it.

In addition, different informants may describe diverging views of children's behavior because children may respond to different demand features (positive or negative parenting behaviors, the commanding voice of a father, lax or strict enforcement of rules in school settings) in different conditions and also have the opportunity to engage in different sets of antisocial behaviors across different settings. For example, a child at home alone is not able to engage in bullying and does not have groups of peers with whom he or she must compete for desired resources. On the other hand, a child may be more likely to show defiance and noncompliance when dealing with only one adult authority figure compared to confronting a number of teachers and school administrators.

When obtaining parental reports, it is also important to remember that children's antisocial behavior is often influenced by parental antisocial traits and that parents' report of negative children's behavior may be influenced by their own antisocial personality traits or poor parenting behavior, whether through willful deception or impaired ability to recognize their role in the onset of antisocial behavior. For example, a parent who reports that a child spontaneously erupts in fits of antisocial behavior suggestive of a volatile negative affect may not recognize that his or her own irritability contributed to the context in which the conflict arose.

DEVELOPMENTAL PROCESSES AND PARENTAL PERCEPTIONS

Further assessment complications are that, as children age and as they progress into CD symptoms, parents often become less aware of the frequency or severity of their CD behaviors. Parents have been found to be more perceptive of problems associated with ODD than with CD behaviors (Teagle, 2002). Likewise, a diagnosis of ODD has been found to be associated with greater caregiver strain than a diagnosis of CD (Bussing, Gary, et al., 2003; Bussing, Zima, et al., 2003). Further suggestive of the greater salience of ODD over CD is the finding that ODD but not CD was associated with involvement in mental health treatment during the prior year (Bussing, Zima, et al., 2003). Because very little service use by children with antisocial behavior is self-motivated, it is likely that the greater burden parents experience with ODD symptoms is driving greater service use.

The greater burden that parents feel with ODD may be due to the interpersonal nature of the symptoms of this disorder. On the other hand, as children age, they tend to become engaged in antisocial behaviors that are more covert and are carried out in the community, outside the awareness of parents. Thus, those conducting assessments must keep in mind the developmental stage of the child and probe carefully when there are parental reports of the absence of a symptom. In terms of the etiology of APD, the transition from ODD to CD is a crucial point not only because it represents a worsening progression, but also because it appears to be associated with the dropping out of the parent as a key agent for change. If parents are less likely to seek treatment for their child's CD symptoms, this means that other elements of the system (school personnel or the police) are going to be required to become more involved. This will likely occur either by pushing the parents for change or assuming responsibility for intervening with the child. Until community sanctions begin to occur, for those whose parents do become less motivated to seek help the processes that propel them toward APD are more likely to continue unabated.

METHODS OF ASSESSMENT

The assessment of APD and its childhood precursors is not markedly different from the assessment of other types of psychopathology. By and large, it relies on self-report and the report of other available informants, such as parents and teachers. Evidence suggests that the reliability of unstructured clinical assessments for personality disorders ranges from poor to fair, and that reliability is improved with the use of structured clinical interviews (Zimmerman, 1994). There are a number of well-established and validated measures of antisocial behavior in childhood, and they typically have been designed to yield diagnostic information consistent with the symptoms of the *DSM* (for reviews, see Dishion, French, & Patterson, 1995; Frick & O'Brien, 1995; Hinshaw & Zupan, 1997).

The most reliable and comprehensive measures for assessing these disorders remain the structured clinical interview. As noted, the assessment of adults relies heavily on self-report. Two specific measures are among the most commonly used adult structured clinical interviews: the Diagnostic Interview Schedule (DIS; Robins et al., 2000; Robins, Helzer, Cottler, & Goldring, 1989) and the Structured Clinical Interview for *DSM-IV* Personality Disorders (SCID-II; First, Gibbon, Spitzer, Williams, & Benjamin, 1997). The DIS has been demonstrated to have adequate reliability for the assessment of APD and for individual items (Cottler et al., 1998); it has been updated for *DSM-IV* (Robins et al., 2000) and has been adapted for administration via computer (Helzer & Robins, 1988). The SCID-II for *DSM-IV* has achieved excellent interrater reliability (Maffei et al., 1997) for the assessment of APD.

There are several structured clinical interviews for the assessment of the psychopathological precursors to APD in childhood. The Diagnostic Interview Schedule for Children (Shaffer, Fisher, Lucas, Dulcan, & Schwab-Stone, 2000) is a structured clinical interview that has shown moderate to good reliability for parents and children, particularly for CD, good measures of validity, and for which computerized versions have been developed (Shaffer et al., 2000). For reviews of this and other structured interview measures of child psychopathology, see the special section of the *Journal of the American Academy of Child and Adolescent Psychiatry* (McClellan & Werry, 2000).

Self-administered measures have also been developed. In general, they are less comprehensive and are appropriate for screening purposes or as aids to other diagnostic procedures. For adults, the Millon Clinical Multiaxial Inventory II (Millon, 1997) is a self-report inventory that focuses on capturing underlying antisocial personality traits; it thus demonstrates low agreement with APD as measured by the SCID (Messina, Wish, Hoffman, & Nemes, 2001). A number of rating scale-based measures have been developed for screening children's psychopathology, generally for use by multiple informants. They offer a less comprehensive evaluation of disorders but provide greater efficiency for screening for potential markers of disorder and for obtaining reports from multiple informants. For a review of rating scales, see Kamphaus and Frick (2002).

Because most measures of childhood psychopathology are designed to assess the *DSM* disorders of ODD and CD, among other disorders, they fail to comprehensively assess antisocial personality features, as these traits are not included among the symptoms. The Antisocial Process Screening Device (Frick & Hare, 2001) was developed to measure antisocial processes in childhood akin to those assessed by the PCL-R (Hare, 1991). One scale assesses CU traits and has been found to be the most stable dimension of the measure (Frick et al., 2005). Others have used the California Child Q-Set (e.g., Lynam, 1997; Piatigorsky & Hinshaw, 2004) or selected items from the Child Behavior Checklist (e.g., Loeber et al., 2002). Given that the emerging literature has suggested that psychopathy, and CU traits in particular, may provide important information regarding the course and outcomes of antisocial traits through childhood, it is very important that researchers begin to employ a consistent construct using reliable measures.

INTERVENTION STRATEGIES

Very little literature exists describing specific effective treatment methods for APD, and those that do exist are of limited utility due to suspect methodological strategies (for reviews, see Andrews, 1991; Reid & Gacono, 2000). However, there is ample evidence in support of several treatment models for ODD and CD. Reviews of this literature are available (Brestan & Eyberg, 1998; Kazdin & Weisz, 1998; Nock, 2003; Webster-Stratton & Taylor, 2001). The review by Nock is noteworthy in particular because it represents an effort to employ a novel strategy for a systematic literature review, referred to as a "progress review," in which the evidence for psychotherapeutic interventions is evaluated in the context of an a priori set of questions that move beyond whether there is evidence that the intervention is effective to considerations of the available evidence about which treatment components are necessary or useful, which mechanisms of change are activated, for whom the intervention is most useful, and under what conditions the intervention works. The understanding of which specific components of treatment mediate outcomes and for whom and under what circumstances treatment is effective is not only essential for improving therapy for children with ODD and CD, but in the absence of a strong literature base on the treatment of APD, such knowledge will help to guide potential intervention strategies for adults.

The present discussion does not include a comprehensive review of the literature on treatment of antisocial conditions of childhood, but instead identifies intervention targets for change and strategies to achieve change that are commonly employed and have at least moderate empirical support regarding their efficacy, discusses examples of specific intervention methods developed around these strategies, and considers the implications for treating APD that are raised by the elements that are and are not typically included in current intervention strategies. These strategies can be organized around the level at which change is sought: the individual, the parent or family, and the larger environment in which the child lives.

Interventions with the Individual

Although the natural inclination when presented with antisocial behavior is to consider ways to elicit change from within the individual, it is also generally the case that the child showing antisocial behavior has little desire or motivation to change on his or her own. A number of theories about child-situated deficits or limitations have driven a variety of different strategies for change, each with very different implications for treatment. These theoretical models include propositions that children's antisocial behavior is driven by learned behavior (such as being reinforced for engaging in antisocial behavior); specific atypical cognitive processes, including a tendency to attribute hostile motivations to others' behavior (Dodge, Price, Bachorowski, & Newman, 1990) or a deficiency in the ability to generate multiple solutions to problems; or an impairment in the ability to regulate emotions and behavior, associated with a tendency to respond in an impulsive or hot-headed manner to provocations.

As a result, interventions designed around these theoretical models focus on skill-building exercises in these areas. They may include efforts to alter cognitive processes so that children challenge their own presumptions about hostile motivations of others, gain the ability to generate prosocial responses to problems and anticipate the effects of their actions, interrupt impulsive decision-making processes, more accurately identify others' feelings, or reevaluate the circumstances around their own distressing or negative mood conditions to reduce their impact on decision making or behavior.

Among the strategies commonly used to achieve these goals with children and adolescents are conducting role-play activities, in which scenarios are acted out that lead to selection and implementation of prosocial solutions and which also challenge antisocial thinking by eliciting from the child a discussion of the undesirable outcomes that might likely result from employing antisocial strategies. Other strategies include training the child to identify thoughts that commonly occur to him or her in challenging situations and that lead to antisocial behavior. These are critically evaluated on their merits, and children are trained to weigh evidence for and against the legitimacy of thoughts that presume hostility on the part of others or that presume negative personal attributes on the part of the child (such as "I'm dumb" or "Nobody likes me"). Children are taught to substitute contrasting thoughts that are more consistent with available evidence and that are likely to reduce hostile or antisocial behavior. The child is also taught to use self-statements as a means of exerting conscious control over behaviors and emotions. Self-statements are thoughts that may involve reminders of steps in a process or of positive personal characteristics.

Increasing a child's control of his or her body is often a strategy for change. Children are taught to use relaxation techniques, which serve multiple purposes. First, relaxation is regarded as incompatible with tension, which is often an indicator of physiological arousal or anger and often precedes an aggressive response. It is both a cue to an emotional state that might otherwise occur without conscious awareness and a potential point for intervention. Second, engaging the mind in self-directed relaxation efforts will interrupt the cognitive processes that might lead a child to escalating hostile attributions and motivations for aggressive reactions.

A key element of APD that has not been typically integrated into child-focused interventions is interpersonal callousness. In part, this is due to the fact that aspects of antisocial personality, such as callousness, have not been listed among the symptoms of ODD or CD. It is also the case that the evidence for the role of CU traits has only begun to accrue in recent years and has likely not yet been incorporated into any treatment models for ODD and CD. Frick (2001) has described, in theory, how CU traits could be addressed in treatment models. He describes intervention strategies based on developmental models of CD, in which CU features are particularly associated with a specific childhood-onset pathway for CD, which he distinguishes from a childhood-onset, primarily inattentive pathway and an adolescent-onset pathway. Frick proposes that each pathway will be associated with different impairments, requiring differing intervention strategies.

Hawes and Dadds (2005) have identified the dampening impact that CU features may have on typically effective treatment methods for conduct problems. Those higher in CU traits showed overall poorer outcomes and showed a lower responsiveness than other children to specific treatment components. No specific interventions have yet been developed to address CU traits. Efforts have been described in the juvenile justice literature to enhance empathy, such as through the use of reenactments and perspective-taking activities, in regard to specific criminal behaviors (e.g., Pithers, 1994). Chalmers and Townsend (1990) described a perspective-taking intervention strategy for girls. In general, these types of interventions have not been subjected to adequate empirical scrutiny to establish their effectiveness and document the degree to which any changes are maintained in other contexts.

PARENT-FOCUSED INTERVENTION STRATEGIES

A number of strategies for changing antisocial behavior focus on improving parental competencies and increasing positive parenting behaviors (see Kazdin, 1997, for a review). These are based on basic behavioral principles (Skinner, 1938), on knowledge of risk factors within the parenting domain (see Burke, Loeber, & Birhamer, 2002), and on models developed by Patterson (Snyder & Patterson, 1995), which describe a coercive process by which parenting behaviors elicit or enhance antisocial behavior by unintentionally reinforcing the use of noxious, manipulative, or even intimidating behaviors on the part of the child. Strategies for change involve direct instruction to parents regarding behavioral principles and parenting practices that eliminate the reinforcement of antisocial behavior and increase the likelihood of compliant and prosocial behavior. These strategies are referred to generally as parent management training (PMT). Specific intervention strategies include training in the consistent and effective use of time-out procedures and other disciplinary strategies; developing a behavioral program with specific goals and systematic monitoring, along with the tracking of accumulated points or tangible secondary reinforcers; structuring simple opportunities for compliance and reinforcement; and increasing the frequency with which parents spontaneously notice and reinforce appropriate behavior. Parents may also be given training and practice in communication styles that will improve cooperation and mutual positive regard, training in negotiation strategies that are developmentally appropriate for a given child, and education in reasonable expectations for children's behavior at different developmental stages.

Other intervention strategies involving parents are focused more on the family as a whole and concentrate on the dynamics among all family members, the roles that they play within the family, and the function that the child's behavior serves for the family. Strategies involve family therapy sessions aimed to address communications between family members; reframing problems within the family to allow for more productive and cooperative solutions; examining, discussing, and modifying family dynamics; and providing direct education, opportunities for skills development, and training in positive reinforcement of desired behaviors.

ENVIRONMENTAL INTERVENTIONS

Recognizing that conduct problems arise as a result of a wide array of risk factors (e.g., Burke, Loeber, & Birhamer, 2002), researchers have designed interventions to comprehensively address children's conduct problems through in-home and community-based child and family services. These services are individualized to the specific concerns of the child and provide more focus on addressing barriers to success within systems in a wide range of social ecology (e.g., the individual, family, peer groups, schools, neighborhoods; Bronfenbrenner, 1979). Parents may be provided assistance to address problems with substance abuse or psychiatric concerns, as well as issues such as unemployment or marital conflict that tend to impact child and family functioning. Efforts to remove children from deviant peer groups and link them with more positive peer relationships are utilized. Interventions for issues in other community settings, such as school, neighborhood, or work, are implemented in a fashion tailored to the specific needs of the child. Strategies identified for children and for parents earlier in the chapter are also used.

The methodology for the delivery of services is very different from other strategies. Not only are the services provided in the home and community, but they are provided by an integrated therapy team with therapy and case management responsibilities, are available as needed on a 24-hour basis, and typically have daily contact with the child and family.

An alternative community-based strategy is to place the child in a tightly controlled community. The most ubiquitous and enduring such intervention for antisocial behavior is detention or physical restriction, such as incarceration in jails or placement in restrictive juvenile group residences or inpatient facilities. Placing antisocial persons in a restrictive setting decreases the opportunity for them to commit antisocial behavior in the public at large, although they may continue to commit antisocial behavior inside the facility. Typically, however, little change in the behavior of an individual arises due to incarceration alone. For juveniles, intervention efforts during incarceration or detention typically involve other strategies for change, as described earlier. Given the nature of the setting, these are most commonly child-focused strategies for change.

SPECIFIC TREATMENT MODELS

A number of specific models have been designed and implemented around the strategies just outlined. Cognitive-behavioral therapy (CBT) is a general treatment approach that has been incorporated into several intervention models specifically targeting antisocial behavior (see Southam-Gerow, 2003). Brestan and Eyberg (1998) identified several specific CBT-related programs among the "probably efficacious" treatments identified through their review, including anger control training with stress inoculation (Feindler, Marriott, Iwata, & Adelphi, 1984), anger coping therapy (Lochman & Lenhart, 1993), problem-solving skills training (Kazdin, Siegel, & Bass, 1992), and rational-emotive therapy (Block, 1978). Nock (2003) concludes that, among a number of CBT packages, there are noteworthy differences in the components they include, that mediational tests of the mechanisms of change for specific components need to be conducted, and that long-term effects of CBT interventions remain to be examined.

The evidence suggests that CBT is effective (Brestan & Eyberg, 1998), if perhaps modestly so (Nock, 2003; Southam-Gerow, 2003). Its effectiveness is increased when CBT is used in conjunction with other treatment components, such as in combination with PMT (Kazdin, Esveldt-Dawson, French, & Unis, 1987; Webster-Stratton, 1996) or as part of a larger multisystemic program (Webster, Augimeri, & Koegl, 2002) or multisystemic therapy (MST; Henggeler, 1997).

Specific PMT treatment programs have also been developed; two PMT programs were the only therapy models identified as "well established" (Brestan & Eyberg, 1998) for the treatment of conduct problems in children. First, parent training interventions based on Patterson and Gullion's (1968) *Living with Children* were so identified. These interventions focus on training parents in the application of basic behavioral principles, reinforcing desirable behavior, and extinguishing or punishing undesirable behaviors. The intervention has been examined in a number of studies with both boys and girls across a broad range of ages and in a variety of settings (see Brestan & Eyberg, 1998). The other well established parent management strategy is the videotape-modeling parent training strategy employed by Webster-Stratton (1996), which is delivered to parents in groups, with a therapist-led discussion component.

Another intervention technique is the use of direct feedback to parents during play activities with children. Often, a "bug in the ear" communication system is used, with parents wearing an earpiece receiver. The clinician can observe parents and children from behind a one-way mirror and can give guidance and feedback to parents immediately. The parent-child interaction training (Eyberg, Boggs, & Algina, 1995) model utilizes this technique and was characterized by Brestan and Eyberg (1998) as probably efficacious. Typically, this strategy is used for younger children. Like CBT interventions, PMT models are often delivered in combination with other types of strategies.

One parent-focused prevention project that should be noted is the home nursing visitation program developed by Olds and colleagues (1997). Children of at-risk pregnant mothers showed marked long-term lower rates of arrest and running away and lower alcohol consumption. The program was delivered by nurses via home visits during pregnancy (an average of nine visits) and during early childhood (an average of 23 visits up to the child's second birthday). The intervention effort focused on providing educational and informational interventions as well as linking mothers with health and human services. Targeted concerns were (a) maternal health-related behaviors, (b) parenting and child care behaviors, and (c) family planning, educational achievement, and occupational development of the mother.

Functional family therapy typifies the outpatient family therapy intervention strategy. Modes of delivery for the intervention may include delivery by one- or two-person teams in the clinic or in the home. It uses an individualized family-focused approach and has been shown to reduce recidivism and prevent delinquency (Alexander, Sexton, & Robbins, 2002). Evidence for MST (Henggeler, 1997) has supported its use for serious antisocial and delinquent adolescents. It has been used to address antisocial behavior as well as substance use (Henggeler, 1997; Henggeler, Clingempeel, Brondino, & Pickrel, 2002).

Inpatient treatment may be used to address emergent situations, particularly when threats of harm occur or to interrupt significant aggressive or destructive episodes. However, inpatient treatment has not been demonstrated to lead to significant or lasting change in antisocial behavior over time. Given the typical brevity of treatment and the primary focus on the individual, inpatient services lack many of the elements of other effective treatments. Partial hospitalization is often employed as a step down from or an alternative to inpatient hospitalization. These programs generally involve programming that includes individual and group therapy activities, pharmacotherapy, and other therapeutic activities. However, participants do not reside at the facility. Such programs typically are provided for a longer duration than inpatient stays and are thus able to implement interventions that focus on skill building with greater attention and practice. However, these interventions have also not yielded satisfactory evidence of lasting change in ODD or CD.

For adolescents who show persisting and generally severe antisocial behavior that is not responsive to parent interventions, residential treatment facilities, group homes, or treatment foster care placements are often employed. These programs may involve individual therapy, such as CBT, pharmacotherapy, and group therapy activities, but generally do not involve PMT or significant family therapy activities and do not focus on addressing barriers to progress for an individual adolescent in the community.

PHARMACOTHERAPY

The evidence in support of most medications for the treatment of ODD and CD is limited and relies on only one or two randomized clinical trials. Evidence supporting the use of risperidone to reduce noncompliant and aggressive behavior among low-IQ youth has been found in a double-blind placebo-controlled study (Aman, De Smedt, Derivan, Lyons, & Findling, 2002) and in an open-label trial with no control group (Croonenberghs, Fegert, Findling, De Smet, & Van Dongen, 2005). However, adverse events were frequently reported in the sample. A common target of medication-based interventions for conduct problems is aggressive behavior in general. Previous support, although quite limited, was found for the use of lithium and haloperidol for the treatment of aggressive children.

There are a number of conditions that often co-occur with ODD and CD and for which there is greater support for the use of medications. Attention-Deficit/Hyperactivity Disorder is often comorbid with ODD and CD and may hasten the onset of CD symptoms (Loeber et al., 1995) among those with ODD. Stimulant medication is a key component of treatment for ADHD (MTA Cooperative Group, 1999) and, in combination with psychosocial treatments, is associated with reductions in comorbid conduct problems and ADHD (J. M. Swanson et al., 2001).

In a review of the literature regarding pharmacotherapy for APD, Sanislow and McGlashan (1998) found that the evidence was limited, both in terms of the number of studies (four) and the poor methodology of those that were available. As with the literature pertaining to childhood disorders, there was a bias evident among the studies to examine aggressive behavior rather than to study pharmacotherapy for the diagnostic criteria. Sanislow and McGlashan concluded that a significant reduction in aggressive behaviors was associated with lithium treatment. Clearly, there is a need for more rigorous studies of the effects of medication on ODD, CD, and APD and for studies to consider the effects of medications on the full set of criteria rather than examining aggression in particular.

RESISTANCE AND BARRIERS TO TREATMENT

Resistance to treatment is high among those showing antisocial behavior. Children and adolescents with these disorders are generally low in motivation to change and are often oppositional to authority figures.

Low rates of involvement in services are evident, and children with disruptive behavior problems are often not aware of or interested in changing their own behavior. Parental awareness and involvement in services also fluctuate over time and show developmentally based change as well. Parents have been found to be more perceptive of problems associated with ODD than CD (Teagle, 2002). A diagnosis of ODD, and not of CD, has been found to be associated with greater caregiver strain (Bussing, Gary, et al., 2003; Bussing, Zima, et al., 2003). Likewise, ODD but not CD was associated with involvement in mental health treatment during the prior year (Bussing, Zima, et al., 2003).

Kazdin (2000) found that parents' perceptions of barriers to participation in treatment predicted treatment acceptability (which was, in turn, related to therapeutic change) beyond that accounted for by socioeconomic disadvantage, parental psychopathology, or severity of child dysfunction. Parental expectancies about the structure and effectiveness of therapy predict attendance and premature termination from therapy (Miller & Prinz, 2003; Nock & Kazdin, 2001). The manner in which parents conceptualize the nature of children's behavioral problems also influences help seeking and engagement in treatment (Morrissey-Kane & Prinz, 1999). Angold and colleagues (1998) showed that both the level of impairment and the severity of symptoms predicted parental burden, and that parental burden mediated the effect of symptom severity on children's mental health service use. Further, symptom severity was a stronger predictor than parental burden of the use of school services. Ethnic differences have been found in perceived barriers to help seeking, with Caucasians reporting fewer perceived barriers than minority group members (Takeuchi, Leaf, & Kuo, 1988).

Much of the existing literature on parental cognitions describes participation in treatment subsequent to initial engagement in services. However, parental cognitions regarding treatment will also influence decision making about seeking help well before services are sought. Parents differ in the timing in which they seek help for behavioral problems (e.g., Burns et al., 2001) and may not ultimately seek treatment at all (Farmer, Burns, Phillips, Angold, & Costello, 2003; Stouthamer-Loeber,

Loeber, & Thomas, 1992). Logan and King (2001) describe a model of help seeking that focuses on the role of parents in facilitating adolescent help-seeking behaviors. The model incorporates elements of Prochaska and DiClemente's (1982) stages of change model to help describe the movement of parents through stages involving the development of awareness of the problem, recognizing the psychological nature of the problem, determining that the severity of the problem warrants attention, beginning to develop the intention to seek mental health services, and subsequently attempting to seek and secure mental health services.

Determining Treatment Outcomes

Treatment outcomes are typically assessed by reductions in parent-reported symptoms or by reductions in incidents of aggression or delinquent behavior. Measurement instruments are typically the same as those used for assessment (described earlier), with lowered symptom counts used as a marker for change. Ratings can be obtained from other informants as well, such as teachers, which will provide evidence of generalization of change across settings.

Part of the difficulty of assessing change for these disorders is that some symptoms typically occur at low rates, making it occasionally difficult to determine whether desistance in a given behavior has occurred or whether the behavior will be shown again in time. Other symptoms require a certain context and may not occur if the opportunity for that behavior is absent. For example, truancy is not possible when school is not in session, and defiance may differ between parents if one parent is more lax and less likely to place demands on the child than the other.

Further, a number of nonclinical indicators may be incorporated into the assessment of change. Recidivism rates are commonly used when antisocial behavior is framed in the context of delinquency. Other measures of change might include rates of disciplinary referrals (e.g., suspensions, detentions) in school or frequency of positive involvement in family activities, among appropriate peer groups, or in positive, prosocial activities in school. Such markers would depend on measurements taken at the initial assessment and over time during treatment for the ability to compare pre- and posttreatment rates. Sociometric rating techniques might be used, which would provide ratings within peer groups that would suggest how a child's behavior is perceived by peers. However, these types of ratings would be complicated to implement in most clinical contexts.

FOLLOW-UP PLANS AND POSTTREATMENT PROBLEMS

Some evidence has been found to suggest that the use of booster sessions helps to maintain improvements over longer periods (Eyberg, Edwards, Boggs, & Foote, 1998). A pretreatment assessment of barriers would suggest potential pitfalls to be addressed as treatment ends, such as access to prosocial community activities.

A primary posttreatment concern for conduct problems is the fact that children and adolescents typically return to the same peer group, school, and community activities after treatment and are at risk to fall into the same behavioral patterns and influences that existed prior to treatment. This is particularly the case for treatment strategies that do not incorporate attention to peer and community activities. Children with conduct problems also often have developed a reputation with peers and adults, who may tend to expect and perhaps unintentionally elicit antisocial behavior as a result of the child's prior behavior patterns.

CONCLUSIONS

Antisocial Personality Disorder is a disorder of particular concern because it represents individuals with chronic histories of causing harm and suffering to others, with a high potential for committing future antisocial and violent behavior. Like other personality disorders, APD captures persisting interpersonal problems that are associated with impairment to the individual across a number of domains. It is distinct, however, in that it can be diagnosed only after the age of 18 and incorporates a requirement that an Axis I disorder (CD) be present earlier in the individual's development. It is arguably focused more on behavioral referents than on personality features, in contrast to both other Axis II disorders and previous conceptualizations of APD. Antisocial Personality Disorder excludes a number of personality features that have been historically associated with the disorder and that continue to be included in alternative constructs such as psychopathy. Despite these important distinctions, APD and psychopathy are often conflated.

From the perspective of childhood precursors and development toward APD, there is a large literature base pertaining to ODD and CD that presumably applies to the development of APD. Much is known about risk factors and comorbid conditions of CD, and increasingly elaborate developmental models based on this knowledge have been developed, with empirical support accruing over recent years. Nevertheless, key questions about the development from ODD and CD have not been satisfactorily resolved. Whereas a number of risk factors have been identified, adequate person-oriented prediction models have not been developed, leading to blind spots in the prediction of which children and adolescents will progress to higher levels of antisocial behavior and, more glaringly, what happens to those who do not.

Most relevant to discussions of these models as etiological explanations for APD, the symptoms of CD are exclusively behavioral in nature. What is the impact of this? First, to the degree that personality features exist distinct from behaviors, predictive models based exclusively on behavioral indicators will correctly identify only a portion of those who will go on to show APD in adulthood. Second, the absence of personality features in childhood diagnoses of antisocial behavior has shaped the research questions, data, and constructs used in the bulk of the available literature and in the development of assessment tools and interventions for CD. The combination of this absence and a *DSM-IV* (American Psychiatric Association, 1994) diagnostic directive that a diagnosis of ODD is not given when CD is present has significantly hamstrung efforts to explain and understand a condition that is already acknowledged to be highly heterogeneous. There is also a marked absence in the most commonly employed models of treatment of any significant strategies to explicitly address callousness, remorse-lessness, and smooth and glib manipulation of others (but see Frick, 2001). Our standard child and adolescent diagnostic assessment tools do not assess these features. If they in fact do have prognostic and therapeutic importance, this deficiency will have to be corrected.

Emerging evidence suggests that CU features indicate those CD cases more likely to show severe and persistent antisocial behavior. There is some evidence that these features may help to distinguish those with CD who are likely to go on to meet criteria for APD (Loeber et al., 2002), although further studies should seek to confirm this. The fact that CU traits share conceptual similarities with aspects of antisocial personality found among the symptoms of APD suggests a potential continuity from childhood to adulthood. It remains to be seen whether the development of such antisocial personality features from childhood through adulthood might be interrupted through targeted interventions, and what type of interventions would be most effective for this. If it is the case that antisocial behavior develops secondary to antisocial personality (e.g., Cooke et al., 2004), it follows that the ability to modify antisocial personality would allow interventions to be delivered earlier in the developmental course and would help to reduce antisocial behavior.

Existing intervention strategies have nevertheless been demonstrated to be reliable and successful for reducing ODD and CD symptoms for many children. These include parent management strategies, cognitive-behavioral therapy methods, and multimodal treatment strategies. Medication treatments are effective in reducing comorbid symptoms, such as ADHD and depression, which may improve outcomes for ODD and CD. Medications may also help to reduce aggressive behaviors, but no medications have been identified as reliably useful for lowering most symptoms of CD directly.

Many children with ODD or CD fail to be identified or referred for mental health services. Parents may be more aware of ODD symptoms and less likely to be motivated to seek services for CD, despite the increasing severity of symptoms. Children may be identified and referred by school personnel, juvenile justice and law enforcement personnel, or by medical service providers if not by their parents. The development and dissemination of improved screening models may help to increase the frequency with which children with ODD or CD, or perhaps with associated antisocial personality features, are identified and linked with appropriate services. Improved early screening methods could help to reduce the overall severity and costs of antisocial behavior.

RECOMMENDATIONS

Increased attention must be given to the relationships between CU traits in the development of childhood antisocial psychopathology and later adult APD. It may be necessary to include these features as part of the diagnostic criteria. Researchers must routinely examine ODD and CD separately in the investigation of developmental models of psychopathology. It is very likely that when ODD symptoms are present along with CD symptoms, in contrast to CD symptoms alone, clinicians should be concerned about different etiologies and different targets for intervention, should be mindful of different concerns regarding potential comorbid conditions, and should be considering different prognoses. This will not be clear until researchers regularly provide information about these disorders distinctly. As evidence emerges to support the clinical utility of distinguishing between the two, the diagnostic prohibition against assigning both ODD and CD diagnoses should be lifted. Furthermore, the most useful research findings will come from prospective data sets with suitable proportions of distinct groups of children and adolescents with antisocial behavior, CU traits, and ADHD and other disorders.

Services researchers should structure their investigations of interventions with an intention to fulfill the goals suggested by the progress review of Nock (2003). They should attempt to identify which specific components of current and future treatments are effective and which are not, what conditions influence treatment effectiveness, and which children benefit most from which interventions. These findings should be used to help refine targeted treatment efforts, matching children's needs with specific treatment strategies, and should be used to shape interventions to address parental expectations about therapy.

REFERENCES

Achenbach, T. M., & Edelbrock, C. S. (1983). *Manual for the Child Behavior Checklist and Revised Child Behavior Profile.* Burlington: University of Vermont.

Alexander, J. F., Sexton, T. L., & Robbins, M. S. (2002). The developmental status of family therapy in family psychology intervention science. In H. A. Liddle, D. A. Santisteban, R. F. Levant, & J. H. Bray (Eds.), *Family psychology: Science-based interventions* (pp. 17–40). Washington, DC: American Psychological Association.

Aman, M. G., De Smedt, G., Derivan, A., Lyons, B., & Findling, R. L. (2002). Double-blind, placebo-controlled study of risperidone for the treatment of disruptive behaviors in children with subaverage intelligence. *American Journal of Psychiatry, 159*(8), 1337–1346.

American Psychiatric Association. (1980). *Diagnostic and statistical manual of mental disorders* (3rd ed.). Washington, DC: Author.

American Psychiatric Association. (1987). *Diagnostic and statistical manual of mental disorders* (3rd ed., rev.). Washington, DC: Author.

American Psychiatric Association. (1994). *Diagnostic and statistical manual of mental disorders* (4th ed.). Washington, DC: Author.

American Psychiatric Association. (2000). *Diagnostic and statistical manual of mental disorders* (4th ed., text rev.). Washington, DC: Author.

American Psychological Association. (2006). *PsycInfo.* Washington, DC: Author.

Andrews, G. (1991). Treatment outlines for antisocial personality disorder. *Australian and New Zealand Journal of Psychiatry, 25,* 541–548.

Angold, A., & Costello, E. J. (1996). The relative diagnostic utility of child and parent reports of oppositional behaviors. *International Journal of Methods in Psychiatric Research, 6,* 253–259.

Angold, A., Costello, E. J., & Erkanli, A. (1999). Comorbidity. *Journal of Child Psychology and Psychiatry, 40*(1), 57–87.

Angold, A., Messer, S. C., Stangl, D., Farmer, E. M. Z., Costello, E. J., & Burns, B. J. (1998). Perceived parental burden and service use for child and adolescent psychiatric disorders. *American Journal of Public Health, 88,* 75–80.

Arseneault, L., Kim-Cohen, J., Taylor, A., Caspi, A., & Moffitt, T. E. (2005). Psychometric evaluation of 5- and 7-year-old children's self-reports of conduct problems. *Journal of Abnormal Child Psychology, 33,* 537–550.

Barkley, R. A., Fischer, M., Smallish, L., & Fletcher, K. (2004). Young adult follow-up of hyperactive children: Antisocial activities and drug use. *Journal of Child Psychology and Psychiatry, 45*(2), 195–211.

Barry, C. T., Frick, P. J., DeShazo, T. M., McCoy, M. G., Ellis, M., & Loney, B. R. (2000). The importance of callous-unemotional traits for extending the concept of psychopathy to children. *Journal of Abnormal Psychology, 109*(2), 335–340.

Beyers, J. M., Bates, J. E., Pettit, G. S., & Dodge, K. A. (2003). Neighborhood structure, parenting processes, and the development of youths' externalizing behaviors: A multilevel analysis. *American Journal of Community Psychology, 31,* 35–53.

Block, J. (1978). Effects of a rational-emotive mental health program on poorly achieving disruptive high school students. *Journal of Counseling Psychology, 25,* 61–65.

Block, J., & Block, J. H. (1980). *The California Child Q-Set.* Palo Alto, CA: Consulting Psychologists Press.

Blumstein, A., Cohen, J., Roth, J. A., & Visher, C. A. (1986). *Criminal careers and "career criminals."* Washington, DC: National Academy of Sciences.

Brestan, E. V., & Eyberg, S. M. (1998). Effective psychosocial treatments of conduct-disordered children and adolescents: 29 years, 82 studies, and 5,272 kids. *Journal of Clinical Child Psychology, 27*(2), 180–189.

Brody, G. H., Ge, X., Conger, R., Gibbons, F. X., Murry, V. M., Gerrard, M., et al. (2001). The influence of neighborhood disadvantage, collective socialization, and parenting on African American children's affiliation with deviant peers. *Child Development, 72*, 1231–1246.

Bronfenbrenner, U. (1979). Contexts of child rearing. *American Psychologist, 34*, 844–850.

Brook, J. S., Whiteman, M., Finch, S. J., & Cohen, P. (1996). Young adult drug use and delinquency: Childhood antecedents and adolescent mediators. *Journal of the American Academy of Child and Adolescent Psychiatry, 35*, 1584–1592.

Burke, J. D., Loeber, R., & Birhamer, B. (2002). Oppositional defiant disorder and conduct disorder: Pt. II. A review of the past 10 years, 1–61. *Journal of the American Academy of Child and Adolescent Psychiatry, 41*, 1275–1293.

Burke, J. D., Loeber, R., & Lahey, B. B. (2003). Course and outcomes of oppositional defiant disorder and conduct disorder. In C. Essau (Ed.), *Conduct and oppositional defiant disorders: Epidemiology, risk factors and treatment* (pp. 61–94). Mahwah, NJ: Erlbaum.

Burke, J. D., Loeber, R., & Lahey, B. B. (in press). Adolescent Conduct Disorder and interpersonal callousness as predictors of psychopathy in young adults. *Journal of Clinical Child and Adolescent Psychology.*

Burke, J. D., Loeber, R., Lahey, B. B., & Rathouz, P. J. (2005). Developmental transitions among affective and behavioral disorders in adolescent boys. *Journal of Child Psychology and Psychiatry, 46*(11), 1200–1210.

Burke, J. D., Loeber, R., Mutchka, J. S., & Lahey, B. B. (2002). A question for DSM-V: Which better predicts persistent conduct disorder, delinquent acts or conduct symptoms? *Criminal Behavior and Mental Health, 12*(1), 37–52.

Burns, B. J., Lansverk, J., Kelleher, K., Faw, L., Hazen, A., & Keeler, G. (2001). Mental health, education, child welfare, and juvenile justice service use. In R. Loeber & D. P. Farrington (Eds.), *Child delinquents: Development, intervention and service needs.* Thousand Oaks, CA: Sage.

Bussing, R., Gary, F. A., Mason, D. M., Leon, C. E., Sinha, K., & Garvan, C. W. (2003). Child temperament, ADHD, and caregiver strain: Exploring relationships in an epidemiological sample. *Journal of the American Academy of Child and Adolescent Psychiatry, 42,* 184–192.

Bussing, R., Zima, B. T., Gary, F. A., Mason, D. M., Leon, C. E., Sinha, K., et al. (2003). Social networks, caregiver strain, and utilization of mental health services among elementary school students at high risk for ADHD. *Journal of the American Academy of Child and Adolescent Psychiatry, 42*(7), 842–850.

Cadoret, R. J., Yates, W. R., Troughton, E., Woodworth, G., & Stewart, M. A. (1995). Genetic-environmental interaction in the genesis of aggressivity and conduct disorders. *Archives of General Psychiatry, 52,* 916–924.

Caspi, A., McClay, J., Moffitt, T. E., Mill, J., Martin, J., Craig, I. W., et al. (2002). Role of genotype in the cycle of violence in maltreated children. *Science, 297*(5582), 851–854.

Chalmers, J. B., & Townsend, M. A. (1990). The effects of training in social perspective taking on socially maladjusted girls. *Child Development, 61*(1), 178–190.

Cleckley, H. (1941). *The mask of sanity: An attempt to reinterpret the so-called psychopathic personality.* St. Louis, MO: Mosby.

Connor, D. F. (2002). *Aggression and antisocial behavior in children and adolescents.* New York: Guilford Press.

Connor, D. F., Steingard, R. J., Cunningham, J. A., Anderson, J. J., & Melloni, R. H., Jr. (2004). Proactive and reactive aggression in referred children and adolescents. *American Journal of Orthopsychiatry, 74,* 129–136.

Cooke, D. J., & Michie, C. (2001). Refining the construct of psychopathy: Towards a hierarchical model. *Psychological Assessment, 13*(2), 171–188.

Cooke, D. J., Michie, C., Hart, S. D., & Clark, D. A. (2004). Reconstructing psychopathy: Clarifying the significance of antisocial and socially deviant behavior in the diagnosis of psychopathic personality disorder. *Journal of Personality Disorders, 18*(4), 337–357.

Cottler, L. B., Compton, W. M., Ridenour, T. A., Ben Abdallah, A., & Gallagher, T. (1998). Reliability of self-reported antisocial personality disorder symptoms among substance abusers. *Drug and Alcohol Dependence, 49*(3), 189–199.

Croonenberghs, J., Fegert, J. M., Findling, R. L., De Smet, G., & Van Dongen, S. (2005). Risperidone in children with disruptive behavior disorders and subaverage intelligence: A 1-year, open-label study of 504 patients. *Journal of the American Academy of Child and Adolescent Psychiatry, 44,* 64–72.

Dishion, T. J., French, D. C., & Patterson, G. R. (1995). The development and ecology of antisocial behavior. In D. Cicchetti & D. Cohen (Eds.), *Manual of developmental psychopathology* (pp. 421–471). New York: Cambridge University Press.

Dobkin, P. L., Tremblay, R. E., Masse, L. C., & Vitaro, F. (1995). Individual and peer characteristics in predicting boys' early onset of substance abuse: A 7-year longitudinal study. *Child Development, 66,* 1198–1214.

Dodge, K. A., Lochman, J. E., Harnish, J. D., Bates, J. E., & Pettit, G. S. (1997). Reactive and proactive aggression in school children and psychiatrically impaired chronically assaultive youth. *Journal of Abnormal Psychology, 106,* 37–51.

Dodge, K. A., Price, J. M., Bachorowski, J., & Newman, J. P. (1990). Hostile attributional biases in severely aggressive adolescents. *Journal of Abnormal Psychology, 99,* 1–8.

Dowson, J. H., Sussams, P., Grounds, A. T., & Taylor, J. C. (2001). Associations of past conduct disorder with personality disorders in "non-psychotic" psychiatric inpatients. *European Psychiatry, 16*(1), 49–56.

Eyberg, S. M., Boggs, S. R., & Algina, J. (1995). Parent-child interaction therapy: A psychosocial model for the treatment of young children with conduct problem behavior and their families. *Psychopharmacology Bulletin, 31*(1), 83–91.

Eyberg, S. M., Edwards, D., Boggs, S. R., & Foote, R. (1998). Maintaining the treatment effects of parent training: The role of booster sessions and other maintenance strategies. *Clinical Psychology: Science and Practice, 5,* 544–554.

Farmer, E. M., Burns, B. J., Phillips, S. D., Angold, A., & Costello, E. J. (2003). Pathways into and through mental health services for children and adolescents. *Psychiatric Services, 54,* 60–66.

Feindler, E. L., Marriott, S. A., Iwata, M., & Adelphi, U. (1984). Group anger control training for junior high school delinquents. *Cognitive Therapy and Research, 8,* 299–311.

First, M. B., Gibbon, M., Spitzer, R. L., Williams, J. B. W., & Benjamin, L. S. (1997). *Structured clinical interview for* DSM-IV *Axis II personality disorders.* Washington, DC: American Psychiatric Press.

Frances, A. J. (1980). The *DSM-III* personality section: A commentary. *American Journal of Psychiatry, 137,* 1050–1054.

Frick, P. J. (2001). Effective interventions for children and adolescents with conduct disorder. *Canadian Journal of Psychiatry, 46*(7), 597–608.

Frick, P. J., Cornell, A. H., Barry, C. T., Bodin, S. D., & Dane, H. E. (2003). Callous-unemotional traits and conduct problems in the prediction of conduct problem severity, aggression, and self-report of delinquency. *Journal of Abnormal Child Psychology, 22,* 457–470.

Frick, P. J., Cornell, A. H., Bodin, S. D., Dane, H. E., Barry, C. T., & Loney, B. R. (2003). Callous-unemotional traits and developmental pathways to severe conduct problems. *Developmental Psychology, 39*(2), 246–260.

Frick, P. J., & Hare, R. D. (2001). *The Antisocial Process Screening Device (APSD).* Toronto, Ontario, Canada: Multi-Health Systems.

Frick, P. J., Lahey, B. B., Loeber, R., Tannenbaum, L., Van Horn, Y., Christ, M. A. G., et al. (1993). Oppositional defiant disorder and conduct disorder: A meta-analytic review of factor analyses and cross-validation in a clinic sample. *Clinical Psychology Review, 13,* 319–340.

Frick, P. J., & O'Brien, B. S. (1995). Conduct disorders. In R. T. Ammerman & M. Hersen (Eds.), *Handbook of child behavior therapy in the psychiatric setting* (pp. 199–216). New York: Wiley.

Frick, P. J., O'Brien, B. S., Wootton, J. M., & McBurnett, K. (1994). Psychopathy and conduct problems in children. *Journal of Abnormal Psychology, 103,* 700–707.

Frick, P. J., Stickle, T. R., Dandreaux, D. M., Farrell, J. M., & Kimonis, E. R. (2005). Callous-unemotional traits in predicting the severity and stability of conduct problems and delinquency. *Journal of Abnormal Child Psychology, 33*(4), 471–487.

Giancola, P. R., & Parker, A. M. (2001). A 6-year prospective study of pathways toward drug use in adolescent boys with and without a family history of a substance use disorder. *Journal of Studies on Alcohol, 62*(2), 166–178.

Greene, R. W., Ablon, J. S., & Goring, J. C. (2003). A transactional model of oppositional behavior: Underpinnings of the collaborative problem solving approach. *Journal of Psychosomatic Research, 55*(1), 67–75.

Greene, R. W., Biederman, J., Zerwas, S., Monuteaux, M., Goring, J. C., & Faraone, S. V. (2002). Psychiatric comorbidity, family dysfunction, and social impairment in referred youth with oppositional defiant disorder. *American Journal of Psychiatry, 159*(7), 1214–1224.

Greene, R. W., & Doyle, A. E. (2000). Toward a transactional conceptualization of oppositional defiant disorder: Implications for treatment and assessment. *Clinical Child and Family Psychology Review, 2,* 129–148.

Gutman, L. M., McLoyd, V. C., & Tokoyawa, T. (2005). Financial strain, neighborhood stress, parenting behaviors, and adolescent adjustment in urban African American families. *Journal of Research on Adolescence, 15*(4), 425–450.

Hare, R. D. (1991). *The Hare Psychopathy Checklist–Revised.* Toronto, Ontario, Canada: Multi-Health Systems.

Hare, R. D., Hart, S. D., & Harpur, T. J. (1991). Psychopathy and the *DSM-IV* criteria for antisocial personality disorder. *Journal of Abnormal Psychology, 100,* 391–398.

Hart, E. L., Lahey, B. B., Loeber, R., & Hanson, K. S. (1994). Criterion validity of informants in the diagnosis of disruptive behavior disorders in children: A preliminary study. *Journal of Consulting and Clinical Psychology, 62,* 410–414.

Hawes, D. J., & Dadds, M. R. (2005). The treatment of conduct problems in children with callous-unemotional traits. *Journal of Consulting and Clinical Psychology, 73*(4), 737–741.

Helzer, J. E., & Robins, L. N. (1988). The diagnostic interview schedule: Its development, evolution, and use. *Social Psychiatry and Psychiatric Epidemiology, 23*(1), 6–16.

Henggeler, S. W. (1997). *Treating serious anti-social behavior in youth: The MST approach* (OJJDP Juvenile Justice Bulletin). Washington, DC: U.S. Department of Justice, Office of Justice Programs, Office of Juvenile Justice and Delinquency Prevention.

Henggeler, S. W., Clingempeel, W. G., Brondino, M. J., & Pickrel, S. G. (2002). Four-year follow-up of multisystemic therapy with substance-abusing and substance-dependent juvenile offenders. *Journal of the American Academy of Child and Adolescent Psychiatry, 41,* 868–874.

Hinshaw, S. P., & Zupan, B. A. (1997). Assessment of antisocial behavior in children and adolescents. In D. Stuff, J. Breiling, & J. D. Mash (Eds.), *Handbook of antisocial behavior* (pp. 36–50). New York: Wiley.

Jensen, P. S., Rubio-Stipec, M., Canino, G., Bird, H., Dulcan, M. K., Schwab-Stone, M. E., et al. (1999). Parent and child contributions to diagnosis of mental disorder: Are both informants always necessary? *Journal of the American Academy of Child and Adolescent Psychiatry, 38,* 1569–1579.

Kamphaus, R. W., & Frick, P. J. (2002). *Clinical assessment of child and adolescent personality and behavior* (2nd ed.). Boston: Allyn & Bacon.

Kazdin, A. E. (1997). Practitioner review: Psychosocial treatments for conduct disorder in children. *Journal of Child Psychology and Psychiatry, 38*(2), 161–178.

Kazdin, A. E. (2000). Perceived barriers to treatment participation and treatment acceptability among antisocial children and their families. *Journal of Child and Family Studies, 9,* 157–174.

Kazdin, A. E., Esveldt-Dawson, K., French, N. H., & Unis, A. S. (1987). Effects of parent management training and problem-solving skills training combined in the treatment of antisocial child behavior. *Journal of the American Academy of Child and Adolescent Psychiatry, 26,* 416–424.

Kazdin, A. E., Siegel, T. C., & Bass, D. (1992). Cognitive problem-solving skills training and parent management training in the treatment of antisocial behavior in children. *Journal of Consulting and Clinical Psychology, 60*(5), 733–747.

Kazdin, A. E., & Weisz, J. R. (1998). Identifying and developing empirically supported child and adolescent treatments. *Journal of Consulting and Clinical Psychology, 66,* 19–36.

Keenan, K., Loeber, R., & Green, S. M. (1999). Conduct disorder in girls: A review of the literature. *Clinical Child and Family Psychology Review, 2*(1), 3–19.

Keenan, K., & Wakschlag, L. S. (2000). More than the terrible twos: The nature and severity of behavior problems in clinic-referred preschool children. *Journal of Abnormal Child Psychology, 28,* 33–46.

Kessler, R. C., McGonagle, K. A., Zhao, S. Y., Nelson, C. B., Hughes, M., Eshleman, S., et al. (1994). Lifetime and 12-month prevalence of DSM-III-R psychiatric disorders in the United States—Results of the national comorbidity survey. *Archives of General Psychiatry, 51,* 8–19.

Kimonis, E. R., Frick, P. J., & Barry, C. T. (2004). Callous-unemotional traits and delinquent peer affiliation. *Journal of Consulting and Clinical Psychology, 72,* 956–966.

Kuhne, M., Schachar, R., & Tannock, R. (1997). Impact of comorbid oppositional or conduct problems on attention-deficit hyperactivity disorder. *Journal of the American Academy of Child and Adolescent Psychiatry, 36*(12), 1715–1725.

Kuperman, S., Schlosser, S. S., Kramer, J. R., Bucholz, K., Hesselbrock, V., Reich, T., et al. (2001). Developmental sequence from disruptive behavior diagnosis to adolescent alcohol dependence. *American Journal of Psychiatry, 158*(12), 2022–2026.

Lahey, B. B., & Loeber, R. (1994). Framework for a developmental model of oppositional defiant disorder and conduct disorder. In D. Routh (Ed.), *Disruptive behavior disorders in childhood: Essays honoring Herb C. Quay* (pp. 139–180). New York: Plenum Press.

Lahey, B. B., Loeber, R., Burke, J. D., & Applegate, B. (2005). Predicting future antisocial personality disorder in males from a clinical assessment in childhood. *Journal of Consulting and Clinical Psychology, 73*(3), 389–399.

Lahey, B. B., McBurnett, K., & Loeber, R. (2000). Are attention-deficit/hyperactivity disorder and oppositional defiant disorder developmental precursors to conduct disorder? In A. Sameroff, M. Lewis, & S. M. Miller (Eds.), *Handbook of developmental psychopathology* (2nd ed., pp. 431–446). New York: Plenum Press.

Lahey, B. B., & Waldman, I. D. (2002). A developmental propensity model of the origins of conduct problems during childhood and adolescence. In B. B. Lahey, T. E. Moffitt, & A. Caspi (Eds.), *Causes of conduct disorder and serious juvenile delinquency* (pp. 1–32). New York: Guilford Press.

Langbehn, D. R., & Cadoret, R. J. (2001). The adult antisocial syndrome with and without antecedent conduct disorder: Comparisons from an adoption study. *Comprehensive Psychiatry, 42*(4), 272–282.

Langbehn, D. R., Cadoret, R. J., Yates, W. R., Troughton, E. P., & Stewart, M. A. (1998). Distinct contributions of conduct and oppositional defiant symptoms to adult antisocial behavior. *Archives of General Psychiatry, 55*, 821–829.

Lochman, J. E., & Lenhart, L. A. (1993). Anger coping intervention for aggressive children—Conceptual models and outcome effects. *Clinical Psychology Review, 13*, 785–805.

Loeber, R. (1982). The stability of antisocial and delinquent child behavior: A review. *Child Development, 53*, 1431–1446.

Loeber, R. (1988). Natural histories of conduct problems, delinquency, and associated substance use: Evidence for developmental progressions. In B. B. Lahey & A. E. Kazdin (Eds.), *Advances in clinical child psychology* (Vol. 11, pp. 73–124). New York: Plenum Press.

Loeber, R., Burke, J. D., & Lahey, B. B. (2002). What are adolescent antecedents to antisocial personality disorder? *Criminal Behavior and Mental Health, 12*(1), 24–36.

Loeber, R., Burke, J. D., Lahey, B. B., Winters, A., & Zera, M. (2000). Oppositional defiant and conduct disorder: Pt. I. A review of the past 10 years. *Journal of the American Academy of Child and Adolescent Psychiatry, 39*, 1468–1484.

Loeber, R., DeLamatre, M., Keenan, K., & Zhang, Q. (1998). A prospective replication of developmental pathways in disruptive and delinquent behavior. In R. Cairns, L. Bergman, & J. Kagan (Eds.), *Methods and models for studying the individual* (pp. 185–215). Thousand Oaks, CA: Sage.

Loeber, R., Green, S. M., Keenan, K., & Lahey, B. B. (1995). Which boys will fare worse? Early predictors of the onset of conduct disorder in a 6-year longitudinal study. *Journal of the American Academy of Child and Adolescent Psychiatry, 34*, 499–509.

Loeber, R., Green, S. M., Lahey, B. B., Christ, M. A. G., & Frick, P. J. (1992). Developmental sequences in the age of onset of disruptive child behaviors. *Journal of Child and Family Studies, 1*, 21–41.

Loeber, R., Green, S. M., Lahey, B. B., & Stouthamer-Loeber, M. (1989). Optimal informants on childhood disruptive behaviors. *Development and Psychopathology, 1*, 317–337.

Loeber, R., Green, S., Lahey, B. B., & Stouthamer-Loeber, M. (1991). Differences and similarities between children, mothers, and teachers as informants on disruptive child behavior. *Journal of Abnormal Child Psychology, 19*, 75–95.

Loeber, R., Wung, P., Keenan, K., Giroux, B., Stouthamer-Loeber, M., Van Kammen, W. B., et al. (1993). Developmental pathways in disruptive child behavior. *Development and Psychopathology, 5,* 101–132.

Logan, D. E., & King, C. A. (2001). Parental facilitation of adolescent mental health services utilization: A conceptual and empirical review. *Clinical Psychology: Science and Practice, 8*(3), 319–333.

Lynam, D. R. (1997). Pursuing the psychopath: Capturing the fledgling psychopath in a nomological net. *Journal of Abnormal Psychology, 106*(3), 425–438.

Lynam, D. R., Caspi, A., Moffitt, T. E., Loeber, R., & Stouthamer-Loeber, M. (in press). Longitudinal evidence that psychopathy scores in early adolescence predict adult psychopathy. *Journal of Abnormal Psychology.*

Maffei, C., Fossati, A., Agostoni, I., Barraco, A., Bagnato, M., Deborah, D., et al. (1997). Interrater reliability and internal consistency of the Structured Clinical Interview for *DSM-IV* Axis II personality disorders (SCID-II), version 2.0. *Journal of Personality Disorders, 11,* 279–284.

Mannuzza, S., Klein, R. G., Abikoff, H., & Moulton, J. L. (2004). Significance of childhood conduct problems to later development of conduct disorder among children with ADHD: A prospective follow-up study. *Journal of Abnormal Child Psychology, 32*(5), 565–573.

Maughan, B., Rowe, R., Messer, J., Goodman, R., & Meltzer, H. (2004). Conduct disorder and oppositional defiant disorder in a national sample: Developmental epidemiology. *Journal of Child Psychology and Psychiatry, 45*(3), 609–621.

McClellan, J. M., & Werry, J. S. (2000). Introduction: Research psychiatric diagnostic interviews for children and adolescents. *Journal of the American Academy of Child and Adolescent Psychiatry, 39*(1), 19–27.

McCord, J. (1991). Competence in long-term perspective. *Psychiatry, 54,* 227–237.

McLoyd, V. C. (1998). Socioeconomic disadvantage and child development. *American Psychologist, 53*(2), 185–204.

Mellsop, G., Varghese, F., Joshua, S., & Hicks, A. (1982). The reliability of Axis II of *DSM-III. American Journal of Psychiatry, 139,* 1360–1361.

Messina, N., Wish, E., Hoffman, J., & Nemes, S. (2001). Diagnosing antisocial personality disorder among substance abusers: The SCID versus the MCMI-II. *American Journal of Drug and Alcohol Abuse, 27*(4), 699–717.

Miller, G. E., & Prinz, R. J. (2003). Engagement of families in treatment for childhood conduct problems. *Behavior Therapy, 34,* 517–534.

Millon, T. (Ed.). (1997). *The Millon inventories: Clinical and personality assessment.* New York: Guilford Press.

Moffitt, T. (1993). Adolescence-limited and life-persistent antisocial behavior: A developmental taxonomy. *Psychological Review, 100*(4), 674–701.

Morrissey-Kane, E., & Prinz, R. J. (1999). Engagement in child and adolescent treatment: The role of parental cognitions and attributions. *Clinical Child and Family Psychology Review, 2*(3), 183–198.

MTA Cooperative Group. (1999). 14-month randomized clinical trial of treatment strategies for attention deficit hyperactivity disorder. *Archives of General Psychiatry, 56,* 1073–1086.

Myers, M. G., Stewart, D. G., & Brown, S. A. (1998). Progression from conduct disorder to antisocial personality disorder following treatment for adolescent substance abuse. *American Journal of Psychiatry, 155*(4), 479–485.

Nock, M. K. (2003). Progress review of the psychosocial treatment of child conduct problems. *Clinical Psychology: Science and Practice, 10,* 1–28.

Nock, M. K., & Kazdin, A. E. (2001). Parent expectancies for child therapy: Assessment and relation to participation in treatment. *Journal of Child and Family Studies, 10,* 155–180.

Olds, D. L., Eckenrode, J., Henderson, C. R., Kitzman, H., Powers, J., Cole, R., et al. (1997). Long-term effects of home visitation on maternal life course and child abuse and neglect: Fifteen-year follow-up of a randomized trial. *Journal of the American Medical Association, 278,* 637–643.

Olweus, D. (1979). Stability of aggressive reaction patterns in males: A review. *Psychological Bulletin, 86,* 852–857.

Pardini, D., Obradovic, J., & Loeber, R. (2006). Interpersonal callousness, hyperactivity/impulsivity, inattention, and conduct problems as precursors to delinquency persistence in boys: A comparison of three grade-based cohorts. *Journal of Clinical Child and Adolescent Psychology, 35,* 45–59.

Patterson, G. R., & Gullion, M. E. (1968). *Living with children: New methods for parents and teachers.* Champaign, IL: Research Press.

Piatigorsky, A., & Hinshaw, S. P. (2004). Psychopathic traits in boys with and without attention-deficit/hyperactivity disorder: Concurrent and longitudinal correlates. *Journal of Abnormal Child Psychology, 32*(5), 535–550.

Pithers, W. D. (1994). Process evaluation of a group therapy component designed to enhance sex offenders' empathy for sexual abuse survivors. *Behavior Research and Therapy, 32*(5), 565–570.

Poulin, F., & Boivin, M. (2000). The role of proactive and reactive aggression in the formation and development of boys' friendships. *Developmental Psychology, 36*(2), 233–240.

Prochaska, J. O., & DiClemente, C. C. (1982). Transtheoretical therapy: Toward a more integrative model of change. *Psychotherapy: Theory, Research, and Practice, 19,* 276–288.

Reid, W. H., & Gacono, C. (2000). Treatment of antisocial personality, psychopathy, and other characterologic antisocial syndromes. *Behavioral Sciences and the Law, 18*(5), 647–662.

Reinecke, M. A. (1995). Comorbidity of conduct disorder and depression among adolescents: Implications for assessment and treatment. *Cognitive and Behavioral Practice, 2,* 299–326.

Ridenour, T. A., Cottler, L. B., Robins, L. N., Compton, W. M., Spitznagel, E. L., & Cunningham-Williams, R. M. (2002). Test of the plausibility of adolescent substance use playing a causal role in developing adulthood antisocial behavior. *Journal of Abnormal Psychology, 111,* 144–155.

Robins, L. N. (1966). *Deviant children grown up: A sociological and psychiatric study of sociopathic personality.* Baltimore: Williams & Wilkins.

Robins, L. N. (1978). Sturdy childhood predictors of adult antisocial behavior: Replications from longitudinal studies. *Psychological Medicine, 8,* 611–622.

Robins, L. N., Cottler, L. B., Bucholz, K. K., Compton, W. M., North, C. S., & Rourke, K. M. (2000). *Diagnostic Interview Schedule for the DSM-IV (DIS-IV).* St. Louis, MO: Washington University.

Robins, L. N., Helzer, J., Cottler, L. B., & Goldring, E. (1989). *The Diagnostic Interview Schedule, Version III-R.* St. Louis, MO.

Robins, L. N., Tipp, J., & Przybeck, T. (1991). Antisocial personality. In L. N. Robins & D. A. Regier (Eds.), *Psychiatric disorders in America: The Epidemiologic Catchment Area study.* New York: Free Press.

Robins, L. N., & Wish, E. (1977). Childhood deviance as a developmental process: A study of 223 urban Black men from birth to 18. *Social Forces, 56,* 448–473.

Rowe, R., Maughan, B., Pickles, A., Costello, E. J., & Angold, A. (2002). The relationship between DSM-IV oppositional defiant disorder and conduct disorder: Findings from the Great Smoky Mountains Study. *Journal of Child Psychology and Psychiatry, 43,* 1–9.

Russo, M. F., Loeber, R., Lahey, B. B., & Keenan, K. (1994). Oppositional defiant and conduct disorders: Validation of the DSM-III-R and an alternative diagnostic option. *Journal of Clinical Child Psychology, 23,* 56–68.

Sampson, R. J., & Laub, J. H. (1993). *Crime in the making: Pathways and turning points through life.* Cambridge, MA: Harvard University Press.

Sanislow, C. A., & McGlashan, T. H. (1998). Treatment outcome of personality disorders. *Canadian Journal of Psychiatry, 43*(3), 237–250.

Shaffer, D., Fisher, P., Lucas, C. P., Dulcan, M. K., & Schwab-Stone, M. E. (2000). NIMH Diagnostic Interview Schedule for Children version IV (NIMH DISC-IV): Description, differences from previous versions, and reliability of some common diagnoses. *Journal of the American Academy of Child and Adolescent Psychiatry, 39*(1), 28–38.

Silverthorn, P., & Frick, P. J. (1999). Developmental pathways to antisocial behavior: The delayed-onset pathway in girls. In D. Cicchetti (Ed.), *Development and psychopathology* (Vol. 11, pp. 101–126). New York: Cambridge University Press.

Simonoff, E., Elander, J., Holmshaw, J., Pickles, A., Murray, R., & Rutter, M. (2004). Predictors of antisocial personality: Continuities from childhood to adult life. *British Journal of Psychiatry, 184,* 118–127.

Skinner, B. F. (1938). *The behavior of organisms: An experimental analysis.* New York: Appleton-Century.

Snyder, J. J., & Patterson, G. R. (1995). Individual differences in social aggression: A test of a reinforcement model of socialization in the natural environment. *Behavior Therapy, 26,* 371–391.

Southam-Gerow, M. A. (2003). Child-focused cognitive-behavioral therapies. In C. A. Essau (Ed.), *Conduct and oppositional defiant disorders: Epidemiology, risk factors, and treatment* (pp. 257–277). Mahwah, NJ: Erlbaum.

Stoolmiller, M., Patterson, G., R., & Snyder, J. (1997). Parental discipline and child antisocial behavior: A contingency-based theory and some methodological refinements. *Psychological Inquiry, 8*(3), 223–229.

Stormshak, E. A., Bierman, K. L., McMahon, R. J., & Lengua, L. J. (2000). Parenting practices and child disruptive behavior problems in early elementary school. *Journal of Clinical Child Psychology, 29,* 17–29.

Stouthamer-Loeber, M., Loeber, R., & Thomas, C. (1992). Caretakers seeking help for boys with disruptive delinquent behavior. *Comprehensive Mental Health Care, 2,* 159–178.

Swanson, J. M., Kraemer, H. C., Hinshaw, S. P., Arnold, L. E., Conners, C. K., Abikoff, H. B., et al. (2001). Clinical relevance of the primary findings of the MTA: Success rates based on severity of ADHD and ODD symptoms at the end of treatment. *Journal of the American Academy of Child and Adolescent Psychiatry, 40*(2), 168–179.

Swanson, M. C., Bland, R. C., & Newman, S. C. (1994). Epidemiology of psychiatric disorders in Edmonton: Antisocial personality disorders. *Acta Psychiatrica Scandinavica* (Suppl. 376), 63–70.

Takeuchi, D. T., Leaf, P. J., & Kuo, H. (1988). Ethnic differences in the perception of barriers to help-seeking. *Social Psychiatry and Psychiatric Epidemiology, 23,* 273–280.

Teagle, S. E. (2002). Parental problem recognition and child mental health service use. *Mental Health Services Research, 4*(4), 257–266.

Vitaro, F., Gendreau, P. L., Tremblay, R. E., & Oligny, P. (1998). Reactive and proactive aggression differentially predict later conduct problems. *Journal of Child Psychology and Psychiatry and Allied Disciplines, 39*(3), 377–385.

Waldman, I. D., & Lilienfeld, S. O. (1991). Diagnostic efficiency of symptoms for oppositional defiant disorder and attention-deficit hyperactivity disorder. *Journal of Consulting and Clinical Psychology, 59,* 732–738.

Waschbusch, D. A., Willoughby, M. T., & Pelham, W. E., Jr. (1998). Criterion validity and the utility of reactive and proactive aggression: Comparisons to attention deficit hyperactivity disorder, oppositional defiant disorder, conduct disorder, and other measures of functioning. *Journal of Clinical Child Psychology, 27*(4), 396–405.

Wasserman, G. A., Miller, L. S., Pinner, E., & Jaramillo, B. (1996). Parenting predictors of early conduct problems in urban, high-risk boys. *Journal of the American Academy of Child and Adolescent Psychiatry, 35,* 1227–1235.

Webster, C. D., Augimeri, L. K., & Koegl, C. J. (2002). The under 12 outreach project for antisocial boys: A research based clinical program. In R. R. Corrado, R. Roesch, & S. D. Hart (Eds.), *Multi-problem violent youth: A foundation for comparing research on needs, interventions, and outcomes* (pp. 1–12). Amsterdam: IOS Press.

Webster-Stratton, C. (1996). Early intervention with videotape modeling: Programs for families of children with oppositional defiant disorder or conduct disorder. In E. D. Hibbs & P. Jensen (Eds.), *Psychosocial* treatment research of child and adolescent disorders: Empirically based strategies for clinical practice (pp. 435–474). Washington, DC: American Psychological Association.

Webster-Stratton, C., & Taylor, T. (2001). Nipping early risk factors in the bud: Preventing substance abuse, delinquency, and violence in adolescence through interventions targeted at young children (0–8 years). Prevention Science, 2(3), 165–192.

Werner, E. E. (2005). What can we learn about resilience from large-scale longitudinal studies? In S. Goldstein & R. B. Brooks (Eds.), Handbook of resilience in children. New York: Kluwer Academic/Plenum Press.

White, H. R., Loeber, R., Stouthamer-Loeber, M., & Farrington, D. P. (1999). Developmental associations between substance use and violence. Development and Psychopathology, 11, 785–803.

Widiger, T. A. (1992). Antisocial personality disorder: DSM-IV in progress. Hospital and Community Psychiatry, 43, 6–8.

Widiger, T. A., Cadoret, R., Hare, R., Robins, L., Rutherford, M., & Zanarini, M. (1996). DSM-IV antisocial personality disorder field trial. Journal of Abnormal Psychology, 1, 3–16.

Widiger, T. A., & Corbitt, E. M. (1993). Antisocial personality disorder: Proposals for DSM-IV. Journal of Personality Disorders, 7, 63–77.

World Health Organization. (1992). International classification of diseases and related health problems (10th ed., Vol. 1). Geneva, Switzerland: Author.

Zimmerman, M. (1994). Diagnosing personality disorders: A review of issues and research methods. Archives of General Psychiatry, 51(3), 225–245.

Zoccolillo, M., Pickles, A., Quinton, D., & Rutter, M. (1992). The outcome of childhood conduct disorder: Implications for defining adult personality disorder and conduct disorder. Psychological Medicine, 22, 971–986.

Zuckerman, M. (1999). Antisocial personality disorder. In M. Zuckerman (Ed.), Vulnerability to psychopathology: A biosocial model (pp. 209–253). Washington, DC: American Psychological Association.

CHAPTER 13

Histrionic
Personality Disorder

THOMAS N. CRAWFORD and PATRICIA R. COHEN

PERSONALITY DISORDERS (PDs) are constellations of symptoms that signal maladaptive ways in which people organize subjective experiences, regulate emotion, and interact with other people. Histrionic PD is indicated when people exaggerate their emotions and go to excessive lengths to seek attention (American Psychiatric Association, 2000). Adults with this Axis II disorder may initially charm new acquaintances by their enthusiasm, liveliness, or flirtatiousness, but these qualities wear thin when expressed as constant demands to be the center of

This research was supported by NIMH grants MH36971 and MH054161 to Dr. Patricia Cohen and by NIDA grant DA03188 to Dr. Judith Brook.

attention. In this chapter, we address how Histrionic PD manifests during childhood and adolescence and hypothesize a developmental model to explain its etiology and developmental course. We describe current diagnostic criteria for Histrionic PD and differentiate them from normal developmental phenomena that could be mistaken for symptoms. We also describe how Histrionic PD overlaps with Borderline and Narcissistic PDs, which together form the Cluster B disorders in the current *Diagnostic and Statistical Manual of Mental Disorders* (*DSM-IV-TR*; American Psychiatric Association, 2000). Although Antisocial PD is also assigned to Cluster B, the *DSM-IV-TR* specifies that this diagnosis cannot be made before age 18. We discuss the clinical significance of Histrionic PD's frequent co-occurrence with Cluster B disorders and a range of other Axis I and Axis II psychiatric disorders. Finally, we review strategies for treating Histrionic PD in children and adolescents.

Insofar as Histrionic Personality Disorder has its conceptual roots in hysteria, it has a very interesting ancestry that extends as far back as ancient Egypt (Alam & Mersky, 1992; Veith, 1965). For centuries emotional disturbances associated with hysteria (loss of reason, volatile emotions, convulsions) were attributed to physical disturbances of the uterus, thus making it an exclusively female affliction. When Freud and early psychoanalysts wrote about hysteria around 1900, they no longer attributed it to physical illness; it was traced instead to memories or desires that people found unacceptable either to themselves or the society around them. When repressed or otherwise made unconscious, these memories or desires were converted into dramatic convulsions, fits, and hysterical paralyses that could not be explained medically. Dissociative symptoms were also prominent in hysterical patients, thus providing another way to keep unacceptable desires or memories from consciousness. By the second half of the twentieth century, psychoanalytic investigators lost interest in hysteria and focused attention on borderline and narcissistic personality pathology instead. Conversion reactions, psychosomatic disturbances, and dissociative symptoms once associated with hysteria are now recorded on Axis I in the *DSM-IV-TR*, and personality disturbances are recorded separately on Axis II. In an effort to eliminate gender bias associated with hysteria, the Axis II disturbance was renamed Histrionic PD.

Current definitions of Histrionic PD in the *DSM-IV-TR* and *International Classification of Diseases* (*ICD-10*) are presented in Table 13.1. It is worth noting that the diagnostic threshold in *DSM-IV-TR* (at least five of eight symptoms) differs from the threshold in *ICD-10* (at least three of six symptoms), thus reflecting how diagnostic decisions are currently based on arbitrary cutoff scores. Given how much prior conceptualizations of this disorder have changed over time, current criteria

Table 13.1

Current Diagnostic Criteria for Histrionic Personality
Disorder in *DSM-IV-TR* and *ICD-10*

DSM-IV, 1994	*ICD-10* Criteria, 1992
Histrionic Personality Disorder (301.50) is characterized by at least 5 of the following:	Histrionic Personality Disorder (F60.4) is characterized by at least 3 of the following:
(1) is uncomfortable in situations in which he or she is not the center of attention	(d) continual seeking for excitement, appreciation by others, and activities in which the patient is the centre of attention
(2) interaction with others is often characterized by inappropriate sexually seductive or provocative behavior	(e) inappropriate seductiveness in appearance or behaviour
(3) displays rapidly shifting and shallow expression of emotions	(c) shallow and labile affectivity
(4) consistently uses physical appearance to draw attention to self	(f) overconcern with physical attractiveness
(5) has a style of speech that is excessively impressionistic and lacking in detail	
(6) shows self-dramatization, theatricality, and exaggerated expression of emotion	(a) self-dramatization, theatricality, exaggerated expression of emotions
(7) is suggestible, that is, easily influenced by others or circumstances	(b) suggestible, easily influenced by others or by circumstances
(8) considers relationships to be more intimate than they actually are	

should not be reified or treated as though they capture something fixed or immutable in the people they describe. Insofar as people with Histrionic PD are highly suggestible, they can be unduly responsive to the other people's expectations, including the clinicians who treat them. Ellenberger (1970) describes how dramatic symptoms encountered in the nineteenth century (e.g., hysterical paralyses, somnambulism) occurred in part because clinicians showed a keen interest in them. When clinicians paid extra attention to hysterical patients, they reinforced specific kinds of symptoms and encouraged them to assume ever more dramatic forms. Once clinicians became more skeptical or lost interest, dramatic conversion reactions occurred with much less frequency. The lesson here is that attention-seeking behavior in histrionic people does not exist in isolation; the people whose attention is being sought (including clinicians) will inevitably influence the form and content of the symptoms.

Despite long-standing interest in Histrionic PD and its historical precursors, there has been little empirical research on the developmental origins of this disorder in childhood and adolescence. In this chapter, we draw on data from the Children in the Community (CIC) study (Cohen & Cohen, 1996), an ongoing longitudinal investigation of 821 children and their mothers who were randomly sampled from two counties in upstate New York. As Co-Principal Investigators of the CIC study, Drs. Patricia Cohen and Judith Brook have accumulated more than 20 years of longitudinal data on Axis II psychopathology; co-occurring Axis I pathology; child and parent personality; parenting and family relationships; social functioning and peer relationships; and environmental factors in the home, school, and neighborhood. Drs. Cohen and Brook surveyed the entire cohort in 1983, 1985 to 1986, 1991 to 1993, and 2001 to 2004, and a new assessment is currently under way. Mothers provided earlier data in 1975 when the children were on average 5.5 years old (Kogan, Smith, & Jenkins, 1977). These longitudinal data provide an unusually rich and comprehensive source of information on the childhood origins and long-term course of *DSM-IV* PDs (Cohen, Crawford, Johnson, & Kasen, 2005).

Personality disorders were first assessed in the CIC sample in 1983, long before any Axis II scales were developed for children or adolescents. An age-appropriate measure of PD was created by selecting a combination of parent- and youth-reported items from existing personality scales (e.g., Gough, 1957; Jackson, 1974; Smith & Fogg, 1979) that matched or closely corresponded to then current *DSM-III* diagnostic criteria. Additional items were drawn from the Personality Diagnostic Questionnaire (Hyler, Rieder, Spitzer, & Williams, 1982) and adapted as necessary to make them age-appropriate. After data collection was complete, a team of clinical researchers reviewed the items and wrote algorithms for Axis II symptom scales and categorical diagnoses. Cohen et al. (2005) provide a detailed history of how CIC scales and algorithms were amended in subsequent prospective assessments and updated to be compatible with *DSM-IV* criteria first published in 1994 and retained in the more recent *DSM-IV-TR*. These combined youth- and parent-reported data provide consistent repeated measures of PD at mean ages 13.7, 16.4, and 22.1.

When interviewed at mean age 33.2, participants were assessed with a newly developed self-report PD measure created to replace the combined parent- and youth-report measure used earlier. Drawing from the same longitudinal protocol, self-report scales and diagnostic algorithms were designed to assess Axis II disorders in adulthood at mean ages 22.1 and 33.2, thereby allowing prospective research across this 11-year interval (Crawford et al., 2005). Slightly abbreviated self-report scales were created for data gathered at earlier assessments. Different versions of the Histrionic PD symptom scales (combined parent- and youth-reports versus self-reports alone) had high correlations at three earlier cross-sectional intervals (mean $r = .69$, range = .58 to .78). In data gathered at mean age 33.2, histrionic diagnoses based on CIC self-report scales were validated against diagnoses derived from the Structured Clinical Interview for DSM-IV Personality Questionnaire. Agreement between diagnoses (kappa = .46) and correlations between corresponding scales ($r = .50$) matched or exceeded agreement between other PD instruments published in the literature (Crawford et al., 2005).

Table 13.2 provides prevalence estimates for Histrionic PD diagnoses by age and gender. Although hysterical symptoms were once thought to afflict only women, there was no evidence of gender differences in diagnoses or mean symptom levels in CIC data. These findings are consistent with results reported for adults (Nestadt et al., 1990). Although *DSM-IV-TR* provides some indication of how male and female patients may differ (e.g., by wearing "macho" clothes versus very feminine attire), writers in the clinical literature have hypothesized further gender differences in how Histrionic PD manifests in boys and girls (Blacker & Tupin, 1991; Kernberg, Weiner, & Bardenstein, 2000). Boys may display hypermasculine interest in fast cars, sports, and so on, and they may seek attention through risk-taking behavior. Girls may attract attention by dressing or behaving in pseudo-feminine or sexually seductive ways. Superficial affect in boys may be accompanied by a tendency to deny feelings; in girls it may manifest in increased emotional reactivity instead. Sexuality serves to gratify dependency needs but may be characterized by promiscuity in boys. Sexuality in girls may be inhibited instead. Once again, these symptomatic expressions in children and adolescents should not be seen in isolation. Symptoms intended to elicit attention or care-giving behavior will inevitably be shaped and reinforced by the people who respond to them.

Table 13.2

Prevalence of *DSM-IV-TR* Histrionic Personality Disorders and Symptoms in a Community Sample

	Subjects (Age in Years)							
	9–12		13–16		17–20		21–24	
	M	F	M	F	M	F	M	F
Diagnostic prevalence	4.6%	5.0%	2.4%	6.0%	2.5%	2.6%	1.9%	1.2%
Mean symptom levels	1.86	1.88	1.82	2.05	1.57	1.64	1.30	1.50
SD	1.45	1.44	1.35	1.48	1.24	1.32	1.17	1.25

Note: N = 821. Prevalence and symptom levels are estimated using 749 participants from the 1983 assessment, 733 from the 1985 to 1986 assessment, and 717 from the 1991 to 1993 assessment.

Table 13.2 suggests that there is a 30% decline in symptoms over time for male adolescents and a 20% decline for female adolescents. However, these gender-specific trajectories are not significantly different. Like most other personality disturbances, Histrionic PD diagnoses and symptoms are normally highest in early adolescence and then decline over time (Bernstein et al., 1993; Harpur & Hare, 1994; Johnson et al., 2000). Reductions in PD symptoms during adolescence and early adulthood may be attributed to the effects of parenting, biological maturation, societal enforcement of adult role expectations, and other normative processes (Stein, Newcomb, & Bentler, 1986). Although mean levels of Histrionic PD declined, the rank-order stability of symptoms was moderately stable ($r = .44$) from mean age 13.7 to 16.4 (Johnson et al., 2000). Stability dropped to .37 across the longer interval from mean age 16.4 to 22.1. In more recent data the stability coefficient was .54 from mean age 22.1 to mean age 33.2 (Crawford et al., 2005). However, these stability estimates do not control for measurement error and thus may underestimate the continuity of histrionic symptoms over time. Crawford, Cohen, and Brooks (2001a) used latent variables in structural equation models to measure the stability of Cluster B symptoms (Histrionic, Borderline, and Narcissistic PDs) in a subsample of youth ages 10 to 14. When latent variables reflecting the "true" variance of Cluster B symptoms were estimated across 2.5 years, their stability in adolescence was notably higher ($r = .73$) than when unadjusted stability estimates were used. Across 9 years stability was .63 and .69 in adolescent boys and girls, respectively.

Given rank-order stability, elevated symptoms relative to the mean are likely to remain high at subsequent assessments even when mean scores decline over time. In other words, high PD symptoms in children and adolescents represent an important risk factor for ongoing personality dysfunction. This may delay or otherwise interfere with the normal personality development expected during adolescence and early adulthood. Although in most cases histrionic symptoms declined over time, approximately 40% of the sample had higher symptoms in earlier adulthood (mean age 22.1) than they did earlier in adolescence (mean age 13.7). Some of this increase may reflect seductive behaviors that occur more frequently in late adolescence than in early adolescence.

CLINICAL ASSESSMENT

Insofar as Axis II criteria do not take developmental considerations into account, clinicians should exercise caution when assessing for PD in children and adolescents. Some behaviors specified as diagnostic criteria may be relatively normal in late childhood and adolescence and may become meaningful as a symptom only when they persist too long into adulthood. Any parent knows that attention seeking is common in childhood. However, excessive attention seeking may occur when the child's dependency needs are thwarted, and excessive demands for attention may come to characterize other relationships in adolescence and early adulthood. Attention seeking might be evident in intensified competition between siblings, especially if parents favor or are perceived to favor a brother or sister. Attention seeking also might become intensified in children with divorced parents who experience stepparents or stepsiblings as rivals.

Clinicians should be careful to distinguish Axis II psychopathology likely to persist over time from more transient disturbances occurring during childhood or adolescence. One way to make this distinction is by noting how much the child's or adolescent's behavior deviates from age norms. For instance, if an 8-year-old girl displays pseudomaturity, acts very grown up, and insists on doing adult things (e.g., having a boyfriend), that set of behaviors departs from normative behavior for children of that age and thus may be symptomatic of Histrionic PD. Symptoms also can be recognized in childhood or adolescent behaviors when they function in maladaptive ways. Seductive dress or flirtatious behavior may be intended primarily to attract attention, but they become maladaptive when they lead others to make unwanted sexual advances. On the other hand, sexually provocative attire could reflect early attempts to express an emerging sexuality without necessarily being a symptom of PD, especially in a social context where sexuality is widely promoted in the media for commercial purposes. Sexually provocative attire also might represent rebellious behavior intended to challenge parental restrictions that adolescents are eager to shed. If provocative dressing or flirtatious behaviors occur in the absence of other symptoms, they may simply be "local" experiences that probably will not persist beyond adolescence. In contrast, when these behaviors co-occur with poorly regulated affect or maladaptive preoccupation with interpersonal relationships, they are more likely to be symptoms of Histrionic PD.

Suggestibility may be more common in adolescence than in adulthood. One of the major tasks of adolescence and early adulthood is the exploration and eventual consolidation of identity (Erikson, 1968). As adolescents "try on" different identities, they may be especially susceptible to the immediate influences of peers, admired teachers, and romantic partners. Youth are also likely to be susceptible to contemporary cultural influences seen on television or other media outlets. Insofar as it may take time for young people to find a comfortable sense of identity, heightened suggestibility probably is an unreliable indicator of PD during adolescence. However, if adolescents place excessive or unwarranted trust in others, it may be symptomatic when it represents an unrealistic wish to be rescued or have unwanted problems magically taken away. In this context, extreme suggestibility may have less to do with identity formation and more to do with unresolved dependency.

Another developmental task of adolescence is to achieve a gradual separation from parents and assume more autonomous functioning during adulthood. Stormy fights between adolescents and parents may appear histrionic but often reflect normative attempts to assert independence. If adolescents are able to assert themselves against their parents at the same time that they can comfortably rely on them for emotional support and guidance, histrionic outbursts are unlikely to persist. However, if there is any significant family disturbance, histrionic arguments may signal risk for Axis II pathology. In divorced families, for instance, youths may feel insecure about their relationship with parents, especially the noncustodial parent. Adolescent daughters from divorced families may act in a precocious and seductive manner to get an absent father's attention, perhaps especially when competitive or jealous feelings exist between that daughter and a new stepmother. Adolescent sons may adopt pseudo-masculine behaviors in their own efforts to get an absent father's attention or approval. Once again, when Axis II symptom criteria are met and also reinforced within a dysfunctional family context, the clinician can recognize them as symptoms likely to persist over time.

Personality disorder symptoms and diagnoses often co-occur in adolescents and adults (Becker, Grilo, Edell, & McGlashan, 2000; Skodol, 2005). As reported in Table 13.3, correlations between continuous measures of histrionic symptoms and other Cluster B symptoms in our epidemiological sample were relatively high (mean $r = .40$, range = .31 to .50), thus justifying the *DSM*'s placement of Histrionic PD together with Antisocial, Borderline, and Narcissistic PD. (Adolescent Antisocial PD symptoms are relevant and informative here, even

Table 13.3

Association between Symptom Criteria for Histrionic
Personality Disorder and Other *DSM-IV-TR* Personality Disorders

	Association with Histrionic Symptoms (Pearson's r) Mean Age (Years)		
	13.7	16.4	22.1
Cluster A Symptoms			
Paranoid PD	.44*	.39*	.38*
Schizoid PD	.14*	.19*	.16*
Schizotypal PD	.38*	.29*	.32*
Cluster B Symptoms			
Antisocial PD	.36*	.33*	.31*
Borderline PD	.49*	.38*	.39*
Narcissistic PD	.50*	.45*	.39*
Cluster C Symptoms			
Avoidant PD	.38*	.31*	.38*
Dependent PD	.34*	.26*	.40*
Obsessive-Compulsive PD	.18*	.07	.13*

*$p < .01$

though categorical diagnoses can be assigned only after age 18.) Cross-sectional associations between histrionic symptoms and Cluster A symptoms (Paranoid, Schizoid, Schizotypal PDs) were lower (mean $r = .30$, range = .14 to .44) but still reflect notable overlap between symptoms. Associations between Histrionic PD and Cluster C symptoms (Avoidant, Dependent, Obsessive-Compulsive PDs) were similar in magnitude (mean $r = .27$, range = .07 to .40). The strength of association between these Axis II constructs appears to be stable over time.

As reported in Table 13.4, co-occurrence between categorically defined PDs appears somewhat different. In addition to reporting the

Table 13.4

Overlap between Histrionic Personality Disorder
and Other Axis II and Axis I Diagnoses

	Mean Age (Years)								
	13.7 ($N = 37$)			16.4 ($N = 17$)			22.1 ($N = 12$)		
	n	Percent (n/N)	Kappa	n	Percent (n/N)	Kappa	n	Percent (n/N)	Kappa
Axis II Disorders									
Paranoid PD	9	24	.20[b]	5	29	.23[b]	1	8	.07
Schizoid PD	2	5	0.02	0	0	−.02	2	17	.18
Schizotypal PD	6	16	0.13[b]	2	12	.06	0	0	−.01
Antisocial PD	—	—	—	—	—	—	1	8	.05
Borderline PD	7	19	.16[b]	4	24	.31[b]	1	8	.05
Narcissistic PD	10	27	.17[b]	4	24	.10	1	8	.09
Avoidant PD	6	16	.12[b]	2	12	.11	1	8	.05
Dependent PD	4	11	.15[a]	0	0	−.01	3	25	.31[b]
Obsessive-Compulsive PD	0	0	−.01	1	6	.09	0	0	−.01
Axis I Disorders									
Anxiety disorders	26	70	.13[b]	11	65	.10[b]	11	92	.07[b]
Mood disorders	10	27	.14[b]	7	41	.11[b]	9	75	.15[b]
Disruptive behavior	22	59	.14[b]	10	59	.09[b]	4	33	.08
Substance abuse	8	22	.17[b]	4	24	.09	3	25	.01

Note: Overlap with Antisocial PD was not estimated at mean ages 13.7 and 16.4 because this disorder cannot be diagnosed before age 18. Mood disorders included major depression, dysthymia, and bipolar disorders. Anxiety disorders included Generalized Anxiety Disorder, Panic Disorder, simple phobia, Social Phobia, Separation Anxiety Disorder, and Obsessive-Compulsive Disorder. Disruptive behavior disorders included Conduct Disorder, Oppositional Defiant Disorder, and Attention Deficit Disorder. Substance abuse disorders included alcohol abuse and marijuana abuse. Where there were fewer than five cases co-occurring with Histrionic PD, the Fisher Exact Test was used to confirm the statistical significance of specific association between diagnoses.

[a] $p < .05$

[b] $p < .01$

percentage of overlapping diagnoses, Table 13.4 provides kappa statistics that take different prevalence rates and chance overlap into account. Diagnoses of Histrionic PD at mean age 13.7 overlapped significantly with diagnoses of all other PDs except Schizoid and Obsessive-Compulsive PD. At later intervals Histrionic PD was associated only with Paranoid, Borderline, and Dependent PDs. (The link between Histrionic and Paranoid PD was unexpected. It could be that they co-occur because both reflect excessive preoccupation with other people; however, in Paranoid PD this preoccupation casts others as hostile antagonists, and in Histrionic PD it casts them as potential rescuers instead.) Although co-occurring diagnoses seem to drop off after early adolescence, this could be a measurement artifact. Specifically, these findings may be influenced by cases that met diagnostic criteria at one assessment but fell just short of that threshold at subsequent assessments. Because correlations reported earlier in Table 13.3 are not susceptible to this threshold effect, they suggest a more stable pattern of associations between symptoms over time.

Co-occurring PDs are problematic insofar as they can make it difficult to differentiate one PD from another or distinguish their unique contribution to maladaptive functioning. Overlap may make it difficult for researchers to differentiate developmental risks for histrionic symptoms from those associated with other PDs. For instance, self-reported histrionic symptoms in CIC data at mean age 16.4 appear related to childhood sexual abuse retroactively reported at mean age 22.1 or 33.2 (standardized $\beta = .11$, $p < .001$). However, this association disappears when borderline symptoms are added as a covariate to the model. The association between childhood sexual abuse and Histrionic PD thus appears to be reflected primarily in its overlap with Borderline PD.

Table 13.4 reports further overlap between Histrionic PD and co-occurring Axis I disorders diagnosed using the Diagnostic Interview Schedule for Children (Costello, Edelbrock, Dulcan, Kalas, & Klaric, 1984). When assessed at three separate ages, a high percentage of people with Histrionic PD had co-occurring anxiety disorders (65 to 92%), mood disorders (27 to 75%), disruptive behavior disorders (33 to 59%), and substance abuse disorders (22 to 25%). To measure the overall association between these variables in the community, kappa statistics take into account both the Axis I diagnoses that overlapped with Histrionic PD along with those that did not. It is worth noting that a large number of Axis I diagnoses did not co-occur with Histrionic PD, and these Axis I disorders are not reported in Table 13.4. However, when Histrionic PD and Axis I disorders did co-occur, kappas indicate the associations between these variables that were statistically significant. In clinical samples, Histrionic PD is likely to have even higher rates of co-occurrence with Axis I and Axis II disorders, especially insofar as the presence of each separate disorder increases the chance that the adolescent is brought in for treatment (Berkson, 1946).

CHILDHOOD AND ADOLESCENT ORIGINS OF HISTRIONIC PERSONALITY DISORDER

Personality emerging in childhood and adolescence is a developmental elaboration of childhood temperament, which Rothbart and Bates (1998) broadly conceptualize as moderately heritable individual differences in reactivity and self-regulation. Differences in reactivity reflect individual variation in the onset, duration, and intensity of affective reactions (e.g., fear, anger, positive affect). Self-regulatory processes include focusing attention, inhibiting inappropriate responses, and planning behaviors that can be used to modulate reactivity (Eisenberg, Fabes, Guthrie, & Reiser, 2000; Eisenberg & Morris, 2002). Based on *DSM-IV-TR* descriptive criteria, the temperament in childhood most likely to be associated with Histrionic PD should be characterized by prominent displays of emotion with rapid onset and short duration. If childhood reactivity is combined with a limited capacity for self-regulation, it may contribute to helplessness and excessive dependency on others to modulate emotional distress that characterizes Histrionic PD.

Bowlby's (1969, 1973, 1980) attachment theory helps to explain the interpersonal origins of Histrionic PD (Bartholomew, Kwong, & Hart, 2001; Bleiberg, 2001; Crawford et al., 2006). According to attachment theory, young children are biologically prepared to seek proximity, signal distress, and enter into reciprocal relationships with caregivers. In turn, caregivers are predisposed to understand and respond to the children's emotional distress by holding, comforting, or acting in other ways to soothe them. Emotional distress is thus "co-regulated" between children and caregivers when the child is unable or only partially able to self-regulate affect (Mikulincer, Shaver, & Pereg, 2003). As a result of repeated interactions, children normally gain subjective experiences of security, restored equilibrium, and satisfaction that are woven into their relationship with caregivers. However, when caregivers are not responsive or available, young children come to feel insecure about the reliability of those caregivers to provide emotional comfort when needed.

Childhood risks for Histrionic PD may be heightened if children are exposed to chronic family dysfunction, divorce, or other forms of interpersonal trauma (Brennan & Shaver, 1998). Insofar as childhood coping resources are immature or fragile, children exposed to family dysfunction or adversity may experience unregulated distress that threatens to overwhelm them. To protect themselves, they may cling to caregivers and become highly anxious when caregivers are absent or emotionally unavailable. Parents may try to compensate for family disturbances by becoming overinvolved with or overprotective of their children. Maternal overinvolvement has been linked with subsequent Histrionic PD in adolescence (Bezirganian, Cohen, & Brook, 1993) and may undermine the child's sense of competence and agency. Children exposed to ongoing family dysfunction may adopt defenses that isolate them from family stressors beyond their control. For instance, young people may learn to deny external problems or internal feelings that otherwise would overwhelm them. Dissociative symptoms serve the same function in more severe cases. Although these defenses may provide necessary protection for the child, they also are likely to interfere with normal personality development if they block or prevent the child from learning how to integrate the subjective experience and the ability to respond to the external world in a flexible and adaptive manner.

Histrionic PD probably has its specific childhood origins in "anxious-ambivalent attachment" (Bartholomew et al., 2001). Caregivers of anxious-ambivalent infants are thought to respond in an inconsistent manner to the child's attachment needs. When experiencing emotional distress, the child feels uncertain about the availability of the caregiver, thus resulting in intensified proximity seeking and heightened anger when that person is unavailable. This anxious-ambivalent behavior reflects a coping strategy that overemphasizes the caregivers and heightens the infant's dependency and also comes at the expense of the child's sense of self-agency (Bleiberg, 2001). Anxious-ambivalent attachment is associated with "hyperactivating strategies" that young people use to elicit care-giving behaviors from parents when needed (Cassidy & Kobak, 1988). Hyperactivating strategies place people constantly on the alert for threats, separations, and abandonment by attachment figures. Although intended to reduce negative affect, hyperactivating strategies often elicit thoughts and expectations that exacerbate emotional distress instead. Furthermore, hyperactivating strategies may lead children and adolescents to place excessive demands on significant others, often leading them to pull away and further reinforce fears of being abandoned.

During adolescence Histrionic PD is likely to manifest in "preoccupied attachment" when teenagers begin to date and enter into early romantic relationships. In the four-category model of attachment styles (Bartholomew & Horowitz, 1991), preoccupied attachment occurs when people experience high attachment anxiety (elevated worry about being abandoned or rejected by others) and low attachment avoidance (limited discomfort about being close to and depending on others). Attachment anxiety may amplify the reactive dimension of temperament associated with Histrionic PD, and low avoidance (i.e., high proximity seeking) represents an interpersonal strategy for reducing that anxiety. The association between Histrionic PD and high anxiety and low avoidance was recently documented in a sample of adolescents (Nakash-Eisikovits, Dutra, & Westen, 2002).

The relational processes that reinforce insecure attachment may be very stable over time (Belsky & Pasco Fearon, 2002), thus resulting in experiences that are overlearned to the point where insecure attachment is simply taken for granted. Insofar as these experiences happen automatically, young people may have no other way of seeing themselves or responding to the interpersonal world around them. However, early attachment insecurity is not immutable. If parents become more sensitive and responsive to their children's attachment needs, attachment security is likely to increase. Depending on partner choices people make when they start dating in adolescence, insecurity in romantic relationships can reinforce or maintain earlier attachment insecurity from childhood. Alternatively, a relationship with a sensitive and responsive romantic partner may offset or reduce insecurity carrying over from childhood.

It is important to emphasize that Histrionic PD is not the only Axis II disorder associated with insecure attachment. For instance, elevated preoccupation with the availability of caregivers or romantic partners is salient in Borderline PD and Dependent PD (Agrawal, Gunderson, Holmes, & Lyons-Ruth, 2004; Livesley, Schroeder, & Jackson, 1990). Even people with Avoidant PD, once they find a romantic partner, can become intensely preoccupied with the availability of that attachment figure. As such, insecure attachment alone cannot explain why Histrionic PD manifests in one adolescent and Dependent or Avoidant PD manifests in another.

We propose that different kinds of PD emerge from insecure attachment based on genetic factors that contribute to individual differences in personality. It is well established in behavioral genetic research that the heritability of normal personality traits ranges between 40% and 60% (Plomin, DeFries, McClearn, & McGuffin, 2001). When PD traits are measured with the Dimensional Assessment of Personality Problems (DAPP; Livesley & Jackson, in press), an empirically defined alternative to *DSM*-defined PDs, heritability of Axis II psychopathology falls within the same basic range as normal personality traits (Livesley, Jang, Jackson, & Vernon, 1993; Livesley, Jang, & Vernon, 1998). Factor analysis was used to identify 18 dimensional constructs underlying PD: affective lability, anxiousness, callousness, cognitive distortion, compulsivity, conduct problems, identity problems, insecure attachment, intimacy problems, narcissism, oppositionality, rejection, restricted expression, self-harm, social avoidance, stimulus seeking, submissiveness, and suspiciousness. In behavioral genetic research these empirically derived dimensions are preferable to *DSM* constructs because they have lower rates of measurement error, thereby increasing the accuracy of heritability estimates.

Figure 13.1 hypothesizes different combinations of heritable personality traits and experiences within the family environment that may increase risk for Histrionic PD. Heritable and environmental risks predispose people to a range of emotions, cognitions, and behaviors associated with a given PD. While increasing susceptibility to PD, these risks should not be seen as predetermining any outcome. As measured on the DAPP, the heritable dimensions most relevant to Histrionic PD include affective lability, narcissism, and insecure attachment (Bagge & Trull, 2003). The affective lability

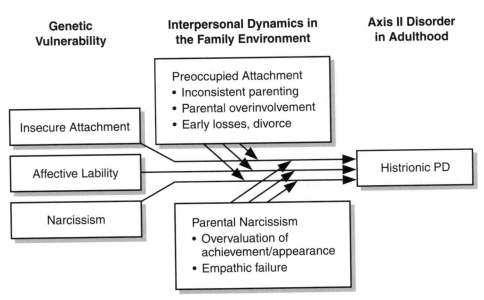

Figure 13.1 Developmental Pathway Model for Histrionic Personality Disorder

dimension encompasses subscales measuring affective overreactivity, hypersensitivity, and labile anger. Narcissism's subscales measure need for adulation, attention seeking, and grandiosity. Insecure attachment on the DAPP encompasses subscales assessing separation protest, feared loss, intolerance of aloneness, and proximity seeking. These three dimensions have high intercorrelations ($r = .46$ to $.50$; Crawford, Livesley, Jang, Shaver, Cohen, & Ganiban, 2007) and load onto a higher order factor indexing emotional dysregulation. Even when variation from this higher order factor is taken into account, genetic factors unique to the individual scales for affective lability, narcissism, and insecure attachment still account for 62% to 66% of their variances (Livesley et al., 1998). Suggestibility is also included on the DAPP but is measured on a subscale from the submissiveness scale, a dimension that pertains both to Histrionic and Dependent PD.

Although genetic effects are well documented in twin studies of adults (see Jang, 2005, for a review), much less is known about genetic influences on these dimensions in children and adolescents. Also, estimates of genetic influences are based on a population average and thus cannot provide reliable clinical information about a specific child or adolescent presenting for treatment. Finally, Rutter et al. (1997) emphasize that heritability estimates typically assume that genetic and environmental effects are separate and thus do not take into account more complex and more plausible interplay between etiological influences that include gene-environment correlations (e.g., circumstances in which genetic factors constitute a risk for exposure to negative environmental factors) and gene-environment interactions (e.g., circumstances in which a combination of genetic liability and environmental hazard presents a powerful risk). Despite these caveats, the available heritability estimates for affective lability, narcissism, and insecure attachment are large enough in magnitude to suggest that genes will have a substantial contribution to Histrionic PD.

Genetic predisposition to Histrionic PD may account for higher levels of affective lability or narcissism in affected children or adolescents when compared with age peers. From this developmental starting point, a variety of pathways leading to pathological and nonpathological outcomes may depend on gene × environment interactions that influence how that genetic predisposition unfolds. For instance, if a young person predisposed to affective lability grows up in an environment that instills anxious-ambivalent attachment, that combination may represent a developmental trajectory leading toward Histrionic PD. If anxious-ambivalent attachment is reinforced in the family but occurs in the absence of any genetic vulnerability to affective lability, our model predicts that anxious-ambivalent attachment would persist but not manifest as Histrionic PD.

This developmental model also hypothesizes that insecure attachment is genetically transmitted from parents to children. At present, however, the twin research that evaluates this hypothesis has been mixed. Insecure attachment in infants and toddlers has not been shown to be heritable (Bakermans-Kranenburg, van IJzendoorn, Schuengel, & Bokhorst, 2004; Bokhorst et al., 2003; O'Connor & Croft, 2001). These studies all had relatively small samples and may have lacked sufficient power to detect any genetic influences that were there. In contrast, self-reported preoccupied attachment styles in adults were shown to be heritable (Brussoni, Jang, Livesley, & MacBeth, 2000). Among the underlying dimensions of preoccupied attachment, anxious attachment is heritable and avoidant attachment is not (Crawford et al., 2007). These outcomes from child and adult twin samples may differ because they pertain to different relationship domains (parent-child relationships versus romantic relationships between adults). Alternatively, the heritable effects of preoccupied or anxious attachment may be evident only in adults because they "switch on" sometime after early childhood.

Childhood pathways to Histrionic PD probably share some of the same heritable risks associated with Borderline PD, thus accounting for some of their diagnostic overlap. Although both PDs are influenced by genetic vulnerability to insecure attachment and affective lability, Borderline PD is influenced by heritable identity disturbances and self-harm that are less salient in Histrionic PD (Bagge & Trull, 2003). Environmental risk for Borderline PD may involve trauma associated with childhood sexual abuse that is less associated with other PDs, including Histrionic PD (Zanarini et al., 1997). Furthermore, attachment in children and adolescents with Borderline PD may be "disorganized." This occurs when children feel a need to avoid an abusive caregiver as a potential source of harm at the same time they seek his or her comfort when feeling afraid (Solomon & George, 1999). Caregivers may have their own history of being abused as children or adolescents (McCloskey & Bailey, 2000; Oates, Tebbutt, Swanston, Lynch, & O'Toole, 1998), and unresolved childhood trauma may interfere with their functioning as parents. When compared with families of youth with Histrionic PD, there may be more interpersonal hostility and open aggression in families of youth with Borderline PD.

Childhood pathways to Histrionic and Narcissistic PD in turn may overlap insofar as both are influenced by genetic predisposition to the narcissism dimension measured on the DAPP. Heritable influences that are more specific to Narcissistic PD are reflected in the callousness dimension (especially subscales for egocentrism, exploitation, interpersonal irresponsibility, lack of empathy, remorselessness) that overlaps more with Antisocial PD than with Histrionic PD (Bagge & Trull, 2003). Whereas the family environment of youth with Histrionic PD may be characterized by preoccupied attachment, the parents of those with Narcissistic PD may have a dismissing attachment style instead (high avoidance and low anxiety). Instead of being anxious about relationships, dismissing parents disparage or distance themselves from the attachment needs of their children.

It is important to emphasize that Figure 13.1 presents a simplified developmental model of Histrionic PD. As indicated, the interplay between genetic and environmental components in this model is likely to be more complex (Rutter et al., 1997). For instance, the same genes for affective lability transmitted from parent to child may also contribute to maladaptive parenting behaviors, thus producing correlated genetic and environmental effects that increase affective lability in children.

Poorly modulated parental affect could provoke sudden changes in emotion in other family members and thus foster emotional reactivity in children. Poorly modulated affect in children could have a similar effect on parents. Heritable narcissism transmitted from parent to child may influence parents who regard children as narcissistic extensions of themselves, thus leading them to reinforce childhood behaviors that attract attention or praise that become so salient in Histrionic PD. Other environmental experiences associated with parental narcissism may include empathic failures toward children, thus limiting parental sensitivity to the emotional needs of the child.

THERAPEUTIC GOALS AND STRATEGIES

Although the CIC study provides invaluable prospective data for investigating the developmental course of PD, it lacks clinical detail needed to illustrate techniques for treating Histrionic PD in children and adolescents. Useful case examples describing psychotherapy with children and adolescents with Axis II disorders in outpatient and residential treatment settings can be found elsewhere (Bleiberg, 2001; Kernberg et al., 2000). We focus here instead on the broad clinical implications of the developmental model presented in this chapter. As indicated, Histrionic PD involves excessive emotional reactivity combined with deficits in self-regulation. Although caregivers might offset limits to a child's capacity for self-regulation through sensitive and responsive parenting, this will not occur reliably in a family environment infused with insecure attachment. When dependency needs go unmet, children may adopt hyperactivating strategies and attention-seeking behaviors to get parents to care for them. Children and adolescents are most likely to be brought in for treatment when maladaptive strategies result in disruptive behavior that is difficult to control.

In the broadest terms, the goals of therapy should include identifying when the child feels attachment insecurity and clarifying what triggers maladaptive strategies intended to reduce it. Over time, therapy can help the child and caregivers to learn new patterns of interacting that foster more effective strategies for modulating affect. As children become more adept at self-regulating affect and attain more competence, their constant need for attention should subside and they should feel less need for someone to take care of them.

Any clinician knows, of course, this is much easier said than done. Children and adolescents with Histrionic PD may be difficult to engage in therapy given their attempts to charm and entertain, their emotional lability, or their unfocused cognitive style. Young people may be accustomed to a dysfunctional interpersonal environment at home and expect similar dysfunction in other relationships, including a relationship with a new therapist. On the other hand, young people with histrionic symptoms usually crave relationships and may respond well to a therapist's warmth and support, thereby providing an initial foundation for a therapeutic alliance. To the extent that narcissistic pathology overlaps with histrionic symptoms, adolescent patients will probably respond over time to empathy and affirmation.

Treatment of Histrionic PD is likely to be further complicated by the presence of comorbid Axis I and Axis II disorders that are common in children and adolescents referred for treatment. If someone presents with severe panic attacks, for instance, it is difficult to address personality disturbances when panic completely overwhelms the child's or adolescent's ability to regulate emotions. Acute Axis I disturbances thus may need to be treated first, even when this task is rendered more difficult by the presence of Axis II disturbances. In some cases, PD symptoms will be secondary to episodic disorders such as Major Depression and may resolve with treatment of that disorder.

To illustrate how treatment strategies for Histrionic PD can be formulated, we selected two adolescents from our sample with "stable" PD, which is our designation for participants who met *DSM-IV-TR* diagnostic criteria twice across a 2.5-year interval (or came within one criterion of the diagnostic threshold at one of those two assessments). These case histories include prospective data gathered on three occasions between 1983 and 1994 and narrative detail drawn from intensive retrospective interviews conducted between 1997 and 1999. We modified the narrative content as needed to preserve the anonymity of our respondents.

Case Illustration

Mark was a preadolescent boy who lived with his parents and an older brother when he was first interviewed. Mother reported that Mark was often upset when she gave attention to other children and that he was happy one moment and sad the next (which we interpret as meeting histrionic criteria 1 and 3). Mark reported that he was often hotheaded or bad-tempered and exaggerated his difficulties (criterion 6) and worried a lot about other people liking him (criterion 7). He indicated that he often lost his train of thought and his mind drifted from one thing to another (our best available match for criterion 5). Mark did not attract attention through flirtation, by the clothes he wore, or by exaggerating how close he was to others—symptoms that are all more likely to manifest later in adolescence and adulthood. Even without these emblematic symptoms of Histrionic PD, *DSM-IV-TR* criteria for the disorder still were met. Although Mark did not have any other PDs diagnosed at that time, he did meet criteria for Conduct Disorder, Oppositional Defiant Disorder, and Separation Anxiety Disorder. Two years later, Mark presented with the same Axis I and II disorders, but his personality pathology intensified and met criteria for Paranoid, Borderline, and Narcissistic PDs.

Because intense and diffuse Axis II pathology is not unusual at this age, it can be difficult to predict the long-term course of childhood or adolescent PD. Multiple Axis I and Axis II pathology is likely to tax if not overwhelm a child's ability to organize or integrate his or her emotional experiences into an emerging personality (Crawford, Cohen, & Brook, 2001b). Mark's emotional vulnerability was further compromised by verbal and physical abuse by his father and by his parents' frequent and sometimes violent arguments prior to their divorce when he was in elementary school. After meeting diagnostic criteria for separation anxiety in preadolescence, Mark's fears about being abandoned evolved and changed form as he grew older. By late adolescence he came to perceive himself as taking care of his mother, in effect replacing his father, instead of depending on her emotionally. Mark continued to live at home with his mother, ostensibly to take care of her through a series of illnesses. This arrangement continued until she eventually insisted that he move out when he was well into his 20s. We know that Mark was in some form of psychotherapy in adolescence but lack information about its focus, duration, or impact. From his narrative interview, we also know that Mark was hungry for contact with someone to talk to during adolescence. It is thus easy to imagine that unresolved dependency issues that were salient throughout Mark's development were discussed at some time in therapy.

Case Illustration

In late adolescence, Mark's histrionic symptoms persisted but were less pronounced. After graduating from high school he developed an interest in body building and started driving a motorcycle, both representing hypermasculine variations of attention-seeking behaviors. He reported having problems modulating his temper at school and at a series of after school jobs. Nevertheless, he asserted that his teachers and employers usually "loved" him despite these frequent problems. His Axis II symptoms were more consistent with Narcissistic PD than the histrionic pathology indicated earlier. Insofar as Mark's personality became organized around suspiciousness and hostility toward others, he also met criteria for Paranoid PD. Among the indicators of his ongoing Axis II pathology, the most salient was his difficulty dating. By age 27 he held out little hope of finding a wife despite his deep desire to be married and have a family.

As argued earlier, family processes that reinforce insecure attachment may be overlearned to the point where they are simply taken for granted. Children and adolescents usually will not be aware of what triggers feelings or cognitions associated with insecure attachment. Being unable to articulate their feelings, they usually act them out instead in their relationships with others. This is illustrated by a female participant in the CIC study whose attention-seeking and competitive behaviors came to define her relationships with caregivers throughout adolescence.

Case Illustration

Linda was the eldest of three full siblings whose parents divorced a year before she was interviewed in early adolescence. Given her difficulty getting along with her mother, she chose to live with her father and his new wife while her two sisters stayed with mother. She felt like an outsider in her father's household and in fact was treated differently from the children from her stepmother's previous marriage. Linda was sent to public school and told by her parents that they could not afford to send her to the private school where her new stepsiblings were enrolled. According to her biological mother, Linda got upset when her mother paid attention to other children (criterion 1) both before and after Linda moved to her father's new household. Each time she was interviewed Linda reported that she had rapidly shifting expressions of emotion (criterion 3) and was often anxious to have other people like her (criterion 7). In the first two interviews she reported that she often lost her train of thought and her mind drifted from one thing to another (criterion 5). Later on in adolescence and early adulthood she reported that she was frequently flirtatious (criterion 2) and often exaggerated her feelings (criterion 6). Linda thus approached criteria for Histrionic PD in early adolescence and met full criteria when interviewed later in adolescence and adulthood. She did not have any co-occurring PDs but did meet criteria for Oppositional Defiant Disorder when assessed in adolescence. After being phobic of strangers throughout early adolescence, she developed a more broadly defined Social Phobia when followed up 2 years later.

When compared with Mark's multiple co-occurring diagnoses, Linda's psychopathology was relatively mild and her Axis II pathology was organized more narrowly around histrionic symptoms. It is noteworthy that both Mark and Linda presented with Oppositional Defiant Disorder, thus suggesting that young people with Histrionic PD may be difficult to engage when brought in for treatment. Histrionic PD in adolescents may be especially linked with oppositional behavior toward adults and even antisocial behavior toward peers that is motivated and reinforced by peer attention, approval, and admiration. It is also notable that Linda chose to follow her father after his divorce, thus paralleling Mark's decision to stay close to his mother well into adulthood. It is unclear whether Linda's decision was motivated by a wish to reject her mother, anxiety about losing her father, or a combination of the two. What appears more certain is that competitive feelings came to define her relationship with her stepmother, perhaps even recapitulating an earlier rivalry with her mother. Although Linda may have succeeded in replacing her mother in a competition for her father, she encountered a new rival when her father remarried. Linda was allowed to stay with her father but was not given the same kind of educational opportunity extended to her stepsiblings. This highly ambivalent acceptance of Linda in her father's new household continued throughout adolescence and probably contributed to the persistence of her histrionic symptoms into adulthood.

When considering the etiological factors specified in Figure 13.1, it is worth noting that psychotherapy does not directly target heritable effects even when they contribute substantially to Axis II pathology. Instead, psychotherapy focuses more on disturbances in how people perceive themselves, how they organize subjective experience of emotion, how they integrate different (sometimes conflicting) aspects of themselves into a coherent whole, and how they experience relationships with significant others. In an important way, therapy targets and tries to change maladaptive ways in which people regulate their emotional experiences internally and through interpersonal relationships. For instance, therapy with Linda might help her talk through difficult relationships with her mother and stepmother to help her become more aware of how these conflict-laden relationships play out in an automatic and recurring manner. Once people become aware of what leads them to act in maladaptive or self-defeating ways, they are more able to decide whether to continue that behavior or find new ways of interacting with others. Therapy also assists people to recognize and address emotional problems, thereby lessening the need to deny or repress them in ways that may interfere with personality maturation and integration in childhood and adolescence.

Some interventions may target specific maladaptive beliefs or cognitions associated with Histrionic PD. A core assumption of histrionic adults is that they are unable to take care of themselves (Beck, Freeman, Davis, & Associates, 2004). This assumption gives rise to maladaptive beliefs ("I need others to take care of me" and "I must make them notice me and like me") that motivate ongoing attempts to seek out and enter into dependent relationships. In children and adolescents, such beliefs and assumptions pertain in a very immediate way to the dependent relationship they have with caregivers. Maladaptive cognitions may ultimately be traced to preverbal mental representations of self and other (internal working models) hypothesized in attachment theory (Bretherton & Munholland, 1999; Fonagy, Steele, & Steele, 1991). Infants and children are thought to internalize the parent-child relationship in the form of lasting expectations of whether or not attachment figures will be available or helpful, especially in stressful or traumatic situations. Based on these experiences, young children internalize beliefs about whether they are worthy of love and whether others can be trusted to take care of them when needed (Shaver, Collins, & Clark, 1996). Internal working models reflect a cognitive dimension of attachment that may be more susceptible to change in psychotherapy (Bowlby, 1988; Brisch, 2002; Slade, 1999; Sperling & Lyons, 1994; West & Keller, 1994) than the heritable effects hypothesized in Figure 13.1.

Therapy may need to address insecure attachment associated with Histrionic PD at the level of interpersonal processes within the family, either through family therapy or collateral meetings with the parents. It is crucial to recognize that caregivers may be overwhelmed by their child's behavioral problems in ways that may interfere with their ability to function as effective parents. Mark's mother met with a mental health care provider for approximately 6 months to discuss his behavior problems in junior high school. Other parents may be less effective as parents if they become depressed about realignments in families as a result of divorce. Linda's mother sought help from a psychologist and a psychiatrist for about a year after her daughter decided to live with her father and new stepmother.

METHODS FOR EVALUATING TREATMENT OUTCOMES

In the CIC study we used combined parent and youth reports to measure change in childhood and adolescent PD. Most children are able to provide data on their own characteristics and problems by age 9 or 10. Before that age we have relied on parent reports to measure emotional problems and risks for later psychopathology. We generally consider any symptomatic report to be valid provided that there is evidence of associated impairment. If only a single informant can be used, adolescents are better informants about their emotions. They also acknowledge behaviors that may be unknown to the parent. For a more detailed discussion of these assessment issues, see Cohen and Crawford (2005).

The Millon Adolescent Clinical Inventory (MACI) is a well-known instrument modeled on the Millon Clinical Multiaxial Inventory (MCMI) designed for adults (see Davis, Woodward, Goncalves, Meagher, &

Millon, 1999). Intended for adolescents as young as 13, the MACI uses 160 self-report items to measure personality disorder constructs congruent with *DSM*-defined PDs but also reflecting Millon's (1990) theory of personality. The MACI measures Histrionic PD with its Dramatizing Scale, Borderline PD with its Borderline Tendency Scale, Narcissistic PD with its Egotistic Scale, and Antisocial PD with its Unruly Scale. The MACI test is geared to a sixth-grade reading level and generally takes about 20 minutes for most patients to complete.

Other instruments are available for parent and clinician reports, but they have not been widely used. The Coolidge Personality and Neuropsychological Inventory for Children (Coolidge, 1998) is a parent report instrument used to assess all *DSM-IV* Axis II disorders in children and adolescents from 5 to 17 years old. The Shedler-Westen Assessment Procedure—200 for Adolescents (SWAP-200-A; Westen, Shedler, Glass, & Martens, 2003) is a Q-sort instrument designed for clinicians to use to assess Axis II pathology in adolescents seen in treatment. Rather than assigning scores for individual items on Likert-style rating scales, Q-sort methods ask clinicians to array items from the most descriptive of the adolescent to the least descriptive. Until recently our own CIC PD scales have been used solely for our longitudinal research. We recently adapted our *DSM-IV* scales and diagnostic algorithms (Crawford & Cohen, 2006) for use by anyone interested in using them. The validity of selected scales from this instrument is currently being evaluated.

CONCLUSIONS

This chapter presented a developmental model of genetic and environmental influences that are hypothesized to form childhood pathways to Histrionic PD. There is abundant evidence of insecure attachment's association with psychopathology in children and adolescents (see Greenberg, 1999, for a review) and compelling evidence documenting the heritability of PD in adults (Jang, 2005; Jang & Vernon, 2001; Livesley et al., 1998), along with some preliminary evidence in children (Coolidge, Thede, & Jang, 2001). However, there is a gap in the existing literature addressing how these respective influences interact or overlap. We have been unable to investigate this developmental model empirically in the CIC study because the DAPP did not exist when we started assessing PD and our nontwin sample does not allow estimates of genetic effects. Nevertheless, we hope our conceptual model will be useful for future research.

Whatever may account for the origins of Histrionic PD, prospective CIC data show that childhood elevations in symptoms of this disorder represent specific long-term risks for depression (Johnson, Cohen, Kasen, & Brook, 2005) and substance abuse (Cohen, Chen, Crawford, Gordon, & Brook, in press). When adolescent Histrionic, Borderline, and Narcissistic PDs are combined, these Cluster B disorders predict a wide range of Axis I and Axis II disorders in adulthood (Johnson et al., 1999; Kasen, Cohen, Skodol, Johnson, & Brook, 1999). Adolescent Cluster B disorders were also associated with sustained elevations in conflict between romantic partners from age 17 to 27 (Chen et al., 2004) and had an inverse association with intimacy as young people entered adulthood (Crawford, Cohen, Johnson, Sneed, & Brook, 2004).

These prospective findings make it clear that Histrionic PD in adolescence represents a long-term risk for psychopathology and interpersonal impairment. However, there remain many questions about the construct validity of this and other PD constructs in the *DSM* (First et al., 2002). Because empirical support is weakest for defining PDs as categorically defined disorders, we recommend that the *DSM-V* specifies Axis I and Axis II disorders as dimensional constructs instead. At present there is a debate about whether diagnostic constructs should be transformed into dimensional scales based on existing *DSM* criteria or if other dimensional models, including the DAPP, should be adopted as a more accurate and clinically useful alternative (Widiger & Simonsen, 2005). Rather than selecting one approach and rejecting the other, we recommend that the *DSM-V* introduce dimensional definitions in a manner that allows the field to transition from familiar but flawed Axis II constructs to newer alternatives that have better empirical support.

Based on the many redefinitions and reconceptualizations of hysteria that have occurred over the centuries, it is important to remember that our current approach to defining PD will inevitably change. We hope it will also improve as we gain a clearer understanding of its etiology and developmental course.

REFERENCES

Agrawal, H. R., Gunderson, J., Holmes, B. M., & Lyons-Ruth, K. (2004). Attachment studies with borderline patients: A review. *Harvard Review of Psychiatry, 12*, 94–104.

Alam, C. N., & Mersky, H. (1992). The development of the hysterical personality. *History of Psychiatry, 3*, 135–165.

American Psychiatric Association. (1994). *Diagnostic and statistical manual of mental disorders* (4th ed.). Washington, DC: Author.

American Psychiatric Association. (2000). *Diagnostic and statistical manual of mental disorders* (4th ed., text rev.). Washington, DC: Author.

Bagge, C. L., & Trull, T. J. (2003). DAPP-BQ: Factor structure and relations to personality disorder symptoms in a non-clinical sample. *Journal of Personality Disorders, 17*(1), 19–32.

Bakermans-Kranenburg, M. J., van IJzendoorn, M. H., Schuengel, C., & Bokhorst, C. L. (2004). The importance of shared environment in infant-father attachment: A behavioral genetic study of the Attachment Q-Sort. *Journal of Family Psychology, 18*(3), 545–549.

Bartholomew, K., & Horowitz, L. (1991). Attachment styles among young adults: A test of a four-category model. *Journal of Personality and Social Psychology, 61*, 226–244.

Bartholomew, K., Kwong, M. J., & Hart, S. D. (2001). Attachment. In W. J. Livesley (Ed.), *Handbook of personality disorders* (pp. 196–230). New York: Guilford Press.

Beck, A. T., Freeman, A., Davis, D. D., and Associates. (2004). *Cognitive therapy of personality disorders* (2nd ed.). New York: Guilford Press.

Becker, D. F., Grilo, C. M., Edell, W. S., & McGlashan, T. H. (2000). Co-morbidity of borderline personality disorder with other personality disorders in hospitalized adolescents and adults. *American Journal of Psychiatry, 157,* 2011–2016.

Belsky, J., & Pasco Fearon, R. M. (2002). Early attachment security, subsequent maternal sensitivity, and later child development: Does continuity in development depend on continuity in caregiving? *Attachment and Human Development, 4,* 361–387.

Berkson, J. (1946). Limitations of the application of fourfold table analysis to hospital data. *Biometrics, 2,* 47–53.

Bernstein, D. P., Cohen, P., Velez, C. N., Schwab-Stone, M., Siever, L. J., & Shinsato, L. (1993). Prevalence and stability of the *DSM-III-R* personality disorders in a community-based survey of adolescents. *American Journal of Psychiatry, 150,* 1237–1243.

Bezirganian, S., Cohen, P., & Brook, J. S. (1993). The impact of mother-child interaction on the development of borderline personality disorder. *American Journal of Psychiatry, 150,* 1836–1842.

Blacker, K. H., & Tupin, J. P. (1991). Hysteria and hysterical structures: Developmental and social theories. In M. J. Horowitz (Ed.), *Hysterical personality style and the histrionic personality disorders* (pp. 17–66). New York: Aronson.

Bleiberg, E. (2001). *Treating personality disorders in children and adolescents: A relational approach.* New York: Guilford Press.

Bokhorst, C. L., Bakermans-Kranenburg, M. J., Fearon, R. M. P., van IJzendoorn, M. H., Fonagy, P., & Schuengel, C. (2003). The importance of shared environment in mother-infant attachment security: A behavioral genetic study. *Child-Development, 74*(6), 1769–1782.

Bowlby, J. (1969). *Attachment and loss: Vol. 1. Attachment.* New York: Basic Books.

Bowlby, J. (1973). *Attachment and loss: Vol. 2. Separation.* New York: Basic Books.

Bowlby, J. (1980). *Attachment and loss: Vol. 3. Loss, sadness, and depression.* New York: Basic Books.

Bowlby, J. (1988). *A secure base: Clinical implications of attachment theory.* New York: Basic Books.

Brennan, K. A., & Shaver, P. R. (1998). Attachment styles and personality disorders: Their connection to each other and parental divorce, parental death, and perception of parental caregiving. *Journal of Personality, 66,* 835–878.

Bretherton, I., & Munholland, K. A. (1999). Internal working models in attachment relationships: A construct revisited. In J. Cassidy & P. R. Shaver (Eds.), *Handbook of attachment: Theory, research, and clinical applications* (pp. 89–114). New York: Guilford Press.

Brisch, K. H. (2002). *Treating attachment disorders.* New York: Guilford Press.

Brussoni, M. J., Jang, K. L., Livesley, W. J., & MacBeth, T. M. (2000). Genetic and environmental influences on adult attachment styles. *Personal Relationships, 7,* 283–289.

Cassidy, J., & Kobak, R. R. (1988). Avoidance and its relation to other defensive processes. In J. Belsky & T. Nezworski (Eds.), *Clinical implications of attachment* (pp. 300–323). Hillsdale, NJ: Erlbaum.

Chen, H., Cohen, P., Johnson, J. G., Kasen, S., Sneed, J., & Crawford, T. N. (2004). Adolescent personality disorders and conflict with romantic partners during the transition to adulthood. *Journal of Personality Disorders, 18*(6), 507–525.

Cohen, P., Chen, H., Crawford, T. N., Gordon, K., & Brook, J. S. (in press). Personality disorders in early adolescence and the development of later substance use disorders in the general population [Special issue]. *Drug and Alcohol Addiction.*

Cohen, P., & Cohen, J. (1996). *Life values and adolescent mental health.* Mahwah, NJ: Erlbaum.

Cohen, P., & Crawford, T. (2005). Developmental issues. In J. M. Oldham, A. E. Skodol, & D. Bender (Eds.), *Textbook of personality disorders* (pp. 171–185). Washington, DC: American Psychiatric Publishing.

Cohen, P., Crawford, T. N., Johnson, J. G., & Kasen, S. (2005). The Children in the Community Study of developmental course of personality disorder. *Journal of Personality Disorders, 19*(5), 466–486.

Coolidge, F. L. (1998). *Coolidge Personality and Neuropsychological Inventory for Children manual: CPNI.* Colorado Springs, CO: Author.

Coolidge, F. L., Thede, L. L., & Jang, K. L. (2001). Heritability of personality disorders in childhood: A preliminary investigation. *Journal of Personality Disorders, 15*(1), 33–40.

Costello, A. J., Edelbrock, C. S., Dulcan, M. K., Kalas, R., & Klaric, S. H. (1984). *Testing of the NIMH Diagnostic Interview Schedule for Children (DISC) in a clinical population* (Final report to the Center for Epidemiological Studies, National Institute for Mental Health). Pittsburgh, PA: University of Pittsburgh.

Crawford, T. N., & Cohen, P. (2006). *Adolescent Personality Disorder Scales.* New York: New York State Psychiatric Institute.

Crawford, T. N., Cohen, P., & Brook, J. S. (2001a). Dramatic erratic personality disorder symptoms: Pt. I. Continuity from early adolescence into adulthood. *Journal of Personality Disorders, 15,* 319–335.

Crawford, T. N., Cohen, P., & Brook, J. S. (2001b). Dramatic erratic personality disorder symptoms: Pt. II. Developmental pathways form early adolescence to adulthood. *Journal of Personality Disorders, 15,* 336–350.

Crawford, T. N., Cohen, P., Johnson, J. G., Kasen, S., First, M. B., Gordon, K., et al. (2005). Self-reported personality disorder in the Children in the Community sample: Convergent validity and prospective validity in late adolescence and adulthood. *Journal of Personality Disorders, 19*(1), 30–52.

Crawford, T. N., Cohen, P., Johnson, J. G., Sneed, J. R., & Brook, J. S. (2004). The course and psychosocial correlates of personality disorder symptoms in adolescence: Erikson's developmental theory revisited. *Journal of Youth and Adolescence, 33,* 373–387.

Crawford, T. N., Livesley, W. J., Jang, K. L., Shaver, P. R., Cohen, P., & Ganiban, J. (2007). Insecure attachment and personality disorder: A twin study of adults. *European Journal of Personality, 21,* 191–208.

Crawford, T. N., Shaver, P. R., Cohen, P., Pilkonis, P. A., Gillath, O., & Kasen, S. (2006). Self-reported attachment, interpersonal aggression, and personality disorder in a prospective community sample of adolescents and adults. *Journal of Personality Disorders, 20,* 331–353.

Davis, R. D., Woodward, M., Goncalves, A., Meagher, S. E., & Millon, T. (1999). Treatment planning and outcome in adults: The Millon Clinical Multiaxial Inventory-III. In M. E. Maruish (Ed.), *The use of psychological testing for treatment planning and outcomes assessment* (2nd ed., pp. 1051–1081). Mahwah, NJ: Erlbaum.

Eisenberg, N., Fabes, R. A., Guthrie, I. K., & Reiser, M. (2000). Dispositional emotionality and regulation: Their role in predicting quality of social functioning. *Journal of Personality and Social Psychology, 78,* 136–157.

Eisenberg, N., & Morris, A. S. (2002). Children's emotion regulation. In R. Kail (Ed.), *Advances in child development and behavior* (Vol. 30, pp. 90–229). Amsterdam: Academic Press.

Ellenberger, H. (1970). *The discovery of the unconscious: The history and evolution of dynamic psychiatry.* New York: Basic Books.

Erikson, E. H. (1968). *Identity: Youth and crisis.* New York: Norton.

First, M. B., Bell, C. B., Cuthbert, B., Krystal, J. H., Malison, R., Offord, D. R., et al. (2002). Personality disorders: A research agenda for addressing crucial gaps in DSM. In D. J. Kupfer, M. B. First, & D. A. Regier (Eds.), *A research agenda for DSM-V* (pp. 123–199). Washington, DC: American Psychiatric Press.

Fonagy, P., Steele, H., & Steele, M. (1991). Intergenerational patterns of attachment: Maternal representations during pregnancy and subsequent infant-mother attachments. *Child Development, 62,* 891–905.

Gough, H. G. (1957). *The California Psychological Inventory.* Palo Alto, CA: Consulting Psychologists Press.

Greenberg, M. (1999). Attachment and psychopathology in childhood. In J. Cassidy & P. R. Shaver (Eds.), *Handbook of attachment: Theory, research, and clinical applications* (pp. 469–496). New York: Guilford Press.

Harpur, T. J., & Hare, R. D. (1994). Assessment of psychopathy as a function of age. *Journal of Abnormal Psychology, 103,* 604–609.

Hyler, S. E., Rieder, R., Spitzer, R., & Williams, J. (1982). *The Personality Diagnostic Questionnaire* (PDQ). New York: New York State Psychiatric Institute.

Jackson, D. N. (1974). *Personality research form.* Goshen, NY: Research Psychologists Press.

Jang, K. L. (2005). *The behavioral genetics of psychopathology: A clinical guide.* Mahwah, NJ: Erlbaum.

Jang, K. L., & Vernon, P. A. (2001). Genetics. In W. J. Livesley (Ed.), *Handbook of personality disorders* (pp. 177–195). New York: Guilford Press.

Johnson, J. G., Cohen, P., Kasen, S., & Brook, J. S. (2005). Personality disorder traits associated with risk for unipolar depression during middle adulthood. *Psychiatry Research, 136,* 113–121.

Johnson, J. G., Cohen, P., Kasen, S., Skodol, A. E., Hamagami, F., & Brook, J. S. (2000). Age-related change in personality disorder trait levels between early adolescence and adulthood: A community-based longitudinal investigation. *Acta Psychiatrica Scandinavica, 102,* 265–275.

Johnson, J. G., Cohen, P., Skodol, A. E., Oldham, J. M., Kasen, S., & Brook, J. S. (1999). Personality disorders in adolescence and risk of major mental disorders and suicidality during adulthood. *Archives of General Psychiatry, 56,* 805–811.

Kasen, S., Cohen, P., Skodol, A. E., Johnson, J. G., & Brook, J. S. (1999). Influence of child and adolescent psychiatric disorders on young adult personality disorder. *American Journal of Psychiatry, 156,* 1529–1535.

Kernberg, P. F., Weiner, A. S., & Bardenstein, K. K. (2000). *Personality disorders in children and adolescents.* New York: Basic Books.

Kogan, L. S., Smith, J., & Jenkins, S. (1977). Ecological validity of indicator data as predictors of survey findings. *Journal of Social Science Research, 1,* 117–132.

Livesley, W. J., & Jackson, D. N. (in press). *Manual for the Dimensional Assessment of Personality Problems—Basic Questionnaire (DAPP-BQ).* London, Ontario, Canada: Research Psychologist Press.

Livesley, W. J., Jang, K. L., Jackson, D. N., & Vernon, P. A. (1993). Genetic and environmental contributions to dimensions of personality disorder. *American Journal of Psychiatry, 150,* 1826–1831.

Livesley, W. J., Jang, K. L., & Vernon, P. A. (1998). The phenotypic and genetic architecture of traits delineating personality disorder. *Archives of General Psychiatry, 55,* 941–948.

Livesley, W. J., Schroeder, M. L., & Jackson, D. N. (1990). Dependent personality disorder and attachment problems. *Journal of Personality Disorders, 4,* 131–140.

McCloskey, L. A., & Bailey, J. A. (2000). The intergenerational transmission of risk for child sexual abuse. *Journal of Interpersonal Violence, 15,* 1019–1035.

Mikulincer, M., Shaver, P. R., & Pereg, D. (2003). Attachment theory and affect regulation: The dynamics, development, and cognitive consequences of attachment-related strategies. *Motivation and Emotion, 27,* 77–102.

Millon, T. (1990). *Toward a new personology: An evolutionary model.* New York: Wiley.

Nakash-Eisikovits, O., Dutra, L., & Westen, D. (2002). Relationship between attachment patterns and personality pathology in adolescents. *Journal of the American Academy of Child and Adolescent Psychiatry, 41,* 1111–1123.

Nestadt, G., Romanoski, A. J., Chahal, R., Merchant, A., Folstein, M. F., Gruenberg, E. M., et al. (1990). An epidemiological study of histrionic personality disorder. *Psychological Medicine, 20,* 413–422.

Oates, R. K., Tebbutt, J., Swanston, H., Lynch, D. L., & O'Toole, B. I. (1998). Prior childhood sexual abuse in mothers of sexually abused children. *Child Abuse and Neglect, 22,* 1113–1118.

O'Connor, T. G., & Croft, C. M. (2001). A twin study of attachment in preschool children. *Child Development, 72,* 1501–1511.

Plomin, R., DeFries, J. C., McClearn, G. E., & McGuffin, P. (2001). *Behavioral genetics* (4th ed.). New York: Freeman.

Rothbart, M. K., & Bates, J. E. (1998). Temperament. In W. Damon & N. Eisenberg (Eds.), *Handbook of child psychology: Social, emotional, and personality development* (5th ed., pp. 105–176). New York: Wiley.

Rutter, M., Dunn, J., Plomin, R., Simonoff, E., Pickles, A., Maughan, B., et al. (1997). Integrating nature and nurture: Implications of person-environment correlations and interactions for developmental psychopathology. *Development and Psychopathology, 9,* 335–364.

Shaver, P. R., Collins, N. L., & Clark, C. L. (1996). Attachment styles and internal working models of self and relationship partners. In G. J. O. Fletcher & J. Fitness (Eds.), *Knowledge structures in close relationships: A social psychological approach* (pp. 25–61). Mahwah, NJ: Erlbaum.

Skodol, A. E. (2005). Manifestations, clinical diagnosis, and comorbidity. In J. M. Oldham, A. E. Skodol, & D. Bender (Eds.), *Textbook of personality disorders* (pp. 57–87). Washington, DC: American Psychiatric Publishing.

Slade, A. (1999). Attachment theory and research: Implications for the theory and practice of individual psychotherapy with adults. In J. Cassidy & P. R. Shaver (Eds.), *Handbook of attachment: Theory, research, and clinical applications* (pp. 575–594). New York: Guilford Press.

Smith, G. M., & Fogg, C. P. (1979). Psychological predictors of early use, late use, and nonuse of marijuana among teenage students. In

D. B. Kandel (Ed.), *Longitudinal research on drug use* (pp. 101–113). Washington, DC: Hemisphere-Wiley.

Solomon, J., & George, C. (1999). *Attachment disorganization.* New York: Guilford Press.

Sperling, M. B., & Lyons, L. S. (1994). Representations of attachment and psychotherapeutic change. In M. B. Sperling & W. H. Berman (Eds.), *Attachment in adults: Clinical and developmental perspectives* (pp. 331–347). New York: Guilford Press.

Stein, J. A., Newcomb, M. D., & Bentler, P. M. (1986). Stability and change in personality: A longitudinal study from early adolescence to young adulthood. *Journal of Research in Personality, 20,* 276–291.

Veith, I. (1965). *Hysteria: The history of a disease.* Chicago: University of Chicago Press.

West, M., & Keller, A. (1994). Psychotherapy strategies for insecure attachment in personality disorders. In M. B. Sperling & W. H. Berman (Eds.), *Attachment in adults: Clinical and developmental perspectives* (pp. 313–330). New York: Guilford Press.

Westen, D., Shedler, J., Glass, S., & Martens, A. (2003). Personality diagnoses in adolescence: *DSM-IV* Axis II diagnoses and an empirically derived alternative. *American Journal of Psychiatry, 160,* 952–966.

Widiger, T. A., & Simonsen, E. (2005). Alternative dimensional models of personality disorder: Finding a common ground. *Journal of Personality Disorders, 19*(2), 110–130.

Zanarini, M. C., Williams, A. A., Lewis, R. E., Reich, R. B., Vera, S. C., Marino, M. F., et al. (1997). Reported pathological childhood experiences associated with the development of borderline personality disorder. *American Journal of Psychiatry, 154*(8), 1101–1116.

CHAPTER 14

Obsessive-Compulsive Personality Disorder: Developmental Risk Factors and Clinical Implications

MARTIN E. FRANKLIN, JOHN C. PIACENTINI,
and CARLA D'OLIO

As PART of the routine screening procedure for our clinical and research programs for pediatric Obsessive-Compulsive Disorder (OCD), one of the first orders of business is to ask the parent who has called to describe the child's symptoms. Once these symptoms have been described, the telephone screener then must make a judgment as to whether the parent's description is in the ballpark with respect to the symptom picture sounding like obsessions and compulsions. Assuming that the description passes this initial test, the caller is then scheduled to bring the child to the clinic for a formal diagnostic interview for OCD and for related problems. Most of the time the trained screener has a relatively easy time determining whether the symptoms fall under the diagnostic umbrella of OCD (e.g., obsessions about germs and associated hand-washing rituals). In support of this claim, the rate of failure to diagnose a patient as actually having OCD following this telephone screening procedure was less than 10% for the Pediatric OCD Treatment Study (Franklin, Foa, & March, 2003; POTS Team, 2004)—but of course there are exceptions. In our 2 decades of interviewing children and adolescents for entry into OCD clinical and research programs, one of the diagnostic boundary issues where we have found this initial screening process to yield a good number of false positives is when it comes to ruling out symptoms of Obsessive-Compulsive Personality Disorder (OCPD). This may strike some readers as somewhat curious, given that it is not customary to diagnose youth with Axis II psychopathology and that some in the field have come to believe that Axis II psychopathology is not prominent in children and adolescents, yet we encounter these traits on a somewhat regular basis when doing our work with OCD. It is this overlap that made the opportunity to write about the development of OCPD in youth intriguing to us, and we have endeavored here to discuss the early signs of a stable interpersonal style characterized by inflexibility, inappropriate attention to detail, and so on, that we have encountered it in clinical practice.

In this chapter, we explore the symptoms of OCPD from a developmental perspective, first pointing out where they do and do not resemble OCD and other disorders in which inflexibility can be central, such as OCD and Asperger's Disorder, then consider how symptoms of OCPD may emerge over the course of development. We focus a good deal of our discussion on what has come to be known as "maladaptive perfectionism," which, although it does not appear to be a risk factor specific to the development of OCPD, is certainly a fundamental part of the OCPD style that can later seriously compromise the individual's ability to function effectively in the world and get along well with other people. Convergent with the broader theme of this book, it is our belief that OCPD symptoms do not emerge wholly formed in adulthood without significant roots in childhood and adolescence; we also discuss in some detail how some of the symptoms of OCPD represent desired traits in youth and are thus reinforced by parents, teachers, coaches, and peers. Ever the interventionists, we also summarize the literature on treatment of OCPD and make some specific suggestions for possible earlier intervention strategies that may prove useful in combating maladaptive perfectionism, which we view as a key risk factor for the development of this often debilitating interpersonal style.

OBSESSIVE-COMPULSIVE PERSONALITY DISORDER: DIAGNOSTIC CONSIDERATIONS

A diagnosis of OCPD requires at least four of the following:

1. Is preoccupied with details, rules, lists, order, organization, or schedules to the extent that the major point of the activity is lost.
2. Shows perfectionism that interferes with task completion.
3. Is excessively devoted to work and productivity to the exclusion of leisure activities and friendships (not accounted for by economic necessity).
4. Is overconscientious, scrupulous, and inflexible about matters of morality, ethics, or values (not accounted for by cultural or religious identification).
5. Is unable to discard worn-out or worthless objects even when they have no sentimental value.
6. Is reluctant to delegate tasks or to work with others unless they submit to exactly his or her way of doing things.

7. Adopts a miserly spending style toward both self and others; money is viewed as something to be hoarded for future catastrophes.

8. Shows rigidity and stubbornness.

As elaborated on in the fourth edition, text revision of the *Diagnostic and Statistical Manual of Mental Disorders* (*DSM-IV-TR*; American Psychiatric Association, 2000, p. 671), individuals with OCPD will often make considerable attempts to maintain control of their day-to-day lives via careful attention to rules, procedures, lists, and so on, often without taking into consideration the effect this may have on other people. As is the case for most of the *DSM-IV* disorders, a diagnosis of OCPD also requires that these preoccupations are serious enough to cut across multiple domains; that is, they are not specific to only certain settings, such as military school or a home in which adherence to rigid rules is required to keep the peace. Individuals with OCPD are likely to expend a great deal of energy paying extraordinary attention to details; they are excessively careful and spend time repeatedly checking for mistakes. With this last symptom in particular it is important to determine whether obsessions about harm are present, as this may better fall under the OCD diagnosis. If these individuals do make a mistake, they are exceptionally self-critical, overemphasizing the magnitude of their error. The interpersonal aspect of OCPD is often demonstrated when others make mistakes: Individuals with OCPD are judgmental and harsh in response to others' seeming lack of care about the quality of what they do. When such opinions are shared with the person who made the mistake, conflict may result, especially among classmates, siblings, and other youth who may not appreciate this seemingly extreme feedback.

As indicated by *DSM-IV*, individuals with OCPD are extremely perfectionistic and adhere to unrealistically high standards for performance (criterion 1). Due to the value they place on these often unattainable standards, these individuals are wrought with anxiety and distress and often unable to complete projects because every part must be perfect (criterion 2).

In addition, individuals with OCPD are often excessively dedicated to work and productivity and will typically exclude relationships and leisure activities in the pursuit of the highest levels of productivity (criterion 3). Individuals with OCPD often feel as though they cannot take time out to spend with family or friends or to participate in activities for fun; they may put off vacations or time off due to this drive for productivity and dedication to work, and they often judge others who do not hold such standards as inferior. Individuals with OCPD will be overly conscientious, scrupulous, and inflexible regarding issues such as morality, ethics, and values (criterion 4). They will adhere to strict moral and ethical rules and codes and, perhaps of greater significance, often demand that others follow these same standards. These individuals follow rules and regulations in a literal way and will not allow flexibility in adherence to these rules. In addition, they tend to be unable to discard old or worthless objects (criterion 5), often due to a fear that they never know when they may need them. Individuals with OCPD are often reluctant to delegate tasks to others, which stems from an insistence that everything be done their way (criterion 6). These individuals may refuse help from others because they fear that no one else can do things correctly, and when delegating tasks, they will give thorough, detailed instructions in hopes that others will conform to their way of completing projects. Individuals with OCPD will often be stingy and tightly monitor their money, being sure to save for an imagined future catastrophe (criterion 7). Overall, individuals with OCPD are rigid and stubborn (criterion 8). They often work very hard to do things in what they perceive is the correct way and ignore suggestions and ideas from others.

Grilo, Shea, et al. (2004) investigated the diagnostic efficiency of criteria for OCPD and found that the two most common criteria OCPD individuals met were "reluctance to delegate" and being "rigid and stubborn"; both occurred in 47% of participants. In addition, 43% met criteria for perfectionism. These and other criteria were used as indices for predicting the diagnosis of OCPD at a 24-month follow-up as well. The criterion "preoccupied with details" showed the highest predictive utility for OCPD diagnosis (41% of participants who met this criterion at initial evaluation also met diagnosis for OCPD at follow-up). When Grilo et al. examined the positive and negative predictive probabilities of the OCPD diagnostic criteria jointly, both "rigid and stubborn" (36% of participants who met this criterion also met diagnosis for OCPD) and "reluctant to delegate" (37% of participants who met this criterion also met diagnosis for OCPD) were particularly useful in correctly diagnosing OCPD at 24-month assessment. Individuals with OCPD also tend to plan far ahead and are inflexible and unwilling to make changes if circumstances require flexibility. They are excessively concerned with their own points of view and are unlikely to acknowledge the viewpoints of others, yet they do not recognize this characteristic as maladaptive or negative. The effect of this style on others is often profound and yet is rarely taken into account by individuals with OCPD when opportunities to exercise flexibility arise.

Because personality disorders are, by definition, a result of "long-lasting, stable patterns and characteristics" in individuals, it stands to reason that there will be signs and symptoms of OCPD characteristics throughout childhood and into adolescence. Indeed, the criteria for OCPD suggest a pervasive pattern beginning by early adulthood, suggesting that in at least some cases the pattern is evident *before* early adulthood. Exploring the nature of these characteristics in youth is the central goal of the chapter. In terms of the characteristics of OCPD that have received the most empirical attention to date, perfectionism stands out, especially what has come to be known as maladaptive perfectionism. Although perfectionism is considered a core symptom of the disorder, we have also come to view it as a possible risk factor for the development of the other criteria. We discuss the development of perfectionism and maladaptive perfectionism in youth, following our presentation of a clinical vignette that we hope will give the reader a better sense of what OCPD symptoms may look and feel like in youth.

DESCRIPTION OF OBSESSIVE-COMPULSIVE PERSONALITY DISORDER IN ADOLESCENCE

In this section we provide a detailed clinical vignette in which an adolescent being interviewed for one of our OCD programs describes and demonstrates symptoms that are more convergent with the diagnosis of OCPD. We chose this as the context for a description of these characteristics in youth because this is the primary setting in which we have encountered these symptoms, and also because distinguishing OCD from OCPD is an important clinical task that has implications for treatment and for the expectation of treatment outcome. We take issue with the *DSM-IV* language that describes this particular differential as "usually easily" distinguished (American Psychiatric Association, 2000, p. 671), as that has not been our experience, especially in youth where personality disorder diagnosis is rarely made clinically and hence the referral questions are often couched in terms of evaluation and treatment of OCD. It is also the case in pediatric OCD that the clear intrusive and ego-dystonic obsessions that can make this differential easier are not as evident as they are in adults. This developmental difference most likely reflects the clinical observation that obsessional content typically becomes more elaborate over the course of the illness (e.g., Rapoport, 1991). Moreover, when the somewhat common pediatric OCD subtype of "Not Just Right" OCD (e.g., Coles, Heimberg, Frost, & Rheaume, 2003; Coles, Heimberg, Frost, & Steketee, 2005) is taken into consideration, the differentiation between OCD and OCPD symptoms in youth becomes even more difficult. Our case example illustrates these issues plainly. To disguise the identity of the youth we have encountered in this context, we have intentionally created a composite in which the case details have been altered to protect confidentiality but the tenor of the discussions has been left intact to give the reader a clinical feel for the interpersonal style and symptoms of the patient. It should be noted that although OCD and OCPD can co-occur, the extant epidemiological literature suggests that this is not common.

Case Illustration

Julianne was a 15-year-old female who had been referred to one of our OCD treatment programs by a local school psychologist who had been asked to consult on the case due to Julianne's increasing difficulties in completing homework assignments despite clear academic competence in the subject matter. During the initial telephone screening process, Julianne's mother (Alice) reported that the main problems she saw were her daughter's tendency to do academic work to the exclusion of almost all other activities; inflexibility with respect to schedules, time, and family activities; her unwillingness to discard old notes and tests from previous years of classes; and her refusal to allow other people to help her when she got behind on chores or academic work. These problems had increased significantly since she began her freshman year at an academically challenging high school, to the point where in the past several months she had broken off all ties with her grade school friends and had been involved in several disagreements with teachers over grades and homework assignments. More recently, Julianne had become unwilling to turn in homework assignments that hadn't been completed "thoroughly enough."

As is our regular practice when screening for OCD and other psychiatric symptoms, the intake clinician met Julianne and her mother together, but directed questions primarily to Julianne given her age (Piacentini, March, & Franklin, 2006). After the initial greeting and orientation to the intake process, the intake clinician began by reviewing the telephone screening information with Julianne, which prompted the following exchange.

THERAPIST: So from what I gather, Julianne, it's been difficult recently for you to complete your homework in a way that you feel it's been done thoroughly, even though you're spending more and more time on academics.

JULIANNE: Well, one could look at it that way, but then again there are other perspectives.

THERAPIST: What's your perspective?

JULIANNE: My perspective is that I attend one of the most prestigious and academically challenging high schools in the region, and that as the semester moves forward the work requires more and more time and effort to do it all properly.

THERAPIST: So the workload increases over time, but the demand for doing it well doesn't change?

JULIANNE: Yes, there are cumulative effects over the course of the semester, and my mother and father don't seem to understand that in order to continue to meet the high standards set by the teachers and to meet my own standards that this level of effort is simply what it takes to achieve.

THERAPIST: So you're not really seeing the devotion to school above all else as problematic?

JULIANNE: No of course not, why would I?

ALICE: But Julianne, you haven't seen your friends from last year in months, and you've spent the last three weekends working morning, noon, and night up in your room.

JULIANNE: Well, Mother, those friends for the most part chose other paths, and they simply don't shoulder the same weight of academic responsibilities that I do. I just can't afford to take the time out from my studies to see them, and even when I run into them it seems there is less and less to say.

ALICE: Of course there's less to say, Julianne, because you haven't had any shared experiences with them since last summer.

JULIANNE: I just don't understand why you don't see my devotion to my school-work as laudable—most parents would be proud that their child was taking school seriously and thinking ahead about the future.

ALICE: We are proud of you, dear, but we remembered you as being happier in your old school, less preoccupied with work all the time, more willing to relax.

JULIANNE: But there is no time to relax if I'm going to remain at the top of this class—these are the very best and brightest students in the whole city, every-one was a grade school valedictorian or academic award winner of some kind—if I let my effort slide then my class rank will slide along with it, which will compromise my future goals. They're goals we've had together, Mom, and now it sounds like you are trying to say that I'm wrong for trying to achieve them.

ALICE: That's not what I'm saying, Julianne, but I am trying to point out that the way you're coming at the schoolwork might even prevent you from achieving your goals.

JULIANNE: How so?

ALICE: Well, you haven't been turning in your homework assignments recently, and presumably you'll lose some points for being late.

JULIANNE: Points that I'll make up for doing the assignment properly. Plus, Mom, you wouldn't even believe how many of my classmates hand in slovenly, half-written material simply to get it done on time—all but a few of us take these assignments seriously, and we still wind up with the better grades. The teach-ers don't take it seriously enough, if you ask me—some of the people who hand in this low-quality work still wind up on the honor roll somehow. I wish they valued the quality more, but then again, it's not just their standards I'm trying to meet anyway.

From this exchange it becomes evident quickly that the patient does not view the amount of effort she is putting into her academic work as excessive, nor does she be-lieve that it is acceptable to turn in homework that has not been completed thor-oughly. In cases like this it is important to examine whether the student has any rereading or rewriting rituals that are adding to the length of the assignments, or whether any learning problems might account for the seemingly inordinate amount of time it takes her to study and complete assigned work. In this case, no previously identified learning problems were reported on the Conners-March Developmental Questionnaire (Conners & March, 1996), and thus the clinician pressed on to learn more about how study time and homework assignments were being approached. It is also clear from the transcript that Julianne's style of interaction, vocabulary, and the seriousness with which she takes the discussion is not characteristic of what most adolescents her age might sound like. Clearly she is a highly intelligent young person, but the interactional style is also more telling.

THERAPIST: So I gather, Julianne, that you don't see the devotion to schoolwork as problematic?

JULIANNE: No, of course not, and I don't know why anyone else would. After all, isn't the point of going to a school like this to do your very best to excel?

THERAPIST: It does sound like there's an emphasis on academic excellence there.

JULIANNE: Yes, there is—at our school the real stars are the people who achieve in the classroom, not those who waste half of their time running after a stupid ball on a field.

THERAPIST: So the strong emphasis on academic achievement was part of the appeal for you?

JULIANNE: It was—I was tired of being teased at my old school for taking my work seriously, and now I am in an academic environment where I don't have to hide my ambitions any more. I do well, I want to do well, and I want that to be important to the people who run the school, the teachers, and to my fellow students as well.

THERAPIST: It sounds like it is there, although it also sounds like there are some kids in the school who don't come at it with quite as much gusto as you do.

JULIANNE: There are a few who work as hard as I do, but the majority are willing to settle for good enough, which honestly has surprised me somewhat. I thought everyone would prioritize schoolwork the way that I do, and that hasn't really turned out to be the case. More so than in my elementary school, certainly, but not as much as I expected.

THERAPIST: Can I ask you some questions about how you are studying? For instance, do you find yourself having to reread words or sentences over and over again because of fears that you missed something, or because you're afraid that something bad might happen if you don't?

JULIANNE: No, neither of those. I studied for a history test yesterday, and what I usually do is I read the assigned material first while taking notes, then I'll review my notes for at least 15 minutes, then return to the assigned material again for a second pass to clarify anything that I wasn't sure about or to commit important facts to memory. After I have completed that, I then answer the questions that are included in the chapter itself, go over all of those answers and, assuming that I got them all correct, will then go back again to read the summaries before I move on to the next task. It has nothing to do with fear that bad things are going to happen, or having to reread because I'm not sure—it's simply what a good student should do if he or she wants to master the material.

THERAPIST: How long might that process take for a given subject?

JULIANNE: It depends on the amount of material, but usually three or four hours. That may also be affected by the complexity of the material, too—sometimes it can take twice that amount of time if the chapter is dense.

ALICE: But you didn't tell the doctor when that history test is—tell him when the test is.

JULIANNE: Three weeks from tomorrow.

ALICE: And your cousins were over all the way from Delaware last night, and you barely took the time to say hello to them.

JULIANNE: I did say hello, and we did interact for a few minutes. But what you don't know is that I have two other tests that same week, and if I don't get my preparation in now for history I will be unable to give it the time that it needs in order to do well.

ALICE: You also didn't say that you'd spent another several hours last weekend preparing for the same history test.

JULIANNE: True, but that was reviewing the *class* notes, which is entirely different and also an essential task, since the class material and the book material are not identical.

ALICE: (Exasperated) Now do you see what I mean?

JULIANNE: What, that your daughter is trying to do her best? Mom, why is that such a problem for you? Would you rather I stay out late at night drinking beer on the street corners?

In this exchange the interpersonal effects and costs of Julianne's style become more evident, demonstrated by examples of her essentially ignoring visiting cousins to study for a history test that was 3 weeks away and her considerable inflexibility when her mother pointed out that her exclusive devotion to school may not be a positive trait. The tendency to judge others who do not hold the same exacting standards is also evident in her discussion of some of her classmates' work habits. Her insight is quite poor, yet she does not appear to have obsessions in the formal sense, which are defined as unwelcome or intrusive thoughts or images, so the diagnosis of OCD with poor insight does not appear to be appropriate. Julianne is quite convinced that she is doing exactly what she needs to do to achieve her academic goals, although these goals may not be especially well formed beyond "Excel, and stay at the top of the class." It is likely that the challenging school setting she is in provides ample reinforcement for the perfectionistic style and for her devotion to academics, and that, as is often the case when students are doing their work and maintaining excellent grades, a collective blind eye may be turned to the interpersonal costs associated with this style.

By this point in the interview, it was becoming more clear to the clinician that Axis I OCD was not likely to be the final diagnosis and that the interview time would be more productively spent examining the other symptoms of OCPD that had not as yet been discussed. In our clinics we often use the Structured Clinical Interview for DSM-IV Personality Disorders (SCID II) to conduct this assessment. From this interview and from her mother's additional input it became increasingly clear that Julianne not only likely met criterion 1 (preoccupation with details), 2 (perfectionism that interferes with task completion), 3 (excessive devotion to work), and 4 (overconscientiousness), but that she was hoarding old academic work in case she needed to refer back to her previous years' classwork (criterion 5), was extremely reluctant to delegate tasks at home or at school unless others followed her rigid set of rules in carrying out these tasks (criterion 6), and showed rigidity and stubbornness about sticking to her preset study and personal task lists (criterion 8).

Continuing the interview, the clinician did not identify any learning disorder symptoms that were contributing to the amount of time spent studying; her methods were likely excessive and inefficient, but Julianne was clear that doing less than this would constitute "laziness," which she would declare is a trait that good students should not display. Further discussion with Julianne focused on social aspects of her school and academic life, as it is important to rule out Asperger's Disorder when diagnosing OCPD. The clinician had already decided that this was an unlikely explanation for Julianne's symptoms because her eye contact and demeanor during the interview suggested a socially skilled, if not polished, young woman, at least until the interview turned to challenging her beliefs that her devotion to academics was necessary and justifiable. Moreover, her mother's description of Julianne's social history suggested none of the social difficulties, deficits in reading nonverbal cues, inability to make friendships and to reciprocate socially, and other skill problems that are characteristic of Asperger's Disorder. This is not to say that Julianne's OCPD symptoms were not having a negative effect on her friendships, but rather that she still had the capacity to relate socially to others and could do so quite effectively when she deemed the interactions sufficiently relevant.

DIFFERENTIATING OBSESSIVE-COMPULSIVE PERSONALITY DISORDER FROM ASPERGER'S DISORDER

Asperger's Disorder as defined by the *DSM-IV* includes severe social interaction impairment, as manifested by impairment in the use and interpretation of nonverbal behaviors; failure to maintain peer relationships; a lack of seeking to share enjoyments, interests, or achievements with others; and a lack of social reciprocity. Individuals also display restricted repetitive and stereotyped patterns of behaviors, interests, and activities, including a preoccupation with restricted patterns of interest that are abnormal in intensity or focus; apparently inflexible adherence to specific, nonfunctional routines or rituals; repetitive motor mannerisms; and preoccupation with parts or objects (American Psychiatric Association, 2000). In addition, these disturbances cause clinically significant impairment in areas of functioning, including, but not limited to, social or occupational activities. Individuals with Asperger's Disorder should display no clinically significant delay in language and no delay in cognitive development or development of age-appropriate self-help skills, adaptive behaviors, and curiosity about the environment, and must not meet criteria for another Pervasive Developmental Disorder or Schizophrenia (American Psychiatric Association, 2000).

As noted, the inflexibility and preoccupation with a limited number of topics that is evident in Asperger's Disorder may overlap somewhat with some of the symptoms of OCPD. Children with Asperger's Disorder are commonly of average or above average intelligence and are often quiet and well behaved and thus may also go unnoticed in the classroom (Jackel, 1996). Children with Asperger's Disorder may be (if only slightly) more likely than other perfectionistic youth to be detected as at risk because they are more likely to be noticed in the classroom. According to Jackel (1996), the school environment demands that students cope with changes, varying behavioral expectations, social interactions with peers and adults, and so on. For children with Asperger's, it may be difficult to understand not only their own emotions, but also what is expected of them socially and otherwise in the classroom setting; in contrast, most children with OCPD tendencies are usually not as obviously unable to cope with these demands. Jackel contends that children with Asperger's might be noticed in the classroom due to a lack of ability to focus, being confused, making too literal an interpretation of instructions, or experiencing an overloading of the senses (they may complain of too much noise or too much visual stimulation).

The social impairments displayed by Asperger's disordered individuals are of particular interest when differentiating Asperger's Disorder and Obsessive-Compulsive Personality Disorder. As described earlier, social interaction difficulties and difficulty reading social cues are central to Asperger's. These characteristics might also be evident to an extent in those with OCPD, who are often not aware of the impact of their rigid, logical behavior on others and who may be oblivious to the negative emotions they elicit (Pollack, 1979). Nevertheless, if the task at hand does require social interactions, most individuals with OCPD tendencies possess the capacity to meet these demands, whereas individuals with Asperger's probably do not. The quality of social interactions that are deemed of interest to the person with OCPD may therefore be a useful way to distinguish the two conditions; the amount of limitation of one's interests may be another, in that individuals with Asperger's are much more likely to have focused interests that are not shared by other age peers, such as railway systems and computer games. Individuals with OCPD, though they do tend to focus on work and productivity, do not tend to have the same kind of restrictions that characterize Asperger's.

MALADAPTIVE PERFECTIONISM: THE DEVELOPMENTAL ROOT OF OBSESSIVE-COMPULSIVE PERSONALITY DISORDER?

According to Rice and Preusser (2002), among other theorists, perfectionism comes in two forms: adaptive and maladaptive; clearly the latter form is of greater interest when it comes to thinking about the development of OCPD in childhood or adolescence. Maladaptive perfectionists, as described by Adler (1956), set unrealistic goals, overemphasize order, and are extremely concerned with making mistakes. Additionally, they have an immense fear of criticism from others while simultaneously desperately desiring admiration. They often lack social interest and are self-centered. Hamachek (1978; as cited in Rice & Preusser, 2002) explained this differentiation in terms of normal and neurotic versions of perfectionism. Although adaptive perfectionists will set high standards for themselves, they will also feel positively about their accomplishments and will allow mistakes in their work. Neurotic perfectionists will set similar high standards, yet they will do so in every situation. Also, they commonly create a limited range for themselves in which to define acceptable performance. Neurotic perfectionists have a sense that their work is never good enough and will overemphasize what they do incorrectly compared to what they do right. Although most perfectionists equate their self-worth with work and productivity, normal perfectionists are able to feel satisfaction in their work, whereas neurotic perfectionists are not, and this can sometimes impact self-esteem. Notably, although maladaptive perfectionism has been found to be more associated with OCPD than with OCD in a sample of individuals with eating pathology (Halmi et al., 2005), it is also a known risk factor for psychopathology other than OCPD (Beiling, Israeli, & Antony, 2004). The pathways for the development of OCPD as opposed to other disorders in individuals high in maladaptive perfectionism are not well understood.

As vulnerable children move from childhood through adolescence to adulthood, internal pressures they place on themselves in combination with pressure from teachers and parents for high-quality work and efforts may cause the maladjustment to proliferate. Moreover, because adaptive perfectionism is sometimes considered a desirable trait by adults, this tendency will often be reinforced by parents, teachers, and coaches, which strengthens adherence to exacting standards in the vulnerable child. Accordingly, children and adolescents who show signs of excessive or maladaptive perfectionism are at a particular risk for distress and eventual OCPD diagnosis. Instead of being considered at risk for the development of a disorder associated with substantial functional and role impairment, however, these children might be thought of as model students, and hence may not warrant the attention of a busy teacher in the way that a child with Attention Deficit Disorder might. Therefore, these perfectionistic tendencies in children and adolescents may increase throughout schooling and higher education, and this can lead to more excessive and harmful forms of perfectionism.

The distinction between adaptive and maladaptive perfectionism has been validated in several studies (e.g., Beiling, Summerfeldt, Israeli, & Antony, 2004), and the relationship between maladaptive perfectionism in particular and Axis I psychopathology has been established in a number of adult clinical studies (e.g., Beiling, Summerfeldt, Israeli, & Antony, 2004). Notably, an experimental study conducted with a college sample indicated that not only did individuals high on a measure of maladaptive perfectionism assign higher levels of importance to the assigned writing task and report more negative affect associated with completing it, but it was also the case that their work was judged to be lower in quality than those low on this measure (Frost, Marten, Lahart, & Rosenblate, 1990). In that same study they were also more likely than their nonperfectionistic counterparts to report that they should have done better on the writing assignment; thus, it may be the case that negative affect impacts performance, and imperfection in performance then contributes to taking the next assignment even more seriously, and a vicious cycle is put into motion.

Parental and social influences may also affect this process for better or worse, depending on the kind of feedback the youngster receives. Beiling, Isaeli, and Antony (2003) have extended this experimental work to perfectionism in the classroom and found a relationship between maladaptive perfectionism, failure to achieve academic goals, and negative affect. In our case example, the beginnings of this pattern may be emerging for Julianne: She is beginning to be downgraded for turning in homework assignments late, which then can affect her overall grades, which, given the emphasis she places on academic performance, will surely result in negative affect. Most individuals who see this connection are sufficiently flexible to adjust their approach and turn in less perfect homework on time; individuals with OCPD may not be able to make this kind of adjustment, and thus the negative impact on performance may increase over time.

It may be more useful to think of the goals of the treatment of personality disorders in terms of modifying the personality style to be more adaptive, as opposed to transforming the personality completely. Personality disorders can be conceptualized as extreme versions of more useful characteristics. In OCPD individuals, these characteristics include many very functional traits and behaviors, including being hardworking, having strong moral principles, doing things the "right" way, being orderly, being practical, and being careful and conscientious. Prior research supports the concept that personality disorders may be best understood in terms of being extreme, maladaptive versions of the five-factor personality traits proposed by McCrae and Costa (1990): neuroticism, extraversion, agreeableness, conscientiousness, and openness. From that perspective, OCPD can be understood in terms of the five-factor model as excessive conscientiousness (Widiger, Trull, Clarkin, Sanderson, & Costa, 2002). Conscientiousness can include order (manifested in OCPD as preoccupation with details, rules, lists, orderliness), striving for achievement (in OCPD includes excessive devotion to work and productivity), dutifulness (overconscientiousness and overscrupulousness concerning ethics and morality), and competence (in OCPD, perfectionism). Thus, behaviors of OCPD individuals can be understood in terms of this maladaptive conscientiousness. For these perfectionists, the task may never be complete, self-induced standards are not met, and there is a preoccupation with organization, rules, and details. In addition, OCPD individuals are low on the openness factor of personality, in that rigidity and stubbornness are criteria for this diagnosis. An OCPD individual's stubbornness can be conceptualized as antagonism (or low compliance/agreeableness), and the OCPD individual's tendency to insist that others complete tasks his or her way can be thought of as high assertiveness or extraversion.

STABILITY OVER TIME AND TREATMENT OPTIONS

Because of the enduring and more long-term qualities of personality disorders, and the likelihood of comorbid Axis I diagnoses, it is a given that treatment of personality disorders is a difficult endeavor. Personality disordered patients may also be harder to treat because they are likely to resist changes in behavior; OCPD patients in particular may not see their behavior as problematic (Cottraux & Blackburn, 2000). The degree of persistence of OCPD over time has received some recent empirical attention and has implications for the need to treat this interpersonal style.

Grilo, Shea, et al. (2004) examined the stability and outcome of OCPD along with Schizotypal Personality Disorder (STPD), Borderline Personality Disorder (BPD), and Avoidant Personality Disorder (AVPD) over a 24-month period, assessing participants at baseline and 6-, 12-, and 24-month follow-ups using the DIPD-IV, Diagnostic Interview for *DSM-IV* Personality Disorders-Follow-Along Version (DIPD-FAV), and the Longitudinal Follow-Up Evaluation (LIFE). The stability of the OCPD diagnosis over 24 months was assessed by examining the agreement between DIPD-IV evaluations completed at baseline and 24 months ($k = .35$ for OCPD). In addition, the number and percentage of participants who retained their baseline diagnoses at the 24-month follow-up were reported. Fifty-four of 136 (40%) participants who met criteria for OCPD at baseline also met criteria at 24-month follow-up. These numbers suggest that the OCPD diagnosis is not as stable as previously thought. In addition, remission rates for OCPD symptoms were measured. Remission was defined as both 2 consecutive months and 12 consecutive months with two or fewer criteria as assessed by the DIPD-FAV. Remission rates were 55% and 38% for the 2- and 12-month evaluations, respectively. Not surprisingly, when a more stringent measure of remission was used, lower remission rates were revealed. When comparing OCPD, AVPD, STPD, and BPD to Major Depressive Disorder remission rates, MDD had significantly higher remission rates (shorter time to remission) than did the personality disorder groups (which were collapsed together). This finding lends support for the contention that personality disorders are more stable and enduring patterns of maladaptive behavior than depression, but that they may not be completely stable over time. In addition, the mean proportion of criteria met by the personality disorder groups was assessed at the four time points. Results indicated a significant effect for time across the four personality disorder groups, suggesting stability. Proportions of criteria met by these groups were reported, and means for OCPD were as follows: .65 (baseline assessment), .50 (6-month assessment), .43 (12-month assessment), and .36 (24-month assessment). This suggests that there is a decrease in

OCPD severity over time. Overall, these data reveal mixed results and suggest that OCPD and other personality disorders are moderately stable over time, though severity levels are likely to vary. Thus, although there is evidence of remission for some individuals, a fairly large proportion of individuals with OCPD maintain the diagnosis over time; for those whose symptoms do not remit, there are several treatments that have been brought to bear.

Although many different therapeutic approaches have been tried with OCPD, cognitive therapy has received some recent empirical support in the treatment of this disorder. The cognitive model requires that patients (a) are able to identify a problem to work on, (b) are motivated to complete treatment assignments and other treatment techniques, (c) have the ability to practice these techniques, and (d) are able to follow the structure usually associated with cognitive therapy. This structure typically includes an investigation of the patient's core schemas, identifying problems and ranking severity. The main goals are for patients to modify and restructure maladaptive beliefs underlying dysfunctional behaviors; therapists provide patients with support and coping skills and tools to utilize in their daily lives. Additional techniques such as relaxation training can be useful for physical anxiety often associated with OCPD. Also, empathy training and role reversal may be especially important for the OCPD patient who may lose sight of the feelings and emotions of others. It is important that the treatment focus somewhat on social skills training to increase patients' pleasurable experiences and emotional experiences.

The therapeutic alliance may be particularly important in treating OCPD individuals and influencing outcome in a variety of treatment methods (Beck, Freeman, & Davis, 2004). This alliance can fluctuate during the course of therapy; an *alliance rupture* occurs when there is difficulty maintaining a quality alliance. These ruptures are sometimes associated with cognitive therapy methods such as working-through and challenging core interpersonal schemata. In addition, these patients may simply enter a session from negative experiences outside of treatment or a lack of acknowledgment by the therapist of difficulties in their experiences. It has been suggested that repairing these ruptures can be therapeutic as well, providing chances to facilitate change. Strauss et al. (2006) investigated this assertion in cognitive therapy. Sixteen patients diagnosed with OCPD were assessed in an open trial for cognitive therapy for personality disorders, along with 24 AVPD patients. Therapeutic alliance was measured using the California Psychotherapy Alliance Scale (CALPAS: Marmar, Wiess, & Gaston, 1989); personality disorder symptoms were assessed with the Wisconsin Personality Disorders Inventory (WISPI: M. J. Klein et al., 1993) as well as the Structured Clinical Interview for *DSM* Axis I Disorders (SCID), SCID-II (Spitzer, Williams, Gibbons, & First, 1987), and Beck Depression Inventory (BDI: Beck, Ward, Mendelson, Mock, & Erbaugh, 1961). Within-group effect sizes were calculated using a formula of (pretreatment score – posttreatment score)/pretreatment standard deviation. The WISPI, SCID, SCID-II, and BDI were administered at intake, sessions 17 and 34, and posttreatment to assess personality disorder symptomatology, and the CALPAS was administered at various time points during treatment to assess for alliance and rupture-repair episodes.

In terms of symptom status pre- and posttreatment, all 30 entrants met criteria for OCPD or AVPD diagnosis at pretreatment, only 2 of 30 meeting criteria at posttreatment. Despite experiences of rupture-repair episodes (occurring in 14 patients), all reported symptom reduction at or above 50% on the SCID-II. These data suggest that potential rupture-repair episodes do not decrease the quality of the alliance per se, and also lend initial empirical support for this form of cognitive therapy as a treatment for OCPD. Clearly, one of the critical needs in the field is the development of age-downward extension studies examining personality disorder characteristics in youth. The review just discussed is entirely reliant on psychotherapy theory and study with adult samples, and the degree to which the findings from these studies can be extrapolated to children and adolescents remains to be determined.

CONCLUSIONS

As we have discussed, maladaptive perfectionism has been found to be a risk factor for the development of many undesirable traits and for psychiatric symptoms from youth into adulthood, including OCPD. We advocate that this potentially important factor be studied longitudinally in the school context, because the specificity of the relationship between these traits and the development of specific disorders has yet to be clarified. Data from such a study could then be used to help interventionists identify at what point maladaptive perfectionism becomes so severe and pervasive that the rates of conversion from interpersonal style to various disorders associated with functional impairment are sufficiently compelling to warrant intervention. Australian researchers, in particular, have been very successful in adopting and implementing this kind of preventive model for mental health problems (e.g., Dadds et al., 1997), and at this point there is sufficient evidence pointing to maladaptive perfectionism as a factor in great need of further study.

Stemming the Growth of Maladaptive Perfectionism

In thinking about what kind of interventions might prove useful in weakening maladaptive perfectionism and hence reduce the risk for the development of disorders such as OCPD, we suggest the development of some intervention strategies directed at the child, some at the parents, and some at relevant adult role models such as coaches and teachers. For interventions directed at the child, we need to draw on the empirical literature on the treatment of OCPD and other conditions in which perfectionism plays an important role, such as OCD; here we find that cognitive therapies addressing maladaptive cognitions and interpersonal processes have proven useful, as have exposure-based treatments that have allowed patients to violate the rules to determine whether the associated negative affect will habituate. These interventions require a willing participant who recognizes some reason to engage in treatment, and thus may not be suitable for all.

We raised the issue earlier that some parents might wish for the kind of serious attention to studies and following of rules in their children that characterize those with perfectionism, and that in many ways these kinds of youth might fly under the parental radar when it comes to even considering modification of the child's or adolescent's approach to the world and his or her interpersonal style. Moreover, if parents have some of the same traits, it could be that the style gets preferential attention at home and is reinforced over other approaches and styles. Thus, parents of children who are already high on measures of maladaptive perfectionism might be alerted to its being a risk factor for the development of some serious and long-standing problems down the road, and they could be encouraged as part of an intervention program to reinforce flexibility so that the at-risk youngster does not get the message at home that rigidity and inflexibility are desirable. Modeling may also play a role in such an intervention program: Parents of such children and adolescents can be encouraged to point out their own mistakes and to encourage risk taking and creativity with academic work over caution and rigid adherence.

School personnel could be brought in to assist with children and adolescents who show these traits. Teachers could be encouraged to offer more reinforcement for turning in work on time rather than perseverating over completing it perfectly and to emphasize the importance of outside activities, leisure time, and living a balanced life. Clinicians could offer teachers psychoeducation about the potential costs of solitary devotion to work and how to encourage student flexibility in interpreting class instructions. It would also be useful to encourage monitoring of anxiety, depression, and maladaptive perfectionism over the course of time to help determine at what point the youngster has crossed over to needing more help than can realistically be provided in the school context alone. We have endeavored over the past several years to call attention to the potential problem of anxiety and perfectionism whenever we present to school psychologists, guidance counselors, teachers, and administrators, in the hope of encouraging them to identify these children and adolescents earlier in the process so that they can receive the attention and help they may need.

We also wish to clarify that the focus of our concern is on the maladaptive perfectionistic style, not on achievement orientation, diligence, or attentiveness to detail per se. As many studies have demonstrated, adaptive perfectionism can be healthy, can help build self-esteem, and does not carry with it the same risks of the more malevolent version. One of the world's most famous adaptive perfectionists put it this way: Tiger Woods was recently discussing his devotion to the game of golf and his reputation for working tirelessly on his swing and his mental approach to the game, which prompted the reporter to ask whether a great fear of failure was what motivated him to keep this seemingly draconian schedule. Woods responded, "I've never had a fear of failure. I grew up in a house full of love, where I was encouraged to do my best and to do what I love to do, and I knew that nothing I did on a golf course would ever change my parents' love for me. It wasn't ever about fear of failure—it was about enjoying the process of getting better at something I loved to do."

REFERENCES

Adler, A. (1956). The neurotic disposition. In H. L. Ansbacher & R. R. Ansbacher (Eds.), *The individual psychology of Alfred Adler* (pp. 239–262). New York: Harper.

American Psychiatric Association. (2000). *Diagnostic and statistical manual of mental disorders* (4th ed., text rev.). Washington, DC: Author.

Beck, A. T., Freeman, A., & Davis, D. D. (2004). *Cognitive therapy of personality disorders* (2nd ed.). New York: Guilford Press.

Beck, A. T., Ward, C. H., Mendelson, M., Mock, J., & Erbaugh, J. (1961). An inventory for measuring depression. *Archives of General Psychiatry, 4,* 561–571.

Beiling, P. J., Israeli, A. L., & Antony, M. M. (2003). Making the grade: The behavioral consequences of perfectionism in the classroom. *Personality and Individual Differences, 35,* 163–178.

Beiling, P. J., Israeli, A. L., & Antony, M. M. (2004). Is perfectionism good, bad, or both? Examining models of the perfectionism construct. *Personality and Individual Differences, 36,* 1373–1385.

Beiling, P. J., Summerfeldt, L. J., Israeli, A. L., & Antony, A. M. (2004). Perfectionism as an explanatory construct in comorbidity of Axis I disorders. *Journal of Psychopathology and Behavioral Assessment, 26,* 193–201.

Coles, M. E., Heimberg, R. G., Frost, R. O., & Rheaume, J. (2003). "Not just right experiences": Perfectionism, obsessive-compulsive features, and general psychopathology. *Behavior Research and Therapy, 41,* 681–700.

Coles, M. E., Heimberg, R. G., Frost, R. O., & Steketee, G. (2005). Not just right experiences and obsessive-compulsive features: Experimental and self-monitoring perspectives. *Behavior Research and Therapy, 43,* 153–167.

Conners, K., & March, J. (1996). *The Conners/March Developmental Questionnaire.* Toronto, Ontario, Canada: MultiHealth Systems.

Cottraux, J., & Blackburn, I. (2000). Cognitive therapy. In W. J. Livesey (Ed.), *Handbook of personality disorders: Theory, research, and treatment.* New York: Guilford Press.

Dadds, M. R., Spence, S. H., Holland, D., Barrett, P. M., & Laurens, K. (1997). Early intervention and prevention of anxiety disorders: A controlled study. *Journal of Consulting and Clinical Psychology, 65,* 627–635.

Franklin, M., Foa, E., & March, J. S. (2003). The pediatric obsessive-compulsive disorder treatment study: Rational, design, and methods. *Journal of Child and Adolescent Psychopharmacology, 13,* S39–S51.

Frost, R. O., Marten, P., Lahart, C., & Rosenblate, R. (1990). The dimensions of perfectionism. *Cognitive Therapy and Research, 14,* 449–468.

Grilo, C. M., Shea, M. T., Sanislow, C. A., Skodol, A. E., Gunderson, J. G., Stout, R. L., et al. (2004). Two-year stability and change of schizotypal, borderline, avoidant, and obsessive-compulsive personality disorders. *Journal of Consulting and Clinical Psychology, 72,* 767–775.

Grilo, C. M., Skodol, A. E., Gunderson, J. G., Sanislow, C. A., Stout, R. L., Shae, M. T., et al. (2004). Longitudinal diagnostic efficiency of DSM-IV criteria for obsessive-compulsive personality disorders: A 2-year prospective study. *Acta Psychiatrica Scandinavica, 110,* 64–68.

Halmi, K. A., Tozzi, F., Thorton, L. M., Crow, S., Fichter, M. M., Kaplan, A. S., et al. (2005). *International Journal of Eating Disorders, 38,* 371–374.

Jackel, S. (1996). *Asperger's syndrome: Educational management issues.* Retrieved December 12, 2005, from http://www.ozemail.com.au/~prussia/asperfer/teach.htm.

Klein, M. J., Benjamin, L. S., Rosenfield, R., Treece, C., Husted, J., & Greist, J. H. (1993). The Wisconsin Personality Disorders Inventory: Development, reliability, and validity. *Journal of Personality Disorders, 285–303.*

Marmar, C. R., Weiss, R., & Gaston, L. (1989). Toward the validation of the California Therapeutic Alliance Rating System. *Psychological Assessment, 1,* 46–52.

McCrae, R. R., & Costa, P. T. (1990). *Personality in adulthood.* New York: Guilford Press.

Pediatric OCD Treatment Study (POTS) Team. (2004). Cognitive-behavior therapy, sertraline, and their combination for children and adolescents with obsessive-compulsive disorder: The Pediatric OCD Treatment Study (POTS) ramdomized controlled trial. *Journal of the American Medical Association, 292,* 1969–1976.

Piacentini, J., March, J., & Franklin, M. (2006). Cognitive-behavioral therapy for youngsters with obsessive-compulsive disorder. In P. Kendall (Ed.), *Child and adolescent therapy: Cognitive-behavioral procedures* (3rd ed., pp. 297–321). New York: Guilford Press.

Pollack, J. (1979). Obsessive-compulsive personality: A review. *Psychological Bulletin, 86*, 225–241.

Rapoport, J. L. (1991). Recent advances in obsessive compulsive disorder. *Neuropsychopharmacology, 5*, 1–10.

Rice, K. G., & Preusser, K. J. (2002). The adaptive/maladaptive perfectionism scale. *Measurement and Evaluating in Counseling Development, 34*, 210–222.

Spitzer, R. L., Williams, J. B. W., Gibbons, M., & First, M. B. (1987). *Structured Clinical Interview for the DSM-III-R* (SCID, Version 1.0). Washington, DC: American Psychiatric Press.

Strauss, J. L., Hayes, A. M., Johnson, S. L., Newman, C. F., Brown, G. K., Barber, J. P., et al. (2006). Early alliance, alliance ruptures, and symptom change in a nonrandomized trial of cognitive therapy for avoidant and obsessive-compulsive personality disorders. *Journal of Consulting and Clinical Psychology, 74*, 337–345.

Widiger, T. A., Trull, T. J., Clarkin, J. F., Sanderson, C., & Costa, P. T. (2002). A description of the DSM-IV personality disorders with the five-factor model of personality. In P. Costa & T. Widiger (Eds.), *Personality disorders and the five factor model of personality* (2nd ed., pp. 89–99). Washington, DC: American Psychological Association.

CHAPTER 15

The Complex Pathway
from Attachment to
Personality Disorder:
A Life Span Perspective on
Interpersonal Dependency

ROBERT F. BORNSTEIN, EMILY BECKER-WEIDMAN,
COREY NIGRO, REBECCA FRONTERA, and MARK A. REINECKE

DEPENDING ON a caregiver provides a foundation for human development. The human infant is a relatively helpless creature with an extended infancy and childhood. In fact, few species on the planet are as helpless for as long as the human being is. Babies require not only physical care, but also emotional support, protection, and guidance, and as Rusansky-Drob (2005, p. 185) noted:

The inherent helplessness of the human infant places him or her completely at the mercy of a "other" (i.e., the parent), who interprets the infant's needs according to his or her own psychical structure, as well as at the mercy of a wider "other," an inherited language, and culture that preconditions the structures of the individual's unconscious.

For Bowlby (1969), this first interpersonal relationship evolved to ensure the survival of the human infant. As infants (and later toddlers) develop motor, social, and cognitive skills they also acquire language and develop explanatory models to account for their world. The child begins to develop a sense of autonomy and personal agency. It is at this point that children begin to become a more substantial part of the family and society and start to take greater responsibility for themselves within the context of the family. The position of the child in the family context, as Rusansky-Drob (2005) stated, will be a function of the way the caregivers respond to the child's emergence and personhood. Consistent with this, retrospective and prospective studies of parent-child interactions suggest that those parenting styles that cause children to perceive themselves as powerless and vulnerable are associated with higher levels of dependency later in life. As children internalize a mental representation of themselves as weak, powerless, or vulnerable, they come to look to others to provide nurturance, protection, and support. They may, in addition, become preoccupied with fears of abandonment (What will I do if my protectors leave me?), behave in an overtly dependent manner (I need others because I am too weak to take care of myself), and show increased risk for depression, anxiety, and other psychopathologies (Blatt et al., 1994).

The ability to seek support, guidance, and nurturance from others and to depend on them is the catalyst for the ongoing development of cognitive, behavioral, and emotional competencies. Failures in the development of normal dependency and autonomy lead to an inability to organize one's existence without the support and nurturance of caregivers.

The inability to function independent of a caregiver characterizes individuals who are pathologically dependent and who meet the *Diagnostic and Statistical Manual of Mental Disorders* (DSM-IV-TR; (American Psychiatric Association, 2000)) criteria for Dependent Personality Disorder (DPD). These individuals appear to be incapable of making even small decisions without advice and reassurance. When involved in therapy, these patients may view the clinician as a savior, soothsayer, priest, shaman, or pseudo-parent.

In keeping with the *DSM-IV-TR* requirements, dependence is problematic when it is pervasive, persistent, not likely due to a normal developmental stage, not better explained by an Axis I disorder, and has been observed for at least 1 year (American Psychiatric Association, 2000). It is when this dependence becomes an inflexible, self-perpetuating pattern that the adult may be characterized as not merely dependent, anxious, clingy, or helpless, but as having met the diagnostic criteria for DPD. For children, however, being dependent on parents, caregivers, teachers, and others is normal, and in many Western societies children and adolescents maintain an enforced and extended dependency while completing school. Thus, although certain children and adolescents may technically meet many of the criteria for DPD, this dependency is really a component of normative development and sets the stage for a broad range of behaviors focused on relating to others, building attachments, and developing separation and individuation with the same goals in mind (Bowlby, 2005; Wallin, 2007).

As is true of most personality disorders, the antecedents of DPD can be identified in childhood. Although the *DSM-IV-TR* (American Psychiatric Association, 2000, p. 746) permits the assignment of a DPD diagnosis for children, the generally accepted model has been to view DPD as emerging in late childhood or adolescence. However, personality disorders do not appear de novo at 18 years of age, but have their etiological roots early in life (Bernstein, Cohen, Skodol, Bezirganian, & Brook, 1996; Cicchetti & Cohen, 1995; Geiger & Crick, 2001; Millon & Davis, 1995). The developmental pathways that underpin DPD stem from the interaction of temperament, personality, parenting, and culture. Thus, research in child development and attachment can inform our understanding of the development of this and other personality disorders in childhood and adolescence.

In this chapter, we summarize the literature on diagnosis, assessment, prevention, and treatment of DPD in adults. We discuss the origins of DPD during childhood and adolescence, with the aim of linking different research programs and delineating an integrated developmental-cognitive perspective on this topic.

DEPENDENT PERSONALITY DISORDER SYMPTOM CRITERIA

The essential feature of DPD in the *DSM-IV-TR* (American Psychiatric Association, 2000, p. 725) is "a pervasive and excessive need to be taken care of that leads to submissive and clinging behavior and fears of separation, beginning by early adulthood and present in a variety of contexts." The *DSM-IV-TR* lists eight DPD symptoms, five of which must be present to receive the diagnosis: (1) difficulty making decisions without excessive advice and reassurance, (2) needing others to assume responsibility for most major areas of life, (3) difficulty expressing disagreement, (4) difficulty initiating projects or doing things on one's own, (5) going to excessive lengths to obtain nurturance and support, (6) feeling helpless when alone, (7) urgently seeking another source of protection when an important relationship ends, and (8) being preoccupied with fears of being left to care for oneself. Although these symptoms provide a useful index of problematic dependency, the *DSM-IV-TR* DPD criteria are limited in two respects. First, by restricting their focus to the link between dependency and passivity, these symptoms fail to capture the range of presentation styles exhibited by dependent adults (Pincus & Wilson, 2001). Second, these symptom criteria have questionable external validity. Bornstein's (1997) review of evidence for the organization of DPD symptoms indicates that four of these symptoms (1, 5, 6, and 8) have been supported by the results of empirical studies, two symptoms (2 and 7) have never been tested empirically, and two (3 and 4) have been contradicted repeatedly. In other words, the symptom profile of DPD in adults may not cohere as well as expected. Further, there is no evidence that the symptom profile of DPD outlined in the *DSM-IV-TR,* which was created primarily to identify problematic dependency in early and middle adulthood, will provide an accurate picture of problematic dependency in children and adolescents (or, for that matter, in older adults).

Consequently, two issues must be addressed. The first issue is lexical: How should we define criterion terms, and what are their observable indices? The second issue centers on the applicability of the symptom criteria to children and adolescents: How are we to understand the concept of "excessive and pervasive dependency" in the context of emerging autonomy over a developmental phase when some degree of dependency is expected and normal?

The following factors represent some key lexical and practical issues regarding the development of DPD features in children and adolescents, focusing on each *DSM-IV-TR* symptom:

- Individuals with DPD tend to experience difficulty making decisions, excessively seeking advice and reassurance. The question becomes: What constitutes *excessive* in this context? At what point does a child's normal requests for parental or caretaker direction become pathological? This varies by chronological age and maturity, and may be impacted by culture as well.

- Individuals with DPD want others to assume responsibility for major areas of their life. Young children, however, naturally need others to assume responsibility because they cannot make reasonable decisions regarding these issues. For example, children must go to school, be vaccinated, have established bedtimes, and maintain an acceptable level of hygiene. Dependency on a primary caretaker to meet these needs is normative, not problematic.

- Individuals with DPD have difficulty expressing disagreement. However, children are often dissuaded from disagreeing with societal rules and the requirements of schools, religion, or family values. The admonition to "honor thy father and mother" has been a foundation of child rearing for millennia. The ability to appropriately and adaptively disagree with parents or authority figures is a skill acquired over the course of development. Moreover, excessive questioning of authority may in certain instances be seen as an indication of oppositional defiance.

- Individuals with DPD have difficulty initiating projects or doing things on their own. Of course, children are limited by age, ability, experience, and social context in what they are able to initiate. To a great extent they are expected to do as they are told, especially early in life. With increased maturity comes increased ability to initiate.

- Individuals with DPD may go to excessive lengths to obtain nurturance and support. Again, "excessive" must be defined in a developmentally appropriate manner, with reference both to chronological age and emotional maturity. In addition, the impact of culture on nurturance- and support-seeking cannot be ignored.

- Individuals with DPD feel helpless when alone. Children, especially young children, *are* helpless when alone and need an adult to survive. However, most children have some autonomous capabilities and can do certain things without assistance. If the child feels helpless in these age-appropriate skill areas, that may indicate a problem. It is also important to clarify what is meant by "alone" in childhood. Is it being dropped off somewhere without an adult, being left in one's crib while the parents are in another room, or being asked to perform an activity without assistance?

- Individuals with DPD urgently seek another source of protection when an important relationship ends. Given that for many children key relationships revolve around family members and other caregivers, the loss of an important relationship is likely to be frightening and cause the child to move closer to other people within the family system.

- Individuals with DPD are preoccupied with fears of being left to care for themselves. Children (like adults) vary along this dimension, and given the relative helplessness of the child, such fears are not unrealistic. When these fears become a functional impairment, they are maladaptive at any age.

Taken together, it is clear that although applying the DPD diagnostic criteria may be comparatively straightforward in adults, application becomes much more complicated with children and adolescents. The degree to which dependent behaviors are considered appropriate varies across age, and dependent behavior in children should be considered characteristic of a disorder only when it is not developmentally appropriate.

EPIDEMIOLOGY OF DEPENDENT PERSONALITY DISORDER

Dependent Personality Disorder is common among adults in inpatient settings, with prevalence rates between 15% and 25% in psychiatric units, rehabilitation centers, and long-term care facilities (Jackson et al., 1991). The base rate of DPD in outpatients ranges from 0% to 10% (Poldrugo & Forti, 1988), which is similar to rates found in large-scale community surveys (Bornstein, 1996, 1997). Preliminary findings from cross-cultural data suggest that there may be cultural differences in the prevalence of DPD. Studies suggest, for example, that the prevalence rate of DPD may be somewhat higher in Japan than in North America and Western Europe (Behrens, 2004; Johnson, 1993). Women are diagnosed more frequently with DPD than men; a meta-analytic review of findings in this area indicated that the base rate of DPD (collapsing across setting and mode of assessment) is approximately 11% in women and 8% in men (Bornstein, 2005). Although this difference may appear modest, it suggests that women are 40% more likely than men to receive a DPD diagnosis. Preliminary studies with adolescent populations suggest similar prevalence rates and gender differences (Rey, Morris-Yates, Singh, Andrews, & Stewart, 1995) but do not address the question of whether these gender differences are genotypic or sociotypic or reflect a combination of these factors.

COMORBIDITY

Dependency has been linked to a range of psychological disorders (Masling & Schwartz, 1979), with depression and anxiety being two of the most common Axis I disorders associated with dependency and DPD. Nietzel and Harris's (1990) review of the dependency-depression relationship indicated that depression severity is positively correlated with dependent traits in adults and adolescents. Dependency has been linked to a range of anxiety disorders, including Agoraphobia (Chambless, Renneberg, Gracely, Goldstein, & Fydrich, 2000), Social Phobia (Sans & Avia, 1994), Generalized Anxiety Disorder (Jansen, Arntz, Merckelbach, & Mersch, 1994), Panic Disorder (Stewart, Knize, & Pihl, 1992), and Obsessive-Compulsive Disorder (Sciuto et al., 1991). Observed correlations in these studies are typically modest, however, and the designs of these investigations do not allow conclusions to be drawn regarding causal relations between dependency and anxiety.

Some clinicians have conceptualized heightened dependency as a risk factor for Axis I disorders (Blatt & Zuroff, 1992); others advocate a developmental framework to explain how dependency results from, rather than leads to, psychopathology (Saviola, 1981). Research to date supports both perspectives. For the majority of disorders that are comorbid with DPD, dependency appears to act as both diathesis and consequence (see Bornstein, 1992, for a review). Causal relations may differ in different patients. Separating causal relationships between DPD and Axis I disorders requires careful investigation of onset and course of individual symptoms. For each comorbid disorder, it is important to determine whether the dependency was primary (preceded Axis I symptom onset) or secondary (followed Axis I symptom onset).

It appears that most psychiatric patients with pathological dependency are likely to have at least one comorbid condition (Bornstein, 2005, 2007). The issue of differential diagnosis thus becomes important, as many Axis I disorders and other Axis II disorders are associated with increases in dependent behavior.

DIFFERENTIAL DIAGNOSIS

Many individuals display dependent personality traits, but only when these traits are inflexible, maladaptive, and persistent do they constitute a personality *disorder.* Dependent Personality Disorder must therefore be distinguished from dependency arising as a consequence of Axis I disorders or due to a medical condition. This is especially important with children and adolescents when dependent behaviors may be normative or an indirect consequence of other pathology.

For example, some anxiety disorders stem in part from a perception (or misperception) of an impending and imminent danger or threat, leading a child to seek protection from a caregiver. Depression, in context, often stems from the loss of a relationship, prompting a child to seek reassurance and support from others. Both anxiety and depression, then, are intimately related to dependency, and both conditions lead children to endeavor to secure relationships with a protective caregiver. Not surprisingly, anxiety and depression often co-occur with dependent behavior, and it can be difficult to tease the conditions apart.

ASSESSMENT OF DEPENDENCY IN CHILDREN

Dependency in childhood serves an adaptive function by helping create a bond with caregivers and aiding the individual in avoiding harm or danger. Problematic dependency results when this need for attachment is unmet in a healthy manner and the child's "clinginess" disrupts adaptive functioning. In this regard, all behaviors that reflect insecure attachment (including many dependent behaviors) may respond to similar types of interventions.

A child who is overly dependent and for whom that dependency is caused by another condition may require alternative treatments. Difficulty making decisions and other symptoms of problematic dependency can, for example, be associated with Pervasive Developmental Disorder, or with depression or anxiety. In these instances, the primary disorder would need to be addressed.

In summary, it is best to complete an evaluation that includes the following components:

- A through review of personal and family history.
- A mental health assessment to determine which, if any, *DSM-IV-TR* diagnoses are present.
- Screening for various other conditions that may be present and require more specialized evaluation, such as:
  —Neuropsychological issues.
  —Learning and educational disabilities.
  —Sensory-integration issues.
- A review of school records and previous evaluations and treatment records.
- A developmental screening.

THEORETICAL CONCEPTUALIZATIONS OF DEPENDENT PERSONALITY DISORDER

There are a number of theoretical models of dependency, which are reviewed in the following sections.

PSYCHODYNAMIC

In classical psychoanalytic theory, dependency is linked to events occurring during the first months of an infant's life (the "oral" stage of development). In Freud's (1953/1983) model, frustration or overgratification during the oral stage was thought to result in oral fixation and an inability to resolve conflicts regarding dependency and autonomy. Empirical support for the psychoanalytic model of dependency has been, at best, mixed. Although research suggests that early relationships with caregivers may play a role in the etiology of dependent personality traits (Fisher & Greenberg, 1996; Masling, 1986), there is no evidence that the oral fixation (as Freud described it) affects dependency-related behaviors in adolescence or adulthood.

Two theoretical models of dependency evolved from the classical psychoanalytic model: object relations theory (Mahler, Pine, & Bergman, 1975) and attachment theory (Bowlby, 1969; Holmes, 1993). These models both hypothesize that the quality of the infant-caregiver relationship in infancy and early childhood is a primary determinant of dependent traits in adulthood (Ainsworth, Blehar, Waters, & Wall, 1978).

OBJECT RELATIONS THEORY

The object relations model of dependency emphasizes the interpersonal dynamics and enduring relationship patterns that foster and maintain dependent behavior (Fairbairn, 1952; Kernberg, 1975). The early infant-caregiver relationship is seen as a prototype for later interpersonal relationships. Self- and object representations are hypothesized to be internalized during childhood and are seen as playing a central role in personality development (Bornstein, Galley, & Leone, 1986).

Blatt's (1974, 1991) theoretical framework has been the most influential contemporary object relations model of dependency. Blatt (1991) argues that dependent personality traits result from the individual's mental representation of the self as weak and ineffectual. As children internalize a mental representation of themselves as weak they look to others for support and nurturance, become preoccupied by fears of abandonment, behave in an overly dependent way, and show increased risk for dependency-related psychopathology (see Blatt & Homann, 1992, for a review of the research in this area).

ATTACHMENT THEORY

Attachment is an adaptive behavioral system that evolved to ensure the survival of the human infant. When there is separation (or threat of separation) from the primary caregiver(s), the attachment system is activated and attachment behaviors evoked. Specifically, proximity-seeking behaviors are activated so that the child moves toward the primary caregiver, who is experienced as a source of comfort, security, and safety. In this framework *attachment* is a global term that refers to the state and quality of an individual's emotional relationships. *Attachment behavior* is any form of behavior that results in a person's attaining or retaining proximity to some preferred person. It is triggered by separation—or threatened separation—from the attachment figure and is terminated by proximity. The *attachment behavioral system* is a model of the world in which the self, significant others, and their interrelationships are represented and that encodes the particular pattern (secure, avoidant, ambivalent, anxious, disorganized) of attachment shown by the person (Bowlby, 1988).

Attachment theorists have proposed that innate, biological underpinnings of infant-mother relationships serve as determinants of self-concept and as a template for future interpersonal behavior (Bowlby, 1969, 1973, 1980, 2005). Attachment theory postulates that patterns of intimate relationships develop from models developed during infancy and early childhood. These patterns represent stable ways of managing intimacy and interpersonal relationships (Hesse, 1999).

Highly dependent behavior characterizes some forms of attachment (i.e., insecure attachment) in childhood (Waters & Deane, 1985) and during adolescence and adulthood (Livesley, Schroeder, & Jackson, 1990; Sperling & Berman, 1991). Bowlby (1969, 1973) proposed that insecure patterns of attachment emerge when a developing child does not receive consistent and reliable responses or sufficiently empathic care. Subsequent relationship efforts are hindered by the individual's expectations that his or her attachment needs will be unmet, attachment figures will be unresponsive, and security will be limited or lost. The child develops beliefs or assumptions that others will be unresponsive and experiences anxiety about losing an attachment figure (Bowlby, 1973).

In a classic study of attachment styles, Ainsworth et al. (1978) identified three primary types of attachment: secure, avoidant, and resistant. The child with a secure pattern of attachment shows a developmentally appropriate capacity to use the primary caregiver as a source of safety, security, and comfort. When not threatened, such a child can explore the environment independently. The child with an avoidant pattern of attachment shows little distress upon separation from the primary caregiver and manages relationships by not placing large demands on those relationships. This child has learned not to demand too much of the parent in order to maintain a relationship with an often distant or preoccupied adult (Hesse, 1999). The child with a resistant or ambivalent pattern of attachment shows significant distress upon separation from the primary caregiver and is often unable to be comforted by that caregiver. In this manner the child with an ambivalent pattern of attachment keeps the primary caregiver involved.

Later research by Main and Hesse (1990) and others identified a fourth category, disorganized attachment, characterized by the lack of clear, coherent, and predictable attachment behavior. When confronted by a separation, these children appear apprehensive, avoidant, resistant, and confused. They may cry and fall to the floor, or turn in circles while simultaneously approaching the caregiver. Main and Solomon (1986) suggest that this pattern of behavior may stem from inconsistent, unpredictable, or punitive parenting, leading the child to simultaneously feel comforted and frightened by the parent.

Given evidence that early parent-child interactions play a role in the development of dependent traits, might associations exist between early attachment security and vulnerability for DPD? Evidence thus far is mixed. The concepts of attachment and dependency are distinct (Livesley et al., 1990). Moreover, individual differences in attachment and dependency may have different antecedents (Sroufe, Fox, & Pancake, 1983) and correlates (Ainsworth, 1969; Maccoby, 1980) and appear to predict different adult behaviors (Kaul, Mathur, & Murlidharan, 1982; Livesley et al., 1990). Patterns of attachment and states of mind with respect to attachment are theorized to develop during infancy and are seen as reflecting the early infant-caregiver relationship; they appear to be reasonably stable over time (Main & Cassidy, 1988; van IJzendoorn, Schuengel, & Bakermans-Kranenburg, 1999). The behavioral characteristics of insecure attachment and dependency, however, show only moderate overlap conceptually (Ainsworth, 1969, 1972; Waters & Deane, 1985) and empirically (Sears, Rau, & Alpert, 1965; Sroufe et al., 1983; West, Livesley, Sheldon, & Reiffer, 1986). Ainsworth (1972) and Livesley et al. (1990) suggest that dependency and attachment differ in at least two important respects: (1) Attachment behavior is manifested primarily by proximity seeking, whereas dependency is manifested primarily by help seeking; and (2) attachment behaviors are object-specific and are directed toward the same person, whereas dependent behaviors may be directed toward any number of people who represent potential nurturers or protectors. At the same time, attachment behavior evoked by a threat or perceived threat is usually directed toward a specific individual who is perceived as a source of safety and security. In this sense, dependency and attachment may be conceptually and functionally related.

The emphasis of attachment theory on external or internalized attachment figures raises questions about the interplay of attachment security, attachment strategies, and the development of autonomous self-regulation skills. Some authors have proposed that secure attachment, which encourages support from an attachment figure, interferes with the development of autonomy because an attachment figure's support favors reliance on others to mitigate distress at the expense of developing one's self-regulation strategies (Kirkpatrick, 1998). From this perspective, securely attached individuals might be more likely to show traits of dependency and seek support and guidance. Equating secure attachment and dependency, however, is not consistent with the views of most attachment theorists (Bartholomew, 1997; Bowlby, 1969) and is not supported by empirical findings concerning the development of attachment (Sroufe et al., 1983). With this in mind, Mikulincer, Shaver, and Pereg (2003) proposed that secure attachment reinforces children's reliance on external and internalized attachment figures, but also provides a base for the development of self-regulatory skills. Children with secure attachments are more tolerant of separation from attachment figures and are more comfortable exploring their environment on their own, with the attachment figure serving as a secure base. Confident exploration of the environment is important in teaching the child that he or she can be alone in the world and do things without the help of others (Thompson & Zuroff, 1999; Weinfield, Sroufe, Egeland, & Carlson, 1999).

During middle childhood, a secure attachment allows children to explore their world more actively; it moderates distress and allows the child to engage effectively with others (Rubin, Bukowski, & Parker, 1998; Weinfield et al., 1999; Zeifman & Hazan, 1997). Engaging in affiliative activities is another important step to achieving autonomy and integrating one's self-concept (Berlin & Cassidy, 1999). During adolescence, securely attached individuals are able to develop mutually beneficial partnerships with peers in which they are able to be a source of comfort and learn how to regulate others' distress (Furman & Wehner, 1994; Zeifman & Hazan, 1997). This, in turn, strengthens their sense of mastery and teaches them new skills that can be applied to regulating their own distress. These adolescents become more confident that they will be able to handle stressful situations without the help of others.

Empirical findings show that adults who scored lower on attachment anxiety or avoidance and who may have the most secure attachment patterns also had the lowest scores on measures of DPD, as well as scales assessing emotional and instrumental dependency (Alonso-Arbiol, Shaver, & Yarnoz, 2002; Brennan & Shaver, 1998). These findings imply that, at least for adults, a secure attachment style is associated with support seeking, but also with establishing the self as a support figure. Securely attached individuals appear to be flexible, relying on attachment figures or their own coping skills when faced with distress.

Whereas secure attachment seems to serve as a foundation for the development of autonomy, an insecure attachment may place individuals at risk for developing DPD (Livesley et al., 1990). Studies with adults show that an insecure attachment style persists over time (Feeney & Noller, 1990). High levels of insecure attachment in the first years of life are associated with a variety of dependent traits later in childhood (Sroufe et al., 1983) and early adulthood (Sperling & Berman, 1991).

Behavioral and Social Models

Behavioral and social learning theorists propose that dependent behaviors are learned and that people exhibit dependent behaviors because those behaviors are rewarded, were rewarded, or are perceived by the individual as likely to elicit rewards (Hull, 1943; Mowrer, 1950). Thus, individual differences in responding result from the varying degrees to which dependent behavior was reinforced during infancy or childhood (Ainsworth, 1969). The social learning model hypothesizes that as the primary caregiver provides biological and psychological gratification to the infant, he or she comes to be associated with pleasurable experiences and becomes a secondary reinforcer. To the extent that the child's beliefs and expectations regarding the caregiver's nurturing behavior generalizes to others, dependent behavior will be exhibited in other relationships. Even if dependent behavior was first acquired in the child's early interactions with caregivers, the behavior must be reinforced in other relationships or it will eventually be replaced by other strategies. As children are likely to be rewarded for showing dependent behavior in some relationships but not others, an intermittent or variable reinforcement pattern is established—a pattern that makes dependent behavior highly resistant to extinction (Bhogle, 1983; Turkat, 1990). From this perspective, dependent behavior need not be directly reinforced to be maintained. To the extent that the child sees other children being rewarded for dependent behaviors, that child is more likely to exhibit those behaviors. This vicarious reinforcement is especially strong if the child admires the person exhibiting the dependent behavior (Bandura, 1978). Modeling (i.e., imitating others) can also play an important role in shaping and maintaining dependent traits. Modeling may be particularly strong for young children, who are often exposed to fictional characters (such as female figures in fairy tales) who exhibit high levels of dependency (Bandura, 1977).

COGNITIVE MODELS

In recent years, there has been increasing emphasis on the role of cognitive processes as mediators of dependent behavior (Abramson, Seligman, & Teasdale, 1978; Mischel, 1973; Mischel & Peake, 1982). As a consequence, many social learning theorists have come to view dependency in terms of a cognitive (or attributional) style in which the person perceives himself or herself as powerless, helpless, and unable to influence the outcome of events in a positive way.

Cognitive therapy is based on the understanding that thoughts, emotions, and behaviors transactionally influence one another over time. Individuals are constantly appraising situations, and these spontaneous appraisals (automatic thoughts) play a role in shaping the person's emotional and behavioral response to a situation. The individual interprets current experiences on the basis of beliefs and assumptions learned through previous experience. These core beliefs or schemas lie dormant until activated by a relevant situation (Beck & Freeman, 1990; Beck, Freeman, Davis, & Associates, 2004). The model does not claim that cognitions cause pathology directly, but views cognition as an important influence on how individuals respond to events.

Beck and Freeman (1990) presented an early cognitive model for understanding and treating personality disorders. As in cognitive models of depression and anxiety, an emphasis was placed on the central role of early schemata and core beliefs. The model offers a genetic and evolutionary view in which different personality types reflect alternative behavioral, cognitive, and emotional strategies that were adaptive at some point in the child's development, but are no longer adaptive. Beck and Freeman (1990) and Beck et al. (2004)

view personality disorders as reflecting the activation of overdeveloped or underdeveloped adaptive strategies. In DPD, for example, help seeking is overdeveloped and autonomy or self-sufficiency is underdeveloped.

Cognitive models conceptualize dependency as the product of maladaptive schemas (i.e., tacit beliefs about the self and others) that cause patients to doubt their abilities, belittle their skills, and exaggerate the imagined consequences of not being perfect (Ball & Young, 2000). Maladaptive schemas not only decrease self-esteem and increase anxiety, but they also lead to an array of cognitive distortions that strengthen the person's negative views of the self, world, and future. Three schema-based cognitive processes are seen as playing a role in the dynamics of dependency: (1) automatic thoughts (i.e., reflexive thoughts that are cued by perceived or anticipated failure), (2) negative self-statements (i.e., self-blaming statements that exacerbate the patient's lack of self-confidence), and (3) attributional bias (i.e., a skewed interpretive style whereby the patient punishes himself or herself for perceived failures but cannot accept credit for successes). A core schema in dependency is "I am unlovable." The accompanying assumptions or propositional beliefs are "If I don't please people, they will reject me and I will be alone," and its converse, "If I please others, they will stay with me and I can feel secure."

Building on earlier work by Beck and Freeman (1990), Young and Lindemann (1992) proposed a multifaceted cognitive-behavioral model of personality disorders that emphasized the role of early maladaptive schemas (EMS) and compensatory strategies used to regulate them. Young (1994) delineated three processes that may serve to maintain schemas: schema maintenance, schema avoidance, and schema compensation. *Schema maintenance* involves selective attention to confirmatory information and the neglect of other evidence to ensure the stability of the dysfunctional schema. The persistence of self-defeating behaviors also contributes to schema maintenance through repetition of negative experiences. Schemas associated with negative affect tend to be avoided. *Schema avoidance* strategies may be cognitive (thought blocking), affective (psychosomatic symptoms, psychic numbing), or behavioral. *Schema compensation* involves the activation of cognitive or behavioral patterns that are the opposite of what would be expected. For example, an excessively dependent person may develop self-protective strategies of excessive autonomy and refuse to accept help.

A primary goal of cognitive therapy is cognitive restructuring: altering dysfunctional thought patterns that foster self-defeating behavior. In the case of dependency, cognitive restructuring focuses on strengthening the patient's beliefs of self-efficacy, especially those related to interpersonal situations (Overholser & Fine, 1994). To accomplish this, therapist and patient work collaboratively to explore (a) the development of maladaptive dependency-related schemas, (b) processes that maintain them over time, (c) avoidance strategies used by the patient to escape schema-triggered anxiety, and (d) compensatory strategies used to manage negative emotions when they cannot be avoided (Ball, 1998; Young, 1994).

Early experiences, including those associated with attachment security, are seen as contributing to later dependent behavior. These experiences are believed to lead to the development of specific tacit beliefs or schema. These cognitive structures are formed in response to early experiences and influence the motivations, behaviors, and affective responses of the dependent person in predictable ways. An underlying perception of the self as weak and in need of guidance from others will have motivational effects. These beliefs motivate the person to seek guidance, support, and protection from others, producing a pattern of dependent behavior. Dependent persons will behave in ways that serve to maximize the probability that they will obtain the guidance and nurturance they desire. Finally, a self-representation as powerless and meek will have affective consequences. The individual comes to fear abandonment and becomes acutely sensitive to signs of interpersonal rejection or loss.

The negative view of the self may be fostered by a child's experience of the caregiver's responsiveness. A responsive caregiver teaches the child that he or she is effective and worthy of care. A rejecting or inconsistent caregiver, in contrast, leads the child to believe that he or she is ineffective and unlovable (Sroufe, 1990). As the child develops, cognitive processes serve as vulnerability factors for developing DPD. The child may become sensitive to social cues that serve to decrease his or her sense of self-efficacy. Feelings of inadequacy contribute to a cycle of failure, serving to reinforce the child's negative views of his or her ability (Geiger & Crick, 2001). Negative self-concept may also contribute to a dependent person's feared loss of support. The individual may come to believe that revealing his or her opinions may damage close relationships (Gilligan, 1982).

From a cognitive-behavioral perspective, and consistent with attachment theory, DPD can be understood as stemming from the development and activation of specific beliefs, attributions, expectations, perceptual and memory processes, and adaptive strategies in specific social situations. When dependent persons' behaviors in different situations and settings are interpreted in the context of their underlying assumptions and beliefs (e.g., a view of the self as powerless and ineffectual; others can provide needed guidance and protection) and goals (i.e., the desire to be guided and supported by others), apparent inconsistencies disappear. To the extent that the dependent person's cognitive constructs are elucidated, our ability to understand and predict behavior of dependent children and adolescents in different contexts is likely to increase.

The observations that dependent individuals can be passive in some settings and assertive or even aggressive in others can be reconciled by examining their underlying motives in different situations. The central goal that underlies much of the dependent individual's behavior is the maintenance of a protective, nurturing, and supportive relationship. Dependent individuals often yield to group pressure (Masling et al., 1986), except when doing so would alienate them from a respected authority figure (Bornstein, Leone, & Galley, 1987). Given dependent persons' strong motivation to obtain and maintain supportive relationships, inconsistencies in their behavior can be understood: Depending on the situation, dependent persons will tend to exhibit behaviors they believe will maximize the likelihood of obtaining and maintaining a protective, supportive relationship. When assertive, active behavior will achieve these goals, the dependent person acts accordingly. Dependent persons will exhibit passive behavior, however, when they believe that is more likely to elicit support. Each kind of behavior is an attempt to fulfill the dependent person's goal of obtaining and maintaining the supportive, protective relationships they desire.

Compliant behavior, from this perspective, may be understood as a "self-presentation" strategy rather than a genuine lack of assertiveness. It is intended to make certain kinds of impressions on others to achieve the dependent person's goals. The dependent person anticipates that passive, helpless behavior may, in some circumstances, elicit support and nurturance from others. Studies confirm that passive behavior does serve as a social cue and can elicit support from others (Baker & Reitz, 1978; Berkowitz & Daniels, 1963, 1964; Harris & Ho, 1984; Taylor, Messick, Lehman, & Hirsch, 1982). Whether this knowledge is implicit or explicit is a question that has not yet been addressed.

The cognitive model of dependency may be better able than psychoanalytic, object relations, or social learning models to account for the diversity of behaviors that are exhibited by dependent persons in various situations and settings. Conceptualizing dependent patients in terms of their "core" motivation can be more helpful in reconciling the wide range of behaviors exhibited. Dependency-related cognitions may play a role in determining the motivations, behaviors, and affective responses of dependent persons. Cognitive models, then, may also be better able to account for recent findings on associations between cognitive style and dependency.

THE COGNITIVE-INTERACTIONIST MODEL

Bornstein (1992, 1993, 1996) combined key elements of extant psychodynamic, cognitive, and attachment-based models of dependency in developing a cognitive-interactionist (C-I) model of interpersonal dependency. His C-I model of dependency includes four primary components:

1. *Cognitive.* A central element in dependency is the perception of oneself as powerless and ineffective, along with the belief that others are powerful and effectual. The C-I model holds that dependency-related motivations, behaviors, and emotional responses result from the dependent person's "helpless" self-concept.

2. *Motivational.* Dependent individuals have a strong desire for guidance, approval, and support from others. These desires can sometimes affect behavior without the conscious awareness of the individual.

3. *Affective.* Dependent individuals may become anxious in situations where they are required to be autonomous, especially when their actions will be evaluated by an authority figure. This anxiety may present as school refusal in children or agoraphobia in adolescents.

4. *Behavioral.* Dependent individuals use a variety of relationship-promoting self-preservation strategies to strengthen bonds with others. These include ingratiation, supplication, exemplification, self-promotion, and intimidation.

The C-I model hypothesizes that three factors contribute to the creation of the dependent person's helpless self-schema: overprotective or authoritarian parenting, gender role socialization, and cultural attitudes. The model argues that variations in the level of self-schema activation will influence motivation, behaviors, and affect in predictable ways. Events that activate the self-schema (e.g., failure, rejection) will increase the motivation to seek support and protection from others, increase relationship-facilitation self-presentation behaviors, and increase fears of abandonment or negative evaluation by others (Bornstein, 2005).

The C-I model acknowledges that dependent individuals show a broader range of social behaviors than was earlier thought, and accounts for individual differences in the expression of DPD. In many situations, dependent patients are passive and compliant. When confronted by a threat (e.g., the loss of a relationship), however, they can become assertive or even aggressive to ensure that they are not abandoned. Integrative models accommodate the range of passive and active behaviors exhibited by dependent persons by recognizing that these behaviors serve a common goal of strengthening ties to others (Bornstein, 1995; Pincus & Wilson, 2001). It is noteworthy that cognitive elements play a central role in this model, which posits that dependency-related motivations, behaviors, and affective responses stem from a schema of the self as powerless and ineffectual. Further, events that activate this self-schema cause state-related variations in dependent behavior. A patient's affective responses can themselves prime the dependent self-schema, producing feedback loops that increase dependency-related responding.

Although the results of this review offer some support for the psychoanalytic, object relations, social, and attachment models of dependency, these models are limited in their ability to account for the diverse behaviors displayed by individuals with DPD in different situations and across settings. However, the C-I model succeeds in drawing dependency's core components into a cohesive picture. The model recognizes the importance of early experience and the role of cognition in shaping dependency-related behavior and places the individual in the context in which this behavior is exhibited. As a result, the C-I model provides underlying consistency to the apparent inconsistency in the behaviors exhibited in different settings—something no other theoretical model fully accomplishes.

A LIFE SPAN PERSPECTIVE ON DEPENDENT PERSONALITY DISORDER

Although early experiences may lay the groundwork for the development of dependent personality traits, later life events shape, reinforce, and consolidate these traits and influence their expression. Understanding the development of dependency across the life span is important for several reasons. First, changing manifestations of dependency have implications for diagnosis and assessment. The clinician must take into account the impact of patient developmental level when attempting to assess or diagnose DPD. Second, factors implicated in vulnerability for DPD may serve as targets of clinical intervention and help determine the focus of treatment. From this perspective, interventions should be linked, conceptually and therapeutically, to a model that explains how the problematic dependency developed over time.

DEPENDENT PERSONALITY DISORDER AS A PERVASIVE LIFE THEME

Until the middle of the past century, developmental theorists tended to view infants as passive recipients of a caregiver's love and nurturance. Psychologists now realize that infants play an active role in eliciting and shaping a variety of caregiver behaviors and that they actively attempt to understand events as they occur (Greenspan, 1989; Stern, 1985). Nonetheless, the first months of life represent a period of maximum dependency on others. Infants are all but completely reliant on caregivers for protection, nurturance, affirmation, and support. Even in early and middle adulthood, when people are generally most self-sufficient, dependency issues arise in relationships. Dependency-related dynamics affect interactions with family, friends, lovers, and colleagues, often in very different ways (Baumiester & Leary, 1995; Behrends, 2004; Fu, Hinkle, & Hannah, 1986).

Different phases of life present unique interpersonal challenges and opportunities, which cause dependency-related dynamics to change as well. Blatt (1990, 1991; Blatt & Shichman, 1983) and others (Franz & White, 1985), building on Erikson's (1950) psychosocial stage model, conceptualize personality development in terms of a lifelong dialectic involving interpersonal relatedness (i.e., dependency, connectedness) and self-definition (i.e., independence, autonomy). Blatt's (1990) dialectic makes explicit the ongoing, lifelong tension between tendencies toward dependency and autonomy.

Methods we use to obtain nurturance and support also change as we mature, and strategies that were appropriate at age 5 become inappropriate at age 25. Indeed, one key feature of healthy dependency is the ability to determine which strategies are optimal for obtaining the desired response in the short term while strengthening long-term bonds with potential caregivers (Cross, Bacon, & Morris, 2000; Lee & Robins, 1995, 1998).

With this as context, the following sections outline the changing expression of dependency across the life span. The evolution of dependency from infancy to adolescence is discussed, focusing on factors that shape the dependent individual's beliefs, motives, and behaviors. Individual differences in dependency and DPD are multiply determined, and the changing manifestations of dependency across the life span reflect a complex array of internal and external factors. Dependent patients present in a diverse array of styles because each patient has a unique constellation of internal and external processes that influence personality development and behavior.

INFANTILE DEPENDENCY

Recent research findings suggest that dependent personality traits may be influenced by genetic factors (Livesley, Jang, Jackson, & Vernon, 1993). Pooled results from twin studies assessing the heritability of dependency show that approximately 30% of the variance in self-report dependency scores is attributable to genetic factors (Coolidge, Thede, & Jang, 2000; Dworkin, Burke, Maher, & Gottesman, 1976; Gottesman, 1966; O'Neill & Kendler, 1998; Torgersen et al., 2000).

PARENTING CONTRIBUTIONS

Relations also may exist between early mother-infant interaction and later dependency. Early research investigated relations between infant

584 PERSONALITY DISORDERS IN CHILDHOOD AND ADOLESCENCE

feeding, weaning, and later dependency (Goldman-Eisler, 1951; Hein-stein, 1963; Sears et al., 1965; Sears, Whiting, Nowlis, & Sears, 1953). Results, however, were mixed, with some studies finding a relation-ship between these variables and later dependency (Heinstein, 1963) and others finding no consistent relationship (Sears et al., 1965). Moreover, most of these studies used mothers' retrospective reports of infant-caregiver interactions. Given the methodological limitations of research in this area, it is difficult to draw firm conclusions regarding the relation of feeding and weaning to later dependency.

More consistent findings came from later studies examining the influence of the overall quality of the infant-caregiver relationship on later dependent behavior. Overprotective parenting may be ex-pected to lead to higher levels of dependency, as an overprotective style may lead children to view themselves as vulnerable and weak; consistent with this, a number of studies have found significant cor-relations between maternal protectiveness and children's depen-dency (Finney, 1961; Gordon & Tegtmeyer, 1983; Hatfield, Ferguson, & Alpert, 1967; Kagan, Moss, & Sigel, 1960). Studies that use retro-spective reports from parents and their adult children produced re-sults that were consistent with these findings (Ojha & Singh, 1988; Parker & Lipscombe, 1980). In a similar manner, several studies found that parental authoritarianism predicts later dependency in childhood (Baumrind, 1971; Bhogle, 1983; McPartland & Epstein, 1975; Roe & Siegelman, 1963; Winder & Rau, 1962) and adolescence (McCranie & Bass, 1984; Vaillant, 1980), in part because children of authoritarian parents come to feel that they must accede to others' demands rather than act independently. Consistent results in this area were obtained despite the fact that many studies used different measures and experimental methodologies, with samples drawn from different groups (i.e., American, Indian, and British). The cross-cultural and cross-methodological consistency attests to the robustness and generalizability of these findings.

The hypothesis that the dependent person is motivated to obtain and maintain nurturing, protective relationships is consistent with the observation that certain parenting styles predict levels of dependency in childhood and adolescence. Early relationships with caregivers play a central role in the construction of the self-concept (Bandura, 1977). Children of overly protective parents, as a consequence, may come to believe that they cannot function independently without the guidance and protection of others, particularly authority figures (Baumrind, 1973). Inasmuch as early relationships create a child's expectations for future interpersonal relationships (Bornstein et al., 1986; Waters & Deane, 1985), parental overprotectiveness may lead to the child's expecting that he or she will be nurtured or cared for by others. Parental authoritarianism, similarly, may lead the child to believe that the way to maintain relationships with others is to acquiesce to their requests, expectations, and demands (Baumrind, 1971; Maccoby, 1980).

Taken together, these findings suggest that early parenting practices—specifically, parental overprotectiveness and authoritarianism—serve to reinforce dependent behaviors in children and prevent the child from developing beliefs and expectations that facilitate independent, autonomous behavior. Both types of parenting styles inhibit the child from engaging in the kind of trial-and-error learning that is necessary for developing a sense of independence, mastery, and competence. Results of studies show that parental reinforcement of dependent behavior (or punishment of independent behavior) during early childhood predicts level of dependency in later childhood or adolescence (Finney, 1961; Fu et al., 1986; Fu, Kelso, & Moran, 1984; J. McCord, McCord, & Thurber, 1962; Sears et al., 1965; Sroufe et al., 1983).

Although research indicates that parental authoritarianism and overprotection predict the development of dependent behaviors in children, the possibility also exists that dependent behaviors in children may serve to encourage and reinforce overprotective, dependency-fostering behavior in parents. In other words, parenting style and childhood dependency may be transactionally related. Certain infantile temperament variables (e.g., low soothability) elicit parenting behaviors that foster dependency (e.g., overprotectiveness). The parent whose child is easily upset and difficult to soothe may come to view that child as fragile and weak, resulting in an overprotective parenting style (Bornstein, 1992, 1993). Several studies indicate that dependent behaviors shown in children elicit strong protective behaviors in parents (Hunt, Browning, & Nave, 1982; Marcus, 1975, 1976). Other studies suggest that a child's dependent behavior increases parental demands (Maccoby, 1980). These results suggest that the relationship of child dependency and parental behavior is characterized by mutual influence and reciprocal reinforcement.

CHILDHOOD DEPENDENCY

As children grow, they internalize schemas of social interactions (what developmental theorists call *internal working models*). These schemas become more organized, integrated, and articulated over time, reflecting the child's ongoing interactions with caregivers and developing cognitive skills. The child begins to conceptualize the self and interpersonal world in increasingly subtle and complex ways (Blatt, 1990; Tabin, 1985).

By middle childhood, dependent children have internalized a representation of themselves as weak and ineffective, as well as the belief that others are powerful and may protect them (Bornstein, 1996). These schemas ultimately evolve into a complex array of underlying assumptions about interpersonal exchanges which reflect a common set of underlying goals, affect qualities, and desired or feared outcomes (Abelson, 1981; Singer & Salovey, 1990). The dependent child's tacit relationship assumptions reflect the underlying goals of help- and support-seeking, an affect tone of anxiety and insecurity, a desired outcome of obtained support, and a feared outcome of rejection or abandonment.

FAMILY CONTRIBUTIONS

The most important interpersonal dynamics that shape a child's beliefs and assumptions are those that take place within the family. Relationship styles are strongly influenced by the family system in which they are embedded (Brock & Barnard, 1988; Epstein, Schlesinger, & Dryden, 1988). In understanding the development and treatment of dependency it is important to consider family roles, expectations, values, and assumptions.

Interpersonal dynamics within the family can combine to create and preserve dependent behavior. Intrapersonally, the child's insecure attachment and helpless self-schema lead the child to focus on maintaining relationships with powerful others rather than building internal coping resources. Interpersonally, family roles and expectations may reinforce the child's dependency in an effort to maintain a balanced family system. The interlocking system is an additional resistance that can undermine a child's progress.

CHILDHOOD ABUSE AND NEGLECT

Research shows that childhood physical or sexual abuse can lead to increased dependency during adolescence and adulthood. Under some circumstances, the experience of abuse, particularly when repetitive, can engender pervasive feelings of powerlessness and vulnerability (Hill, Gold, & Bornstein, 2000). Findings are mixed, however, in that some studies suggest that early and severe emotional deprivation may also lead to decreased dependency in the child (W. McCord & McCord, 1956).

ADOLESCENT DEPENDENCY

The transition to young adulthood is often conflictual, as the individual struggles with increasing internal pressure to separate from the family yet feels unable to manage the challenges of independence. The adolescent is no longer a child, but not yet comfortable in adult roles. This ambivalence is coupled with physiological changes and social demands, often causing unpredictable, impulsive behavior (Bornstein, 2005).

Adolescents who have a greater degree of autonomy (e.g., those with a secure attachment style and healthy relationship schemas) may transition into adolescence with relative ease. The dependent adolescent, however, often shows less adaptive responses to the challenges of this transition period. This may result in increased peer-group dependency (Bornstein, 2005). Even relatively autonomous adolescents show some degree of peer-group dependence as a means for transitioning from familial dependence to mature adulthood (Steinberg & Silverberg, 1986; Zirkel, 1992), but highly dependent adolescents differ in the intensity and rigidity of their attachment. This may mean submersion in the collective identity of a clique (Marcia, 1993) or a particularly strong bond to a best friend (Hartup, 1989, 1999). In either case, the dependent adolescent shifts familial dependency onto a peer or peer group (Friedlander & Siegel, 1990; Lapan & Patton, 1986).

Another way some overly dependent adolescents cope with this transition is by retreating into more dependent, immature behavior (Galatzer-Levy & Cohler, 1993). These adolescents respond to the stresses of this period by clinging even more tightly to their family and retreating from peers. In this way, the adolescents avoid feelings of anxiety that may accompany increases of autonomy, and focus solely on their desire for dependency. For some highly dependent adolescents, this regression can linger into adulthood (Alperin, 2001; Brock & Barnard, 1988).

Gender Role Socialization

The vast majority of studies investigating gender differences in adult dependency have used self-report measures (i.e., interviews and questionnaires), typically finding higher levels of dependency in women than men (Birtchnell & Kennard, 1983; Chevron, Quinlan, & Blatt, 1978; Conley, 1980; Lao, 1980; Ojha & Singh, 1985; Singh & Ojha, 1987; Vats, 1986). Using questionnaires, gender differences have been found in school-age children of various ages and from a variety of cultures (Chadha, 1983; Ederer, 1988; Ojha &

Singh, 1972). Longitudinal studies of dependency in children typically find little or no difference between boys and girls with regard to dependency levels in early childhood (Maccoby & Jacklin, 1974). Gender differences increase with age (Kagan et al., 1960), with girls almost invariably showing greater dependency than boys by the time they reach school age (Chadha, 1983; Yeger & Miezitis, 1985). It is possible that the increasing gender differences in dependency levels with increasing age is due to gender role socialization. Boys are generally discouraged from expressing openly dependent feelings, whereas passive, dependent behavior has traditionally been regarded as consonant with female behavior (Spence & Helmreich, 1978).

ASSESSMENT OF DEPENDENCY IN ADULTS

Numerous self-report measures of dependency are available for use in clinical settings with adults. More than 35 self-report measures of dependency and DPD have been developed (see Bornstein, 1999, 2005, for reviews). Many of these measures assess dependency along with other traits (e.g., Blatt, D'Afflitti, & Quinlan, 1976; Pincus & Gurtman, 1995). Other self-report dependency scales are embedded in omnibus personality inventories, such as the Minnesota Multiphasic Personality Inventory (Navran, 1954), the Millon Clinical Multiaxial Inventory (Millon, Millon, & Davis, 1994), and the Personality Diagnostic Questionnaire (Davison, Morven, & Taylor, 2001).

Hirschfeld et al.'s (1977) Interpersonal Dependency Inventory (IDI) is one of the most widely used self-report dependency tests and has been validated extensively in inpatient and outpatient settings. The IDI includes 48 self-statements, each of which is rated on a 4-point scale anchored with the terms *disagree* (1) and *agree* (4). The items form three subscales: Emotional Reliance on Others (18 items), Lack of Social Self-Confidence (16 items), and Assertion of Autonomy (14 items). The subscales tap different dependency-related traits, rather than directly assessing DPD symptoms. Although these measures have been extensively validated with adult populations (Fisher & Greenberg, 1985; Masling, 1986; Masling & Schwartz, 1979), little research has been conducted on their validity with children or adolescents. But because there are few measures of dependency designed specifically for children, research on dependency in children and adolescents often uses these adult measures, despite the lack of research supporting their validity for that population.

Questionnaire ratings of dependency should be augmented by the clinical assessment of the patient's perceptions of self and others, coping strategies, and social relationships. Key elements in DPD are perceptions of the self as weak and of others as powerful (Bornstein, 1996; Huprich, 2001; Pincus & Wilson, 2001). Sensitive interviewing about these beliefs and perceptions as well as discussion of how individuals feel when required to behave in an independent manner or when separated from important people in their life can be helpful in this regard.

Although depressed individuals often behave in a dependent manner, and depressive episodes are often precipitated by interpersonal losses or separation, dependency is distinct from hopelessness, helplessness, and depression. It is thus important to distinguish traits of DPD from state-dependent symptoms of dependence that may accompany a depressive episode (see Hirschfeld et al., 1983).

TREATMENT

Although a great deal has been written about psychotherapy with dependent adults, there has been surprisingly little empirical research. Only eight controlled outcome studies have examined the efficacy of psychotherapy for DPD (Bornstein, 2005). Research on treatment of problematic dependency has included both insight-oriented therapy and cognitive or cognitive-behavioral treatments. Results, however, have been modest. Researchers reported small positive effects for time-limited (Alexander & Abeles, 1968) and long-term (Blatt, 1992; Blatt & Ford, 1994) psychodynamic therapy for dependent adult patients with an array of comorbid diagnoses. Five studies investigated the effectiveness of cognitive or cognitive-behavioral treatment for dependency, with two producing positive results (Nelson-Gray, Johnson, Foyle, Daniel, & Harmon, 1996; Rathus, Sanderson, Miller, & Wetzler, 1995) and three yielding non-significant results (Black, Monahan, Wesner, Gabel, & Bowers, 1996; Moore & Blackburn, 1996; Rector, Bagby, Segal, Joffe, & Levitt, 2000). Thus, no single modality has yielded consistently positive results, and data published to date do not provide clear support for a single therapeutic modality in treatment of DPD. These modest treatment efficacy findings, coupled with the multifaceted nature of DPD, suggest that integrated treatment approaches may be needed (Bornstein, 2007).

Overholser and Fine's (1994) four-stage model is perhaps the most fully developed cognitive framework for treatment of dependent patients. This model seeks to build patient confidence and teach social problem-solving skills, while maximizing treatment effectiveness by anticipating potential roadblocks. Overholser and Fine recommend that the therapist take an active stance early in therapy, providing considerable guidance and structure to engage the patient. Patients are taught behavioral skills that enable them to make meaningful changes quickly, thereby increasing their sense of control. As the patient gains trust in the therapist, more responsibility is gradually placed on the patient for structuring treatment. As patients show increased self-efficacy, the focus of treatment shifts to increasing autonomous behavior outside therapy. To facilitate this shift, the therapist uses Socratic methods—active, guided questioning—to help the patient generate solutions and insights (Overholser, 1987). Self-control strategies are also helpful in providing the patient with skills needed to replace reflexive help-seeking behaviors with effective problem solving in high-stress situations. As patients assume a more active role in their outside life, the focus again shifts to practicing relapse prevention techniques to minimize posttherapy backslides. Alternative ways of coping are discussed, and the patient is encouraged to reframe setbacks so minor backslides are not magnified into global failure experiences. Thus, the model is divided into four stages: (1) active guidance, (2) enhancement of self-esteem, (3) promotion of autonomy through problem-solving training, and (4) relapse prevention.

Messer (1992) introduced the concept of assimilative integration as a method for combining treatment strategies to maximize therapeutic outcome. Messer recommended selecting a core therapeutic modality based on the patient's personality and presenting problem, then supplementing this approach with interventions derived from other treatment models. As Beitman (1992) pointed out, the timing of new interventions can be important. The therapist's overarching strategy should be one of engaging patients, providing them with a conceptual framework to understand their current difficulties, and elucidating long-standing patterns in cognition, behavior, and emotional responding. Once these goals have been achieved, the stage is set for therapeutic shifts to be introduced as needed.

Case Example

After Sara was born, her mother, Mrs. Jones, experienced postpartum depression that left her unable to function for several months. Even after the more severe symptoms subsided, Mrs. Jones continued to have difficulty functioning until Sara began day care at age 3.5. During these first 3.5 years Mrs. Jones was barely able to meet Sara's physical needs. Her ability to be emotionally available and responsive to Sara in an attuned manner was significantly impaired. As a result, Sara was a clingy, whiny toddler. She would fret whenever Mrs. Jones was present and would follow her closely and act in a demanding fashion. Sara's pattern of attachment would most likely be classified on the Ainsworth Strange Situation Protocol as insecure-anxious.

As Sara developed, she continued to behave in a clingy, demanding manner. During the second grade, she began to display school avoidance and frequently attempted to stay at home with her mother. During late childhood, she showed notable anxiety symptoms and, later, as a teenager, was clingy with boyfriends and peers. She frequently sought reassurance from her friends, calling them to ask for advice and to have them tell her what to do about friendships. Sara's relationship with her mother was strained. She would alternately seek her mother's approval and then act defiantly when her mother set any limits or boundaries. When threatened with a separation or breach in her relationship with her mother, Sara would respond tearfully and use a variety of behavioral strategies to reengage Mrs. Jones.

These strategies ranged from being hostile and aggressive to being overly compliant and clingy.

Sara's adjustment as a young adult was poor. She had difficulty holding jobs that required autonomy or responsibility. She would frequently ask her supervisors for advice, direction, or approval, to such an extent that she was asked to leave jobs as a sales clerk in a department store, an accounting assistant for a local nonprofit, and a data entry clerk for a local insurance company. Her relationships with men tended to be tumultuous. Sara often found herself dating controlling and abusive men. At other times, her boyfriends would break-off the relationship when Sara's demands and insecurities caused her to require more attention, support, and attention than they were willing or able to provide.

CONCLUSIONS

Dependent Personality Disorder results largely—though not exclusively—from early social processes within the family. Developmental research suggests that the presence of certain risk factors (e.g., authoritarian parenting, unavailable or overprotective caregiver) increases the chances of dependency-related problems in later childhood and adolescence. These risk factors can be balanced by protective factors (e.g., having a positive social orientation, exposure to additional caretakers who model good relationships), which compensate for the negative effects of various risk factors and reduce the chances of developing problematic dependency later in life. More research is needed to identify factors that influence the progression toward later personality disorder so that early interventions based on this sequence of personality development can be designed.

Research on the development of healthy and unhealthy dependency raises questions about contemporary conceptualizations of DPD, which, in the current diagnostic system, cannot be diagnosed until adulthood. Mounting evidence suggests that a broader and more integrative approach to defining and diagnosing DPD should be taken— an approach that incorporates findings regarding the changing expression of dependency across the life span. With this goal in mind, further research into the etiology of DPD and its unique presentation in children and adolescents is needed.

REFERENCES

Abelson, R. (1981). Psychological status of the script concept. *American Psychologist, 36,* 715–729.

Abramson, L. Y., Seligman, M. E. P., & Teasdale, J. D. (1978). Learned helplessness in humans: Critique and reformulation. *Journal of Abnormal Psychology, 87,* 49–74.

Ainsworth, M. D. S. (1969). Object relations, dependency, and attachment: A theoretical review of the infant-mother relationship. *Child Development, 40,* 969–1025.

Ainsworth, M. D. S. (1972). Attachment and dependency: A comparison. In J. L. Gewirtz (Ed.), *Attachment and dependency* (pp. 97–137). Oxford: V. H. Winston & Sons.

Ainsworth, M. D. S., Blehar, M. C., Waters, E., & Wall, S. (1978). *Patterns of attachment: A psychological study of the Strange Situation.* Oxford, England: Erlbaum.

Alexander, J. F., & Abeles, N. (1968). Dependency changes in psychotherapy as related to interpersonal relationships. *Journal of Consulting and Clinical Psychology, 32*(6), 685–689.

Alonso-Arbiol, I., Shaver, P., & Yarnoz, S. (2002). Insecure attachment, gender roles, and interpersonal dependency in the Basque Country. *Personal Relationships, 9,* 479–490.

Alperin, R. (2001). Barriers to intimacy: An object relations perspective. *Psychoanalytic Psychology, 18,* 137–156.

American Psychiatric Association. (2000). *Diagnostic and statistical manual of mental disorders* (4th ed., text rev.). Washington, DC: Author.

Baker, L. D., & Reitz, H. J. (1978). Altruism toward the blind: Effects of sex of helper and dependency of victim. *Journal of Social Psychology, 104,* 19–28.

Ball, S. A. (1998). Manualized treatment for substance abusers with personality disorders: Dual focus schema therapy. *Addictive Behaviors, 23,* 883–891.

Ball, S. A., & Young, J. E. (2000). Dual focus schema therapy for personality disorders and substance dependence. *Cognitive and Behavioral Practice, 7,* 270–281.

Bandura, A. (1977). Self-efficacy: Toward a unifying theory of behavior change. *Psychological Review, 84,* 191–215.

Bandura, A. (1978). The self system in reciprocal determinism. *American Psychologist, 33,* 344–358.

Bartholomew, K. (1997). Adult attachment processes: Individual and couple perspectives. *British Journal of Medical Psychology, 70,* 249–263.

Baumiester, R., & Leary, M. (1995). The need to belong: Desire for interpersonal attachment as a fundamental human motivation. *Psychological Bulletin, 117,* 497–529.

Baumrind, D. (1971). Current patterns of parental authority. *Developmental Psychology, 4*(1, Pt. 2), 1–103.

Baumrind, D. (1973). Will a day care center be a child development center? *Young Children, 28,* 154–169.

Beck, A., & Freeman, A. (1990). *Cognitive therapy of personality disorders.* New York: Guilford Press.

Beck, A. T., Freeman, A., Davis, D., & Associates (2004). *Cognitive therapy of personality disorders* (2nd ed.). New York: Guilford Press.

Behrens, K. (2004). A multifaceted view of the concept of amae: Reconsidering the indigenous Japanese concept of relatedness. *Human Development, 47,* 1–27.

Beitman, B. D. (1992). Integration through fundamental similarities and useful differences among the schools. In J. C. Norcross & M. R. Goldfried (Eds.), *Handbook of psychotherapy integration* (pp. 202–230). New York: Basic Books.

Berkowitz, L., & Daniels, L. R. (1963). Responsibility and dependency. *Journal of Abnormal and Social Psychology, 66,* 429–436.

Berkowitz, L., & Daniels, L. R. (1964). Affecting the salience of the social responsibility norm: Effects of past help on the response to dependency relationships. *Journal of Abnormal and Social Psychology, 68,* 275–281.

Berlin, L., & Cassidy, J. (1999). Relations among relationships: Contributions from attachment theory and research. In J. Cassidy & P. Shaver (Eds.), *Handbook of attachment: Theory, research, and clinical applications* (pp. 688–712). New York: Guilford Press.

Bernstein, D., Cohen, P., Skodol, A., Bezirganian, S., & Brook, J. (1996). Childhood antecedents of adolescent personality disorders. *American Journal of Psychiatry, 153,* 907–913.

Bhogle, S. (1983). Antecedents of dependency behavior in children of low social class. *Psychological Studies, 2,* 92–95.

Birtchnell, J., & Kennard, J. (1983). What does the MMPI Dependency Scale really measure? *Journal of Clinical Psychology, 39,* 532–543.

Black, D. W., Monahan, P., Wesner, R., Gabel, J., & Bowers, W. (1996). The effect of fluvoxamine, cognitive therapy, and placebo on abnormal personality traits in 44 patients with panic disorder. *Journal of Personality Disorders, 10,* 185–194.

Blatt, E. (1992). Factors associated with child abuse and neglect in residential care settings. *Children and Youth Services Review, 14,* 493–517.

Blatt, S. J. (1974). Levels of object representation in anaclitic and introjective depression. *Psychoanalytic Study of the Child, 29,* 107–157.

Blatt, S. J. (1990). Interpersonal relatedness and self-definition: Two personality configurations and their implications for psychopathology and psychotherapy. In J. L. Singer (Ed.), *Repression and dissociation: Implications for personality theory, psychopathology, and health* (pp. 299–335). Chicago: University of Chicago Press.

Blatt, S. J. (1991). A cognitive morphology of psychopathology. *Journal of Nervous and Mental Diseases, 179,* 449–458.

Blatt, S. J., D'Afflitti, J. P., & Quinlan, D. M. (1976). Experiences of depression in normal young adults. *Journal of Abnormal Psychology, 85,* 383–389.

Blatt, S. J., & Ford, R. Q. (1994). *Therapeutic change: An object relations perspective.* New York: Plenum Press.

Blatt, S. J., Ford, R. Q., Berman, W. H., Cook, B., Cramer, P., & Robins, C. (1994). *Therapeutic change: An object relations perspective.* New York: Plenum Press.

Blatt, S. J., & Homann, E. (1992). Parent-child interaction in the etiology of dependent and self-critical depression. *Clinical Psychology Review, 12,* 47–91.

Blatt, S. J., & Shichman, S. (1983). Two primary configurations for psychopathology. *Psychoanalysis and Contemporary Thought, 6,* 187–254.

Blatt, S. J., & Zuroff, D. C. (1992). Interpersonal relatedness and self-definition: Two prototypes for depression. *Clinical Psychology Review, 12,* 527–562.

Bornstein, R. F. (1992). The dependent personality: Developmental, social, and clinical perspectives. *Psychological Bulletin, 112,* 3–23.

Bornstein, R. F. (1993). *The dependent personality.* New York: Guilford Press.

Bornstein, R. F. (1995). Active dependency. *Journal of Nervous and Mental Diseases, 183,* 64–77.

Bornstein, R. F. (1996). Beyond orality: Toward an object relations/interactionist reconceptualization of the etiology and dynamics of dependency. *Psychoanalytic Psychology, 13,* 177–203.

Bornstein, R. F. (1997). Dependent personality disorder in the *DSM-IV* and beyond. *Clinical Psychology: Science and Practice, 4,* 175–187.

Bornstein, R. F. (1999). Dependent and histrionic personality disorders. In T. Millon, P. H. Blaney, & R. D. Davis (Eds.), *Oxford textbook of psychopathology* (pp. 535–555). Oxford: Oxford University Press.

Bornstein, R. F. (2005). *The dependent patient: A practitioner's guide.* Washington, DC: American Psychological Association.

Bornstein, R. F. (2007). Dependent personality disorder: Effective time-limited therapy. *Current Psychiatry, 6,* 37–45.

Bornstein, R. F., Galley, D. J., & Leone, D. R. (1986). Parental representations and orality. *Journal of Personality Assessment, 50,* 80–89.

Bornstein, R. F., Leone, D. R., & Galley, D. J. (1987). The generalizability of subliminal mere exposure effects: Influence of stimuli perceived without awareness on social behaviour. *Journal of Personality and Social Psychology, 53,* 1070–1079.

Bowlby, J. (1969). Disruption of affectional bonds and its effects on behavior. *Canada's Mental Health Supplement, 59,* 12.

Bowlby, J. (1973). *Separation: Anxiety and anger.* New York: Basic Books.

Bowlby, J. (1980). *Attachment and loss.* New York: Basic Books.

Bowlby, J. (1988). *A secure base.* New York: Basic Books.

Bowlby, J. (2005). *The making and breaking of affectional bonds.* New York: Routledge.

Brennan, K., & Shaver, P. (1998). Attachment styles and personality disorders: Their connections to each other and to parental divorce, parental death, and perceptions of parental caregiving. *Journal of Personality, 66,* 835–878.

Brock, G., & Barnard, C. (1988). *Procedures in family therapy.* Boston: Allyn & Bacon.s

Chadha, N. K. (1983). A study of dependence-proneness and test-anxiety in school going children. *Indian Psychological Review, 24,* 34–38.

Chambless, D., Renneberg, B., Gracely, E., Goldstein, A., & Fydrich, T. (2000). Axis I and II comorbidity in agoraphobia: Prediction of psychotherapy outcome in a clinical setting. *Psychotherapy Research, 10,* 279–295.

Chevron, E. S., Quinlan, D. M., & Blatt, S. J. (1978). Sex roles and gender differences in the experience of depression. *Journal of Abnormal Psychology, 87,* 680–683.

Cicchetti, D., & Cohen, D. (Eds.). (1995). *Developmental psychopathology: Vol. 1. Theory and methods.* New York: Wiley.

Conley, J. J. (1980). Family configuration as an etiological factor in alcoholism. *Journal of Abnormal Psychology, 89,* 670–673.

Coolidge, F., Thede, L., & Jang, K. (2000). Heritability of personality disorders in childhood: A preliminary investigation. *Journal of Personality Disorders, 15,* 33–40.

Cross, S., Bacon, P., & Morris, M. (2000). The relational-interdependent self-construal and relationships. *Journal of Personality and Social Psychology, 78,* 791–808.

Davison, S., Morven, L., & Taylor, P. J. (2001). Examination of the screening properties of the Personality Diagnostic Questionnaire 4 (PDQ-4) in a prison population. *Journal of Personality Disorders, 15,* 180–194.

Dworkin, R., Burke, B., Maher, B., & Gottesman, I. (1976). A longitudinal study of the genetics of personality. *Journal of Personality and Social Psychology, 34,* 510–518.

Ederer, E. (1988). Dysthymia, psychosocial dependency, and self-esteem in 10-year-old boys and girls: An empirical contribution to clinical personality research. *Studia Psychologica, 30*(3), 227–235.

Epstein, N., Schlesinger, S., & Dryden, W. (1988). *Cognitive-behavioral therapy with families.* New York: Brunner & Mazel.

Erikson, E. (1950). *Childhood and society.* New York: Norton.

Fairbairn, W. (1952). *An object relations theory of personality.* New York: Basic Books.

Feeney, J., & Noller, P. (1990). Attachment style as a predictor of adult romantic relationships. *Journal of Personality and Social Psychology, 58,* 281–291.

Finney, J. C. (1961). Some maternal influences on children's personality and character. *Genetic Psychology Monographs, 63,* 199–278.

Fisher, S., & Greenberg, R. (1985). *The scientific credibility of Freud's theories and therapy.* New York: Columbia University Press.

Fisher, S., & Greenberg, R. (1996). *Freud scientifically reappraised: Testing the theories and therapy.* New York: Wiley.

Franz, C., & White, K. (1985). Individuation and attachment in personality development: Extending Erikson's theory. *Journal of Personality, 53,* 224–256.

Freud, S. (1983). An outline of psychoanalysis. In J. Strachey (Ed. & Trans.), *The standard edition of the complete psychological works of Sigmund Freud* (Vol. 23, pp. 141–279). London: Hogarth Press. (Original work published 1953)

Friedlander, M., & Siegel, S. (1990). Separation-individuation difficulties and cognitive-behavioral indicators of eating disorders among college women. *Journal of Counseling Psychology, 37,* 74–78.

Fu, V. R., Hinkle, D. E., & Hanna, M. A. (1986). A three-generational study of the development of individual dependency and family interdependence. *Genetic, Social, and General Psychology Monographs, 112,* 153–171.

Fu, V. R., Kelso, G. B., & Moran, J. D. (1984). The effects of stimulus dimension and mode of exploration on original thinking in preschool children. *Educational and Psychological Measurement, 44,* 431–440.

Furman, W., & Wehner, E. A. (1994). Romantic views: Toward a theory of adolescent romantic relationships. In R. Montemayor, G. R. Adams, & T. P. Gullotta (Eds.), *Personal relationships during adolescence* (pp. 168–195). Thousand Oaks, CA: Sage.

Galatzer-Levy, R., & Cohler, B. (1993). *The essential other: A developmental psychology of the self.* New York: Basic Books.

Geiger, T., & Crick, N. (2001). A developmental psychopathology perspective on vulnerability to personality disorders. In R. E. Ingram & J. M. Price (Eds.), *Vulnerability to psychopathology* (pp. 55–102). New York: Guilford Press.

Gilligan, C. (1982). *In a different voice: Psychological theory and women's development.* Cambridge, MA. Harvard University Press.

Goldman-Eisler, F. (1951). The problem of "orality" and of its origin in early childhood. *Journal of Mental Science, 97,* 765–782.

Gordon, M., & Tegtmeyer, P. F. (1983). Oral-dependent content in children's Rorschach protocols. *Perceptual and Motor Skills, 57,* 1163–1168.

Gottesman, I. (1966). Genetic variance in adaptive personality traits. *Journal of Child Psychology and Psychiatry, 7,* 199–208.

Greenspan, S. (1989). *The development of the ego.* New York: International University Press.

Harris, M. B., & Ho, J. (1984). Effects of degree, locus, and controllability of dependency, and sex of subject on anticipated and actual helping. *Journal of Social Psychology, 122,* 245–255.

Hartup, W. (1989). Social relationships and their developmental significance. *American Psychologist, 44,* 120–126.

Hartup, W. (1999). Friendships and adaptation across the lifespan. *Current Directions in Psychological Science, 8,* 76–79.

Hatfield, J. S., Ferguson, L. R., & Alpert, R. (1967). Mother-child interaction and the socialization process. *Child Development, 38,* 365–414.

Heinstein, M. (1963). Behavioral correlates of breast-bottle regimes under varying parent-infant relationships. *Monographs of the Society for Research on Human Development, 28,* 1–61.

Hesse, E. (1999). The Adult Attachment Interview: Historical and current perspectives. In J. Cassidy & P. Shaver (Eds.), *Handbook of attachment* (pp. 395–433). New York: Guilford Press.

Hill, E., Gold, S., & Bornstein, R. (2000). Interpersonal dependency among adult survivors of childhood sexual abuse in therapy. *Journal of Child Sexual Abuse, 9,* 71–86.

Hirschfeld, R. M., Klerman, G. L., Clayton, P. J., Keller, M. B., McDonald-Scott, P., & Larkin, B. H. (1983). Assessing personality: Effects of the depressive state on trait measurement. *American Journal of Psychiatry, 140,* 695–699.

Hirschfeld, R., Klerman, G., Gough, H., Barrett, J., Korchin, S., & Chodoff, P. (1977). A measure of interpersonal dependency. *Journal of Personality Assessment, 41,* 610–618.

Holmes, J. (1993). *John Bowlby and attachment theory.* New York: Rutledge.

Hull, C. (1943). *Principles of behavior.* New York: Appleton-Century-Crofts.

Hunt, E., Browning, P., & Nave, G. (1982). A behavioral exploration of dependent and independent mildly mentally retarded adolescents and their mothers. *Applied Research in Mental Retardation, 3,* 141–150.

Huprich, S. (2001). Object loss and object relations in depressive personality analogues. *Bulletin of the Menninger Clinic, 65,* 549–559.

Jackson, H., Whiteside, H., Bates, G., Bell, R., Rudd, R., & Edwards, J. (1991). Diagnosing personality disorders in psychiatric inpatients. *Acta Psychiatrica Scandinavica, 83,* 206–213.

Jansen, M., Arntz, A., Merckelbach, H., & Mersch, P. (1994). Personality disorders and features in social phobia and panic disorder. *Journal of Abnormal Psychology, 103,* 391–395.

Johnson, F. (1993). *Dependency and Japanese socialization.* New York: New York University Press.

Kagan, J., Moss, H., & Sigel, I. (1960). Conceptual style and the use of affect labels. *Merrill-Palmer Quarterly, 6,* 261–276.

Kaul, V., Mathur, P., & Murlidharan, R. (1982). Dependency and its antecedents: A review. *Indian Educational Review, 17,* 35–46.

Kernberg, O. (1975). *Borderline conditions and pathological narcissism.* New York: Aronson.

Kirkpatrick, L. A. (1998). Evolution, pair-bonding, and reproductive strategies: A reconceptualization of adult attachment. In J. A. Simpson & W. S. Rholes (Eds.), *Attachment theory and close relationships* (pp. 353–393). New York: Guilford Press.

Lao, R. C. (1980). Differential factors affecting male and female academic performance in high school. *Journal of Psychology: Interdisciplinary and Applied, 104,* 119–127.

Lapan, R., & Patton, M. (1986). Self-psychology and the adolescent process: Measures of pseudoautonomy and peer-group dependence. *Journal of Counseling Psychology, 33,* 136–142.

Lee, R., & Robins, S. (1995). Measuring belongingness: The Social Connectedness and Social Assurance Scales. *Journal of Counseling Psychology, 42,* 232–241.

Lee, R., & Robins, S. (1998). The relationship between social connectedness and anxiety, self-esteem, and social identity. *Journal of Counseling Psychology, 45,* 338–345.

Livesley, W. J., Jang, K., Jackson, D., & Vernon, P. (1993). Genetic and environmental contributions to dimensions of personality disorder. *American Journal of Psychiatry, 150,* 1826–1831.

Livesley, W. J., Schroeder, M. L., & Jackson, D. N. (1990). Dependent personality disorder and attachment problems. *Journal of Personality Disorders, 4,* 131–140.

Maccoby, E. (1980). *Social development.* New York: Harcourt-Brace.

Maccoby, E., & Jacklin, C. (1974). *The psychology of sex differences.* Stanford: Stanford University Press.

Mahler, M., Pine, F., & Bergman, A. (1975). *Psychological birth of the human infant.* New York: Basic Books.

Main, M., & Cassidy, J. (1988). Categories of response to reunion with the parent at age 6: Predictable from infant attachment classifications and stable over a 1-month period. *Developmental Psychology, 24,* 415–426.

Main, M., & Hesse, E. (1990). Parents' unresolved traumatic experiences are related to infant disorganized attachment status: Is frightened and/or frightening parental behavior the linking mechanism? In M. T. Greenberg, D. Cicchetti, & E. M. Cummings (Eds.), *Attachment in the preschool years: Theory, research, and intervention* (pp. 161–182). Chicago: University of Chicago Press.

Main, M., & Solomon, J. (1986). Discovery of an insecure-disorganized/disoriented pattern. In T. B. Brazelton & M. Yogman (Eds), *Affective Development in Infancy.* Norwood, NJ: Ablex Publishing.

Marcia, J. (1993). The relational roots of identity. In J. Kroger (Ed.), *Discussions on ego identity* (pp. 118–128). Hillsdale, NJ: Erlbaum.

Marcus, R. F. (1975). The child as elicitor of parental sanctions for independent and dependent behavior: A simulation of parent-child interaction. *Developmental Psychology, 11,* 443–452.

Marcus, R. F. (1976). The effects of children's emotional and instrumental dependent behavior on parental response. *Journal of Psychology: Interdisciplinary and Applied, 92,* 57–63.

Masling, J. M. (1986). Orality, pathology, and interpersonal behavior. In J. Masling (Ed.), *Empirical studies of psychoanalytic theories* (Vol. 2, pp. 73–106). Hillsdale, NJ: Erlbaum.

Masling, J. M., & Schwartz, M. (1979). A critique of research in psychoanalytic theory. *Genetic Psychology Monographs, 100,* 257–307.

McCord, J., McCord, W., & Thurber, E. (1962). Some effects of paternal absence on male children. *Journal of Abnormal and Social Psychology, 64,* 361–369.

McCord, W., & McCord, J. (1956). *Psychopathy and delinquency.* Oxford, England: Grune and Stratton.

McCranie, E., & Bass, J. (1984). Childhood family antecedents of dependency and self-criticism. *Journal of Abnormal Psychology, 93,* 3–8.

McPartland, J., & Epstein, J. (1975). *An investigation of the interaction of family and social factor in open school.* Baltimore: Centre for the Social Organization of Schools, Johns Hopkins University.

Messer, S. (1992). A critical examination of belief structures in integrative and eclectic psychotherapy. In J. C. Norcross & M. R. Goldfried (Eds.), *Handbook of psychotherapy integration* (pp. 130–165). New York: Basic Books.

Mikulincer, M., Shaver, P. R., & Pereg, D. (2003). Attachment theory and affect regulation: The dynamics, development, and cognitive consequences of attachment-related strategies. *Motivation and Emotion, 27,* 77–102.

Millon, T., & Davis, R. (1995). The development of personality disorders. In D. Cicchetti & D. J. Cohen (Eds.), *Developmental psychopathology: Vol. 2. Risk, disorder, and adaptation* (pp. 633–676). New York: Wiley.

Millon, T., Millon, C., & Davis, R. (1994). *Millon Clinical Multiaxial Inventory-III.* Minneapolis, MN: National Computer Systems.

Mischel, W. (1973). Toward a cognitive social learning reconceptualization of personality. *Psychological Review, 80,* 252–283.

Mischel, W., & Peake, P. (1982). Beyond déjà vu in the search for cross-situational consistency. *Psychological Review, 89,* 730–755.

Moore, R. G., & Blackburn, I.-M. (1996). The stability of sociotropy and autonomy in depressed patients undergoing treatment. *Cognitive Therapy and Research, 20,* 69–80.

Mowrer, O. (1950). *Learning theory and personality dynamics.* New York: Ronald Press.

Navran, L. (1954). A rationally derived MMPI scale to measure dependence. *Journal of Consulting Psychology, 18,* 192.

Nelson-Gray, R. O., Johnson, D., Foyle, L. W., Daniel, S. S., & Harmon, R., Jr. (1996). The effectiveness of cognitive therapy tailored to depressives with personality disorders. *Journal of Personality Disorders, 10*, 132–152.

Nietzel, M., & Harris, M. (1990). Relationship of dependency and achievement/autonomy to depression. *Clinical Psychology Review, 10*, 279–297.

Ojha, H., & Singh, R. R. (1972). Sex differences in dependence proneness and prestige suggestibility. *Manas, 19*, 9–15.

Ojha, H., & Singh, R. R. (1985). Relationship of marriage-role attitude with dependence proneness and insecurity in university students. *Psychologia: An International Journal of Psychology in the Orient, 28*, 249–253.

Ojha, H., & Singh, R. R. (1988). Childrearing attitudes as related to insecurity and dependence proneness. *Psychological Studies, 33*, 75–79.

O'Neill, F., & Kendler, K. (1998). Longitudinal study of interpersonal dependency in female twins. *British Journal of Psychiatry, 172*, 154–158.

Overholser, J. C. (1987). Facilitating autonomy in passive-dependent persons: An integrative model. *Journal of Contemporary Psychotherapy, 17*, 250–269.

Overholser, J. C., & Fine, M. A. (1994). Cognitive-behavioral treatment of excessive interpersonal dependency: A four-stage psychotherapy model. *Journal of Cognitive Psychotherapy, 8*, 55–70.

Parker, G., & Lipscombe, P. (1980). The relevance of early parental experiences to adult dependency, hypochondriasis and utilization of primary physicians. *British Journal of Medical Psychology, 53*, 355–363.

Pincus, A. L., & Gurtman, M. B. (1995). The three faces of interpersonal dependency: Structural analyses of self-report dependency measures. *Journal of Personality and Social Psychology, 69*, 744–758.

Pincus, A. L., & Wilson, K. R. (2001). Interpersonal variability in dependent personality. *Journal of Personality, 69*, 223–251.

Poldrugo, F., & Forti, B. (1988). Personality disorders and alcoholism treatment outcome. *Drug and Alcohol Dependence, 21,* 171–176.

Rathus, J. H., Sanderson, W. C., Miller, A. L., & Wetzler, S. (1995). Impact of personality functioning on cognitive behavioral treatment of panic disorder: A preliminary report. *Journal of Personality Disorders, 9,* 160–168.

Rector, N., Bagby, R., Segal, Z., Joffe, R., & Levitt, A. (2000). Self-criticism and dependency in depressed patients treated with cognitive therapy or pharmacotherapy. *Cognitive Therapy and Research, 24,* 571–584.

Rey, J. M., Morris-Yates, A., Singh, M., Andrews, G., & Stewart, G. W. (1995). Continuities between psychiatric disorders in adolescents and personality disorders in young adults. *American Journal of Psychiatry, 152,* 895–900.

Roe, A., & Siegelman, M. (1963). A parent-child relations questionnaire. *Child Development, 34*(3), 355–369.

Rubin, K. H., Bukowski, W., & Parker, J. G. (1998). Peer interactions, relationships, and groups. In W. Damon & N. Eisenberg (Eds.), *Handbook of child psychology: Vol. 3. Social, emotional, and personality development* (5th ed., pp. 619–700). New York: Wiley.

Rusansky-Drob, L. (2005). A Lacanian approach. In A. Freeman, M. H. Stone, & D. Martin (Eds.), *Borderline personality disorder: A practitioner's guide to comparative treatments* (p. 185). New York: Springer.

Sans, J., & Avia, D. (1994). Cognitive specificity in social anxiety and depression: Self-statements, self-focused attention, and dysfunctional attitudes. *Journal of Social and Clinical Psychology, 13,* 105–137.

Saviola, M. (1981). Personal reflections on physically disabled women and dependency. *Professional Psychology: Research and Practice, 12,* 112–117.

Sciuto, G., Diaferia, G., Battaglia, M., Perna, G., Gabriele, A., & Bellodi, L. (1991). *DSM-III-R* personality disorders in panic and obsessive-compulsive disorder: A comparison study. *Comprehensive Psychiatry, 32,* 450–457.

Sears, R. R., Rau, L., & Alpert, R. (1965). *Identification and child rearing.* Stanford: Stanford University Press.

Sears, R. R., Whiting, J. W. M., Nowlis, V., & Sears, P. S. (1953). Some child-rearing antecedents of aggression and dependency in young children. *Genetic Psychology Monographs, 47,* 135–236.

Singer, J., & Salovey, P. (1990). Organized knowledge structures and personality: Person schemas, self-schemas, prototypes, and scripts. In M. J. Horowitz (Ed.), *Person schemas and maladaptive interpersonal patterns* (pp. 33–79). Chicago: University of Chicago Press.

Singh, R. R., & Ojha, S. K. (1987). Sex difference in dependence proneness, insecurity, and self concept. *Manas, 34,* 61–66.

Spence, J., & Helmreich, R. (1978). *Masculinity and femininity: Their psychological dimensions, correlates, and antecedents.* Austin: University of Texas Press.

Sperling, M., & Berman, W. (1991). An attachment classification of desperate love. *Journal of Personality Assessment, 56,* 45–55.

Sroufe, L. A. (1990). Considering normal and abnormal together: The essence of developmental psychopathology. *Development and Psychopathology, 2,* 335–347.

Sroufe, L. A., Fox, N. E., & Pancake, V. R. (1983). Attachment and dependency in developmental perspective. *Child Development, 54,* 1615–1627.

Steinberg, L., & Silverberg, S. B. (1986). The vicissitudes of autonomy in early adolescence. *Child Development, 57,* 841–851.

Stern, D. (1985). *The interpersonal world of the infant.* New York: Basic Books.

Stewart, S., Knize, K., & Pihl, R. (1992). Anxiety sensitivity and dependency in clinical and non-clinical panickers and controls. *Journal of Anxiety Disorders, 6,* 119–131.

Tabin, J. (1985). *On the way to self.* New York: Columbia University Press.

Taylor, R., Messick, D., Lehman, G., & Hirsch, J. (1982). Sex, dependency, and helping revisited. *Journal of Social Psychology, 118,* 59–65.

Thompson, R., & Zuroff, D. (1999). Dependent and self-critical mothers' responses to adolescent sons' autonomy and competence. *Journal of Youth and Adolescence, 28*, 365–384.

Torgersen, S., Lygren, S., Oien, P., Skre, I., Onstad, S., Edvardsen, J., et al. (2000). A twin study of personality disorders. *Comprehensive Psychiatry, 41*, 416–425.

Turkat, I. (1990). *The personality disorders: A psychological approach to clinical management.* Elmsford, NY: Pergamon Press.

Vaillant, G. (1980). Natural history of male psychological health: Pt. VIII. Antecedents of alcoholism and orality. *American Journal of Psychiatry, 137*, 181–186.

van IJzendoorn, M., Schuengel, C., & Bakermans-Kranenburg, M. (1999). Disorganized attachment in early childhood: Meta-analysis of precursors, concomitants, and sequelae. *Development and Psychopathology, 11*, 225–250.

Vats, A. (1986). Birth order, sex, and dependence proneness in Indian students. *Psychological Reports, 58*, 284–286.

Wallin, D. J. (2007). *Attachment in psychotherapy.* New York: Guilford Press.

Waters, E., & Deane, K. E. (1985). Defining and assessing individual differences in attachment relationships: Q-methodology and the organization of behavior in infancy and early childhood. *Monographs of the Society for Research in Child Development, 50*, 41–65.

Weinfield, N. S., Sroufe, L. A., Egeland, B., & Carlson, E. A. (1999). The nature of individual differences in infant-caregiver attachment. In J. Cassidy & P. R. Shaver (Eds.), *Handbook of attachment: Theory, research, and clinical applications* (pp. 68–88). New York: Guilford Press.

West, M., Livesley, W. J., Sheldon, A., & Reiffer, L. (1986). The place of attachment in the life events model of stress and illness: Reply. *Canadian Journal of Psychiatry, 31*, 793–794.

Winder, C. L., & Rau, L. (1962). Parental attitudes associated with social deviance in preadolescent boys. *Journal of Abnormal and Social Psychology, 64*, 418–424.

Yeger, T., & Miezitis, S. (1985). Pupil sex as it relates to the pupil-teacher dependency relationship. *International Journal of Women's Studies, 8,* 457–464.

Young, J. (1994). *Cognitive therapy for personality disorders: A schema-focused approach.* Sarasota, FL: Professional Resource Press.

Young, J., & Lindemann, M. (1992). An integrative schema-focused model for personality disorders. *Journal of Cognitive Psychotherapy, 6,* 11–23.

Zeifman, D., & Hazan, C. (1997). Attachment: The bond in pair-bonds. In J. A. Simpson & D. T. Kenrick (Eds.), *Evolutionary social psychology* (pp. 237–263). Hillsdale, NJ: Erlbaum.

Zirkel, S. (1992). Developing independence in a life transition: Investing the self in the concerns of the day. *Journal of Personality and Social Psychology, 62,* 506–521.

CHAPTER 16

Avoidant
Personality Disorder

JOANNA A. ROBIN, SHARON L. COHAN,
JAMES HAMBRICK, and ANNE MARIE ALBANO

THE *DIAGNOSTIC and Statistical Manual of Mental Disorders*, fourth edition, text revision (*DSM-IV-TR*; American Psychiatric Association, 2000) states that the onset of a personality disorder begins in adolescence or early adulthood, yet there is reluctance to diagnose personality disorders in youth under 18. This hesitancy continues among mental health professionals despite the mounting evidence that symptoms of personality disorders are identifiable in adolescents (e.g., Bernstein, Cohen, Skodol, Bezirganian, & Brook, 1996; Westen, Shedler, Durrett, Glass, & Martens, 2003). Longitudinal and epidemiological studies of community samples have reported that approximately 15%

of adolescents meet diagnostic criteria for a personality disorder (Bernstein et al., 1996). Results of a study conducted by Westen and colleagues show that personality pathology can be diagnosed in youth ages 14 through 18. As in studies conducted with adults, Westen et al. found similar patterns of comorbidity among personality disorders in a sample of adolescents.

Earlier identification of personality disorders in youth may clear the way for earlier intervention, which is extremely important given that prospective research studies indicate that adolescents with symptoms of personality disorders are at risk for impairment, distress, and poor adjustment in adulthood (Bernstein et al., 1993; Johnson, Cohen, Skodol, et al., 1999; J. G. Johnson, Smailes, Cohen, Brown, & Bernstein, 2000).

Avoidant Personality Disorder (AVPD), has received considerable attention in the adult literature, but has not been studied extensively in adolescent clinical or community samples. The few studies that have been completed suggest that AVPD begins to develop in adolescence and can be associated with impairment in several domains of functioning. However, others have called into question the validity of the diagnostic criteria in adolescent populations. In the study by Westen and colleagues (2003), a high percentage (30%) of adolescents were diagnosed with AVPD, leading the authors to suggest that the current criteria for AVPD may overpathologize internalizing symptoms in adolescents. Although this result may call into question the sensitivity of the AVPD criteria, it also makes clear that Axis II symptoms and criteria are present among adolescents. Whether a diagnosis of AVPD is applicable for children remains unknown.

Although the field is still in its infancy with regard to the identification and treatment of AVPD in adolescence, research with adults with AVPD provides a framework to understand the development and impairment associated with AVPD. Therefore, we review several studies from the adult AVPD literature, in addition to reviewing research conducted with adolescents. We provide a description of AVPD, including the prevalence, course, associated impairment, and prognosis. We also discuss theories of the etiology of AVPD and provide an overview on the debate regarding the diagnostic overlap between generalized Social Phobia and AVPD. Finally, we discuss implications for treatment of adolescent AVPD.

DESCRIPTION OF AVOIDANT PERSONALITY DISORDER

Personality disorders are defined in the *DSM-IV-TR* (American Psychiatric Association, 2000) as enduring patterns of inner experience and behavior that deviate from the expectations of an individual's culture. These patterns are viewed as inflexible and pervasive across a broad range of personal and social situations, and result in clinically significant distress or impairment in social or occupational functioning. Patients with AVPD report a pervasive pattern of social inhibition and unwillingness to engage in new activities, driven by feelings of inadequacy and hypersensitivity to negative evaluation. Affected individuals appear shy, inhibited, or withdrawn in new situations. They frequently avoid social interactions and close relationships for fear that they will be humiliated or rejected by others.

When AVPD first appeared in *DSM-III* (American Psychiatric Association, 1980), the defining feature of the disorder was a "defensive avoidance of social interactions despite an intense desire for closeness" (Rettew, 2000, p. 284). Social avoidance and emotional distancing continue to be important components of the disorder, but the diagnostic criteria for AVPD now place more emphasis on fear of negative evaluation and discomfort in social situations. *DSM-IV-TR* (American Psychiatric Association, 2000) specifies that at least four out of the following seven criteria must be present for an AVPD diagnosis:

1. The person avoids occupational activities that require significant interpersonal contact, because of fears of criticism, disapproval, or rejection.
2. The person is unwilling to get involved with people unless he or she is certain of being liked.

3. The person shows restraint within intimate relationships because of fear of being shamed or ridiculed.

4. The person is preoccupied with being criticized or rejected in social situations.

5. The person is inhibited in new interpersonal situations because of feelings of inadequacy.

6. The person views himself or herself as socially inept, personally unappealing, or inferior to others.

7. The person is usually reluctant to take personal risks or to engage in any new activities because they may prove embarrassing.

AVOIDANT PERSONALITY DISORDER IN CHILDREN AND ADOLESCENTS

Very little is known about the clinical presentation of AVPD in youth. However, there is some evidence that signs of the disorder are present during early development (Rettew et al., 2003). Avoidant personality traits, such as excessive shyness or fear when the child is in the presence of new people and situations, typically appear in childhood. Some degree of shyness and hesitancy in the face of new stimuli is developmentally appropriate for young children, and occasional avoidant behaviors are not uncommon in children or adolescents. However, when shyness, continual fears of rejection, hypersensitivity to criticism, and social avoidance persist and intensify throughout adolescence, a diagnosis of AVPD may be appropriate.

In the empirical literature, there is a paucity of research on child or adolescent AVPD. There are several reasons for this. First, Westen and colleagues (2003) point out that, with the exception of Borderline Personality Disorder, there are no reliable and valid measures of Axis II pathology in youth. Second, most of the symptoms associated with AVPD are not readily observable, as they involve the child's internal state, and therefore are not easily accessible to others and may often be confusing to adults trying to work with a child.

Kashdan and Herbert (2001) identified several additional obstacles to the diagnosis of Social Phobia in children and adolescents that are most likely to be obstacles in diagnosing AVPD, including (a) level of cognitive development detrimentally affecting the child's ability to accurately report his or her experience; (b) initial symptom manifestation varying greatly as a function of age (e.g., children may appear more sad or irritable, whereas adolescents may exhibit more antisocial behaviors); (c) difficulty ascertaining the boundaries between normal levels of shyness and pathological anxiety, especially in adolescence; (d) difficulty communicating problems simply because the child becomes so anxious that he or she is unable to talk to the clinician; and (e) variance in clinical presentation with regard to number and types of feared situations, level of avoidance of those situations, and resultant disability. Although research has identified these obstacles to making a diagnosis only of Social Phobia, it seems reasonable to extrapolate that these difficulties would be similar or even worse when attempting to diagnose AVPD, given the similarity between the two disorders.

AGE OF ONSET, PREVALENCE, AND GENDER DISTRIBUTION OF AVOIDANT PERSONALITY DISORDER

Despite the obstacles in identifying AVPD in childhood, research suggests that age of onset for this disorder is usually in late childhood and early adolescence. In the absence of intervention, AVPD appears to have a chronic course (e.g., Van Velzen, Emmelkamp, & Scholing, 2000). Avoidant Personality Disorder appears to affect males as frequently as females (Corbitt & Widiger, 1995). Prevalence estimates for *DSM-IV* AVPD range from 2.1% to 2.6% in the general North American adult population (Grant et al., 2004). Recent studies have also reported rates of 5.0% to 6.6% in community samples from Norway (Torgersen, Kringlen, & Cramer, 2001) and Sweden (Ekselius, Tillfors, Furmark, & Fredrikson, 2001).

IMPAIRMENT IN FUNCTIONING

Retrospective research with adults regarding impairment associated with AVPD suggests that impairment is present in adolescence. For example, Rettew and colleagues (2003) examined the childhood histories of adults with AVPD through retrospective report. They found that adults with AVPD were more likely to report less athletic achievement throughout childhood than patients with other personality disorders, or patients with major depression and no personality disorders. Adults with AVPD also reported feeling less popular and participating in fewer hobbies during adolescence than the comparison groups. These findings suggest that these children exhibit deficits in social functioning starting in childhood and that they are likely to avoid participating in both social and nonsocial situations starting at a young age. This study is important in reinforcing the early warning signs of these disorders, although it does suffer from being a retrospective study and therefore nonpredictive and open to memory biases. In addition, the authors note that it is not clear whether these represent risk factors for AVPD or whether these youth may have met partial or even full criteria for the disorder.

Given that the one of the symptoms of AVPD in adulthood is the avoidance of occupational activities because of fear of embarrassment or criticism, this symptom may plausibly relate to avoidance of school-related activities for similar reasons in childhood. Again, although there are no prospective studies regarding school avoidance and AVPD, retrospective research suggests that school avoidance is associated with symptoms of severe social anxiety, which is similar to AVPD. For example, Van Amerigen, Mancini, and Farvolden (2003) reported that adult patients with generalized Social Phobia were more likely to have dropped out of school compared to patients with other types of anxiety disorders. Although the interpretability of the results is limited by the retrospective design, it is likely that if youth with Social Phobia are at high risk for school dropout, children with more severe symptoms and avoidant personality traits may also be at risk for school dropout. Future research with adolescents is needed to determine whether AVPD is such a risk factor.

PROGNOSIS

The presence of AVPD in childhood or adolescence implies that the individual is already thinking in maladaptive ways, is avoiding social situations with peers and adults, and has not developed healthy interpersonal relationships with others. As a result, opportunities to learn and practice social skills that are needed for the transition into adulthood may no longer be available, which may increase the risk of maintaining AVPD into adulthood. Indeed, research by J. G. Johnson, Cohen, Kasen, and Brook (2006) demonstrated that adolescents with personality disorders often have high rates of personality disorder traits in adulthood. Kasen, Cohen, Skodol, Johnson, and Brook (1999) found that the presence of a personality disorder in adolescence, independent of an Axis I disorder, predicted a personality disorder in young adulthood. Chen, Cohen, Kasen, and Johnson (2006) studied the relationship between adolescent personality disorder and quality of life in young adulthood. They found that a diagnosis of a personality disorder in adolescence accounted for impairments in quality of life in young adulthood and that these impairments are more than would be expected by the presence of an Axis I disorder. Unfortunately, these studies did not report on AVPD specifically. This suggests that without proper intervention, personality problems such as AVPD may persist into adulthood.

ETIOLOGY OF AVOIDANT
PERSONALITY DISORDER

CAUSES

The etiology of AVPD has yet to be sufficiently elucidated, but most models suggest that personality pathology is the result of a complex interaction between temperamental vulnerabilities and environmental stressors. As with personality disorders in general, AVPD may be best conceptualized from a biopsychosocial perspective in which risk and vulnerability factors identified at multiple levels of analysis are incorporated into a single model (Paris, 1999, 2003). There is reason to believe that AVPD is influenced by a combination of genetic, temperamental, psychological, and social/environmental factors that are first evident in childhood and adolescence.

Genetic Factors

Studies examining rates of AVPD and social anxiety in the first-degree relatives of affected individuals have provided evidence for the familial aggregation of AVPD (Reich, 1989), which may indicate a significant genetic component to the disorder. For example, Tillfors, Furmark, Ekselius, and Fredrikson (2001) examined family history of excessive social anxiety in a sample of 1,202 adults drawn from the general Swedish population. Individuals with *DSM-IV* diagnoses of Social Phobia or AVPD had greater rates of a positive parental history of social anxiety. Having an affected family member placed these individuals at a two- to threefold increased relative risk for developing Social Phobia and/or AVPD. An even higher rate of relative risk was found by Stein and colleagues (1998) when they interviewed 106 first-degree relatives of 23 patients with generalized Social Phobia (17 of whom also met criteria for AVPD). First-degree relatives of these patients were at approximately 10-fold greater relative risk for Social Phobia and AVPD when compared to first-degree relatives of adults without Social Phobia. Only one study to date has explored the familial nature of AVPD in younger patients. B. A. Johnson and colleagues (1995) used direct interview and family history methodology in a sample of 66 adolescent inpatients and their first-degree relatives. Similar to studies using adult populations, results indicated that the relatives of adolescents with AVPD had significantly higher rates of AVPD than did those of adolescents without AVPD (40% versus 17%).

Increased rates of psychiatric disorders within a family are often taken as evidence of a strong genetic contribution, but environmental factors may also account for this pattern. Because family studies are limited in this respect, twin studies are needed to clarify the relative contributions of genetic and environmental factors in the development of a given condition. A recent twin study by Torgersen and colleagues (2001) indicates that personality disorders have a substantial genetic component. The authors compared prevalence rates of *DSM-III-R* personality disorders in 92 monozygotic and 129 dizygotic twin pairs. Heritability estimates were .60 for personality disorders generally and .28 for AVPD in particular. The authors speculate that the weaker genetic influence found for AVPD relative to other personality disorders may be the result of a cultural effect, which is also responsible for the increased prevalence of AVPD in Scandinavian populations. Additional behavioral genetic studies have examined the heritability of related constructs such as shyness and behavioral inhibition in young children. Warren, Schmitz, and Emde (1999) found that genetic influences accounted for one third of the variance in social anxiety scores in a sample of 7-year-old monozygotic and dizygotic twins. The influence of shared environmental factors was not significant. Higher heritability estimates of approximately .60 were found for social anxiety symptoms in an Italian study of 378 twin pairs between the ages of 8 and 17 years (Ogliari et al., 2006). Other studies have also found substantial heritability of behavioral inhibition in children, a temperament closely related to shyness and social anxiety (DiLalla, Kagan, & Reznick, 1994; Robinson, Kagan, Reznick, & Corley, 1992).

Taken together, these studies suggest that genetic factors play at least a modest role in the development of symptoms associated with AVPD, but more work is needed to determine which genes are associated with AVPD. Preliminary evidence from a study of 156 adult patients with Major Depressive Disorder indicates increased rates of AVPD among individuals with two different dopamine D4 receptor polymorphisms (Joyce et al., 2003). However, the implications of these findings are still unclear. Molecular genetic studies examining other candidate genes, such as the serotonin transporter gene promoter polymorphism, shown in several studies to be associated with increased risk for shyness in children (Arbelle et al., 2003; Battaglia et al., 2005), are also needed to determine the relative influence of specific genetic factors in the development of AVPD.

Temperament Factors

Temperament has long been considered one of the primary factors in the development of personality and personality disorders (Rutter, 1987). The majority of research regarding temperament precursors to social anxiety focuses on behavioral inhibition to the unfamiliar (BI), which was first identified by Kagan, Reznick, and Snidman (1987) in the Harvard Infant Study. Behavioral inhibition is an enduring temperament style in which children display fear, avoidance, or withdrawal from novel people, situations, or objects. The construct overlaps somewhat with extreme shyness but also encompasses inhibition in the presence of novel nonsocial objects such as toys and games. It is thought to reflect a lower threshold for activation in limbic and hypothalamic brain structures such as the amygdala in response to unfamiliar, challenging, or threatening stimuli (Kagan, 1997). There is some evidence to support this notion. For example, in a recent neuroimaging study, adults who had been categorized as inhibited at the age of 2 showed greater amygdala response when presented with novel versus familiar faces (Schwartz, Wright, Shin, Kagan, & Rauch, 2003). Behavioral inhibition is expressed differently at different developmental periods. Behaviorally inhibited infants are characterized by greater irritability than noninhibited infants, toddlers tend to withdraw from unfamiliar people and cling to caregivers, and preschoolers show hesitancy and restraint when interacting with unfamiliar peers or adults. School-age children with BI typically display reticence, introversion, and social withdrawal from peers.

There is increasing evidence that children identified as behaviorally inhibited in the first 3 years of life are at greater risk for anxiety disorders in later childhood (Hirshfeld et al., 1992; Rosenbaum et al., 1993) and for Social Phobia in particular (Biederman et al., 2001). These results come from both prospective and retrospective studies.

For example, Mick and Telch (1998) used retrospective reports of childhood BI to examine the relationship between BI and later anxiety symptomatology in a young adult sample. They found that a history of childhood BI was more strongly associated with symptoms of Social Phobia but not Generalized Anxiety Disorder, suggesting that BI may be a specific risk factor for later social anxiety. Similarly, in a study of 2,242 high school students, Hayward, Killen, Kraemer, and Taylor (1998) found that adolescents who were classified as BI in elementary school were at 4 to 5 times greater risk for developing Social Phobia in adolescence. The authors also examined two different components of BI to better understand the relationship between early temperament and later psychopathology. Of note, self-reported social avoidance in elementary school was a specific predictor for onset of Social Phobia but was not related to depression during adolescence, whereas fearfulness appeared to be a nonspecific factor that increased the risk for both Social Phobia and depression. Results from adult samples using retrospective reports of BI also indicate a specific relationship between inhibited temperament and a lifetime diagnosis of Social Phobia (Gladstone, Parker, Mitchell, Wilhelm, & Malhi, 2005).

In addition, a prospective study by Schwartz, Snidman, and Kagan (1999) investigated the longitudinal relationship between early childhood BI and anxiety disorders in early adolescence. Seventy-nine adolescents who had been classified as either inhibited or uninhibited at 2 years of age were followed up 12 years later. Results from structured interviews indicated that being inhibited as a toddler doubled the likelihood of having generalized Social Phobia in early adolescence. Only 20% of those who were inhibited as toddlers reported never having generalized social anxiety during their lifetime. No association was found between early BI and adolescent rates of specific phobias, separation anxiety, or performance anxiety. In addition, direct interviews with the adolescents indicated some decrement in current social functioning. Adolescents who had been inhibited as children smiled less and made fewer spontaneous comments during one-on-one interviews compared to those classified as uninhibited.

These results indicate that BI is a specific risk factor for adolescent social anxiety, and that reticence and/or social avoidance may be the key components of BI that predispose later development of Social Phobia. Unfortunately, the majority of studies examining temperament precursors to anxiety disorders do not assess avoidant personality traits or Axis II pathology. To date, there have been no studies directly examining the relationship between BI and later AVPD. Although the results from the social anxiety literature are suggestive, future retrospective and longitudinal studies are needed to specifically assess the relationship between BI in and later AVPD.

PSYCHOLOGICAL FACTORS

Very few studies have investigated psychological risk factors for AVPD using prospective data from child and adolescent samples. The Children in the Community study (Cohen, Crawford, Johnson, & Kasen, 2005) is one notable exception. This study followed an epidemiological sample of 800 children (ages 1 to 10 years) for a 20-year period through adolescence and into adulthood. Unfortunately, due to statistical limitations, personality disorders were frequently analyzed as clusters of disorders rather than as individual disorders. The implications for AVPD in particular are therefore limited. As may be expected, substantial comorbidity (50%) was found for Cluster C personality disorder diagnoses (Avoidant, Dependent, and Obsessive-Compulsive Personality Disorder) and Axis I anxiety disorders in adolescence. However, comorbidity with other Axis I disorders was also common. Thirty-four percent of adolescents with Cluster C diagnoses met criteria for disruptive behavior disorders, and 23% met criteria for depressive disorders. In an earlier report using this sample, the authors found that the odds of new onset Cluster C disorders in adulthood were 4 times higher following adolescent anxiety disorders (Kasen et al., 1999). These results suggest that anxiety plays a role in adolescent Cluster C disorders, including AVPD, and it may also be a precursor for later onset Cluster C personality pathology.

As stated previously, the main psychological factor associated with AVPD is social anxiety, with comorbidity rates of 25% to 89% between *DSM-IV* AVPD and generalized Social Phobia (see Rettew, 2000, for a review). Individuals with AVPD are certainly characterized by a high degree of anxiety in social situations, and it may be appropriate to classify AVPD along a continuum with Social Phobia. However, some authors have argued that the pattern of avoidance in AVPD also relates to nonsocial situations and that the disorder is not simply a severe variant of Social Phobia (Rettew, 2000; Taylor, Laposa, & Alden, 2004). Indeed, avoidance of novelty in social and nonsocial situations may be an important additional factor that results in significant impairment for individuals with AVPD (Alden, Laposa, Taylor, & Ryder, 2002). This issue was addressed in a recent study by Taylor and colleagues, who examined associations between AVPD symptoms and nonsocial avoidance in three samples of young adults and an adult clinical sample. Results from a series of studies indicated that AVPD was associated with emotional and novelty avoidance, in addition to avoidance of other nonsocial situations; it was also associated with social concerns about displaying emotions. In the clinical sample, individuals with AVPD reported more negative beliefs about experiencing emotions, avoidance of positive emotions, and social concerns regarding emotional displays relative to community controls. The authors of this report conclude that AVPD is more broadly characterized by a pattern of avoidance that extends beyond social situations to include avoidance of both positive and negative emotions and of novelty in general. These findings are consistent with previous studies that have found high levels of harm avoidance among adults with AVPD (Svrakic, Whitehead, Przybeck, & Cloninger, 1993), but additional studies are needed to determine if youth with AVPD are also characterized by high levels of nonsocial avoidance.

Cognitive theories of AVPD posit that individuals who develop the disorder hold negative beliefs about themselves and are hypersensitive to potential criticism, rejection, and humiliation. Their feelings of inadequacy and interpersonal sensitivity cause them to withdraw and avoid social contact with others (Millon, 1981). According to cognitive theory of personality disorders, individuals with AVPD hold rigid, negative, overgeneralized beliefs about themselves (e.g., "I am defective") and others (e.g., "If people knew the real me, they would reject me"; Beck & Freeman, 1990). Affected individuals develop a pervasive pattern of social, cognitive, and emotional avoidance in order to cope with these painful beliefs. There is some evidence that people who show traits of AVPD selectively attend to information that supports their preexisting negative beliefs, or schema, about themselves and the world. In a study directly investigating the cognitive model, Dreesen, Arntz, Hendriks, Keune, and van den Hout (1999) examined schema-congruent information-processing bias in a sample of 57 young adults who scored either high or low on a measure of *DSM-III-R* personality disorder symptoms. Results indicated that symptoms of AVPD were associated with avoidant beliefs, and avoidant beliefs, but not AVPD symptoms, were associated with schema-congruent information-processing bias on a pragmatic inference task. Low self-esteem was related to the information- processing bias, but Social Phobia and general personality pathology were not. Another study examined the relationship between AVPD symptoms and negative expectancies in a young adult sample. Meyer and Carver (2000) found that pessimistic expectancies were predictive of AVPD symptoms and that this relationship was stronger among individuals who reported sensory-processing sensitivity and those who had greater recall of negative childhood memories. These findings suggest that avoidant beliefs and information-processing bias are important psychological aspects of AVPD. The extent to which these factors are present in childhood and adolescence remains to be seen. Future research is needed to determine the role of cognitive factors in early-onset AVPD.

SOCIAL AND ENVIRONMENTAL FACTORS

Although environmental variables alone cannot account for the development of AVPD in youth, some social and environmental factors have been implicated in the development of the disorder. Most models of AVPD emphasize the role of early family relationships (e.g., history of criticism or rejection by important family members) in the development of avoidant beliefs and behaviors (Beck & Freeman, 1990; Millon, 1981), but few studies have directly examined this hypothesis. There is some evidence that poor parenting places children at increased risk for personality disorders in general, and for AVPD in particular (Cohen et al., 2005). For example, J. G. Johnson, Cohen, Chen, Kasen, and Brook (2006) found that low parental affection or nurturing was associated with elevated risk of AVPD in adulthood. In addition, J. G. Johnson, Cohen, Brown, Smailes, and Bernstein (1999) found that officially reported childhood neglect was a significant predictor of AVPD symptoms in early adulthood, even after controlling for co-occurring personality disorder symptoms. Specifically, childhood emotional neglect appears to be associated with increased risk for AVPD during adolescence and early adulthood (J. G. Johnson et al., 2000).

Studies examining retrospective accounts of childhood experiences have also found an association between AVPD symptoms and negative childhood experiences. For example, Meyer and Carver (2000) found that relative to young adults with other personality disorder symptoms and normal controls, young adults with high rates of AVPD symptoms were more likely to recall experiences of rejection, social isolation, abandonment, and social ineptness when asked to write a narrative description of their childhood. In another retrospective study, Arbel and Stravynski (1991) found that adults with AVPD differed from community controls in their perceptions by reporting a less encouraging home climate growing up and experiencing fewer parental demonstrations of love and pride.

Further support for the notion that negative childhood experiences are associated with AVPD comes from a more recent study by Rettew and colleagues (2003). They examined early social functioning and maltreatment experiences in a sample of 146 adults with a primary diagnosis of AVPD. Compared to adults with a primary diagnosis of Major Depression, adults with AVPD reported higher rates of physical and emotional abuse, but the abuse variables were no longer significant predictors of AVPD after controlling for comorbid conditions like Posttraumatic Stress Disorder. Adults with AVPD rated their parents as less socially skilled and reported fewer positive relationships with noncaretaking adults. These results provide preliminary evidence for the hypothesis that parental modeling of avoidant responses and restricted exposure to social situations may be important risks for later AVPD. However, additional empirical studies are needed to tease out the influence of environmental and social factors in the etiology of AVPD. Longitudinal studies have begun to elucidate some of the prospective risks for AVPD and other personality pathology in youth, but more work focused specifically on AVPD is needed.

DIFFERENTIAL DIAGNOSIS

AVOIDANT PERSONALITY DISORDER OR SOCIAL PHOBIA?

Avoidant Personality Disorder shares a number of features with the generalized subtype of Social Phobia (GSP), leading several researchers to question whether AVPD and Social Phobia are qualitatively different disorders, or if AVPD is best regarded as the extreme end of the social anxiety/shyness continuum (Boone et al., 1999; Ralevski et al., 2005; Van Velzen et al., 2000). Results from several studies indicate that AVPD may reflect a more severe or persistent form of social anxiety (Herbert, Hope, & Bellack, 1992; Holt, Heimberg, & Hope, 1992; Tillfors, Furmark, Ekselius, & Fredrikson, 2004), but others have concluded that there are few clinically meaningful differences between socially phobic individuals and those who carry an additional AVPD diagnosis (Ralevski et al., 2005). The severity continuum hypothesis has been the dominant hypothesis that differentiates these disorders; however, this raises the question of whether severity is sufficient to justify the existence of two separate constructs.

In clinical samples GSP and AVPD are frequently comorbid (Ralevski et al., 2005; Rettew, 2000), and individuals with SP are at a greater than twofold increased risk for AVPD (Dyck et al., 2001). This is not surprising, given that six of the seven *DSM-IV-TR* (American Psychiatric Association, 2000) criteria for AVPD have an interpersonal component, and the most important criterion for both disorders is the same: fear of negative evaluation, leading to debilitating levels of anxiety and avoidance of social situations. Furthermore, GSP and AVPD both exhibit a similarly chronic and unremitting course, making them difficult to differentiate as a function of time course.

RESEARCH ON DIFFERENTIATING SOCIAL PHOBIA
AND AVOIDANT PERSONALITY DISORDER

Despite the substantial overlap between the diagnostic criteria of these disorders, there are avenues for distinction. One avenue is severity. Most of the research in this area has been conducted comparing individuals meeting criteria for SP with AVPD to individuals meeting criteria for SP without AVPD, and this research has been conducted exclusively on adults. Boone and colleagues (1999) found that individuals with comorbid GSP and AVPD reported poorer overall functioning, greater comorbidity of both Axis I and II disorders, higher levels of social and trait anxiety, and higher levels of depression compared with individuals diagnosed with GSP alone.

Similar results were reported by Van Velzen and colleagues (2000), who reported that adults with AVPD had the highest levels of social phobic avoidance, depressive symptoms, neuroticism, introversion, and social and occupational impairment compared with adults with only GSP. Ralevski and colleagues (2005) also reported that individuals with comorbid SP and AVPD report more anxiety and more impairment than individuals with SP alone. Van Velzen and colleagues found that individuals with SP and AVPD were more likely to receive Multiple Personality Disorder diagnoses than individuals with SP but without AVPD.

A second avenue of differentiation between SP and AVPD is situational avoidance. As noted previously, the vast majority of the criteria for AVPD specify interpersonal situations. In a sense, SP covers a broader spectrum of situations, as it incorporates not only social interactions, but performance situations (e.g., public speaking, eating in public, and writing in public). Research suggests that individuals who mainly experience interpersonal anxiety are more likely to have AVPD than individuals who predominantly experience anxiety in performance situations and individuals who predominantly experience anxiety in situations in which they are speaking in front of a group or eating while being observed (Perugi et al., 2001).

Other evidence has suggested that individuals with AVPD may avoid a wider range of situations, beyond merely social interactions. The seventh, noninterpersonally based AVPD criterion in the *DSM-IV-TR* is avoidance of personal risks or engaging in new activities because of fear of being embarrassed. Differential diagnosis between SP and AVPD may be improved by examining avoidance in a range of situations that are not limited strictly to social interaction or social performance. Further research in these areas may benefit in clarifying the borders of these two diagnoses and determining whether the difference is strictly one of severity or if there are in fact qualitative differences between them.

Differential diagnosis of SP and AVPD is dogged by multiple problems, including the difficulty of theoretically or empirically differentiating these two disorders, as well as the paucity of research investigating how these disorders present during adolescence. That said, recent research has begun to suggest promising avenues of research. Late childhood and early adolescence appear to be a critical period for the development of both SP and AVPD. Initial application of Axis II diagnostic criteria to adolescence suggests that the diagnostic picture operates similarly to the way it operates in adulthood, which supports further investigation of avoidant pathology among children and adolescents. Among adults, initial explorations of more careful, focused assessment of types of avoided situations may contribute to clarification of the diagnostic boundaries between these two disorders.

TREATMENT IMPLICATIONS

In the adult literature, studies have shown support for cognitive-behavioral therapy (CBT) for adults with AVPD and Social Phobia. Despite adults with AVPD and Social Phobia having higher pretest anxiety levels compared to adults with Social Phobia without AVPD (e.g., Feske, Perry, Chambless, Renneberg, & Goldstein, 1996; Oosterbaan, van Balkom, Spinhoven, de Meij, & van Dyck, 2002), adults with AVPD do benefit from CBT (e.g., Brown, Heimberg, & Juster, 1995; Van Velzen, Emmelkamp, & Scholing, 1997). Furthermore, Herbert and colleagues (2005) reported that a treatment including social skills training and CBT was more effective than CBT alone when treating adult patients with Social Phobia. Interestingly, a large percentage of the patients in both groups also met criteria for AVPD.

In the child literature, CBT has been shown to be more effective than an attention control condition (e.g., Beidel, Turner, Young, & Paulson, 2005) and a wait-list control condition (e.g., Hayward et al., 2000) in the treatment of Social Phobia. None of these studies reported on whether the children in the study also met criteria for AVPD, making it difficult to determine whether children with comorbid AVPD and Social Phobia will benefit from CBT. However, given the success that CBT has had in reducing symptoms of Social Phobia and research suggesting similar treatment response for adults with AVPD/SP and SP, CBT for adolescent AVPD may yield positive results. Research in this area is needed to determine whether adjustments to CBT protocols need to be made to adequately address the severity of symptoms associated with AVPD, especially as an earlier onset of AVPD may be associated with increased impairment and avoidance. Furthermore, given that adolescents typically live with their family of origin, it may be important to work with parents who may be reinforcing their child's beliefs about the social world and the child's inability to master interpersonal relationships.

CONCLUSIONS

Despite evidence that personality disorders may begin in adolescence or earlier (Bernstein et al., 1996), little is known about AVPD in childhood. Although research suggests that early signs of AVPD can be detected in young children and that AVPD can be diagnosed as early as adolescence, it is unclear whether full-blown AVPD occurs in childhood. Furthermore, the debate in the adult literature regarding the overlap between generalized Social Phobia and AVPD complicates our understanding of personality traits versus disorder in children and adolescence. However, given that symptoms of AVPD may begin to develop in childhood, it is important to identify these symptoms in youth before children develop AVPD. Better identification may lead to interventions that may prevent the worsening of symptoms and solidifying of maladaptive personality traits.

REFERENCES

Alden, L. E., Laposa, J. M., Taylor, C. T., & Ryder, A. G. (2002). Avoidant personality disorder: Current status and future directions. *Journal of Personality Disorders, 16*, 1–29.

American Psychiatric Association. (1980). *Diagnostic and statistical manual of mental disorders* (3rd ed.). Washington, DC: Author.

Arbel, N., & Stravynski, A. (1991). A retrospective study of separation in the development of adult avoidant personality disorder. *Acta Psychiatrica Scandinavica, 83*, 174–178.

Arbelle, S., Benjamin, J., Golin, M., Kremer, I., Belmaker, R. H., & Ebstein, R. P. (2003). Relation of shyness in grade school children to the genotype for the long form of the serotonin transporter promoter region polymorphism. *American Journal of Psychiatry, 160,* 671–676.

Battaglia, M., Ogliari, A., Zanoni, A., Citterio, A., Pozzoli, U., Giorda, R., et al. (2005). Influence of the serotonin transporter promoter gene and shyness on children's cerebral responses to facial expressions. *Archives of General Psychiatry, 62,* 85–94.

Beck, A. T., & Freeman, A. (1990). *Cognitive therapy of personality disorders.* New York: Guilford Press.

Beidel, D. C., Turner, S. M., Young, B., & Paulson, A. (2005). Social effectiveness therapy for children: Three year follow-up. *Journal of Consulting and Clinical Psychology, 73,* 721–725.

Bernstein, D. P., Cohen, P., Skodol, A., Bezirganian, S., & Brook, J. S. (1996). Childhood antecedents of adolescent personality disorder. *American Journal of Psychiatry, 153,* 907–913.

Bernstein, D. P., Cohen, P., Velez, C. N., Schwab-Stone, M., Siever, L. J., & Sinsato, L. (1993). Prevalence and stability of the *DSM-III-R* personality disorders in a community based survey of adolescents. *American Journal of Psychiatry, 150,* 1237–1243.

Biederman, J., Hirshfeld-Becker, D. R., Rosenbaum, J. F., Herot, C., Friedman, D., Snidman, N., et al. (2001). Further evidence of association between behavioral inhibition and social anxiety in children. *American Journal of Psychiatry, 158,* 1673–1679.

Boone, M. L., McNeil, D. W., Masia, C. L., Turk, C. L., Carter, L. E., Ries, B. J., et al. (1999). Multimodal comparisons of social phobia subtypes and avoidant personality disorder. *Journal of Anxiety Disorders, 13,* 271–292.

Brown, E. J., Heimberg, R. G., & Juster, H. R. (1995). Social phobia subtype and avoidant personality disorder: Effect on severity of social phobia, impairment, and outcome of cognitive behavioral treatment. *Behavior Therapy, 26,* 467–486.

Chen, H., Cohen, P., Kasen, S., & Johnson, J. G. (2006). Adolescent Axis I and personality disorders predict quality of life during young adulthood. *Journal of Adolescent Health, 39,* 14–19.

Cohen, P., Crawford, T. N., Johnson, J. G., & Kasen, S. (2005). The Children in the Community study of the developmental course of personality disorder. *Journal of Personality Disorders, 19,* 466–486.

Corbitt, E. M., & Widiger, T. A. (1995). Sex differences among the personality disorders: An exploration of the data. *Clinical Psychology: Science and Practice, 2,* 225–238.

DiLalla, L., Kagan, J., & Reznick, J. (1994). Genetic etiology of behavioral inhibition among 2-year-old children. *Infant Behavior and Development, 17,* 405–412.

Dreesen, L., Arntz, A., Hendriks, T., Keune, N., & van den Hout, M. (1999). Avoidant personality disorder and implicit schema-congruent information processing bias: A pilot study with a pragmatic inference task. *Behavior Research and Therapy, 37,* 619–632.

Dyck, I. R., Philips, K. A., Warshaw, M. G., Dolan, R. T., Shea, M. T., Stout, R. L., et al. (2001). Patterns of personality pathology in patients with generalized anxiety disorder, panic disorder with and without agoraphobia, and social phobia. *Journal of Personality Disorders, 15,* 60–71.

Ekselius, L., Tillfors, M., Furmark, T., & Fredrikson, M. (2001). Personality disorders in the general population: *DSM-IV* and ICD-10 defined prevalence as related to sociodemographic profile. *Personality and Individual Differences, 30,* 311–320.

Feske, U., Perry, K. J., Chambless, D. L., Renneberg, B., & Goldstein, A. J. (1996). Avoidant personality disorder as a predictor for treatment outcome among generalized social phobics. *Journal of Personality Disorders, 10,* 174–184.

Gladstone, G. L., Parker, G. B., Mitchell, P. B., Wilhelm, K. A., & Malhi, G. S. (2005). Relationship between self-reported childhood behavioral inhibition and lifetime anxiety disorders in a clinical sample. *Depression and Anxiety, 22,* 103–113.

Grant, B. F., Hasin, D. S., Stinson, F. S., Dawson, D. A., Chou, S. P., Ruan, W. J., et al. (2004). Prevalence, correlates, and disability of personality disorders in the United States: Results from the National Epidemiologic Survey on Alcohol and Related Conditions. *Journal of Clinical Psychiatry, 65,* 948–958.

Hayward, C., Killen, J. D., Kraemer, H. C., & Taylor, C. (1998). Linking self-reported childhood behavioral inhibition to adolescent social phobia. *Journal of the American Academy of Child and Adolescent Psychiatry, 37,* 1308–1316.

Hayward, C., Varady, S., Albano, A. M., Thienemann, M., Henderson, L., & Schatzberg, A. F. (2000). Cognitive behavioral group therapy for social phobia in female adolescents: Results of a pilot study. *Journal of the American Academy of Child and Adolescent Psychiatry, 39,* 1–6.

Herbert, J. D., Gaudiano, B. A., Rheingold, A. A., Myers, V. H., Dalrymple, K., & Nolan, E. M. (2005). Social skills training augments the effectiveness of cognitive behavioral group therapy for social anxiety disorder. *Behavior Therapy, 36,* 125–138.

Herbert, J. D., Hope, D. A., & Bellack, A. S. (1992). Validity of the distinction between generalized social phobia and avoidant personality disorder. *Journal of Abnormal Psychology, 101,* 332–339.

Hirshfeld, D. R., Rosenbaum, J., Biederman, J., Bolduc, E. A., Faraone, S. V., Snidman, N., et al. (1992). Stable behavioral inhibition and its association with anxiety disorder. *Journal of the American Academy of Child and Adolescent Psychiatry, 31,* 103–111.

Holt, C. S., Heimberg, R. G., & Hope, D. A. (1992). Avoidant personality disorder and the generalized subtype of social phobia. *Journal of Abnormal Psychology, 101,* 318–325.

Johnson, B. A., Brent, D. A., Connolly, J., Bridge, J., Matta, J., Constantine, D., et al. (1995). Familial aggregation of adolescent personality disorders. *Journal of the American Academy of Child and Adolescent Psychiatry, 34,* 798–804.

Johnson, J. G., Cohen, P., Brown, J., Smailes, E. M., & Bernstein, D. P. (1999). Childhood maltreatment increases risk for personality disorders during early adulthood. *Archives of General Psychiatry, 56,* 600–606.

Johnson, J. G., Cohen, P., Chen, H., Kasen, S., & Brook, J. S. (2006). Parenting behaviors associated with risk for offspring personality disorder during adulthood. *Archives of General Psychiatry, 63,* 579–587.

Johnson, J. G., Cohen, P., Kasen, S., & Brook, J. S. (2006). Personality disorders evident by early adulthood and risk for anxiety disorders during middle adulthood. *Journal of Anxiety Disorders, 20,* 408–426.

Johnson, J. G., Cohen, P., Skodol, A. E., Oldham, J. M., Kasen, S., & Brook, J. S. (1999). Personality disorders in adolescence and risk of major mental disorders and suicidality during adulthood. *Archives of General Psychiatry, 56,* 805–811.

Johnson, J. G., Smailes, E. M., Cohen, P., Brown, J., & Bernstein, D. P. (2000). Associations between four types of childhood neglect and personality disorder symptoms during adolescence and early adulthood: Findings of a community-based longitudinal study. *Journal of Personality Disorders, 14,* 171–187.

Joyce, P. R., Rogers, G. R., Miller, A. L., Mulder, R. T., Luty, S. E., & Kennedy, M. A. (2003). Polymorphisms of DRD4 and DRD3 and risk of avoidant and obsessive personality traits and disorders. *Psychiatry Research, 119,* 1–10.

Kagan, J. (1997). Temperament and the reactions to unfamiliarity. *Child Development, 68,* 139–143.

Kagan, J., Reznick, J. S., & Snidman, N. (1987). The physiology and psychology of behavioral inhibition in children. *Child Development, 58,* 1459–1473.

Kasen, S., Cohen, P., Skodol, A. E., Johnson, J. G., & Brook, J. (1999). Influence of child and adolescent psychiatric disorders on young adult personality disorder. *American Journal of Psychiatry, 156,* 1529–1535.

Kashdan, T. B., & Herbert, J. D. (2001). Social anxiety disorder in childhood and adolescence: Current status and future directions. *Clinical Child and Family Psychology Review, 4,* 37–61.

Meyer, B., & Carver, C. S. (2000). Negative childhood accounts, sensitivity, and pessimism: A study of avoidant personality disorder features in college students. *Journal of Personality Disorders, 14,* 233–248.

Mick, M. A., & Telch, M. J. (1998). Social anxiety and history of behavioral inhibition in young adults. *Journal of Anxiety Disorders, 12,* 1–20.

Millon, T. (1981). *Disorders of personality:* DSM-III *Axis II.* New York: Wiley.

Ogliari, A., Citterio, A., Zanoni, A., Fagnani, C., Patriarca, V., Cirrincione, R., et al. (2006). Genetic and environmental influences on anxiety dimensions in Italian twins evaluated with the SCARED questionnaire. *Journal of Anxiety Disorders, 20, 760–777.*

Oosterbaan, D. B., van Balkom, A. J. L. M., Spinhoven, P., de Meij, T. G. J., & van Dyck, R. (2002). The influence on treatment gain of comorbid avoidant personality disorder in patients with social phobia. *Journal of Nervous and Mental Diseases, 190, 41–43.*

Paris, J. (1999). A diathesis-stress model of personality disorders. *Psychiatric Annals, 29, 692–697.*

Paris, J. (2003). *Personality disorders over time: Precursors, course, and outcome.* Arlington, VA: American Psychiatric Publishing.

Perugi, G., Nassini, S., Maremmani, I., Madano, D., Toni, C., Simonini, E., et al. (2001). Putative clinical subtypes of social phobia: A factor analytical study. *Acta Psychiatry Scandinavica, 104,* 280–288.

Ralevski, E., Sanislow, C. A., Grilo, C. M., Skodol, A. E., Gunderson, J. G., Shea, M. T., et al. (2005). Avoidant personality disorder and social phobia: Distinct enough to be separate disorders? *Acta Psychiatrica Scandinavica, 112,* 208–214.

Reich, J. H. (1989). Familiality of DSM-III dramatic and anxious personality clusters. *Journal of Nervous and Mental Diseases, 177,* 96–100.

Rettew, D. C. (2000). Avoidant personality disorder, generalized social phobia, and shyness: Putting the personality back into personality disorders. *Harvard Review of Psychiatry, 8,* 283–297.

Rettew, D. C., Zanarini, M. C., Yen, S., Grilo, C. M., Skodol, A. E., Shea, M. T., et al. (2003). Childhood antecedents of avoidant personality disorder: A retrospective study. *Journal of the American Academy of Child and Adolescent Psychiatry, 42,* 1122–1130.

Robinson, J. L., Kagan, J., Reznick, J. S., & Corley, R. (1992). The heritability of inhibited and uninhibited behavior: A twin study. *Developmental Psychology, 28,* 1030–1037.

Rosenbaum, J. F., Biederman, J., Bolduc-Murphy, E. A., Faraone, S. V., Chaloff, J., Hirshfeld-Becker, D. R., et al. (1993). Behavioral inhibition in childhood: A risk factor for anxiety disorders. *Harvard Review of Psychiatry, 1,* 2–16.

Rutter, M. (1987). Temperament, personality, and personality disorder. *British Journal of Psychiatry, 150,* 443–458.

Schwartz, C. E., Snidman, N., & Kagan, J. (1999). Adolescent social anxiety as an outcome of inhibited temperament in childhood. *Journal of the American Academy of Child and Adolescent Psychiatry, 38,* 1008–1015.

Schwartz, C. E., Wright, C. I., Shin, L. M., Kagan, J., & Rauch, S. L. (2003). Inhibited and uninhibited infants "grown up": Adult amygdalar response to novelty. *Science, 300,* 1952–1953.

Stein, M. B., Chartier, M. J., Hazen, A. L., Kozak, M. V., Tancer, M. E., Lander, S., et al. (1998). A direct-interview family study of generalized social phobia. *American Journal of Psychiatry, 155,* 90–97.

Svrakic, D. M., Whitehead, C., Przybeck, T. R., & Cloninger, C. R. (1993). Differential diagnosis of personality disorders by the seven-factor model of temperament and character. *Archives of General Psychiatry, 50,* 991–999.

Taylor, C. T., Laposa, J. M., & Alden, L. E. (2004). Is avoidant personality disorder more than just social avoidance? *Journal of Personality Disorders, 18,* 571–594.

Tillfors, M., Furmark, T., Ekselius, L., & Fredrikson, M. (2001). Social phobia and avoidant personality disorder as related to parental history of social anxiety: A general population study. *Behavior Research and Therapy, 39,* 289–298.

Tillfors, M., Furmark, T., Ekselius, L., & Fredrikson, M. (2004). Social phobia and avoidant personality disorder: One spectrum disorder? *Nordic Journal of Psychiatry, 58,* 147–152.

Torgersen, S., Kringlen, E., & Cramer, V. (2001). The prevalence of personality disorders in a community sample. *Archives of General Psychiatry, 58,* 590–596.

Van Amerigen, M., Mancini, C., & Farvolden, P. (2003). The impact of anxiety disorders on educational achievement. *Journal of Anxiety Disorders, 17,* 561–571.

Van Velzen, J. M., Emmelkamp, P. M. G., & Scholing, A. (1997). The impact of personality disorders on behavioral treatment outcome for social phobia. *Behavioral Research and Therapy, 35,* 889–900.

Van Velzen, J. M., Emmelkamp, P. M. G., & Scholing, A. (2000). Generalized social phobia versus avoidant personality disorder: Differences in psychopathology, personality traits, and social and occupational functioning. *Journal of Anxiety Disorders, 14,* 395–411.

Warren, S. L., Schmitz, S., & Emde, R. N. (1999). Behavioral genetic analyses of self-reported anxiety at 7 years of age. *Journal of the American Academy of Child and Adolescent Psychiatry, 38,* 1403–1408.

Westen, D., Shedler, J., Durrett, C., Glass, S., & Martens, A. (2003). Personality disorders in adolescence: *DSM-IV* Axis II diagnoses and an empirically derived alternative. *American Journal of Psychiatry, 160,* 952–966.

CHAPTER 17

Negativistic Personality Disorder in Children and Adolescents

GINA M. FUSCO and ARTHUR FREEMAN

Negativists seem to find the "dark lining in the silver cloud."
—Millon (1969, p. 288)

PERHAPS THE best description of the dynamics of passive aggression was offered by Eric Berne in his classic *Games People Play* (1963). He described the passivity part of the syndrome as a thin social veneer that covers and obscures aggression and anger. To the world, the individual appears calm and passive; anger and aggression emerge in apparently reasonable and agreeable behaviors that on the surface have a socially accepted rationale. For the individual who is passive-aggressive, there is rarely openly expressed anger or rage; rather, the individual will in-directly disagree to subtly sabotage the efforts of others, or refuse to act, all in a seemingly agreeable manner. These individuals are in a constant battle between obedience to and defiance of authority (Mil-lon, Davis, Millon, Escover, & Meagher, 2000, p. 472). Their behaviors may, in fact, hurt or humiliate others but leaves the passive-aggressive individual with plausible deniability. "What do you mean?" "Me? Angry?" "Oh no, don't be silly!" If directly confronted about their be-haviors, typical responses are laden with incredulous resentment, all the while proclaiming their innocence and justification of their actions. Some responsibility for their dilemmas may be evident, but they will "set up counter arguments to nullify any positive suggestion, such that no beneficial change occurs" (Stone, 1993a, p. 361). However, when the passive veneer is more directly or broadly exposed, the underlying anger wells up through the scratch and floods the area, and what be-fore was passive now becomes direct aggression.

The quiet, withdrawn, and seemingly agreeable child may suddenly become obstinate and contrary or may express anger directly. The dis-plays of anger may quickly subside to be replaced by the more stylistic negativism. Millon (1981) and McCann (1988, 1999) state that the Passive-Aggressive Personality Disorder (PAPD; also termed the Nega-tivistic Personality Disorder [NegPD]; Millon et al., 2000, p. 472) in adults may be the result of the developmental progression of childhood Oppositional Defiant Disorder (ODD). McCann (1988, p. 175) states, "As such, there may be specific genetic and/or metabolic factors con-tributing to a lifelong pattern of erratic moods and edgy irritability," however, these views must be considered "speculative" given the lack of empirical evidence supporting this contention. The PAPD diagnosis, the precursor for NegPD, was lacking in empirical diagnostic reliability and internal consistency. Therefore, Millon suggested the more di-mensional construct of the NegPD rather than the purely behaviorally bound PAPD syndrome. Fine, Overholser, and Berkoff (1992) similarly suggested that the PAPD diagnosis would be a more useful diagnosis within a dimensional approach. Millon provided a review of the proposed revised diagnostic labels to PAPD to include either retaining and expanding the original PAPD, Oppositional Personality Disorder, or NegPD (Millon, 1993a, 1993b). The negativistic label, however, provided a much more holistic conceptualization, capturing what Millon suggested was a "behaviorally less overt and indirectly expressed adult variant of the child/adolescent 'oppositional defiant disorder'" (p. 84). The diagnostic label Passive-Aggressive/Negativistic Personality Disorder was selected to represent the more holistic and broader elements of the greater pattern (Millon et al., 2000). For ease of use, we use the term Negativistic Personality Disorder (NegPD).

Although the criteria for NegPD overlap significantly with ODD, Rey, Morris-Yates, Singh, Andrews, and Stewart (1995) note that the diagnosis of ODD in childhood does not increase the likelihood of NegPD in adulthood. Specifically, oppositional children demonstrate resistance to external demands, argumentativeness, hostility, defiance, and irritability (American Psychiatric Association, 2000). When comparing ODD with adults with NegPD, overlapping traits are evident, such as resistance to authority, argumentativeness, mood lability, and hostile defiance. Although many traits may superficially appear similar, a subset of children with passive aggressiveness not only present with symptoms consistent with ODD, but present with additional negativistic traits to create a more complex and vexing constellation of symptoms. These include a more salient mood component, intense ambivalence, feelings of being misunderstood, and, unlike the child with ODD, resistance demonstrated through largely passive means.

Passive-aggressive children present frustrating and challenging behaviors to parents, siblings, teachers, and peers. Millon (1969, p. 289) notes that those children with more trait-based negativistic personality constructs seem to shift "with ease" and greater frequency to a sullen passive-aggressive position. Forgetfulness, apparent confusion, apparent sensory failure, or verbal agreement without follow-through are the norm, rather than a momentary reaction or a fleeting defiant stance. The pervasiveness of these behaviors exceeds normal developmental childhood rebelliousness. The passive or covert-type behaviors create a no-win scenario for others as passive aggressiveness creates the unenviable predicament of punishing a child for "forgetting," or reacting angrily to the child's all too frequent complaint, "But I didn't hear you!" This style is not limited to or emblematic of any particular group. Long and Long (2001, p. 2) state, "Passive aggressive behavior exists in all civilized cultures and at every socioeconomic level."

The fate of the diagnosis remains unclear, but studies have recently supported the retention of the diagnosis (Joiner & Rudd, 2002; Vereycken, Vertommen, & Corveleyn, 2002; Wetzler & Morey, 1999). Characteristics specific to NegPD involve a pattern of passive resistance to external demands for adequate social and occupational performance which manifest as procrastination, resistance to authority, argumentativeness, protests, and obstructiveness. Overall, these individuals resist carrying out their obligations. Deadlines are seldom met, and missing them may even be blamed on forgetfulness (Ottaviani, 1990). As the behaviors are largely passive, social and vocational relationships suffer due to the tremendous frustration these behaviors evoke in others. Worsening and further sabotaging the situation, these individuals often seek others' assistance and guidance, all the while thwarting the suggestions that are given (Fusco, 2004). Although they may wish to be close to and comforted by others, their intense "active ambivalence" (Millon & Davis, 1996) while opposing and rejecting the same individual (Fusco, 2004) eventually ends in failure as others withdraw in frustration. Analogies can be made to Yalom's (1985) "help rejecting complainer," Groves's (1976) "manipulative help rejectors," and Freeman's (2006, personal communication) "helpless narcissist."

The model proposed by Millon et al. (2000) is a more dimensional view that has added the additional clinical domains of resentfulness, an interpersonally contrary style, a cognitively skeptical view, a discontented self-image, vacillating objects, poor displacement mechanisms, a divergent disorganization, and an irritable mood. Associated within these domains are feelings of being misunderstood, an intense ambivalence, and sullenness (Millon & Davis, 1996). This dimensional construct permits better diagnostic discrimination and a holistic assessment, key for clinically informed treatment plans (Fusco, 2004).

Social impairment exists as the NegPD individual is "unstable and erratic . . . easily nettled, offended by trifles . . . can readily be provoked into being sullen and contrary" (Millon, 1969, p. 289). Inwardly, NegPD individuals may see themselves as entitled to better treatment. Their behavior, however, is inconsistent, angry, and irritable and they almost seem to revel in their obstinate interpersonal style. There is a consistent unwillingness to fulfill the expectations of others, even if those expectations are consonant with the expectations and demands of the individual (Wetzler & Morey, 1999). Interestingly, Stone (1993a) describes a child's rebelliousness to a parent as analogous to the NegPD personality's defiance of authority. The persistence of these childlike behaviors is sometimes referred to in adulthood as an "emotionally immature" personality (Millon & Davis, 1996). Overwhelming dependency needs alternate and vacillate between a powerful resentment of authority and need for greater autonomy (Millon, 1993a, 1993b). Trapped somewhere between their intense dependency needs while resenting direction and guidance, they suffer an exquisite anguish of never feeling content or satisfied. They exist in a highly charged emotional state unable to move beyond their own inertia (Fusco, 2004). This ever-present lack of contentment can emulate symptoms of depression and dysphoria for both ODD and NegPD inasmuch as depression, dysthymia, and dysphoria include the inability to perform simple tasks as one of the diagnostic hallmarks.

Strongly held, compelling, and powerful schema dictate that direct assertion may be dangerous or catastrophic. This distortion is a product of the individual's believing that following a request or demand of another results in a loss of self-esteem or autonomy. Similar to narcissism is the associated and more catastrophic belief that if one follows a demand, one then subjugates oneself to another. In this way, NegPD individuals avoid being controlled, though they never quite take ownership of their opposition to the request or the position of others (Fusco, 2004). In fact, external demands are predictably viewed as an affront and as offensive (Fusco, 2004). Individuals with this pattern start and stall their way through life, creating a path of "unfinished business" (Wetzler & Morey, 1999, p. 57). The notion and the patterns of passive aggressive or negativistic behavior have been described from a range of theoretical perspectives (Frances & Widiger, 1987; Gorton & Akhtar, 1990; Helgeland, Kjelsberg, & Torgesen, 2005; Levy et al., 1999; Magnavita, 1993a, 1993b, 1994; Millon, 1999; Perry & Flannery, 1982; Whitman, Trosman, & Koenig, 1954; Widiger & Frances, 1985; Zeman & Shipman, 1996).

RESEARCH AND EMPIRICAL DATA

Several authors (McCann, 1988; Millon, 1993a, 1993b) have noted that little empirical research has been completed with the NegPD as the primary focus of the studies. However, both McCann and Millon state that this is largely due to the restrictive criteria of the original PAPD diagnosis, which generated no empirical studies. Until recently, only two studies specifically examined the PAPD. Within the past few years, however, additional studies have been completed that attempt to either validate the diagnosis or examine its characteristics.

Fossati et al. (2000) assessed the *Diagnostic and Statistical Manual of Mental Disorders* (*DSM-IV*) PAPD psychometric properties and comorbidity patterns. Of a sample of 379 in- and out-patients admitted to the Medical Psychology and Psychotherapy Unit of the Scientific Institute di San Raffaele of Milan, Italy, 47 subjects (12.3%) received a *DSM-IV* diagnosis of NegPD with 89.4% receiving an additional PD diagnosis. In particular, the authors note that a significant correlation existed with the Narcissistic Personality Disorder (NarPD), and that the NarPD was the only *DSM-IV* personality disorder significantly predictive of the NegPD diagnosis. In addition, there was no significant association between PAPD and other Cluster C personality disorders. Characteristics such as grandiosity and interpersonal exploitation of others were the most predictive narcissistic criteria of the NegPD diagnosis. The authors therefore suggest that PAPD is a subtype of NarPD rather than its own distinctive personality disorder (Fossati et al., 2000).

Vereycken et al. (2002) investigated personality disorders of young men with chronic authority conflicts using the Millon Clinical Multiaxial Inventory I (MCMI-I; Millon, 1983). The authors compared personality disorder diagnoses between young men with chronic and acute authority conflicts and a normal control group. Results indicated that NegPD was overrepresented among young men with chronic authority conflicts (28 of 41) and was clearly distinctive from other personality disorders. The authors therefore concluded that the diagnosis was a useful, valid, and reliable diagnostic category. Regarding treatment, the study suggests that due to the high probability of PAPD characteristics evident in young men with chronic authority conflicts, treatment will be difficult (Vereycken et al., 2002).

Bernstein et al. (1993) examined the prevalence and stability of *DSM-III-R* personality disorders within a large group of adolescents from a community-based sample. Randomly selected adolescents were assessed at three different time intervals. Diagnoses of personality disorder symptoms peaked at age 12 for boys and age 13 for girls. For both girls and boys, the intensity and prevalence of personality symptoms declined thereafter. However, those diagnosed with NegPD showed the most social dysfunction, as demonstrated by the highest expulsion and suspension rates from school. Actual prevalence numbers of those children with passive-aggressive personality traits or disorder are variable. Bernstein et al. indicated that within this large sample of adolescents (733), approximately 8.3% of boys and 5.3% of girls showed significant passive-aggressive symptoms at ages 11 to 14; on retest at ages 15 to 17, 5% of boys and 4.9% of girls showed symptoms; and at final retest at ages 18 to 21, 3.9% of boys and 3.6% of girls showed symptoms. These results indicate that in early adolescence boys may be more likely to demonstrate defiance or oppositional behaviors, but as their age progresses, girls and boys are relatively similar. Overall, 6.0% of males and 4.7% of females met criteria for PAPD (Bernstein et al., 1993). Similarly, the Rey et al. (1995) study demonstrated that of a large clinical population of adolescents (with disruptive and emotional disorders), 6% were diagnosed with PAPD as young adults. Prevalence rates for adult NegPD within patient populations range from 10% to as high as 52% (cited in McCann, 1999). When comparing data to the ODD literature, similar trends exist. Oppositional Defiant Disorder is diagnosed in males slightly more often than in females. Sex differences do not usually present until after age 6 for disruptive behavior disorders, when more boys show overt forms of disruptive behavior (Loeber, Burke, Lahey, Winters, & Zera, 2000).

ETIOLOGY OF PASSIVE-AGGRESSIVE CHILDREN

Millon (1981) suggests numerous contributing factors to the development of the passive-aggressive personality in children. Millon (1981) and McCann (1988) speculate that "difficult to schedule" infants may exhibit their erratic mood pattern throughout their lives. Thought of as "fretful" and "nervous" children, they may actually create or increase inconsistent or ambivalent responses from their parents. At times, the parents may be easy to please, and at other times difficult to the point of exhaustion. Parents may demonstrate intense inconsistency, which the child models and then incorporates and integrates as polarized positions within his or her own personality. Millon writes, "His erraticism and vacillation, his tendency to shift capriciously from one mood to another, may be viewed as mirroring the varied and inconsistent reinforcements to which he was exposed" (1969, p. 287). Never quite knowing how a parent may respond, and therefore never quite knowing what to anticipate, the child learns to reflect parental ambivalence and inconsistency. Consequences are not learned inasmuch as the child is unable to anticipate the outcomes of actions in a consistent fashion or come to positive and rewarding resolutions in interactions. These children may present with a "bewildered failure to understand" their predicament and dependently seek direction and guidance (Stricker, 1983, p. 15). Developmentally, Millon suggests that those children who become passive-aggressive are unable to resolve Erikson's (1950) conflicts of trust versus mistrust, competence versus doubt, and initiative versus guilt. They continue to deal with interactions and potential conflicts as polar, which then becomes central to their actions. These unresolved conflicts create ambivalent, opposing self- and other appraisals and pervasive indecisiveness, eventuating in unstable and erratic emotional states that are then seen as the child's "personality." Struggles occur both within the children and without as to whether to seek reinforcements or settle for less than they want (or believe that they deserve), whether to be dependent or independent, and whether to seek reward or avoid punishments. Millon (1981, p. 265) writes, "Thus, 'irregular' children may set into motion erratic and contradictory reactions from parents that serve, in circular fashion to reinforce their initial tendency to be spasmodic and variable." In essence, these children are "double handicapped": They were not the recipients of external control, and therefore they never integrated internal control (Millon, 1981).

From the interpersonal perspective, Benjamin (1996) captures the essential nature of the negativist. She writes, "There is a tendency to see any form of power as inconsiderate and neglectful . . . (the individual) fears control in any form and wishes for nurturant restitution" (p. 272). Additionally, there is the sense that others are given recognition and accolades, but the negativists are not noticed, not awarded, and all too often overlooked. The result is anger and resentment of others' accomplishments as they feel "cheated and robbed" of their due (Benjamin, 1996, 2002). Children with passive aggressiveness often belittle, disregard, or minimize the achievements of other children. They become incensed at how other children, whether siblings or peers, seem to successfully progress through life. Negativistic children remain so focused on the "slight" they have received that they hardly move forward at all.

Psychodynamically, Stricker (1983) notes that the passive-aggressive personality begins with a failure of the parenting object to meet the dependency needs of the child. This results in intense frustration, insecurity, and anxiety. Often an atmosphere of demanding and unsympathetic parenting attitudes is prevalent. The implicit and explicit message the child receives is that he or she is not safe to express anger, and therefore must inhibit angry emotions, which are seen as negative or bad. Stricker (1983, p. 11) writes, "The frustration of dependency is accompanied by parenting which is so threatening that the child does not dare to express feelings directly." However, by indirectly expressing their anger, these children are able to discharge emotions causing irritation and frustration without the obvious consequences of expressing direct anger. However, a pattern emerges in which they are reluctant or unable to take ownership of their actions or emotions due to the indirect discharge of their anger. Because their early dependency needs were not met, their low self-esteem is compounded by not understanding how their own emotions and behaviors have a cause and effect on their internal and external environment (Stricker, 1983).

These children need to constantly align with one parent against the other, never living in their own experience (Millon, 1969, 1981). Millon (1969, 1981; Millon et al., 2000) has also speculated that family dynamics that include a child who experiences an extreme form of being "replaced" by a younger sibling creates vulnerabilities that contribute to passive-aggressive actions and personalities. Children who experience being neglected or tossed aside at the birth of a sibling experience parental affections as being withdrawn. In the extreme example, the child who had previously experienced an intense close symbiotic bond or "specialness" (Bonds-White, 1983) with the mother is forced to now share that special bond with the intruding sibling and subsequently feels a dramatic loss and absence of the primary attachment figure. This creates intense anxiety and anger. Similar to narcissism, the child's specialness is no longer the focus of the family's attention. However, with the birth of a sibling, the child is also put into a conundrum. Angry at the loss of parental attention and affection, yet thrown into the position of being the older caretaking "big brother or sister," these children experience intensified conflicting emotions and exist in a situation in which they have little control. An all too common experience is the older sibling giving the baby a hug that causes the baby to cry. The parental response is "Don't hug the baby so hard." If they could, these children would love the baby to death. Their life has "turned sour" (Millon et al., 2000, p. 477). Unable to overtly express their anger at the infant or the parents, they build resentment. They begin their quest to "recapture" the closeness or bond they perceive they have lost. As the primary attachment with the parents can never be truly recapitulated, these children perpetually experience extreme disappointments in relationships. Bonds-White notes that passive-aggressive individuals often begin their life embraced as a special, almost objectified child that is deprived of self-differentiation.

REFERRALS FOR TREATMENT

Extrapolating from the literature on ODD, reviews of diagnostic studies of personality disorders in adolescents, and anecdotal material, the passive-aggressive child will likely present for treatment as a result of external pressures or complaints. These may include difficulty in task completion, difficulty in completing or refusal to complete assignments, or to meet the expectations of parents or teachers. These children may demonstrate perpetual passive defiance. They often have difficulties with peer relationships, social situations, and with situations that require compliance or working as a member of a group or team. They may be known as difficult or at times as "ornery" children who vacillate in their mood, is at times irritable and at other times sad. Homework may be a series of debating the requirements of the assignment rather than sincere efforts to complete it. Easily mislabeled as learning disabled or having Attention-Deficit/Hyperactivity Disorder (ADHD), which shares many of the same characteristics, the child may be referred for psychological evaluation. An authority figure, for example a teacher or a job supervisor (for adolescents), may instigate the referral. Malinow (1981, p. 128) writes that the teacher may "even have been directly involved in frustrating and conflict-laden situations" with the individual. Indeed, Hardt (1988, p. 13) writes, "In the classroom, the passive-aggressive child uses many tactics that are apt to drive any teacher crazy."

Berres and Long (1979) suggest the following behaviors are consistent with passive-aggressive children: (a) selective vision: "I didn't see it!"; (b) selective hearing: "I didn't hear you!"; (c) slow-down tactics or purposefully stalling when doing tasks: "I'm moving as fast as I can"; (d) losing objects: "But I can't find it!"; (e) being a destructive volunteer who helps but sabotages: "I didn't mean to step on it, I was just trying to help"; and (f) not asking for help: "You didn't help me so I couldn't do it!" All of these behaviors allow the children to express their anger indirectly while appearing to be socially appropriate, apologetic, or even baffled and confused by the teacher's or parent's frustration. As passive-aggressive children have a negativistic view flavored with sarcasm that permeates their interactions, the teacher-pupil relationship suffers as well as their relationships with their peers. These children may use what we would term "apologetic sarcasm" to excuse their lack of performance, for example, "I could have gotten it done if you weren't so busy with the baby," or "I know that you don't have time to help me, not with all of the other kids in the class."

Turkat (1990, p. 87) provides an alarming and potentially lethal example of adolescent passive aggressiveness: "an insulin-dependent diabetic adolescent who deliberately 'forgets' to monitor her blood glucose." Normal adolescents may in fact resent the obligation of taking daily medications because an authority figure has asked them to do so. This resentment is compounded in passive-aggressive children. The result may be an ongoing adversarial interaction with parents and with treating physicians.

Long and Long (2001) suggest that passive-aggressive behaviors exist along a continuum, with sporadic developmentally "normal" atypical responses standing as polar opposites to a stable personality pattern. For example, children may respond in a situational and atypical way to what they perceive to be unreasonable adult requests or demands; they may respond in a way appropriate to their developmental stage; they may respond in way that is characteristic of a cultural norm; or their response may be in keeping with a more entrenched personality style as an internalized way of life. Long and Long identify five levels of passive-aggressive behaviors:

Level 1, temporary compliance: The child verbally agrees to follow through with a demand or a request but delays in completing the request or simply "forgets." This type of behavior is the most common passive-aggressive behavior and includes manifestations questioning sensory ability ("I didn't see/hear it"), simply "forgetting" things, procrastination, and dawdling.

Level 2, intentional inefficiency: This is a more sophisticated form of passive-aggressive behavior. The child completes the requested task, but does so in such a way that the product or behavior is either unacceptable or angers and provokes the adult. The result does not meet the expectations of the request. Examples include thwarting help when it is given, not paying attention to what was asked, creating more problems when attempting to help the adult, and speaking very softly or slowly when others are rushed.

Level 3, letting a problem escalate: This occurs when a child does not share information that would prevent a problem from worsening or escalating, or even preventing the problem. The child silently appears to be enjoying the satisfaction garnered from the stress or anguish of another (e.g., not informing someone of an important phone call). Manifestations of this level of passive aggression include not sharing where lost things may be or preventing someone from avoiding an embarrassing situation (e.g., a food particle left on someone's chin after lunch).

Level 4, hidden but conscious revenge: This is a deliberate getting back or vengeful behavior. The child is determined to harm a parent, teacher, or peer through retaliatory means such as spreading rumors, stealing objects, or thwarting another's productivity through sneaky means. The child does not approach the individual directly, but through covert means, and causes some form of distress (e.g., hiding keys, scaring an individual, or causing a prized object to be lost). Additional retaliatory behaviors could occur that also foster group support and peer status, such as sticking one's tongue out behind the teacher's back or making an obscene gesture.

Level 5, self-depreciation or pathological passive-aggressive behaviors: These are the result of retaliatory behaviors that are so offensive that the child invariably self-destructs through alienation or rejection from others. The behaviors ultimately are self-defeating in nature, analogous to Millon et al.'s (2000) self-defeating "self-perpetuating pattern." Examples include doing poorly in school to thwart parents' desire to send him or her to a chosen college; not being clean, not showering, and having noticeable body odor; and dressing so outrageously inappropriately that opportunities may be missed. The authors suggest that this form of passive-aggressive behavior is the most serious and pathological and requires psychological intervention (Long & Long, 2001).

ASSESSMENT

It is often difficult to get a clear diagnostic picture of passive-aggressive individuals, as they "present vaguely" (Turkat, 1990, p. 88). Their answers may be confusing, meandering, and almost non-goal-directed, making assessment very challenging. For example, when asked a very direct question such as "Is the sky blue?," they may answer in a truthful but cantankerous way, "No. It's raining today so the sky is gray." If asked "Are you doing well in school?," they may respond "How do you define 'doing well'?" or "Why is that important?" or "How is this important to the evaluation?" This can lead to tangential discussions defining particular words or constructs. The assessment can lead to a frustrating puzzle of incomplete answers laden with inconsequential details. Andrews (1991, p. 410) describes passive-aggressive individuals as "both frustrated and frustrating." Compounding the irritable nature of their response is the possibility of a mocking or sarcastic tone. Passive-aggressive children retain their self-percept of autonomy by avoiding direct answers and therefore not acquiescing to the authority figure (Fusco, 2004).

Assessment of children requires the therapist to be skillful and knowledgeable regarding development. As certain behaviors are typically more normal at different developmental stages, it is imperative that the assessment consider development and age appropriateness versus inappropriate behaviors. It is imperative that a comprehensive evaluation occurs, one in which all aspects of the child's life are examined. This includes information from the family, teachers, and primary care physician. Because some children claim that they haven't seen, for instance, the missing object or heard the teacher's request, the obvious first step is to ensure that no physical disabilities exist. For example, if a child has a visual or auditory deficit, his or her behavior, which is viewed by elders and authorities as oppositional, may be more parsimoniously explained. Physical problems that are related to neurological problems should be ruled out before a negativistic cast is put on the behavior. This can occur through a comprehensive physical examination with the family physician. For example, a 7-year-old boy was referred for an evaluation of cognitive ability. He was being considered for retention for a second year in kindergarten or a referral to a class for special needs children. He was the youngest of eight children. His score on the intellectual assessment was an IQ of 62. A second measure was administered with a resulting IQ of 64. Although it seemed clear that the boy was cognitively impaired, his overall language use and behavior seemed unusual. While turning away from the child to retrieve another test, the examiner asked the child a question to which the child did not respond although previously responding to examiner questions. The examiner then tried covering his mouth and the child was asked a series of questions. The child did not respond. When this finding was shared with the boy's mother, her response was that the boy was just being obstinate. When he did not respond at home, she found that when she would grab him by the arms and yell at him she could break through his negativistic behavior.

An audiological examination found the boy to have a 90% deficit in each ear. When aided, the boy was able to progress in school.

DEVELOPMENTAL CONSIDERATIONS

Overdiagnosing or pathologizing benign developmentally appropriate passive-aggressive behavior can occur if the clinician does not conceptualize the behavior within a developmental perspective. Bonds-White (1983) provides a review of the progression of a passive-aggressive personality structure through a developmental lens.

TODDLERHOOD

Development for a 2-year-old typically involves testing limits, battling wills with caretakers, and beginning to interact with the environment as a differentiated individual. For the "terrible twos" the most frequent word is "NO." This is used whether or not the child wishes the opportunity offered. Ideally, parents and caretakers provide a safe and protective atmosphere within which the child builds confidence to move toward the outside world, thereby helping to resolve the Ericksonian crisis toward the building of initiative.

In the genesis of the passive-aggressive personality, the child experiences a mother who has created a sense of "omnipotence" or overprotection (Bonds-White, 1983). Mothers may even "restrict mobility" as a form of protection for the child rather than encouraging and praising the toddler for physical curiosity in exploring the world. Opposed to the sent message that the child is helpless, the mother simultaneously conveys the idea that a very dangerous world awaits the child just outside the door of the family home. Ill-equipped to navigate this potentially malevolent world, the child must restrict his or her independence and thus remain intensely dependent on the powerful mother. These children are caught in a cycle where they are prevented from experiencing independence or risk challenging their mother and possibly losing her affection; in this way, early ambivalence and a restriction of self are created.

EARLY CHILDHOOD, 3 TO 7 YEARS

During this time, differentiation from the primary attachment figure normally occurs (Bonds-White, 1983). The child has progressed to feeling comfortable enough to socialize with others (peers, siblings, parents) in various forms of play and in social and emotional interactions. Play is a key component of this age and creates the working template by which daily life is constructed. For children who will be passive aggressive, individuation has not occurred; instead, they remain caught in a helpless position. They must feel what their mother feels, and receive mother's affection by remaining attached to her in an infantile position. This translates to doing little or nothing. Play, therefore, may be restricted to interacting only with mother or being left on their own. Depersonalized play such as drawing by themselves, walks with adults, playing alone with dolls or action figures, or making up games on their own are examples of their isolation. Isolative and socially limited play limits their ability to experience the boundaries of what is possible and permissible through "sociodramatic" play (p. 52). The play is not an active, engaging skill-building of competencies or opportunity to test their own strengths, but is passive and directed toward "entertaining mother" (p. 52). A feeling of superiority infiltrates the activity (Bonds-White, 1983), which encourages and fans the flame of a growing narcissistic flair. Indeed, isolative and socially remote play interferes with creating empathy and an understanding of others as components of a developing personality. Teachers may notice a child who is not socializing with peers, seems almost infantile in emotional interactions, and seeks attention from the authority figure but through negative means (e.g., defiance). Simple tasks are not followed through, and the child requires constant redirection.

LATENCY AGE: 7 TO 13 YEARS

At this point in development, children begin to challenge themselves in school and, ideally, to master tasks and experience varied competencies. They begin to take ownership of their accomplishments and achievements. Children whose personality is evolving in a passive-aggressive direction remain dependent (not pursuing independent activities), while at the same time mother is claiming reward or recognition for whatever achievements the child does incur (e.g., a mother taking credit for her child's performance in a choir). There may even be envy or resentment on the parent's behalf of the child's accomplishments. There is little reinforcement of independent problem solving or thinking skills, thus confirming their perception and feelings of helplessness. Messages from parents may be that the children are ineffectual or not able to have an effect on their environment (Bonds-White, 1983). Powerful feelings of dependency are contradicted with intense feelings of resentment, anger, and a felt lack of recognition. A child at this stage may begin to express anger at peers receiving recognition or respect for achievements and consequently feeling misunderstood or overlooked. As anxiety is often present with PAPD, these children may manifest more somatic complaints. They may experience intense frustration and be prevented from expressing their anger; they seem to have a broody, pessimistic edge beyond normal transient mood shifts. The older child may also be struggling with mood changes as a result of hormonal surges related to puberty.

ADOLESCENCE

Adolescence is a time of normal rebelliousness. Developmentally, children have achieved vast physical, intellectual, and sexual growth. However, they continue to remain largely dependent on their parents because of limited financial resources and personal freedom (Bonds-White, 1983). In addition, laws may require that the adolescent remain in school. Adolescents are typically searching and discovering themselves (their identity) through experiencing independence in so-cial, scholastic, and interpersonal relationships. Adolescents with a developing passive-aggressive personality will likely have difficulty creating and maintaining relationships and difficulty progressing with formal study or training in a vocation. Stone (1993a, p. 362) writes that these adolescents will often "[defeat their own] goals just to get back at the parents . . . which happens to be the very thing [they] always wanted to do." They will demonstrate a high level of competitiveness and may even be spiteful toward those who achieve more than they do. They will belittle those who may be able to expe-rience intimacy, and in a stubborn angry way not be open to examin-ing how their behaviors contribute to their isolation or marginalized social life. Time management and realistic goal-setting is difficult for these adolescents, thereby creating obvious challenges when plan-ning for future vocational activities or applying to colleges (Bonds-White, 1983). School policies, restrictions, and rules may be difficult for the passive-aggressive student to accept. Violations of these rules may lead to suspensions or expulsions. Schema related to being spe-cial and misunderstood propel anger and hostility toward others who are moving ahead in various areas. Time may be spent arguing and debating the purpose, value, meaning, rationale, and goals of what others accept as normal everyday routine (e.g., arriving at school at a certain time). These traits carry over into adulthood, as passive-aggressive individuals appear to have difficulty in owning or under-standing the impact their obstinate and oppositional style creates in their lives.

Studies have indicated that passive-aggressive individuals have a higher likelihood of substance use (Small, Small, Alig, & Moore, 1970), disruptive disorders in adulthood (Johnson, Cohen, Skodol, et al., 1999), and an association with suicidality and hopelessness (Joiner & Rudd, 2002). As teenagers have access to cars, medication, and other means of self-injury, careful consideration of high-risk variables is paramount for evaluation of these adolescents. Assessment instruments that identify potential substance abuse and personality characteristics will assist the clinician in treatment planning.

DIFFERENTIAL DIAGNOSIS

Currently, if a patient meets criteria for NegPD, the diagnosis is formally categorized on Axis II, NOS (not otherwise specified). Evaluation for associated high-risk behaviors such as suicidality, homicidality, or substance abuse must occur. Careful attention to these symptoms is warranted. Additional Axis I symptoms that may be apparent include those consistent with anxiety disorders. These may be present during times that directly challenge the patient to be assertive or respond to an external demand or when forced to choose a specific course of action.

The NegPD diagnosis can be difficult to discriminate from other personality disorders. Millon and Davis (1996, p. 560) state, "With exception of the borderline, it alone among the personality disorders possesses the entire mixture of traits seen more consistently and with less diversity among other types. This very heterogeneity and changeability are among its distinguishing hallmarks." Currently, NegPD is presumed to exist within the Cluster C spectrum of personality disorders, with the cardinal underlying trait of anxiety as its defining feature. In keeping with the existing nomenclature, the NegPD presentation would also include features of the other three personality disorders included in Cluster C: Dependent, Obsessive-Compulsive, and Avoidant (American Psychiatric Association, 2000). Dependency needs are prevalent, and obsessive-compulsive features are manifested as an inordinate attention to detail, tangentiality, and perfectionism. These individuals tend to become lost in the minutiae; in effect, they cannot see the forest for the trees. This short-sightedness impedes progress in completing tasks and challenges. Small battles are waged while the overall war is lost (Fusco, 2004). Avoidant features are also present: Conflict is often avoided due to intense fears of rejection, and many tasks will not be attempted without a guarantee that success will occur.

Some authors have hypothesized a connection with narcissism and question the validity of PAPD remaining within the Cluster C personality disorder categories given its commonality in traits with narcissism (Fossati et al., 2000). Rey et al. (1995) studied the continuity between psychiatric disorders in adolescents and personality disorders in young adults and noted that adolescents with ODD showed a preponderance of Cluster B disorders as adults, rather than the anxiety-based Cluster C disorders. Many individuals with NegPD show features of Cluster B personality disorders. Narcissism is manifested in individuals' considerable focus on their plight and misfortune, with a concomitant inability to empathize with others and an intense feeling of being misunderstood by others (Fossati et al., 2000). Fossati's study suggests that the negativistic attitude of PAPD does not stem from the conflict between autonomy and dependence, as proposed by Millon (1969), but rather is based on a narcissistic personality structure. The narcissism is manifested as grandiosity and the exploitation of others. They are outraged by external demands and having to meet the expectations and obligations of others (Fossati et al., 2000). Differentiation can be made between the two disorders, as the narcissistic individual typically will not demonstrate exaggerated dependency needs, and if in disagreement with an authority figure or external demand will likely not express this difference of opinion in a passive way. Narcissists consider themselves the authority and may be vocal and energetic in their protest. The passive-aggressive attempts to thwart the demands of others more quietly. Although those with Borderline Personality Disorder also demonstrate severe ambivalence and vacillation, they experience more radical cognitive extremes, extreme shifts in affectivity, and more severe behavioral conflicts than those with NegPD (Millon & Davis, 1996).

The differentiation of NegPD and ODD is seen in the way defiance is demonstrated. For children who have ODD, defiance is not subverted or passive. Additionally, intense dependency needs, sullenness of mood, and intense ambivalence are more prevalent with the NegPD child or adolescent. Children with Conduct Disorder violate the rights of others and are involved in physical fighting, whereas the passive-aggressive child will passively cause problems. Loeber et al. (2000) indicated that ODD may often be a precursor to CD, which may later lead to Antisocial Personality Disorder (APD). McCann (1999) notes that common traits of defiance and oppositionality exist with NegPD and APD. Malinow (1981) suggests that there is an overlap with APD, but that the passive-aggressive individual is able to reality test, so is able to remain just within the bounds of what is socially and legally acceptable.

NegPD personality symptoms in childhood and adolescence have been demonstrated to be associated with ADHD (Fischer, Barkley, Smallish, & Fletcher, 2002), violent acts as adults (Johnson, Cohen, Smailes, et al., 2000), and increased risk for disruptive disorders as adults (Johnson, Cohen, Skodol, et al., 1999). Studies examining the issue of abuse have indicated that childhood maltreatment increases the risk for personality pathology in adulthood. Drake, Adler, and Valliant (1988) in a study of a community sample of men demonstrated that nearly two thirds met criteria for PAPD or Dependent Personality Disorder, and that family instability and lack of parental affection and supervision during adolescence was found. In a more contemporary study, Johnson, Cohen, Brown, Smailes, and Bernstein (1999) examined a community sample of youths and their mothers from two counties in New York. The sample was administered psychosocial and psychiatric interviews at four different time intervals over an 18-year period. Results indicated that children with documented child abuse or neglect were more than 4 times more likely to be diagnosed with personality disorders during early adulthood. Specifically, childhood neglect was associated with higher symptom levels of PAPD. The authors suggest that given the strength of the data related to neglect, further research needs to be conducted to examine the effects of neglect on childhood development. In a follow-up study further examining neglect, the authors indicate that specifically childhood supervision neglect was associated with increased risk for passive-aggressive and Cluster B personality disorders during early adulthood (Johnson, Smailes, Cohen, Brown, & Bernstein, 2000). Knutson (1999) reviewed risk factors of children who were neglected. In sum, his review indicated that mothers of neglected children demonstrated an anxious-resistant type of attachment, and that children who were neglected showed more difficulty engaging in the school setting, common elements of a passive-aggressive child. Ratican (1992) also reviewed literature suggesting that child sexual abuse may be an etiological factor in adult passive-aggressive pathologies. The Johnson, Cohen, Skodol, et al. (1999) study did not indicate an association with child sexual abuse and adult passive-aggressive personality; rather, only Borderline Personality Disorder was significant.

TREATMENT

The passive-aggressive child presents many challenges to the therapeutic relationship. Gardner (1975, p. 42) writes that the passive-aggressive child lives by the statement, "What he wants me to do is the very thing I will not do." These children are very difficult to engage in therapy as any request becomes the "cue to do nothing." Additionally, passive-aggressive children are able to kill two birds with one stone by sitting silently in treatment: Not only are they frustrating to the therapist, but they know that their parents are paying for their treatment. Gardner writes that in such sessions, the therapist essentially becomes "an ally in the child's acting out" (p. 42). In 1989, the *Task Force Report to the American Psychiatric Association* (American Psychiatric Association, 1989) described the central problem in psychotherapy with passive-aggressive individuals as "the negative transference to the therapist and the resistance to the requirements of the therapy" (p. 2786). The Task Force found that this resistance in treatment is displayed in myriad ways, including being tardy, being silent for prolonged periods, becoming oppositional, dropping out at high rates, and exhibiting increasing passive resistance to the therapy and to change (American Psychiatric Association, 1989). Children may in fact be referred for treatment due to the defiant nature of their behaviors both at home and at school. Stone (1993b, p. 308) writes that PADP "seldom lead[s] to residential treatment or to incarceration." Typically, the behavioral manifestations do not warrant higher levels of care unless there are comorbid conditions that warrant further services. This includes knowledge that the adult NegPD population has been associated with high levels of suicidality and hopelessness (Joiner & Rudd, 2002) and substance abuse (Small et al., 1970).

Beck, Freeman, Davis, and associates (2004) suggest that, in the cognitive-behavioral treatment of PAPD, a collaborative approach be utilized to identify automatic thoughts and schema related to dysfunctional behaviors and inappropriate expressions of anger. The major focus of the treatment is to challenge basic beliefs and thought patterns of how the self, others, and the world are perceived. By modifying these irrational beliefs, a change in emotion or affect states will occur (Beck, Freeman, et al., 1990).

Prout and Platt (1983) define the behavioral conceptualization of the characteristics of the PAPD patient and the expression of passive-aggressive nonassertive behaviors as being largely interpersonal in nature and involving the dishonest expression of feelings and thoughts. In addition, unassertive behaviors are largely socially inappropriate and demonstrate a lack of concern for others. Unassertive communication may be expressed verbally or nonverbally, such as in loudness and tone of voice, fluency of spoken words, eye contact, facial expressions, body posture, and lean of body toward or away from the other (Prout & Platt, 1983).

TREATMENT WITH A COGNITIVE-BEHAVIORAL APPROACH

The cognitive profile of NegPD includes core beliefs, conditional assumptions, and compensatory strategies that are consistent with retaining autonomy, negativism, ambivalence, resistance, and an inability to meet the expectations of others (Fusco, 2004). Automatic thoughts reflect "negativism, autonomy, and desire to follow the path of least resistance" (Ottaviani, 1990, p. 336). Powerful guilt-inducing schema such as "It is not acceptable to express my desires and anger directly" inhibit direct expression of hostility and anger (Burns & Epstein, 1983, p. 73). A pervasive skepticism and pessimism pervade core beliefs and schema and thus impacts how NegPD individuals view themselves, others, and the world and all its challenges. They seem to have a negative filter cast across any and all situations. They view requests from others as invasive, intrusive, and offensive, even in the face of evidence that following or completing these requests may be beneficial to them. Wanting to be in favor with authority figures (dependency and acknowledgment) remains in direct contradiction to their belief that to remain autonomous they must circumvent or ignore the rules. As a means of managing this ambivalence, independence is maintained by using passive behaviors that do not directly confront or challenge the authority. If the authority figure is not challenged, they retain control (Fusco, 2004). Burns and Epstein (1983) state that with the emotional activation of anger, powerful cognitive factors create distortions related to entitlement ("If they don't do what I want, they don't love me"), reciprocity ("They owe me!"), and conflict phobia ("I shouldn't express my anger"), preventing resolution of underlying conflict. Typical distortions include overgeneralizing, "should" statements, mind reading, emotional reasoning, labeling, personalization, and disqualifying the positive; these distortions appear as feelings of being slighted and misunderstood and as an externalization of blame (Burns & Epstein, 1983). Among adolescents, powerful schema prevent their progression and transition to mature and independent thinking. Instead, independence is demonstrated by an ongoing refusal to meet others' demands through superficial cooperation. Compliance is synonymous with a loss of control and freedom and is associated with a loss of autonomy, a position they are unable to tolerate. Continually feeling as if they are being put upon, they deem requests from others as offensive and demonstrate that others are incapable of understanding their more noble intentions. Typical core beliefs are listed in Table 17.1.

CONDITIONAL BELIEFS

Conditional beliefs of NegPD patients are largely expressed in terms of remaining superficially compliant, all the while convinced that their means of handling situations is the best, obvious, and most

Table 17.1
Comparison of Oppositional Defiant Disorder and Passive-Aggressive Personality Disorder

Oppositional Defiant Disorder	Passive-Aggressive Personality Disorder
A. A pattern of negativistic, hostile, and defiant behavior lasting at least 6 months, during which four(or more) of the following are present: 1. Often loses temper 2. Often argues with adults 3. Often actively defies or refuses to comply with adults' requests or rules 4. Often deliberately annoys people 5. Often blames others for his or her mistakes or misbehavior 6. Often touchy or easily annoyed by others 7. Often angry or resentful 8. Often spiteful or vindictive	A. A pervasive pattern of negativistic attitudes and passive resistance to demands for adequate performance, beginning by early adulthood and present in a variety of contexts as indicated by four (or more) of the following: 1. Passively resists fulfilling social and occupational tasks 2. Complains of being mistreated by others 3. Is sullen and argumentative 4. Unreasonably criticizes and scorns authority 5. Expresses envy and resentment toward those apparently more successful 6. Voices exaggerated and persistent complaints of personal misfortune 7. Alternates between hostile defiance and contrition
B. The disturbance in behavior causes clinically significant impairment in social, academic, or occupational functioning. The behaviors do not occur exclusively during the course of a psychotic or mood disorder.	B. Does not occur exclusively during major depressive episodes and is not better accounted for by Dysthymic Disorder.
C. Criteria are not met for Conduct Disorder, and, if the individual is age 18 or older, the criteria are not met for Antisocial Personality Disorder.	

unique way. Successful management of a situation thus requires shallow acquiescence (Fusco, 2004).

Typical conditional beliefs are listed in Table 17.2.

COMPENSATORY BELIEFS

Compensatory beliefs include themes of remaining in the favor of the authority figure by superficially conforming. For children, this may be a pattern of agreeing to do something (e.g., temporary compliance) but never following through. However, if superficial conformity becomes problematic in any situation, individuals then rely on the belief that an extreme injustice has occurred. They are convinced they are not being recognized or appreciated for the unique and special contribution they are making, nor are others capable of understanding them. There is a narcissistic quality to their compensatory strategies that can appear as a protective mechanism to avoid or avert rejection. However, the intense rage that accompanies these beliefs somewhat contradicts the notion that these beliefs are protective in their function, instead of the result of a narcissistic injury (Fusco, 2004).

COLLABORATION

The core beliefs of the passive-aggressive individual makes collaboration difficult. Actually identifying the problem in question will need to be a collaborative venture. Identifying the problem may mean to children that they must agree with the therapist, thereby acquiescing to the authority. Therefore, aligning with the child's felt distress, not the imagined slight, is imperative. Kaplan, Sadock, and Grebb (1994, p. 747) state that the therapist must take care not to "become enmeshed in trying to assuage the patients' many claims of unjust treatment" and to be wary of the juxtaposition "To fulfill their demands is often to support their pathology but to refuse their demands is to reject them."

Ottaviani (1990) writes that the very first step is to actively engage them in the therapeutic process by focusing on collaborative empiricism. As the primary core belief of NegPD individuals is to not follow

Table 17.2
Clinical Domains of the Negativistic (Passive-Aggressive) Prototype

Behavioral Level

Expressively resentful: Resists fulfilling expectancies of others, frequently exhibiting procrastination, inefficiency, and obstinacy, as well as oppositionalism and irksome behaviors; reveals gratification in demoralizing and undermining the pleasures and aspirations of others.

Interpersonally contrary: Assumes conflicting and changing roles in social relationships, particularly dependent and contrite acquiescence and assertive and hostile independence; conveys envy and pique toward those more fortunate, as well as acting concurrently or sequentially obstructive and intolerant of others, expressing either negative or incompatible attitudes.

Phenonmenological Level

Cognitively skeptical: Cynical, doubting, and untrusting, approaches positive events with disbelief, and future possibilities with pessimism, anger, and trepidation; has a misanthropic view of life, whines and grumbles, voicing disdain and caustic comments toward those experiencing good fortune.

Discontented self-image: Sees self as misunderstood, luckless, unappreciated, jinxed, and demeaned by others; recognizes being characteristically embittered, disgruntled, and disillusioned with life.

Vacillating objects: Internalized representations of the past comprise a complex of countervailing relationships, setting in motion contradictory feelings, conflicting inclinations, and incompatible memories that are driven by the desire to degrade the achievements and pleasures of others, without necessarily appearing so.

Intraspsychic Level

Displacement mechanism: Discharges anger and other troublesome emotions either precipitously or by employing unconscious maneuvers to shift them from their instigator to settings or persons of lesser significance; vents disapproval by substitute or passive means, such as acting inept or perplexed, or behaving in a forgetful or indolent manner.

Divergent organization: A clear division in the pattern of morphologic structures such that coping and defensive maneuvers are often directed toward incompatible goals, leaving major conflicts unresolved and full psychic cohesion often impossible because fulfillment of one drive or need inevitably nullifies or reverses another.

Biophysical Level

Irritable mood: Frequently touchy, temperamental, and peevish, followed in turn by sullen and moody withdrawal; often petulant and impatient, unreasonably scorns those in authority and reports being annoyed easily or frustrated by many.

Source: "Negativistic Personality Disorders: The Vacillating Pattern" (p. 550), by T. Millon and R. Davis, in *Disorders of Personality: DSM-IV and Beyond,* T. Millon (Ed.), 1996, New York: Wiley.

the dictates of an authority figure, the therapeutic process becomes challenging. They may believe that the therapist is trying to tell them what to do and how to do it and that they are being required to change. It is therefore imperative that *they* make the commitment to the therapeutic process and become actively involved in the progress and process of therapy. This requires ongoing diligence on the part of the therapist to ensure that the child maintains some of the control in the therapeutic relationship. Frequent checking and confirming is crucial to ensure that these patients do not feel railroaded into complying with the therapist's requests. If they assume that the therapist is controlling the session or requesting compliance, they may passively resist the process, such as "forgetting" to do homework, being silent during sessions, not showing up, or canceling the session (Fusco, 2004).

Collaboration must also be maintained with the family and the school. This may be very difficult as the family is often entangled systematically in reinforcing the negative passive-aggressive behaviors. School personnel may be frustrated with the child's behavior and focus less on the child's strengths and more on his or her negativistic contributions to the classroom. Areas where the behavior manifests itself must be identified in the event that the behaviors are a situational response rather than a personality trait. The reason for referral must be carefully examined.

From a cognitive perspective, automatic thoughts must be consistently identified both within the session and between sessions. Ottaviani (1990) suggests that when an affective shift occurs in the session, the therapist must be sure to examine the thoughts related to this shift. The therapist must be able to challenge the patient's distorted beliefs related to being controlled by providing evidence that the patient has collaborated throughout the process and has not been requested or dictated to do something. The therapist and patient must then work together to identify those cognitions that are blocking or preventing task completion (Ottaviani, 1990).

As NegPD patients become aware of the affective shifts they experience (self-monitoring) in reaction to others, associated automatic thoughts related to being taken advantage of, being misunderstood, or attempting to be controlled are more easily identified and therefore challenged. Children may be more readily able to identify those situations in which they received a punishment (something concrete) and didn't understand why they experienced the consequences they received. Identifying how anger, disappointment, and other emotional states actually feel (e.g., physiological reactions) provides a valuable gateway to their associated automatic thoughts and their underlying core beliefs. Putting words to emotions will be key as passive-aggressive individuals struggle with alexithymia. They typically are unclear as to what their distress is actually related to, only that they are in distress. Early homework assignments should include documenting and collecting automatic thoughts, particularly after experiencing an intense emotion. Ottaviani (1990) suggests that to encourage compliance with these assignments, dysfunctional thought recording should be presented as a no-lose assignment. Not only does the assignment allow for a connection between their thoughts and how they may feel, but it can identify those areas that contribute to any depression or anxiety they may be experiencing (Ottaviani, 1990). Assignments for children must be gauged to their developmental level, including a more behavioral approach for younger children, while tapping into more of the abstract thinking that exists for the adolescent.

FAMILY THERAPY

Family therapy or systems therapy will be a necessary component of most treatments with a negativistic child or adolescent. Kaslow (1983) describes the pattern of families where resistance is an undercurrent that emerges indirectly rather than directly. Circular in nature, the passive aggressiveness of one individual influences how others within the system respond. Passive withholding or covert undermining of others is a powerful and controlling facet within the family, and it is ultimately a successful maneuver. Stone (1993a) implicates parental overcontrol and nagging as significant family dynamics that are present with passive-aggressives. As a means of staging a protest in "the unending power struggles with one's parents," the child develops "face-saving techniques" (p. 361). A thorough understanding of the communication dynamic and pattern within the family is imperative.

Kaslow (1983) notes that positive reinforcement for the adolescent can contradict the parental dictate "Don't cause trouble." Kaslow further suggests that family therapy address the "functional autonomy" of the behavior or the actual function the behavior serves. Therapy needs to focus on identifying the pattern established in communicating frustration and anger, appropriate outlets for anger, boundaries, and recognition of each person's contribution to the entire family system. Anger should be allowed to be expressed in a direct form and worked through as a process. Overlapping behaviors that may manifest in the school or relationships can therefore be addressed.

Many passive-aggressive individuals will approach therapy as a "battleground" (Kaplan, Sadock, & Grebb, 1994). Stone (1993a, p. 361) writes, "The PAPD . . . will set up counter arguments to nullify any positive suggestion . . . constituting a major impediment to treatment." Therapy often becomes "a matter of managing oneself" (Andrews, 1991, p. 410). Marquoit (2004, p. 177) notes that the passive-aggressive student has the ability to inflame and antagonize even trained professionals to react with "ineffective punitive responses." Intense confrontation therefore is unlikely to have a positive outcome. Beck, Freeman, Davis, and associates (2004) note that the therapist must avoid challenging dysfunctional beliefs and behaviors too aggressively or prematurely, as direct confrontation may activate compelling core schema related to authority figures. Attempts to lull the therapist into competitive squabbling, voicing frustration with endless detail-laden descriptions of slights, and provocative challenges must be resisted. Focusing on the emotional and deleterious effects this form of social behavior incurs is likely to be more beneficial.

Burns and Epstein (1983, p. 84) list common tipoffs that the patient may be developing negative feelings and reactions toward the therapist to include: "forgetting appointments, homework"; not allowing the therapist to make an obvious point; using sarcasm; being late; complaining; stating "No one understands!"; requesting referral to another therapist; giving "Yes, but . . ." answers; appearing to be upset but refusing to talk about it; and coming to therapy intoxicated or inappropriately dressed.

As a means of avoiding struggles, Reid (1988) suggests that clear rules of therapy should be written, outlining expectations of the therapy, scheduling, and the time frame of treatment. This should be completed early in the therapy, and most important, the therapist needs to consistently adhere to the limitations that have been set. Again, this process (list) must be completed collaboratively, checking with each point that a mutual understanding exists and that there is agreement to the structure and limits of the therapeutic process. Passive-aggressive behaviors such as showing up late for a session due to automatic thoughts related to "nobody's going to tell me when to arrive" provide ample in vivo opportunity to address, challenge, and dispute these distortions.

Bonds-White (1983, p. 60) suggests a sequence of powerful "permission giving" statements that the therapist can build within the therapy, such as "You can think and solve problems"; "You can succeed"; "You can enjoy your success"; "You can maintain your boundaries"; "You belong to yourself"; "You are a feeling human being." Burns and Epstein (1983, p. 86) suggest using the "disarming technique," which basically acknowledges the grain of truth in patients' statements even if part of the material is distorted. In this way, patients are disarmed from engaging the oppositional position and may be more open to talking about feelings.

Throughout treatment, remaining consistent, objective, and empathic with the NegPD individual must be maintained by the therapist. The therapist can get caught in an almost impossible battle that is waging within these patients that presents as *please help me/screw you* behaviors (Fusco, 2004, p. 357). Their caustic interactions can prove to be tiring, and at times are offensive. Their continued ambivalence causes frequent starts and stops throughout therapy. As patients slowly become more comfortable (dependent) with suggestions from the therapist, underlying ambivalence can cause an erratic shift, leading to a rejection or setback of the treatment process (oppositional). The therapist needs to consistently identify the dysfunctional thoughts related to these shifts and forge ahead, challenging these distortions. Although it can appear that these patients revel in their misery, they experience great discomfort, angst, and sadness in their plight (Fusco, 2004).

SPECIFIC INTERVENTIONS

Social skills training is a vital aspect of treatment of NegPD children. Many of their interactions are fraught with negativism, poor boundaries, caustic interactions, and an argumentative style. Role-playing situations in which they felt overlooked or slighted may assist in demonstrating socially sabotaging exchanges that result in alienation. Modeling by the therapist also provides a powerful example of managing and tolerating frustration in an adaptive and healthy way.

As several of the proposed diagnostic symptoms involve hostility, the passive-aggressive needs to learn appropriate discharges of anger, hostility, and, in particular, resentment. Ottaviani (1990) suggests that therapists need to assist those with NegPD to manage and examine their means of "getting back" at others that are perceived to have received recognition and validation. Associated themes such as "They should be punished" and "No one really understands" should be challenged (Ottaviani, 1990). This may be difficult to do, as it requires a focus on their own performance and behaviors rather than their perceived lack of acceptance and acknowledgment. This taps into the narcissistic quality of the NegPD individual's core beliefs consisting of compelling schema related to injustice and the feelings of being misunderstood. Strategies of treatment of Narcissistic Personality Disorder should also be reviewed (Fusco, 2004).

Turkat (1990) suggests that when emotionally triggered, these individuals may have even more difficulty expressing aggression directly. Due to their core beliefs that others may be attempting to control or devalue them, the emotional response of anger often drives the behavioral response to a situation. Often a cognitive interpretation of the situation does not occur; rather, reactions are derived from the immediate visceral response. A cost-benefit analysis can assist in identifying the advantages and disadvantages of their impulsive reactions and the benefit of examining the relationship between their core beliefs and their associated emotional responses (Fusco, 2004).

TEACHER INVOLVEMENT

Understanding how a child is behaving in the school setting versus the home setting is vital to understand whether the behaviors are situational or part of the child's personality. Additionally, if a child is experiencing intense difficulties at school, collaborative and cooperative involvement of the teacher and the school counselor can provide a consistent delivery of the treatment plan. Hardt (1988) suggests that it is imperative that the teacher is able to recognize passive-aggressive behaviors and to be able to place the behaviors in the context in which they occur.

Hardt (1988) suggests several tactics to managing passive-aggressive children in the classroom. She suggests teacher modeling of appropriate discharge of anger and of positive teacher-peer interactions. Teachers should model messages such as "It's okay to be wrong," show feelings, and give encouragement to others. Specific strategies may include cooperative learning projects that are mastery-oriented, thus encouraging and promoting self-esteem. In extreme examples (more of the personality), children should be referred to the school psychologist for further assessment and evaluation. Teacher reactions are very important and provide valuable opportunities to model positive behaviors.

MAINTAINING PROGRESS

Maintaining therapeutic gains may be difficult due to a relapsing to core beliefs related to adhering to plans, following others' suggestions, or general compliance with structure. Situations that may place the individual under the direction of an authority figure can activate these schema and can quickly thwart any therapeutic process gained. Creating a list prior to termination that identifies triggers or situations that easily activate maladaptive schema helps to proactively manage the situation in a healthy way. Millon (1969) first suggested that their "anticipation of disappointment" means that passive-aggressives are waiting for the proverbial other shoe to drop. Therefore, the therapist should help these patients identify those situations in which they anticipate difficulty where none may actually exist. Returning for follow-up visits to review their behaviors or problem areas can help in retaining alternative productive means of managing difficult situations.

REFERENCES

American Psychiatric Association. (2000). *Diagnostic and statistical manual of mental disorders* (4th ed., text rev.). Washington, DC: Author.

Andrews, G. (1991). Treatment outlines for avoidant, dependent and passive-aggressive personality disorders. *Australian and New Zealand Journal of Psychiatry,* 404–411.

Beck, A., Freeman, A., Davis, D., Pretzer, J., Fleming, B., Simon, K., et al. (2004). *Cognitive therapy of personality disorders* (2nd ed.). New York: Guilford Press.

Beck, A., Freeman, A., Pretzer, J., Fleming, B., Davis, D. D., Simon, K. M., et al. (1990). *Cognitive therapy of personality disorders.* New York: Guilford Press.

Benjamin, L. S. (1996). *Interpersonal diagnosis and treatment of personality disorders.* New York: Guilford Press.

Benjamin, L. S. (2002). *Interpersonal diagnosis and treatment of personality disorders* (2nd ed.). New York: Guilford Press.

Berne, E. (1967). *Games people play.* New York: Ballantine Books.

Bernstein, D., Cohen, P., Velez, C. N., Schwab-Stone, M., Siever, L., & Shinsato, L. (1993). Prevalence and stability of the *DSM-III-R* personality disorders in a community-based survey of adolescents. *American Journal of Psychiatry, 150*(8), 1237–1243.

Berres, M., & Long, N. (1979). The passive aggressive child. *Pointer, 34,* 27–31.

Bonds-White, F. (1983). A transactional analysis perspective on passive-aggressiveness. In R. Parsons & R. Wicks (Eds.), *Passive aggressiveness: Theory and practice* (pp. 44–71). New York: Brunner/Mazel.

Burns, D., & Epstein, N. (1983). Passive-aggressiveness: A cognitive-behavioral approach. In R. Parsons & R. Wicks (Eds.), *Passive aggressiveness: Theory and practice* (pp. 72–97). New York: Brunner/Mazel.

Drake, R., Adler, D., & Valliant, G. (1988). Antecedents of personality disorders in a community sample of men. *Journal of Personality Disorders, 2,* 60–68.

Erikson, E. (1950). *Childhood and society.* New York: Norton.

Fine, M., Overholser, J., & Berkoff, K. (1992). Diagnostic validity of the passive aggressive personality disorder: Suggestions for reform. *American Journal of Psychotherapy, 46*(3), 470–484.

Fischer, M., Barkley, R., Smallish, L., & Fletcher, K. (2002). Young adult follow-up of hyperactive children: Self-reported psychiatric disorders, comorbidity, and the role of childhood conduct problems and teen CD. *Journal of Abnormal Child Psychology, 30*(5), 463–476.

Fossati, A., Maffei, C., Bagnato, M., Donati, D., Donini, M., Fiorilli, M., et al. (2000). A psychometric study of *DSM-IV* passive-aggressive (negativistic) personality disorder criteria. *Journal of Personality Disorders, 14*(1), 72–86.

Frances, A., & Widiger, T. (1987). A critical review of four *DSM-III* personality disorders: Borderline, avoidant, dependent, and passive-aggressive. In G. Tischler (Ed.), *Diagnosis and classification in psychiatry: A critical appraisal of* DSM-III (pp. 269–289). Cambridge, England: Cambridge University Press.

Fusco, G. (2004). Passive-aggressive (negativistic) personality disorder. In A. Beck, A. Freeman, & D. Davis (Eds.), *Cognitive-behavioral therapy of personality disorders* (2nd ed., pp. 341–361). New York: Guilford Press.

Gardner, R. (1975). *Psychotherapeutic approaches to the resistant child.* New York: Aronson.

Gorton, G., & Akhtar, S. (1990). The literature on personality disorders, 1985–1988: Trends, issues, and controversies. *Hospital and Community Psychiatry, 41*(1), 39–51.

Groves, J. (1976). Taking care of the hateful patient. *New England Journal of Medicine, 298,* 883–887.

Hardt, J. (1988). How passive aggressive behavior in emotionally disturbed children affects peer interactions in a classroom setting. *Disabilities and Gifted Education, U.S. Department of Education.*

Helgeland, M., Kjelsberg, E., & Torgersen, S. (2005). Continuities between emotional and disruptive behavior disorders in adolescence and personality disorders in adulthood. *American Journal of Psychiatry, 162*(10), 1941–1947.

Johnson, J., Cohen, P., Brown, J., Smailes, E., & Bernstein, D. (1999). Childhood maltreatment increases risk for personality disorders during early adulthood. *Archives of General Psychiatry, 56*(7), 600–606.

Johnson, J., Cohen, P., Skodol, A., Oldham, J., Kasen, S., & Brook, J. (1999). Personality disorders in adolescence and risk of major mental disorders and suicidality during adulthood. *Archives of General Psychiatry, 56*(9), 805–811.

Johnson, J., Cohen, P., Smailes, E., Kasen, S., Oldham, J., Skodol, A., et al. (2000). Adolescent personality disorder associated with violence and criminal behavior during adolescence and early adulthood. *American Journal of Psychiatry, 157*(9), 1406–1413.

Johnson, J., Smailes, E., Cohen, P., Brown, J., & Bernstein, D. (2000). Associations between four types of childhood neglect and personality disorder symptoms during adolescence and early adulthood: Findings of a community-based longitudinal study. *Journal of Personality Disorders, 14*(2), 171–188.

Joiner, T., & Rudd, M. (2002). The incremental validity of passive-aggressive personality symptoms rivals or exceeds that of other personality symptoms in suicidal patients. *Journal of Personality Assessment, 79*(1), 161–170.

Kaplan, H., Sadock, B., & Grebb, J. (1994). *Kaplan and Sadock's synopsis of psychiatry* (7th ed.). Baltimore: William & Wilkins.

Kaslow, F. (1983). Passive-aggressiveness: An intrapsychic, interpersonal, and transactional dynamic in the family system. In R. Parsons & R. Wicks (Eds.), *Passive aggressiveness: Theory and practice* (pp. 134–152). New York: Brunner/Mazel.

Knutson, J. (1999). Psychological characteristics of maltreated children: Putative risk factors and consequences. *Annual Review of Psychology, 46,* 401–431.

Levy, K., Becker, D., Grilo, C., Mattanah, J., Garnet, K., & Quinlan, D. (1999). Concurrent and predictive validity of the personality disorder diagnosis in adolescent inpatients. *American Journal of Psychiatry, 156*(10), 1522–1528.

Loeber, R., Burke, J., Lahey, B., Winters, A., & Zera, M. (2000). Oppositional defiant and conduct disorder: Pt. I. A review of the past 10 years. *American Academy of Child and Adolescent Psychiatry, 39*(12), 1468–1484.

Long, N., & Long, J. (2001). *Managing passive aggressive behavior of children and youth at school and home.* Austin, TX: ProEd.

Magnavita, J. (1993a). The treatment of passive-aggressive personality disorder: Pt. I. A review of current approaches. *International Journal of Short-Term Psychotherapy, 8,* 29–41.

Magnavita, J. (1993b). The treatment of passive-aggressive personality disorder: Intensive short-term dynamic psychotherapy: Pt. II. Trial therapy. *International Journal of Short-Term Psychotherapy, 8*(93), 93–106.

Magnavita, J. (1994). The process of working through and outcome: Pt. III. The treatment of passive-aggressive personality disorder with intensive short-term dynamic psychotherapy. *International Journal of Short-Term Psychotherapy, 9,* 1–17.

Malinow, K. (1981). Passive-aggressive personality. In J. Lion (Ed.), *Personality disorders diagnosis and management* (revised for *DSM-III*; 2nd ed., pp. 121–132). Baltimore: Williams & Wilkins.

Marquoit, J. (2004). Reclaiming the passive aggressive youth. *Reclaiming Children and Youth, 13*(3), 177–180.

McCann, J. (1988). Passive-aggressive personality disorder: A review. *Journal of Personality Disorders, 2*(2), 170–179.

McCann, J. (1999). Obsessive-compulsive and negativistic personality disorders. In T. Millon, P. Blahney, & R. Davis (Eds.), *Oxford textbook of psychopathology* (pp. 585–604). New York: Oxford University Press.

Millon, T. (1969). *Modern psychopathology: A biosocial approach to maladaptive learning and functioning.* Philadelphia: Saunders.

Millon, T. (1981). Passive-aggressive personality: The negativistic pattern. In T. Millon (Ed.), *Disorders of personality* DSM-III: *Axis II* (pp. 244–272). New York: Wiley.

Millon, T. (1983). *Manual for the Millon Clinical Multiaxial Inventory-I (MCMI-I).* Minneapolis, MN: National Computer Systems.

Millon, T. (1993a). *Millon Adolescent Clinical Inventory (MACI) manual.* Minneapolis, MN: National Computer Systems.

Millon, T. (1993b). Negativistic (passive-aggressive) personality disorder. *Journal of Personality Disorders, 7*(1), 78–85.

Millon, T. (1999). *Personality-guided therapy* (pp. 558–587). New York: Wiley.

Millon, T., & Davis, R. (1996). Negativistic personality disorders: The vacillating pattern. In T. Millon (Ed.), *Disorders of personality:* DSM-IV *and beyond* (pp. 541–574). New York: Wiley.

Millon, T., Davis, R., Millon, C., Escovar, L., & Meagher, S. (2000). *Personality disorders in modern life.* New York: Wiley.

Ottaviani, R. (1990). Passive-aggressive personality disorder. In A. Beck & A. Freeman (Eds.), *The cognitive behavioral treatment of personality disorders* (pp. 333–348). New York: Guilford Press.

Perry, J., & Flannery, R. (1982). Passive-aggressive personality disorder treatment implications of a clinical typology. *Journal of Nervous and Mental Diseases, 170*(3), 164–173.

Prout, M., & Platt, J. (1983). The development and maintenance of passive-aggressiveness: The behavioral approach. In R. Parsons & R. Wicks (Eds.), *Passive aggressiveness: Theory and practice* (pp. 25–43). New York: Brunner/Mazel.

Ratican, K. (1992). Sexual abuse survivors: Identifying symptoms and special treatment considerations. *Journal of Counseling and Development, 71*(1), 33–39.

Reid, W. (1988). *Personality disorders: The treatment of psychiatric disorders revised for the* DSM-III-R (pp. 339–351). New York: Brunner/Mazel.

Rey, J., Morris-Yates, A., Singh, M., Andrews, G., & Stewart, G. (1995). Continuities between psychiatric disorders in adolescents and personality disorders in young adults. *American Journal of Psychiatry, 152*(6), 895–900.

Small, I., Small, J., Alig, V., & Moore, D. (1970). Passive-aggressive personality disorder: A search for a syndrome. *American Journal of Psychiatry, 126*(7), 973–983.

Stone, M. (1993a). *Abnormalities of personality.* New York: Norton.

Stone, M. (1993b). Long-term outcome in personality disorders. *British Journal of Psychiatry, 162*, 299–313.

Stricker, G. (1983). Passive-aggressiveness: A condition especially suited to the psychodynamic approach. In R. Parsons & R. Wicks (Eds.), *Passive-aggressiveness: Theory and practice* (pp. 5–24). New York: Brunner/Mazel.

Turkat, I. (1990). Personality disorders. In I. Turkat, (Ed.), *The personality disorders: A psychological approach to clinical management* (pp. 55–89). New York: Pergamon Press.

Vereycken, J., Vertommen, H., & Corveleyn, J. (2002). Authority conflicts and personality disorders. *Journal of Personality Disorders, 16*(1), 41–51.

Wetzler, S., & Morey, L. (1999). Passive-aggressive personality disorder: The demise of a syndrome. *Psychiatry, 62*(1), 49–59.

Whitman, R., Trosman, H., & Koenig, R. (1954). Clinical assessment of passive-aggressive personality. *Archives of Neurology and Psychiatry, 72,* 540–549.

Widiger, T., & Frances, A. (1985). The *DSM-III* personality disorders. *Archives of General Psychiatry, 42,* 615–623.

Yalom, I. (1985). *The theory and practice of group psychotherapy* (3rd ed.). New York: Basic Books.

Zeman, J., & Shipman, K. (1996). Children's expression of negative affect: Reasons and methods. *Developmental Psychology, 32*(5), 842.

CHAPTER 18

Development and Treatment of Personality Disorder: Summary

MARK A. REINECKE and ARTHUR FREEMAN

PERSONALITY DISORDERS are, by definition, chronic and pervasive patterns of cognition, affect, behavior, and circumstance. Whether these patterns combine to form a "condition" is dependent on many factors. The manifestations of the patterns are, however, recurrent and may define an individual throughout his or her life. They often impair relationships, creativity, and productivity, and can extract a toll on individuals and their families. Although significant progress has been made during recent years in understanding the characteristics, concomitant problems, and course of personality

681

disorders, there is relatively little we can say with confidence about the developmental psychopathology of these disorders, their treatment, or prevention. Like many complex conditions, personality disorders appear to be determined by complex factors—biological, environmental, social, cognitive, and developmental—all playing a role in various combinations and permutations. The ways in which these factors interact over the course of development, however, are poorly understood. Research on the development of externalizing behavior disorders among youth suggests that genetic vulnerabilities and stressful life events may place youth at risk for later psychopathology, and that children's temperament types may elicit different types of behavior from caregivers (Shiner & Caspi, 2003). Might similar processes be at play in the development of personality disorders? We can offer surmise, hypotheses, clinical experience, and case studies to fill the gaps in our knowledge. More simply, we don't know. In many ways, what we don't know about the development and prevention of these conditions is less than what we do know.

That said, cognitive and developmental psychopathology models have provided a foundation for a large body of work directed toward identifying and understanding vulnerability for psychopathology. In early work in this area, researchers relied on cross-sectional designs and retrospective self-report to examine factors associated with risk for developing these conditions. Several factors, including early abuse and neglect, parent-child interaction difficulties, and parental psychopathology, were identified as nonspecific vulnerability factors. During recent years, investigators have employed more sophisticated methodologies—often based on longitudinal designs—as a means of elucidating the complex interplay of factors placing youth at risk. Further, professionals are willing to entertain the notion and discuss the multiple and complex problems that are involved in the recognition, assessment, treatment, and postintervention of these disorders. As the chapters of this volume attest, important progress has been made. What, then, can be said with confidence about personality disorders, their development, and their treatment?

WHAT DO WE KNOW?

First, the precursors of adult personality disorders can be identified among children and adolescents, as can be the disorders. As noted in the *DSM-IV-TR* general diagnostic criteria for personality disorders, an individual must manifest an enduring, inflexible, and pervasive pattern of maladaptive behavior, mood, and cognition that "is stable and of long duration, and it's onset can be traced back *at least* to adolescence or early adulthood." Although questions can be raised with regard to the definition of terms such as "stable," "enduring," and "long duration," and hence with whether we can (or should) make a diagnosis of a personality disorder during childhood or adolescence, the important point still remains—enduring symptoms that come to characterize personality disorders can often be observed among youth. Further, the specific criteria speak of patterns that are in place by early adulthood. This has typically been interpreted at age 18. However, only in the diagnosis of Antisocial Personality Disorder is age 18 specified. The term "by early adulthood" suggests that it might start earlier. In the demographic data regarding personality disorders, *DSM-IV-TR* states, "Personality Disorder categories may be applied to children or adolescents in those relatively unusual instances in which the individual's particular maladaptive personality traits appear to be pervasive, persistent, and unlikely to be limited to a particular developmental stage or an episode of an Axis I disorder. It should be recognized that the traits of a Personality Disorder will often not persist unchanged into adult life. To diagnose a Personality Disorder in an individual, under 18 years of age, the features must have been present for at least a year. The one exception to this is Antisocial Personality Disorder, which cannot be diagnosed in individuals under age 18 years" (*DSM-IV-TR*, p. 687). Further, *DSM-IV-TR* states, "The features of a personality Disorder usually become recognizable during adolescence or early adult life" (p. 688).

Evidence suggests that it is possible to reliably identify symptoms and antecedents of personality disorders among adolescents (Bernstein et al., 1993; Cohen, Crawford, Johnson, & Kasen, 2005). Olin et al. (1997) found that teacher ratings of adolescents who were subsequently diagnosed as Schizotypal Personality Disorder found that analogs of the adult disorder were obvious in late childhood or early adolescence. These included greater passivity, less socially engaged, more sensitive to criticism, and responded with an apparent nervousness, but were not rated by the teachers as anxious children.

Second, personality disorders, like many forms of psychopathology, appear to be multiply determined. As noted, personality disorders appear to reflect the transaction of biological, environmental, sociocultural, and developmental factors. The possibility exists that different personality disorders will have different developmental trajectories, reflecting the interaction of different risk and resilience factors. Relationships between specific factors (such as parental psychopathology, early abuse or neglect, temperament, genetic vulnerability) and the emergence of personality disorders are reasonably well established. For example, victims of early childhood sexual abuse, physical abuse, or neglect are four times more likely to be diagnosed with a personality disorder by early adulthood (Johnson et al., 2000).

The mechanisms by which they serve to place youth at risk, however, are not known. One of the best ways to develop a prevention or early intervention program for personality disorders is to identify key discriminating characteristics of youth who will develop a personality disorder and determine how those features differ from those seen in children who are not likely to develop a personality disorder. Controlled cross-sectional research examining personality characteristics, temperamental traits, social behavior, neuropsychological functioning, genetics, neuroendocrine functioning, cognitive patterns, and psychophysiological differences can then be used to identify concomitants of personality disorders. The difficulty, of course, is that we cannot draw causal inferences from the differences observed using cross-sectional designs. There is, however, an alternative. By identifying children who are at-risk for personality disorders or who manifest early "prodromal" symptoms, and following them longitudinally, it may be possible to develop a clearer understanding of the development of these conditions. It is worth acknowledging that many early symptoms or "markers of risk" may be subtle. They may appear as temperamental characteristics rather than frank symptoms and may fluctuate in intensity over time. Childhood and adolescence are periods of cognitive, social, and emotional change—the concrete of personality may have been poured, but it's not set. Longitudinal research with at-risk and normative samples that systematically assesses multiple risk factors is needed.

At the same time, not all children who manifest these risk factors develop a personality disorder. Protective factors serve to insulate children, and so ameliorate this risk. Protective factors, like risk factors, also may be biological, social, cognitive, or environmental. Their specific nature and how they function, however, are not well understood. Life presents children, like adults, with problems. Traumatic events can tax their ability to cope, leaving them overwhelmed and vulnerable. Many things can go wrong over the course of development. Normative development, as such, involves acquiring an ability to flexibly respond to novel, shifting challenges. Resilience in the face of change and adversity may, in some ways, be seen as the converse of vulnerability for a personality disorder. Whereas the individual with a personality disorder manifests rigid, maladaptive patterns of perceiving and interpreting events, affective instability, dysfunctional relationships, and deficits in impulse control, the resilient individual manifests flexible patterns of perceiving others and resolving problems; affective stability; an ability to trust others and to resolve interpersonal difficulties; and the capacity to delay gratification and to tolerate frustration, ambiguity, and anxiety. How, then, can we understand the development of resilience? Several factors may play a role. We would propose that resilience is founded on a sense of security and the ability to trust others. We believe that the presence of a consistently safe and supportive early environment is critical. At the same time, resilience requires exposure to relationships that support the development of adaptive social skills and effective affect regulation. Finally, resilience is founded on a sense of personal efficacy, control, and agency. Taken together, this provides the individual with a stable sense of self-worth. We do not wish to imply that adverse life events and early parent-child problems are the source of personality disorders. They are but one set of factors that contribute to risk. Rather, we are proposing that protection from adverse life events, along with reliable, predictable, responsive, and supportive parenting, may serve as a socioenvironmental protective factor.

Third, our understanding of risk and resilience may allow us to develop prevention strategies. Based on what we know, efforts might usefully be directed toward (a) identifying children at risk for trauma and abuse and providing effective interventions, (b) providing parents with guidance in nonpunitive childrearing practices, (c) intervening with at-risk parents and their infants to facilitate the development of a secure attachment relationship, (d) providing psychoeducational assistance for parents of children with difficult temperament, (e) explore the possibilities of respite services or in-home services for parents of children with difficult temperament, and (f) offering psychoeducational and psychotherapeutic assistance to parents who manifest disabling psychopathology. Parental depression, alcohol or substance abuse, psychosis, and personality disorders all appear to contribute to an increased risk of personality disorders among children. Providing parents with effective treatment will help them and their children.

Fourth, there is considerable symptomatic overlap between personality disorders. Not surprisingly, many individuals manifest symptoms of more than one disorder. The diagnosis of Personality Disorder-Not Otherwise Specified is, in many clinics, quite common. Along the same lines, diagnostic comorbidity is not unusual. A substantial percentage of adolescents with Anorexia Nervosa or Bulimia, for example, meet criteria for a personality disorder (Herzog, Keller,

Lavori, Kenny, & Sacks, 1992; Herzog, Keller, Sacks, Yeh, & Lavori, 1992). Anxious and depressed youth frequently manifest symptoms of personality disorders, such as heightened dependency, affective lability, and impaired interpersonal functioning. Symptomatic overlap and comorbidity present a serious challenge for the validity of our current diagnostic taxonomy and impede research into the developmental psychopathology of specific personality disorders.

Fifth, strategic, structured psychotherapy appears to be effective for alleviating symptoms of personality disorders among adults. Dialectical Behavior Therapy (DBT; Linehan, 1993; Linehan, Armstrong, Suarez, Allmon, & Heard, 1991; Linehan, Heard, & Armstrong, 1993), Schema Therapy (Giesen-Bloo, van Dyck, Spinhoven et al., 2006; Nordahl & Nysaeter, 2005; Young, 1990), and a psychodynamically-based partial hospitalization program (Bateman & Fonagy, 1999) all have received some empirical support. It is worth noting that, of these, only DBT has been found to be efficacious in independent randomized controlled trials. Although there are several promising therapies, only DBT can, at this point, be considered to be an empirically supported treatment. To our knowledge, no studies have been conducted focusing explicitly on the prevention or treatment of personality disorders among children or adolescents. Unfortunately, we know relatively little about how to prevent or treat personality disorders among youth. The challenge and opportunity will be to refine and replicate outcome studies with promising treatment protocols and to modify strategies found to be effective with adults for use with younger individuals.

Sixth, the experimental literature on the development, prevention, and treatment of personality disorders (other than BPD and ASPD) is small. This, however, is not surprising. Patients with Borderline Personality Disorder behave in ways that truly frighten friends and family members. They often are emotionally labile, and frequently cut themselves and threaten suicide. Along the same lines, antisocial youth attract the attention of parents, school officials, and police. While parents and teachers may ruefully accept a teenager who is painfully shy and withdrawn with schoolmates and strangers, or who obsessively organizes his room and is excessively devoted to his schoolwork, they will immediately seek treatment for their impulsive, labile, self-destructive, or aggressive teen. These are the teens who attract our clinical and research attention. They become the "squeaky wheel" that gets the grease. Our understanding of the developmental trajectories for the other personality disorders, and the factors that contribute to their stability over time, is quite limited.

Seventh, not all disorders are created as equal. For some children and adolescents, a particular disorder may cause significant and severe personal discomfort and dysfunction. Their pain is noted and may be related to self-destructive behavior. For other children and adolescents, the behavioral pattern is ego-syntonic and the "distress," if any, comes from family members, peers, or school personnel. For still others, the style is, at this point, functional. Their behavior may even earn them rewards or attention, academic success, or peer envy. In fact, few individuals in the child's life may be distressed by the behavioral pattern. Finally, there are those children and adolescents for whom nobody is watching, and nobody cares. Their disorder or maladaptive pattern may be excused, ignored, or written off with the comment, "What do you expect from one of *them?*"

Eighth, the severity of the disorder differs. A mild manifestation may (or may not) be noticed, may (or may not) be functional, might be seen as a personal style, without prejudice. A moderate manifestation has likely been noticed. The notice comes from the pattern being dysfunctional and reflective of an impaired personal "style." Severity and impact of the resulting problems depend, as noted earlier, on the parents, teachers, and other school personnel. When there is a severe manifestation, we can be reasonably sure that it has frequently come to the notice of school personnel or the criminal justice system and been documented. The impairment in function is moderate to severe and causes significant conflict.

Ninth, given the antipathy and reluctance on the part of many mental health professionals to use the personality disorder diagnosis, euphemisms may be used that obscure the problems and reduce the likelihood of research. The reluctance may be based on several factors, including:

1. The child's personality is still forming and that to label it as "disordered" gives the impression that the personality of the child is fully formed and encased in stone.
2. "Inappropriate" labeling with such a foreboding diagnosis may lead to caregivers, therapists, and teachers giving up on the child.
4. The personality disorder diagnosis will be applied inappropriately to culturally different groups.
5. The behavioral notion that "personality" does not exist absent the specific behaviors, therefore there can be no "personality disorder."
6. This would be too weighty and stigmatizing a diagnosis for a child.

Tenth, given the potential countertransference to many of these disorders, the children, and their families, treatment can be negatively impacted by the negative and powerful reactions that can be elicited.

FUTURE DIRECTIONS: WHAT DO WE NEED TO KNOW? WHAT DO WE NEED TO DO?

Several important issues deserve immediate attention. These issues, once resolved, will provide a foundation for research into the prevention and treatment of personality disorders among youth. First, it is worth acknowledging that significant concerns exist with the *DSM-IV-TR* nosology. The reliability and validity of the diagnostic criteria for several personality disorders has not been firmly established. Moreover, relatively little work has been completed on the validity of these diagnostic criteria among youth. Put simply, it is difficult to investigate vulnerability or to develop treatment programs without a clear phenotype. Symptomatic overlap between disorders and diagnostic comorbidity only exacerbate this problem. Careful, systematic research on the reliability and validity of our categorical taxonomy, and the stability of symptoms and diagnoses over time, are needed.

An alternative solution may be to adopt a dimensional approach. An emerging body of evidence suggests that several temperament dimensions (i.e., shyness/behavioral inhibition, impulsivity) may have genetic or neurochemical substrates and that these characteristics may be stable over time. It has been proposed that personality disorders are "maladaptive exaggerations of normal traits" (Paris, 2003, p. xvii). These temperamental characteristics may be seen as serving as a foundation for the development of personality disorders. Along similar lines, it has been suggested that personality disorders are stable over time and across settings as underlying personality traits (e.g., neuroticism, extraversion, openness, agreeableness, conscientiousness; Roberts & DelVecchio, 2000), and that relationships may exist between these traits and specific personality disorders (Trull & McCrae, 1994; Warner et al., 2004). Research on the development of personality traits during childhood and adolescence and their relationship to personality disorders is warranted.

Second, the *DSM-IV-TR* definitions are unclear, and a lexicon for *DSM* needs to be developed. Terms such as "stable" or "unstable," while *generally* understood, do not allow for the specificity needed to develop diagnoses over groups, ages, and gender.

Third, although a large number of instruments have been developed for the diagnosis and assessment of personality disorders and personality traits among adults (for a review, see Clark & Harrison, 2001), relatively few instruments have been developed for use with children and adolescents. In addition to diagnostic interviews that can be administered to youth and their parents, there is a need for self-report instruments, trait-based interviews, measures that can be completed by other respondents (such as teachers), and instruments and techniques that are sensitive to subclinical or prodromal symptomatology.

Fourth, relationships between personality traits and diagnostic categories are not at all clear. Although associations have been found between the Big-Five personality dimensions and personality disorders, there is no sharp line distinguishing normative traits from clinical disorders. Further research is needed to determine if it is more reasonable to view personality disorders as qualitatively distinct phenomena (a medical model), or as a variant of a normative developmental process. Personality and temperament traits (e.g., impulsivity, behavioral inhibition, lability, neuroticism) also may be polygenetic and multiply determined.

As noted, a range of factors appears to interact over time in contributing to risk for personality disorders. As Glen Gabbard (2005) noted, "virtually all major psychiatric disorders are complex amalgams of genetic diatheses and environmental influences" (p. 648). So too with personality disorders. Genes function in interaction with an environment. They are indissociably linked and cannot be disengaged conceptually or empirically. A fuller understanding of vulnerability for personality disorders will require us to step beyond the traditional Cartesian duality of "mind" and "brain," and to attend to the ways in which genetic vulnerabilities and environmental experiences interact in contributing to risk. It will be important, as well, to determine the points over the course of development at which environmental events have their most significant effect.

Fifth, a substantial body of evidence indicates that early environmental stress can affect neuroendocrine functioning and neurological development. At the same time, childhood experiences can affect the development of cognitive and social skills. Although a body of research suggests that it is the ongoing accumulation of negative life events and vulnerability factors that place individuals at risk for psychopathology (i.e., it is the amount that counts), recent research by Caspi and colleagues (2003) indicates that the timing of stressful life events also may be important. There may, in a sense, be critical periods during which youth are most sensitive to the deleterious effects of specific risk factors. Timing may not be everything, but it is an important thing.

In addition to work on the classification, assessment, and diagnosis of personality disorders among youth, there is a need for a synthetic model of etiology. This model will, we suspect, integrate findings from behavioral genetics and developmental neuroscience with research in

cognitive psychology and developmental psychopathology. It is our belief that therapeutic models in clinical psychology and psychiatry
should be informed by research on normative child development.

Sixth, we should be careful that our clinical observations and theories do not bias our perceptions. We should not reify our models (or
our diagnostic schemes). They are simply templates for understanding
change and continuity over the course of development, and guides for
our interventions. As noted at the outset, two of the defining characteristics of personality disorders are that they are stable and maladaptive. These, however, are relative terms. Is the observed stability and
organization of personality disorders a characteristic of the child, their
environment, or the observer? Are the behaviors maladaptive in the
context in which they were acquired and in which the child now lives?

Seventh, there is a need for protocols and research on each of the
childhood personality disorders. It would then be essential to manual-
ize evidence-based treatment protocols and disseminate them broadly.
We need to know what the best treatment possibilities are, what works
best and for whom, under what specific circumstances, who would
need to be involved, what would be the optimal time frame for treatment, and whether treatment exacerbates the problems.

Eighth, the types of treatments that are recommended by our contributors are expensive. Who will pay the bills for the research and for the
interventions? We do not, at this point know what the costs and investments would be. These investments would include staff time, personal
investments by patients and their caregivers, and financial support for
the clinical research. The answer to the accountants who watch over
psychotherapy may be determined by whether we, as a community,
would rather treat the 25-year-old woman who has had multiple hospitalizations, lives a challenged and unhappy life, has few supports and
significant relationships, and may be misusing drugs or have treated
her as a child and adolescent. Ideally, these children need to be diagnosed very early so that they can receive the best, most intensive, and
most appropriate care. Early detection and intervention may limit the
chronicity of the disorder allowing clinicians to take a more preventative stance. We can initiate therapy for the child, request/require

parental involvement, request school or agency intervention, and develop opportunities for postintervention over the years. This early identification and intervention may halt or limit traumatic experiences.

Ninth involves running afoul of the oft-cited, but little demonstrated notion of "cure." We do not know what would be a reasonable outcome for treatment. We do not know how Axis I and Axis II disorders exacerbate one another over the course of development. Further, we do not know how personality dimensions and Axis II disorders may serve as substrates for the development of Axis I problems. We know that there may be many concomitants, but how they play one against the other is still largely unknown.

Tenth, it is worth noting that psychotherapy with personality disorders can be effective, at least under some circumstances. Meaningful change is possible. Moreover, longitudinal research indicates that not all individuals who meet criteria for a personality disorder will meet criteria several years later. Symptoms of personality disorders tend to ebb and flow over time. Personality traits also appear to be somewhat malleable. Although the concrete of vulnerability may be poured during childhood, it may never fully set. There is, then, reason for hope.

Given the costs and consequences of developing a personality disorder, the major question raised is whether we can afford *not* to treat these children.

REFERENCES

Bateman, A., & Fonagy, P. (1999). Effectiveness of partial hospitalization in the treatment of borderline personality disorder: A randomized controlled trial. *American Journal of Psychiatry, 156,* 1563–1569.

Bernstein, D., Cohen, P., Velez, C., Schwab-Stone, M., Siever, L., & Shinsato, L. (1993). Prevalence and stability of the DSM-III personality disorders in a community-based survey of adolescents. *American Journal of Psychiatry, 150,* 1237–1243.

Caspi, A., Sugden, K., Moffitt, T., Taylor, A., Craig, I., Harrington, H., et al. (2003). Influence of life stress on depression: Moderation by a polymorphism in the 5-HTT gene. *Science, 301*(5631), 386–389.

Clark, L., & Harrison, J. (2001). Assessment instruments. In W. Livesley (Ed.), *Handbook of personality disorders* (pp. 277–306). New York: Guilford Press.

Cohen, P., Crawford, T., Johnson, J., & Kasen, S. (2005). The children in the community study of developmental course of personality disorders. *Journal of Personality Disorders, 19,* 466–486.

Gabbard, G. (2005). Mind, brain, and personality disorders. *American Journal of Psychiatry, 162,* 648–655.

Giesen-Bloo, J., van Dyck, R., Spinhoven, P., van Tilburg, W., Dirksen, C., van Asselt, T., et al. (2006). Outpatient psychotherapy for borderline personality disorder: Randomized trial of schema-focused therapy vs. transference-focused psychotherapy. *Archives of General Psychiatry, 63,* 649–658.

Herzog, D., Keller, M., Lavori, P., Kenny, G., & Sacks, N. (1992). The prevalence of personality disorders in 210 women with eating disorders. *Journal of Clinical Psychiatry, 53,* 147–152.

Herzog, D., Keller, M., Sacks, N., Yeh, C., & Lavori, P. (1992). Psychiatric comorbidity in treatment-seeking anorexics and bulimics. *Journal of the American Academy of Child and Adolescent Psychiatry, 31,* 810–818.

Johnson, J. G., Cohen, P., Smailes, E., Kasen, S., Oldham, J. M., Skodol, A. E., et al. (2000). Adolescent personality disorders associated with violence and criminal behavior during adolescence and early adulthood. *The American Journal of Psychiatry, 157*(9), 1406–1412.

Linehan, M. (1993). *Cognitive-behavioral treatment of borderline personality disorder.* New York: Guilford Press.

Linehan, M., Armstrong, H., Suarez, A., Allmon, D., & Heard, H. (1991). Cognitive-behavioral treatment of chronically parasuicidal borderline patients. *Archives of General Psychiatry, 48,* 1060–1064.

Linehan, M., Heard, H., & Armstrong, H. (1993). Naturalistic follow-up of a behavioral treatment for chronically parasuicidal borderline patients. *Archives of General Psychiatry, 50,* 971–974.

Olin, S., Raine, A., Cannon, T., Parnas, J., Schulsinger, F., & Mednick, S. (1997). Childhood precursors of schizotypal personality disorder. *Schizophrenia Bulletin, 23*(1), 93–103.

Paris, J. (2003). *Personality disorders over time: Precursors, course, and outcome.* Washington, DC: American Psychiatric Publishing.

Roberts, B., & DelVecchio, W. (2000). The rank-order consistency of personality traits from childhood to old age: A quantitative review of longitudinal studies. *Psychological Bulletin, 126,* 3–25.

Shiner, R., & Caspi, A. (2003). Personality differences in childhood and adolescence, measurement, development, and consequences. *Journal of Child Psychology and Psychiatry, 44,* 2–32.

Trull, T., & McCrae, R. (1994). A five-factor perspective on personality disorder research. In P. Costa & T. Widiger (Eds.), *Personality disorders and the five-factor model of personality* (pp. 59–71). Washington, DC: American Psychological Association.

Warner, M., Morey, L., Finch, J., Gunderson, J., Skodol, A., Sanislow, C., et al. (2004). The longitudinal relationship of personality traits and disorders. *Journal of Abnormal Psychology, 113,* 217–227.

Young, J. (1990). *Cognitive therapy for personality disorders: A schema-focused approach.* Sarasota, FL: Professional Resource Exchange.

Author Index

Subject Index